HENRY DARGER

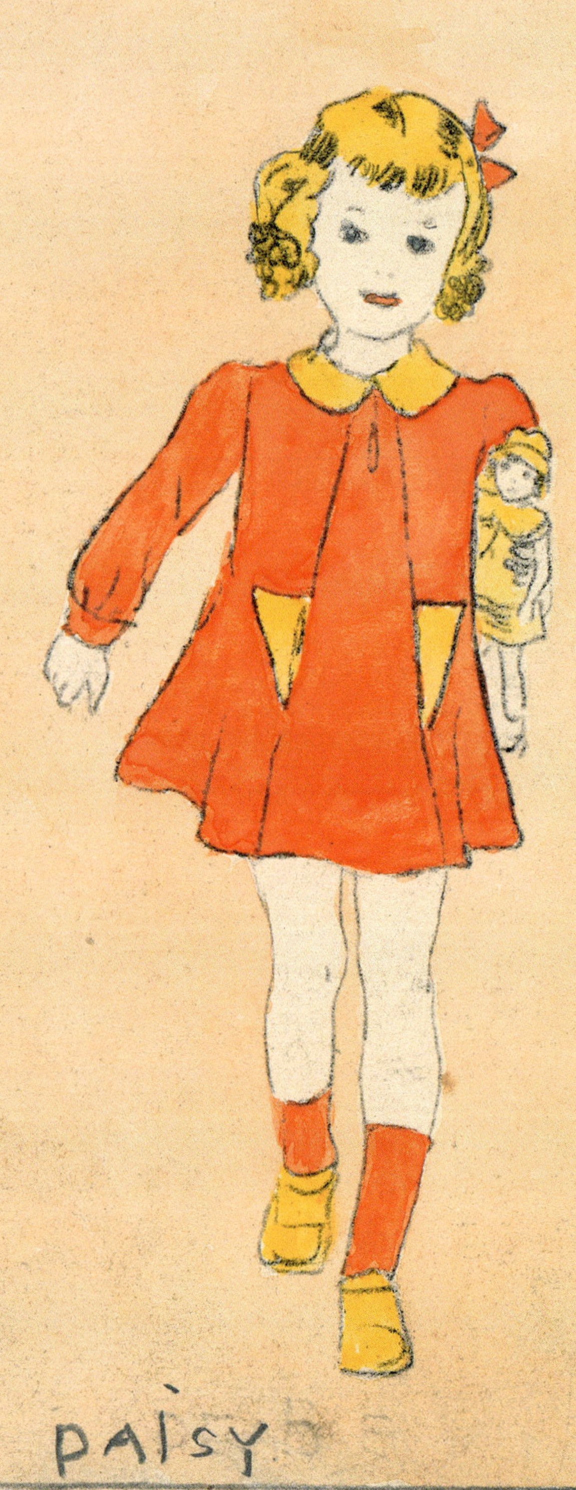

PAISY

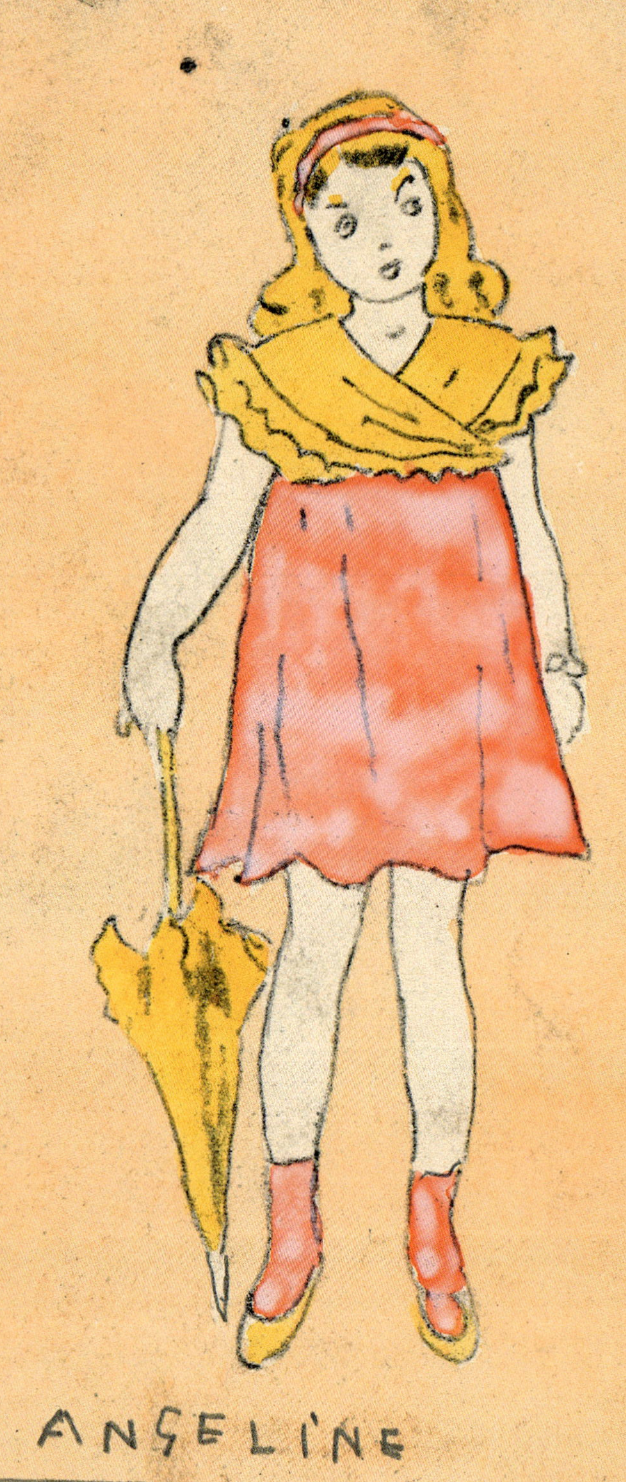

ANGELINE

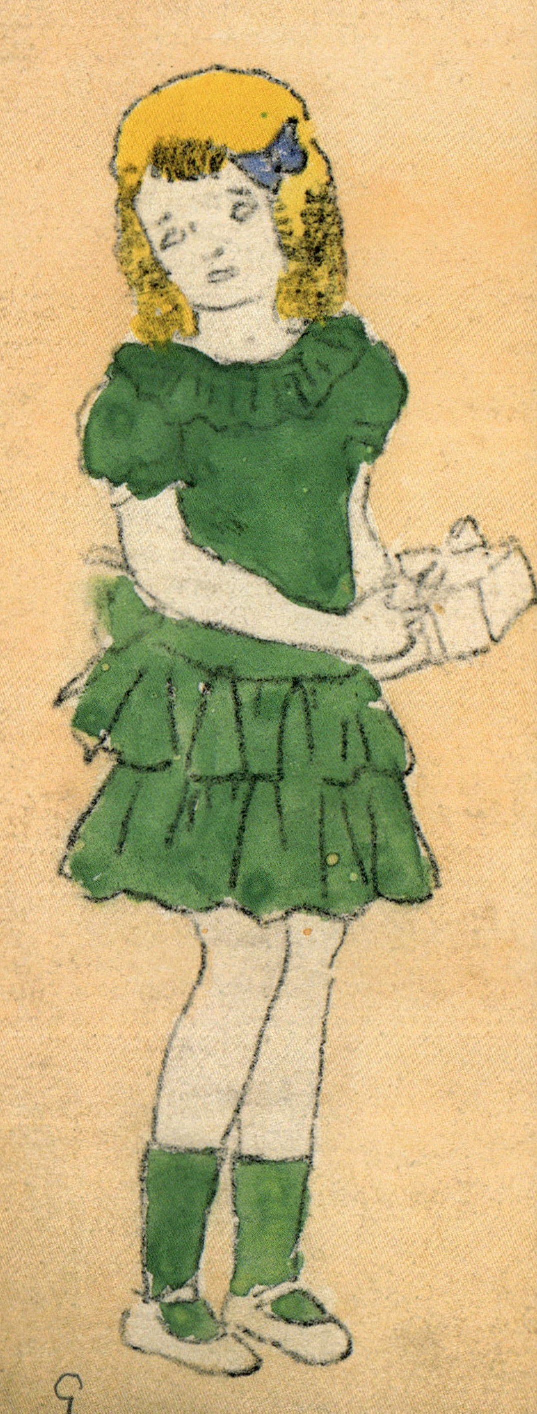

9

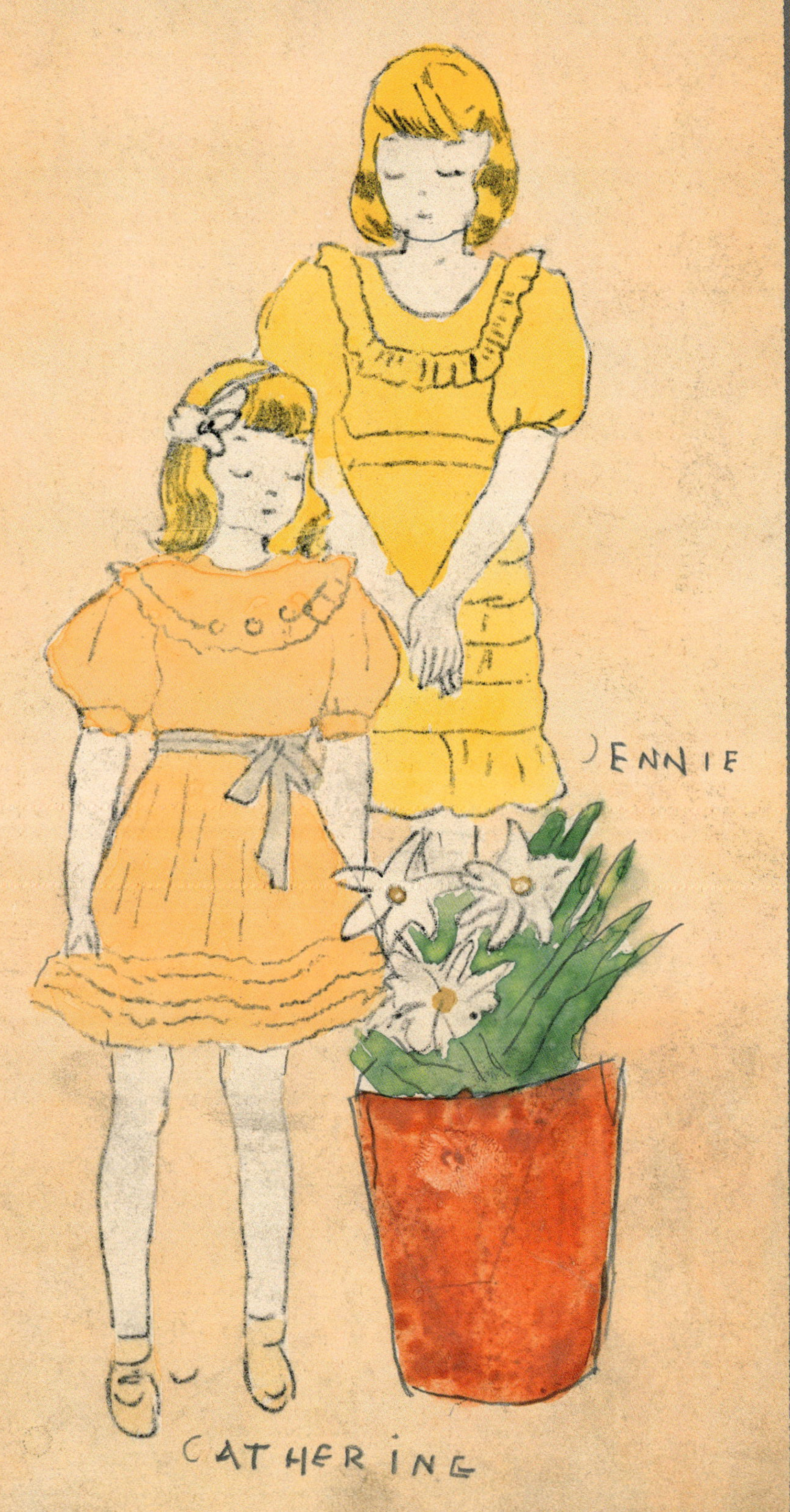
JENNIE
CATHERINE

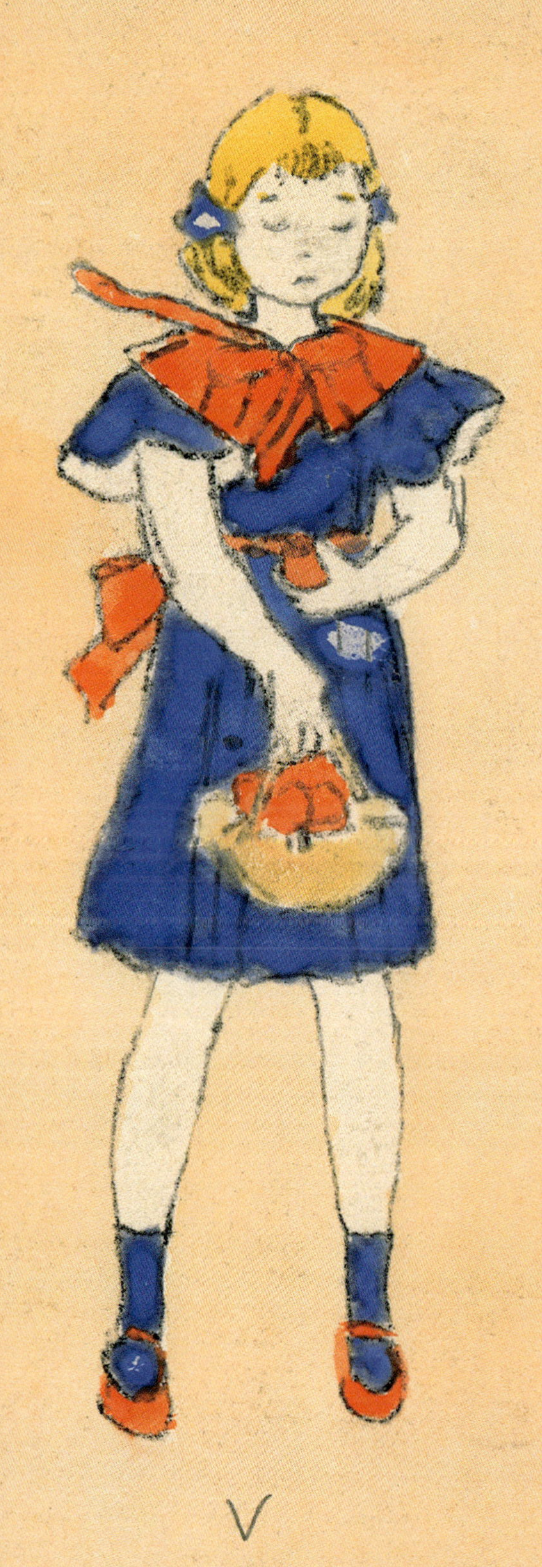
V

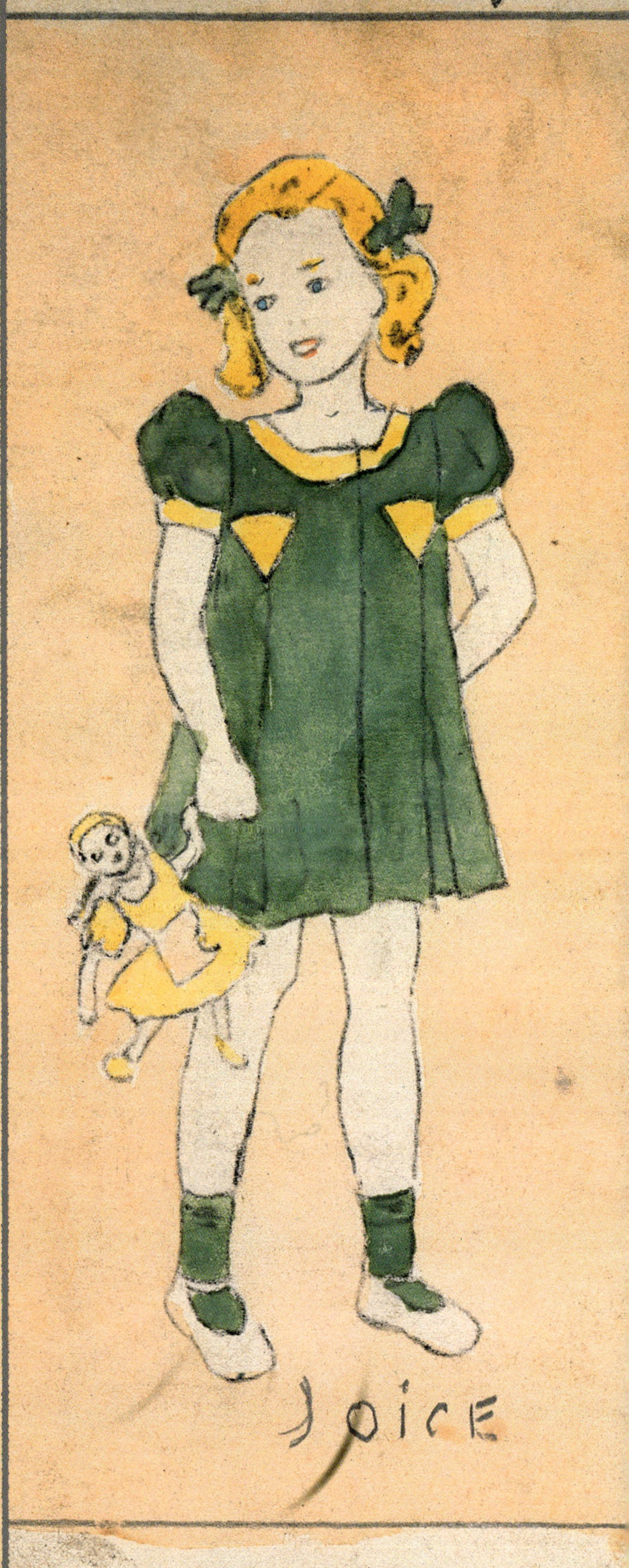
JOICE

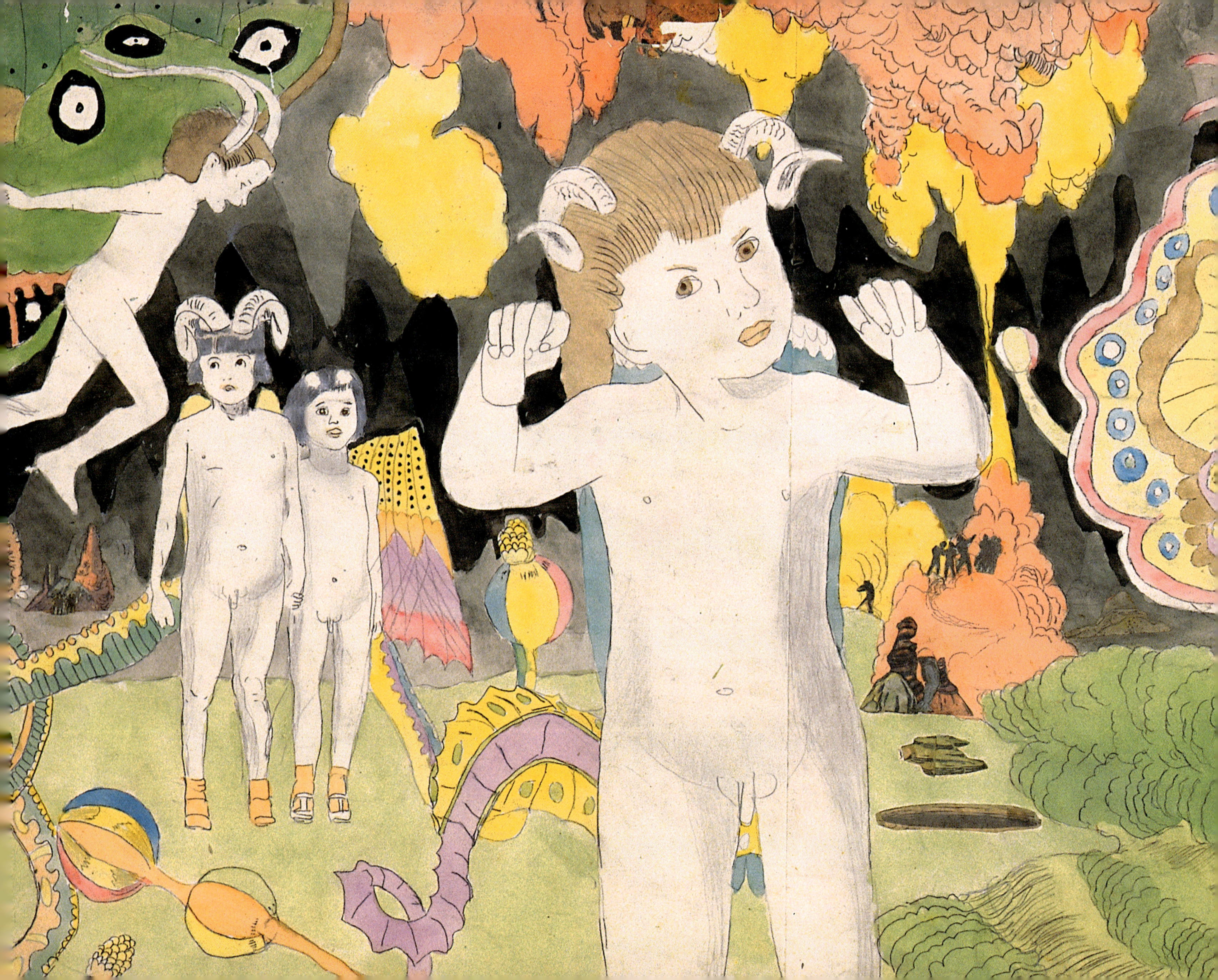

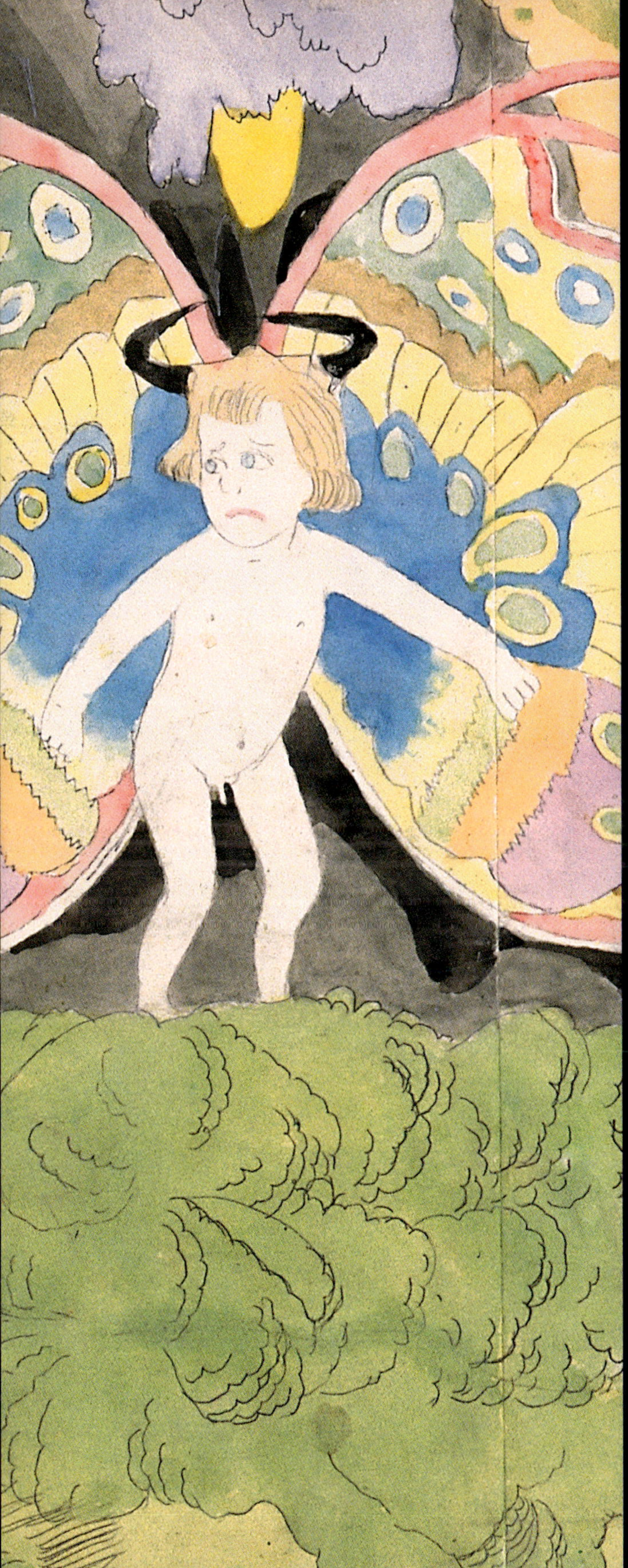

HENRY DARGER

Edited and with an introduction by

KLAUS BIESENBACH

Contributions by

BROOKE DAVIS ANDERSON, MICHAEL BONESTEEL
AND CARL WATSON

with

HENRY DARGER'S *The History of My Life*

Prestel

MUNICH LONDON NEW YORK

IN COOPERATION WITH THE AMERICAN FOLK ART MUSEUM, NEW YORK

4th edition 2023 © 2009, Prestel Verlag, Munich · London · New York
for the text "American Innocence," © 2009, Klaus Biesenbach · for the text "An Artist's
Studio at 851 Webster Avenue," © 2009, Brooke Davis Anderson · for the excerpt from
Girls on the Run by John Ashbery, © 1999, John Ashbery; reprinted by permission of
Georges Borchardt, Inc., and Carcanet Press Ltd. on behalf of the author
for illustrations of works by Henry Darger, © Kiyoko Lerner

Published by Prestel, a member of Penguin Random House Verlagsgruppe GmbH
Neumarkter Strasse 28, 81673 Munich

www.prestel.com
Library of Congress Control Number: 2019939554

Editorial direction: Christopher Lyon
Design: Mark Melnick · Origination: Reproline Mediateam
Production: Amanda Freymann, Nele Krüger and Friederike Schirge
Editorial assistance: Ryan Newbanks · Editor: Eve Sinaiko
Research assistant to Klaus Biesenbach: Alexander Kauffman
Printed and bound by DZS Grafik, d.o.o., Ljubljana
Printed in Slovenia

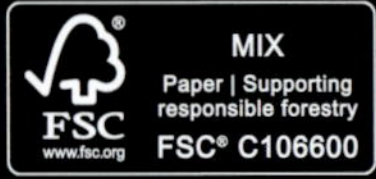

Penguin Random House Verlagsgruppe FSC® N001967
Paper: Galaxi supermat 150 g/m²

ISBN 978-3-7913-8583-9
For their advice and kind assistance in helping to realize this book,
the publisher wishes to thank Kiyoko Lerner, Andrew Edlin and the staff of the
Edlin Gallery, New York, and the American Folk Art Museum, New York.

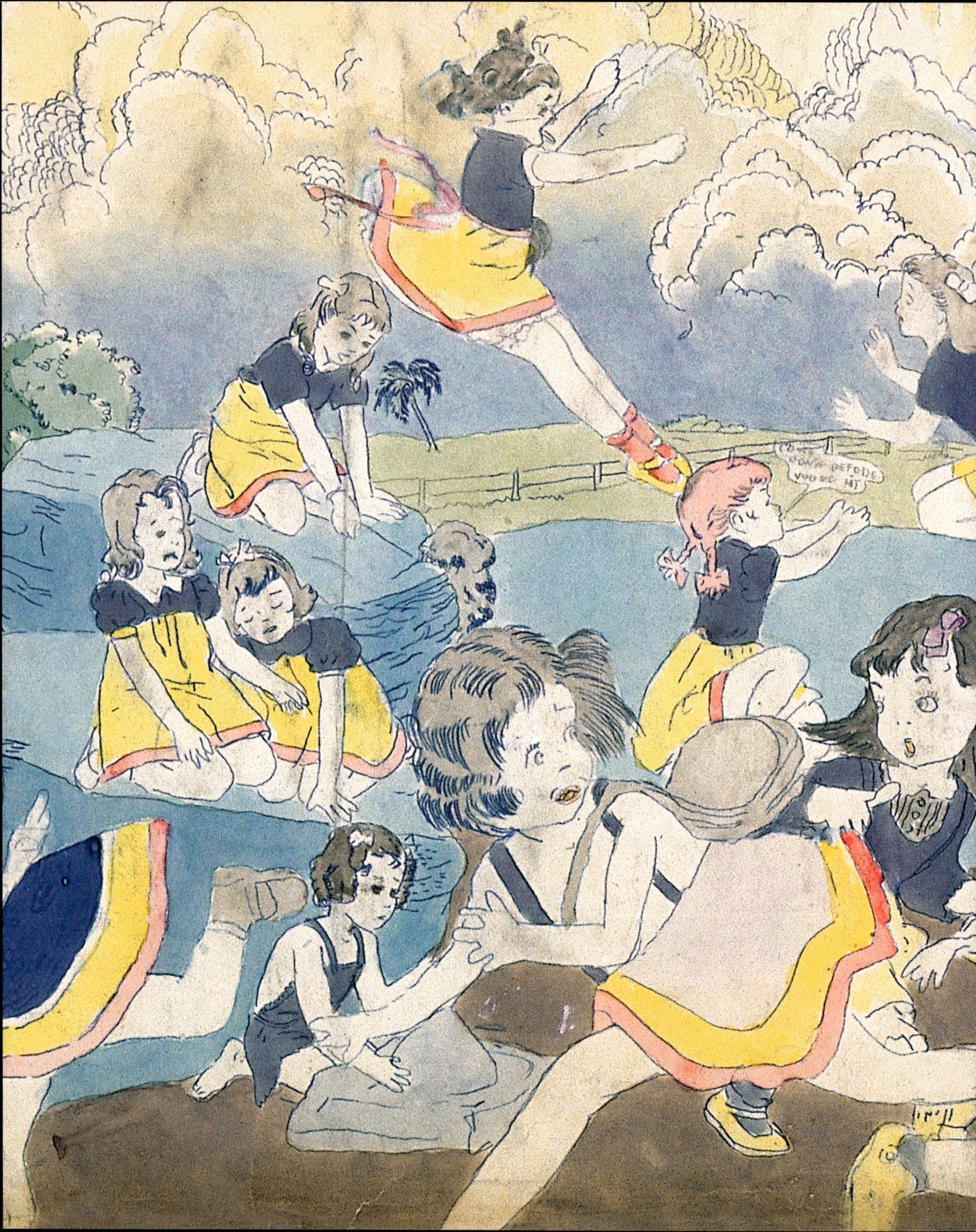

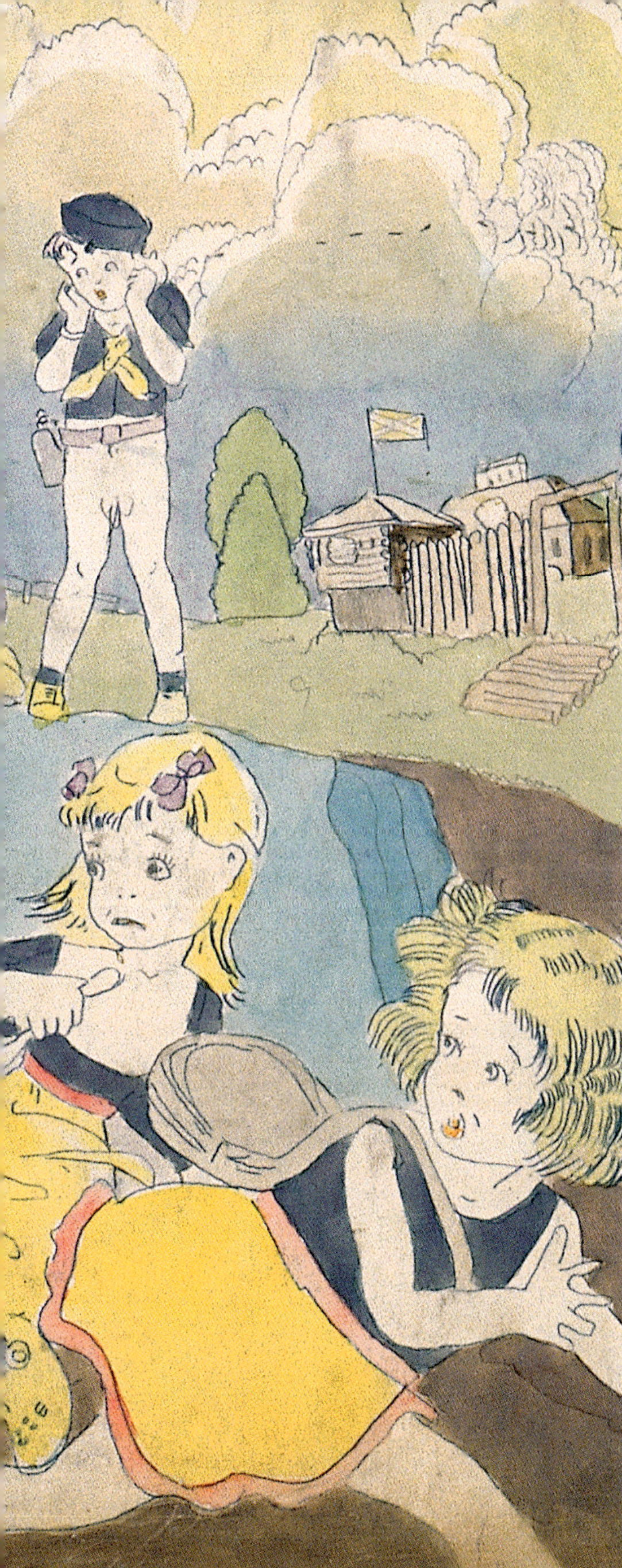

GIRLS ON THE RUN

after Henry Darger

A great plane flew across the sun,

and the girls ran along the ground.

The sun shone on Mr. McPlaster's face, it was green like an elephant's.

Let's get out of here, Judy said.

They're getting closer, I can't stand it.

But you know, our fashions are in fashion

only briefly, then they go out

and stay that way for a long time. Then they come back in

for a while. Then, in maybe a million years, they go out of fashion

and stay there.

Laure and Tidbit agreed,

with the proviso that after that everyone would become fashion

again for a few hours. Write it now, Tidbit said,

before they get back. And, quivering, I took the pen.

Drink the beautiful tea

before you slop sewage over the horizon, the Principal directed.

OK, it's calm now, but it wasn't two minutes ago. What do you want me to do, said Henry,

I am no longer your serf,

and if I was I wouldn't do your bidding. That is enough, sir.

You think you can lord it over every last dish of oatmeal

on this planet, Henry said. But wait till my ambition

comes a cropper, whatever that means, or bursts into feathered bloom

and burns on the shore. Then the kiddies dancing sidewise

declared it a treat, and the ice-cream gnomes slurped their last that day.

—**John Ashbery**, excerpt from *Girls on the Run* (1999)

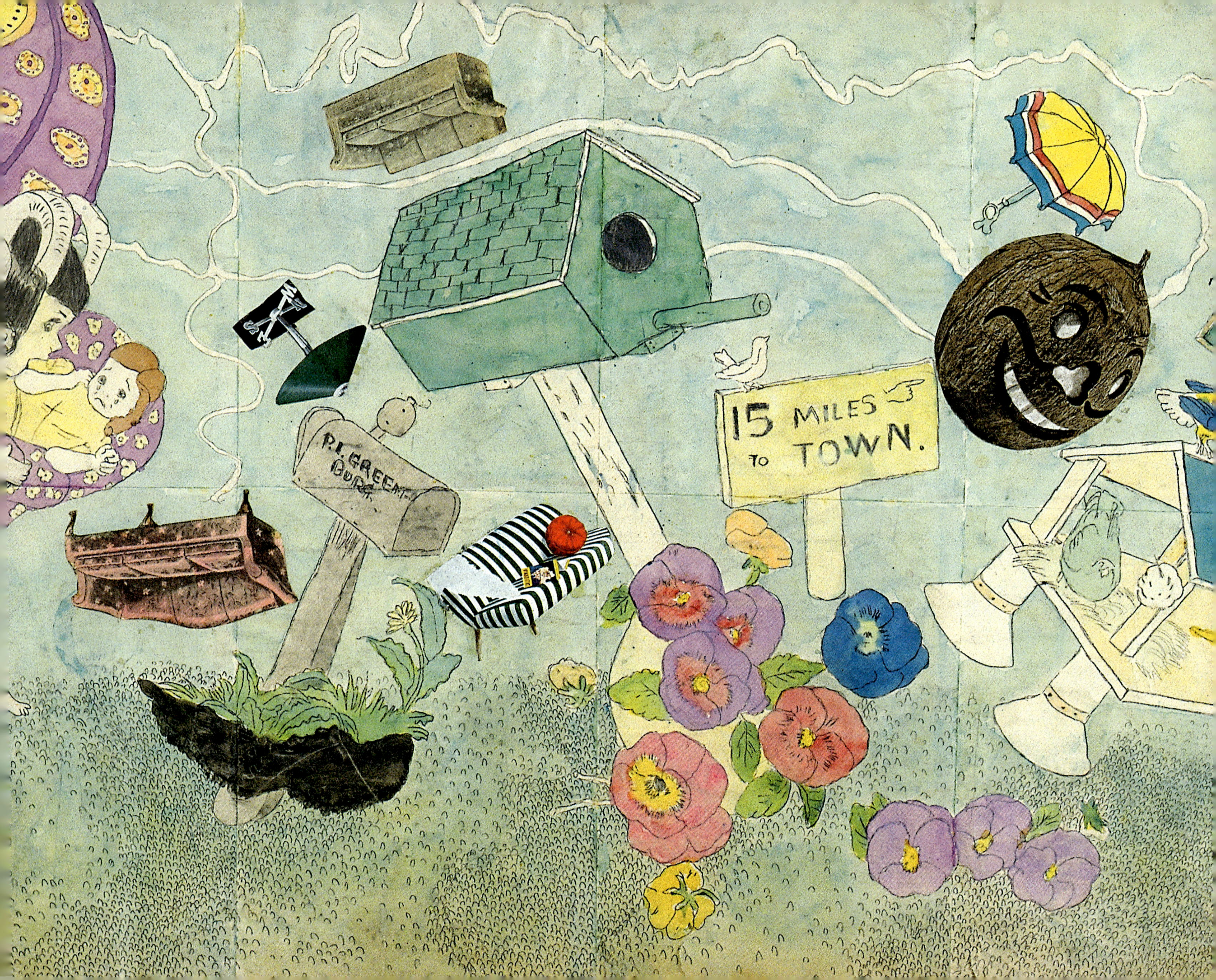

P.T. GREEN
DUFF
15 MILES
TO TOWN.

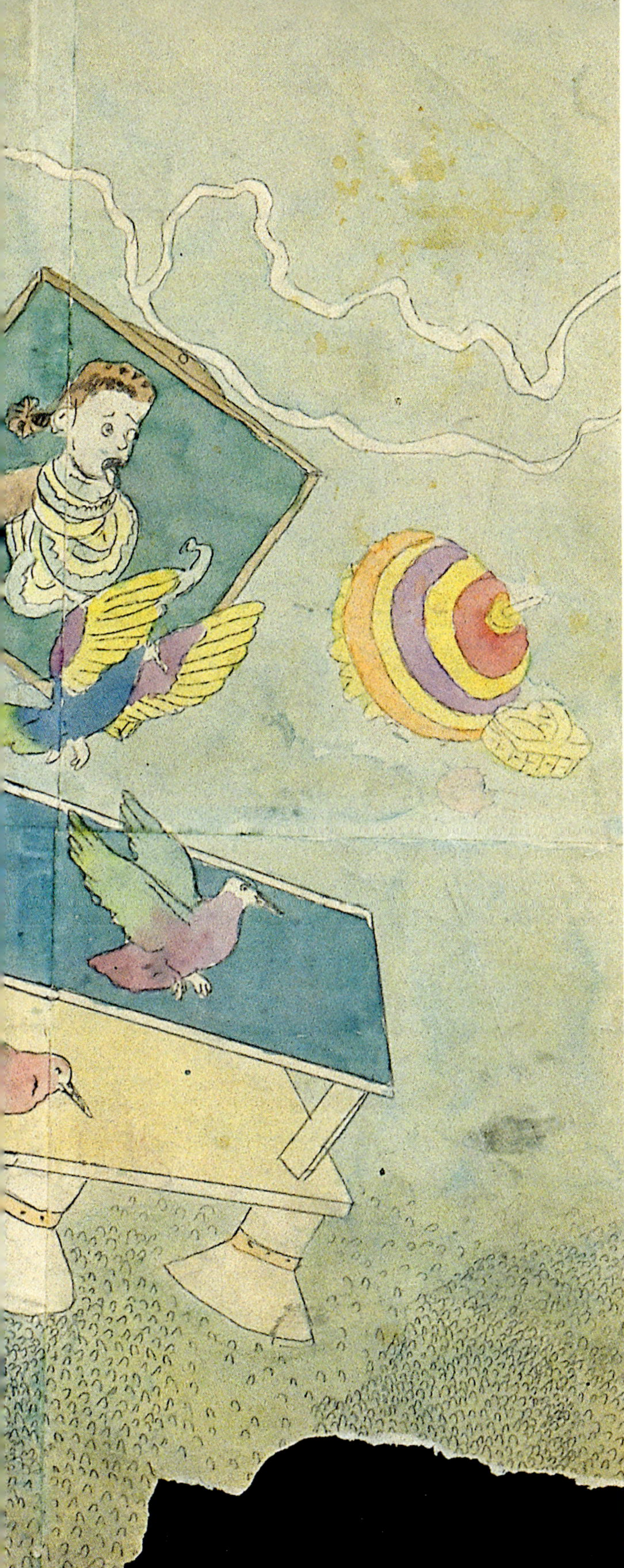

CONTENTS

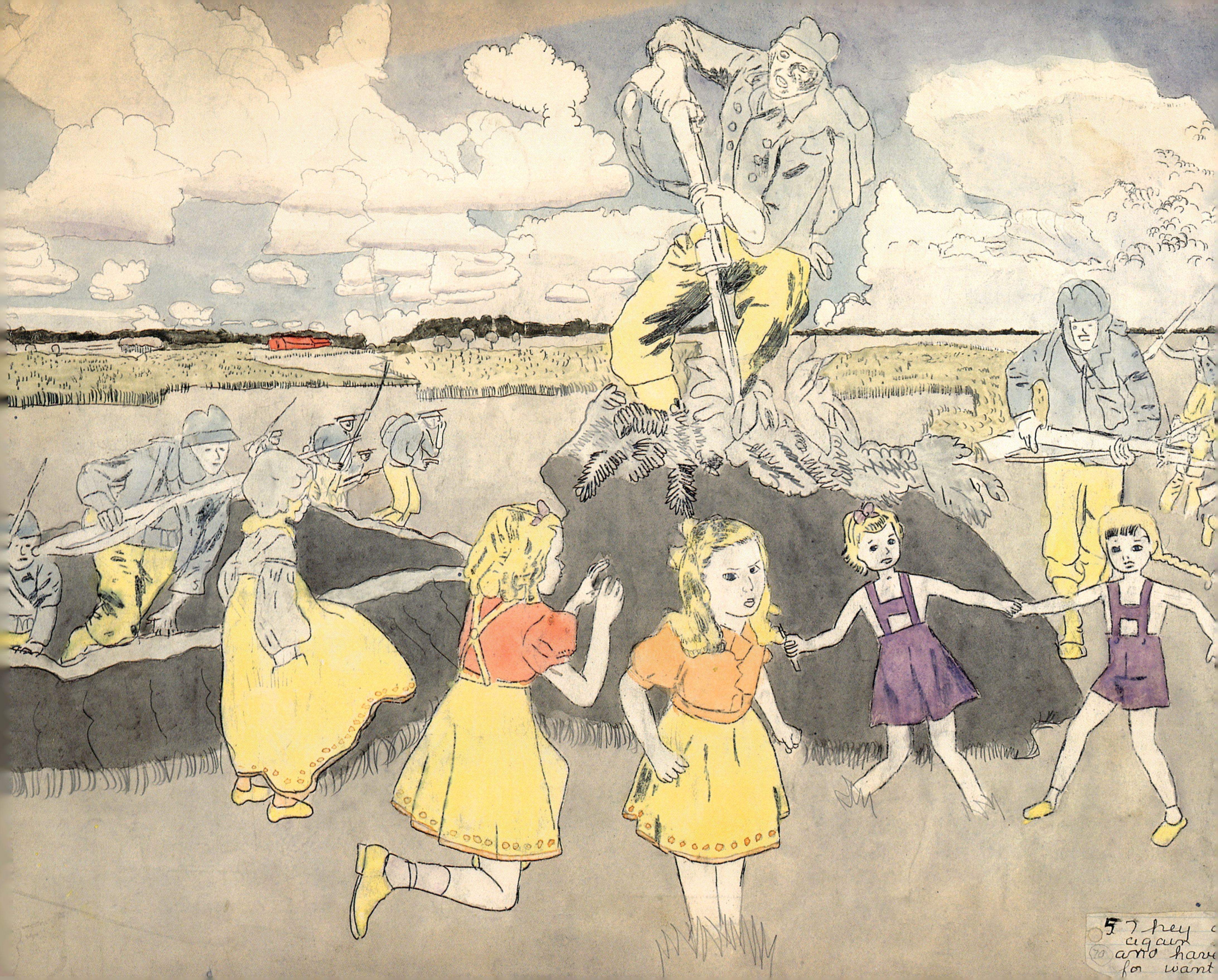
5 They
again
and have
for want
70

American Innocence

KLAUS BIESENBACH

1: POINTS OF DEPARTURE

In her video *We Are All Made of Stars* (2002), Laurel Nakadate puts herself in the hands of truck drivers: waiting at a truck stop, scantily clad, she follows them into their cabs, protected only by her innocence and a small video camera recording the situation.

I first experienced Nakadate's work in 2004 when, as one of a team of curators from P.S. 1 Contemporary Art Center in New York City and the Museum of Modern Art, I was researching the second *Greater New York* exhibition, held at P.S. 1 in 2005. To prepare for this overview of emerging talent in the five boroughs, we visited hundreds of young artists' studios in the greater New York area. It was extraordinary to note how many of them were aware of Henry Darger's work, as Nakadate was, talked about Darger, pinned up images of his work, or even directly referred to him in their own artworks.

Henry Darger continues to be regarded as an "outsider" artist. I am not going to attempt to prove that he was not, but instead describe Darger in his motivations and his inspirations, explain when and how he worked, and point to other artists who lived and worked through the same decades and had the same points of departure or used similar source material. Which artists arrived at similar results? Or contrary ones?

There are parallels between Darger and his better-known, more widely accepted contemporaries. As much as Darger was outside of the typical social class that artists very often come from, as much as he was outside of the educational trajectories that artists normally go through, as much as he was outside of a family structure or conventional value system, he nevertheless created a body of work that resonates with what we now see as primary themes and concerns of artists in recent decades.

One must look at common motifs in Darger's work, such as those derived from his beloved *Uncle Tom's Cabin, Heidi,* and the Oz books by L. Frank Baum. One must also consider Darger's obsessiveness and compulsions, from his interminable, numbingly detailed battle descriptions and casualty lists for the civil war that is the subject of his vast unfinished novel, *In the Realms of the Unreal,* to the hundreds of pages of weather reports he compiled late in his life.

An overview of recent art production inspired by Henry Darger's work or reflecting his imagery will shed light on his continuing impact. Why is Darger so relevant today? Perhaps it is because his focus on war and violence, belief and despair, and the heaven and hell of human interaction seem all too contemporary and speak to the deepest anxieties of our media-driven society.

Obsessed with ideas of vulnerability and protection, control, power, and freedom, Henry Darger thought about adoption and slavery. *In the Realms of the Unreal* is the history of an epic war fought between an alliance of four great

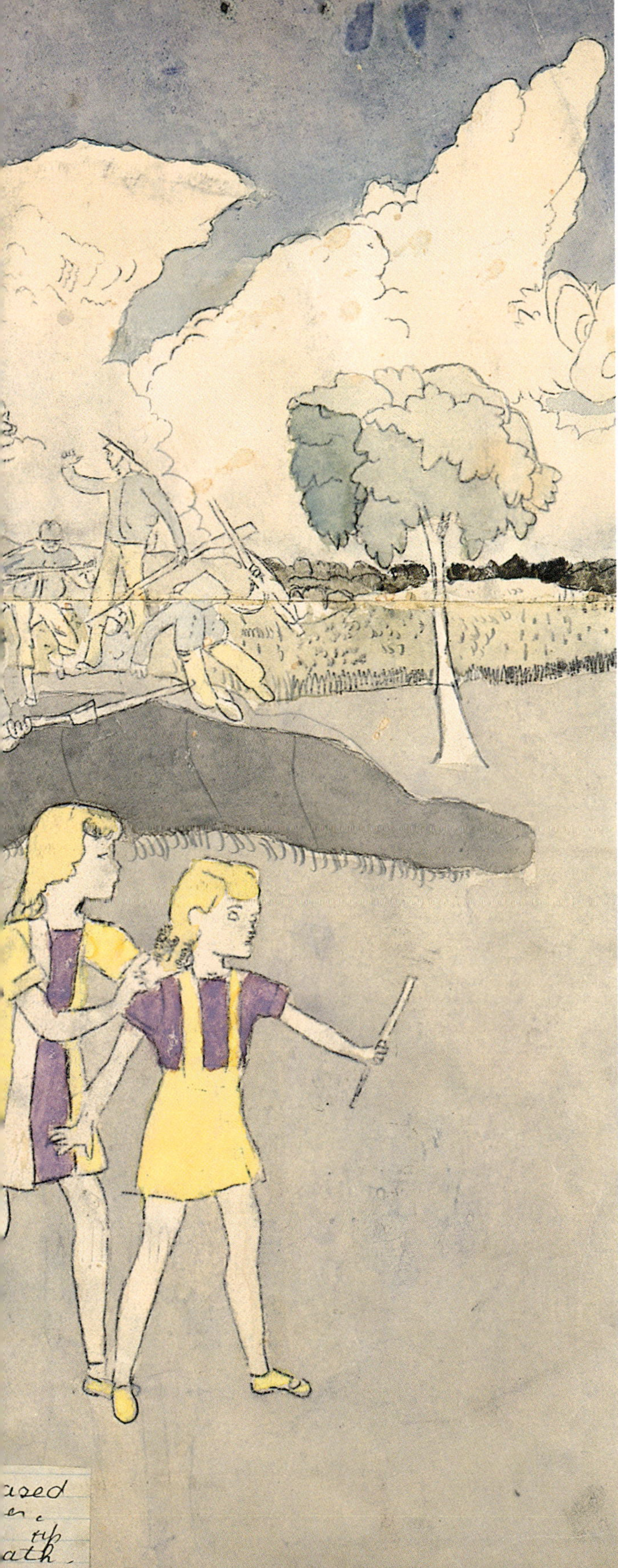

Catholic nations, led by Abbieannia, and an evil empire, Glandelinia, that practices child slavery. The heroines of the novel are the seven innocent, prepubescent Vivian sisters, daughters of the emperor of Abbieannia, who help to free kidnapped children enslaved in Glandelinia, a nation of corrupt, evil adults.

When Darger, born in 1892, was still a baby, his mother died in childbirth. Arriving in the absence of his mother, Darger's new baby sister did not trigger normal feelings of sibling jealousy. There was no mother to fawn over the new infant. In a way, he suffered an exchange of his sister for his mother. However, soon after her birth his sister too was taken from him, given up for adoption, leaving Darger doubly disappointed, doubly frustrated. Perhaps Darger's life would have had a very different trajectory if he too had been adopted. When his father, who was fifty-two when Henry was born, became too lame to work and was admitted to St. Augustine Home for the Aged, the child was placed in the care of a Catholic boys' home. In his autobiography, Darger recalls nearly being adopted by a female relative who accompanied his father on a visit to the boys' home. Darger reports that "without a court order," the administrator, Father Meaney, "could not grant the request."[1] Later, from the time he was in his mid-twenties and for a dozen or so years thereafter, Darger prayed to adopt a child, but it is not known whether he took concrete steps to actually do so.[2]

Given up by his father, denied the possibility of being adopted or adopting a child himself, Darger would spend much of his life creating—and defending—imagined children. His work begs the questions, Who "owns" the child and its labor? Who defends the child's innocence and life? The American Dream, understood as a positive, shared, but still individual goal in the American mentality, could only be attained by reestablishing a certain state of innocence after colonialism and widespread slave labor laid the foundation of this country's economic

success. Darger's interest in Harriet Beecher Stowe's *Uncle Tom's Cabin* and his extensive knowledge about the American Civil War demonstrate his awareness of the history of slavery in the United States and its circumstances. In *Realms,* one sect of Glandelinians, known as the Hooded Gargolian Kurds, is explicitly compared to the Ku Klux Klan.[3] Borrowing from *Uncle Tom's Cabin*, Darger introduces as a character Stowe's own Evangeline St. Clare, the angelic little girl who befriends Tom. Appearing unexpectedly in Darger's novel, she explains that she has just escaped from the Glandelinians and recalls, "I . . . lived with my father for ten years and saw all kinds of slavery among the poor colored, and they killed poor old Uncle Tom. I'm the same little Eva you have read about and have become a Catholic two months ago. The child slavery here is worse than the slavery of the poor creatures in the United States." To explain the appearance of little Eva, Darger reimagines her death in Stowe's novel. "Did you not die from consumption?" asks one of Darger's generals. "I did not die but fainted when the sickness got at its worst." and Darger adds, "(BEG PARDON TO THE WRITER OF UNCLE TOM'S CABIN)."[4]

Despite his deep love of and fascination with recorded history, Darger was wary of it. He discovered early on, when he encountered conflicting accounts of Civil War casualties, that history can be unreliable. Writing his autobiography, Darger, then in his mid-seventies, remembered: "I once told my teacher, but the one, Mrs. Dewey at the Skinner school, that I believed no one truthfully knew the losses in the battles of wars (including our Civil War), because each history told different losses, and I had the histories and other stories to prove it, and let her see and go over them."[5]

The creator of *Realms*, however, a long, all-consuming text, seemed to tolerate inconsistencies in his own war history up to a point, despite his painstakingly assembled lists of battles, characters, and casualties, and this actu-

ally tells us something about his working method. For example, one of the protagonists, a boy named Schoefield Penrod, is inspired by Booth Tarkington's Penrod novels, which follow the boy-hero Penrod Schofield, growing up in the Midwest before World War I. When we first meet Schoefield in *Realms*, he is introduced as a French-Canadian: the Glandelinians call him the "black haired little Frenchie Imp, Schoefield Penrod." Later in the story it is explained that he is "not a Canadian as many thought he was," but a native of Abbieannia.[6] Another of Darger's heroes, Walter Starring, is depicted in a collage-drawing as a little boy. However, in the text he is described as a scientist and general commanding his own armies. Some time after a massive explosion sends a large part of the city of Abieann into the ocean, Starring dives down to explore the ruins and account for lives lost. Darger explains the boy's seemingly adult abilities with a single sentence: "Walter Starring was more of a man than a boy, despite his young age and five feet tall."[7]

Darger's reliance on found materials in the creation of his art, and on characters and texts adapted from published sources in the writing of his novel, persistently forced him to reconcile depictions or statements and plot points that seemed inconsistent or even contradictory. This basic challenge is the cause of the convoluted structure, as it required Darger to move episodes around in his attempts to rationalize the narrative, and may have led to the ultimate abandonment of the novel. Darger bound the first seven volumes of *Realms*, but did not finish binding the remaining eight. As Michael Bonesteel has suggested, a likely reason "is that the reshuffling of episodes had caused a chronological nightmare that he was never going to resolve."[8]

The weather journals Darger maintained for exactly a decade, from 1957 to 1967, reveal his continuing obsession with inconsistencies. Recording conditions at predetermined times each day, Darger vigorously disputed daily newspaper weather predictions, basking in the weatherman's mistakes and carefully noting them in the journals.

Darger compares his task of writing the history of the Glandeco-Angelinian War to Glinda the Good Witch's keeping of her record book in the Oz books by L. Frank Baum. Darger's private library included first editions of *The Wonderful Wizard of Oz* and its thirteen sequels.[9] A model for his own fantasy universe, Baum's series imagines histories of nations with their own flags and maps. The prominent illustrations featured in the Oz series as storytelling tools likely influenced Darger's own decades-long illustration project, in which the text is embellished and rewritten through illustration.

While a devoted fan of Oz, Darger was conscious of his own work's departure from Baum's utopian landscapes. In volume VII he writes, "I have read many of the beautiful Oz books, and have read that in that kind of a country no one, whether man, woman, or children, or beasts, ever become sick or die. . . . This is one of the reasons Oz was a fairy land."[10] Darger suggests that his universe is more like the real world, full of death and destruction. He continues, "I was just wondering lately what would the people of Oz do if their country had been somewhere in Calverinia . . . and Glinda would see in her great record book, 'Great Glandelinian army advancing on the Emerald City. Rebel army pursuing Angelinians. Glandelinian army one hundred million strong.' "[11]

The publication in 1900 of Baum's first Oz book, *The Wonderful Wizard of Oz*, illustrated by W. W. Denslow, marks a time at the opening of the twentieth century when many new utopian ideas took hold of the American imagination through technical inventions and intriguing fiction. The second volume of the Oz series, *The Marvelous Land of Oz* (1904), illustrated by John R. Neill, drew on such a utopian dream.[12] Although the Oz books were banned by many libraries in the 1920s (one cited reason being the ambiguous political world view they commu-

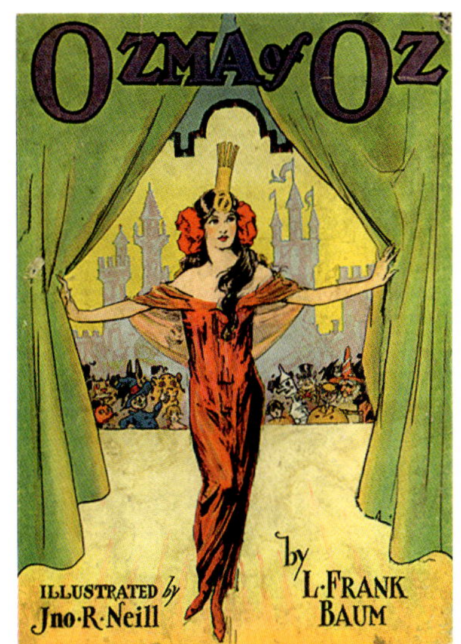

Above: **John R. Neill,** cover illustration for *Ozma of Oz* by L. Frank Baum, 1907. *Below:* **John R. Neill,** illustration for *The Magic of Oz* by L. Frank Baum, 1919

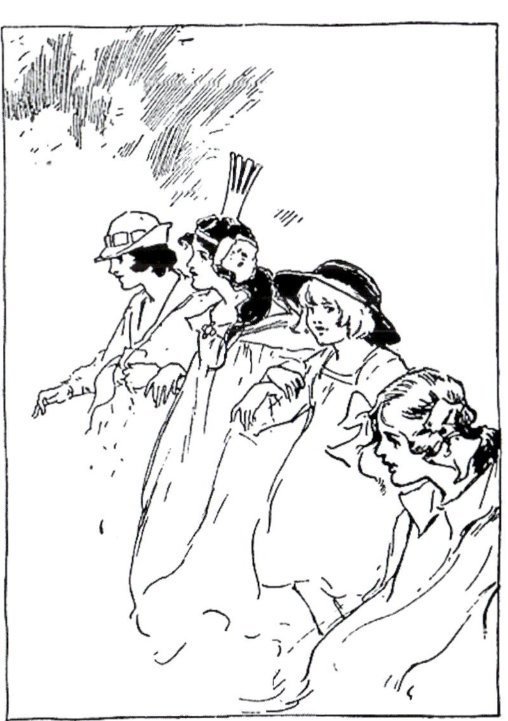

nicated to young readers), many fell in love with Baum's imaginary world, infused with the author's own experiences living on the American frontier, in the Dakota Territory in the 1880s. In this second volume about Oz, a powerless little boy, Tip, is eventually revealed to be a girl called Ozma, the rightful ruler of Oz, who had been transformed into a boy by the witch Mombi when she was an infant. His destiny is to be Ozma, the "transsexual" queen of Oz. The seemingly bizarre sexual confusion of Darger's characters thus may not have seemed so strange to the legions of American readers who grew up with the Oz series. This tale also features an all-girl Army of Revolt, anticipating Darger's intrepid soldier girls, as well as benevolent dictators and bewitched creatures. Baum was married to Maud Gage, daughter of the radical feminist activist Matilda Joslyn Gage, and his mother-in-law's politics find their way into Oz and, through the beloved books, into Darger's *Realms*, albeit at a far remove.

—

Darger closely guarded his privacy, only allowing guests into his art- and junk-filled room when absolutely necessary. When he moved out of his apartment on the North Side of Chicago and into St. Augustine's Home for the Aged in November 1972, his landlord, the artist Nathan Lerner, found Darger's artworks in the two-room apartment at 851 W. Webster Avenue, where he had lived since 1931. David Berglund, a young student helping clear out the apartment, had already removed piles of trash from the compulsive collector's home when he came across three immense hand-bound albums, each approximately two feet high and roughly twelve feet wide, containing the panoramas and polyptychs for which Darger is now famous. Within old trunks he found the story these drawings illustrate, in fifteen volumes totaling more than fifteen thousand typewritten pages. This immense novel provided a context for the dozens of framed collages and painted photographs on the walls, found and altered pictures de-

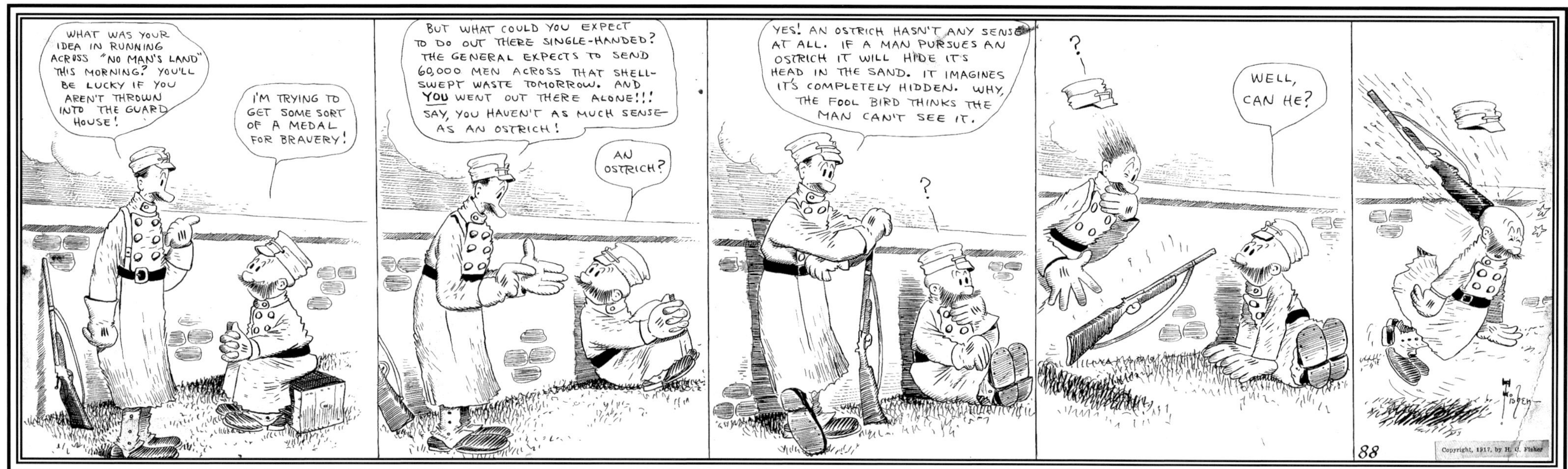

Bud Fisher, *Mutt and Jeff* daily comic strip, December 28, 1917

picting battles, generals, and little girls. Darger's collection of photographs, found during daily searches through the neighborhood, included the images of nude and dead children that are so common in his watercolors.[13]

Even in the confusion of the apartment, overflowing with piles of old newspapers and magazines, the Lerners immediately recognized an enormously ambitious body of work. Darger's long-term commitment to the fictional world of his novel—imagining and recording its front-page news, its obituaries, and even its weather—seemed to rival Baum's or J. R. R. Tolkien's degree of immersion in the fictive worlds they created. Darger's engagement with printed media, through the daily newspapers, magazines, paperbacks, and cartoons he found, scavenging the streets and trashcans of his neighborhood, is revealed in the pastiche of character types and storybook clichés in his novel. Darger borrowed as well from comic books and children's adventure serials, filling his novel with outrageously named characters and a brilliant patchwork of genres.

Yet the Lerners soon found that Darger emerges as a far more creative, prolific, and somehow sensitively disturbing artist in what could be called the parallel pictorial world he created, the erratic narrative of the hundreds of watercolor and pencil drawings, often with collage elements, that illustrate—or extend—the written world of *In the Realms of the Unreal*.[14] Illuminating dense, often meandering prose, the drawings cover the front and back of hundreds of long, pieced-together paper pages, usually two feet in height and some extending to twelve feet in length. Disregarding the constraints of traditional art-making, Darger developed his own style: uncannily complex watercolor and collage tableaux, incorporating hand-drawn, photographically reproduced, enlarged, and traced figures and landscape elements, repurposed from found source material, including comic strips, advertisements, and coloring books.

Darger never trained as an artist. His formal education ended at age twelve, when he was abruptly sent to the Asylum for Feeble-Minded Children in Lincoln, Illinois. An early reader, he had skipped from first to third grade upon entry to St. Patrick's Catholic School. When he was eight, his father became ill and entered a home for the aged. Darger was sent to a Catholic boys' home, the first of many interruptions in his education. After causing frequent disruptions in his classes with outbursts and aggressive behavior, he was deemed "feeble-minded" by a Chicago physician and sent to the Lincoln asylum. Though he described his five years there positively in his autobiography, Darger attempted two escapes following the news of his father's death in 1907. His third escape was successful. At age seventeen, he ran away with two other boys, catching a train to Decatur, Illinois. From Decatur, Darger walked the approximately 175 miles to Chicago, alone. In his autobiography, he recalls the journey's many days and nights.

One may imagine this trip as the source of Darger's intimate familiarity with extreme weather conditions. Arriving in Chicago, he obtained the first of many menial jobs in Chicago's Catholic hospitals and started writing his history of the imagined Glandeco-Angelinian War, which would become *In the Realms of the Unreal*. He was drafted to fight in World War I in 1917, offered a chance to experience the fierce combat he wrote about, but only got as far as basic training at a base in Texas. He was discharged in 1918 for "eye trouble," returning home to Chicago.

It is believed that Darger worked for approximately twenty years writing *Realms* and spent nearly five decades illustrating it. During the time that he worked on his illustrations, he was his own teacher, explorer, inventor, and researcher of those techniques most comfortable and effective for use in his daily work. He was a pioneer, exploring new technologies for his artistic ends. His figures are the products of an encyclopedic collection of clippings, photographic reproductions, and tracings. He made thick, numbered files of his materials, pasted newspaper comic strips such as *Little Annie Rooney* and *Mutt and Jeff* into the pages of old phone books, and repurposed the strong cardboard covers of children's coloring books as reference files containing clippings of poses and facial expressions, landscape elements, and so on. For the most part, Darger labeled the scrapbooks by subject, for example, identifying one volume as "Pictures of Fires big or small in which Firemen or persons lose their lives." Reflecting his preoccupation with American wars, Darger approached his fictional world as a historian detailing the battles of the Glandeco-Angelinian War. As a child, he had been fascinated by the details of Revolutionary and Civil War skirmishes, reciting dates and casualty figures. When he imagined his own war, fought over the right to kidnap and enslave children, he recorded every detail, created extensive lists of casualties for each battle, and painted the flags and portraits of the generals.

Darger adopted an institutional routine, with the hospital, his workplace, and the church as the important sites of his life. Remembering that confinement in an asylum shaped him as well, the next stage in the critical evaluation of Darger's work should be informed by Michel Foucault's examinations of the power institutions wield in shaping discourse. Often, before and after his work as a hospital janitor, he attended Catholic Mass in his local church. After retiring in 1963 due to extreme leg pain, he attended Mass and Communion every day, recording each visit in his diary.[15] If we were able to look at the imagery that surrounded him in the architectural environment of the church sanctuary, we would likely see a nearly nude person being crucified, winged creatures, and aureoles surrounding other figures' heads. We also might see in the stained-glass windows the dense color composition prevalent in Darger's work, which displays many reds and yellows, and, especially in the later work, presents very little unused space.

In a recent documentary on Andy Warhol, his screen-printed portraits are compared to the grid of icons he used to look at every Sunday morning attending Mass in his local church in Pittsburgh.[16] While this speculation provokes an intriguing stream of speculation, the parallels seem even more evident in Darger's work, since religious iconography is directly reflected in the repertoire of Christian motifs in *Realms*.

His apartment must have been a dense world of images, with its collection of framed, unframed, and cut-out pictures, small figurines standing on his mantel, his own works in progress, and the innumerable piles of newspapers, magazines, illustrated children's stories, and found photographs he accumulated, creating the setting of an artist's studio as image archive.

Examples of magazines and a painting manual featuring reproductions of fine art found in his apartment suggest Darger's non-hierarchical approach to images. The manual, *A Step-Ladder to Painting*, published in 1939, includes black and white reproductions of well-known paintings by Rembrandt, Titian, Cézanne, Eakins, and others. Michael Bonesteel has recognized the presence of a photographic reproduction of a nineteenth-century American landscape painting in Darger's *At Jennie Richee*. *While sending warning to their father watch night black cloud of coming storm through windows* (see pages 144–45). In this watercolor, the girls watch a lightning storm from three large windows. While two of the windows reveal a typical Darger storm, a third one, at the left, is actually a clipping of a painting by the artist Martin Johnson Heade. Darger's reproduction of *Thunder Storm on Narrangansett Bay* (1868) appeared in the February 1945 issue of *Ladies' Home Journal*, not long after the work was rediscovered and featured in an exhibition at the Museum of Modern Art on the Hudson River School.

———

After Darger's death, Nathan Lerner showed his work to unsuspecting friends and visiting curators, who had actually come to Webster Avenue to see Lerner's own important photography, beginning with work from the 1930s and including his influential experimental photos produced at the New Bauhaus and Chicago's Institute of Design, as well as in New York in the early 1940s.[17] Esther Sparks, head of the Prints and Drawings Department at the Art Institute of Chicago at the time, was one of the first curators to see Darger's preserved apartment and the expansive repository of watercolors. Darger's work was introduced to the public at Chicago's Hyde Park Art Center in 1977. Fifteen years later, it traversed the globe in the 1992 group show *Parallel Visions*, traveling to the Los Angeles County Museum of Art, Madrid's Museo Nacional Reina Sofía, Basel's Kunsthalle, and Tokyo's Setagaya Art Museum. The watercolors made headlines in a 1996 solo show at the Collection de l'art brut in Lausanne, Switzerland, where a large selection remains on permanent view. Also in 1996 a substantial survey, *The Unreality of Being*, was

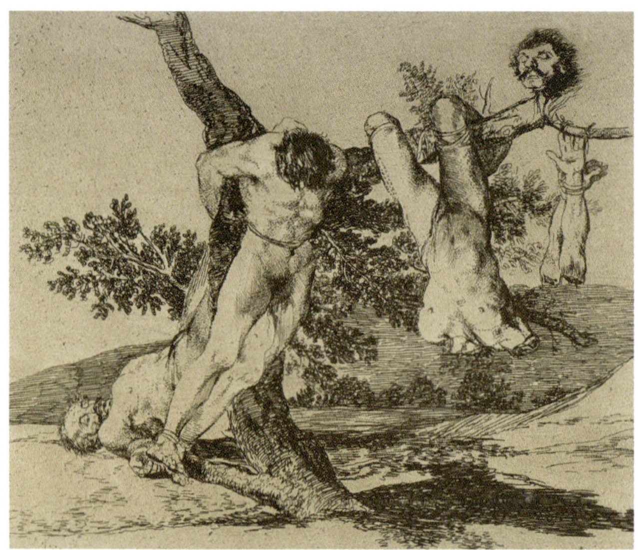

Francisco de Goya, *Grande hazaña! Con muertos!* (Heroic feat! Against the dead!)
[Disasters of War], plate 39, 1810–20. Etching and lavis, 6 ⅛ x 8 ⅛ in.
S. P. Avery Collection, The New York Public Library

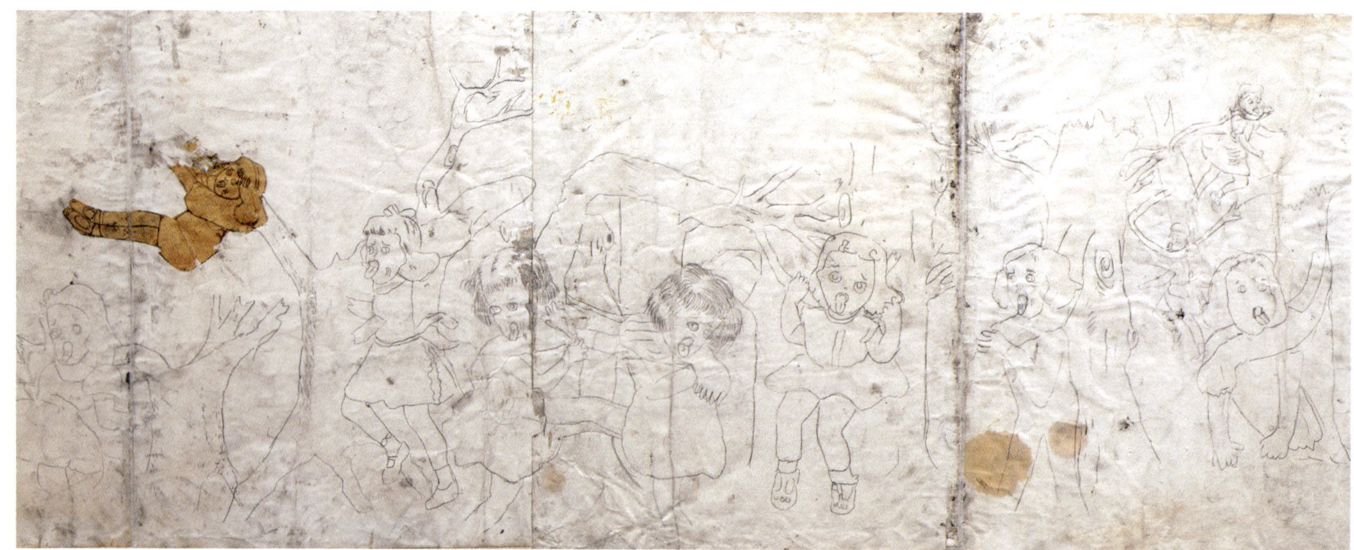

Henry Darger, Untitled (detail). Pencil and collage on pieced paper,
24 ½ x 102 in. Collection de l'art brut, Lausanne

organized by Stephen Prokopoff, director of the University of Iowa Museum of Art, where the exhibition of sixty-three watercolors originated. It traveled to the American Folk Art Museum in New York in 1997. Kiyoko Lerner donated Darger's manuscripts and personal archive, including the ephemera found in his room, to the museum in 2000. The opening of this new resource coincided with the first English-language publication of Darger's writing. The endlessly fascinating collection of excerpts, edited and introduced by Michael Bonesteel, provides a view into Darger's decades of work. The art historian and psychologist John MacGregor's seven-hundred-page critical study, published in 2002, breaks the life and works down to thematic chapters that provide a framework for understanding Darger. The award-winning 2004 documentary film *In the Realms of the Unreal*, by Jessica Yu, brought Darger to a much larger audience.

As the first retrospective in New York of Darger's work, *The Unreality of Being* became a pilgrimage site for art-

ists familiar with Darger's watercolors only from reproductions and those previously unaware of the artist. It was here that the artist Tony Oursler introduced me to Darger and I first became intrigued by his work. At that time, Oursler had just created several sculptural video installations that dealt with multiple personality disorder, split personalities, and the "acting out" or visualization of traumatic experiences. I remember looking at the polymorphous, hermaphroditic children with long hair, dressed like little girls, and instantly recalling some of Jake and Dinos Chapman's sculptures that had recently been on view in an exhibition at the Institute of Contemporary Arts, London.

In 2000, P.S. 1 Contemporary Art Center, an affiliate of the Museum of Modern Art, organized the exhibition *Disasters of War*, juxtaposing a selection of Darger's watercolors and the cycle of etchings by Francisco de Goya titled Disasters of War as well as *What the Hell I–IX*, Jake and Dinos Chapman's large-scale photographs of their 1999 sculp-

ture *Hell*. Part of the Saatchi collection, the sculpture was famously destroyed in 2004 in a fire at an East London art storage warehouse. *Hell*, a diorama populated by thirty thousand two-inch figures, portrayed Nazis and mutant warriors engaging in apocalyptic battle scenes. It was originally displayed in nine glass vitrines assembled in the shape of an inverted swastika.

Visiting the Chapmans in their London studio when preparing the show, I saw the artists and a few assistants painting by hand each individual face of the thousands of soldiers in the apocalyptic, panoramic sculpture. Jake Chapman mentioned that the consuming process of working on the piece was like writing a monumentally long text or working on the detailing of a gigantic print pattern.

Even more shocking than the notorious Chapman piece were the Disasters of War. *Los Desastres de la Guerra* is the title that the Academy of San Fernando gave to Goya's set of eighty prints depicting horrors of the 1807–14 Peninsular War, in which Spain fought for its independence against

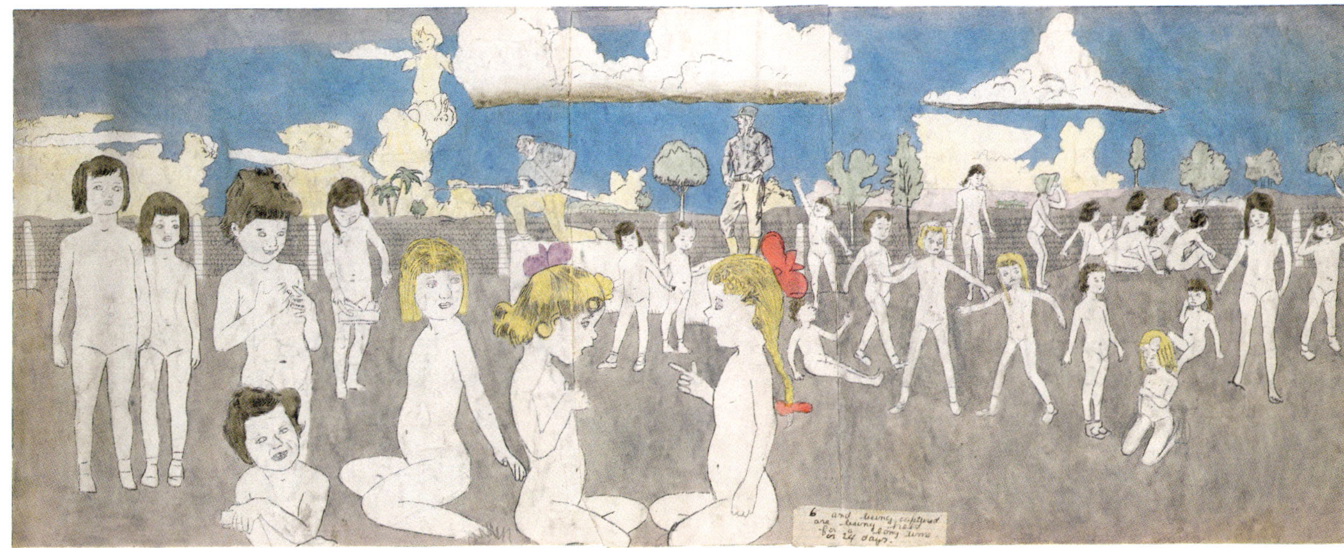

Henry Darger, *At Jennie Richee. They are placed in concentration camp with crowd of child prisoners.*
Watercolor, pencil, and carbon tracing on pieced paper, approx. 19 x 48 in. Collection Kiyoko Lerner

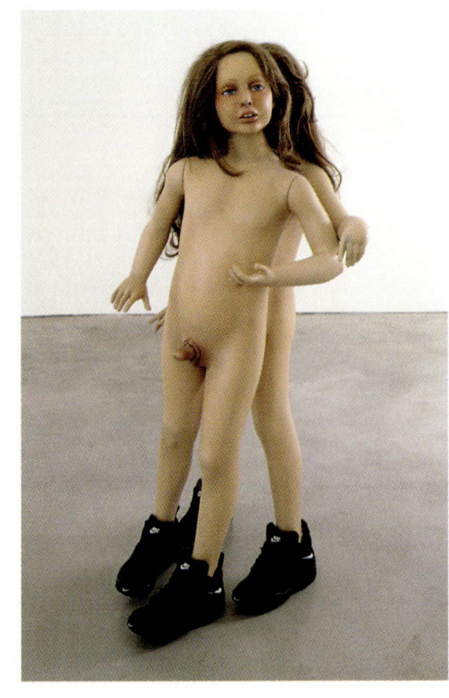

Jake & Dinos Chapman, *Shuffle,* 1996.
Fiberglass resin and paint. 50 x 24 x 23 in.

Napoleon's armies. Published by the Academy in 1863, the prints were labeled by Goya as "Fatal consequences of the bloody war in Spain against Bonaparte and other striking *caprichos*."[18] They depict a great deal of spilled blood on both sides. The viewer witnesses executions of monks and women raped amid corpses. In some prints, the Spanish are the victims, in others, the French. The socialist historian Gwyn A. Williams describes the depiction of graphic brutality in the prints as conveying the absurdity of war: "The impression is of mountains of corpses, flight, wrecked groups of wounded; people are almost portrayed as victims of natural disaster."[19] Accordingly Goya seemed perfect company for Darger. The graphic nature of Darger's violence is only heightened by his seeming naiveté. For example, Darger does not appear to have understood rape, explaining it as an act of disembowelment.[20]

At P.S. 1, Darger's watercolors, Goya's prints, and the Chapmans' photographs shared the third-floor galleries, three large rooms with dark blue exhibition walls. In Darger's writing and watercolors, brutal violence is often juxtaposed with playful pastoral scenes. Drawing from accounts of some of the bloodiest wars in American history, Darger painted executions and dead soldiers. Hangings and strangling of young girls, their figures adapted from coloring books, and epic battles accompanied by mounds of bleeding corpses convey war's senselessness. As in Goya's prints, the startlingly horrific violence is deeply alienating and at the same time affecting. John MacGregor describes the role of violence in the artist's oeuvre: "While Darger's vision of war incorporates elements of romanticism and patriotic idealism, even allowing for occasional humor, his ultimate objective is the portrayal of a world wracked and torn, of civilization destroyed, earth in upheaval, and mankind inundated with its own blood."[21]

After the Chapman photographs finally arrived at P.S. 1, many viewers commented that this was the first exhibition that showed Darger within the canon of the fine arts, in a historical framework embracing Goya's prints but also contemporary practice. The P.S. 1 exhibition had originated at KW Institute for Contemporary Art in Berlin, where the press feedback was immense and the audience extraordinarily large. The Darger portion of the exhibition toured to Sweden, Japan, Poland, and Switzerland, among other countries, and a modest book was published that reproduced the watercolor panoramas in a cartoonish, quasicinematic, animation-like way, emphasizing Darger's fictive realm rather than the materiality of the works as art objects, thus allowing insight into a very complex, intricately detailed visual world.

The book explicitly aimed to place Darger outside of the outsider context. "Perhaps it is not so much a matter of whether or not Darger belongs in the Outsider art category, but more a matter of whether that category can truly contain him," Michael Bonesteel had written in the introduction to his survey of Darger's work.[22] Following the unexpected discovery of Darger's stockpile of diaries, manuscripts, and illustrations, and the first exhibitions of his work, Darger was only gradually recognized as one of America's most important self-taught artists. This is perhaps surprising; at first glance, Darger's biography is that of the consummate outsider. He suffered a difficult and lonely childhood without the benefits of a stable family life or complete formal education. He spent his adult life transcribing the world of his imagination, working menial jobs and keeping mostly to himself. He painted without any formal training, inventing new techniques as his work required them. He was eccentric and self-involved in the eyes of neighbors, who remember him talking loudly late at night, alone in his third-floor apartment. For Darger, talking in voices was a way of having company.

Darger can now be found in catalogs and exhibitions of American outsider artists alongside Joseph Elmer Yoakum, whose landscapes in pencil, pastels, and watercolors share a certain kinship with Darger's expansive landscapes, and J. Richardson, whose Civil War drawings, dating from the early 1920s, resemble Darger's war scenes.[23] However, as the range of his watercolors and the sensibility revealed by his autobiography suggest, Darger does not quite conform to the conventions of the outsider artist, and some of the earliest writing on his work struggled with its characterization as outsider art.[24]

Darger was certainly not outside American popular culture; he read every newspaper, magazine, paperback, and comic he could get his hands on. Like so many of his contemporaries, he clipped pictures of celebrities from newspapers and magazines, incorporating the visage of the star football quarterback Joe Namath into one collage. Far from the romantic image of the solitary artist working from his imagination in isolation, Darger had an insatiable appetite for the novels of Charles Dickens and L. Frank Baum. Drawing on works from the whole spectrum

of late nineteenth- and early twentieth-century popular literature, many of the passages in *Realms* read as the work of a hyperaware media flâneur or (early) data dandy, digesting his culture through the act of daily recording and fictionalizing.

As an adult poring over newspapers for material, Darger read horrific accounts of World War I, the sinking of the Titanic, the Great Depression, World War II, the bombings of Dresden and Coventry and the detonation of the atomic bombs over Hiroshima and Nagasaki, and the assassination of John F. Kennedy. One cannot imagine that the extreme violence and national pain described in the newspapers did not find their way into Darger's imagination. One watercolor depicting kidnapped children contained by a high barbed-wire fence is ominously titled, *At Jennie Richee. They are placed in concentration camp with crowd of child prisoners* (page 17). His descriptions of child slavery lack the humor of his other chapters. He explains that the rise of child slavery in his imagined world "drove many to insanity, and also hundreds to commit suicide. Mothers fearing the horrors of child slavery, and that their own would be victims, murdered their own children and then themselves," returning to the double loss he suffered as a child, torn from both mother and sister.[25]

The full extent of Darger's sources will never be known. The materials discarded as trash before the discovery of his artwork cannot be recovered. The songs and poems Darger invented in *Realms* reflect his appreciation of popular music. But Darger's extensive phonograph collection, never cataloged, was sold.[26]

The poet John Ashbery, whose 1999 book-length poem *Girls on the Run* (the opening lines appear on page 7) was inspired by a visit to Darger's 1996 exhibition in Lausanne, *Dans les royaumes de l'irréel*, identified with Darger's interest in little girls. Interviewed in 1999, Ashbery seemingly channels Darger, recalling, "I was fascinated by little girls when I was a little boy, and their clothes and their

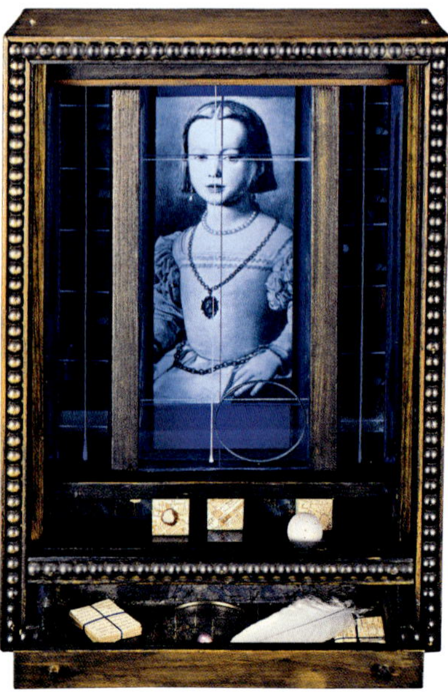

Joseph Cornell, *Medici Princess.* Painted wood, photomechanical reproductions, painted and colored glass, painted paper, string, cork, metal rings, plastic balls, and a feather, in glass-faced, painted wood box, 17 ⅝ x 12 ¼ x 4 ¾ in. Hirshhorn Museum and Sculpture Garden, Smithsonian Institution, Washington, D.C., Museum Purchase, 1979

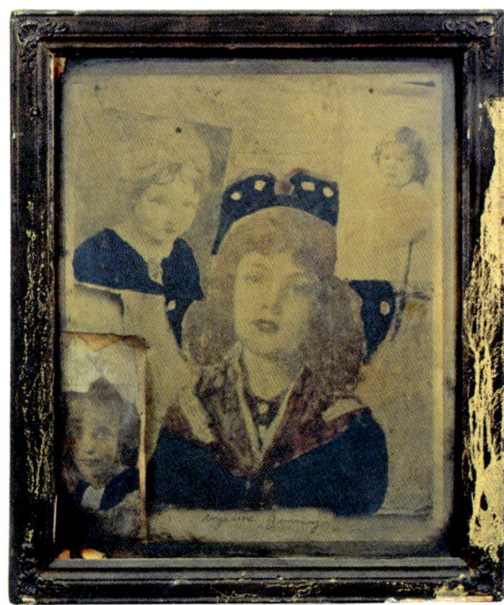

Henry Darger, *Angeline Jennings.* Watercolor, pencil, collage, and carbon tracing on paper, 12 ½ x 10 ½ in. Intuit Center for Creative and Outsider Art, Chicago

games and their dolls appealed to me much more than what little boys were doing. Therefore I was sort of ostracized." The poet, who has also made found image collages for decades (exhibited for the first time in 2008 at Tibor de Nagy Gallery), explained the role of children's literature and comics in his early life: "I read Nancy Drew books and the Oz books and comics like 'Little Orphan Annie.' I use a lot of imagery from comic strips like 'Popeye' and so on, because lying on the floor looking at these huge colored comic supplements was the first literary and visual art experience I ever had, and in a way it has somehow remained one of the strongest influences."[27]

The Abstract Expressionist Adolph Gottlieb described a similar artist's education in a 1967 interview. Asked if there was any exposure to art in his family background, he replied, "Not at all. No, I was brought up with comic strips and the Gibson books on the library table. Charles Henry Gibson. . . ." The interviewer, Dorothy Seckler, asks: "Where did you begin? By copying any of these things?" "Oh sure," answers Gottlieb, "I copied Mutt and Jeff."[28] A long-running daily comic strip created by Bud Fisher in 1907, *Mutt and Jeff* is prominent in Darger's collection of cut-out comic strips. The bumbling friends also appear as characters in *Realms*. Though unrelated to the comic-strip figures, they are often compared to them. In one passage, Darger even suggests that his Mutt and Jeff characters, Professional International Spies known as Mr. Mutt and Mr. Jeff, inspired Bud Fisher to create his strip.[29]

When considering the canon of twentieth-century American art, one has to ask why the untrained Darger is more often than others considered an outsider. If the word "outsider" is replaced by the term "self-taught," as a first step, and as a second the word "self-taught" is replaced by "autodidact," the whole discourse shifts. Then we might look at the oeuvres of Joseph Cornell or Jean-Michel Basquiat. Like Darger, Cornell and Basquiat never graduated from high school and never formally studied art. In any

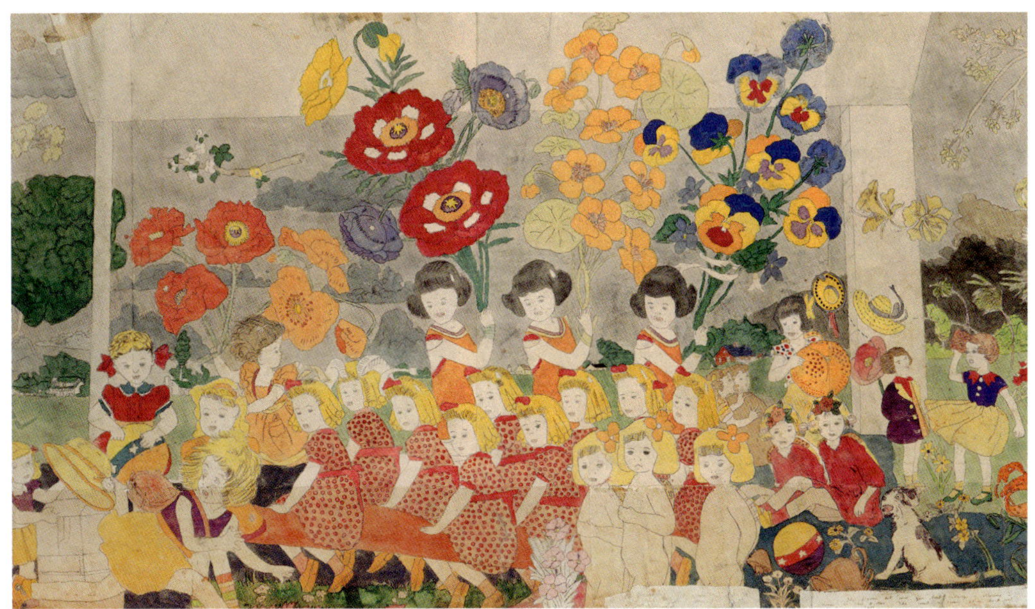

Henry Darger, *[Storm] brewing. This is not a strawberry the little girl is carrying. It comes from a paradise tree . . .* (detail). Watercolor, pencil, carbon tracing, and collage on pieced paper, 30 x 125 in. Collection de l'art brut, Lausanne

aspect of his life, Darger seemed most engaged with the world around him through his art. He was an outsider as a poor custodian working at Chicago hospitals. Few noticed him working long hours and obsessively performing repetitive tasks like wrapping bandages. Barely making a living, he poured every spare cent into his art-making. All of his life, Darger existed just beyond traditional institutions like school and family, growing up with very little of either. He depended on regular church attendance for a weak association to a world he had committed to in his mind and art but had little contact with in his everyday life.

Joseph Cornell's life mirrors Darger's in certain aspects, though, unlike Darger's, Cornell's artworks were widely exhibited during his lifetime. It is in his emergence as an artist that Cornell is most like Darger. As a child, Cornell, born in 1903, was extremely protective of his youngest brother, Robert, who suffered from cerebral palsy. When Cornell was fifteen, his father died of a red-blood-cell disease diagnosed as "pernicious anemia," and the tight-knit upper-middle-class family had to come to terms with its

reduced circumstances. Responding to this trauma, Cornell became meditative and withdrew from age-appropriate activities. Describing a Houdini-inspired magic show Joseph performed for his family four months after his father's death, the biographer Deborah Solomon writes, "Already he had taken refuge in what might be called a fantasy of eternal innocence, imagining a world untouched by time or adult experience."[30] At the urging of his father's former employer, Joseph entered the Phillips Academy, the prestigious preparatory school in Andover, Massachusetts. Enrolled from age fourteen to eighteen, Cornell never graduated and unlike his ambitious peers, he did not apply to colleges in his third year.

The earliest known work by Cornell is a *Mutt and Jeff* cartoon drawn in the margins of a letter sent to his brother Robert while Joseph was away at school. While Darger's interest in comics is shared by Cornell, he developed a mature technique that had little in common with Darger's. Both may have scavenged publications for images to incorporate in their art, but Darger was primarily a draftsman who sometimes employed collage and Cornell almost never drew. Cornell's well-known boxes generate a shallow depth through their actual interiors, while Darger depicts illusionistic space, sometimes deeply receding, in his watercolors.

The Japanese artist Yayoi Kusama lived and worked in New York from 1956 to 1973. A friend of Joseph Cornell, and his "lover" at one time, she suffers from hallucinations, translating them into large-scale sculpture and installations, as well as paintings and drawings. While living in New York she would work obsessively, day and night, for extended periods. Her symbolic order, derived from her visions, involves the repetition of polka dots, transforming a cute, decorative gesture into an obsessive, viruslike motif. Like that of Cornell and Darger, Kusama's art has been rapidly assimilated into art history. Asked by the interviewer Grady Turner how she may have been affected by being eclipsed by male artists like Claes Oldenburg, Warhol, or Lucas Samaras, working in the American Pop movement at the same time as she did, Kusama replied, "Those male artists are simply imitating my illness." She recalled that Oldenburg's wife admitted to borrowing one of Kusama's ideas for Oldenburg's entry in a 1962 group show at the Green Gallery.[31] The Pop movement itself was defined by appropriation, although not necessarily of this kind. Nevertheless, Kusama thrived on the energy of New York and its rapidly changing art scene as it responded to American popular culture.

One must not forget that Henry Darger was a contemporary of Walt Disney and a witness to the rise of Mickey Mouse. Disney was an artist and entrepreneur who changed the perception of American pop culture and had a lasting effect on how the visual world of the twentieth century evolved; his cell animation style is reimagined in Darger's repetition of figures in a single plane. A watercolor like *[Storm] brewing . . .* (see page 19) is animated by an entire sequence of action beneath the ominous rain clouds. Darger populated the scene with many girls, though the horizontal tableau also can be read left to right like the Eadweard Muybridge photographic motion studies that gave birth to modern animation.

Born in 1901, Walt Disney also never completed his formal education, leaving school at sixteen to enlist in World War I. Rejected because he was under-age, he joined the Red Cross, driving an ambulance in France and witnessing the war's worst horrors. Returning home, he started his first company, making animated commercials and beginning his revolutionary series of innovative contributions to the animation and movie world. Returning to our title, "American Innocence," one may imagine that without Disney an entire spectrum of current practice is scarcely imaginable, from the surgically self-designed figure of Michael Jackson (who in some mug shots published when he was accused of child molestation looks like a three-dimensional portrait of Mickey Mouse) to an artist like Laurel Nakadate. In Jeff Koons's *Michael Jackson and Bubbles,* Jackson is redone in porcelain as a giant plaything with his arm around Bubbles, a monkey. Like the giant castle that welcomes visitors to Walt Disney's theme parks, Koons's sculpture evokes America's libidinous fascination with the big toy. The coloring-book imagery of Darger's watercolors similarly recalls the libidinous character of a toy object, instantly associating his project with the children's activity of filling in coloring-book pages, yet on an epic scale.

Walt Disney acquired the rights to eleven of Baum's Oz books in 1954. He sought repeatedly to make film adaptations of them over the rest of his career, beginning many versions that were later abandoned. *The Rainbow Road to Oz,* Disney's most nearly realized Oz adaptation, would have starred the child actors of the Mickey Mouse Club. Annette Funicello was set to play Ozma.

The question of film's influence on Darger's work is largely speculative. Looking at one watercolor in which the Vivian girls try to escape by rolling themselves in floor rugs, Michael Bonesteel points to a similar scene in the 1925 film adaptation of the comic strip *Little Annie Rooney,* starring Mary Pickford. The female protagonists of *Realms,* particularly Annie Aronburg, with their curly blond locks and eternally adolescent faces, remind one of Pickford and Shirley Temple, stars with whom America had its own obsession. One might consider Darger's worshiping of little girls as an antecedent of the child beauty pageants, objectifying girls as young as four or five, that became notorious with the murder of JonBenét Ramsey in 1996. Darger explicitly mentions Charlie Chaplin and Ben Turpin in *Realms.*[32] One prominent reference to motion pictures may indicate Darger's awareness of early pornographic media, including film reels. Describing the treatment of pretty women and children enslaved by the Glandelinians, Darger writes that despite being "worse than the vilest villains, . . . none of the Glandelinians tried to force their love on the pretty women and girls as is written in other books and particularly in moving pictures stories."[33]

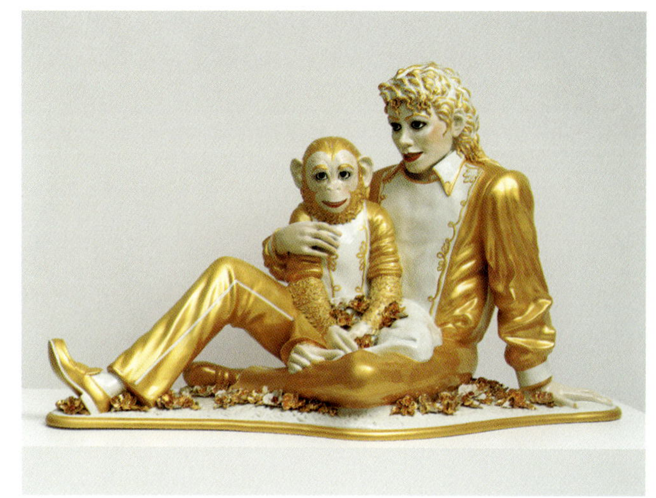

Jeff Koons, *Michael Jackson and Bubbles,* 1988.
Porcelain, 42 x 70 ½ x 32 ½ in.

Much of the hardship in *Realms* was created by Darger in response to the loss of an image, a photograph reproduced in a newspaper. The character of the tragic heroine Annie Aronburg is based on Elsie Paroubek, a kidnapped and later murdered girl whose picture, clipped from the paper, Henry Darger cherished and lost. John MacGregor presents evidence that Darger covered his walls with newspaper stories of kidnapped and murdered children.[34] The violent details of the children's deaths in *Realms* suggest that he may have embellished newspaper accounts with his own frequent visions of disembowelings and beheadings.

A collage-drawing fragment of Glandelinian soldiers infiltrating downtown Chicago is one of the few depictions of Chicago's architecture in his art. Despite the fact that Henry Darger lived in Chicago for most of his life, the vast majority of his depictions do not reflect the vertical nature of the city. Along with the urban view reproduced on this page, *At Battle of Mic-Hollester Run . . .* (see page 48) is a rare example in his work of a vertically oriented watercolor. During Darger's lifetime his native city pioneered the building of skyscrapers. Darger must have seen them on the horizon from his apartment on Chicago's North Side, whose porch looked south toward the Loop. But in his illustrations, verticality is limited to gigantic flowers, the stalactites and stalagmites in the few depictions of caves, and the jagged flashes of lightning he renders in scenes with storms.

This again tells us something about the connection between Darger's working methods and his compositions. Because of the processes he used to reproduce his figures, it was extremely difficult for Darger to compose in perspectival depth, since that would have required the capacity to flexibly scale the figures at an array of sizes. But he had no practical way of doing this. He didn't have the confidence to draw figures freehand, and his method of photographically scaling them was laborious and expensive, requiring that he send material out for photo-processing and enlarging. Thus he was forced to adopt a shallow horizontal format that would permit him to present many figures at just a few standard sizes across an entire composition.

Although the narrative panoramic format of his watercolor tableaux may be a byproduct of necessity, it nevertheless suggests an affinity with cinematic vision, which may help to explain our attraction to his work. When he repeatedly uses the stenciled, photocopied, and traced motif of a specific girl in one scene, the sheer multiplication of the image with minor variations, often lined up or staggered, necessarily reminds the viewer of techniques of stop-motion film animation, in which continuous movement is created by filming the same figures repeatedly, with slight changes from one image to the next. The dominant role that cinematic narrative and imagery, loops, repetition, and exaggeration play in today's society has certainly contributed to making Darger more of an insider as all too many (media) images battle for more than short-lived attention.

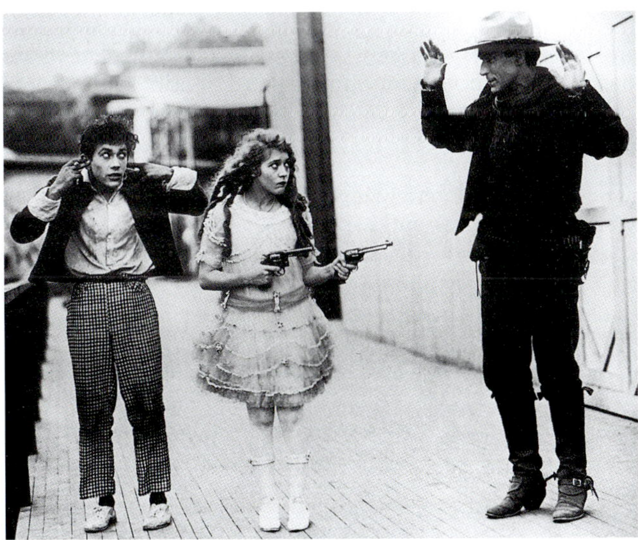

Jack and Mary Pickford with the cowboy star William S. Hart in *Heart o' the Hills*, 1919, directed by Sidney A. Franklin

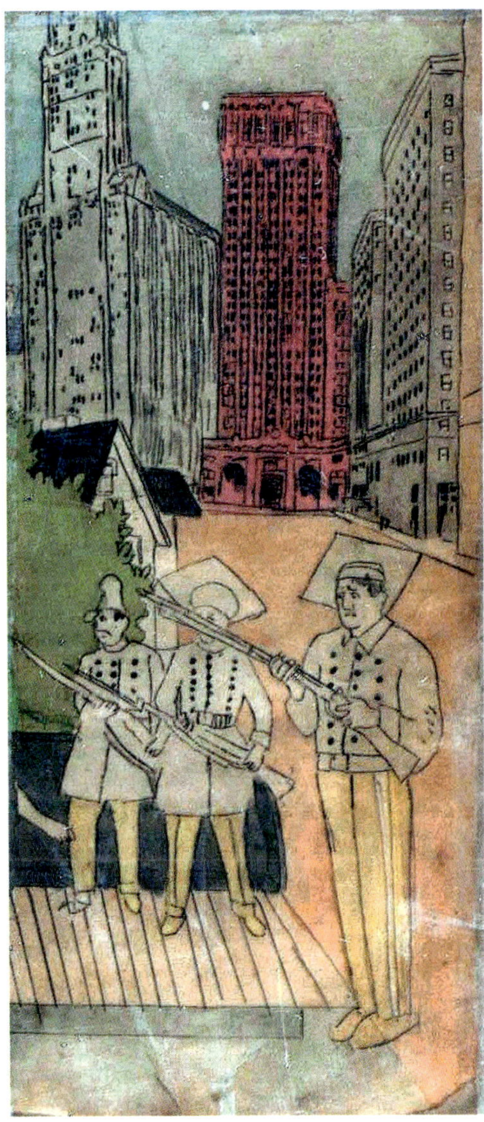

Henry Darger, Untitled (Glandelinian soldiers in downtown Chicago). Pencil with collage on paper, 22 x 9 ¾ in. Private collection

Sean Landers, *Fart*, 1993 (detail). Oil on canvas, 84 x 112 ½ in.

2: CONNECTIONS

Obsession

Henry Darger's writing and illustrating projects, devoted to illuminating an imagined world, consumed practically his entire adult life. Based on the records he kept, he rarely went a day without writing or painting. Nathan Lerner, in his foreword to John MacGregor's 2002 study of Darger, describes this manic private life: "Every minute counted for him, and he did something, not necessarily something of any importance, but he just worked!"[35] Listing Darger's furious activity—scavenging, cutting and collaging, creating scrapbooks, recording the inaccuracies of daily meteorological reports, finding string to wind into balls, writing, rewriting, and illustrating— Lerner concludes, "Somewhere he got the idea that you must not waste a minute." So much so that if he could not

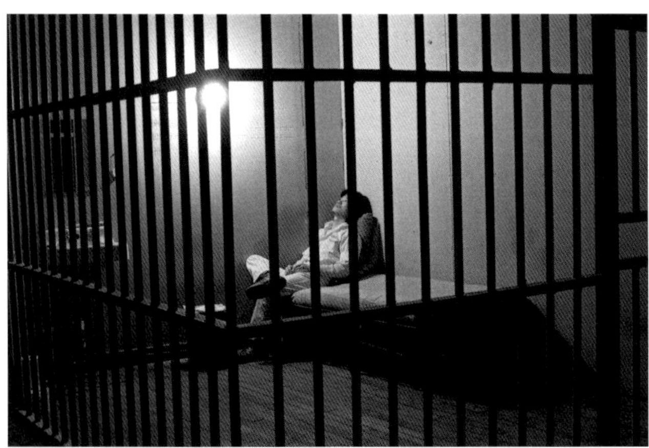

Tehching Hsieh, *One Year Performance 1978–1979*. Life image.

find anything else to do, Darger would "take out the Bible and just start copying it."[36]

Darger filled every waking moment before and after his hospital work with these endless tasks. After describing the conclusion of the war, completing *In the Realms of the Unreal*, and binding the typewritten draft in 1932, he returned to the text, rearranging and adding to the narrative over many years.

Darger wrote that he didn't want to grow up, and he seemingly got stuck in the process of working on his major work. Like a tape recording on a multiple-decade loop, he didn't finish *Realms*, choosing instead to rewrite and recombine, creating alternative plots and endings. In 1963, the deteriorating condition of his legs and his poor eyesight, which had been the ostensible reason for his dismissal from the army during World War I, finally made it impossible for him to continue working. It was as if his life had been moving in cinematic slow motion. One may imagine that as long as Darger didn't finish, he might remain the child he wished to be. To identify with the poor girls in his writings, he needed to give them penises in his depictions of them. For this lonely man, art-making was a way of living.

The daily necessity of simply dealing with life as a period of time to be spent can produce innovative artistic strategies. The Taiwanese-American artist Tehching Hsieh has only made eight works over his career, five of which were one-year-long performances between 1978 and 1986. In an interview with Adrian Heathfield, he discusses the long duration of his works: "It doesn't really matter how I spend time: time is still passing. Wasting time is my basic attitude to life; it is a gesture of dealing with the absurdity between life and time."[37] If one were to watch one of these performances unfold over a year, one would be painfully aware of watching life itself transpire. Earlier in the same interview, Tehching expresses the basic premise underlying all of the One Year perfor-

22

mances: "life as a life sentence."[38] Darger's obsession with all-encompassing tasks can at times remind one of Sisyphus. One might look at his weather journal, maintained daily for ten years, and consider it a waste of time. But as Tehching explains, living itself is an act of wasting time. One merely chooses activities to fill it with, Darger's being no more arbitrary than any other.

Darger started his daily weather journal late in life, maintaining it for a decade from December 31, 1957, to December 31, 1967. The American artist Ad Reinhardt decided to create only sixty-by-sixty-inch monochrome black paintings for the last decade of his life, from 1957 to his death in 1967. From 1966 to the present, the artist On Kawara has created Date Paintings. Each white-on-black painted date is the same format and each is completed on the date depicted. An ongoing project born in 1969 out of his work on the Date Paintings, Kawara's *One Million Years* records sequential years in book form, currently spanning twenty volumes. Like *In the Realms of the Unreal, One Million Years* could span any number of volumes, relinquishing any structure that requires an end. To mark the passing of time in such a purposeful way is an unusual practice in a society that is characterized by attention-deficit disorder.

Other examples of long-term strategies include those of the German artist Hanne Darboven. In a representative work, *7 Tafeln, II* (7 Panels, II) of 1972/73, she drew the same wavy lines on every line of 245 pages of paper. The pencil lines form an index of the artist living; they are simply the evidence of her living, breathing, being in time. The Polish-French artist Roman Opalka has been working solely on the painting series *OPALKA 1965/1-∞* since 1965. For this epic work, he began counting aloud in Polish in 1965. Each day he loads a paintbrush with white paint and records his counting across the canvas until the paint thins. He then reloads the brush and starts with the next number in the sequence. Today, he has passed five million and will continue until his death. Daily photographs, sound recordings of his counting, and the canvases are all part of the counting project.

Sean Landers's work in the 1990s can be seen as the uncontrollable byproduct of male hysteria, as that term is described by Arthur and Marilouise Kroker.[39] It fits with Darger's incessant drive to work. In his text paintings and videos dating to the early nineties, Landers's stream-of-consciousness ramblings, at once embarrassingly intimate and distant, reveal an artist struggling with the act of making art. "Now I'm a happy victim of my own charade," he wrote in the painting *The Booby*, an oil on linen piece from 1998. "I figure that it's better to be a sucker who makes something than a wise guy who is too cautious to make anything at all."[40]

Disasters

All of this scenery of disaster may seem interesting, and worth exploring for, by many, I suppose, but it has left me a forlorn melancholic feeling, something of a feeling that tells of a sad occurrence of a dreadful event of the past which the world itself could not atone for.
—Henry Darger[41]

Much of *In the Realms of the Unreal*, and in fact Darger's entire oeuvre, literary and visual, is devoted to describing disasters or weather or disasters caused by weather. *The History of My Life*, Darger's handwritten autobiography, begun in his mid-seventies, is well over five thousand pages long (see pages 281–313). Just over two hundred of the pages address Darger's life. On manuscript page 206, he finishes his life story and without interruption begins weaving a fantasy involving a tornado named Sweetie Pie that destroys real and imagined locations. His obsession with the apocalyptic storm is all-consuming.

As MacGregor notes, Darger's writing style undergoes a transformation in the description of Sweetie Pie. Stuck on an endless loop, he returns on page after page to "the same events, images, the same questions and concerns, as though, caught in the tornado's rotating funnel, he is spiraling wildly out of control."[42]

Having read Baum's Oz books, Darger knew that extreme weather conditions could play a transformative role in fiction. In Darger's landscapes, as in J. M. W. Turner's, weather is inscribed with emotion and personality. Darger carried this belief in nature over into reality. The Sweetie Pie tornado is a natural event he supposedly witnessed in spring 1906. As the story of the storm balloons with more and more of Darger's imagination, it reflects his late-life concerns. In this way, it might be more autobiographical than any factual account could be.

In the Bible, a change in the weather can be evidence of God's presence. Storms and natural disasters punish sinners in Genesis, as when God destroys Sodom and Gomorrah. "Then the Lord rained upon Sodom and upon Gomorrah brimstone and fire from the Lord out of Heaven" (Genesis 19:24). As MacGregor writes, the tornado's "wholesale destruction of religious institutions, churches, convents, and orphanages, along with the clergy and children who occupy them" prompts Darger to ask, "Why did the Good God allow the most greatest tornado catastrophe, the most destructive the world has ever seen?"[43] Throughout his life, Darger verbally questioned and argued with God. Neighbors recall hearing him yelling and cursing alone in his room. In his writing, the weather is a powerful force often equated with God. He writes in his diary, "Bad and insulting toward God because He is holding back the rain." He blamed God for his own misfortune and declining health, recording in his April 16, 1968, diary entry: "Had trouble again with the twine. Mad enough to wish I was a bad tornado. Swore at God. Yet go to three morning masses. Only cooled down

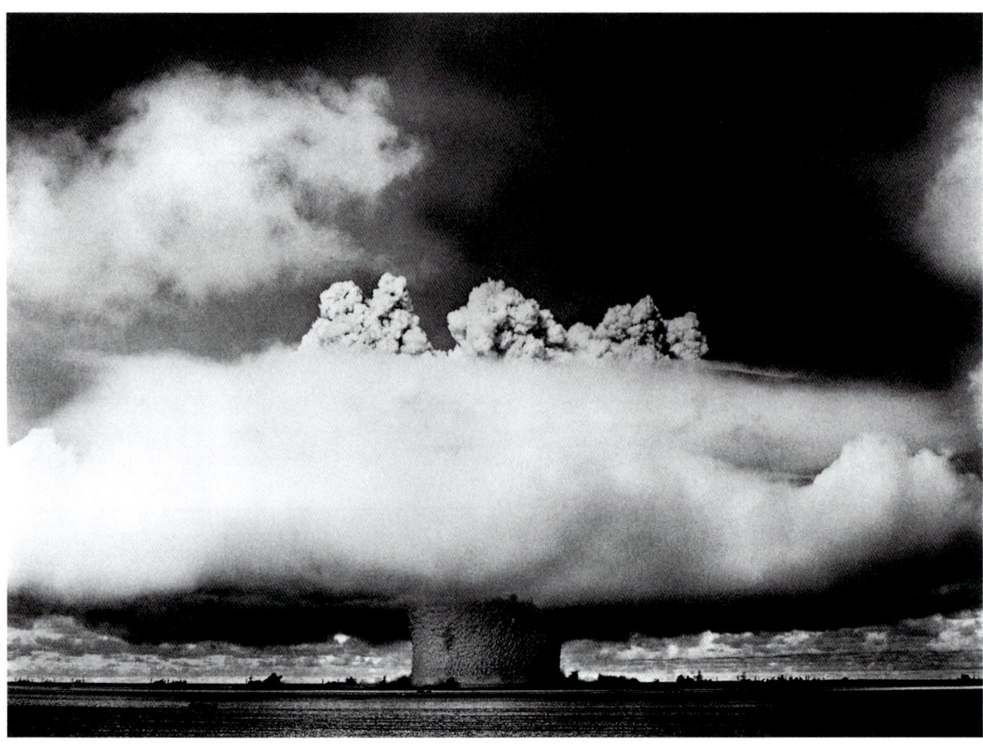

Bruce Conner, *Crossroads,* 1976.
35mm film, black and white
with sound, 36 min.

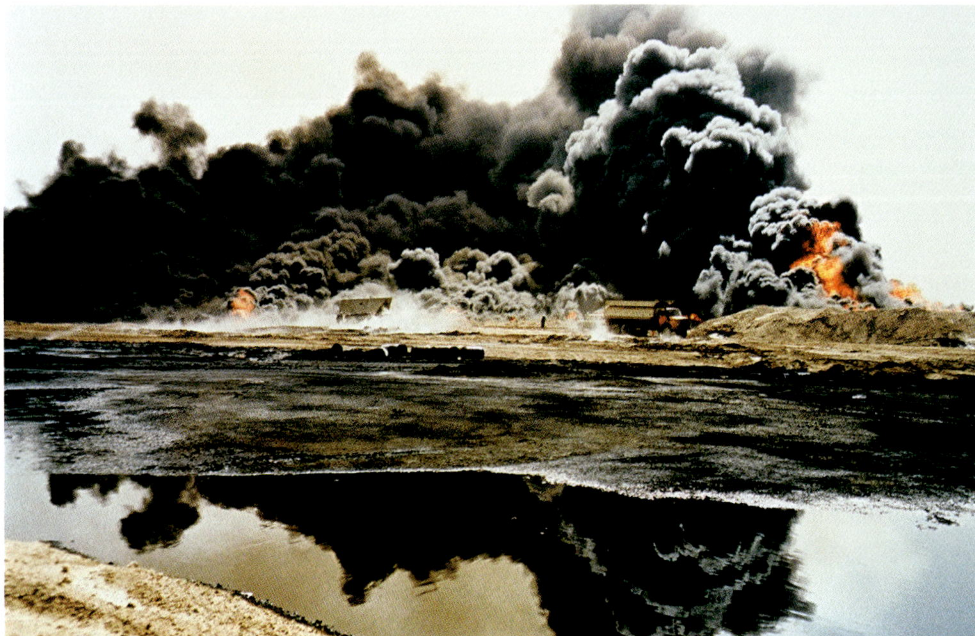

Werner Herzog, *And a Smoke Arose—*
Lessons of Darkness, 1992.
16mm film transferred to DVD,
sound, color, 5 min.

by late afternoon. Am I a real enemy of the cross or a very very Sorry Saint?"[44] This diary entry dates from the time he wrote his autobiography, his final literary effort. He records working on it through 1971, and the incomplete manuscript was left behind when he moved to St. Augustine's Home for the Aged in 1972.

Born in MacPherson, Kansas, in 1933, the artist Bruce Conner spent his childhood amid farmland threatened by extreme weather, from dangerous tornadoes to droughts. In *Crossroads* (1976), Conner loops United States government archival footage of the nuclear bomb tests at Bikini Atoll. The mushroom cloud grows to enormous proportions and then disappears twenty-seven times in Conner's editing, somehow removing the sense of reality. Like Darger's endless loop of Sweetie Pie, whose destruction is described for thousands of pages, Conner's appropriation of the footage, repeating the bomb's detonation at different angles and speeds, makes for a mesmerizing, dislocating film. Having lived through the period when Hiroshima and Nagasaki were bombed and read the newspaper reports of the consequent devastation and death, Darger may have internalized the destructive power of the mushroom cloud. His nickname for the tornado, Sweetie Pie, is, like "Little Boy," the bomb dropped on Hiroshima on August 6, 1945, an eerily endearing name for an instrument of mass death. The artist Robert Longo, whose studio is located in Lower Manhattan, created huge black charcoal drawings of mushroom clouds, recapturing the blasts that were reported to the world through black-and-white newspaper photographs. While not animated like Conner's film, Longo's drawings inevitably recall the clip in the viewer's mind, even seeming to flicker.

In the New Museum of Contemporary Art's 2008 exhibition *After Nature,* a postapocalyptic landscape as seen through smoke-filled air was projected on a large central screen. The work was Werner Herzog's *And a Smoke Arose—Lessons of Darkness* (1992), composed from aerial footage of a very real landscape, the flaming oil fields of Kuwait in the wake of the first Gulf War. Even with that knowledge, we can barely believe that we are watching a real place and not a computer-generated graphic. Herzog's footage, displayed during the more recent war in Iraq, emerged as a damning postscript to it. As if he or she were a soldier in an invading army surveying damage, the viewer is taken on an aerial tour of hell on earth. One can see reflections of Darger's own ideas of war in the burning landscape. In *Realms,* General Hanson Vivian explains to war correspondents covering what might appear as a noble fight for freedom, "Hell has no place here, and if it was here, it would literally flee from the horrors of this greatest of wars."[45]

Restagings

Dead Troops Talk (a vision after an ambush of a Red Army patrol, near Moqor, Afghanistan, winter 1986), a large-scale photo work by the Canadian artist Jeff Wall, presented as a transparency in a light box, appears at first glance to be an amazing piece of war photojournalism, the aftermath of a deadly ambush of a Red Army patrol. The figures vaguely recall art-historical poses and the rock-strewn, nearly monochromatic setting highlights the red blood trickling down the faces and uniforms of the soldiers. However, moving in closely, one becomes aware of the macabre surrealism of Wall's staged scene: the casualties have come to life and appear to be talking with one another. The result of an elaborate production process involving sets, makeup, costumes, and actors, the work is a digital collage of small, staged shots. Wall, like Darger, builds his monstrous scene from his memory and imagination. He has internalized the conventions of war photography and military violence and created this absurdist tribute.

The Vietnamese-American artist An-My Lê's photographs of the Iraq War are in a similar mode. Her putative documentary photographs of Iraq are shot in California at

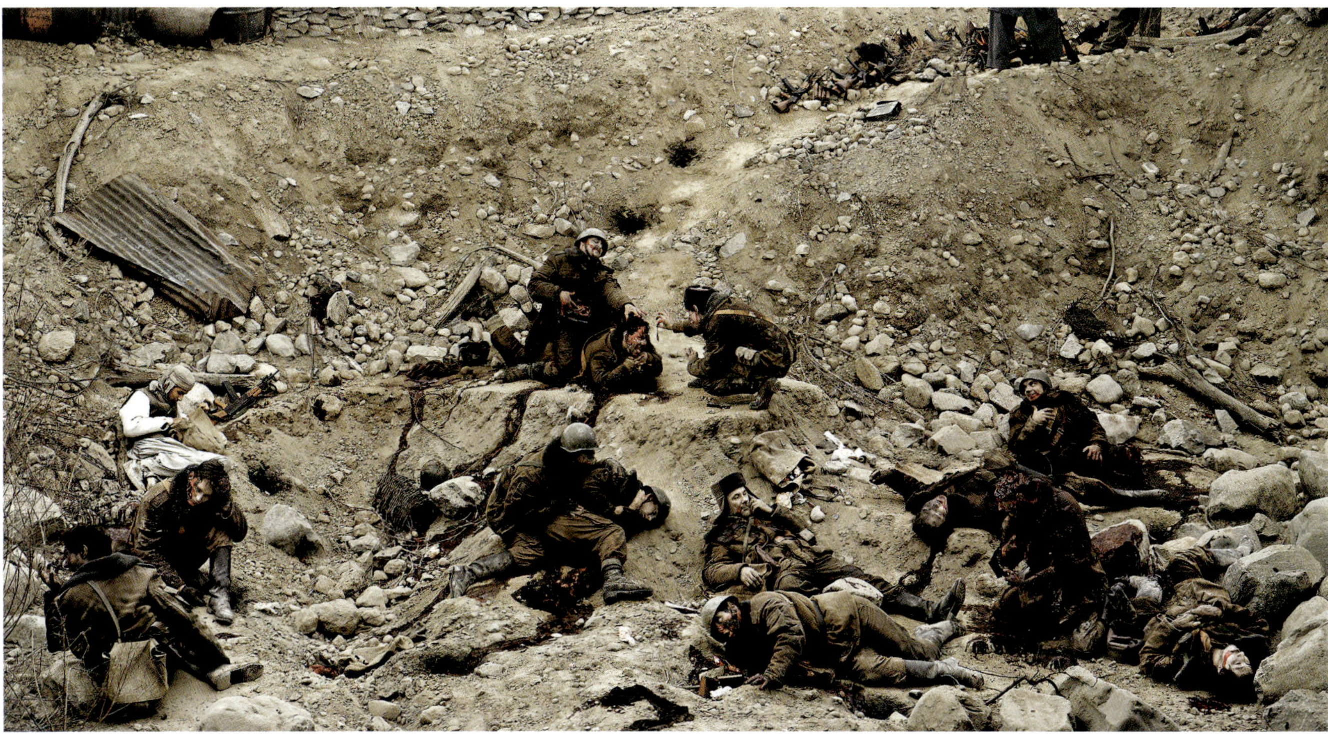

Jeff Wall, *Dead Troops Talk (a vision after an ambush of a Red Army patrol, near Moqor, Afghanistan, winter 1986),* 1992. Transparency in lightbox, 90 ⅛ x 164 ⅛ in.

a simulated Iraqi village built for U.S. military training. Her 2006 exhibition *Small Wars* at the Museum of Contemporary Photography in Chicago took the Vietnam, Iraq, and Afghanistan wars as its subject, wars that have changed our relationship to the kind of graphic violence depicted in Darger's work. Heavily photographed and televised, recent wars brought into American homes violent images far more traumatizing than Darger's brutal visions.

Most of the children's stories found in Darger's extensive library feature girl protagonists. Among his favorites were the Heidi series by the Swiss children's author Johanna Spyri. He was apparently drawn to the precocious Heidi, an orphaned girl who is passed from her aunt to her grandfather, and he modeled aspects of his Vivian girls on her. Darger's work exploits the clichés of late nineteenth- and early twentieth-century children's literature and his library reflects a keen appreciation of such narratives. Paul McCarthy and Mike Kelley attack the conventions of such stories in *Heidi: Midlife Crisis Trauma Center and Negative Media-Engram Abreaction Release Zone* (1992). In this installation-video work the artists stage an adaptation of the narrative of Heidi living with her grandfather, exaggerating latent taboo themes of childhood sensuality and incest. The matter-of-fact depiction of family dysfunction and child exploitation in *Heidi* deconstructs the ideals inscribed in the Alpine setting of Heidi's life with her grandfather. The staging of the performance was purposefully low-tech. McCarthy describes it as more like a puppet show than a traditional film, explaining that the intention is to highlight the illusionary aspect of film.

The cinematic appropriation and animation of fictional female protagonists emerges again in the French artist Pierre Huyghe's work with the figure known as Annlee. Collaborating with Philippe Parreno in 1999, Huyghe purchased the copyright to an anime figure from the Japanese agency Kworks, part of an industry in Japan that sells imaginary prefigured characters to be used for publication and animation in advertisements, comics, video games, and other formats. Huyghe and Parreno used her in their project *No Ghost Just a Shell,* in which the artists invited others to incorporate the character in projects. Bought and sold, Annlee lives and dies at the will of her owners. Huyghe set out to create a life to combat the short-term nature of creation in a haunting echo of the way our own lives take on meaning through work. Darger's need to create speaks to this as well. Exhibited in 2002–3, *No Ghost Just a Shell* charted Annlee's movement through the works of artists including Dominique Gonzalez-Foerster and Liam Gillick. Seeing the same figure appear in the very different contexts of these artists' work comments on the very act of cultural appropriation and collage and what can be gained and lost in this process. By bringing together the Annlee-based works, Huyghe and Parreno create a collective work of art—a life cobbled together for the virtual girl. Annlee gives a name to the mass of visual information changing hands as an artist transforms found objects and images.

Other prominent contemporary painters come to mind for their use of found figures and illustration modes based in popular culture. Richard Prince's *Nurse Paintings,* gestural appropriations of nurses depicted on the covers of pulp-fiction paperback books from the 1950s and 1960s, speaks to the life of these cultural objects blown up and worked into an artist's symbolic order. Seeing the sexualized nurses on the canvas, we realize that the web

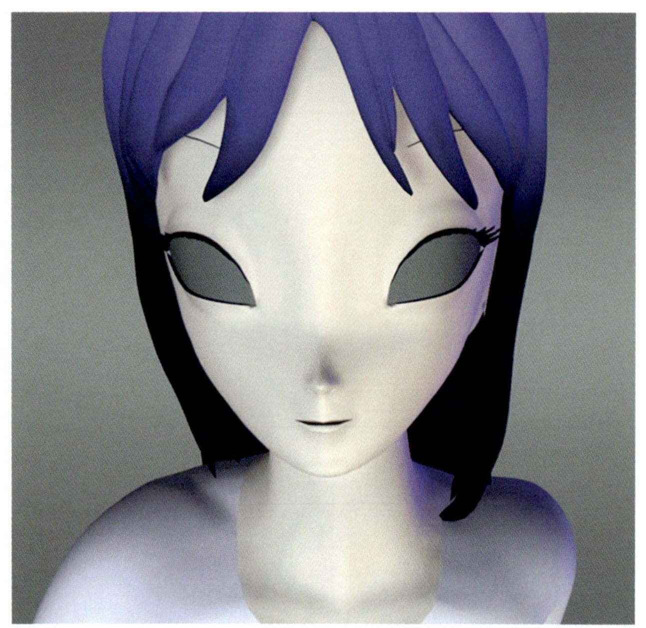

Pierre Huyghe, *Two minutes out of time,* 2000. Beta digital, 4 min.

of social constructions represented by these fetish images has become the subject of Prince's work. The German painter Neo Rauch's work continues this legacy of the cartoon. Born in Leipzig in 1960, Rauch marries the Socialist Realism typical of the former Eastern Bloc with the cartoon sensibility of capitalistic Western consumer culture, creating something that could be playfully called Cartoon Realism. The space of Rauch's paintings is that of cartoons. His surreal costumed characters share Darger's coloring-book aesthetic. Like Rauch, Darger does not create convincing three-dimensional relationships between the figures in his landscapes. Any reality in his watercolors is subjugated to the whims of his imagination.

The influence of newspaper comic strips on Darger is paralleled by their concurrent emergence in the work of some of the most influential artists of the later twentieth century, Robert Rauschenberg, Roy Lichtenstein, and Andy Warhol. Rauschenberg's Red Paintings (1953–54) are visibly grounded in layers of cut-out comic strips; Andy Warhol and Roy Lichtenstein's early canvases are hand-painted fragments of comic strips featuring the likes of Dick Tracy and Donald Duck. Darger's attraction to the comic strip as a powerful vehicle for storytelling approaches Lichtenstein's well-known experiments with enlarging single panels of printed comics.

Obsession, disasters, and the reworking of popular images all come together in the legacy of Andy Warhol. Darger's ceaseless appetite for collecting and the decades-old refuse found in his room didn't nearly approach the collecting mania of Warhol, who filled 610 standard-size cardboard boxes with ephemera over thirty years, making no distinction between trash and things of value such as letters and works of art. And while Darger and Warhol may seem not to have much in common, both used newspapers as source material, combing the pages for accidents, murders, and other disasters. Warhol got his start in New York as a commercial illustrator in the 1950s. His illustrations for Nelson Doubleday's 1958 Best in Children's Books series feature innocent children and have remarkable watercolor effects. Just four years later, in the summer of 1962, Warhol used an image of a plane crash from the front page of a local paper for his first disaster painting, *129 Die in Jet.* During the following three years, he created work based on newspaper images of car crashes, race riots, electric chairs, and celebrities. Darger's obsession with the loss of his cut-out newspaper photo of the murdered Elsie Paroubek speaks to the power of such images—a power that Warhol also perceived in reproducing Marilyn Monroe's image soon after she died. Like Jake Smith's devotion to the actress Maria Montez, Joseph Cornell's obsession with Lauren Bacall, and Warhol's fascination with Monroe, Darger's desire to protect the young girl Elsie Paroubek is channeled into his art.

To demonstrate the obvious, one may type the phrase "American beauty" into the Google search engine and it receives nearly 132 million hits.[46] The search for "American dream" returns about 65 million. The search for "American innocence" returns slightly more than 1 million, less than 1 percent as many hits as "American beauty."

The movie *American Beauty* (1999) paints a depressing picture of American society at the end of the twentieth century, as a place of crisis and despair, longing and avoidance, and, in the end, lust and murder. The pursuit of individual happiness has become a search for what one might or might not want. It seems as if the American dream has come to a dead end. Modest wealth, a house, a car, a family are not enough any more. The individual search for self-expression leads to alienation, a state in which one wants to change body and mind, career and goals.

In the movie, a father shaken by midlife crisis is longing for the love of the underage friend of his daughter. The pursuit of happiness leads him to an insane admiration of adolescence, youth, and innocence. But in a certain way he only reflects tendencies in an American society obsessed by youth and seduction. The public's gaze is currently fixed on the Disney kids, the Olsen twins, whose infantile lives were broadcast nonstop, *American Idol,* and Disney's Hannah Montana, alias Miley Cyrus (who, by the way, returns over 50 million Google hits). These children are exposed to and owned by the public in a more radical way than was the child star Shirley Temple, who reigned in Darger's middle age.

Desire in a certain way anticipates consumption, which, if not balanced by other cultural forces, can lead to a hedonistic, apolitical, overly individualistic society in which nothing but personal well-being counts. In the early 1990s the idea of an "end of history" was much discussed. The fall of the Berlin Wall and the collapse of the Eastern Bloc supposedly had brought the region, if not the world, to a peaceful mix of democratic, liberal consumer societies. But the subsequent conflicts in Rwanda and Yugoslavia, to name only two of many, raised doubts. In the new millennium, the attacks of September 11, 2001, on the United States, and the repressive reactions that followed them, created new global political and economic tensions.

In 2008 the Western nations that share a capitalist, market-oriented culture precipitated a worldwide economic meltdown that has reminded many of the collapse of the former Eastern Bloc. On the cultural scene recently, discourse has been increasingly concerned with art and artists who deal with the consequences of recent history, who depict war and violence, corruption and exploitation. Child labor, slavery and sex trafficking, war camps and refugees, brutal torture, mutilation, and public humiliation appear daily on the news—not to mention cataclysmic weather events such as tsunamis, earthquakes, epic hurricanes, and global warming. Darger's work, speaking to our deepest anxieties as a world community, remains strikingly current.

As the media play such a powerful role in contemporary society, it is important that Darger's work and life are media-compatible. Jessica Yu's award-winning documentary *In the Realms of the Unreal* (2004) provides views of Darger through his voluminous work that stand in sharp contrast to the fragmented glimpses of the man gleaned from recollections of neighbors and acquaintances. The film reveals discrepancies even in interviewees' pronunciation of Darger's name, some using a hard "g" and others the soft "g," which seems to underscore the subjectivity of their impressions. His life story lends itself to oral history, making Darger a contemporary legend whose personality and work merge into a single entity. Some think he was a violent madman while others believe he was just an ordinary hospital custodian, making art to pass the time.

Darger's work has had the same divergent impact, representing different things to different contemporary artists. Picasso is supposed to have said, "Good artists borrow, great artists steal," but artists unaware of one another's work may be impressed by comparable ideas and images. Darger certainly has had a direct influence on the artistic production of the last decade or so, but artists may also have arrived at similar depictions and concerns in their work without being aware of him. Instead, an artist may have a common interest (the Wizard of Oz, Mutt and Jeff, etc.) or share the same artistic affinities and obsessions that connect Darger with so many artists today.

In 2008 the American Folk Art Museum organized the exhibition *DARGERism: Contemporary Artists and Henry Darger*, seeking to illuminate this dialogue between contemporary art and Darger. Selecting art by younger artists whose work in one way or another reflects Darger's, the curator Brooke Davis Anderson sought to highlight the artist's legacy in work by Robyn O'Neil, Grayson Perry, Paula Rego, Michael St. John, Trenton Doyle Hancock, Jefferson Friedman, Anthony Goicolea, Amy Cutler, Justin Lieberman, Justine Kurland, and Yun-Fei Ji. One might have added Melissa Brown and others to this list.

The dialogue between contemporary art informed by Darger and our view of Darger as it is informed by contemporary art can be investigated by placing the artists involved in a larger generational, cultural context to identify overlap and difference, similar points of departure and crass discrepancies. Grayson Perry's ceramic objects have classical forms contrasting with their contemporary subject matter. Representations of Perry as Claire, his female alter ego, recur throughout this imagery, which also approaches such difficult motifs as sadomasochism. When he received the Turner Prize in 2003, he accepted it dressed as Claire. Included in the *DARGERism* exhibition was a glazed urn covered in religious iconography, including a little girl seemingly being offered up as a sacrifice;

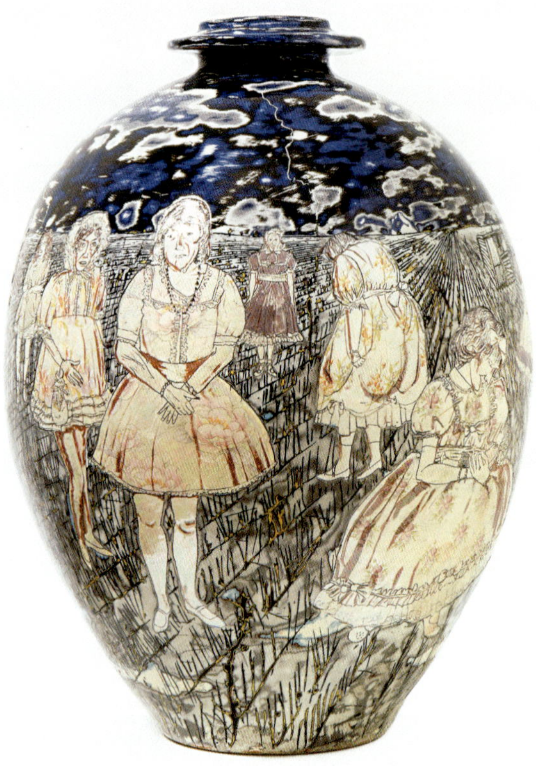

with a bow in her hair and a little pink dress, she could have come straight out of Darger's oeuvre.

"Henry Darger is my favorite artist," Perry has said. "I have spent a life long playing out of his world and tried to emulate his technique."[47] When Perry was seven years old, his father left home. To escape from a difficult family situation involving his stepfather's violence, Perry would retreat for safety to his bedroom or his father's shed, where he became absorbed in the imagery of his thoughts and fantasies. He took an interest in drawing and building model airplanes, both of which were to become themes of his work. He began dressing as a woman publicly at the age of fifteen. Perry studied fine art at Portsmouth Polytechnic and took evening pottery lessons. The themes and techniques of Perry's work connect him to Darger, but there is more to the bond than that. Seeing Darger's work early, at a 1979 exhibition in London, Perry grew to identify with the artist who "retreated to an imaginary world."

The international exposure of Darger in exhibitions, publications, and the media over the last decade and a half has influenced many young artists. Like Perry, who credits Darger with giving him "permission to make works principally motivated by my obsessions and my inner imaginative world," younger artists draw on both the art and the story of the man. Darger's pervasive influence can be seen in the young artist group shows named after him, and in the songs and poetry that have been dedicated to him. Like Mutt and Jeff finding roles in *Realms*, Darger has been incorporated into popular culture and appears as a character in fictional works.

Songs based on Darger's life and work include "The Ballad of Henry Darger" (2001) by Natalie Merchant, "Segue: In the Realms of the Unreal" (2006) by . . . And You Will Know Us by the Trail of the Dead, "The Vivian Girls Are Visited in the Night by Saint Dargarius and His Squadron of Benevolent Butterflies" (2006) by Sufjan Stevens, and "The Vivian Girls" (1979) by Snakefinger. Neil Gaiman's hugely popular Sandman graphic novel series includes an episode in *Endless Nights* in which a janitor character describes his project to "chronicle the Sky-Boys and their journey through Hells Infinite," which is six thousand pages long. The Dog & Pony Theatre Company's 2008 production of Devon de Mayo's *As Told by the Vivian Girls* is based on Darger's text. In Dog & Pony's staging, audience members wear paper Vivian girl masks and choose the actions of the play's characters. John Ashbery's 1999 *Girls on the Run*, mentioned above, draws on Darger's Vivian girls and reimagines their universe. Jesse Kellerman's 2008 mystery novel *The Genius* features a reclusive artist inspired by Darger. When the artist's drawings, recovered from boxes of refuse in his apartment, go on sale, a policeman recognizes the depicted children as possible murder victims.

Darger only became influential after his death and after the efforts of Nathan and Kiyoko Lerner and many devoted curators and writers researching his life and works. Today his themes and imagery are much more digestible, nearly common, decades after he moved out of the Chicago apartment where he did most of his work. Documentary images of history unfolding and the immense flood of created, animated, and recorded images in the mass media have exposed us to every kind of disturbing picture. That the imagery in Darger's work still retains some shock value, in a time when the artist Damien Hirst works with real sliced-in-half animal corpses, begs further investigation. That the "look into the body" as depicted by early paintings of medical operations is ubiquitous today does nothing to lessen the hit. Darger, Hirst, and the Chapmans have the ability to edit and single out the monstrous in their imagery so that it stays with the viewer. In Hirst's *The Virgin Mother*, installed at Lever House in New York, one senses echoes of Darger's most effective illustrations. Hirst's large-scale anatomical model of a pregnant woman is Dargeresque

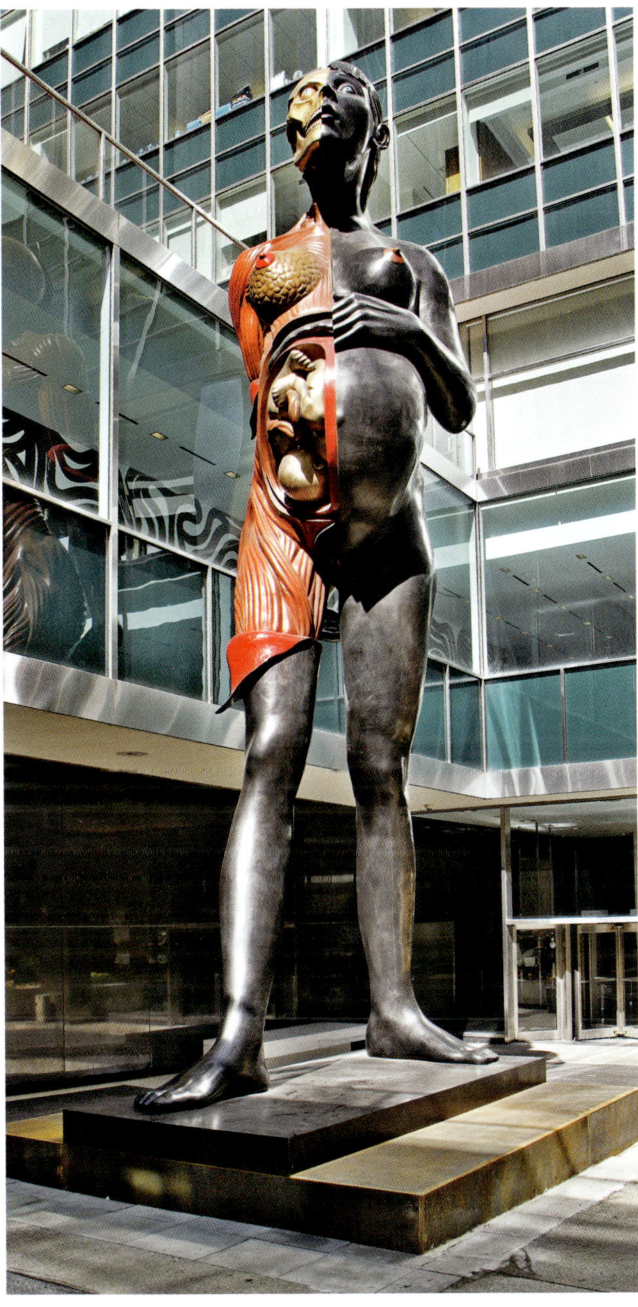

Damien Hirst, *The Virgin Mother*, 2005.
Bronze, 33 ft., 7 in. x 15 ft., 2 in. x 6 ft., 9 in.

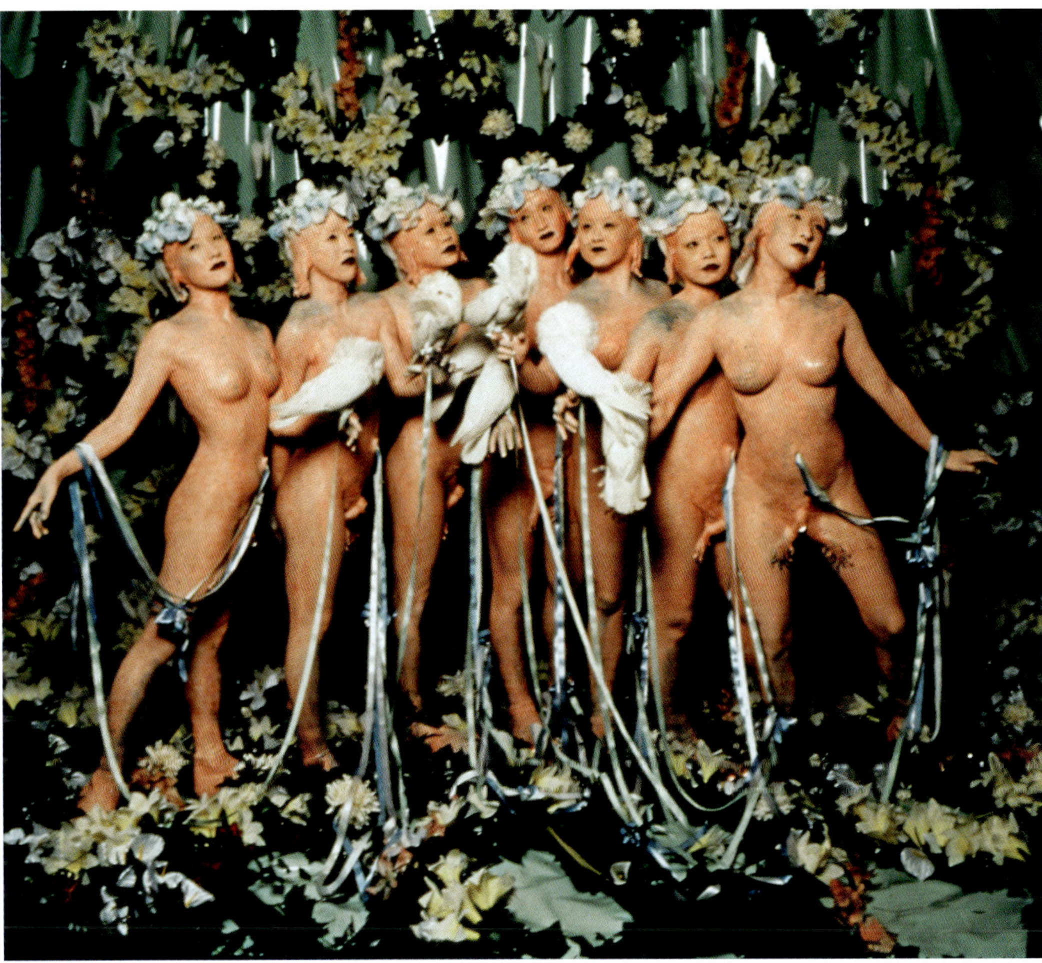

Matthew Barney, *Cremaster 5*, 1997. Production still

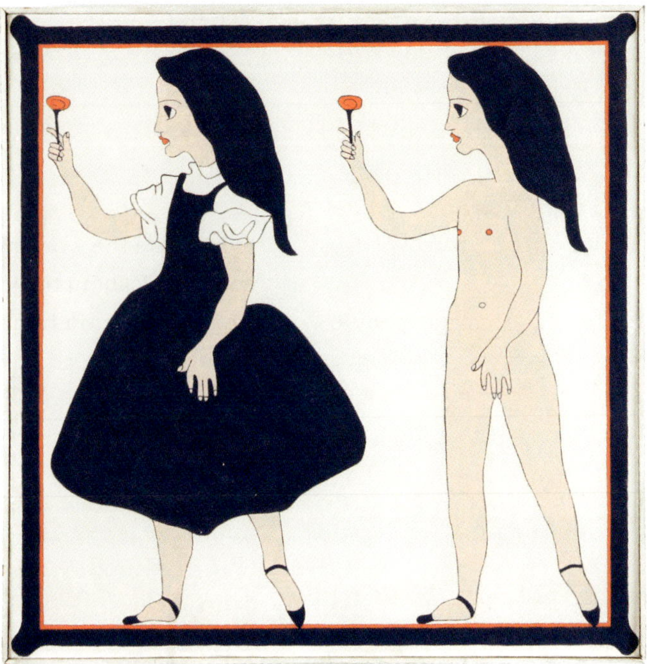

John Wesley, *Little Alice*, 1965.
Acrylic on canvas, 24 x 24 in.

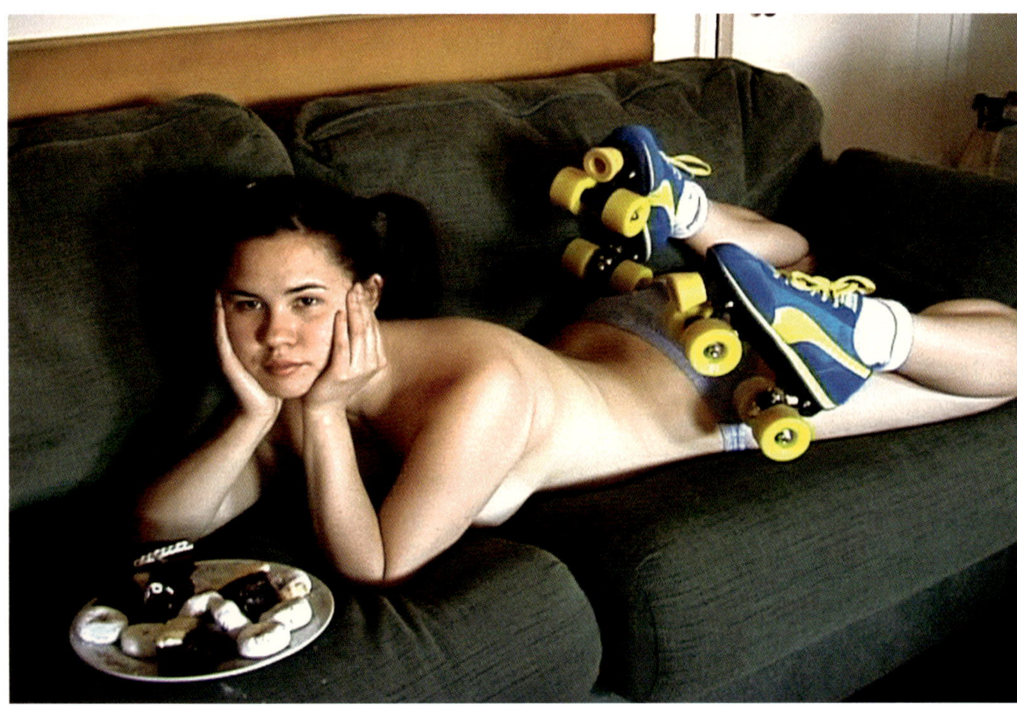

Laurel Nakadate,
We Are All Made of Stars, 2002.
Five-channel video,
17 min., 20 sec.

because our mind associates the cut-open female body with the brutal scenes of crucifixions, disembowelments, and mutilations in Darger's watercolors. When the toy-like, innocent, cartoonish quality of the bodies collides with immediate, brutal violence the effect is unbearable.

Realms once thought to be limited to children alone—graphic novels, Japanese manga, and the video-game industry, rivaling film—are influencing artists, filmmakers, and musicians. Imagery that is cartoonish or gamelike is one of the dominant visual languages of today. The scale of invention required to create the immersive world of new games seems almost to require a confusion of life and imagination on the massive scale achieved by Darger. He would change the names on letters and photos to match his fictive stories. The world of *In the Realms of the Unreal* is meticulously crafted through the accumulation of details and characters. Dargereque images seem to galvanize how we perceive our times. Darger's winged, dragonlike Blengins and tree-flowers now seem to rival the hybrid creatures of Matthew Barney's world. In *Cremaster 5*'s famous scene filmed at the Gellért Thermal Baths in Budapest, Barney presents the Füdór Sprites, creatures that are half flower and half human, and look frighteningly real (page 29). This aesthetic is now the cutting edge, even on a global level.

On the other hand, Darger's work can appear strangely reminiscent of a long-lost era in America. The sexual and media revolution and the liberalization of Western society, the mass accessibility of porn and brutality in all its specific niches, distributed first through video and then through the Internet and gaming culture, make Darger's hermaphroditic, militaristic protagonists seem as tame as children's-book illustrations again in the eyes of an increasingly jaded general public.

The veteran painter John Wesley plays off illustrational styles, subtly mixing "past and present Americana" but with a sexual charge, as critic Roberta Smith has said. Like Darger's watercolors, Wesley's paintings hover in an alien time, somehow both a part of the confusions of the modern world and outside its ever more frenetic pace. Often relegated to Pop art, Wesley's work has less to do with consumerism than with the Dargeresque themes of innocence and fantasy.

Returning to the first image of this essay, that of Laurel Nakadate in her truck-stop scenario, one encounters the idea of innocence embedded in the work of a truly American artist. Born in Austin, Texas, and raised in Ames, Iowa, her mother is American and father Japanese-American. Nakadate shoots video on unsure ground when she follows leering men back to their homes, inviting them to take part in her art projects. We note that she purposefully invites their gaze to shoot her work and wonder, Who is it that is really approaching whom? As she bridges Japanese and American culture in her own biography, Nakadate investigates the dance of innocence and seduction both in Japanese culture (in works such as *Love Hotel*) and American daily life.

Nakadate commented recently, "I am drawn to people who live alone and have complicated stories to tell. Henry Darger's work has haunted and inspired me. I often think of Darger, working alone in his world—in secret and with such urgency and dedication. In my photographs and videos, I work with men who live alone and keep to themselves. We perform stories that are one part fact and one part fiction. We write these stories together. I have often taken on the character of a young, curious, and brave girl to navigate the worlds of these men and make these videos. I think about the Vivian girls. I think about American stories of men in hiding, and men who hide secret fantasy lives, and girls in ruffles, and pretend wars, and heroic motions taken to try and save the day. I think about

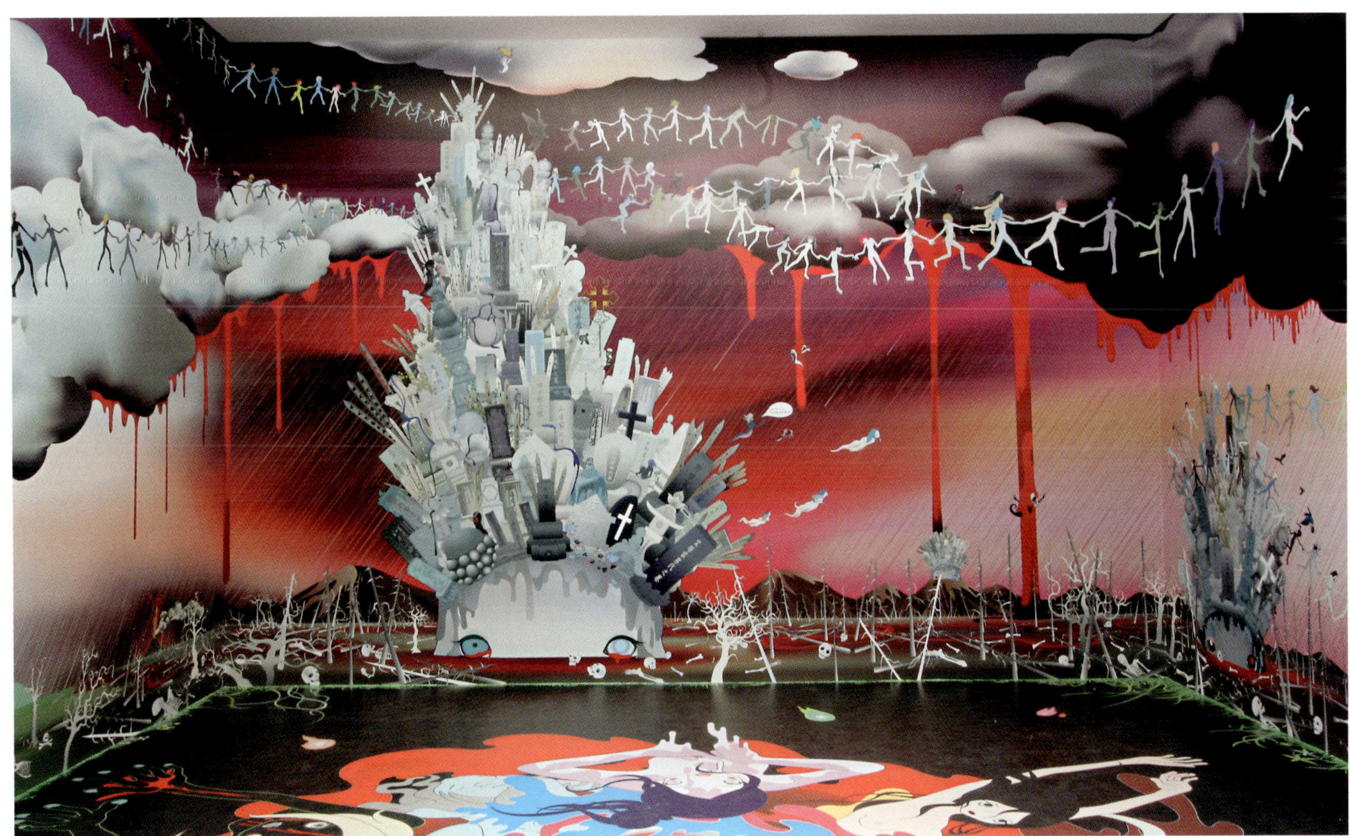

Chiho Aoshima, installation view, *Asleep, Dreaming of Reptilian Glory*, 2005, Blum & Poe, Los Angeles. Floor: *Gushing Zombies*, 2005. Digital print on vinyl, 24 ft., 10 in. x 19 ft., 10 in. Wall: *Graveheads*, 2005. Inkjet print on paper, 13 ft., 7 in. x 83 ft., 7 in.

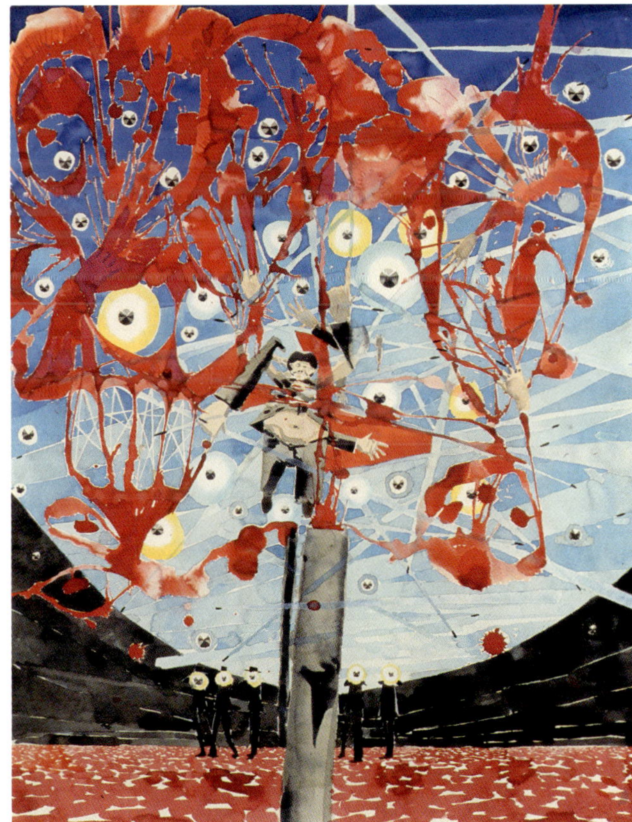

Barnaby Furnas, Untitled (Execution), 2003. Watercolor and ink on paper, 25 x 20 in.

beauty, terror, and glee. I think about how in our secret rooms, everything is possible and sometimes the tour guides are young, knowing girls, and sometimes they are men with amazing, dark, and delightful secrets."[48]

Nakadate's girly look reminds the viewer of the photographs of girls in school uniforms, with short dresses and socks, by the acclaimed Japanese artist Nobuyoshi Araki. The grown-ups gazing onto these female "children" seem to have control over the objects of these depictions. But these children gain some reciprocal power in the twisted relationship. There is a crossover between photographic depictions of Japanese schoolgirls with various sexual undertones and the overwhelming success of Takashi Murakami and a younger generation of artists who work with cartoon imagery and translate their toylike characters into paintings, sculptures, installations, and videos.

Murakami was trained in the school of traditional Japanese painting known as *Nihonga*, a nineteenth-century mixture of Western and Eastern styles. But the prevailing

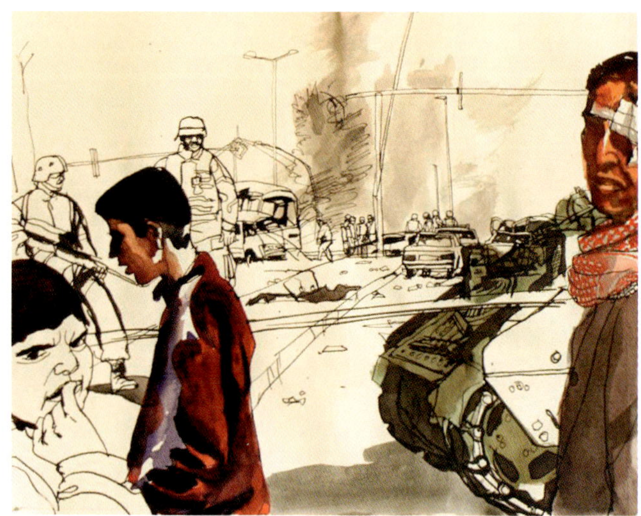

Steve Mumford, *The aftermath of the bombing on January 18th, 2004, at the Coalition Provisional Authority main gate. Twenty nine people were killed in the explosion,* 2004. Watercolor and ink on paper, 11 x 14 in.

popularity of anime and manga directed his interest toward the art of animation because, as he has said, "it was more representative of modern-day Japanese life." American popular culture in the form of animation, comics, and fashion is among the influences on his work. As curator of *Little Boy: The Arts of Japan's Exploding Subculture*, Murakami, in collaboration with New York's Japan Society and the Public Art Fund, explored the notion of the innocent girl-child, playing with toys and being a toy, without pubic hair or mature sexual desires. With that show of contemporary Japanese art, Murakami described a certain compulsive national innocence as a regression following the trauma of World War II. Murakami mostly selected artists who share his devotion to cartoon, animation, and manga culture. The imagery of their work suggests that many of the artists also share Henry Darger's sensibility, even if they were not influenced by his watercolors.

For example, Chiho Aoshima is known for her large-scale murals portraying otherworldly landscapes comprised of candy-colored vegetation and creatures. Without any formal art training, Aoshima uses a vocabulary that integrates traditions of Japanese scroll painting with contemporary manga aesthetics. Her subject matter is full of apocalyptic and grotesque imagery. *Graveheads* (2005), one such work, features a wall painting in which dark rain clouds drip with blood (page 31). A mountainous cemetery juts into a sky filled with little girls holding hands who snake across the wall. Throughout the work, young girls are depicted in desperate and surreal circumstances, in a world of unease. Aya Takano is influenced by both Japanese manga and American science-fiction imagery. An artist, illustrator, and writer, she depicts her fictive world across media. In her visual work, the heroines are drawn with exaggeratedly large eyes and are often partially or completely nude. They are placed in cold, eerie cityscapes, sharing scenes with neon signs and corporate logos but rarely with other humans. Darger's work in watercolor is

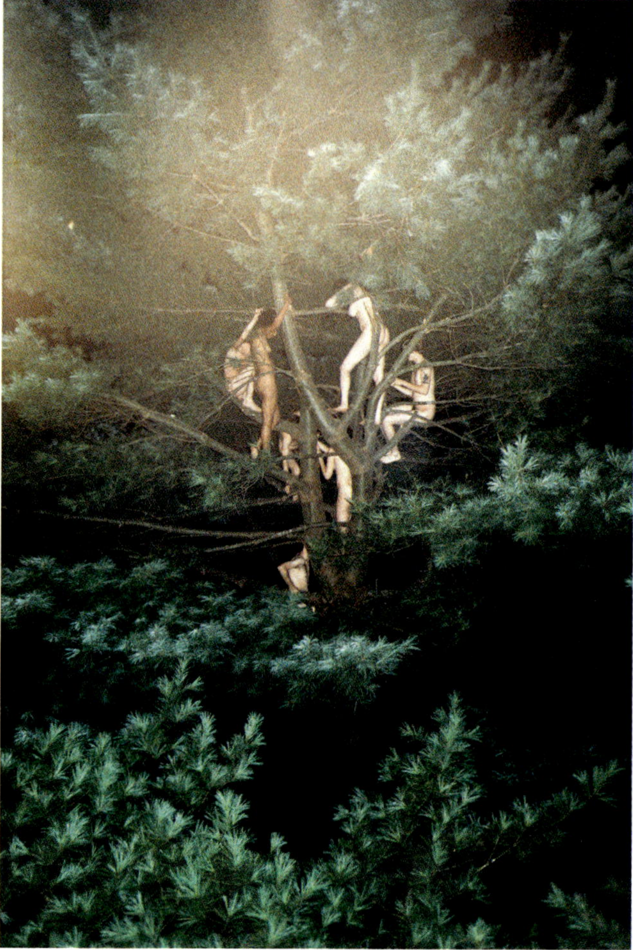

Ryan McGinley, *Tree #3*, 2003. C-print, 72 x 48 in.

directly tied to his fiction; similarly, Takano's acrylic-on-canvas paintings are in their own way a component of her massive, serialized publications. But comparing a seemingly typical Japanese innocence with the idea of American innocence is not enough. The exhibition's title, *Little Boy*, encouraged the viewer to approach Murakami's universe through the memory of the trauma of defeat in World War II and the mass destruction and annihilation caused by the detonation of the atomic bomb dropped on Hiroshima.

During Darger's life, the American military forcefully engaged in violent foreign wars whose bloody photographs were recorded in the newspapers that he read every day. This experience certainly informed the graphic violence of his narratives and illustrations. In a parallel internalization of such disaster visions, the artist Barnaby Furnas beautifully portrays explosions. He began his career as a graffiti artist and creates his own paints from mixtures of pigment and urethane. Poised between figuration and geometric abstraction, his scenes of cataclysmic explosions and battles are treated with seductive violence in fractured, flattened compositions. Body parts are scattered in scores of fragments and fountains of blood and other corporal fluids abound, while divine halos of yellow and white pierce the horizon. In Untitled (Execution) (2003), a firing-squad victim is obliterated in a sea of fireworks (page 31). In *Dead Red I* and *The Dead Sea*, scenes have been distilled to a completely abstract sea of red. Furnas's imposing scale has an epic quality and yet also retains an element of slapstick.

Steve Mumford visited Iraq a number of times beginning in 2003 and was able to accompany American military units. He made disturbingly beautiful watercolors of the daily life of American soldiers in Baghdad and the Iraqi countryside (opposite). Mumford's works on paper are in stark contrast with the unimaginable mass of photographs that soldiers take with their cell phones or small digital cameras and send all over the world to their friends, relatives—or, in the case of the infamous Abu Ghraib photos, to the press. Darger's imagery looks so contemporary because we are in times of war again and it is everywhere.

Darger's *In the Realms of the Unreal* is more than a war

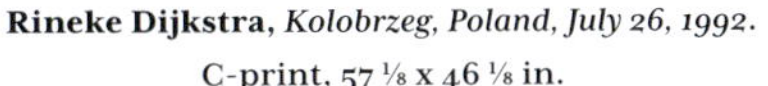

Rineke Dijkstra, *Kolobrzeg, Poland, July 26, 1992*.
C-print, 57 ⅛ x 46 ⅛ in.

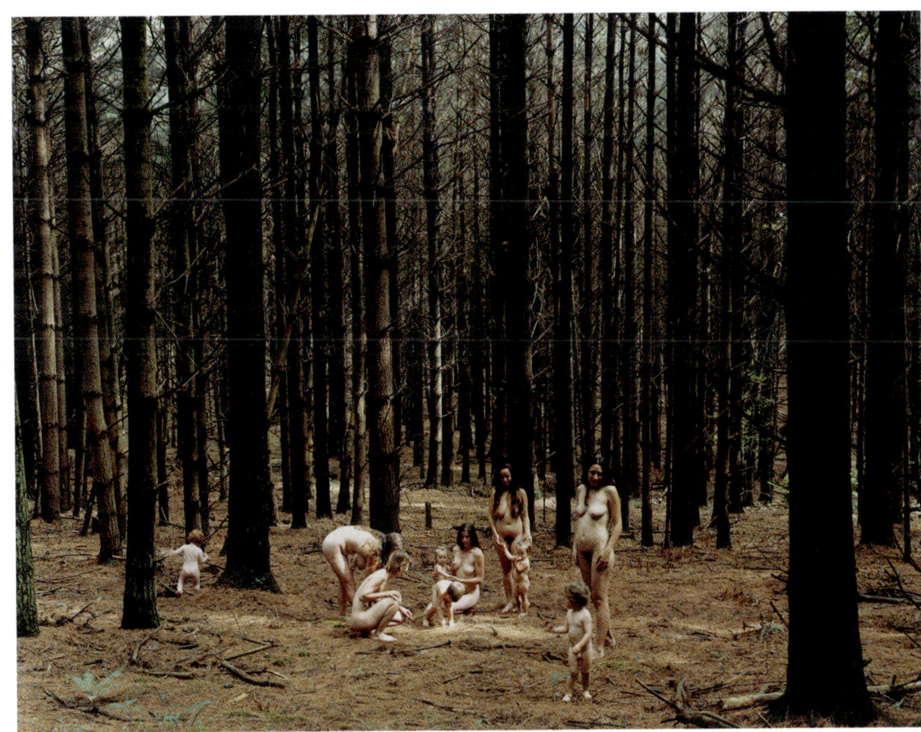

Justine Kurland, *Pine Forest*,
2005. C-print, 30 x 40 in.

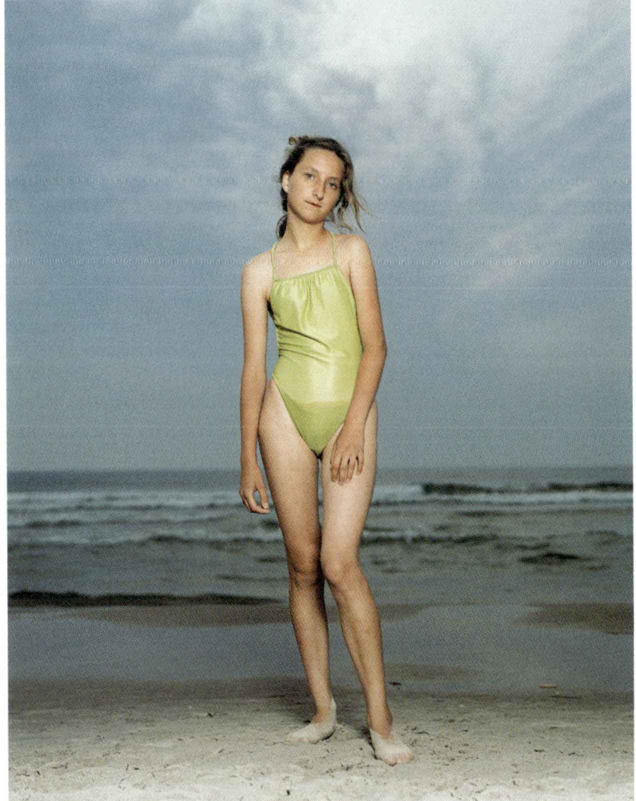

history. It is the story of the Vivian girls, his prepubescent, angelic protagonists. His is a study of the pull between adolescence and maturity as he depicts his girl-heroines and boy-heroes grappling with the adult violence of war. A recent generation of photographers, including Yale graduates Anna Gaskell and Justine Kurland, has marked this moment in the fragility of youth with a theatrical materiality of the body. Gaskell puts blue pinafore dresses and white tights on the young girl subjects of her photographic portraits, so that they are reminiscent of Dorothy in *The Wizard of Oz*. Like those of Nakadate and Darger, her protagonists enter intimate, potentially dangerous situations. In Untitled #73 (resemblance) (2001), a young girl is about to give mouth-to-mouth resuscitation to another; the line between injury and physical experimentation is blurred.

In Justine Kurland's female-populated landscapes, mothers and their seraphic children roam the woods, cross creeks, and hold clandestine meetings, together forming a secret world (page 33). In *New York* (2001), a group of young women lie in a field; they could be cloud-gazing, or lifeless. Many of Kurland's elaborately staged photographs allude to a brutal act committed within or by the group depicted, but not seen in the picture. The images play with a before and after, with the tension of the moment. Her settings, barren, rocky landscapes and country roads edged with wildflowers, recall Darger, and suggest a Technicolor theatricality that contrast with the intimacy of the fragile scenes. Other artists working with similar motifs include Katy Grannan and Malerie Marder.

If an audience listens to a piano concert, but the pianist is not visible, will the audience know if the pianist is male or female? The work of Gaskell, Kurland, Grannan, and Marder brings the question of an artist's gender into focus. The huge discrepancy between Darger's sensibility and that of Kurland, for example, is due in large part to his gender.

At first glance, the nymphets in Sally Mann's black-and-white portrait photographs appear to the Darger reader as reincarnations of the Vivian girls. Capturing an ill-defined moment between childhood and adulthood, Mann photographed twelve-year-old girls in poses that suggest a sexuality that is at once assumed and scandalous. The girls' facial expressions sensitively convey the unease and fragility of adolescence. Darger's own Vivian girls ride this line, as they are described at play in one scene and brutally killing enemy soldiers in the next. Suggestions of sexuality between the girls and the enemy Glandelinians and boy-heroes are muddied by Darger's

Marcel Dzama, *You gotta make room for the new ones*, 2005.
Ink and watercolor on paper; overall drawing dimensions: 14 x 22 in.

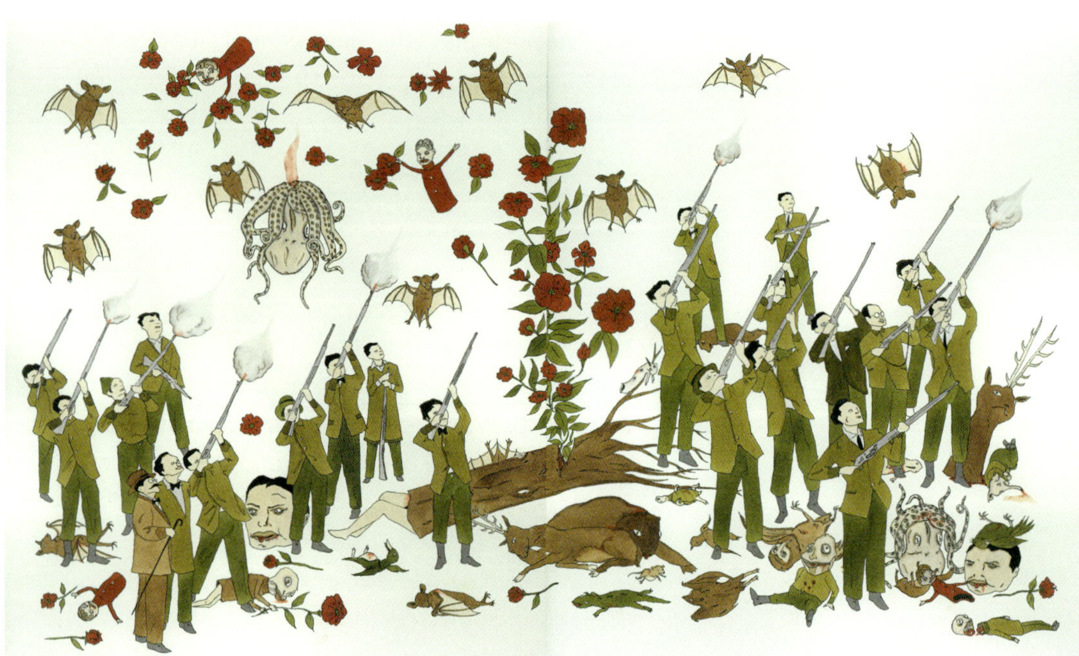

Dasha Shishkin, *It Takes Money to Feed Pretty Women*, 2009.
Acrylic and ink on panel, 12 x 12 in.

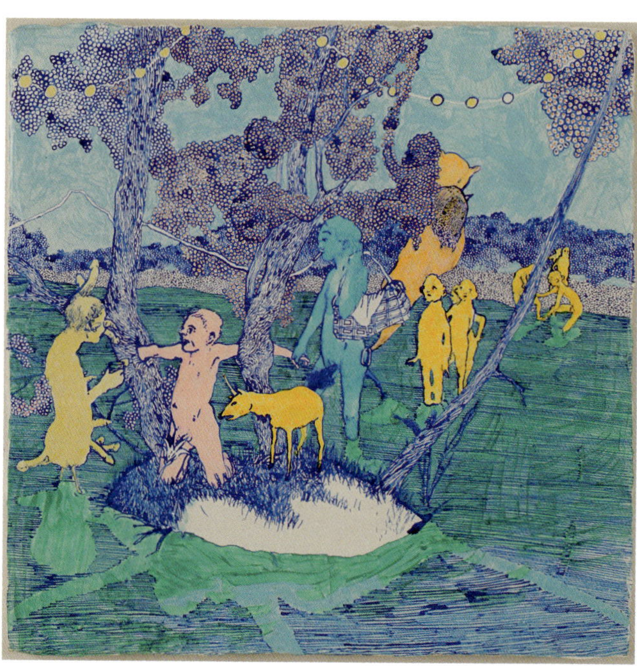

own unease with the subject. *Immediate Family*, Mann's series of photographs taken between 1984 and 1991, portrays her own young children growing up. Posing nude or partially nude, they become the subjects of elaborate narratives of childhood, vulnerability, of innocence in America, invited by Mann's depictions of sensuality and suggestive titles like *Popsicle Drips* or *Dirty Jessie*.

Mann depicts a fragile beauty, whereas Rineke Dijkstra, in a much more matter-of-fact, constructed, and composed image-making process visualizes the fragile intimacy between the photographer and her model. Some principal actors in her photographic portraits play multiple roles, further confusing identity and reality. The works often function in series, as she looks at groups of adolescents, young people at clubs, on beaches, at war. Her strictly composed images feature subjects standing, face to the camera, against a minimal background, their humanity fully exposed (page 33).

Ryan McGinley's works seems to depict real life. He captures images of young people in natural environments: nude bodies are glimpsed between trees, lying down in clearings, and so on (page 32). His pastoral, often magically removed atmospheres show a nearly genderless paradisiacal state, before regular daily routine, aging, and alienation set in. Alienation and the pain of growing up is also a central motive in the work of Sue de Beer. She focuses on subtle details in her diaristic video works. In *Disappear Here* (2004), the camera focuses in on a young girl's swinging ponytail and the back of her knees. In de Beer's more grisly works, violent scenes are constructed with palpable gore. One photographic work depicts the aftermath of the artist "giving birth to herself." The two-channel installation *Hans und Grete* incorporates elements of the story of the Baader-Meinhof gang in the tortured psychological dramas of its teenage characters.

Like de Beer, Laura Parnes is primarily known for her experimental videos and installations. She appropriated Kathy Acker's 1984 novel *Blood and Guts in High School*. The novel imagined the sexual life of an outsider, Janey Smith, beginning with an incestuous relationship at the age of ten. Parnes reimagines Janey through a video series that explores chapters in her life between 1978 and 1982. Set in New York at a time when Reagan was coming into power and punk was emerging, each episode presents a day in Janey's life, interrupted by news events that surreally fuse with her personal experience. The installation includes life-size portraits of the many sides of Janey's personality, as well as a display of Parnes's interpretive material based on Acker's novel. The animation of a literary text is central to Darger's illustration project. Largely pursued after the completion of the text of *Realms*, the watercolors are Darger's way back into his story, often used as storytelling tools in themselves. Adding more and more elements to his novel through illustration, Darger further populates his video-gamelike universe.

Darger's endless exploration of a fictive world, recognized by Grayson Perry as an early formative influence, is also found in the book-illustration aesthetic of Marcel Dzama (opposite). Originally from Winnipeg, Dzama began creating artwork as part of the Royal Art Lodge collective, which existed between 1996 and 2008. The Royal Art Lodge itself had a fictional figurehead named Professor Arthur Royale. Dzama's repertoire of characters

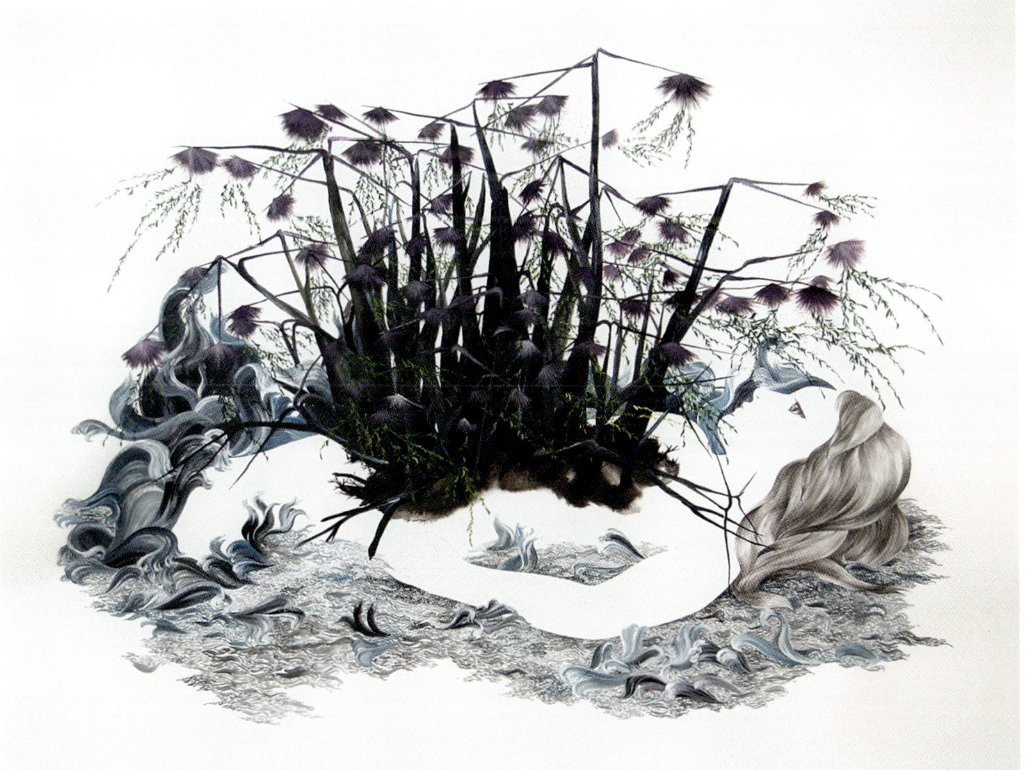

Min Kim, *Black Forest*, 2006. Pencil, watercolor, and gouache on paper, 38 x 50 in.

consists of young girls and boys, women and men, bats, half-human trees, floral wreaths, soldiers at attention and at the front lines, and vampires. His images juxtapose brutal punishment (hangings from gallows, hooded figures or executioners, their faces concealed) with ornate filigree against a mostly bare background. Like Darger's ensemble, the protagonists in Dzama's works on paper are always in some kind of uniform (matching outfits). In the work *Last Winter Here* (2004), the scene is cold and dismal; one figure is hanging from a point above the frame and a severed half of a body is left on the ground. Battle scenes such as *Casualties and Hypocrites, The Movement, Scheme of the Circles of Battle, The Avant-Guard Army,* and *Citizens of Regimentation* (2004) treat the subject with somber decorum. Concurrently Dzama's world consists of an idyllic menagerie or parade of nude babies, cryptozoological creatures, and so on. His 2008 diorama, *On the Banks of the Red River*, which consisted of nearly three hundred ceramic figures, features faceless, suited hunt-

ers with bayonets amid a pile of fallen bodies, a backdrop of flowers and bats, and faces with blood dripping from the orifices. His depiction of encampments in his battle scenes reveals the influence of the American Civil War. In an interview with *Newsweek* from 2004, Dzama recalls that he had only learned about Darger a few years earlier after reading repeated comparisons between his work and Darger's. Darger wasn't an influence on Dzama, but it is interesting nonetheless to consider the parallels.

The reemergence of complex symbolic orders in Amy Cutler's watercolors similarly point to Darger as an antecedent. The artist, included in the American Folk Art Museum's *DARGERism* show, suggests an interesting relationship between her cast of characters and architectural structures, whether they are encampments, enclosures, objects, or animals on which her figures lean, ride, idle, and interact. The women who inhabit her world have distorted, elongated features and absurdly long ponytails. In one untitled work from 2008, a row of girls with long locks

of hair share a bed, tucked in neatly like a resting squadron. Like Darger and Barney, she creates hybrid beings.

Born in Moscow, Dasha Shishkin has made a body of work titled *First Sorrow*, inspired by the Kafka story of the same name and referring to the first loss of innocence. The narrative connecting these works centers on concepts of impotence, freedom, and philanthropy. A tawdry cast of characters engages in gymnastic routines, states of emergency, spectacles reminiscent of a Toulouse Lautrec café-concert. Shishkin refers to some of her newer pieces as "colorings," where hues are applied as if in a coloring book. The work *Judith and Holofernes* (2007) depicts the artist's rendering of this violent biblical story in which Judith beheads the general. In the more recent work *It Takes Money to Feed Pretty Women* (2009), the loosely drawn faces of young androgynous girls retain a wild preciousness (page 34).

Working in graphite, ink, gouache, and paper, the Korean-American artist Min Kim places her young female

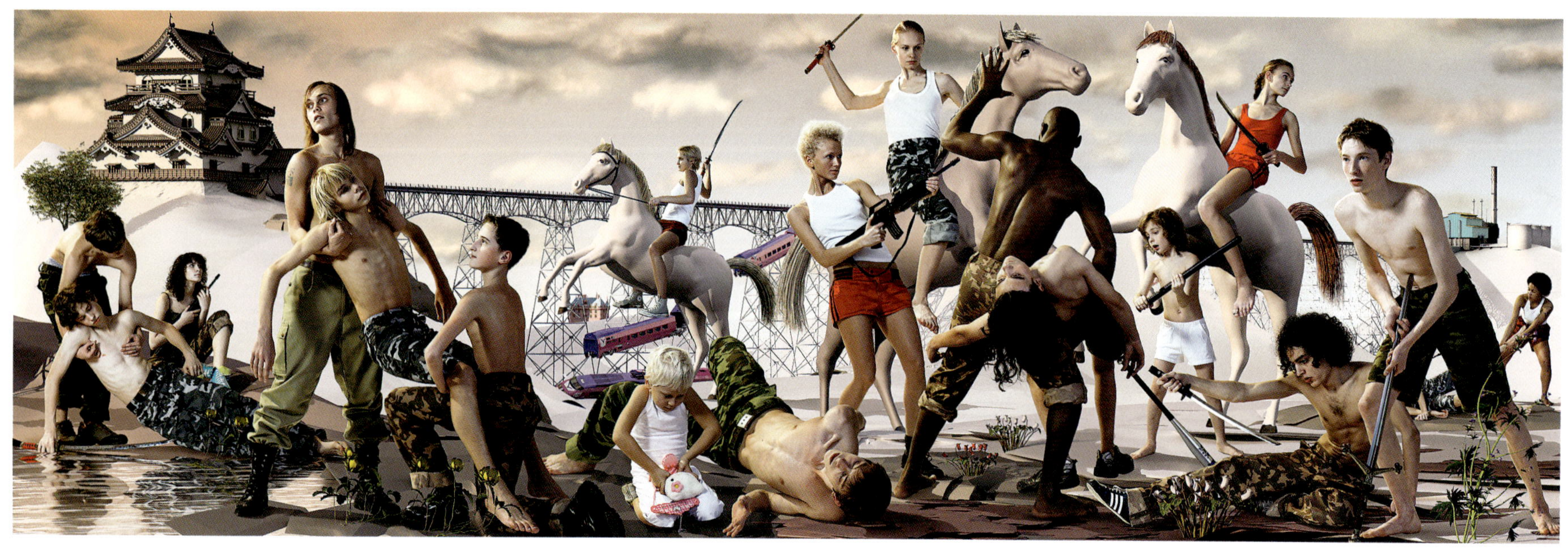

AES+F Group, *Last Riot*, Panorama #4, 2007. Lambda print on paper, 94 x 33 in.

protagonists in surreal collages of giant animals and alien fauna. The girls of his images are monochromatic, set among wildly colored scenery that seems to be consuming the empty-faced innocent children (page 35). Asked about Darger in an interview published in *Useless* magazine, Kim replied that she admired how "nothing in his work is superfluous." "Everything he did in his work came from a necessity to tell an important story that was very personal to him."[49] Kyung Jeon, who grew up in New Jersey, shrouds playful scenes of childlike figures with darker narratives of physical suffering and sexual deviancy. Using traditional rice paper and ornate geometrical patterns inspired by Korean craft, Jeon's compositions are defined by a flattening of perspective, figures floating in space. Her protagonists are like mischievous apparitions, engaging in acts of violence and earthly pleasure. Evocative of Japanese animation, the figures have a Pop cuteness but harbor the potential for real damage. In *One-Fingered Duel* (2007), a shirtless, pigtailed girl impales the stomach of a small boy with a long, pointed weaponlike appendage as an audience of stuffed animals looks on.

The Russian artist collective AES+F's three-channel video works *Last Riot* and *Last Riot 2* take place in a three-dimensional landscape that, while not created in the medium of Darger's work, reimagines the artist's themes and obsessions. AES formed in 1987, a collaboration of the artists Tatiana Arzamasova, Lev Evzovich, and Evgeny Svyatsky. The photographer Vladimir Fridkes became the F when he began working with them on select projects in 1995. *Last Riot* places live actors, young, fresh-faced teenagers, in a computer-animated panorama. While it depicts a narrative of Armageddon, populated by partially undressed children and teenagers wielding swords and automatic weapons, the work retains the feeling of a fairy tale. Featured in the Russian Pavilion of the 2005 Venice Biennale, *Last Riot*, set to the music of Wagner, joins history painting with the hysteric violence of video games.

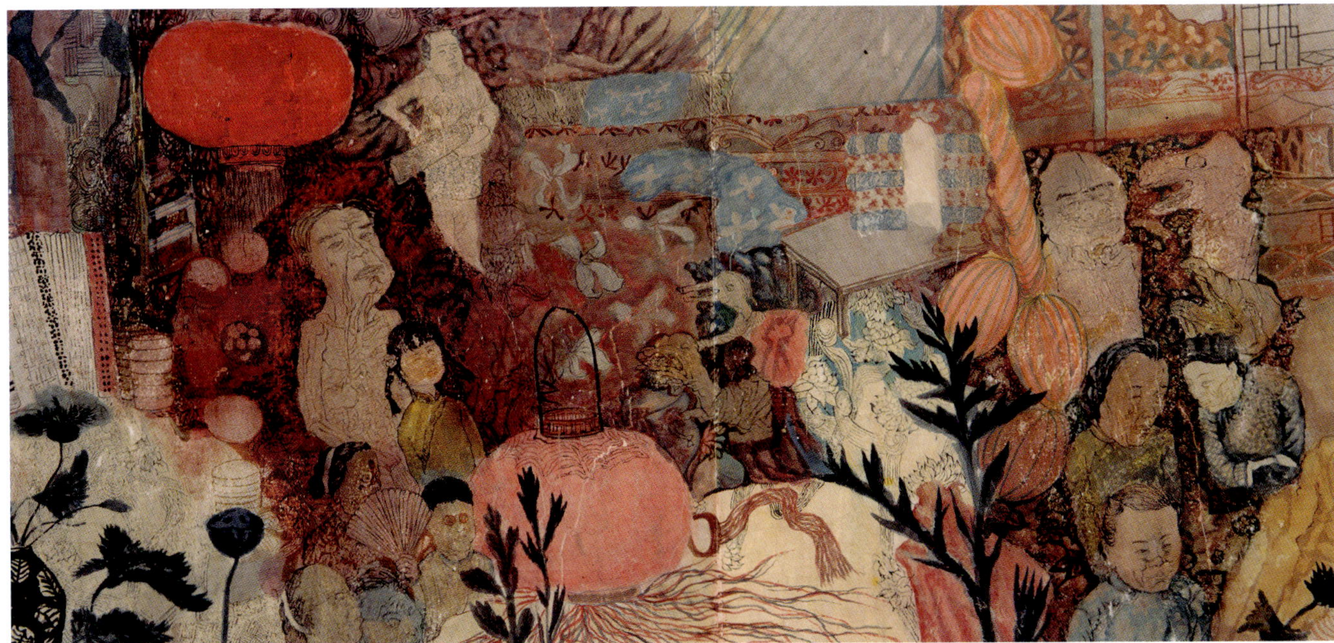

Yun-Fei Ji, *The Wedding Ballad* (detail), 2002.
Mineral pigments and ink on mulberry paper, 25 x 171 in.

The epic, exaggerated scale of the battle contrasts with a fantasy setting of miniature castles, volcanoes, and mountains that recalls Oz. AES+F's landscapes vary as widely and rapidly as Darger's, with snow-topped mountains joining sand storms and wind-swept canyons. Darger's anticipation of video-game imagery is revealed is this work, whose computer-generated environments are evocative of second-life constructs.

That AES+F, working out of Moscow, can enter a dialogue with a reclusive hospital janitor in Chicago, long dead, through a video on view the Russian Pavilion of the Venice Biennale, suggests the truly decentralized world of art today. Yun-Fei Ji, who studied at the Central Academy of Fine Arts, Beijing, and the University of Arkansas, did a residency in Rome, and now works in Brooklyn, exemplifies this important global quality of art today. It is

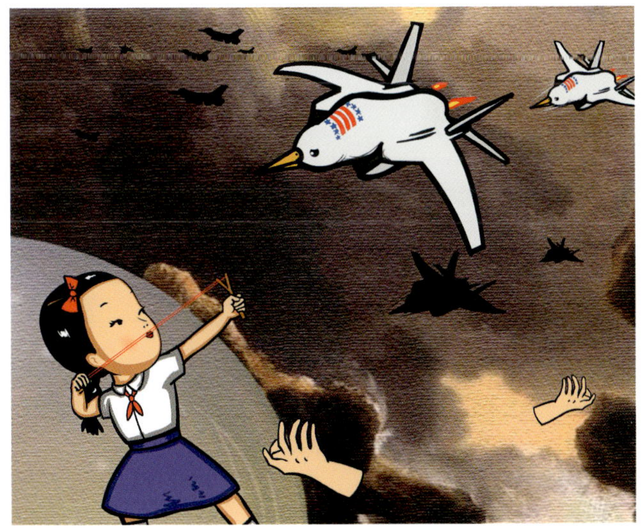

Bu Hua, *Savage Growth*, 2008. Animation, 3 min., 52 sec.

globally informed and should be globally understood. Featured in *DARGERism*, Ji's paintings are characterized by the themes of life and death, often depicting hovering ghosts. Ji, who has visited the reconstruction of Darger's apartment at Intuit: The Center for Intuitive and Outsider Art in Chicago, has explained, "I grew up with ghost stories—I know the dead are present among the living."[50] His flattening of layers and perspective evokes both ancient Chinese scroll painting and Darger's compositions. He paints on handmade rice paper with translucent ink or paint based on natural pigments, using ancient techniques, including calligraphy, to address the failure of the Communist utopia in China.

While traveling might be the only way of keeping an overview of what is happening in this ever-expanding contemporary art scene, biennials have become both a production tool and a focal point of new artistic practice. Looking at the installation *Security* by Jane Alexander at the São Paulo Biennale in 2006, a work that addressed the situation of prisoners in South Africa, the viewer was reminded of the U.S. prison at Guantanamo Bay, Cuba. All references seemed to be multilayered. The first Athens Biennale, titled *Destroy Athens,* occurred in 2007. Each day of the Biennale carried a subtitle. Day five, which was known as ". . . the bombing and total demolition of the Parthenon which has literally choked us . . ." featured two artists, Vassilis Karouk and Martin Skauen, who evoked Darger, Bosch, or Goya, or all of them at the same time, with similar depictions of violence and destruction.

A year later the Shanghai Biennale featured the Chinese artist Bu Hua, who creates short animated sequences using Flash, a digital platform popular for integrating animation in websites. Her video *Savage Growth* stars a little pony-tailed girl wearing a blue skirt (page 37). She chases after flying birds that begin to resemble airplanes as she begins shooting them down with a slingshot. Bu Hua uses surreal imagery to convey the madness of the rapid growth of Chinese cities. She naturally uses cartoonlike imagery, because it is a language she is influenced by that seems universally understandable. Hua makes the protagonist look powerless at first, an insignificant figure among the masses of China, only a little girl. But then she takes control; she becomes a warrior shooting airplanes from the sky.

Toward the end of Darger's life, the United States was struggling with its longstanding role as the "good" superpower. There had always been a bad counterpart: the Germans, the Japanese, and later the Soviet Union. The leading good countries in Darger's narrative, Angelinia and Abbieannia, begin with "A," like America. In recent years, especially after the debacle of the presidency of George W. Bush, the Iraq War, and the nation's failure to protect New Orleans from Hurricane Katrina, the question arises: is America still the leading, capable superpower, and is it still good?

The promise of the well-meaning, caretaking, peacekeeping nation seems at risk, if not lost. In this scenario Darger's work once again looks timely. A "protector of children," as Nathan Lerner called him, with good intentions, Darger cannot stop himself from imagining

Amy Wilson, *A Glimpse of What Life in a Free Country Could Be Like #6*, 2004.
Watercolor and pencil on paper, 6 x 24 in. One of a suite of seven drawings

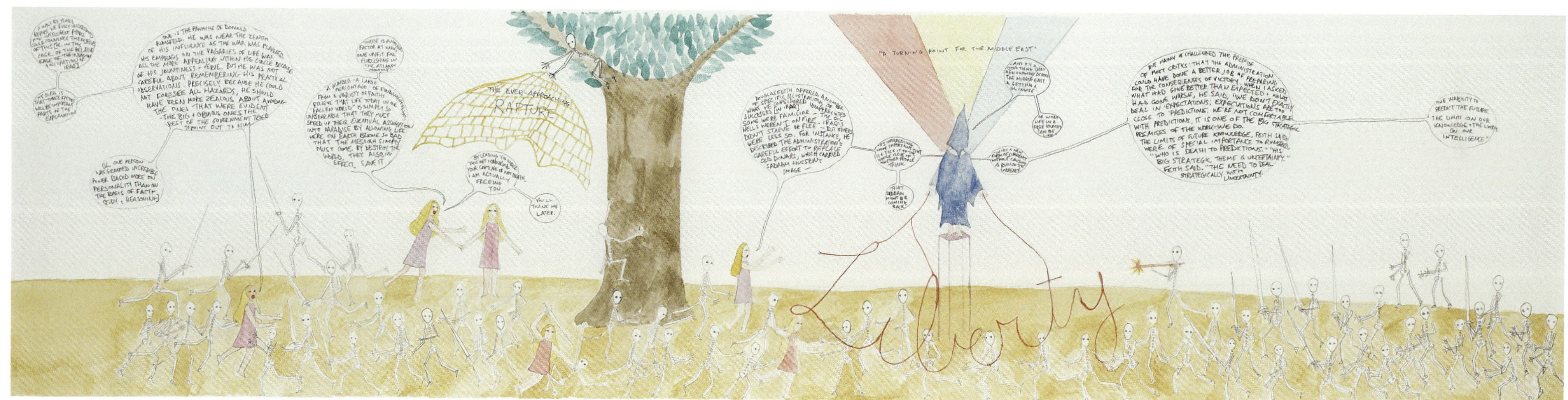

gruesome deaths in war and slavery for many of his characters, as indicated in the pages and pages of casualty records he maintained for his fictional world.

In *A Glimpse of What Life in a Free Country Could Be Like*, a 2004 set of seven drawings by the artist Amy Wilson, little girls traveling through an imagined landscape converse in stream-of-consciousness dialogues through text bubbles. The work was compared with Darger's watercolors in nearly every review. Wilson recognizes the influence of Henry Darger, naming him as a source of her imagery in a statement about her work from 2004 to 2005.[51] She places the titles of her paintings in fictive labels, little *cartellini*, at the top of her collages and watercolor works on paper. Wilson's work from this period is strongly horizontal, recalling Darger's long paintings on pieced paper. The politically charged title, *A Glimpse of What a Free Country Could Be Like,* belies the content of the drawings' texts, transcribed from political events occurring as Wilson created the drawings. In 2005, the Drawing Center was being considered for inclusion in a cultural hub then being planned for the International Freedom Center at Ground Zero (the site of the World Trade Center). The *New York Post* attacked the plan, choosing to reproduce one of Wilson's drawings from the series, which featured the hooded prisoner figure from the Abu Ghraib photographs, which sparked a controversy. The Drawing Center was excluded from the Ground Zero site.

Paul Chan, who has organized or participated in high-profile public art projects in recent years, explicitly refers to Darger in his earlier pieces. Projected onto a translucent screen hung from the ceiling in an exhibition space, Chan's *Happiness (Finally) after 35,000 Years of Civilization (After Henry Darger and Charles Fourier)* looks like a framed, double-sided scroll. This 2003 animated video tribute to Darger and the French socialist philosopher Charles Fourier places the Vivian girls in a Dargeresque horizontal plane, caught up in scenes that recall the sex and violence both latent and realized in Darger's work, directly bringing Darger into the present. As Chan told one interviewer, "I'm not Darger. But I can ask, What if Darger had a G5 [computer], and an MFA, and were still alive?"[52] Fourier's vision of hedonism and Darger's imagined wars meet in Chan's frame, reigniting the American search for utopia.

In 2002 Chan was part of the American aid group Voices in the Wilderness that broke United States sanctions and federal law by working in Baghdad before the U.S. invasion and occupation. In 2004 he garnered police attention for *The People's Guide to the Republican National Convention*, a free map distributed throughout New York City, where the election-year convention was to be held, to help protesters to get in or out of the way of it. More recently, Chan collaborated with the Classical Theatre of Harlem and Creative Time to produce a site-specific outdoor presentation of Samuel Beckett's play *Waiting for Godot* in New Orleans in the aftermath of Hurricane Katrina. His sincere and serious, unironic and not at all cynical gestures remind us of our responsibilities as individuals, as citizens, as artists, and as consumers.

After all, American innocence does not exist.

Paul Chan, *Happiness (Finally) after 35,000 Years of Civilization (after Henry Darger and Charles Fournier)*, 2000–3.
Mini PC, installation instructions, sparkle vellum screen, and equipment specification, 17 min., 20 sec.

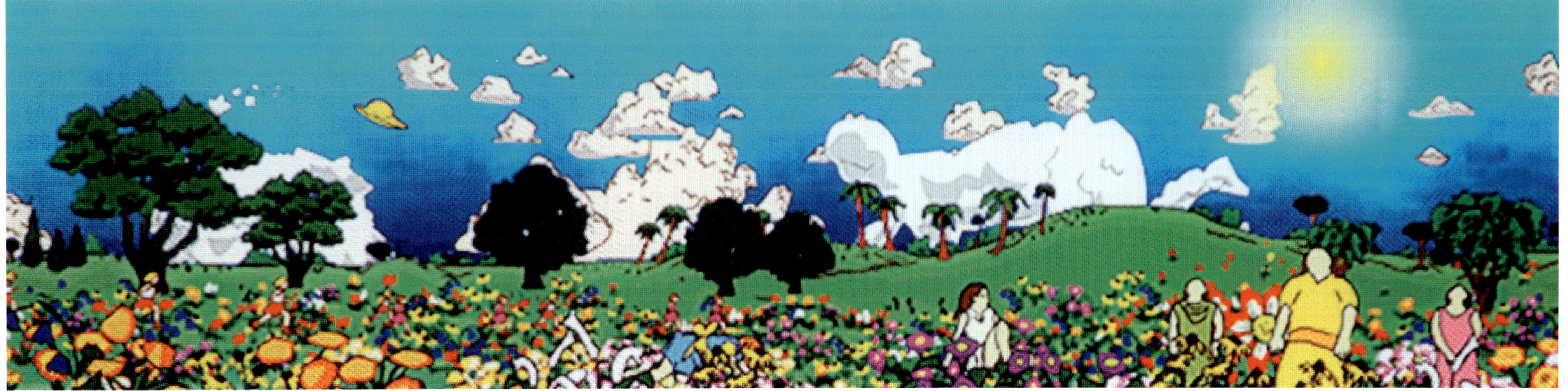

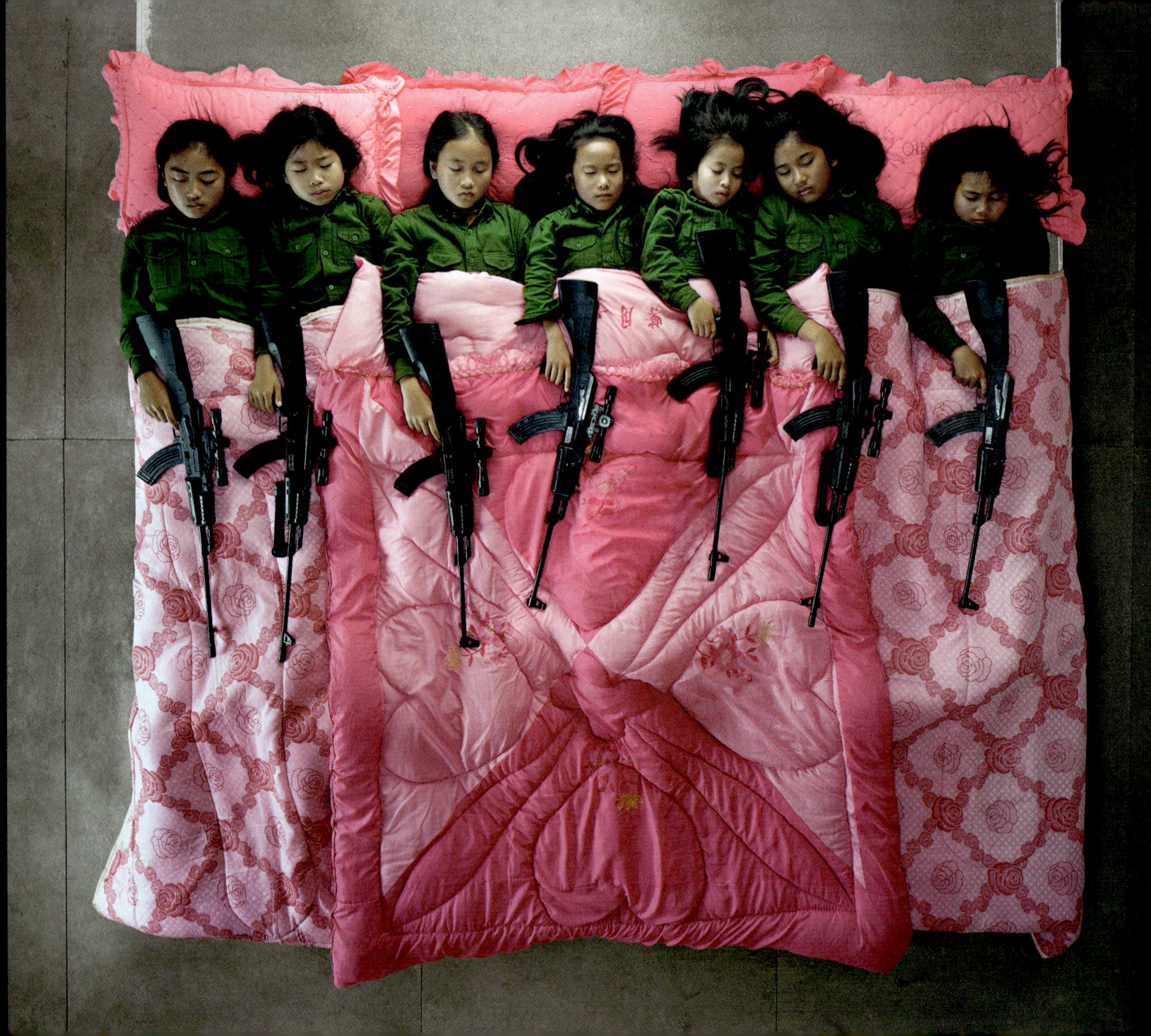

The International Labour Organization, a specialized agency of the United Nations, estimates there are more than 80 million children under the age of fourteen engaged in hazardous work, many in situations of virtual slavery, in clothing and shoe sweatshops, as child soldiers, in agriculture, brick-making, fishing, domestic service, or as child sex workers. The ILO considers that 8.4 million children are in the unconditional worst forms of child labor, which would include situations akin to slavery.[53]

Notes

1. John MacGregor, *Henry Darger: In the Realms of the Unreal* (New York: Delano Greenidge, 2002), 42.

2. MacGregor, *Henry Darger: In the Realms of the Unreal*, 67.

3. Michael Bonesteel, *Henry Darger: Art and Selected Writings* (New York: Rizzoli, 2000), 23.

4. MacGregor, *Henry Darger: In the Realms of the Unreal*, 100–1.

5. Henry Darger, *The History of My Life*, manuscript, ca. 1968–72, 19.

6. MacGregor, *Henry Darger: In the Realms of the Unreal*, 262.

7. Ibid, 253.

8. Bonesteel, *Henry Darger: Art and Selected Writings*, 19.

9. MacGregor, *Henry Darger: In the Realms of the Unreal*, 99. Baum wrote fourteen Oz novels; a large number of additional books were later written by other authors (see note 12).

10. Ibid.

11. Ibid.

12. John R. Neill illustrated thirty-nine of the forty canonical Oz books. After the first fourteen by Baum, these were written by Ruth Plumly Thompson and finally by Neill himself.

13. Darger's collection of photographs may not have seemed out of place in turn-of-the-century America. Portraits of nude or near-nude children were less scandalous in the late nineteenth and early twentieth centuries. In the Victorian era, a post-mortem portrait may have been the only photo ever taken of a person, particularly a child. Photographers took care to pose the corpses as if they were still living, sometimes sitting them up in chairs, eyes closed, hands crossed in their laps. Many of these photographs captured images of babies who had died, dressed in their christening outfits.

14. The exact number of artworks made by Darger is not presently known, and awaits the thorough inventory of a catalogue raisonné. Many of Darger's watercolors are two-sided; others are polyptychs, and scholars approach the counting of these in different ways. The American Folk Art Museum counts two-sided works and those with a multipart format as single artworks, arriving at an estimate that Darger made more than three hundred of these; other scholars consider each unit as a separate work. The drawings (called "tracings" by MacGregor) number in the hundreds.

15. MacGregor, *Henry Darger: In the Realms of the Unreal*, 81.

16. *Andy Warhol: A Documentary Film*, directed by Ric Burns, broadcast by the Public Broadcasting Service on September 20 and 21, 2006 (produced by Steeplechase Films, High Line Productions, Daniel Wolf, and Thirteen/WNET, 2006).

17. The Institute of Design was founded by László Moholy-Nagy as the New Bauhaus in 1937. Nathan Lerner became its interim director following Moholy-Nagy's death in 1946. It became part of the Illinois Institute of Technology in 1949, and Lerner left the school to open a design office in Chicago. After retiring from his design business, Lerner resumed his photography career in the 1960s, working both in black-and-white and color.

18. Gwyn A. Williams, *Goya and the Impossible Revolution* (New York: Pantheon Books, 1976), 142.

19. Ibid.

20. Bonesteel, *Henry Darger: Art and Selected Writings*, 34, n. 19.

21. MacGregor, *Henry Darger: In the Realms of the Unreal*, 202.

22. Bonesteel, *Henry Darger: Art and Selected Writings*, 17.

23. Frank Maresca, Roger Ricco, and Lyle Rexer. *American Self-taught: Paintings and Drawings by Outsider Artists*. (New York: Knopf, 1993), 191–92.

24. See the extensive quotation from a 1979 article by Jack Burnham in Bonesteel, *Henry Darger: Art and Selected Writings*, 16–17.

25. Bonesteel, *Henry Darger: Art and Selected Writings*, 91.

26. MacGregor, *Henry Darger: In the Realms of the Unreal*, 681, n. 47.

27. "The Way We Live Now: 4-4-99—Questions for John Ashbery; A Child in Time," *New York Times*, Sunday, April 4, 1999, sec. 6, 15.

28. Adolph Gottlieb interview, October 25, 1967, Archives of American Art, Smithsonian Institution, Washington, D.C.

29. MacGregor, *Henry Darger: In the Realms of the Unreal*, 251.

30. Deborah Solomon, *Utopia Parkway: The Life and Work of Joseph Cornell* (New York: Farrar, Straus and Giroux, 1997), 20.

31. Grady Turner, "Yayoi Kusama," *Bomb* 66 (Winter 1999).

32. Bonesteel, *Henry Darger: Art and Selected Writings*, 30.

33. MacGregor, *Henry Darger: In the Realms of the Unreal*, 545.

34. Ibid., 597.

35. Ibid., 5.

36. Ibid.

37. Adrian Heathfield and Tehching Hsieh, *Out of Now: The Lifeworks of Tehching Hsieh* (London: Live Art Development Agency, 2009), 334.

38. Ibid., 324.

39. See Arthur and Marilouise Kroker, *The Hysterical Male* (London: Macmillan, 1991).

40. Quoted in Beatrix Ruf, ed., *Sean Landers* (Zurich: JRP Ringier Kunstverlag, 2004), 97.

41. MacGregor, *Henry Darger: In the Realms of the Unreal*, 255.

42. Ibid., 434.

43. Ibid.

44. Bonesteel, *Henry Darger: Art and Selected Writings*, 251.

45. Ibid., 227.

46. Google search results as of May 24, 2009.

47. Unpublished wall text for the exhibition *DARGERism: Contemporary Artists and Henry Darger*, American Folk Art Museum, New York, April 15–September 21, 2008.

48. Nakadate, correspondence with the author, May 20, 2009.

49. Conrad Macellus Ventur, "In New York Min Kim Depicts the Endangered Fantastic," *Useless* no. 4, 41.

50. Carly Berwick, "Before the Deluge," *ArtNews*, September 2003

51. www.amy-wilson.com/statement1.php, accessed May 22, 2009.

52. "Paul Chan," by Nell McClister, *BOMB* 92 (Summer 2005).

53. The U.S. Department of State's *Trafficking in Persons Report*, June 2008, contains a similar statement, noting that the ILO "estimates that there are 12.3 million people in forced labor, bonded labor, forced child labor, and sexual servitude at any given time; other estimates range from 4 million to 27 million. Annually, according to U.S. government-sponsored research completed in 2006, approximately 800,000 people are trafficked across national borders, which does not include millions trafficked within their own countries. Approximately 80 percent of transnational victims are women and girls and up to 50 percent are minors." U.S. Department of State, Publication 11407, Office of the Under Secretary for Democracy and Global Affairs and Bureau of Public Affairs.

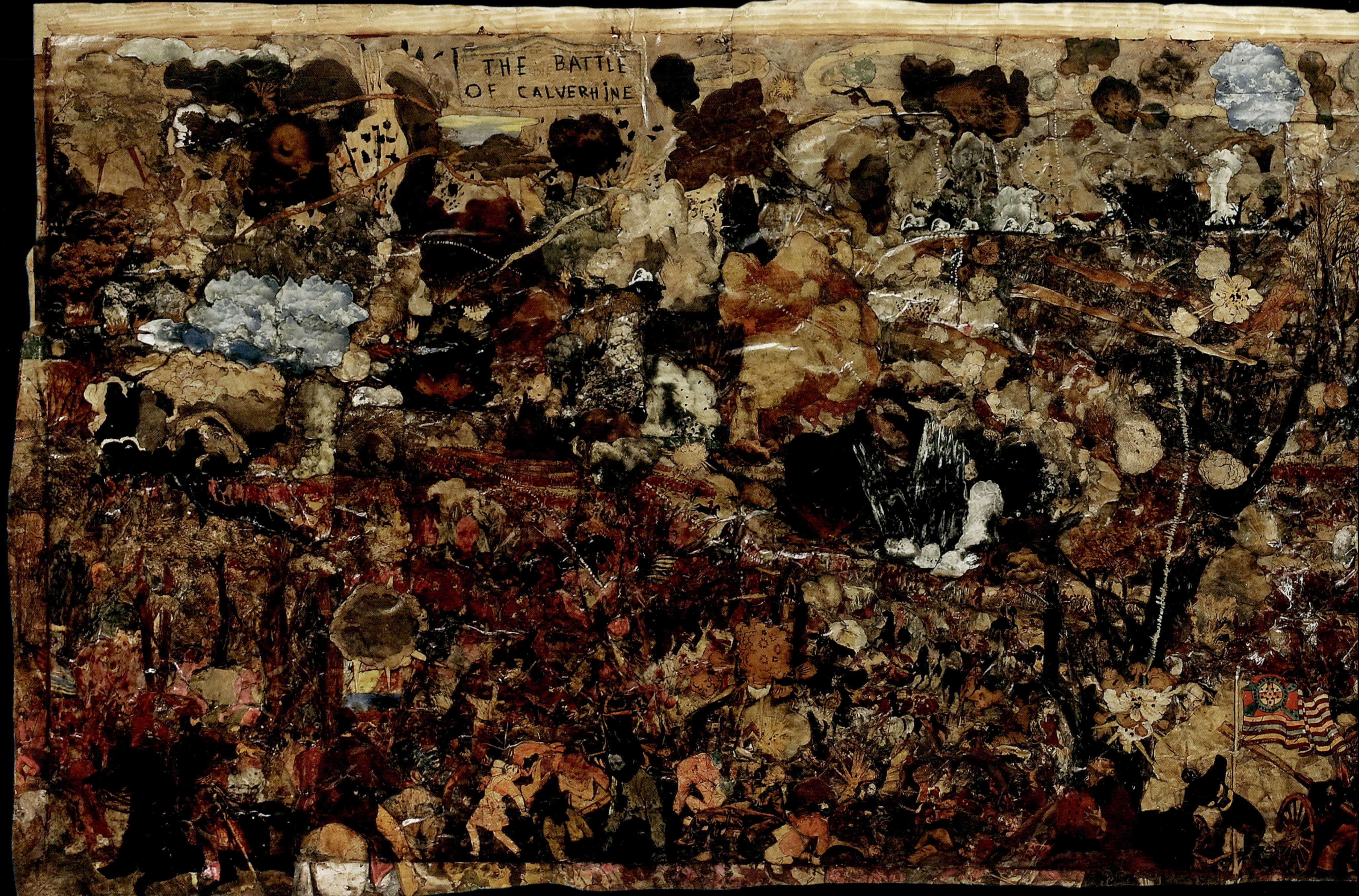

42 | *The Battle of Calverhine.*

Varnished collage, 37 ½ x 116 ⅝ in.

Collection Kiyoko Lerner

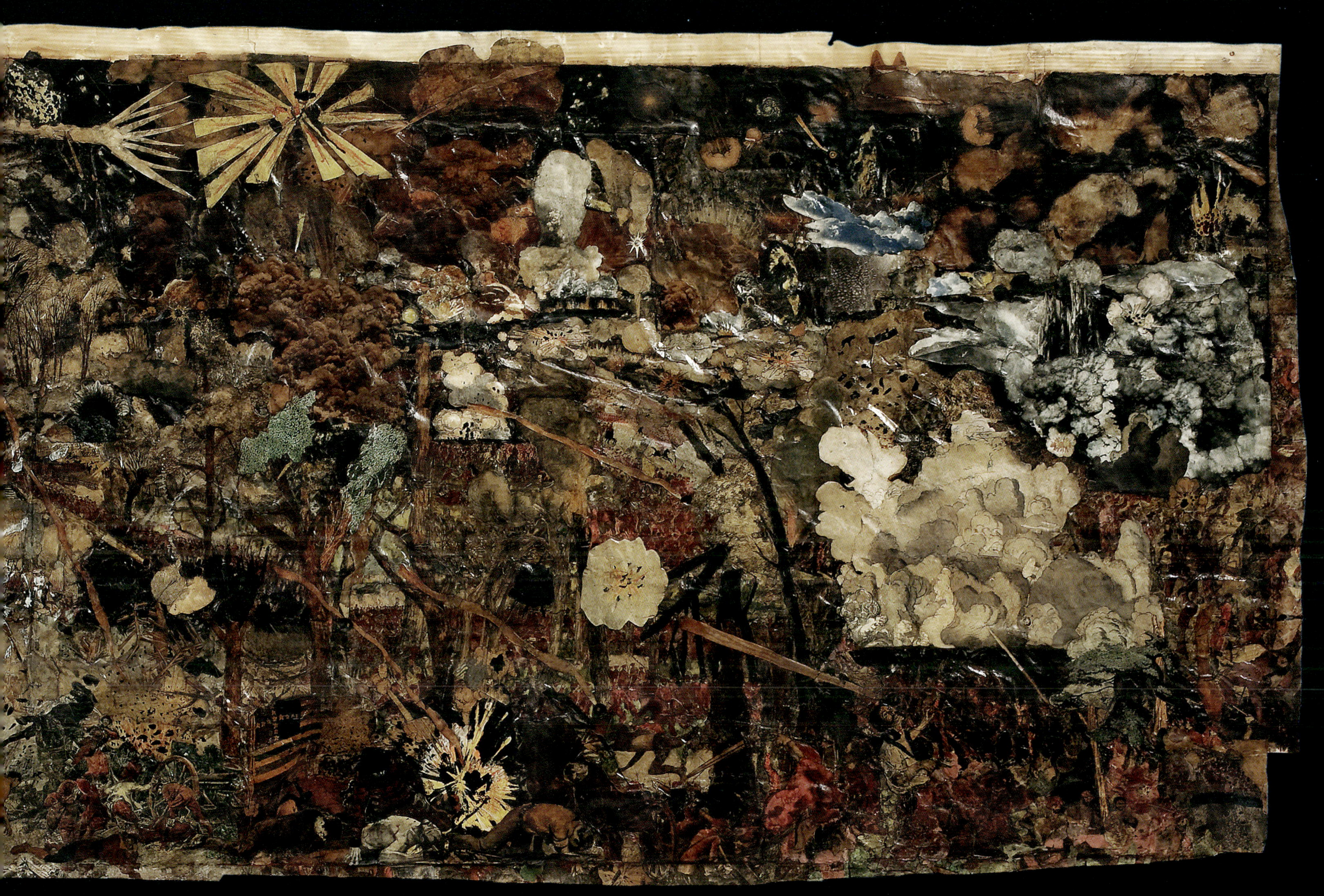

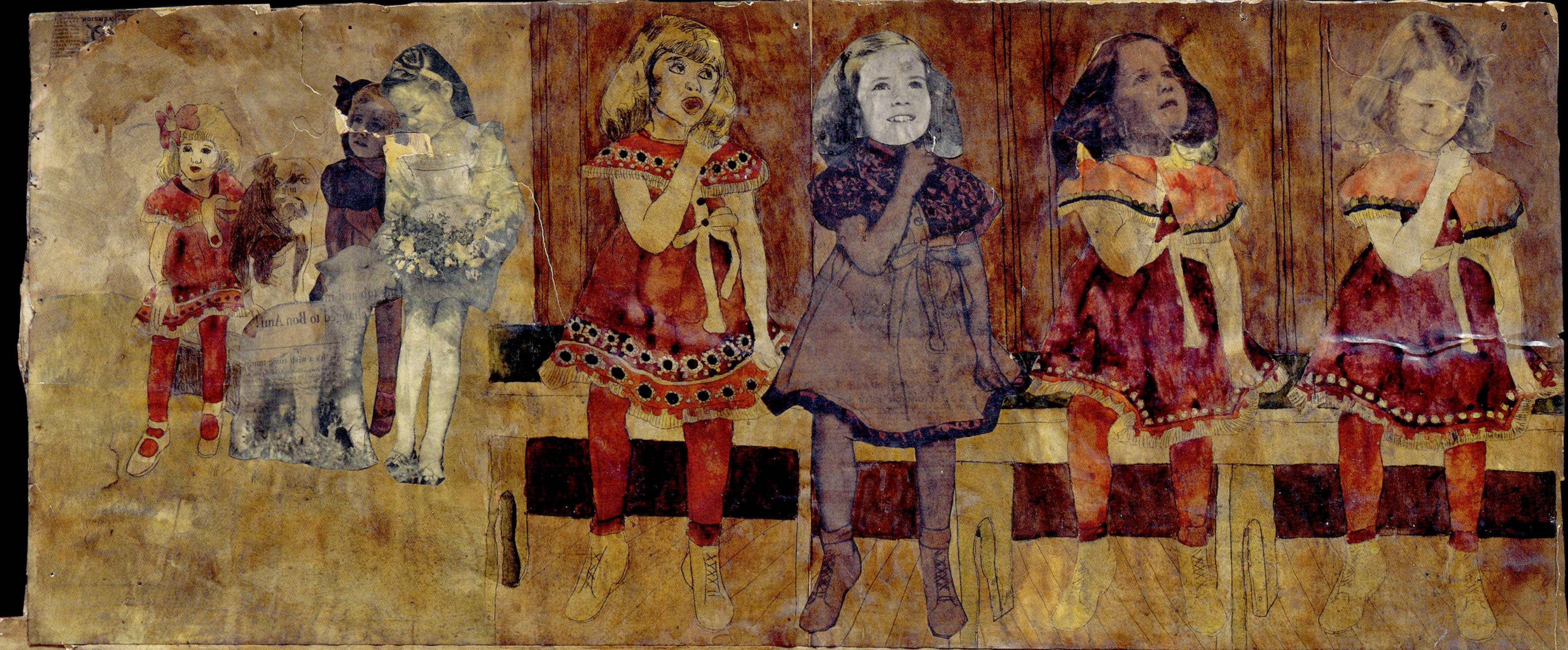

THE VIVIAN PRINEESSES. THESE LITTLE GIRLS PICTURED HERE IN BEST CLOTHES, LOOK HAPPY HERE, BUT WHAT IS WRITTEN OF THEM (HERE) WOULD MAKE THE
OBSERVER. NOT WISH TO BE IN THEIR PLACE. I,LL BET NO SAINT ON EARTH WENT THROUGH A LIFE OF HORROR SUFFERING AND SORROW LIKE THEY DID
JUST BECAUSE THEY ARE GOOD, WICKED FOES, EXILED THEM ON THE DEVILS ISLAND AND A LEPERS ISLE. OTHER THINGS TOLD ABOUT THEM ARE DREADFUL, THE LITTLE GIRLS SHOWN
DIFFERENT POSES, ARE THEY ALSO, BUT IN DISGUISES. THEY ARE VERY BRAVE, HOLY AND VERY FORGIVING THE BOY IN THE PICTURE IS THEIR BROTERER PENROD.
TO KNOW ABOUT THEM PROPERLY. THE OBSERVER WILL HAVE TO READ THE LONG STORIES ABOUT THEM. THEY   BEAUTIFUL

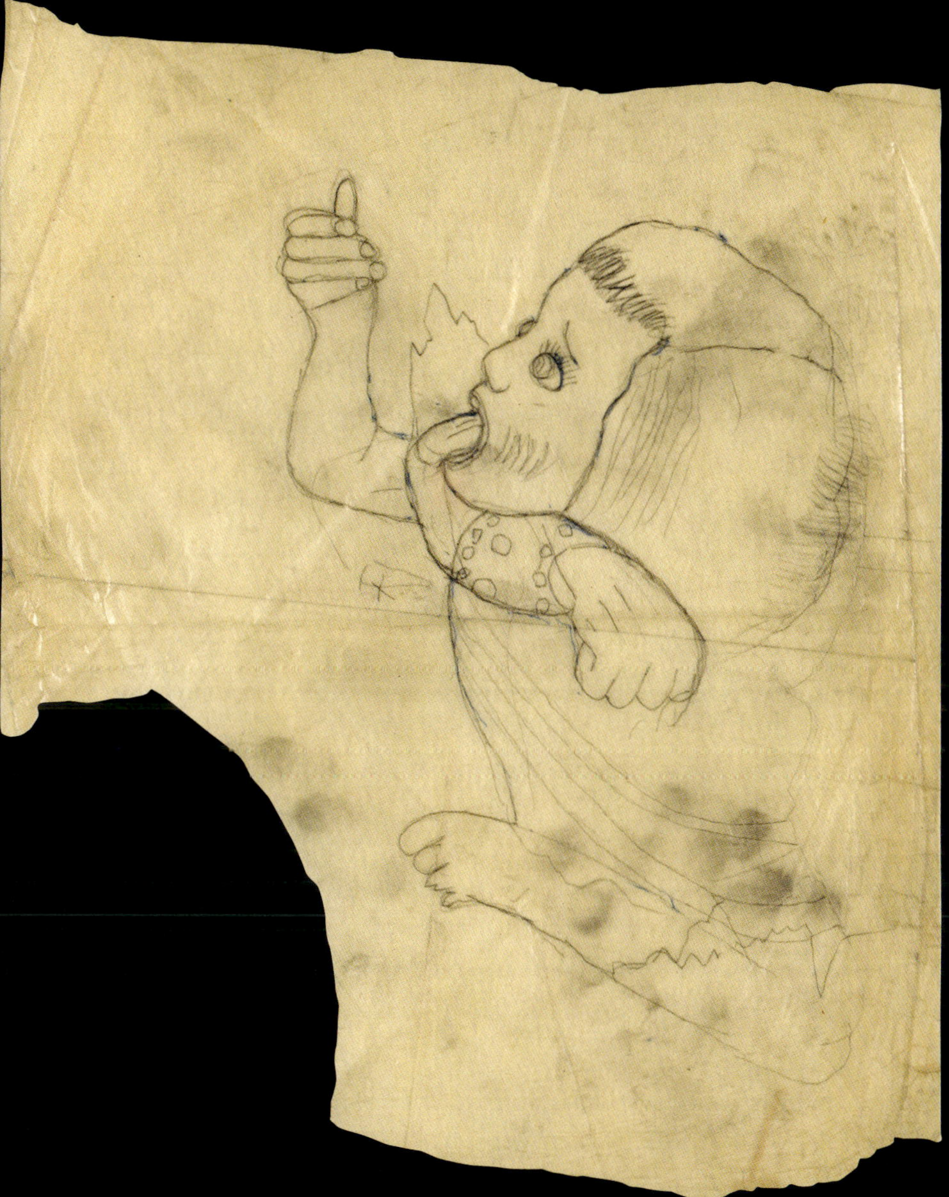

THE ART OF HENRY DARGER

[Sources and Drawings]

A PORTFOLIO

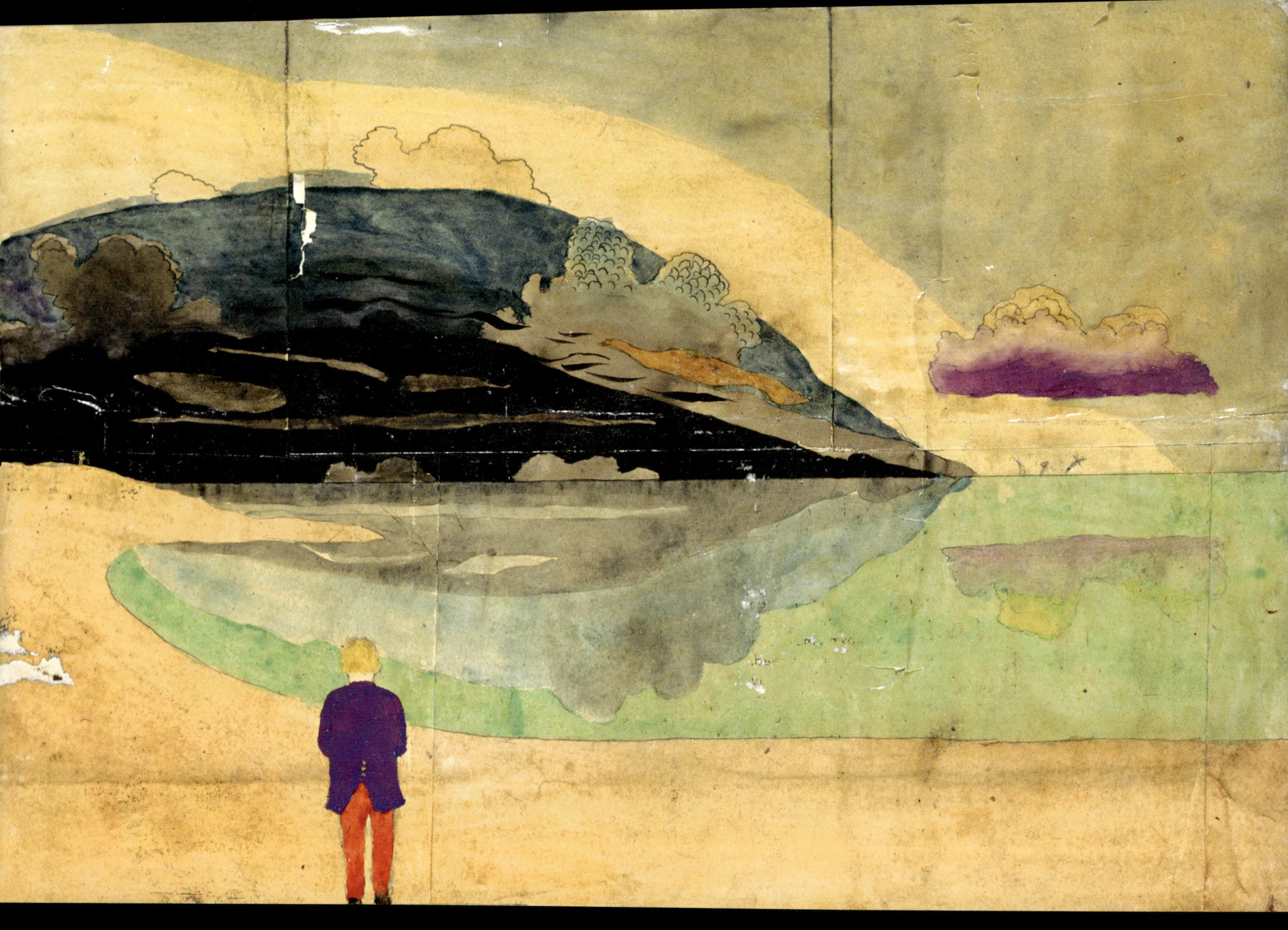

Robert Vivian, his brother going near the see shore . . . (detail).
Watercolor, carbon tracing, and collage on paper, 28 ⅜ x 46 ¼ in.
Collection de l'art brut, Lausanne

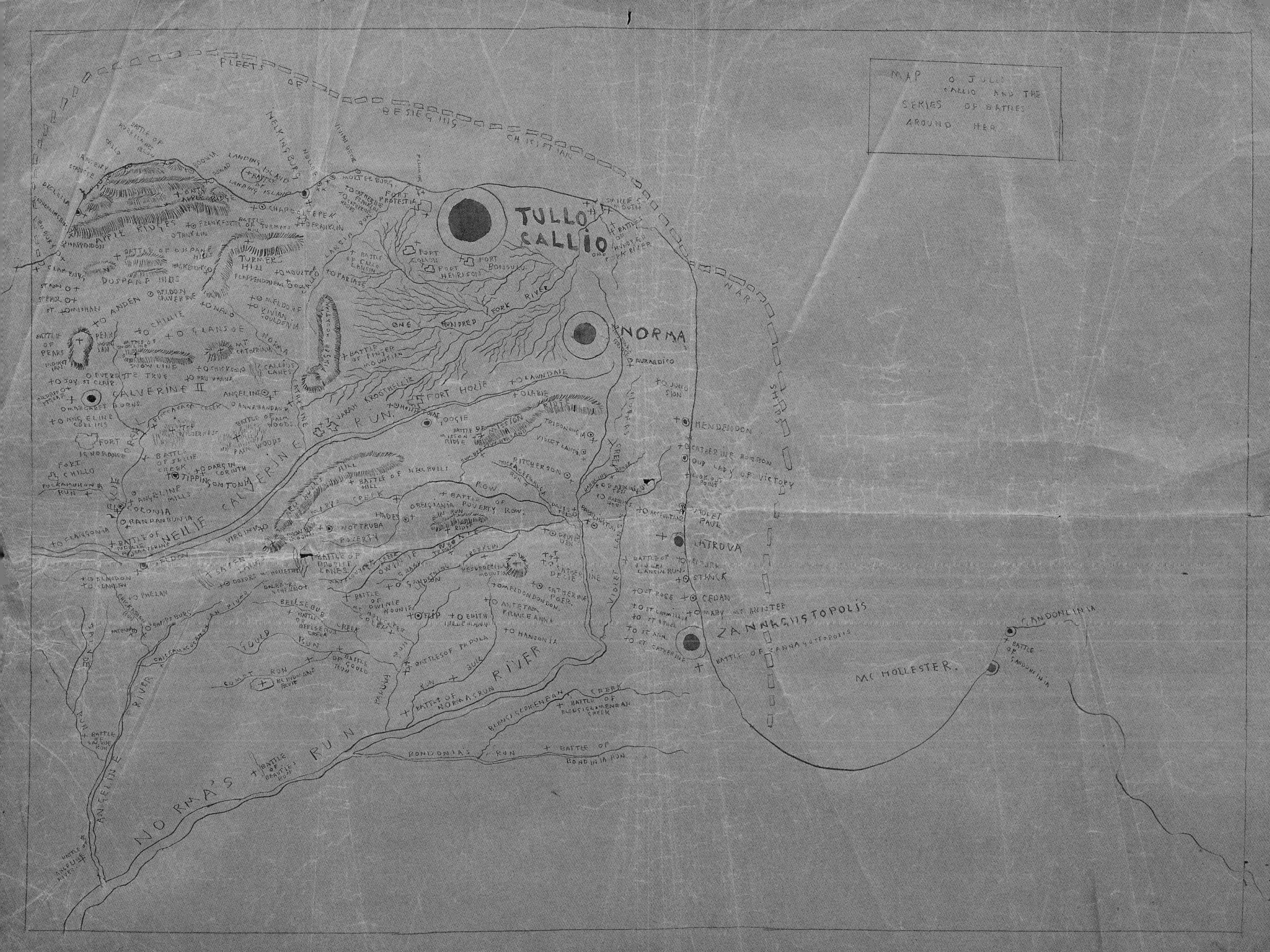

MAP O JULI
CALLIO AND THE
SERIES OF BATTLES
AROUND HER
FLEETS OF
BESIEGING CHRISTIAN
TULLO CALLIO
NORMA
ONE HUNDRED FORK RIVER
TURNERS HILL
DOSPANE HILLS
APPLE RIDGES
CALVERINE II
CALVERINE RUN
FORT HOLLIE
LASTROVA
VIOLET PAUL
HENDENDON
CATHERINE BOGGON
OUR LADY OF VICTORY
BATTLE OF NELLIE
COLONIA
POVERTY ROW
ZANNKGIISTOPOLIS
MC MOLLESTER
CANDONLINIA
BATTLE OF CANDONLINIA
NORMA'S RUN
NORMA'S RIVER
ANGELINE RIVER
BATTLE OF NORMAS RUN
BONDONIAS RUN
BATTLE OF BONDONIA RUN

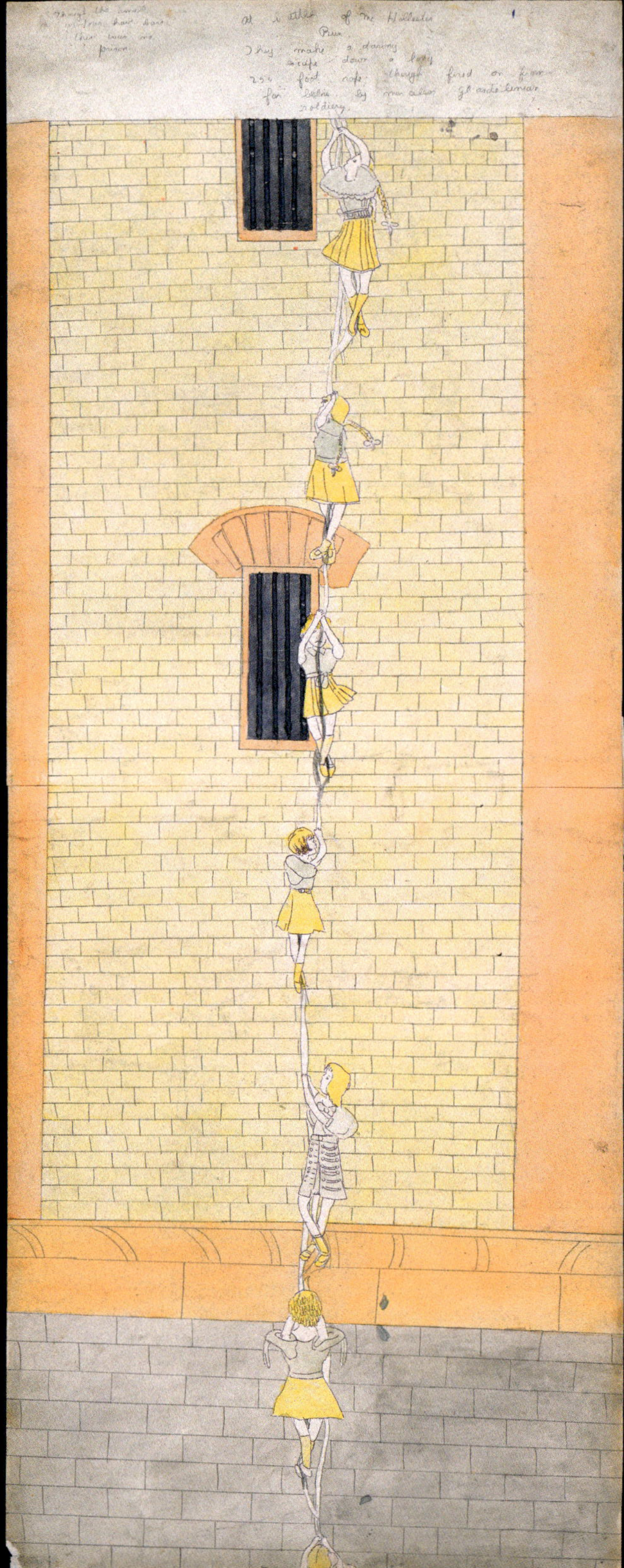

At Battle of Mic-Hollester Run. They make a daring escape
down a long 250-foot rope though fired on
from far below by a merciless Glandelinian soldiery.
Watercolor, pencil, and carbon tracing on pieced paper, 48 x 19 in.
Collection Kiyoko Lerner

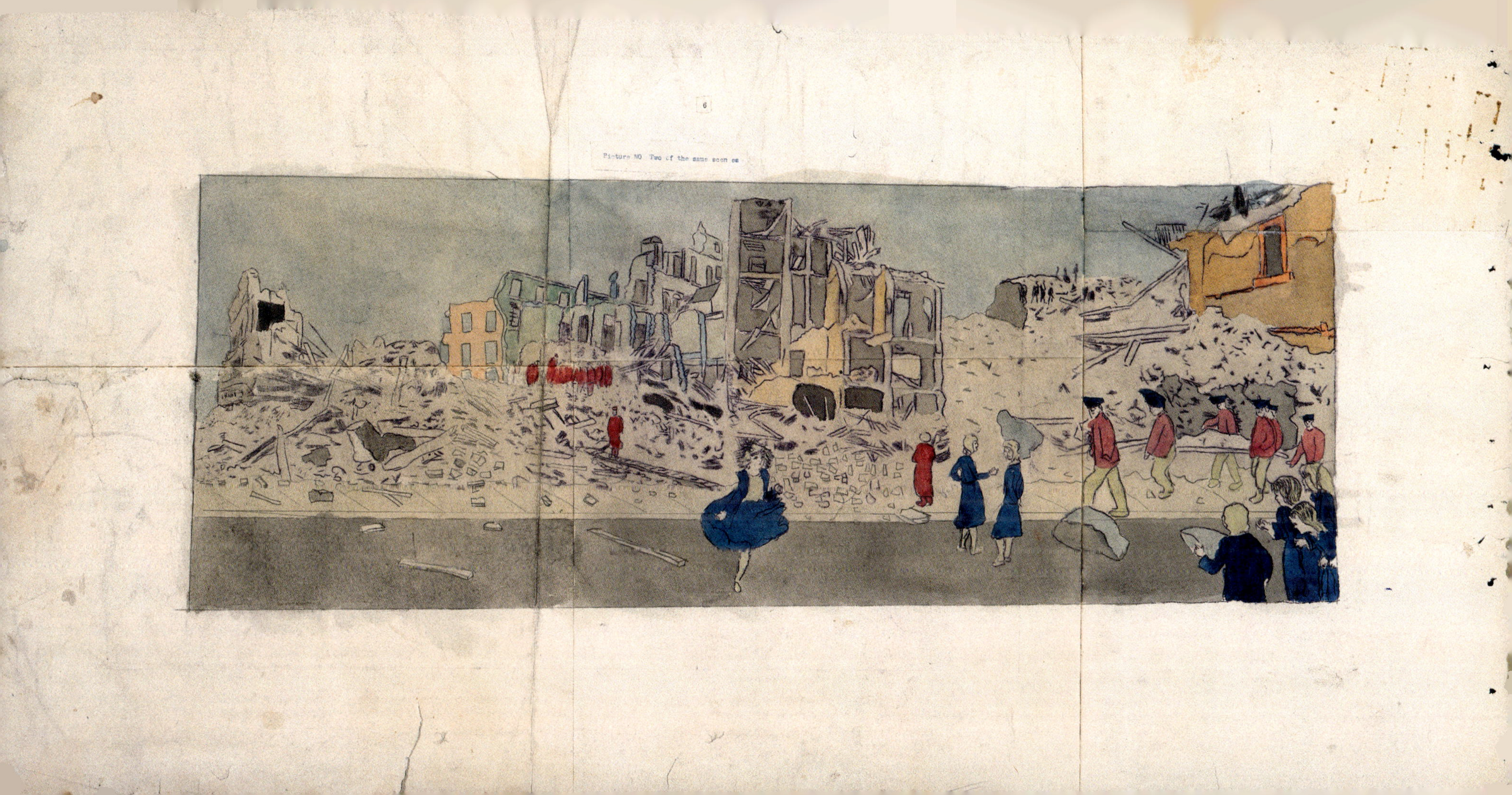

6
Picture NO. Two of the same scene as

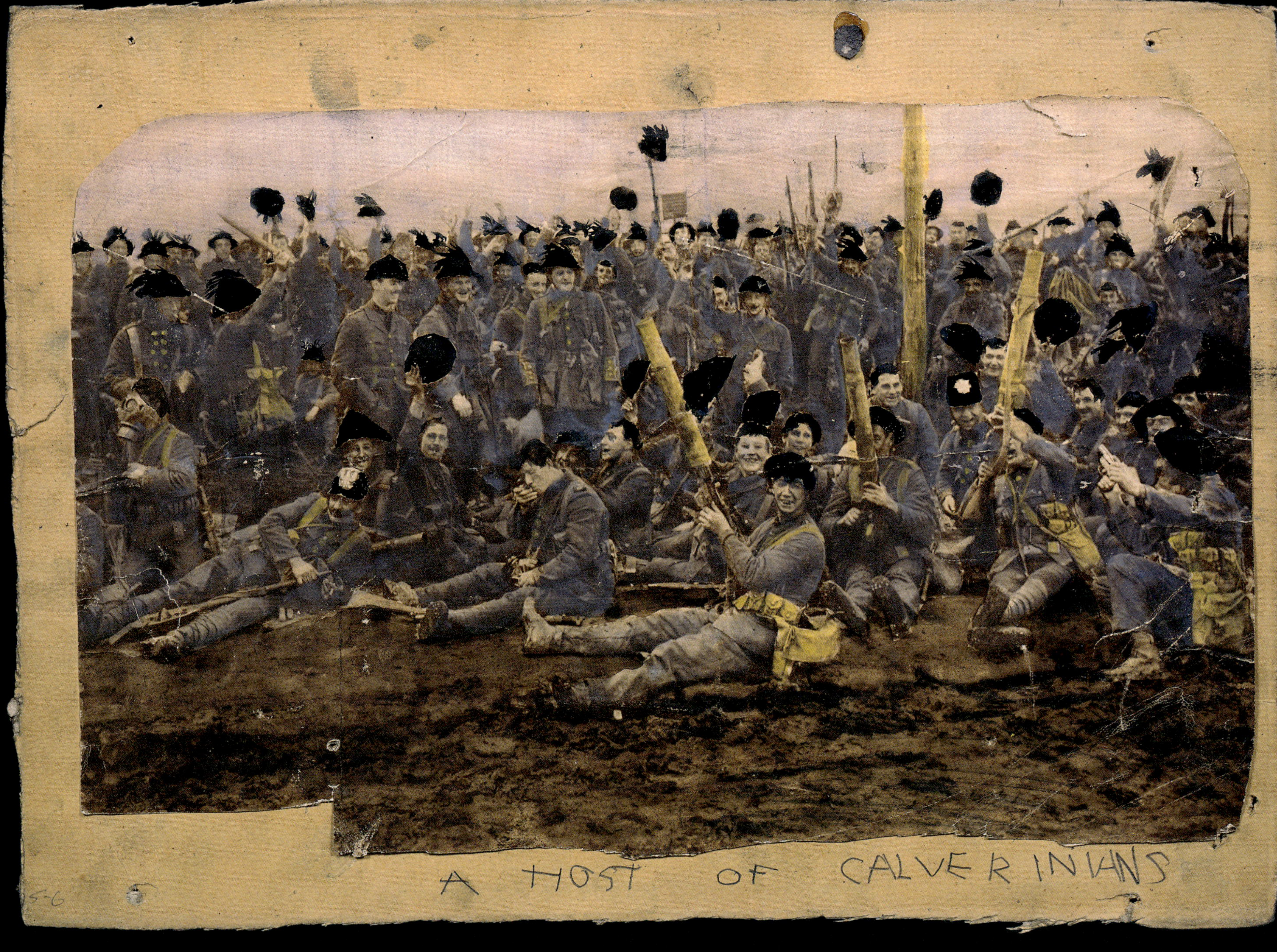

50 | *A Host of Calverinians.*

Sepia-toned photograph with color added by Darger, 11 ½ x 16 in.

Collection de l'art brut, Lausanne

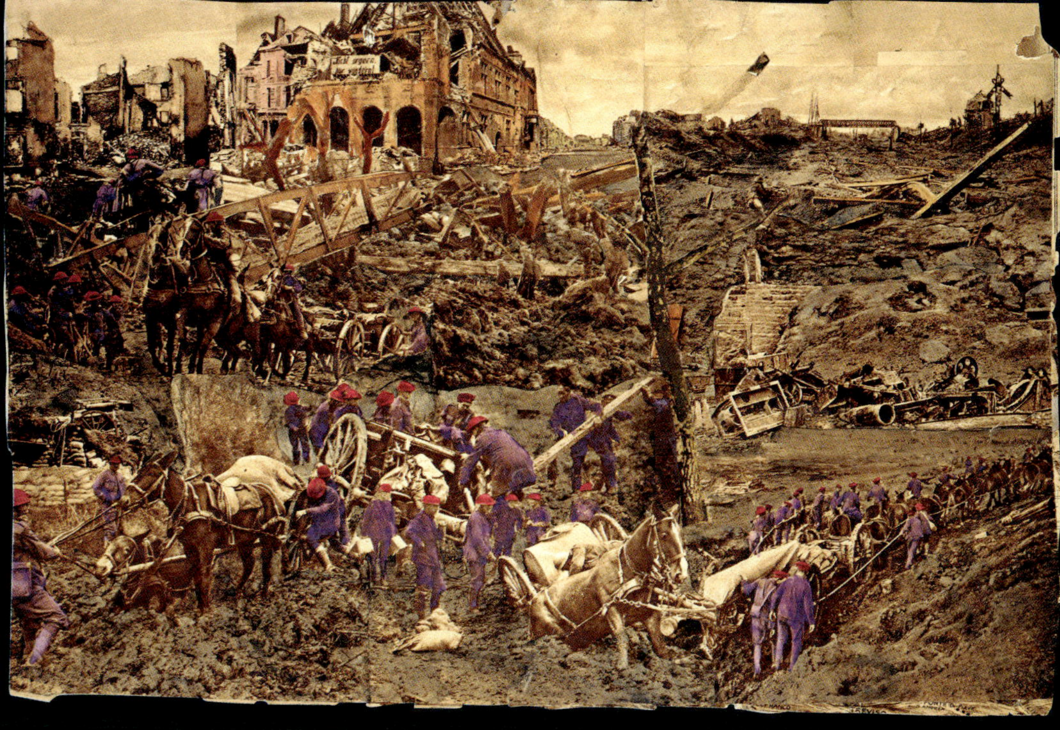

Untitled (Nicht argern, nur wundern!). Collage and watercolor on paper,
15 x 22 ¾ in. Collection de l'art brut, Lausanne

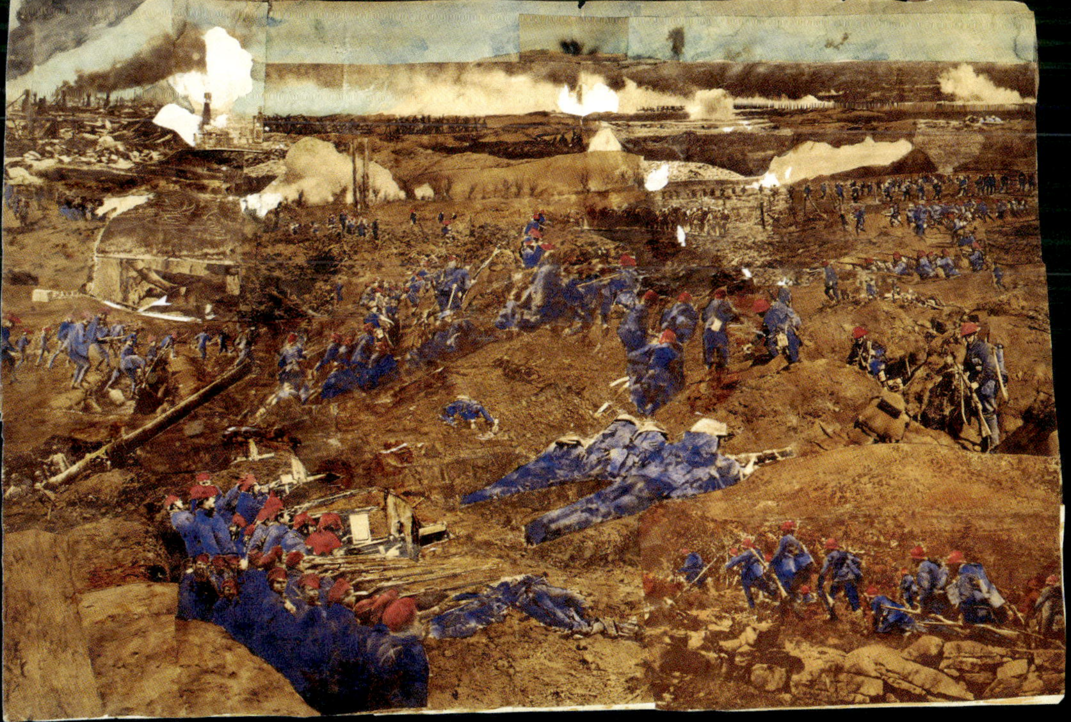

Untitled. Collage and watercolor on paper,
15 ⅝ x 23 in. Collection de l'art brut, Lausanne

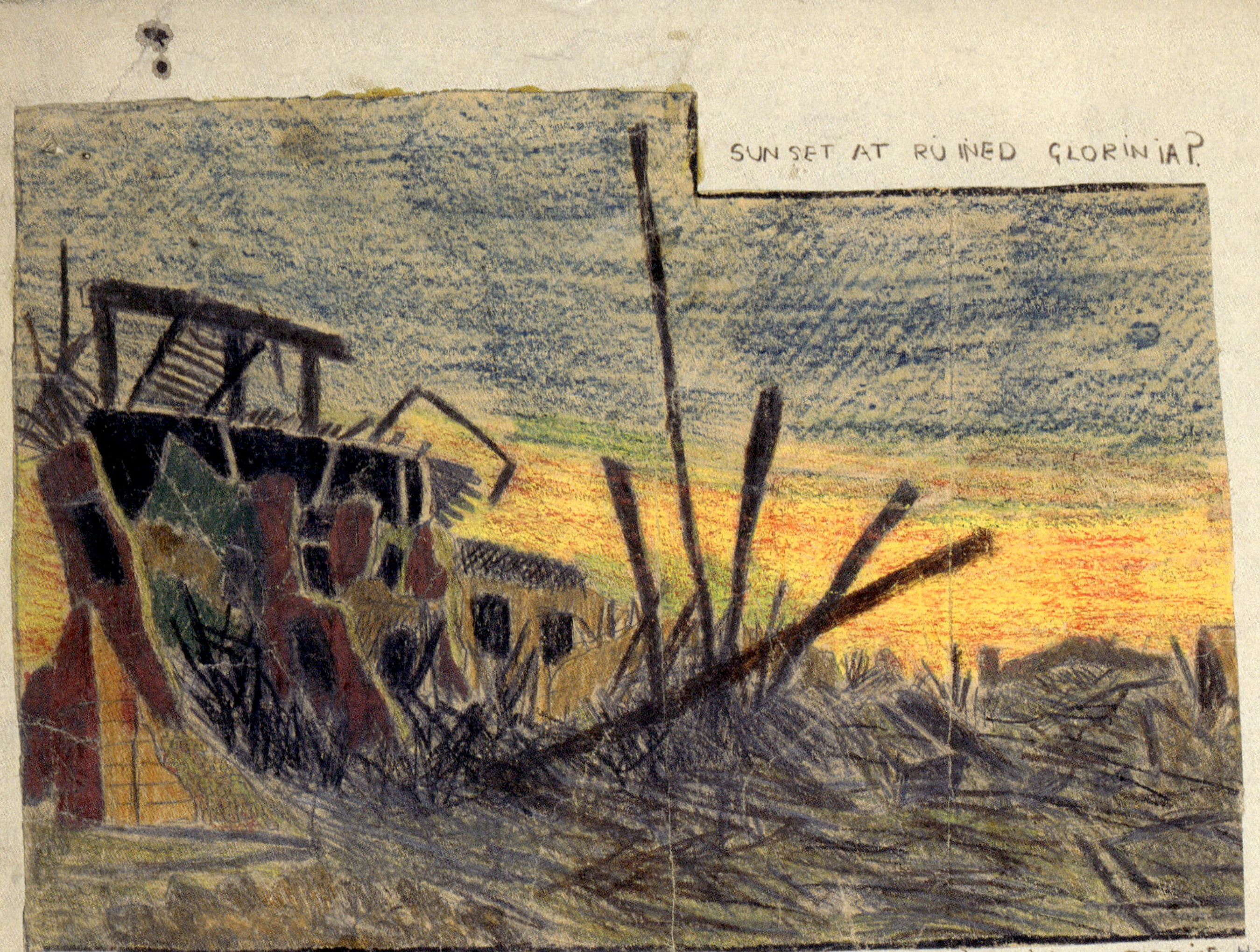

SUNSET AT RUINED GLORINIA?
RUINS OF AKONBURGS MANISON, GLORINIA WHERE THREE OF THE VIVIAN GIRLS CATHERINE HETTIE DAISY WERE TAKEN. THIS IMMENSE STRUCTURE HAVING BEEN A BLOCK LONG AND FIVE STORIES HIGH. IT FAIRLY CAVED IN AT THE SUDDEN CONCUSSION OF THE CANNONADING ON THE Mc HOLLESTER, STANCK, WHITE ROSE AND CARNATION RIDGES DURING THE BATTLE OF GLORINIA. OVER SIX HUNDRED PEOPLE WERE KILLED IN THIS BUILDING, THE MANISON CAVING IN SO QUICKLY THAT NONE OF ITS TENANTS ESCAPED. ONLY THE REMAINING WALLS SEEN IN THE PICTURE HELD FIRM. THIS BUILDING STOOD ON THE CORNERS OF ALICIE AND Mc HOLLISTER STREET IN THE CITY OF GLORINIA

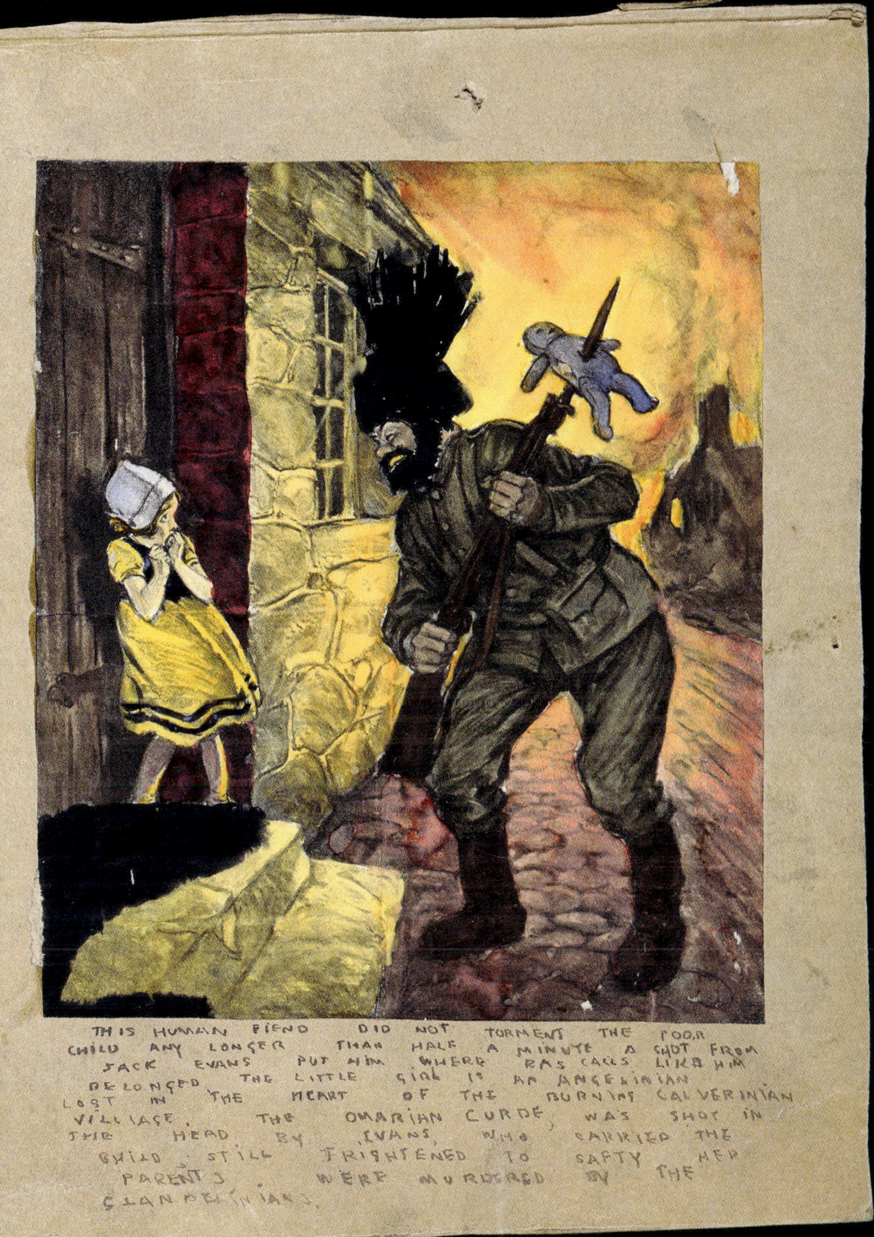

Untitled ("This human fiend . . ."). Watercolor and pencil on clipping of illustration, mounted on cardboard, 16 1/8 x 11 5/8 in. Collection American Folk Art Museum, New York. Gift of Kyoko Lerner

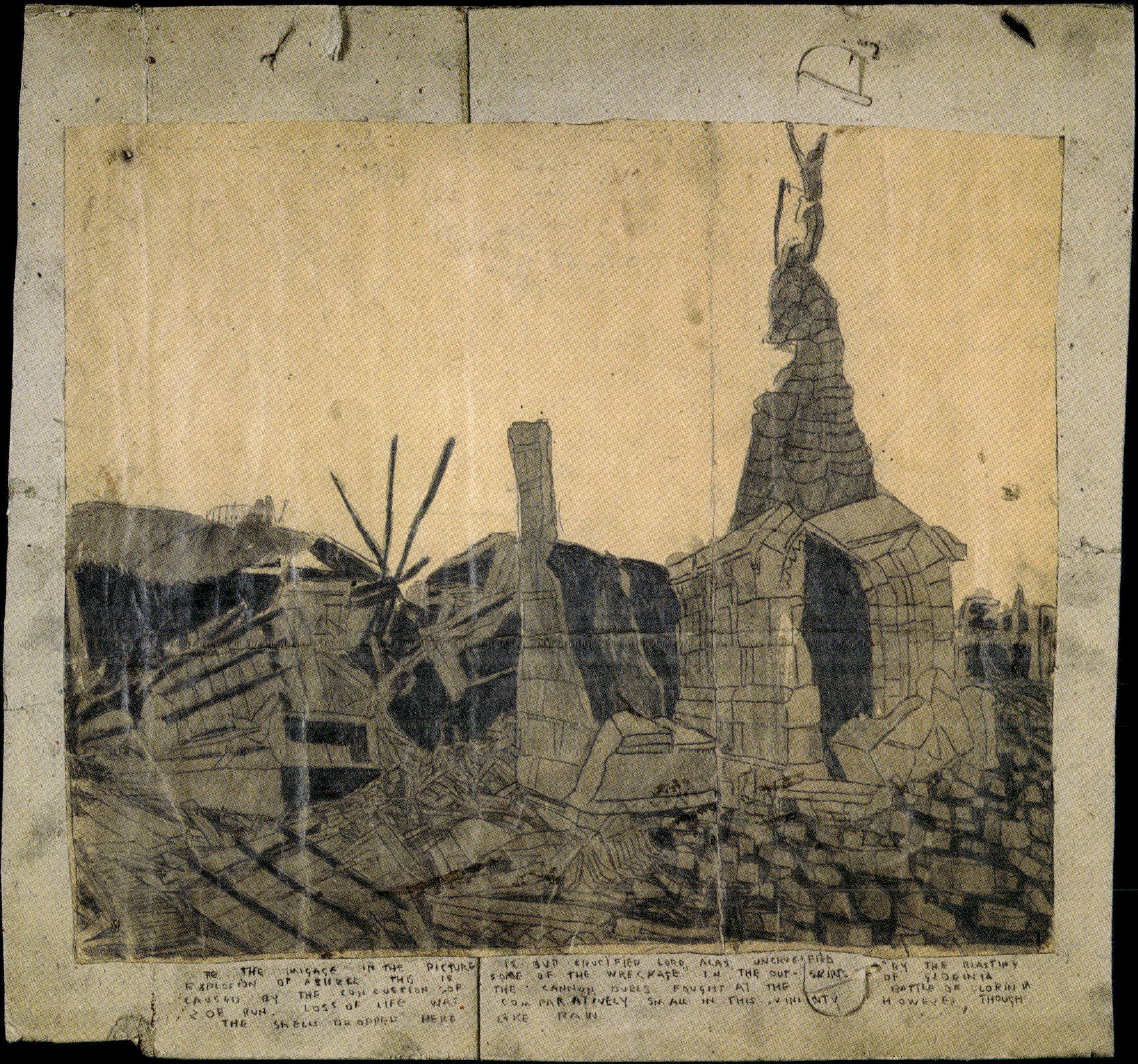

The [image] in the picture is our crucified lord, alas, uncrucified by the blasting explosion of [. . .] this is some of the wreckage in the out-skirts of Glorinian . . . Loss of life was comparatively small in this vinicinity however the shells dropped here like rain. Watercolor and pencil on clipping of illustration, mounted on cardboard, 18 x 18 in. Collection Kiyoko Lerner

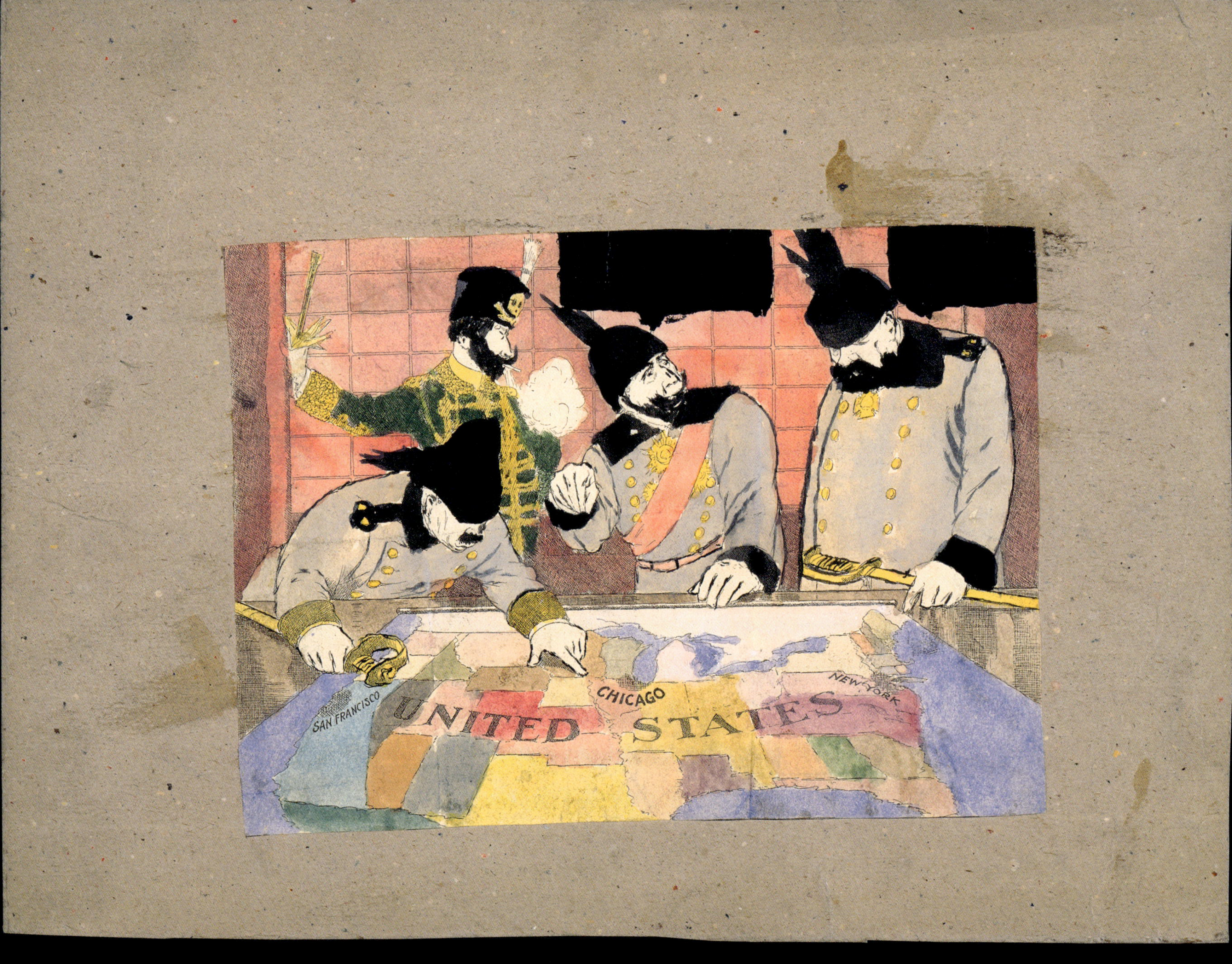

54 | *German General Staff.* Watercolor and pencil
on clipping of illustration, mounted on cardboard, 14 x 18 in.
Collection Kiyoko Lerner

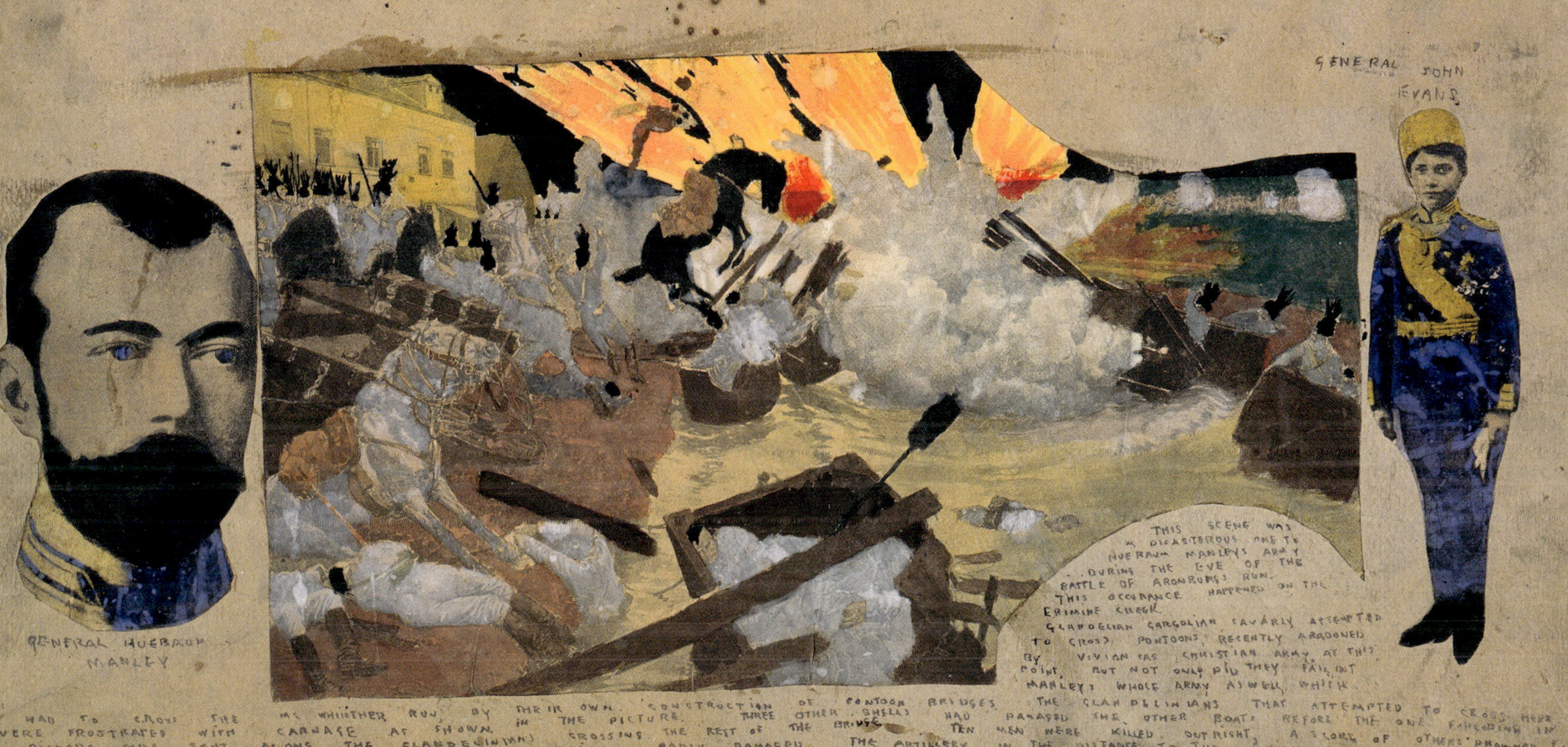

GENERAL JOHN EVANS
GENERAL HUEBAUM MANLEY
THIS SCENE WAS A DISASTEROUS ONE TO HUEBAUM MANLEYS ARMY DURING THE EVE OF THE BATTLE OF ARONRURGS RUN. THIS OCCURANCE HAPPENED ON THE ERMINE CREEK.
GLANDELIAN GARGOLIAN CAVARLY ATTEMPTED TO CROSS PONTOONS RECENTLY ABADONED BY VIVIAN FAS CHRISTIAN ARMY AT THIS POINT, BUT NOT ONLY DID THEY FAIL BUT MANLEYS WHOLE ARMY AS WELL WHICH HAD TO CROSS THE MS WHIITHER RUN BY THEIR OWN CONSTRUCTION OF PONTOON BRIDGES WERE FROSTRATED WITH CARNAGE AS SHOWN IN THE PICTURE. THREE OTHER SHELLS THE PICTURE WAS SENT ACROSS THE GLANDELINIANS CROSSING THE REST OF THE BRIDGE. WOUNDED, TWO HORSES KILLED, AND THE BRIDGE BADLY DAMAGED. WAS DIRECTED BY EVANS WHO IS SEEN IN HIS COLONEL UNIFORM THE GLANDELINIANS THAT ATTEMPTED TO CROSS HERE PASSED THE OTHER BOATS BEFORE THE ONE EXPLODING IN TEN MEN WERE KILLED OUTRIGHT, A SCORE OF OTHERS DROWNED FIVE THE ARTILLERY IN THE DISTANCE TO THE RIGHT FIRING ON THE BRIDGE THOUGH A GENERAL AS HE WAS IT WAS HE THE BROTHER OF JACK EVANS, THE GOARDIAN OF THE VIVIAN GIRLS, WHO STOPPED THE ENEMY FROM CROSSING THE ERMINE CREEK.

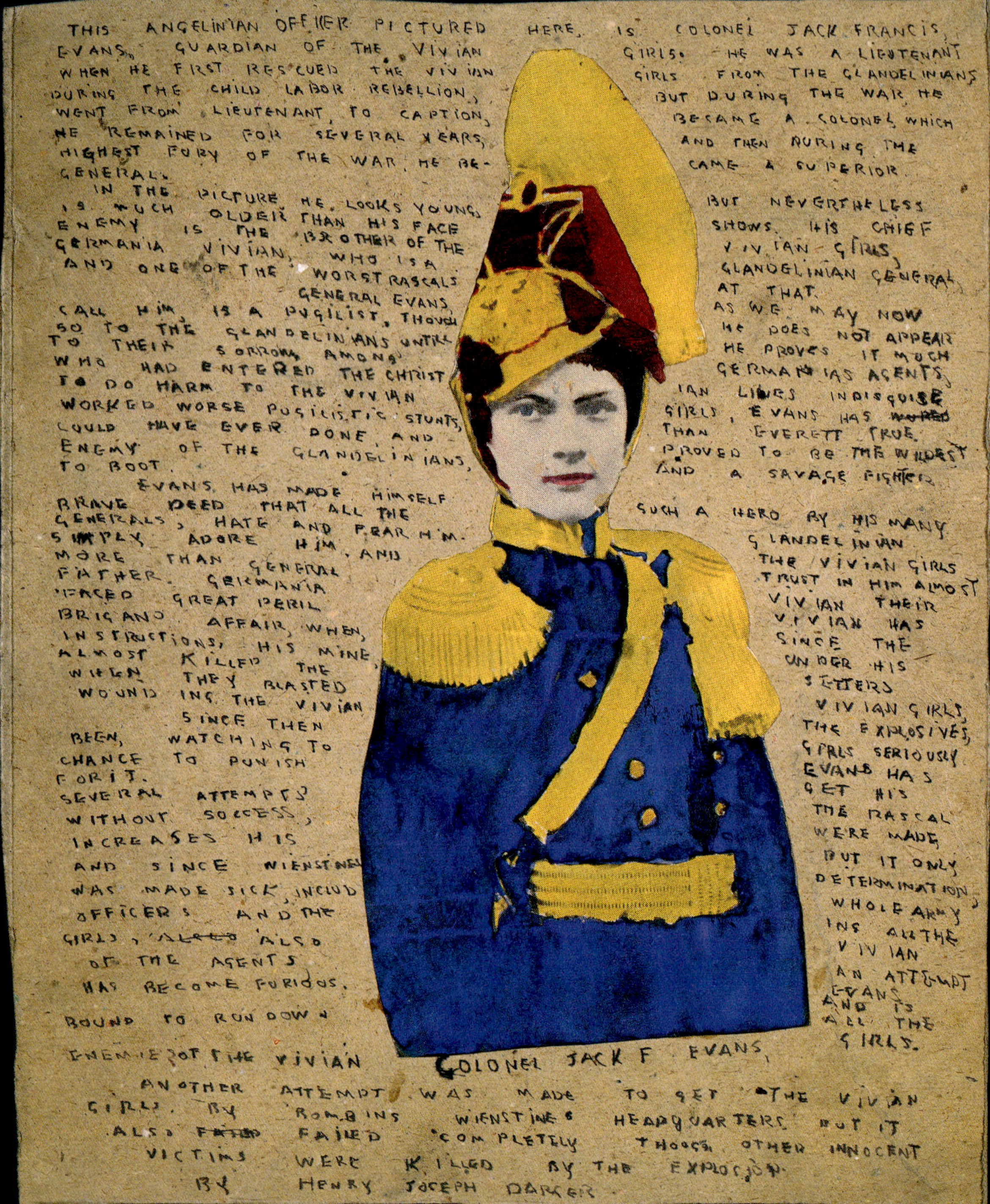

Colonel Jack F Evans.

Watercolor and pencil on clipping of illustration,
mounted on cardboard, 13 ¾ x 11 ½ in.
Collection American Folk Art Museum, New York

THIS ANGELINIAN OFFICER PICTURED HERE, IS COLONEL JACK FRANCIS EVANS, GUARDIAN OF THE VIVIAN GIRLS. HE WAS A LIEUTENANT WHEN HE FIRST RESCUED THE VIVIAN GIRLS FROM THE GLANDELINIANS DURING THE CHILD LABOR REBELLION, BUT DURING THE WAR HE WENT FROM LIEUTENANT TO CAPTION, BECAME A COLONEL WHICH HE REMAINED FOR SEVERAL YEARS, AND THEN DURING THE HIGHEST FURY OF THE WAR HE BE- CAME A SUPERIOR GENERAL.

IN THE PICTURE HE LOOKS YOUNG, BUT NEVERTHELESS IS MUCH OLDER THAN HIS FACE SHOWS. HIS CHIEF ENEMY IS THE BROTHER OF THE VIVIAN GIRLS, GERMANIA VIVIAN, WHO IS A GLANDELINIAN GENERAL AND ONE OF THE WORST RASCALS AT THAT.

GENERAL EVANS AS WE MAY NOW CALL HIM IS A PUGILIST, THOUGH HE DOES NOT APPEAR SO TO THE GLANDELINIANS UNTIL HE PROVES IT MUCH TO THEIR SORROW, AMONG GERMANIAS AGENTS WHO HAD ENTERED THE CHRIST- IAN LINES IN DISGUISE TO DO HARM TO THE VIVIAN GIRLS, EVANS HAS WORKED WORSE PUGILISTIC STUNTS THAN EVERETT TRUE. COULD HAVE EVER DONE AND PROVED TO BE THE WILDEST ENEMY OF THE GLANDELINIANS AND A SAVAGE FIGHTER TO BOOT.

EVANS HAS MADE HIMSELF SUCH A HERO BY HIS MANY BRAVE DEED THAT ALL THE GLANDELINIAN GENERALS, HATE AND FEAR HIM. THE VIVIAN GIRLS SIMPLY ADORE HIM, AND TRUST IN HIM ALMOST MORE THAN GENERAL VIVIAN THEIR FATHER. GERMANIA VIVIAN HAS FACED GREAT PERIL SINCE THE BRIGAND AFFAIR, WHEN UNDER HIS INSTRUCTIONS, HIS MINE LETTERS ALMOST KILLED THE VIVIAN GIRLS WHEN THEY BLASTED THE EXPLOSIVES, WOUNDING THE VIVIAN GIRLS SERIOUSLY SINCE THEN EVANS HAS BEEN WATCHING TO GET HIS CHANCE TO PUNISH THE RASCAL FOR IT. WERE MADE SEVERAL ATTEMPTS BUT IT ONLY WITHOUT SUCCESS, DETERMINATION INCREASES HIS WHOLE ARMY AND SINCE WIENSTINE INS ALL THE WAS MADE SICK, INCLUD VIVIAN OFFICERS AND THE AN ATTEMPT GIRLS, ALSO ALSO EVANS OF THE AGENTS AND IS HAS BECOME FURIOUS. ALL THE GIRLS. BOUND TO RUN DOWN

ENEMIES OF THE VIVIAN COLONEL JACK F EVANS, ANOTHER ATTEMPT WAS MADE TO GET THE VIVIAN GIRLS BY ROMBINS WIENSTINE HEADQUARTERS BUT IT ALSO FAILED FAILED COMPLETLY THOUGH OTHER INNOCENT VICTIMS WERE KILLED BY THE EXPLOSION. BY HENRY JOSEPH DARGER

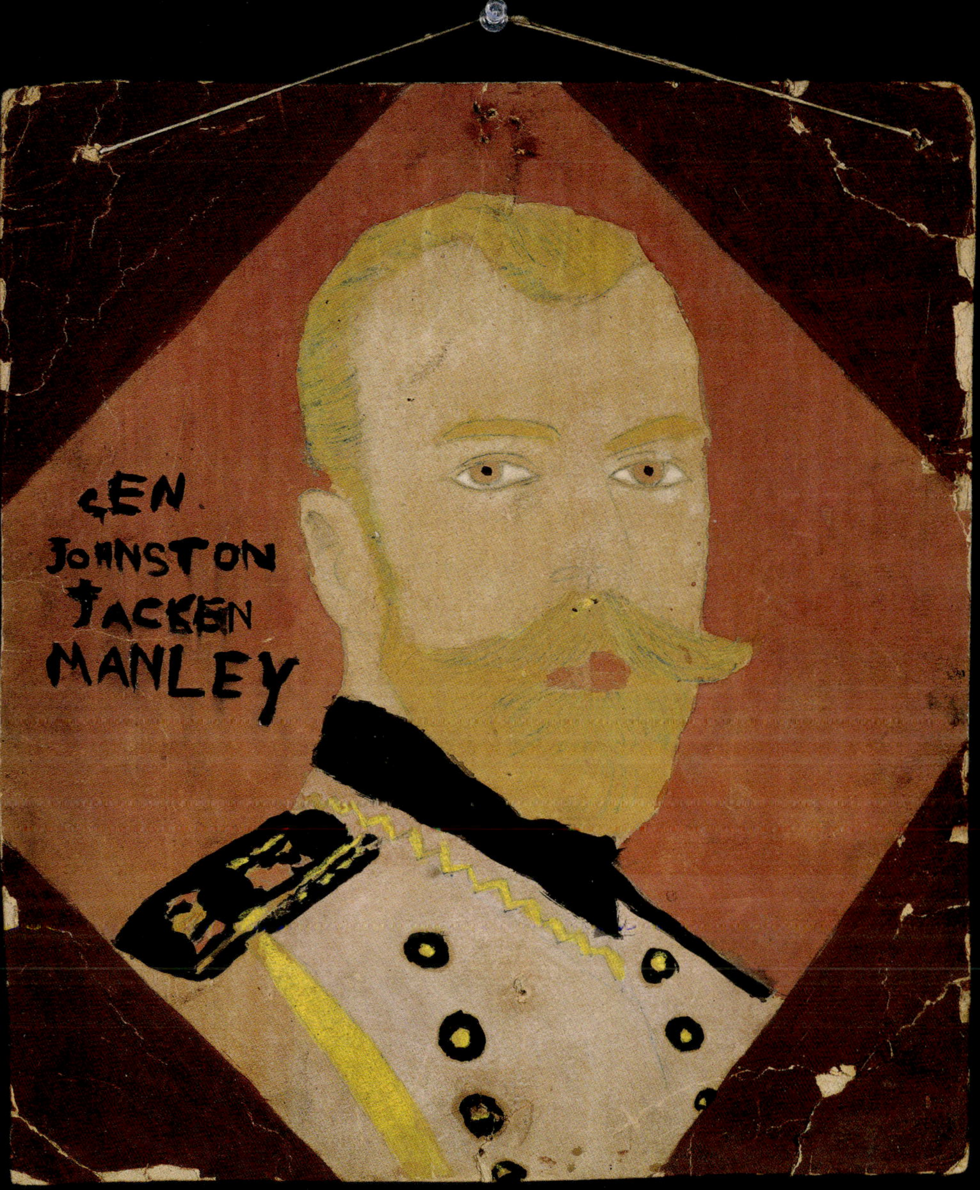

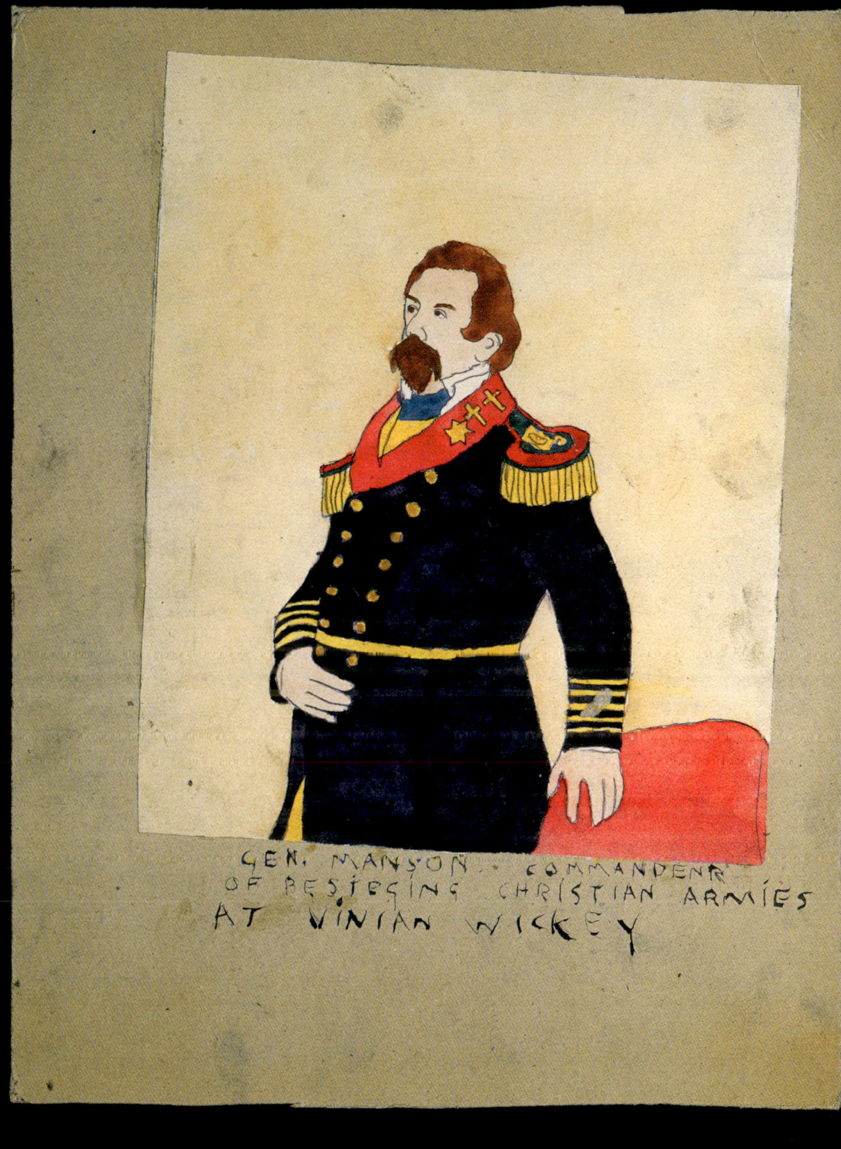

General Johnston Jacken Manley.
Watercolor and pencil on cardboard, 15 x 13 ½ in.
Collection Kiyoko Lerner

General Manson Commander of besieging Christian armies at Vivian Wickey.
Watercolor and pencil on paper mounted on cardboard, 14 ½ x 11 in.
Private collection

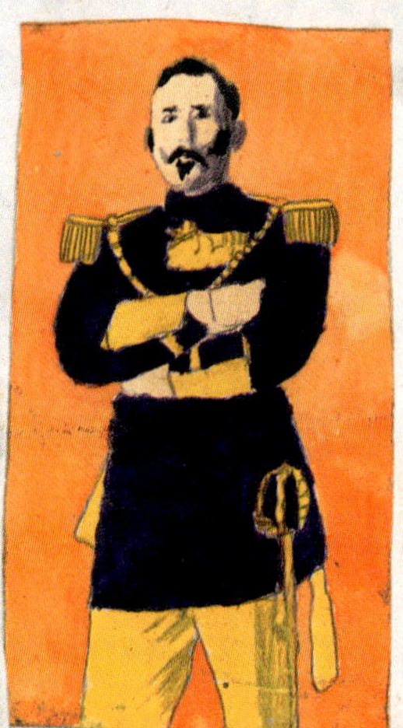

GEN. CONCENTINIAN
ARONBURG. FATHER OF
ANNIE ARONBURG.

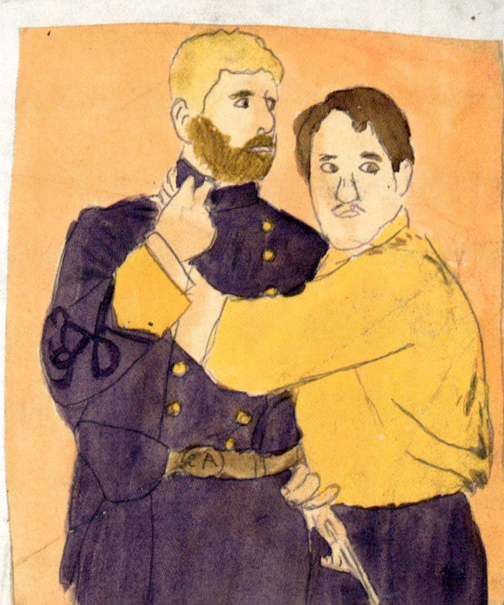

GENERAL NERO AND FRANCIS
VIVIANANNA

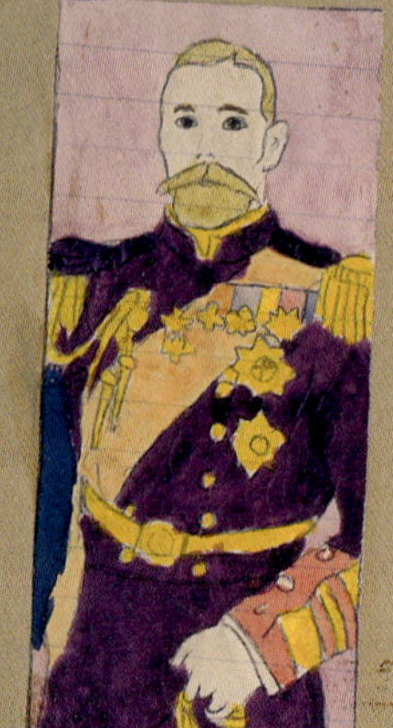

General Robert
Angelic Vivian

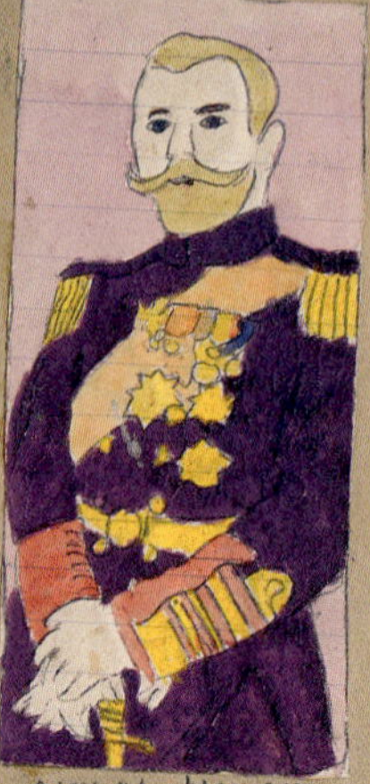

General Hanson
Angelic Vivian

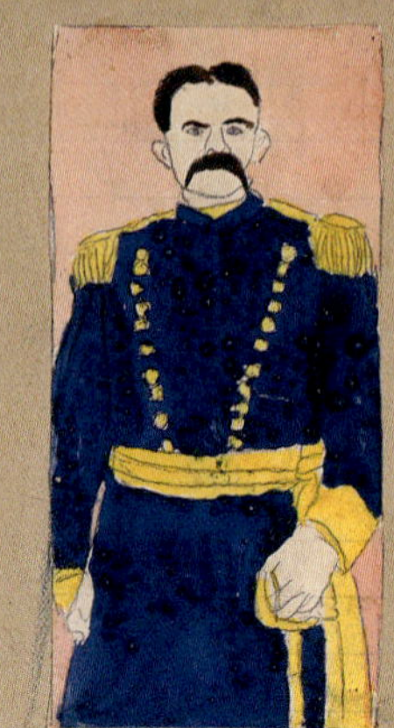

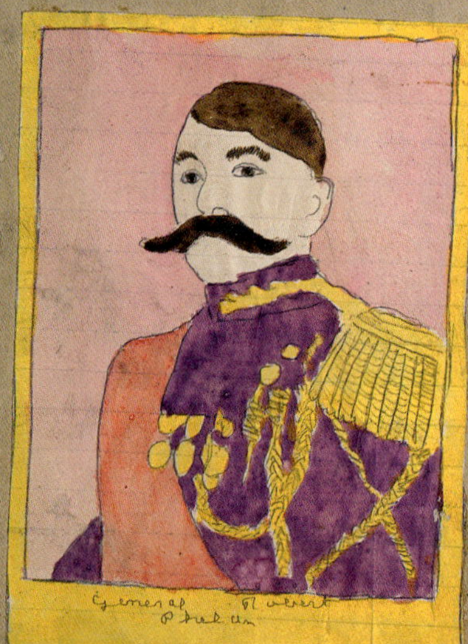

General Robert
Phelan

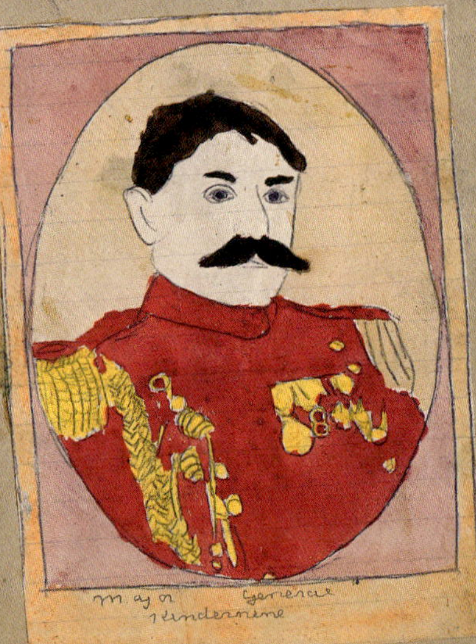

Major Genriene
Vinderviene

5-26
(21)

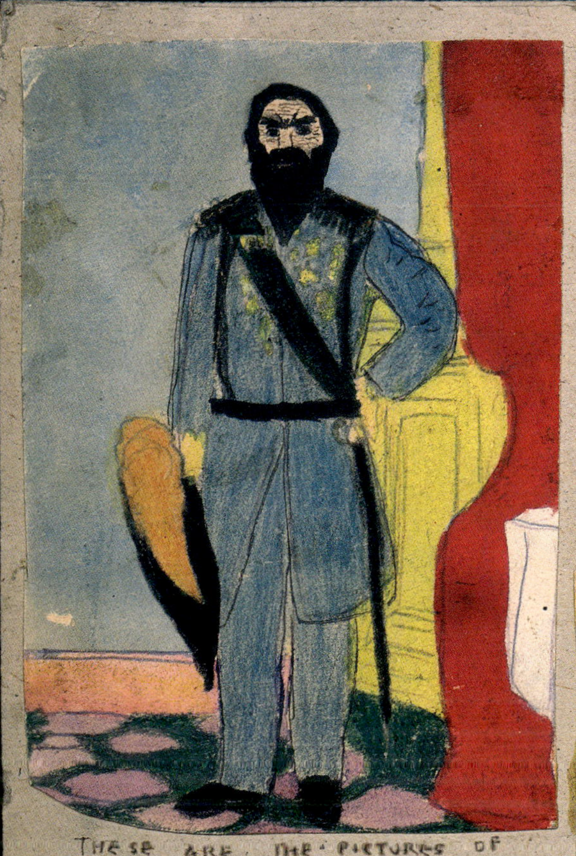
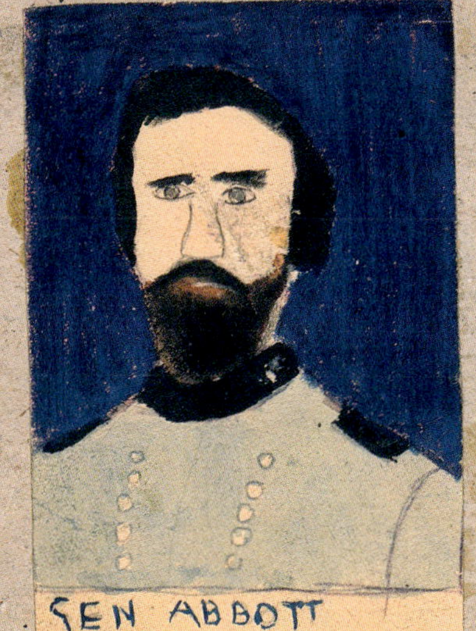

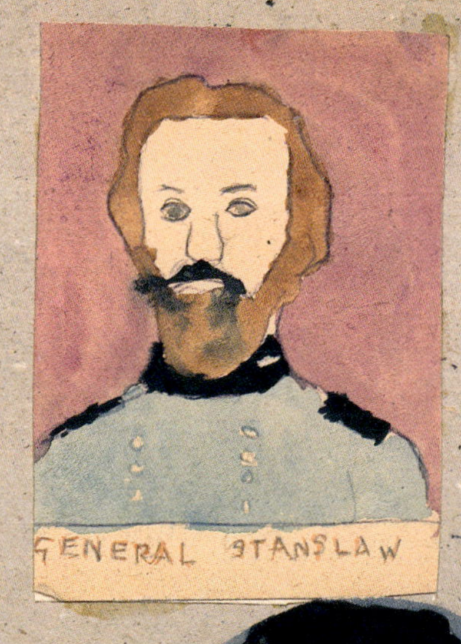

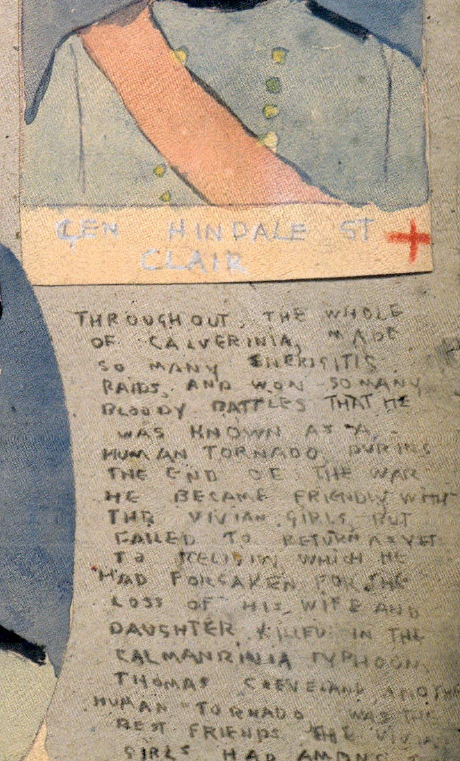

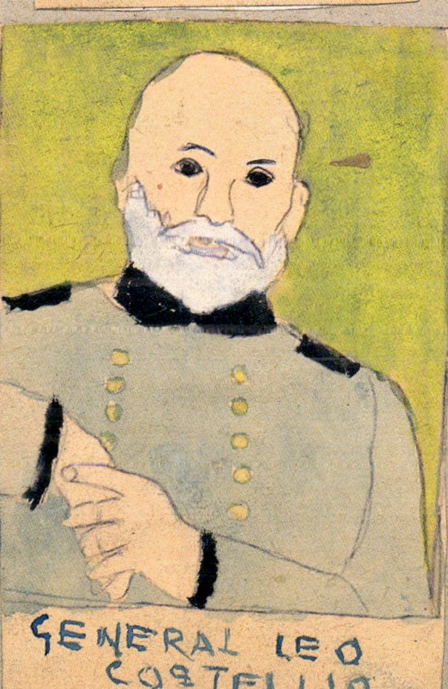

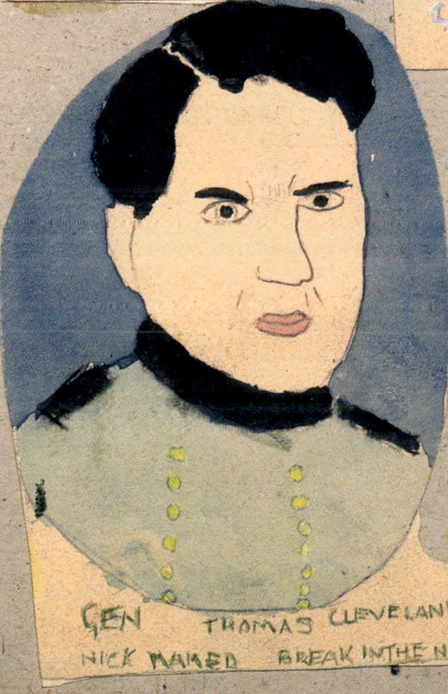

Six Generals: Raymond Richardson Federal, Abbott, Stanslaw, Hindale St. Clair, Leo Costellio, and Thomas Cleveland, nicknamed Break in the Neck. Watercolor and pencil on paper mounted on cardboard, 11 ½ x 17 in. Private collection

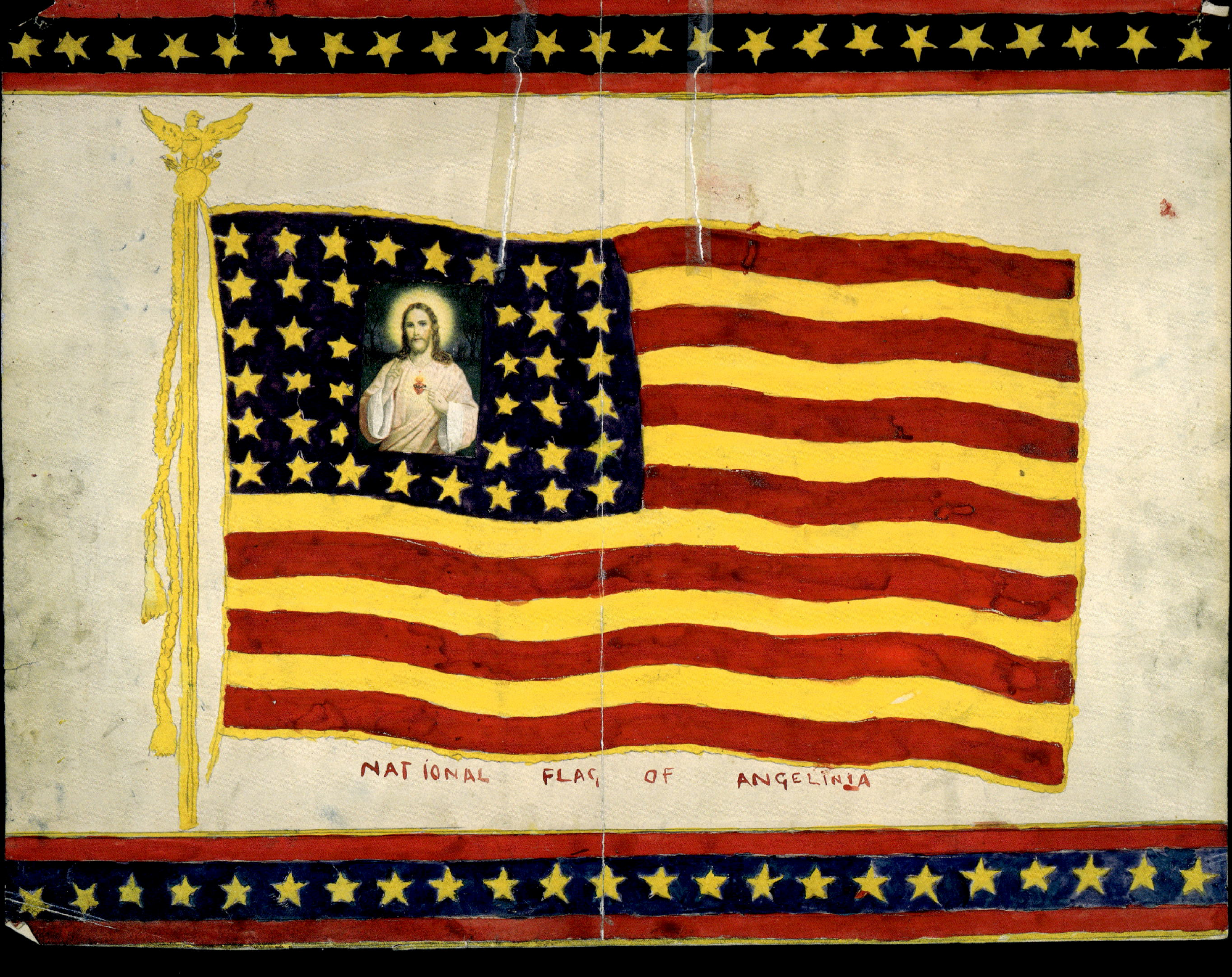

60 | *National Flag of Angelinia.*
Watercolor, pencil, collage, and carbon tracing
on pieced paper, 18 ½ x 24 in. The Museum of Everything

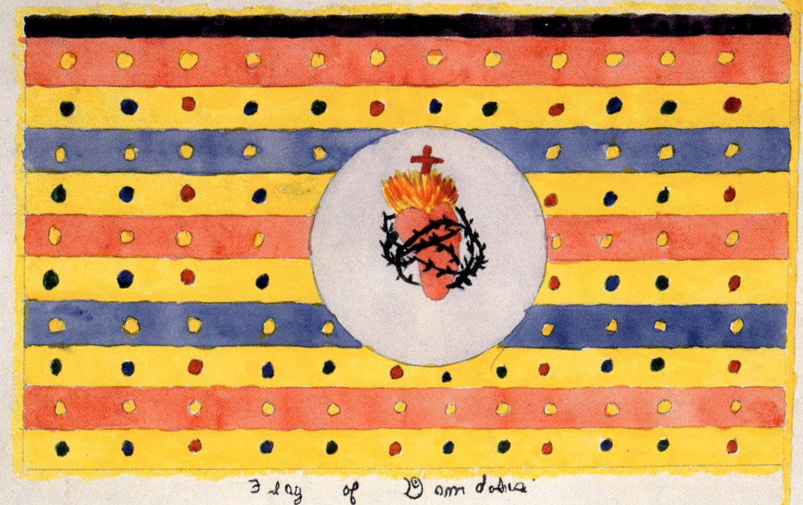

Flag of Damdobia

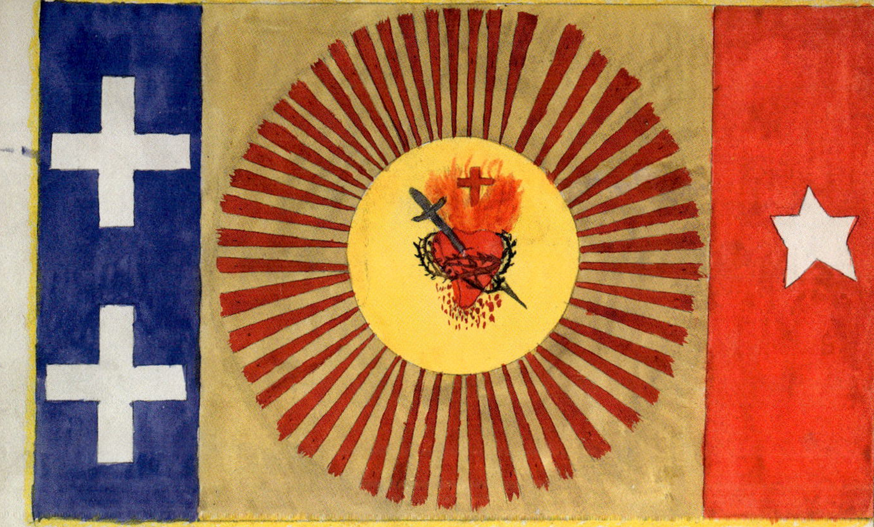

THE MAIN NATIONAL FLAG
OF ABBIEANNIA

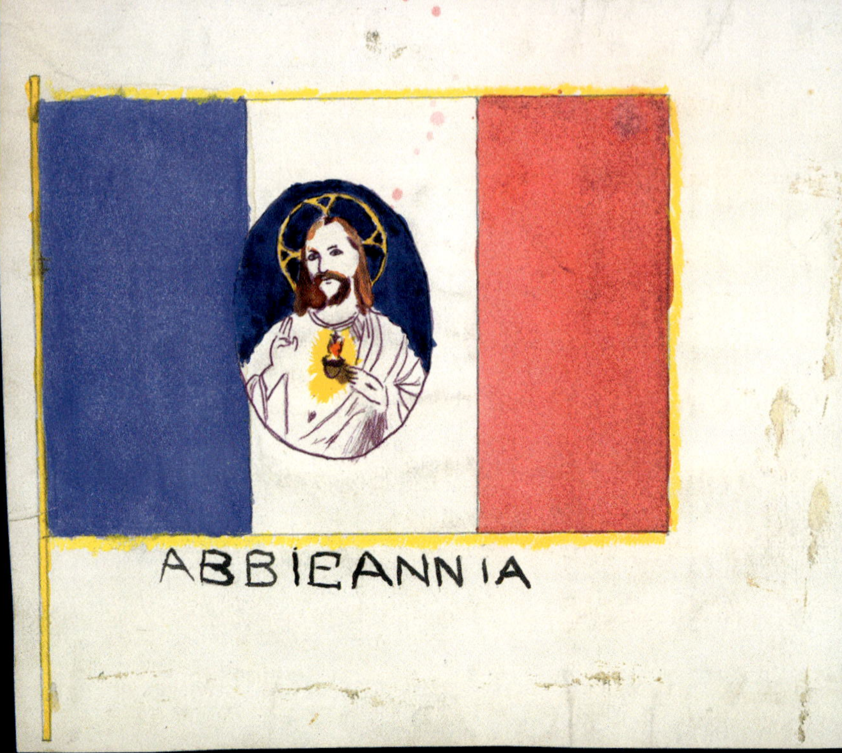

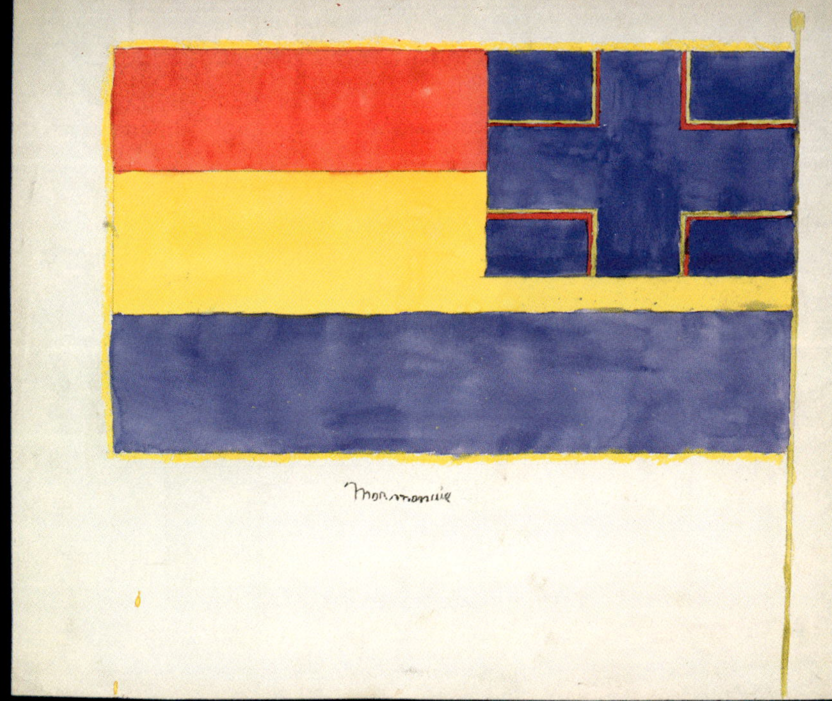

Top row:

Flag of Abbieannia. Watercolor, pencil, and carbon tracing
on paper, 12 x 13 in. Collection Kiyoko Lerner

Flag of Tribongonlia. Watercolor, pencil, and carbon tracing
on paper, 14 x 17 in. Collection Kiyoko Lerner

Flag of Concentinia. Watercolor and pencil on paper,
8 x 9 ½ in. Collection Kiyoko Lerner

Bottom row:

Flag of Morammia. Watercolor and pencil on paper,
14 x 17 in. Collection Kiyoko Lerner

Mc-Hollestinian Flag of Glandelinia. Watercolor and pencil
on paper, 14 x 17 in. Collection Kiyoko Lerner

Flag of Calverinia. Collage, watercolor, and pencil
on paper, 7 x 8 in. Private collection

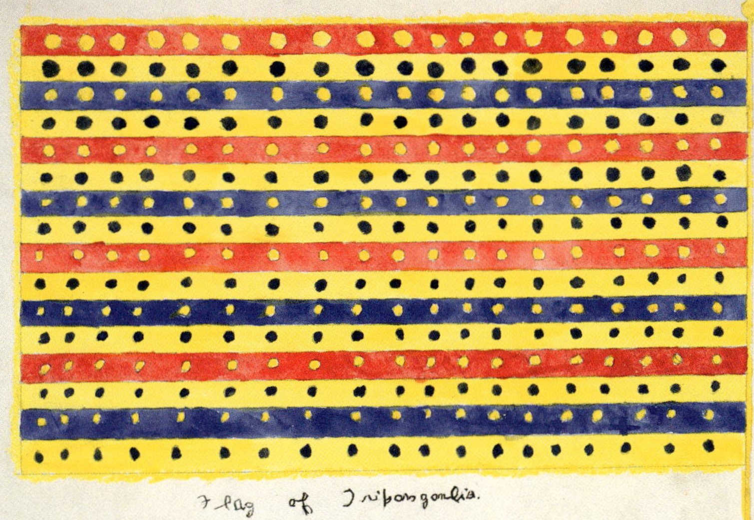

Flag of Tribongonlia.

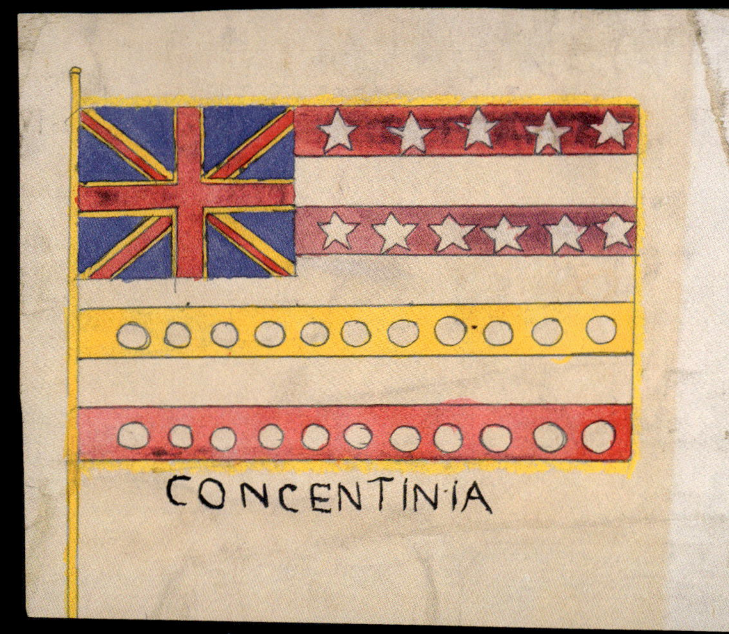

CONCENTINIA

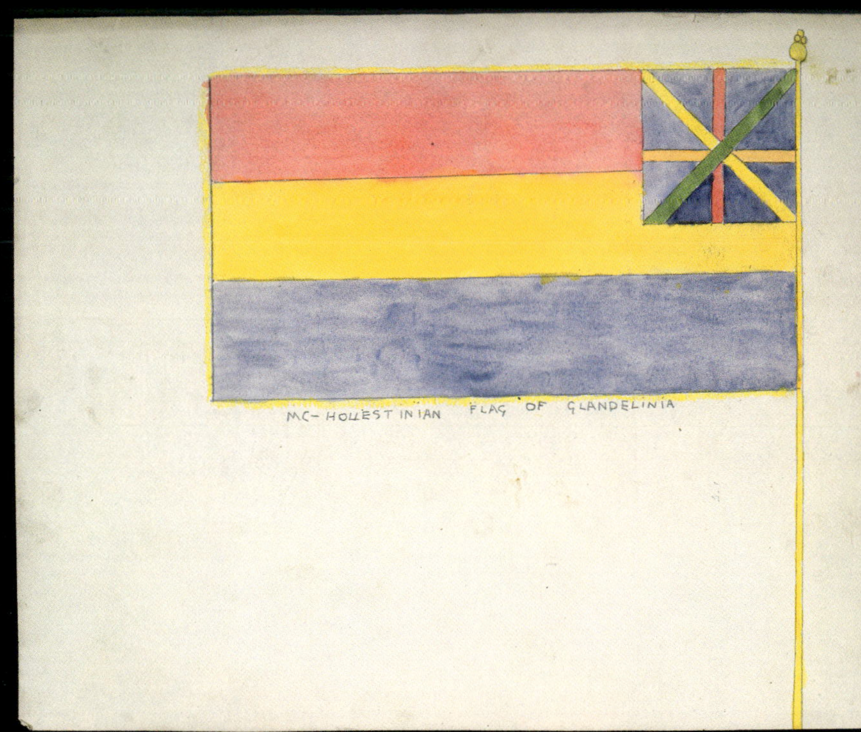

MC- HOLLESTINIAN   FLAG OF GLANDELINIA

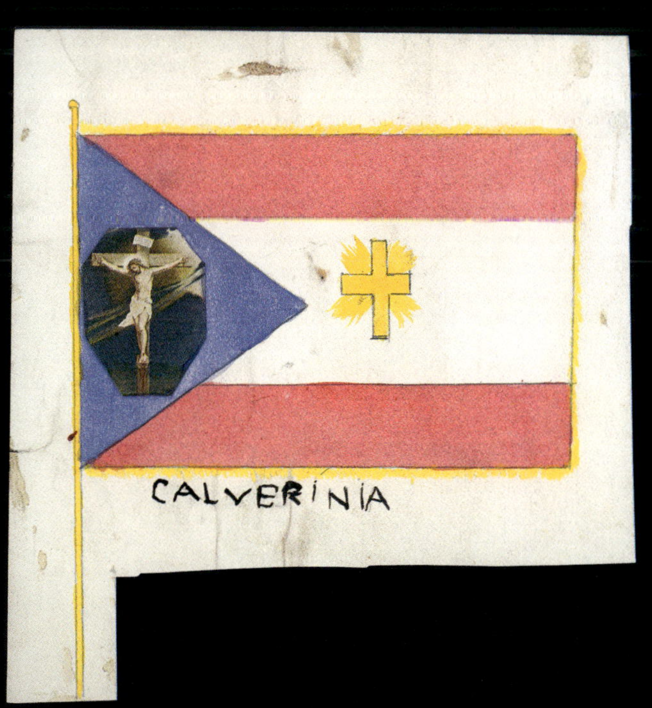

CALVERINIA

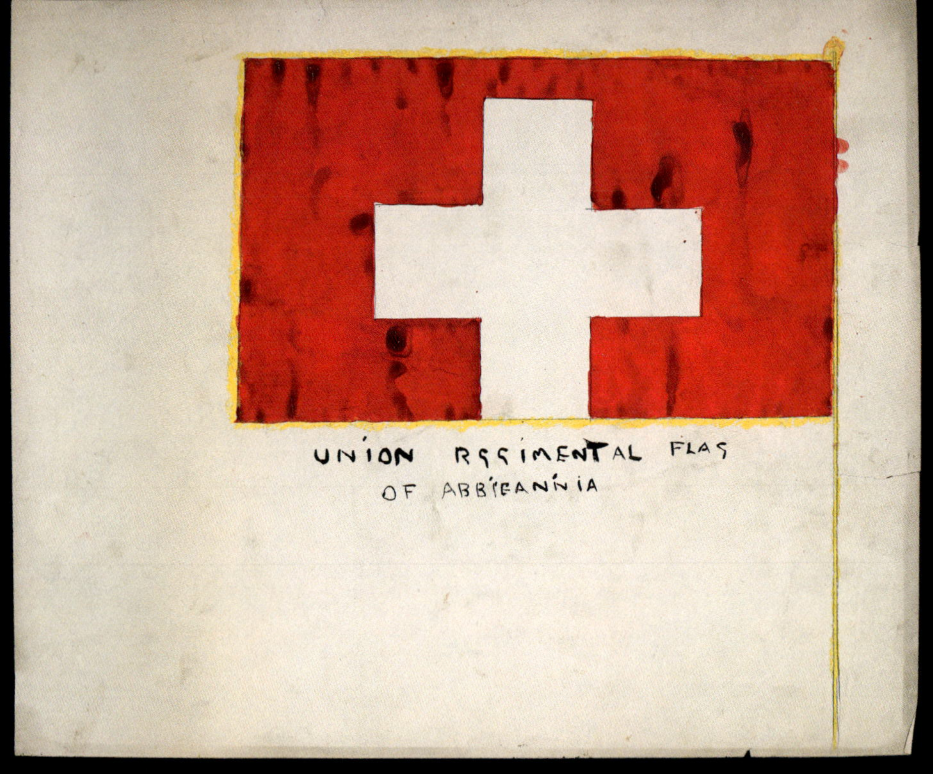

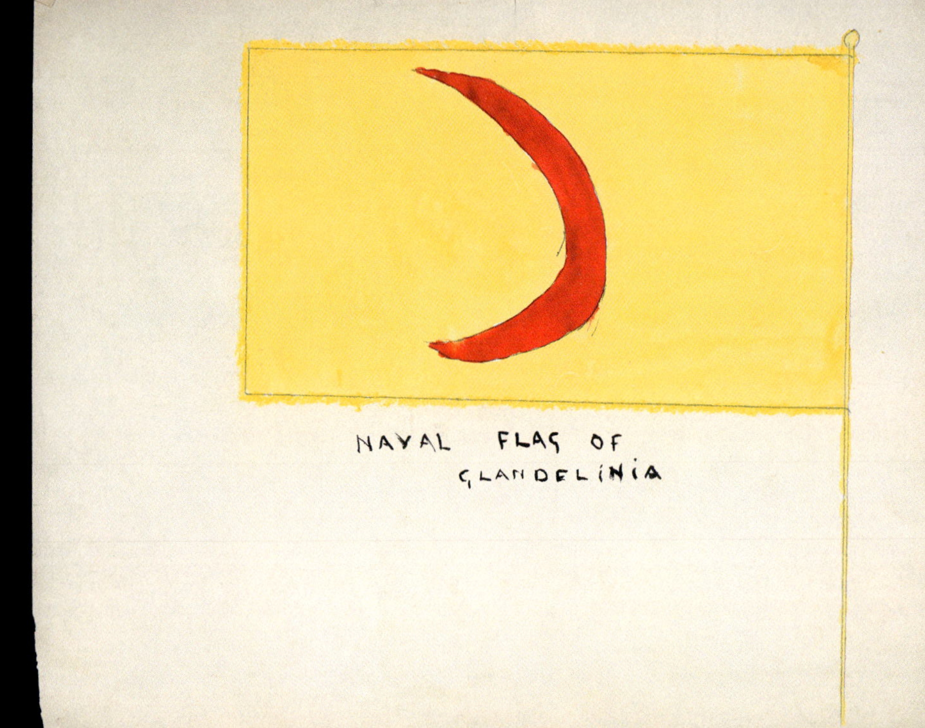

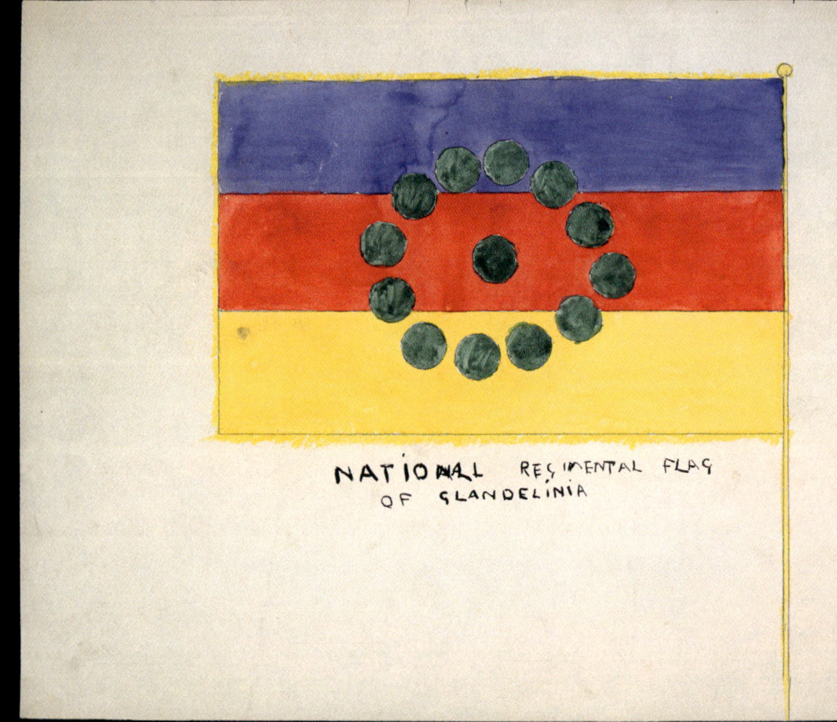

This page (clockwise from above):

Union Regimental Flag of Abbieannia. Watercolor and pencil on paper,
14 x 17 in. Collection de l'art brut, Lausanne

Naval Flag of Glandelinia. Watercolor and pencil on paper,
14 x 17 in. Collection Kiyoko Lerner

National Regimental Flag of Glandelinia. Watercolor and pencil on paper,
14 x 17 in. Private collection

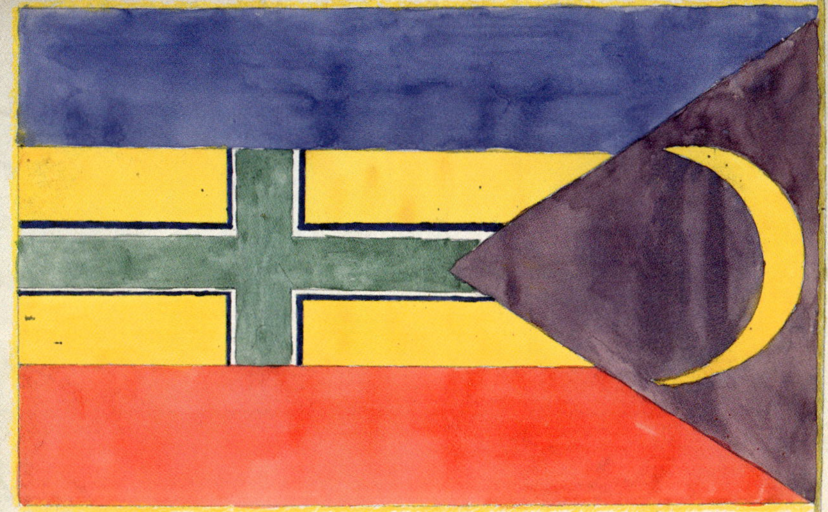

WAR FLAG OF CALVERINIA

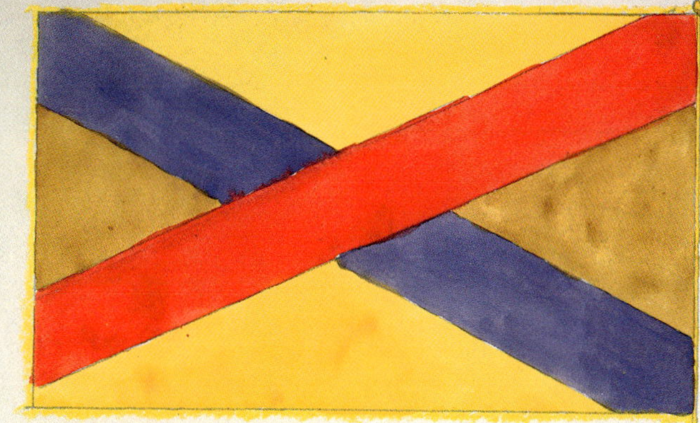

SUB NATIONAL FLAG
OF GLANDELINIA

WITH CROSSES LEFT
OUT ALSO DESIGNS.

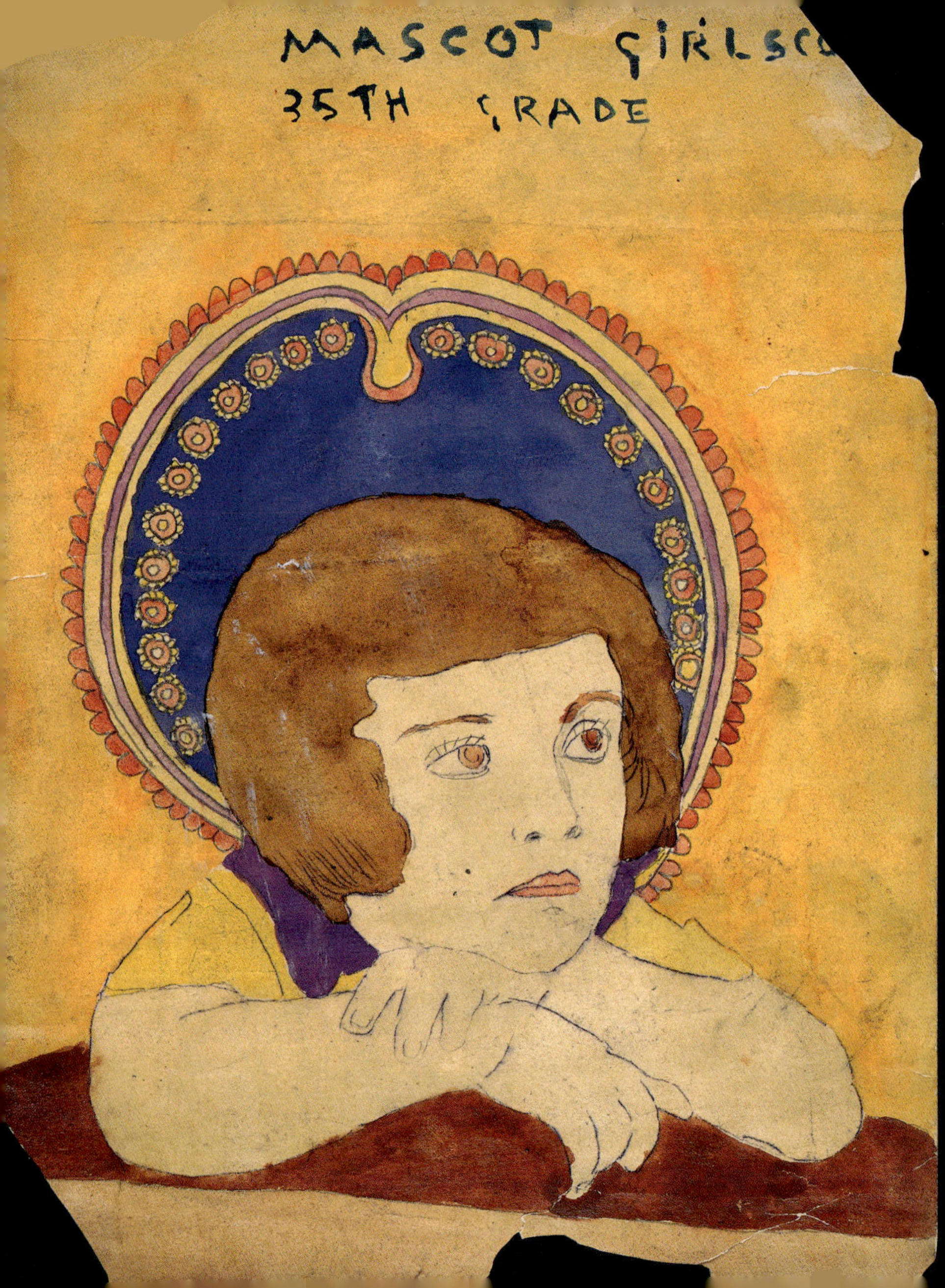

MASCOT GIRLSCO
35TH GRADE
MASCOT GIRLSCOUT 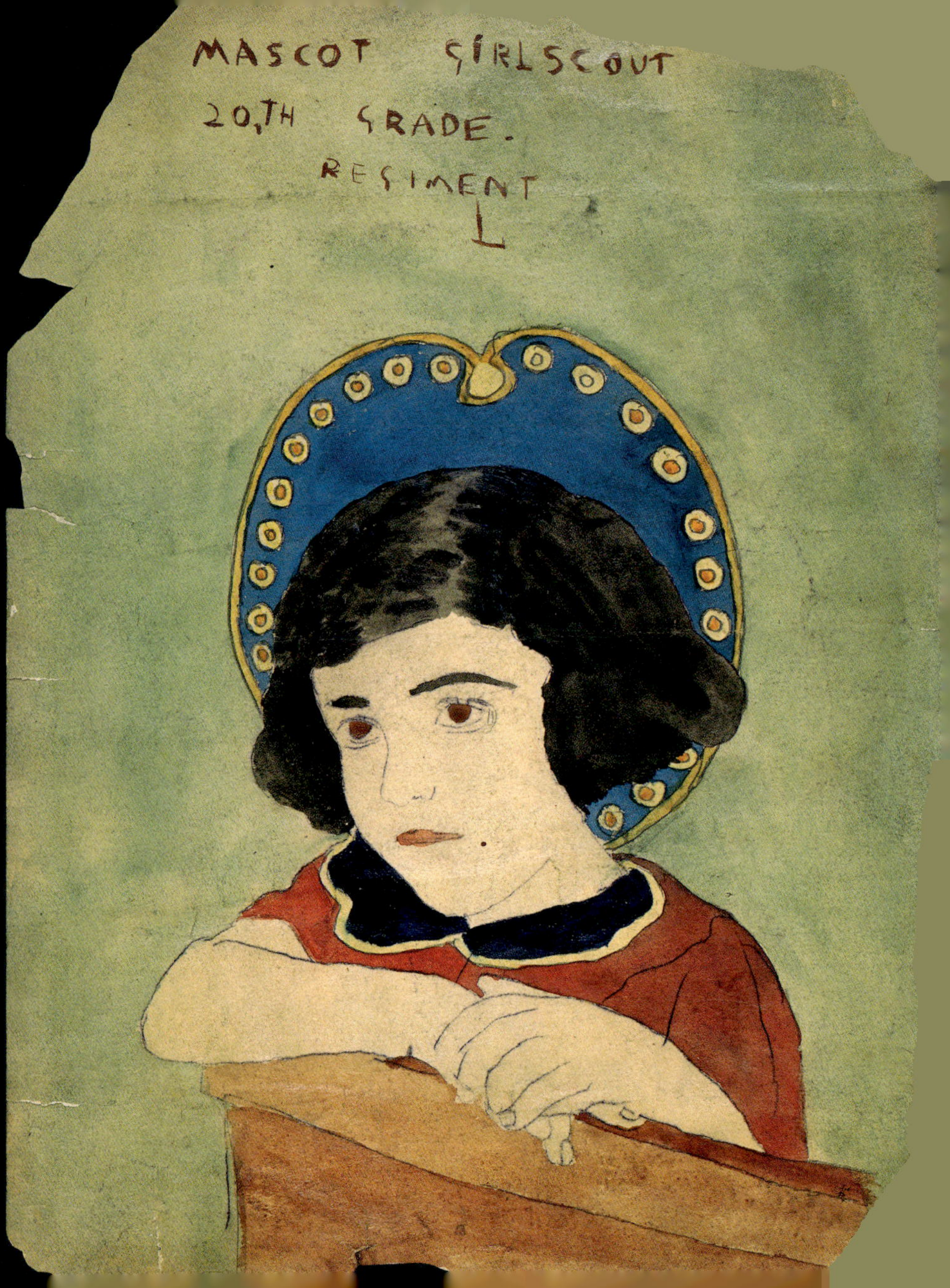
20,TH GRADE.
RESIMENT
L

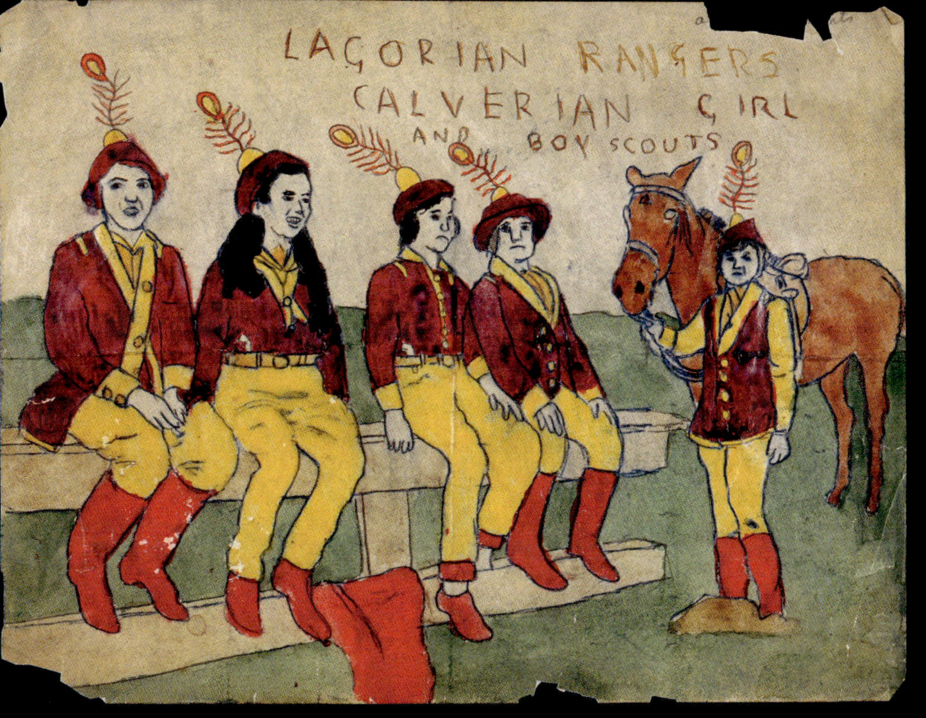

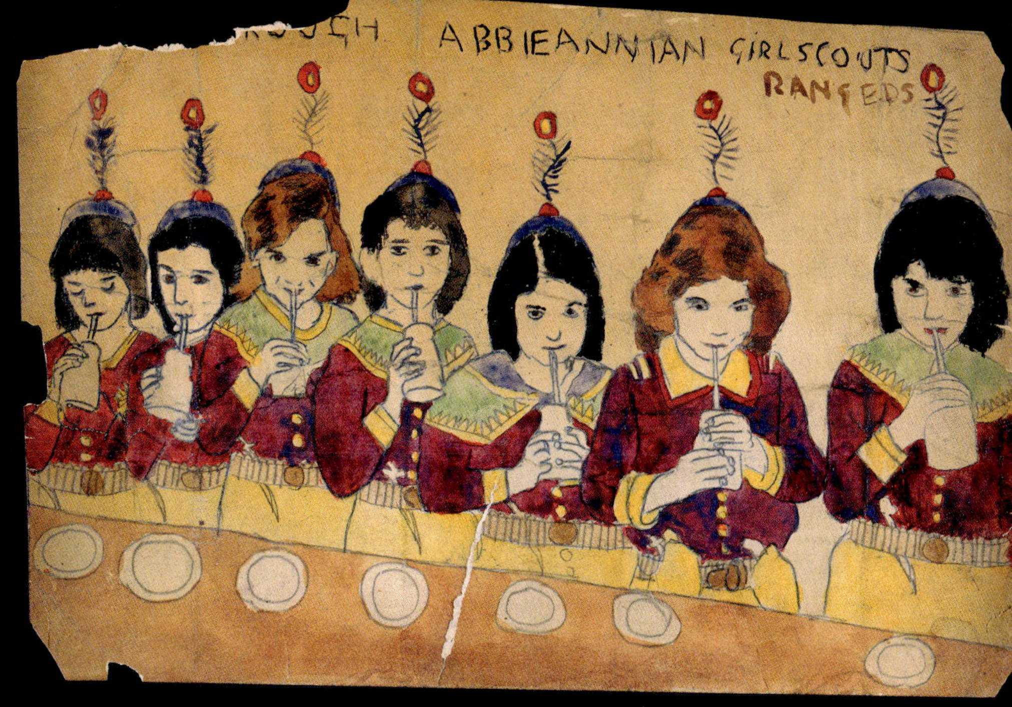

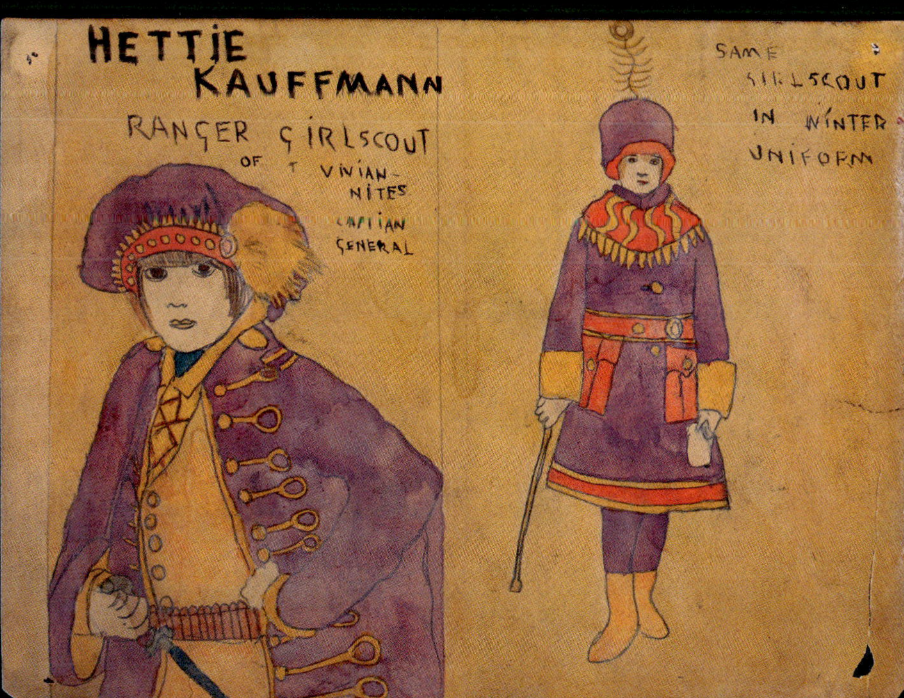

Above left: *Lagorian Rangers, Calverian Girl and Boy Scouts.*
Watercolor, pencil, and carbon tracing on paper, 8 x 12 in.
Collection Justin Silverman

Above right: *[Rough] Abbieannian Girl Scouts Rangers.*
Watercolor, pencil, and carbon tracing on paper, 8 x 12 in.
Private collection, Lausanne

Left: *Hettie Kauffmann Ranger Girl Scout of Vivian-nites*
Captian General. Same Girl Scout in Winter Uniform.
Watercolor, pencil, and carbon tracing on paper, 8 x 12 in.
Collection Kiyoko Lerner

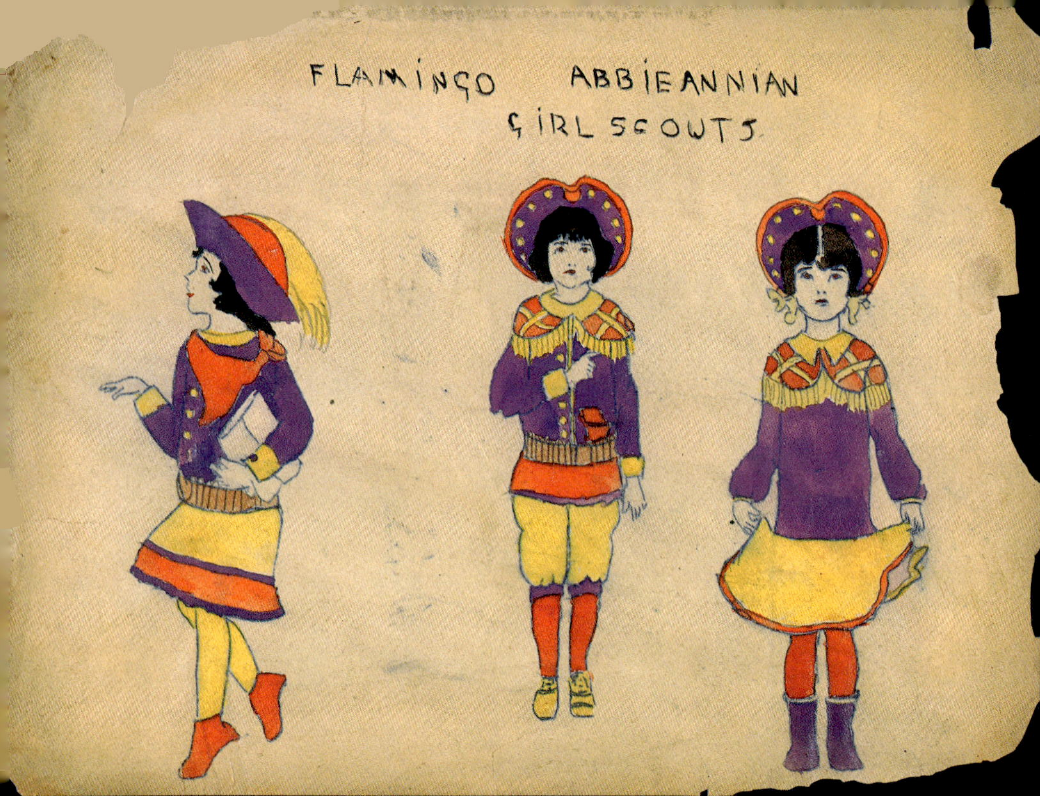

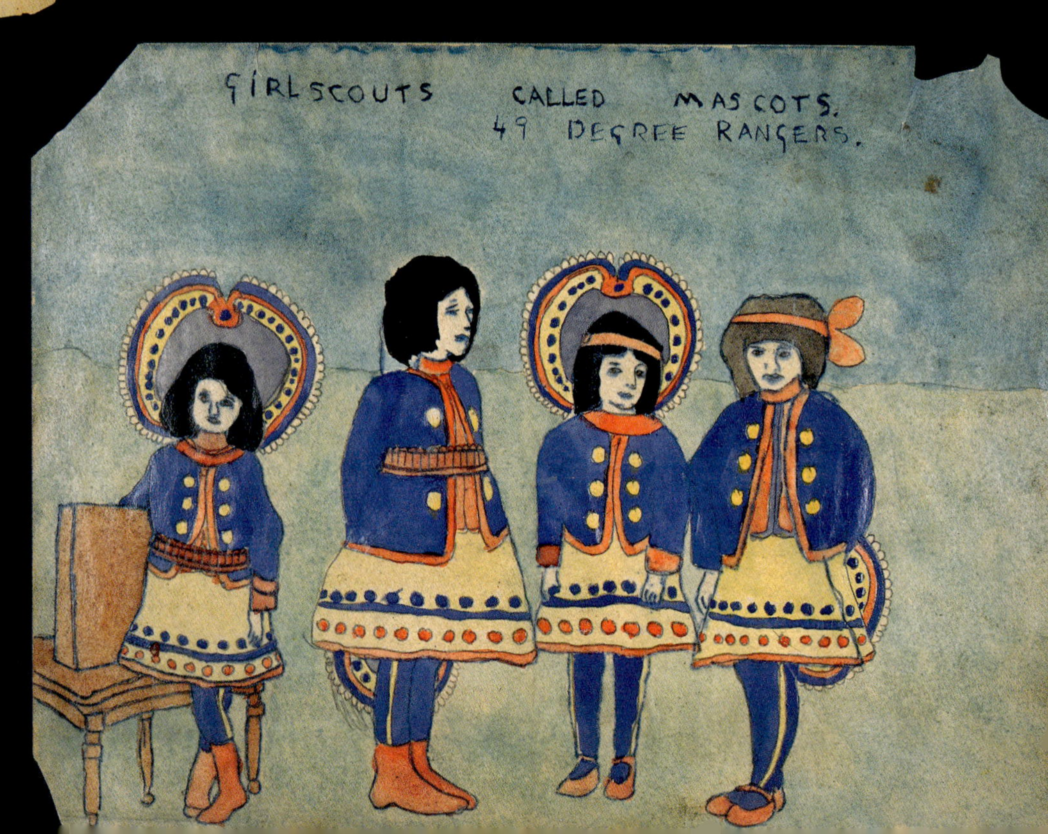

Above: *Flamingo Abbieannian Girl Scouts.* Watercolor, pencil, and carbon tracing on paper, 8 x 12 in. Private collection, Dublin

Below: *Girl Scouts Called Mascots, 49 Degree Rangers.* Watercolor, pencil, and carbon tracing on paper, 8 x 12 in. Collection Kim Manocherian

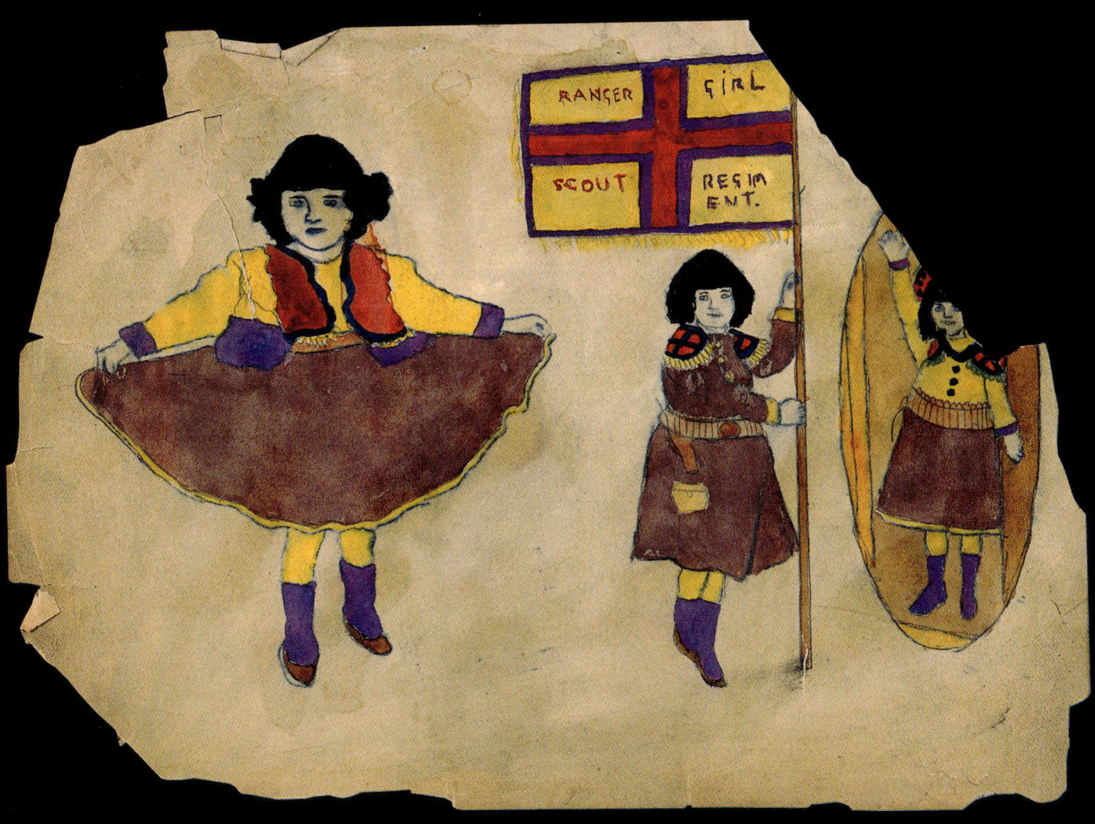

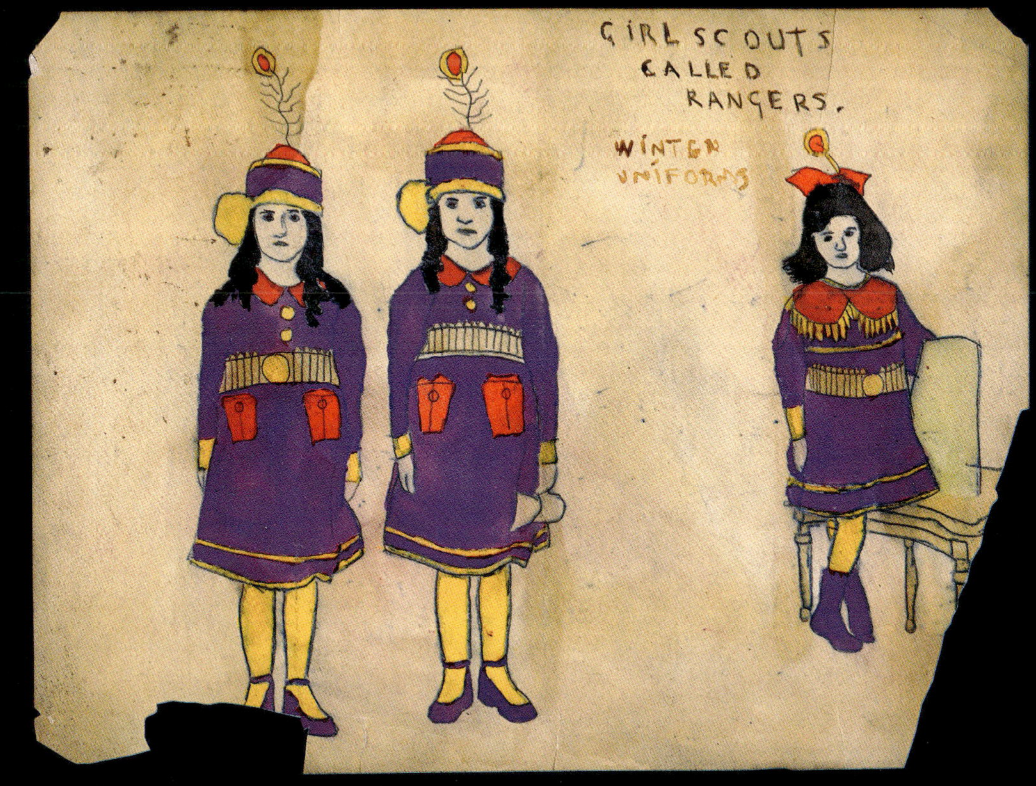

Above: *Ranger Girl Scout Regiment*. Watercolor, pencil, and carbon tracing on paper, 8 x 12 in. Collection Anne-Brigitte Sirois

Below: *Girl Scouts Called Rangers, Winter Uniforms*. Watercolor, pencil, and carbon tracing on paper, 8 x 12 in. Collection Kiyoko Lerner

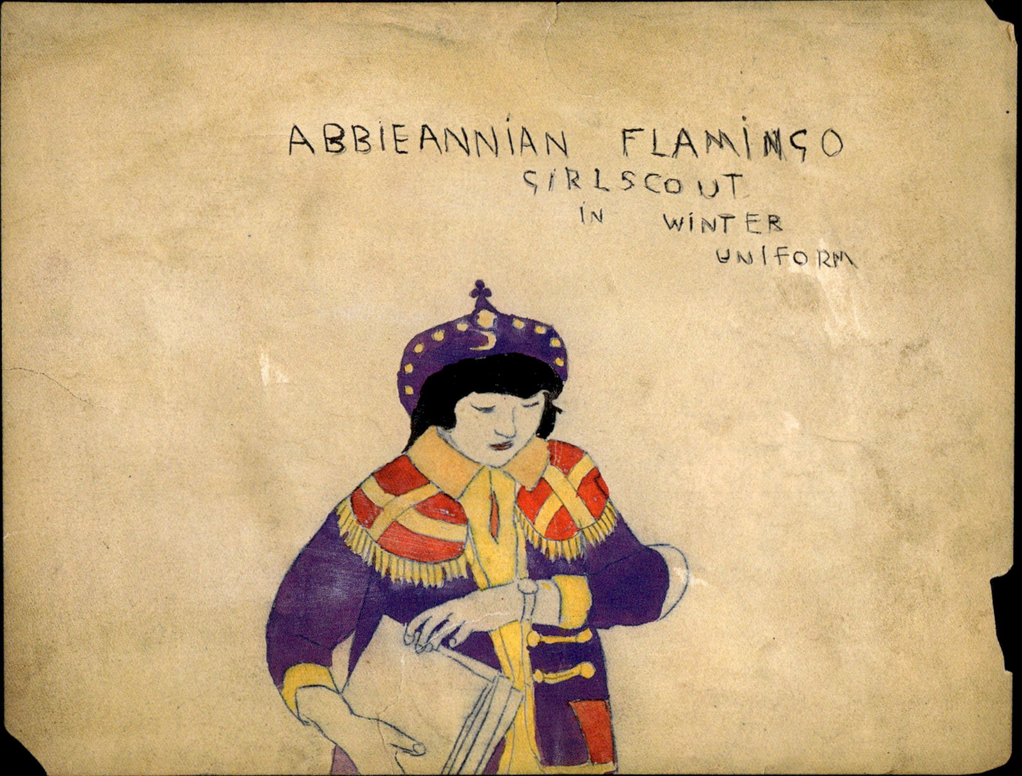

Above: *Abbieannian Flamingo Girl Scout in Winter Uniform.*
Watercolor, pencil, and carbon tracing on paper, 8 x 12 in.
Private collection

Below: *Flanengoe Girl Scouts Thirty Third Degree Rangers.*
Watercolor, pencil, and carbon tracing on paper, 8 x 12 in.
Collection Patricia and Edward DeFranco

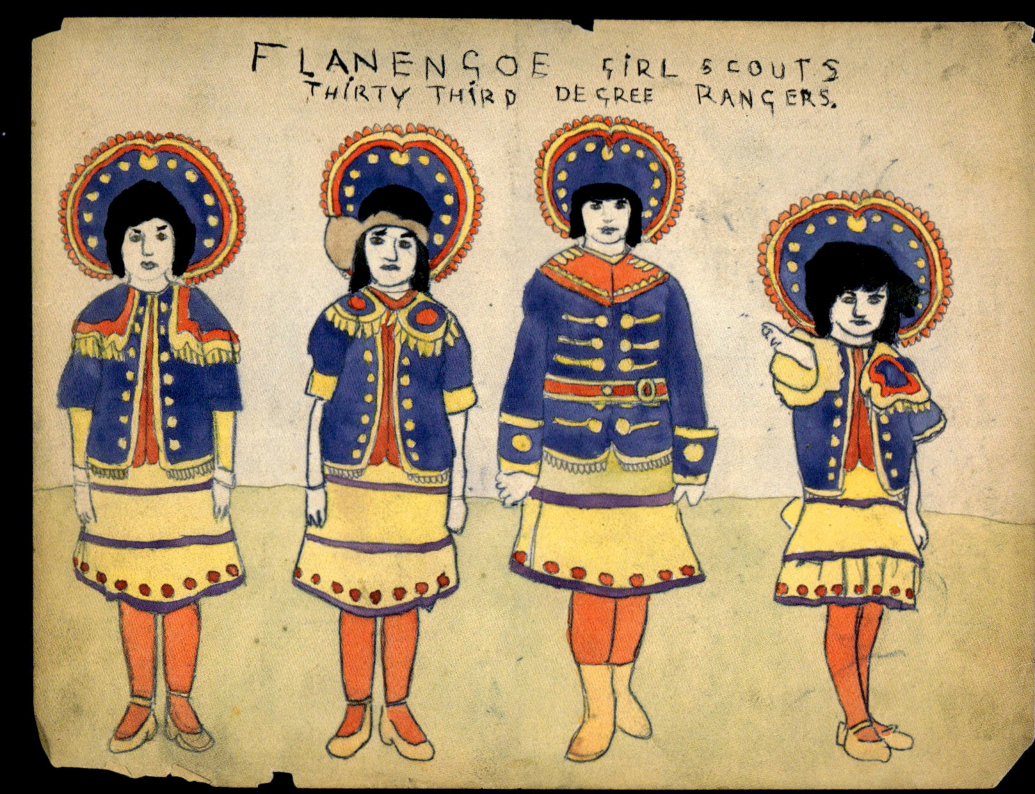

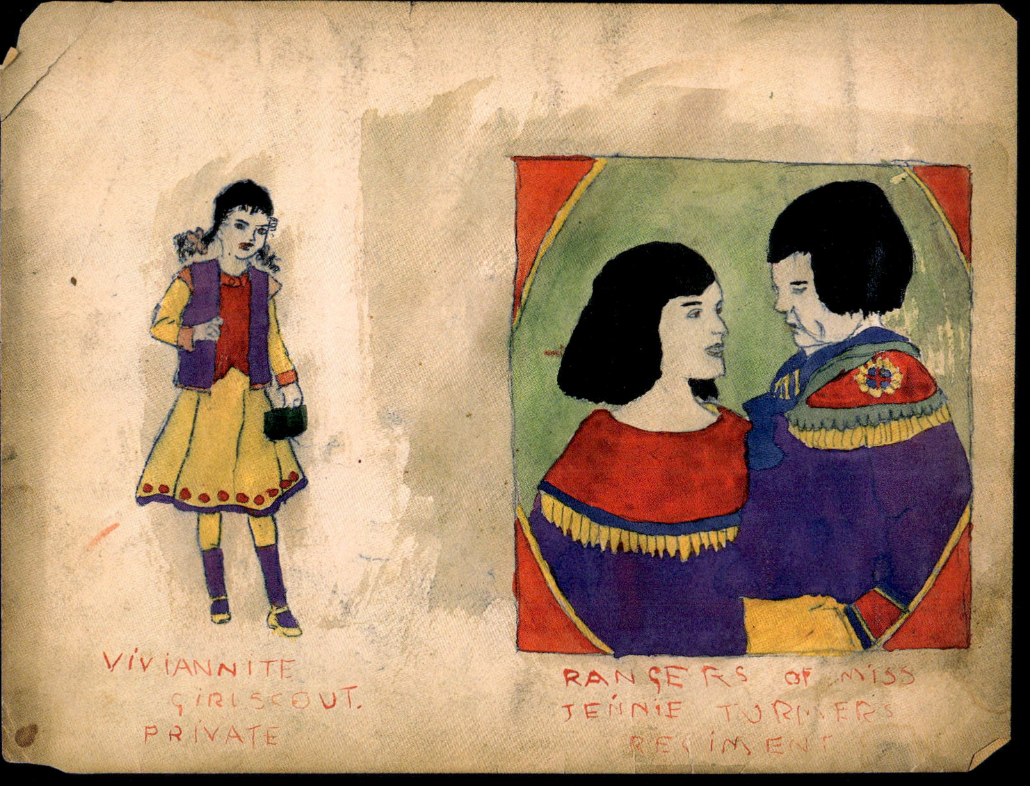

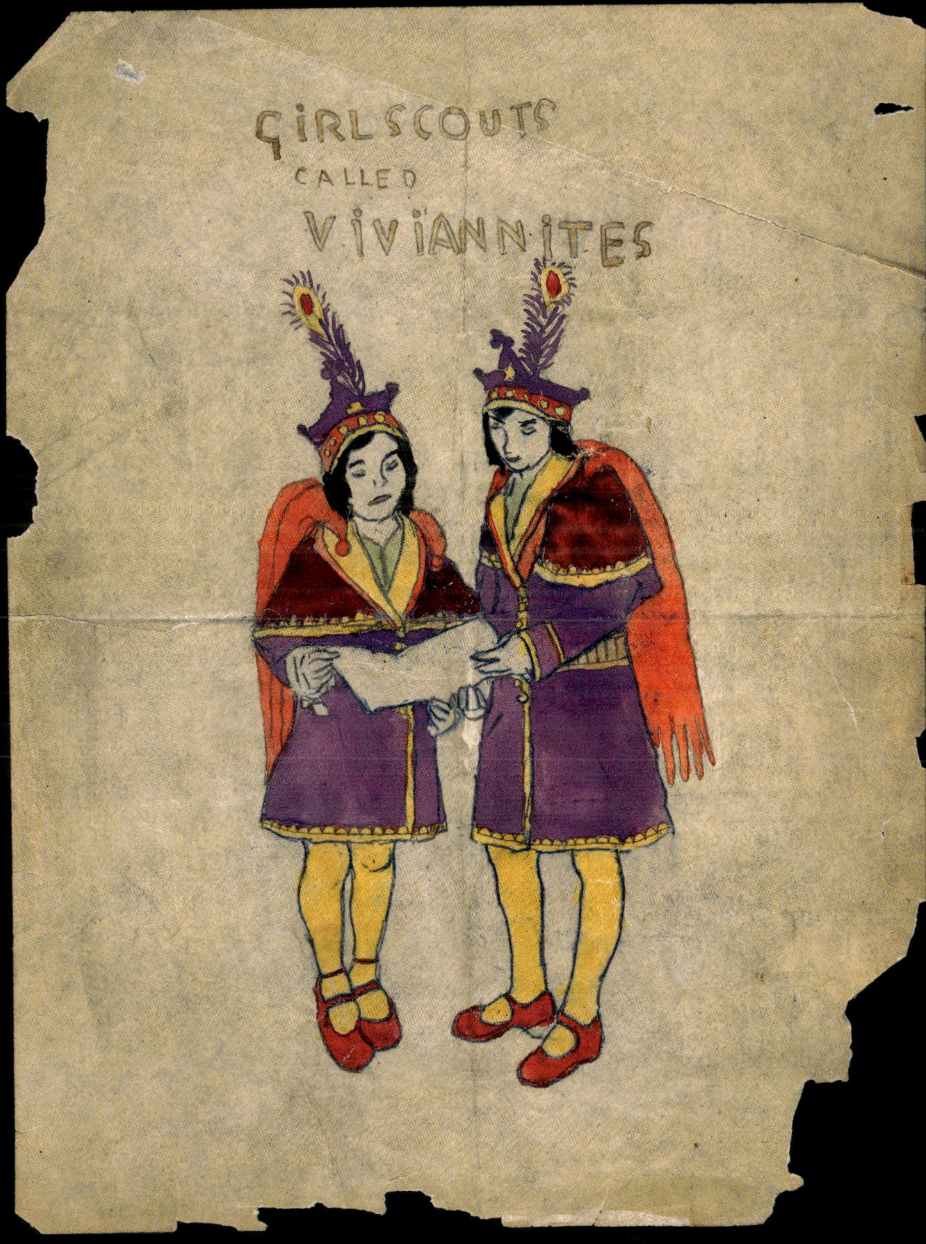

Above: *Viviannite Girl Scout Private. Rangers of Miss Jennie Turmer's Regiment.* Watercolor, pencil, and carbon tracing on paper, 8 x 12 in. Collection Kiyoko Lerner

Below: *Girl Scouts Called Viviannites.* Watercolor, pencil, and carbon tracing on paper, 12 x 8 in. Collection Laurence Marchand

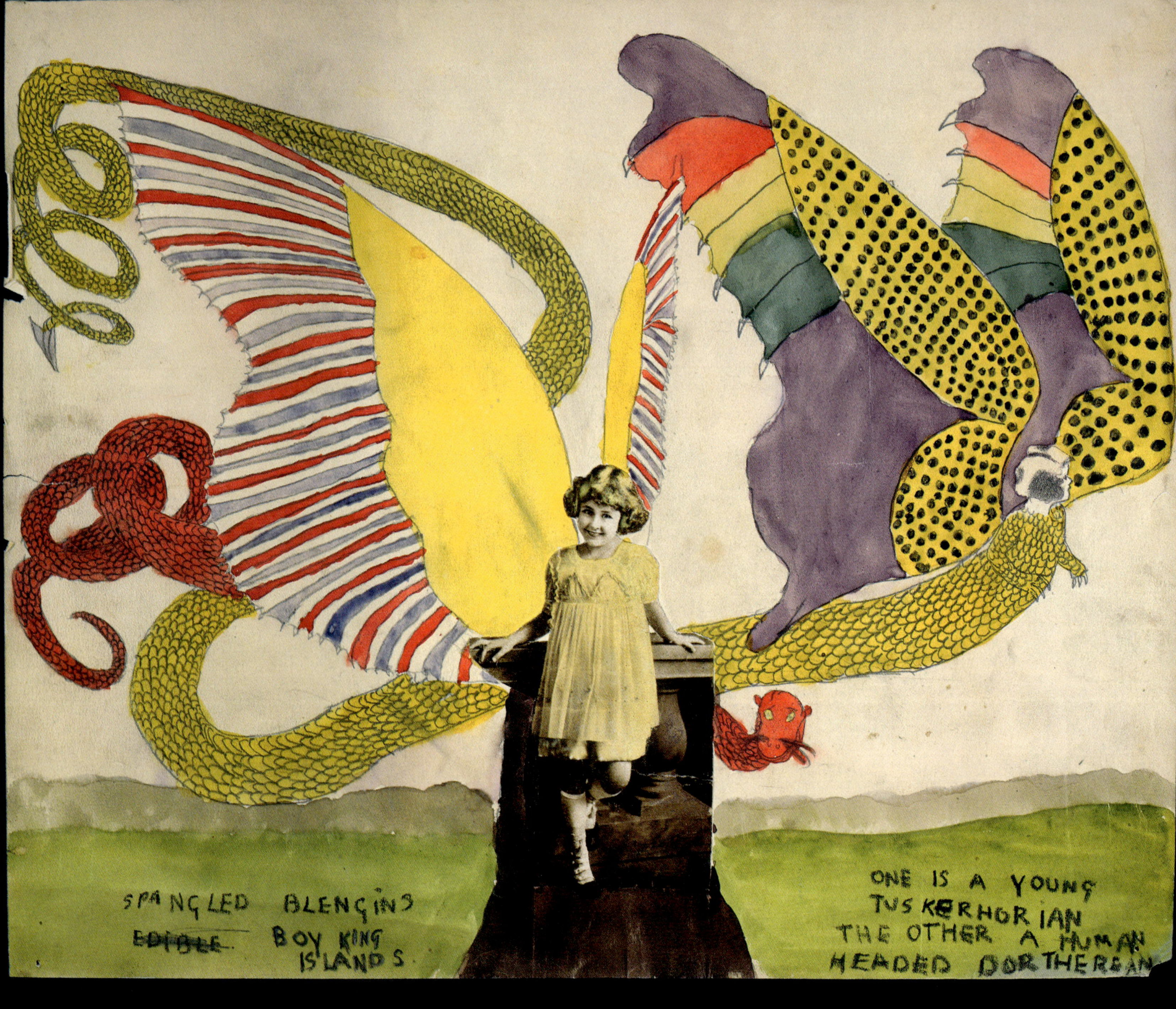

72 *Spangled Blengins. ~~Edible.~~ Boy King Islands. One is a young Tuskerhorian the other a human headed Dortherean.* Collage, watercolor, pencil, and carbon tracing on paper, 14 x 17 in. Collection Kiyoko Lerner

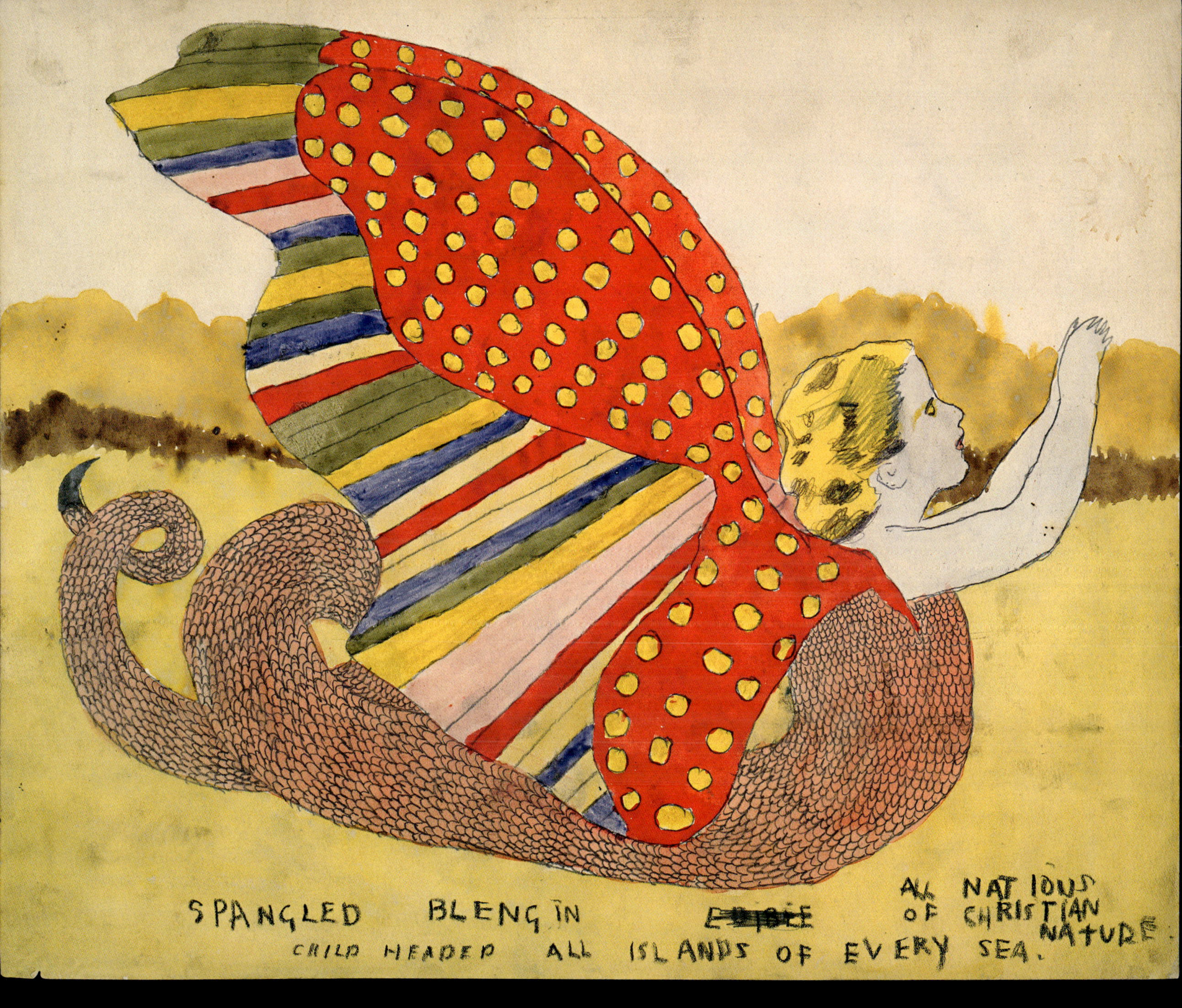

Spangled (Child Headed) Blengin. ~~*Edible.*~~ *All Nations of Christian Nature. All Islands of Every Sea.* Watercolor, pencil, and carbon tracing on paper, 14 x 17 in.

Collection Kiyoko Lerner

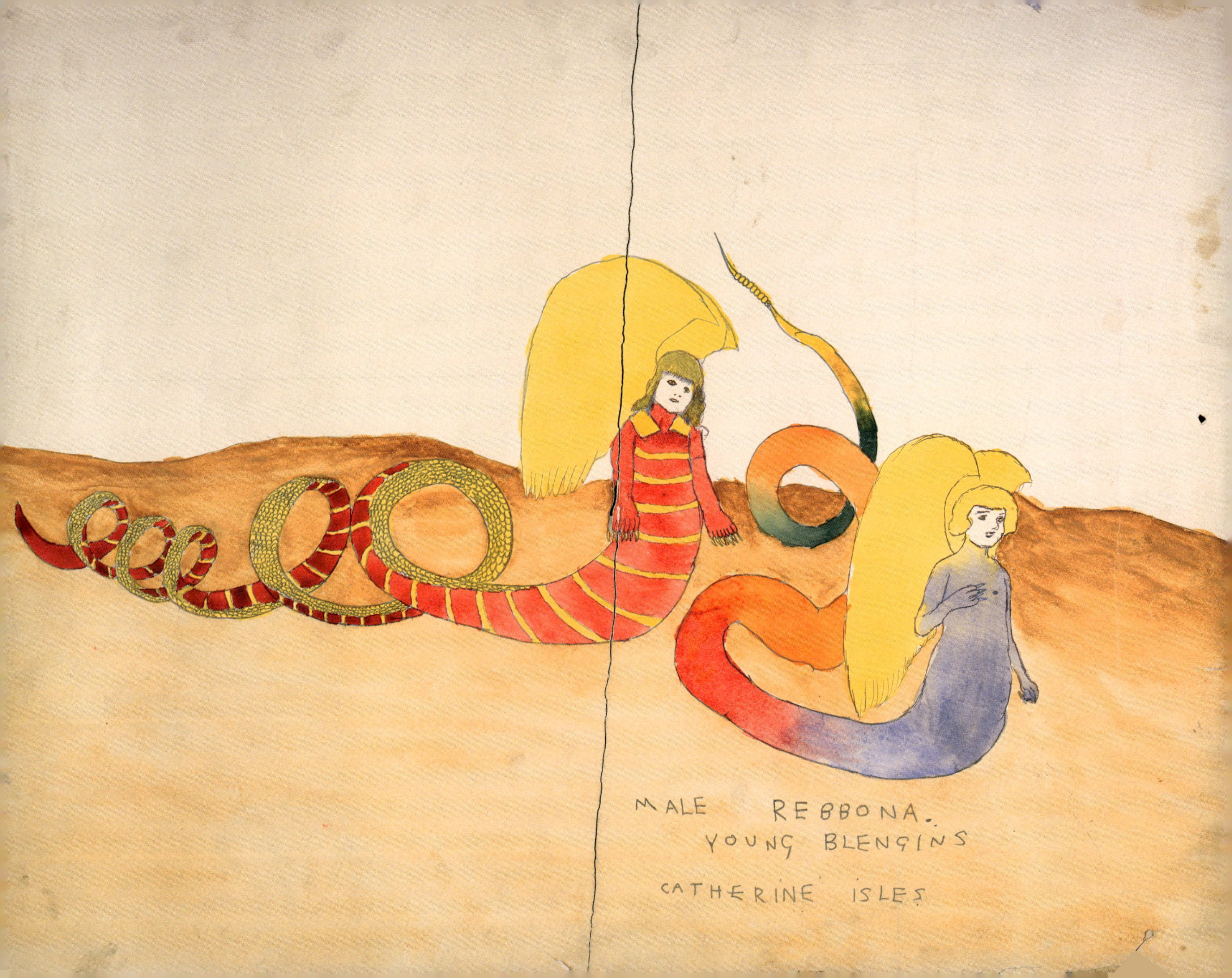
MALE REBBONA.
YOUNG BLENGINS
CATHERINE ISLES

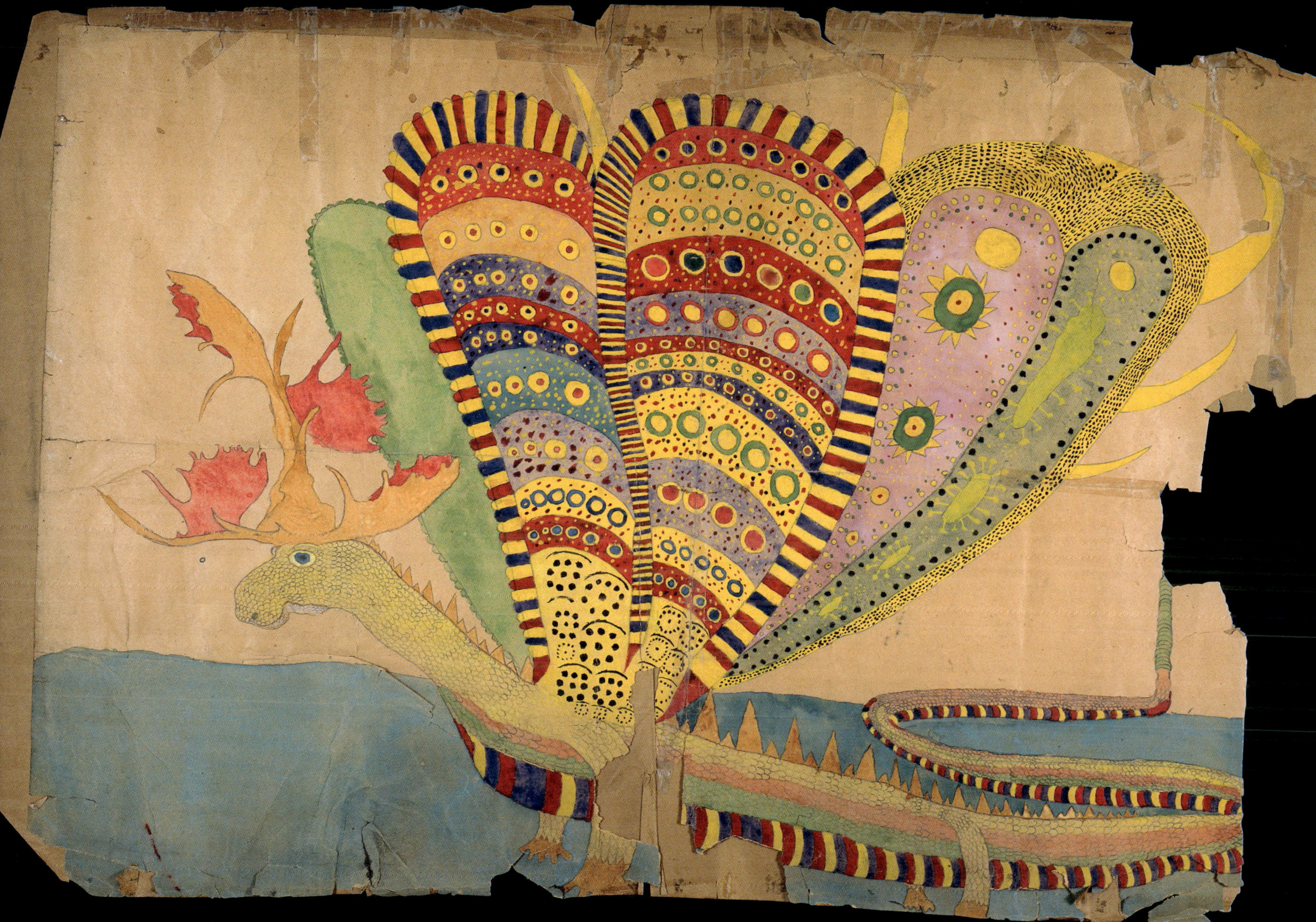

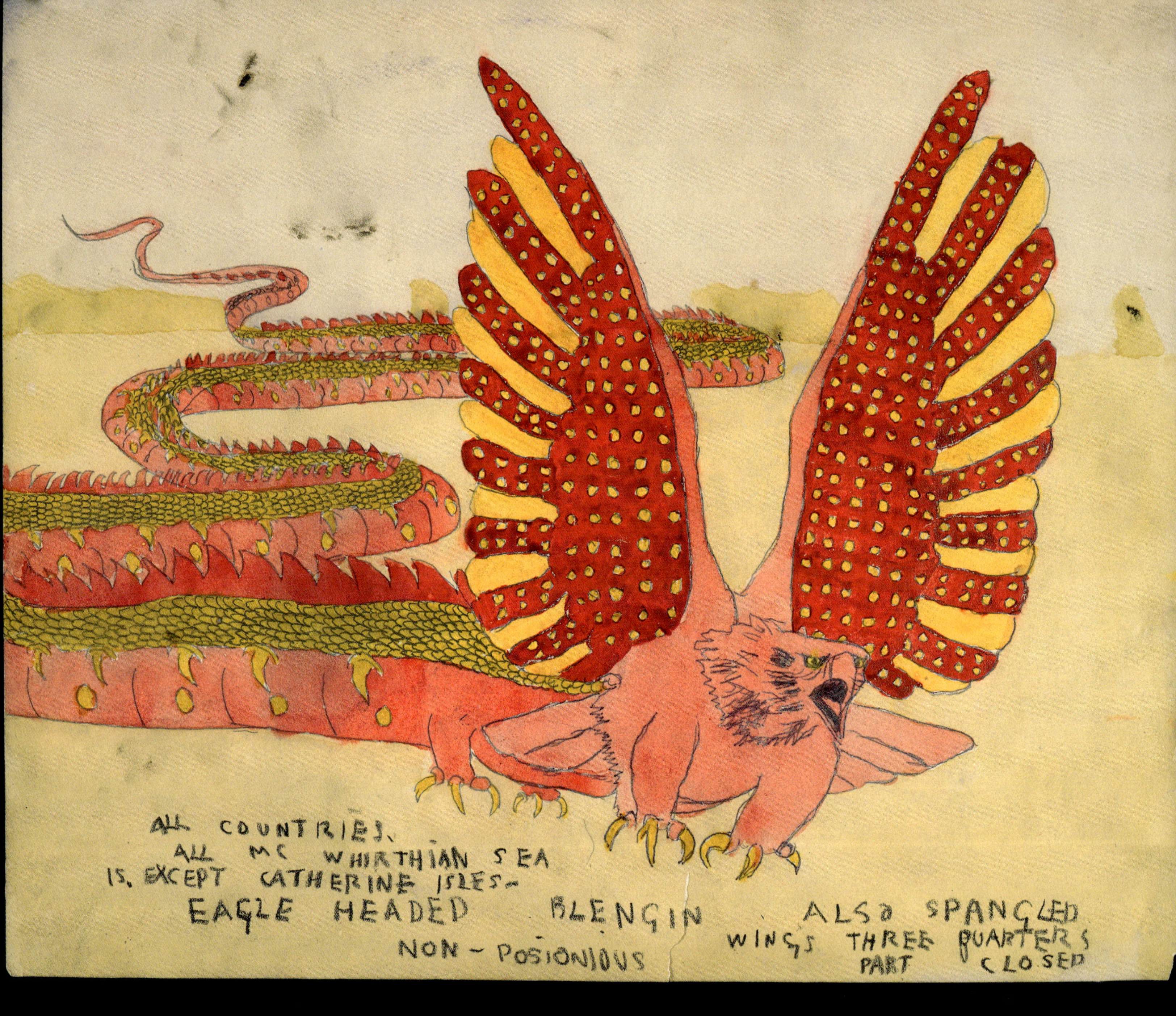

  | *Eagle Headed Blengin, Non-Posionious, also Spangled, Wings Three Quarters Part Closed.*

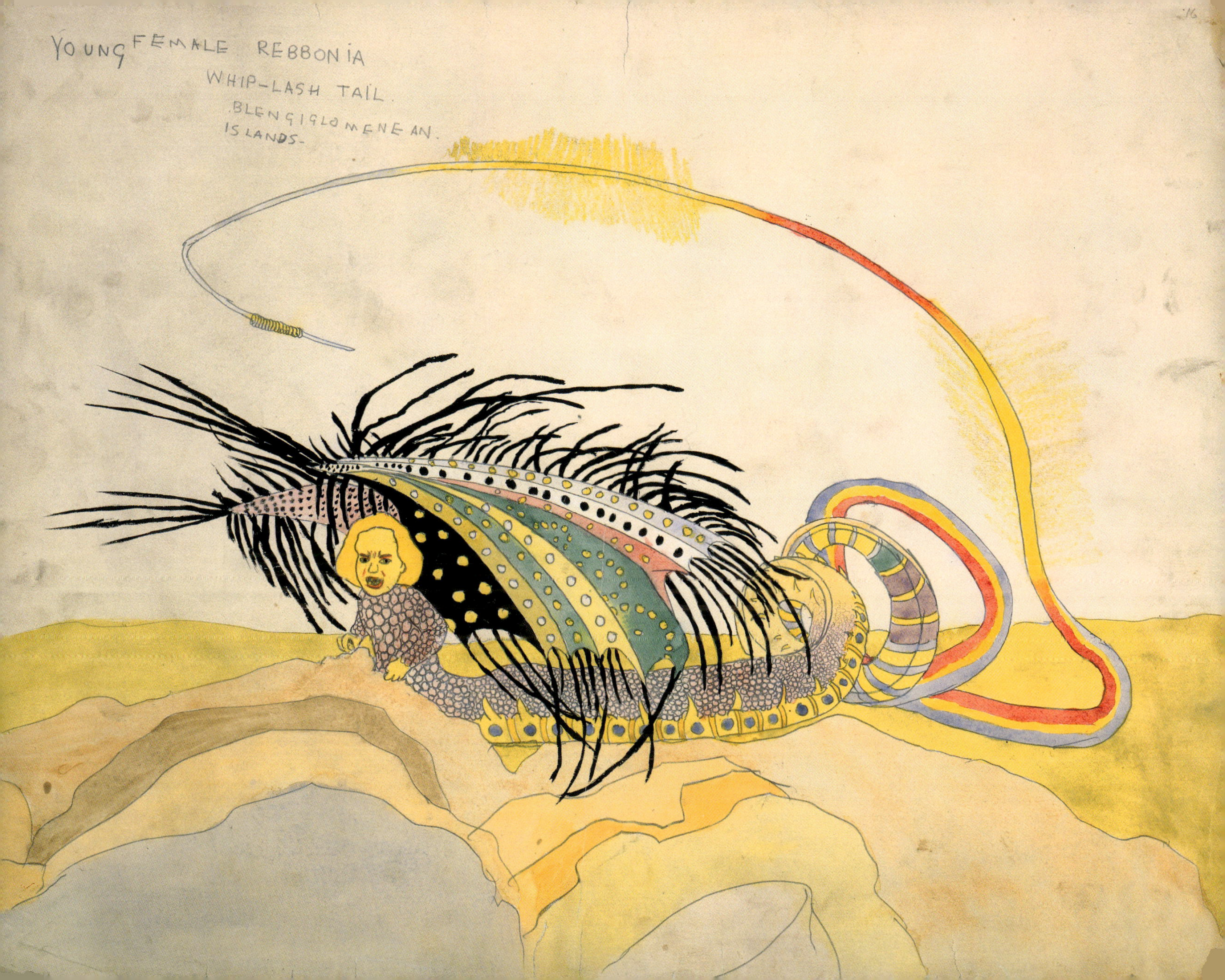

YOUNG FEMALE REBBONIA
WHIP-LASH TAIL.
.BLENGIGLOMENEAN.
IS LANDS-

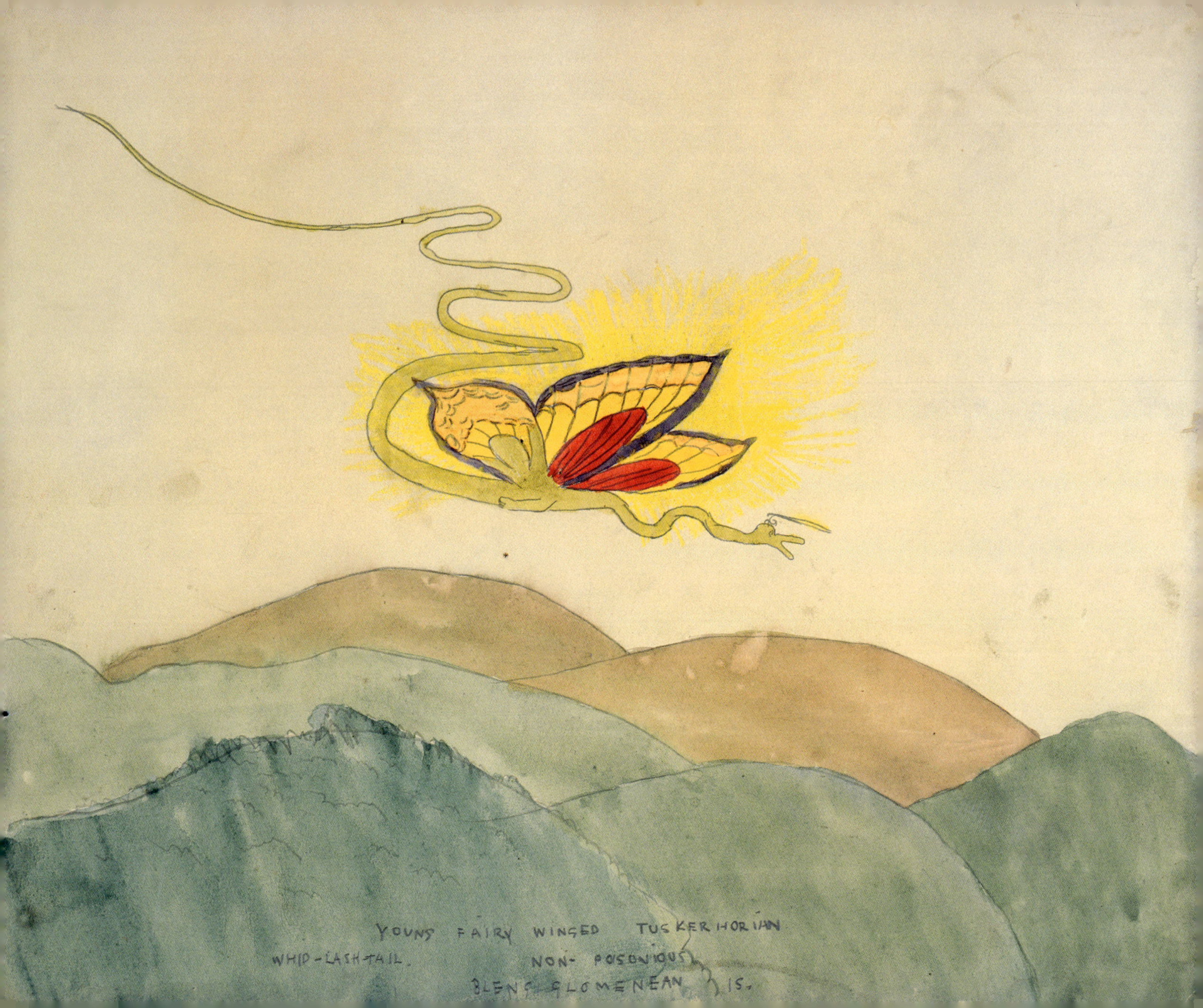
YOUNG FAIRY WINGED   TUSKER HORIAN
WHIP-LASH-TAIL.   NON- POISONOUS)
BLENG GLOMENEAN 15.

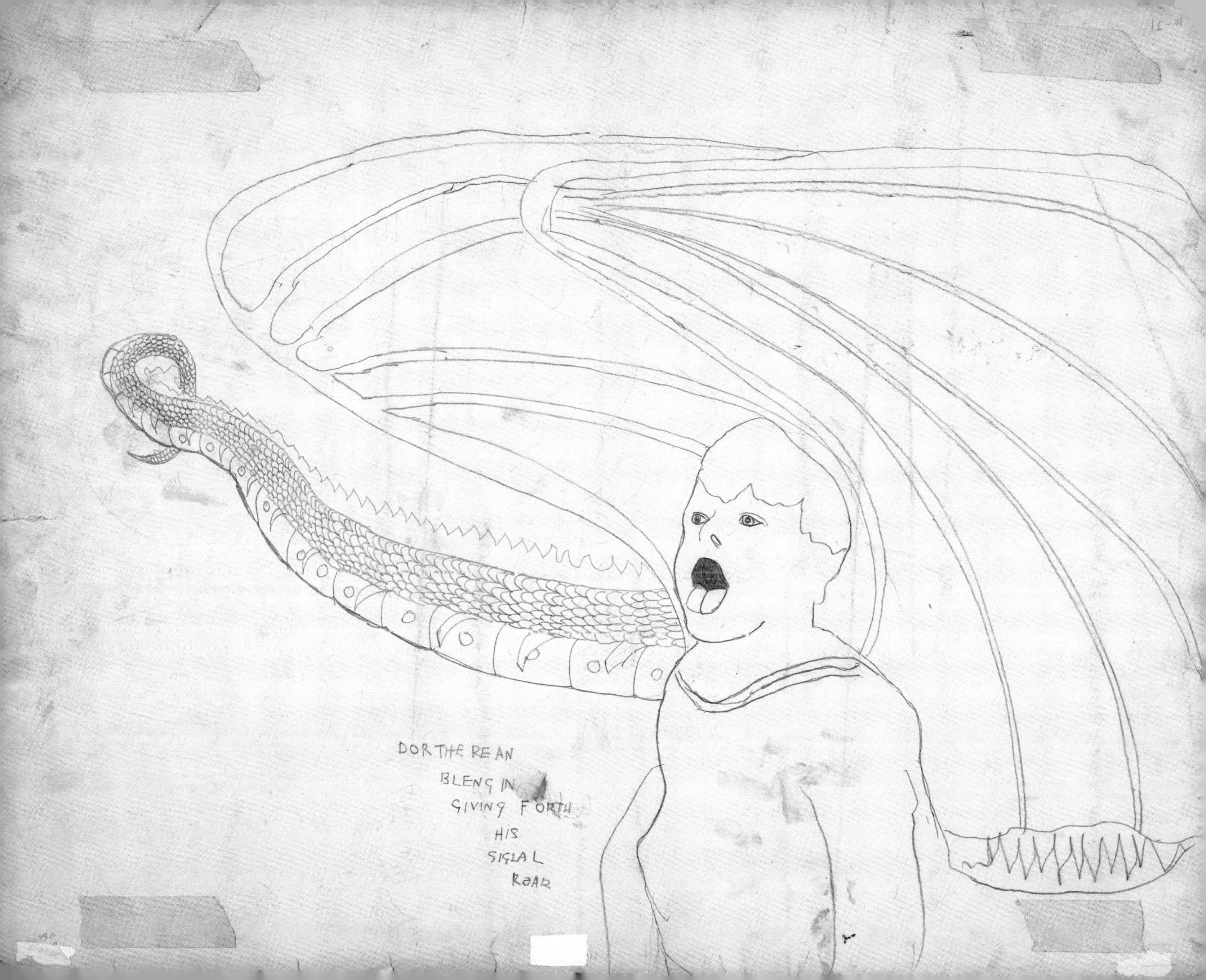
DORTHE REAN
BLENG IN
GIVING FORTH
HIS
SIGLAL
ROAR

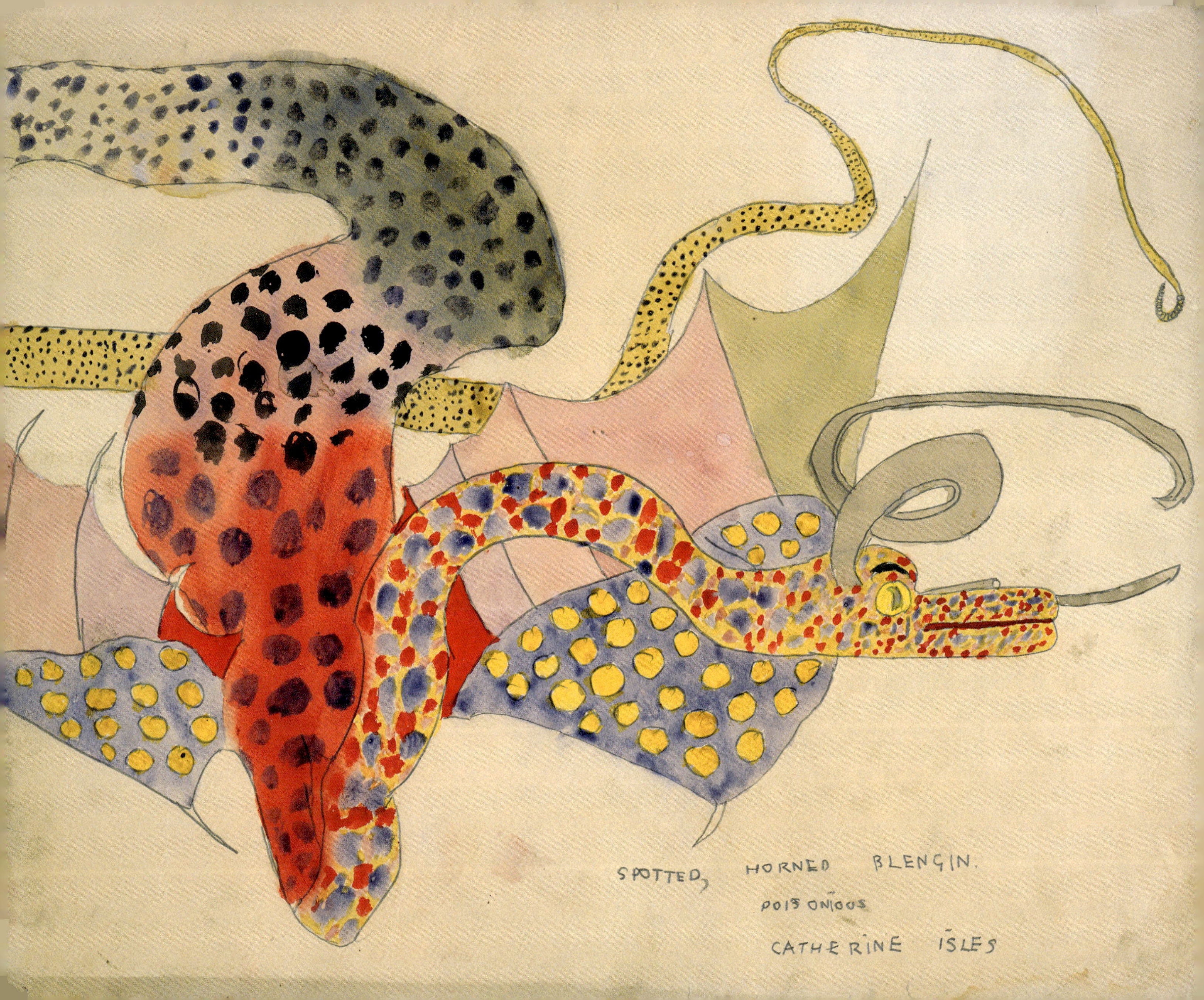

SPOTTED, HORNED BLENGIN.
POISONOUS
CATHERINE ISLES

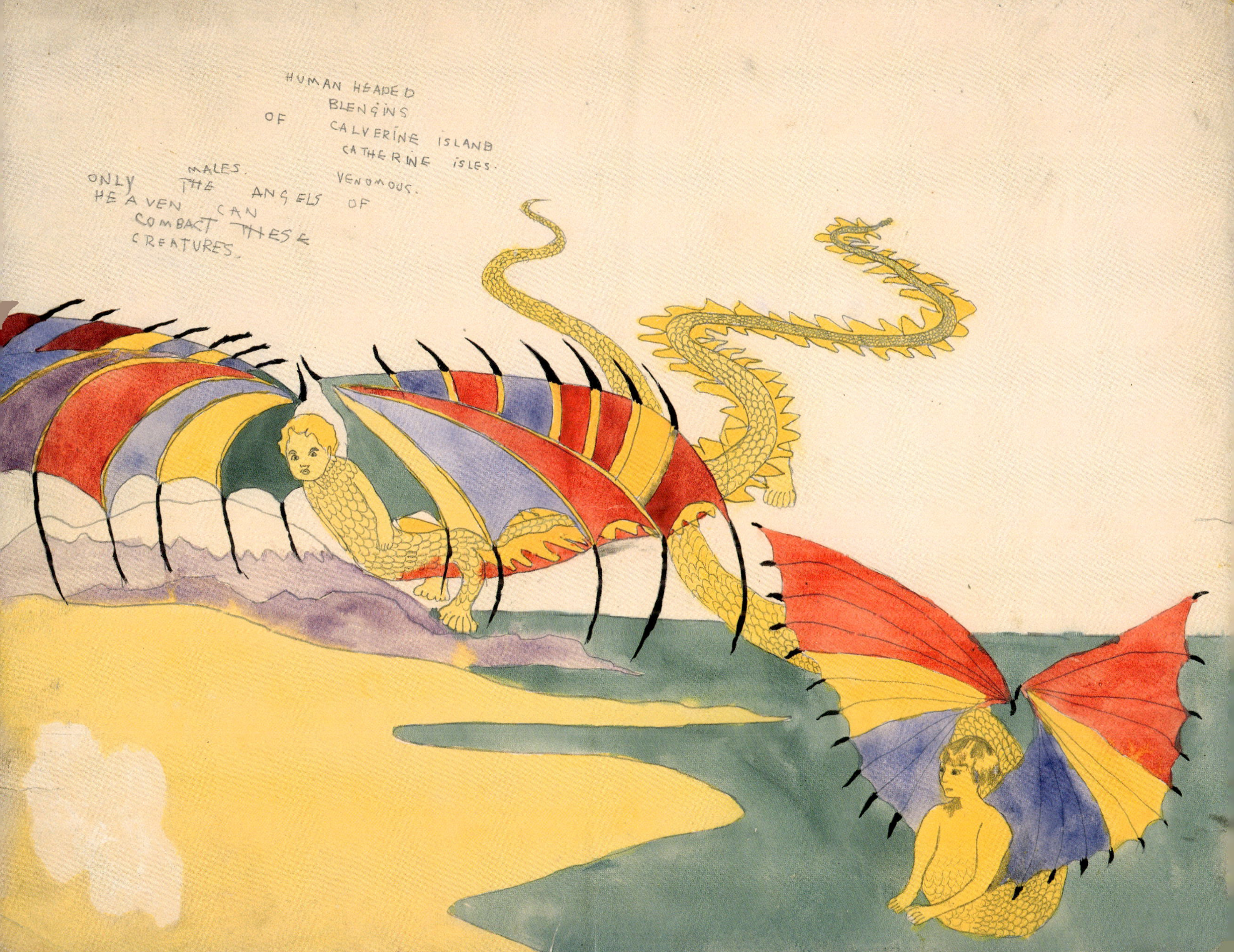
HUMAN HEADED
BLENGINS
OF CALVERINE ISLAND
CATHERINE ISLES.
MALES. VENOMOUS.
ONLY THE ANGELS OF
HEAVEN CAN
COMBACT THESE
CREATURES.

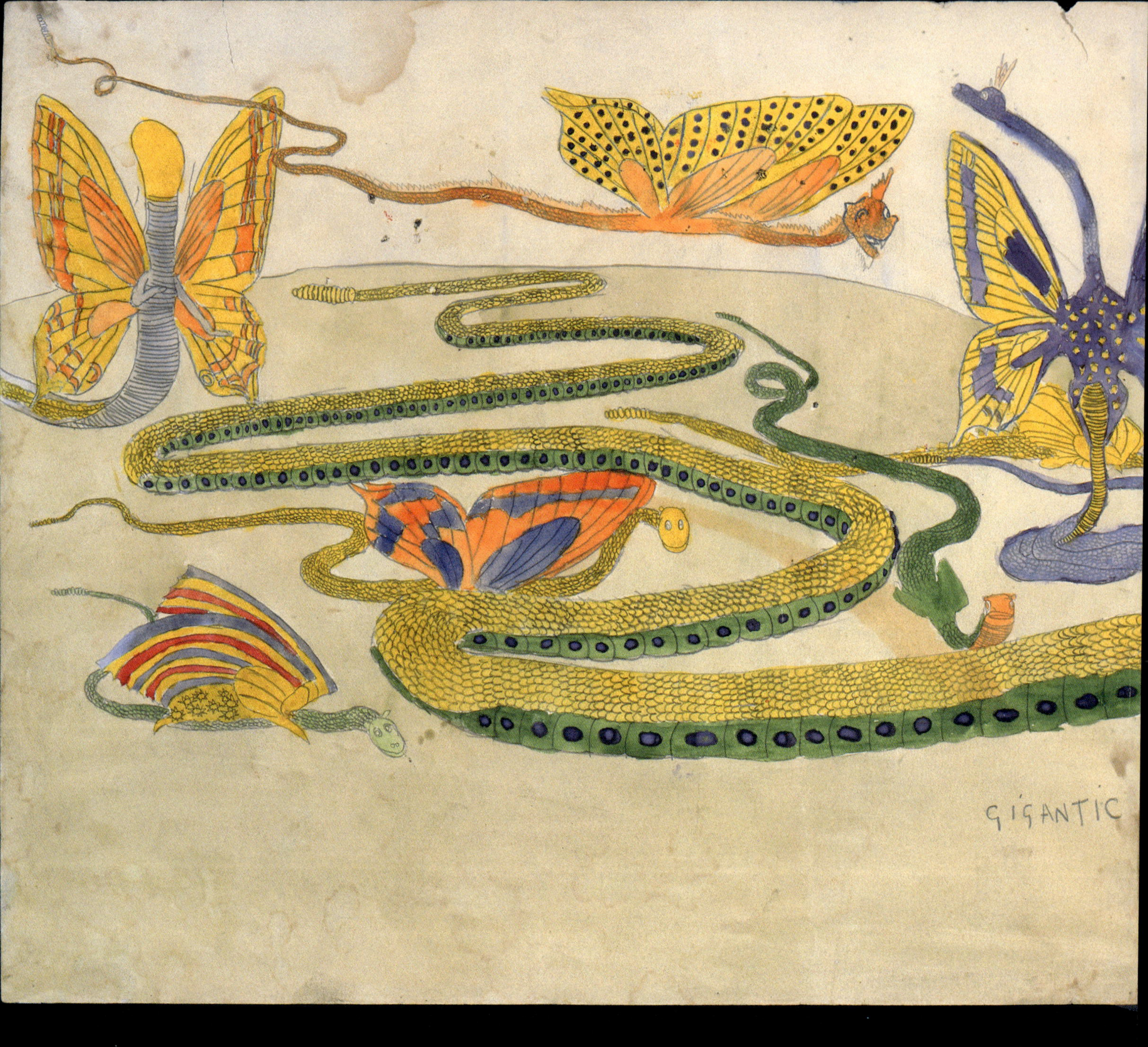

 Gigantic Roverine with Young All Poisonous All Islands of Universan Seas and Oceans. Also in Calverinia, Angelinia and Abbieannia. Watercolor, pencil, and carbon tracing on pieced paper, 14 x 33 ¾ in.

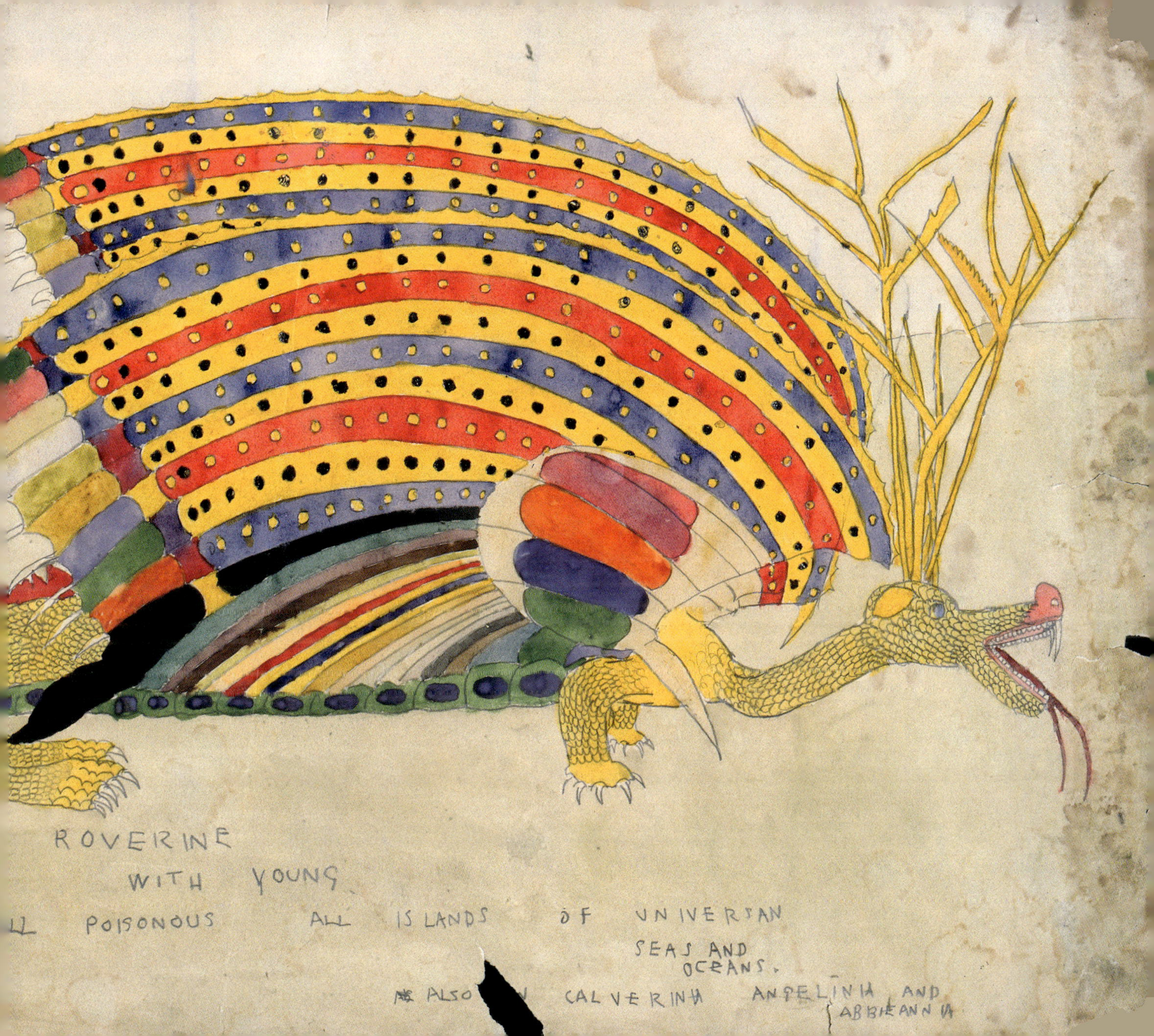
ROVERINE
WITH YOUNG
LL POISONOUS ALL ISLANDS OF UNIVERSAN
SEAS AND
OCEANS.
AS ALSO IN CALVERINIA ANGELINIA AND
ABBIEANNIA

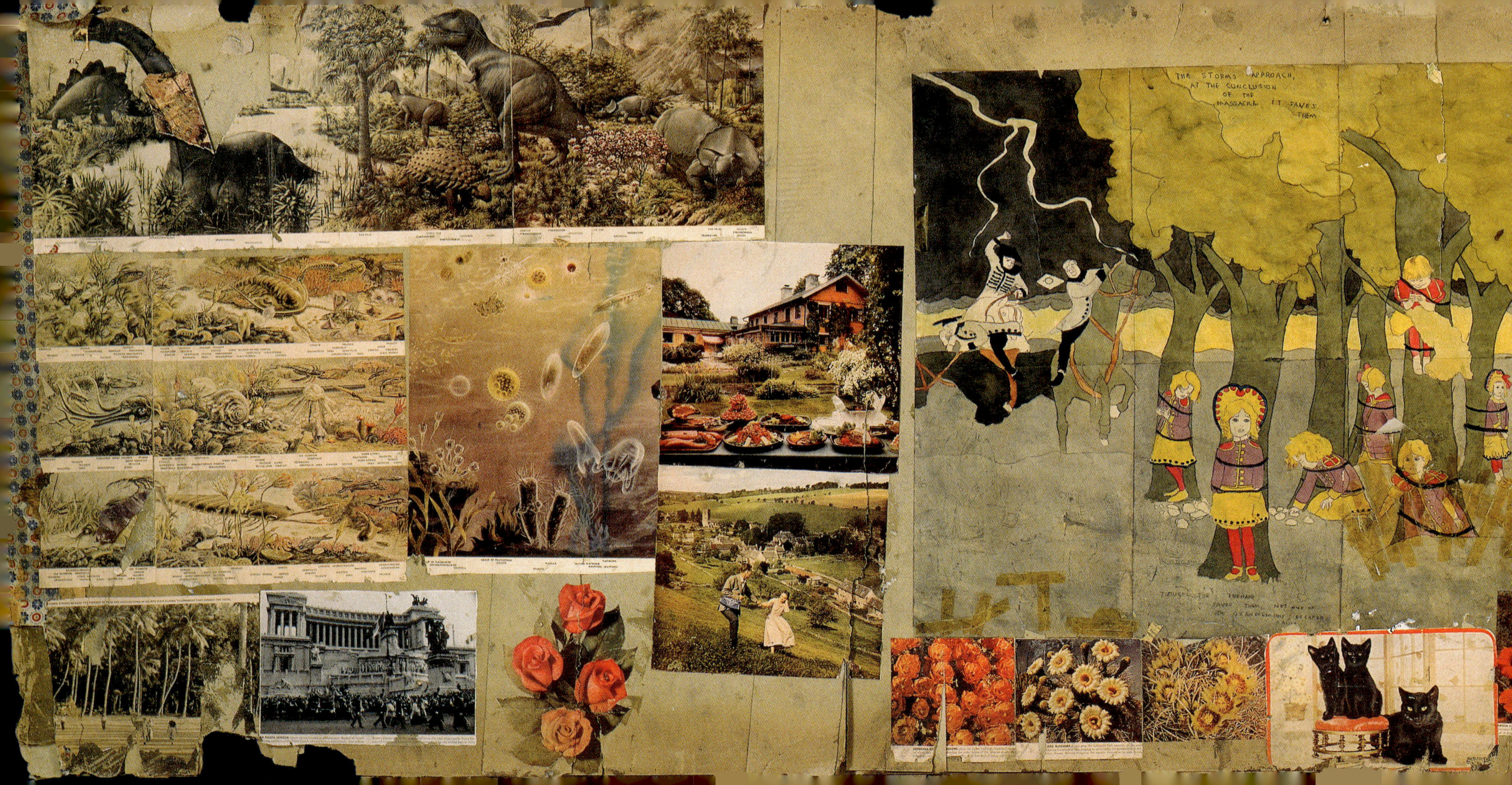

THE STORMS APPROACH,
AT THE CONCLUSION
OF THE
MASSACRE. IT SAVES
THEM.

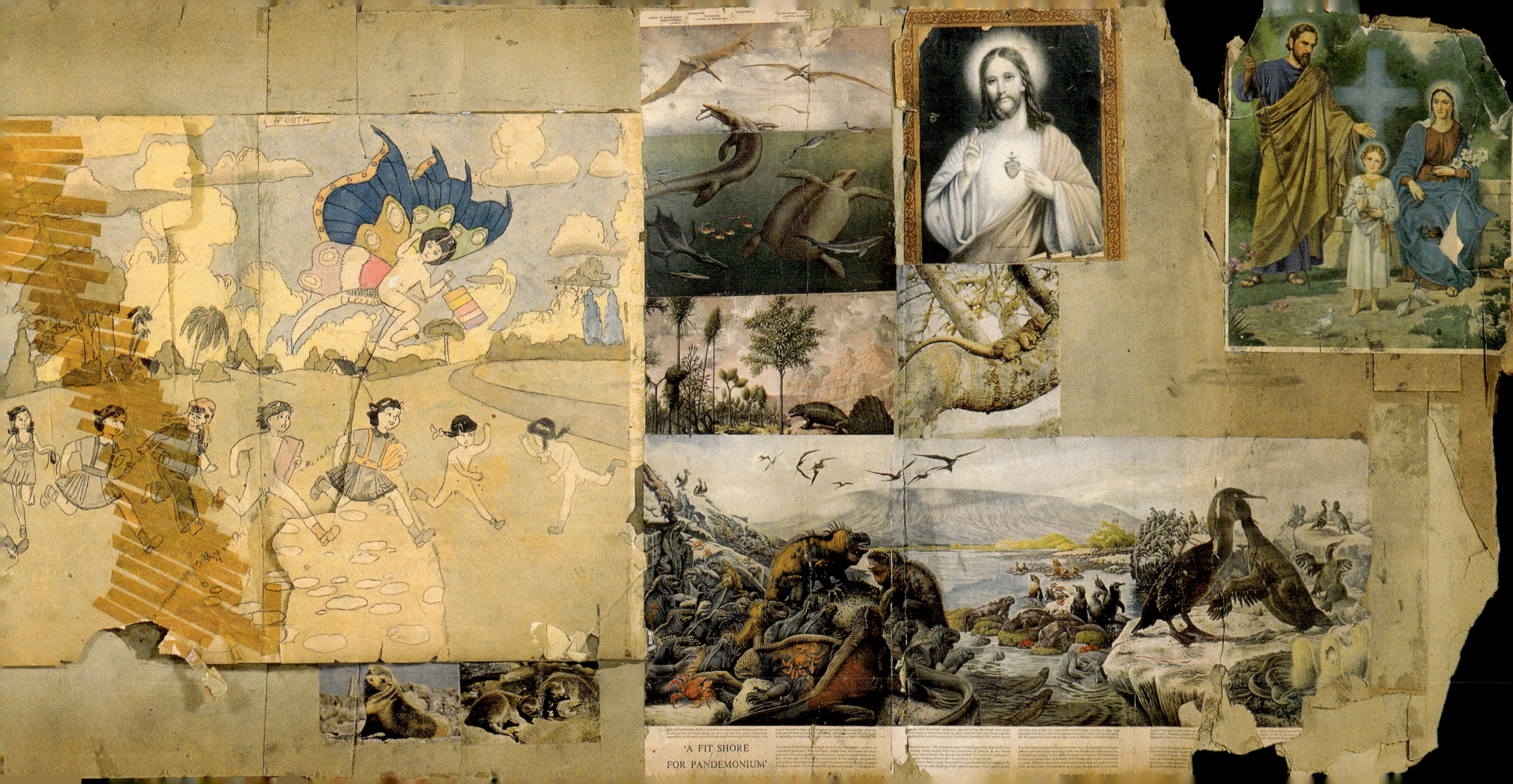

NORTH
'A FIT SHORE
FOR PANDEMONIUM'

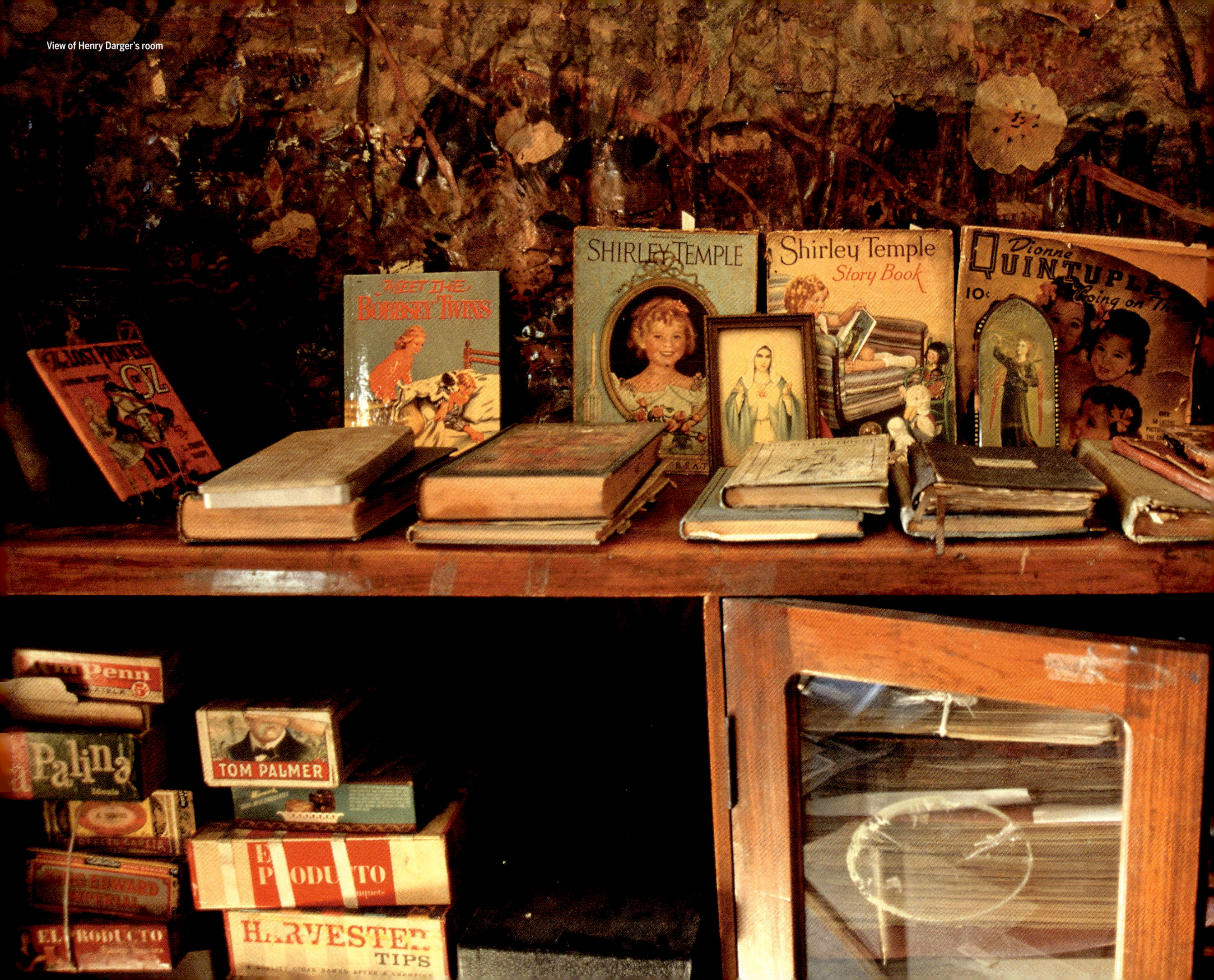

View of Henry Darger's room

An Artist's Studio
at 851 Webster Avenue

BROOKE DAVIS ANDERSON

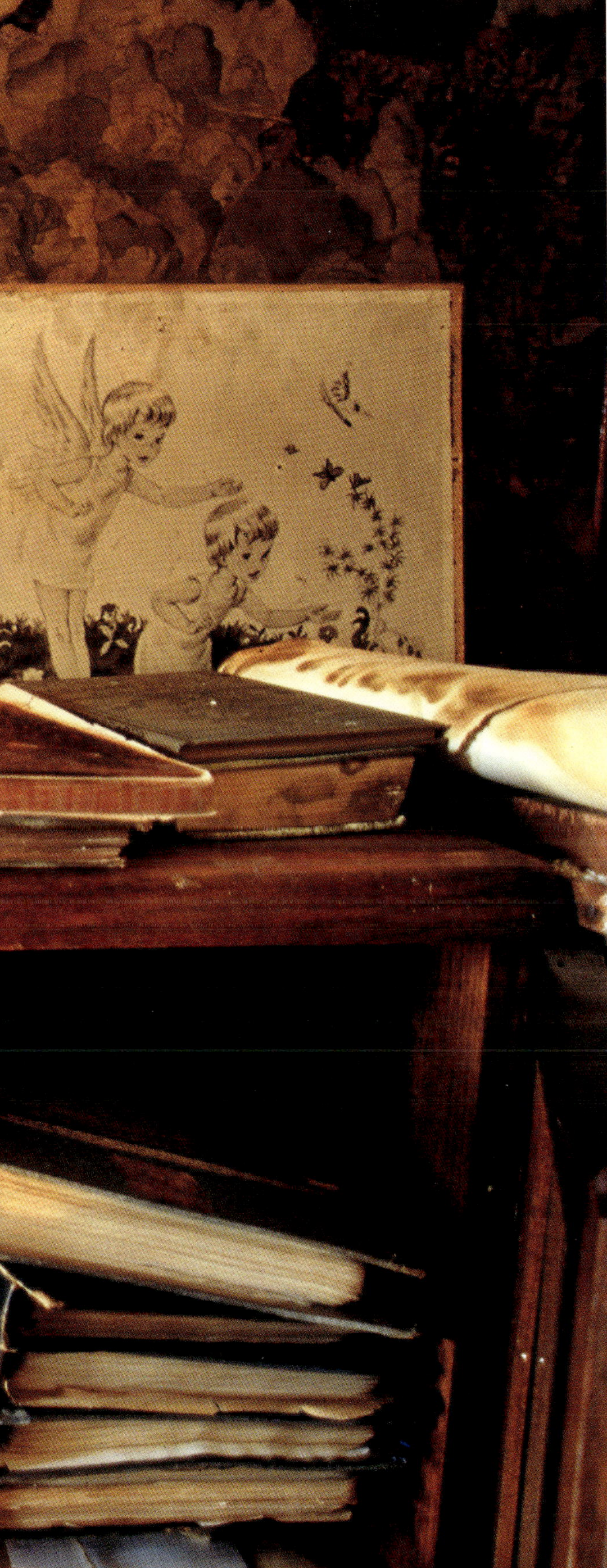

In 2000 the American Folk Art Museum established the Henry Darger Study Center to foster open inquiry and interdisciplinary research into the Chicago artist's life and work. Through a combination of gift and purchase, the museum acquired a substantial group of important paintings, books, and archival material by Darger, one of the most celebrated self-taught artists of our time. This significant addition to the permanent collection establishes the museum as the single largest repository of Darger's works, allowing it to explore one man's creative impulse through regular exhibitions and educational programs.

The effort received substantial encouragement from Kiyoko Lerner, whose husband, Nathan Lerner, discovered and preserved Darger's legacy. Kiyoko Lerner generously gave to the museum the artist's personal archive, including diaries, correspondence, books, photographs, source material, studies, and paper ephemera, as well as the manuscripts and typescripts of his vast literary works, including his masterpiece, *The Story of the Vivian Girls, in What Is Known as the Realms of the Unreal, of the Glandeco-Angelinian War Storm, Caused by the Child-Slave Rebellion* (commonly called *In the Realms of the Unreal*). Because Nathan and Kiyoko Lerner preserved the majority of the contents of the art studio Darger maintained in his room at 851 Webster Avenue, we are able to reconstruct something of this self-taught artist's motivations, intentions, methodologies, and strategies. It is not difficult to imagine a different outcome: all of the contents of Darger's room might have been thrown away at the time of the artist's death.

Many contemporary self-taught artists have been perceived as marginal to society and have been undervalued by their communities; as a result, ephemera relating to their work are easily discarded.[1] While students and scholars, collectors, and enthusiasts never had the opportunity to interview Darger about his intentions and motivations, his techniques and processes, they have a tremendous resource available to them in the Henry Darger Study Center. The Lerners are to be commended for recognizing the value not only of Darger's art, but also of the materials he used to make it.

Henry Darger (1892–1973) created a far-flung imaginary world not unlike that of L. Frank Baum, author of *The Wonderful Wizard of Oz* and its first thirteen sequels or, more recently, J. K. Rowling, who made real the world of one Harry Potter. After writing an epic novel spanning more than fifteen thousand pages, Darger had ambitions to illustrate it. Without the benefit of an education in the arts, the author taught himself how to draw, paint, and collage, as well as compose, color, and animate a surface. Without the tools taught in art school, he equipped himself with motifs and forms and images to successfully depict the narrative of his fantasy world. Without the privilege of instruction from teachers and a classroom of fellow students, Darger began making art around 1915 and continued working until at least the late 1960s, even though he was in poor health at this time. He thus spent decades honing his artistic skills until he was able to achieve sophisticated and realistic representations of his fantasy tale.

The collection at the American Folk Art Museum records the step-by-step processes of appropriation, tracing, and photography employed by Darger over the course of his career, while also illustrating his artistic development. The archival materials reveal Darger as a working artist making complex aesthetic decisions on a daily basis in the course of a lifetime deeply rooted in the American experience of the twentieth century. The collection is thus a primary source for scholars and students of his art; it is also a vital tool for study of one man's creative process, particularly because the artist was never interviewed about his art works, or the story they illustrate and the imaginary characters peopling them. The collection challenges the long-held notion that self-taught artists—also called visionary, outsider, art brut, and vernacular—are isolates without a cultural foundation or visual language. In general, the art world considers art brut a form of expression that is created outside the boundaries of culture. The Henry Darger Study Center Collection invites us to explore how self-taught artists are more commonly our culture-bearers, revealing ideas and concepts about our society.[2]

While Darger's watercolors and manuscripts have been discussed in many publications and exhibitions, the artist's archive remains largely unexplored.[3] In it we may detect Darger's interests and passions, as well as aspects of his daily life. The archive includes 1,574 clippings, 819 photographic enlargements, 210 negatives, and 486 sketches, all revealing his learning curve and shedding light on his artistic process.[4] It also contains his personal papers and library: the former add some flesh to a man who has taken on almost mythic status since his death; the latter brings to light some of Darger's primary inspirations, particularly the Oz series and other illustrated children's books, as well as the remnants of children's coloring books.

Henry Darger was an organized and methodical worker, a master of using every little bit and piece of material. For example, he would deconstruct a coloring book, removing all the sheets he planned to trace (opposite, above left). He would save the rigid cover as a file folder and store clippings inside: pictures of clouds, for example, taken from newspapers and magazines (page 94). When he needed to trace a cloud into a painting, he would go to this folder. He kept a kind of "to do" list in which he wrote out titles of all of the paintings he wanted to make (below right). This journal has not been carefully studied, but it indicates that each title illustrates a particular episode of *In the Realms of the Unreal*. Another document uncovers aspects of his prep work, recording the dates when each painting was made (below left). For example, Darger might write, "Started drawing new picture double number June 18 – finished? July 19." He tracked the time it took to complete a painting, and he also indicated the size, calling a work a "double number," for example, which refers to one of his diptychs.

Throughout the archive there are hints that Darger was aware of high-art traditions. He saved images of well-known historical artworks such as the Ghent Altarpiece, painted by Jan van Eyck in the fifteenth century, and watercolors by John James Audubon from the nineteenth century. His use of a reproduction of the painting *Thunder Storm on Narragansett Bay* by Martin Johnson Heade (1868) is well known (see page 144).[5] In one painting he poses a Blengiglomenean in a standard odalisque posture, echoing the work of such artists as Goya or Manet who were drawn to this classic archetype from the

Pages from Henry Darger's journal detailing painting activity in 1958 and 1959 (left), and to-do list for unfinished paintings (right). Collection American Folk Art Museum, New York. Gift of Kiyoko Lerner

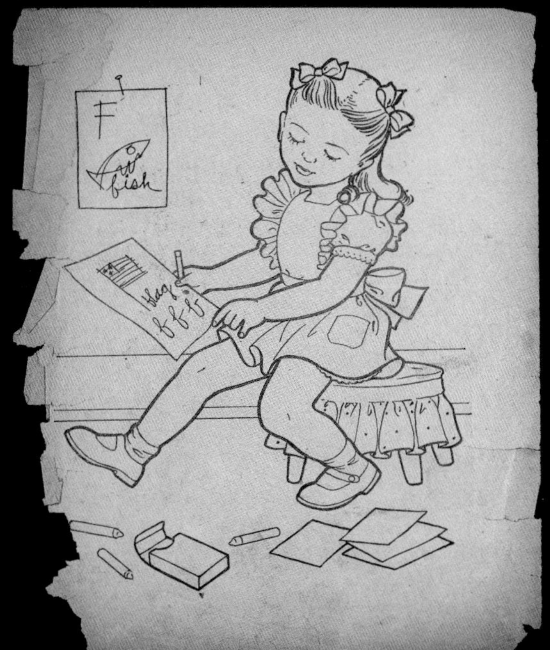
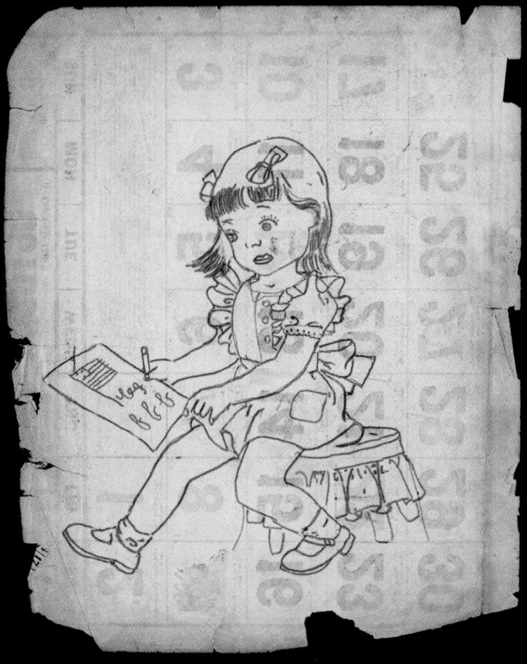

Above left: Coloring book with carbon tracing by Henry Darger, mid-twentieth century. 13 x 10 ½ in.
Above right: Henry Darger, Untitled (girl drawing), after 1954. Paper calendar with pencil and carbon tracing, 13 ¾ x 11 ¼ in.

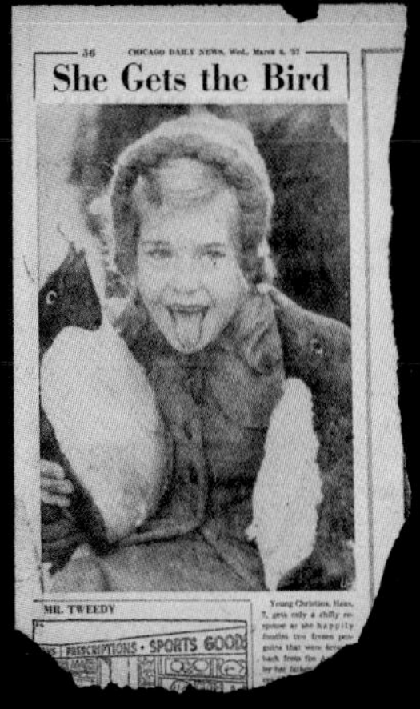

Above: "She Gets the Bird,"
newspaper clipping from *Chicago Daily News*,
March 6, 1957, 11 x 6 ½ in.

Right: Henry Darger, Untitled (two girls being
strangled by soldier), mid-twentieth century.
Pencil on tracing paper, 18 ¾ x 23 ½ in.
All items Collection American Folk Art Museum,
New York. Gift of Kiyoko Lerner

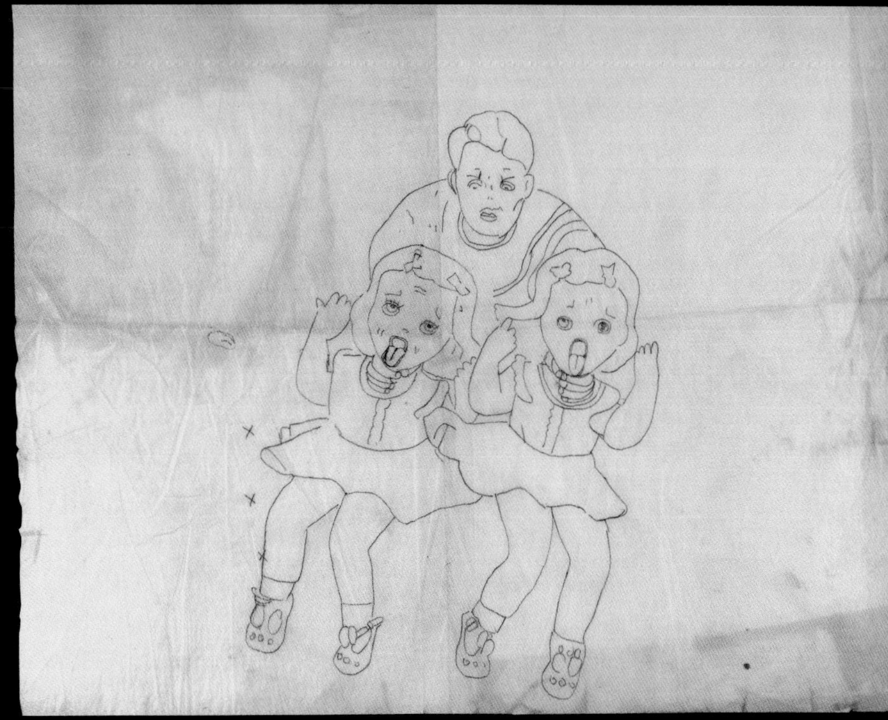

western art history tradition (see pages 196–97). His employment of high-art conventions is also evident in some of the interior scenes in his later work. The artist decorates his interiors with paintings of the Vivian girls and other characters from *In the Realms of the Unreal*, displaying them on the walls of his stagelike spaces.[6] The idea of placing a painting within a painting also may have been suggested by coloring books.

In order to realize his aesthetic vision, Darger invented techniques involving appropriation and collage from popular media: magazines, newspapers, pages from coloring books, newspaper fashion advertisements featuring children, and comic strips. He devised a clever system of enlarging images culled from borrowed sources to achieve a desired scale; he traced parts of these images, using carbon paper to transfer them to the sheet.[7] The artist freely and unapologetically commandeered images, often simply cutting and pasting reproductions directly onto his watercolor paintings. His subjects sometimes are placed in lush fantastical gardens, other times against the backdrop of a menacing storm or of a bloody battleground, painted with dime-store watercolors. Darger's brilliance as an artist rests partly on his ability to make his drawings much more than tracings from borrowed images, an effect achieved through his complex process and confident hand.

Access to this material is aiding scholars and students in constructing a chronology of Henry Darger's oeuvre. While Darger did not date his hundreds of watercolors, recently scholars have proposed a sequence of production that traces an arc of artistic development.[8] The artist started developing a visual language by clipping images from newspapers or magazines and coloring them with paint (pages 50-55), emulating the coloring-book practice. He would typically adhere this altered clipping onto reclaimed shirt board (from a laundry) or cardboard, fixing it for display; such modest works, which embellished

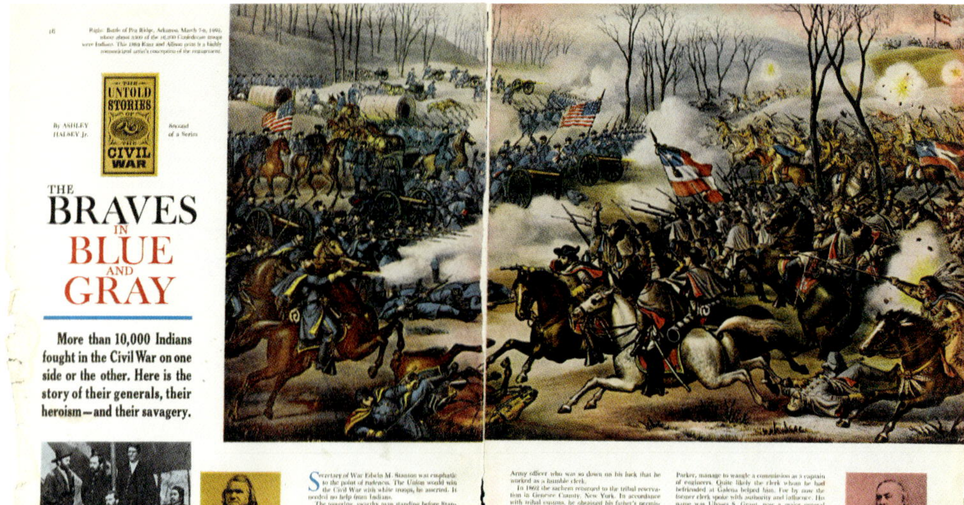

"The Untold Stories of the Civil War, Part II: The Braves in Blue and Gray," clipping from the *Saturday Evening Post*, January 14, 1961, 13 ½ x 20 ¾ in. Collection American Folk Art Museum, New York. Gift of Kiyoko Lerner

his small apartment, were his first attempts at art-making. These early collages, dating to circa 1910–25, remind us that from the beginning this was an artist at work, creating a nurturing studio environment dense with images for inspiration. The Henry Darger Study Center preserves nearly one hundred of these works, most measuring approximately fourteen by sixteen inches and many framed by Christmas Seal stamps or other available decorative elements. Darger sometimes painted the found figures to transform them into his invented characters and creatures, whether Glandelinians and Abbieannians or Vivian girls and Blenginglomeneans. He regularly added handwritten captions to these adapted images, further assimilating them into his fictitious world. These early attempts at creating a visual accompaniment to his written text involved collecting, clipping, and collating a vast array of images from popular media, a process central to understanding Darger's art. He scoured newspapers, magazines, comic strips, and coloring books for appealing pictures. He sometimes purchased but often

found these printed sources, sorting and storing them by theme. The images that survive (many must have been discarded before their importance was realized) reveal the artist's passions: weather, religion, war, and children, all of which are central themes of *In the Realms of the Unreal* and in his paintings as well.

Publications recounting the American Civil War and news coverage of both world wars provided Darger with fodder for his imaginary war story. Because he was reliant on American popular media, his work is inflected with our appetite for national history and traditions and our nation's consumer habits. These sources became the basis for the visual language he developed over the decades, an American mass-media vocabulary at the core of Darger's artistic production.

As his illustrative goals became more ambitious, Darger moved from coloring in clippings to tracing them into original drawings. He most likely started painting in the 1920s, adding watercolor to these drawings. Clearly, his ambition to make large-scale artworks began

fairly early. Following the modest cardboard/collage artworks—his first stage—the artist started to tackle diptychs and triptychs, his second stage. This phase likely dates to the 1930s or 1940s and relies solely on figures repurposed from newspapers and magazines. In this period, Darger's figures are uniform in scale and largely rendered on the frontal plane of the picture, creating a stagelike appearance. Troops of young girls live one-dimensionally in these panels—the background, whether indoors or outdoors, active or serene, is flat and lacks depth. Tracing allowed the artist to construct an environment for his characters. Typically, he created a sandwich of source image, carbon paper, and drawing paper, though many intermediate drawings or sketches survive on wax paper, tracing paper, butcher paper, and various found papers. Upon close inspection, we see that his drawn line is a dark carbon blue, not graphite gray as might be expected. His diptychs and triptychs indicate a frustration at his inability to create a believable three-dimensional space. Henry Darger was facing the dilemma of any artist aiming at realism: how to create a convincing scene on a flat surface. Because most of his figures from source material conform to a scale befitting their original purpose in ads, coloring books, and articles, tracing from them inhibited the artist's aim to make gigantic illustrations—that is, until he incorporated a technique that freed his outsized imagination.

In the mid-1940s Darger began to use a photographic process to aid his painting technique, ushering in the third stage of his artistic career.[9] He delivered his clippings to a nearby drugstore (he used several) in his Lincoln Park neighborhood in Chicago. The artist would request that the druggist send the clipping (a one-inch clipping from the *Little Annie Rooney* comic strip, for example) to Kodak for photographic processing. Following instructions, Kodak would produce an internegative and then make an enlargement from it. The technique cost anywhere from \$2.00 to \$5.00 and Darger purchased more than eight hundred of these. It was not unusual for the artist to pay for several enlargements of a favorite image, either at different scales or cropped in another way.

We will perhaps never know how he arrived at this particular process. Nor can we know what the druggists thought of this man ordering large-scale reproductions of comics, coloring books, and advertisements. By the time Darger happened upon the technique, he was nearing his sixties, living on a modest fixed income and inching toward forced retirement. (This is the period in which he wrote *The History of My Life*, which describes his work and financial condition, but scarcely mentions his art; see pages 281–313.) While Darger had a healthy savings account, it was eventually depleted by, we may presume, the costs of this not-inexpensive photographic process.[10] Despite the financial burden, though, the newfound technique was the solution the artist had been seeking to the perspective puzzle. The ability to enlarge his chosen characters from popular media meant that he could expand his drawings and at the same time attempt more complicated compositions. With the combination of clippings, tracing, and finally photographic enlargement, all integrated by hand painting, he could construct convincing landscapes in which to set his fantastic story *In the Realms of the Unreal*.

The power to control and shift scale allowed Darger to create larger, more intricate scenes on big sheets of paper, and it is these long, scroll-like paintings, extending up to twelve feet wide, that confound and astonish contemporary viewers. The enlargements meant that he could position figures in the front, middle, and rear picture plane (larger figures were closer, smaller ones more distant), constructing a believable landscape and creating the depth and dimension he had so eagerly desired in his flat renderings. Now his images are convincing tableaux with figures populating a place—often he in-

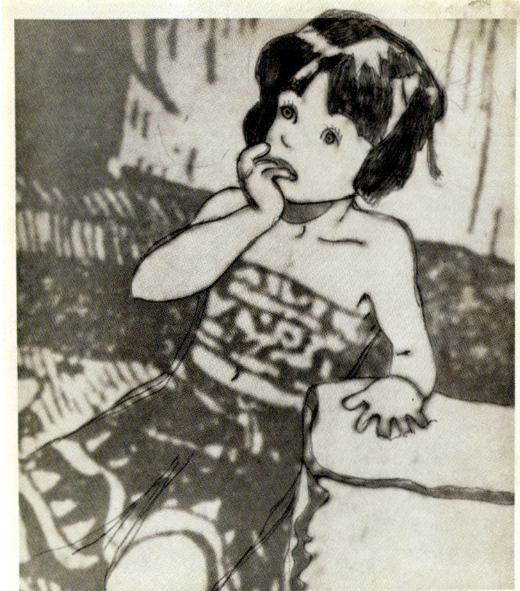
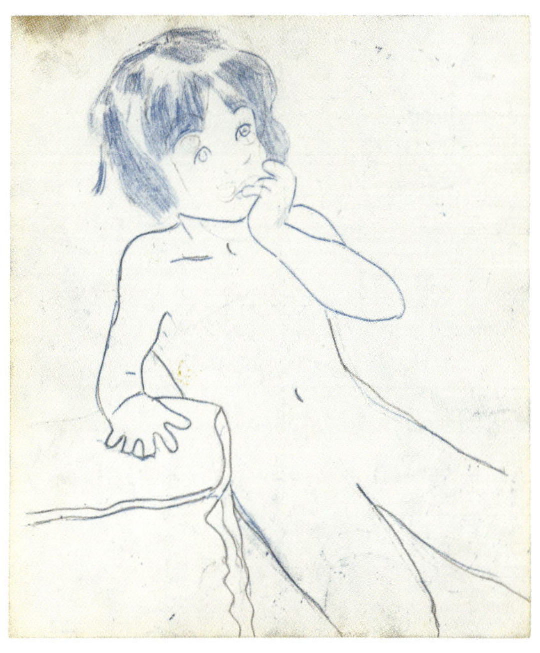

Henry Darger, Untitled (Little Annie Rooney), mid-twentieth century. Views of both sides of a photo enlargement with pencil and carbon tracing, 12 ½ x 11 in. Collection American Folk Art Museum, New York. Gift of Kiyoko Lerner

corporates the same image traced several times from its original source and its enlarged reproduction, producing the effect of a crowd. This new artistic strategy merges with Darger's mature, well-honed sense of color, and his confident line, practiced after years of tracing from popular media sources. These late works—ambitious in scale, subtle in color, and complex in composition—are Darger's most sophisticated and formally exciting paintings.[11]

Henry Darger may not have received a degree in fine arts or have had the privilege of learning in a conventional manner. Nonetheless, from common, everyday sources he learned about the formal elements of art-making (color, line, texture, composition, for example) and taught himself devices to make concrete his own unique visual vocabulary (appropriation, photography, tracing, collage).[12] This toolbox of techniques brings to mind an art-historical movement with which Henry Darger may have been unfamiliar: Pop art. While Darger developed his solutions on his own, starting as early as the mid-1940s, trained artists in Britain and New York in the late 1950s and early

1960s were starting to use similar techniques and appropriate from comparable sources—especially advertising and comics. This overlap of one man's adventures in art-making with an entire school in the hotbed of art-historical discourse indicates the presence of a *Zeitgeist*, a moment when capitalism and an acquisitive population fostered the cultural importance of advertising and marketing: people experienced a sudden flood of mass media. It didn't take long for artists, whether trained or self-taught, to add the culture of commerce to their palette. It is less important to wonder if Darger knew about Pop art or Pop artists knew about Darger (unlikely on both counts) than to point out that all artists—whether working with the advantages of the art world machine or not—are in one way or another responding to the appetites of their communities. Henry Darger, Richard Hamilton, Andy Warhol, and Roy Lichtenstein each was seduced by American culture. Can we not finally acknowledge that the autodidact Henry Darger was looking through a similarly critical eye onto the same landscape?

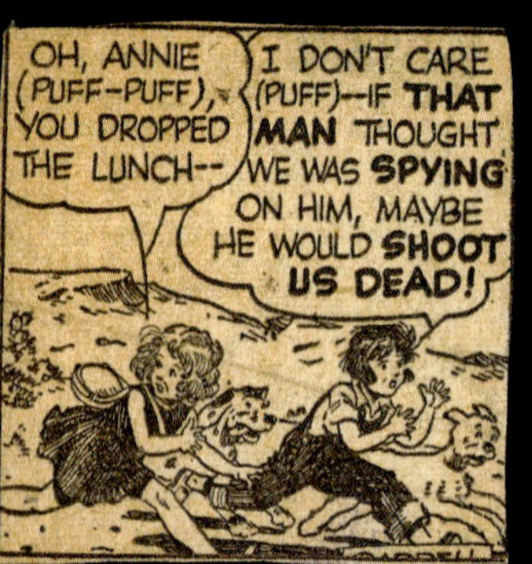

OH, ANNIE (PUFF-PUFF), YOU DROPPED THE LUNCH--
I DON'T CARE (PUFF)--IF THAT MAN THOUGHT WE WAS SPYING ON HIM, MAYBE HE WOULD SHOOT US DEAD!

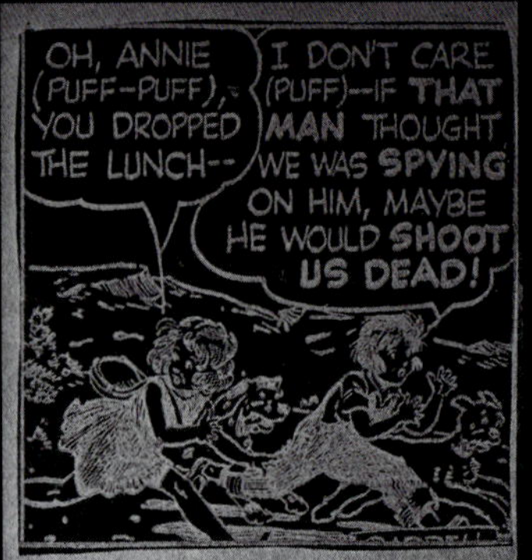

OH, ANNIE (PUFF-PUFF), YOU DROPPED THE LUNCH--
I DON'T CARE (PUFF)--IF THAT MAN THOUGHT WE WAS SPYING ON HIM, MAYBE HE WOULD SHOOT US DEAD!

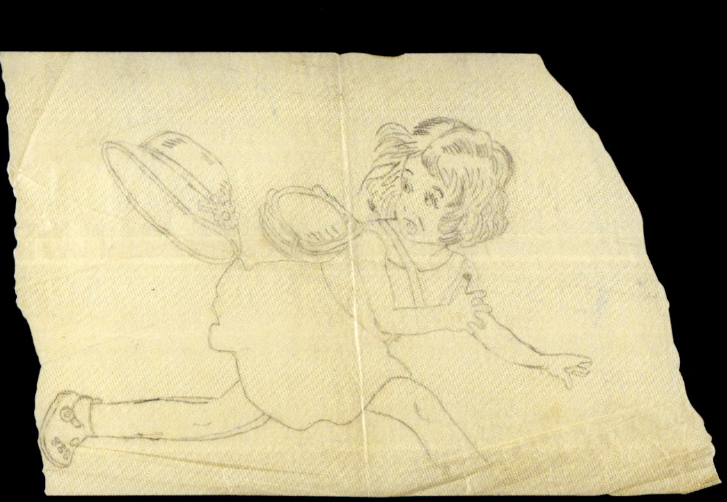

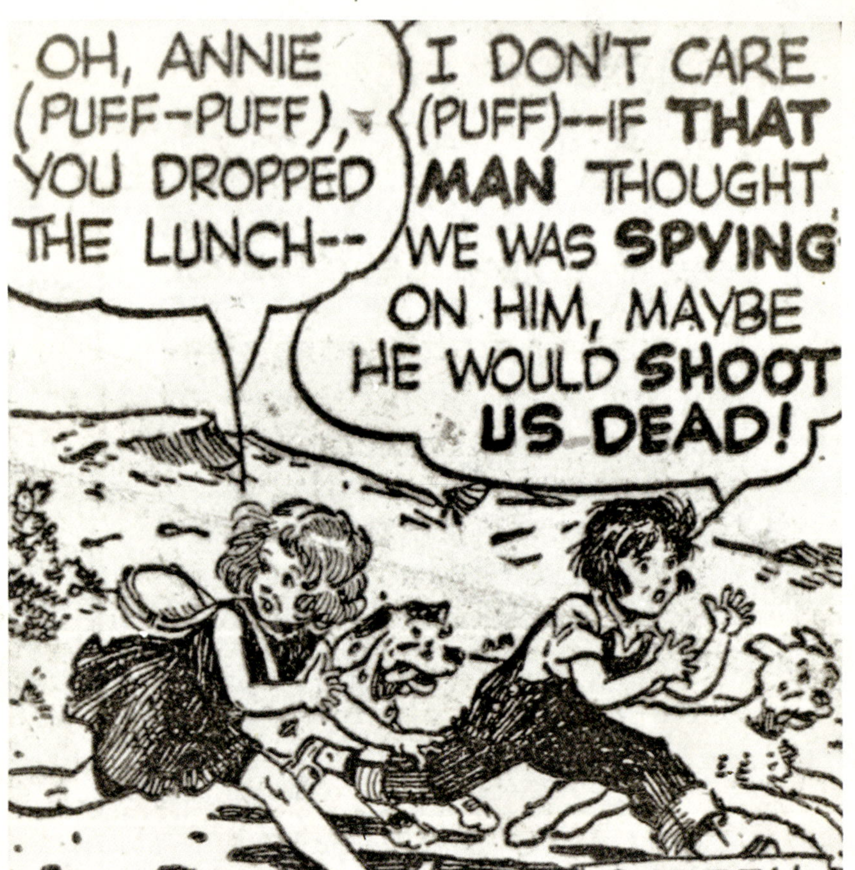

OH, ANNIE (PUFF-PUFF), YOU DROPPED THE LUNCH--
I DON'T CARE (PUFF)--IF THAT MAN THOUGHT WE WAS SPYING ON HIM, MAYBE HE WOULD SHOOT US DEAD!

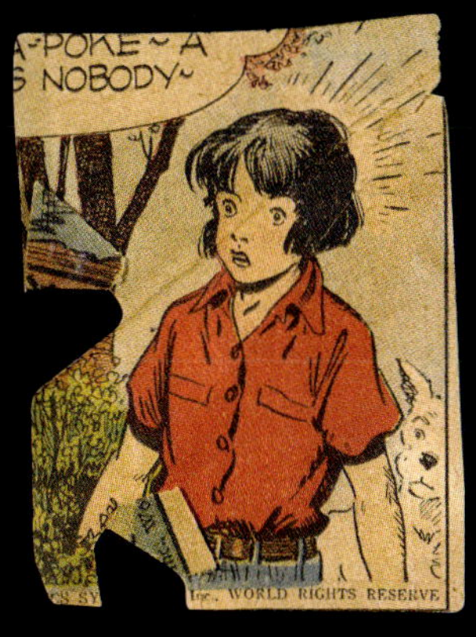

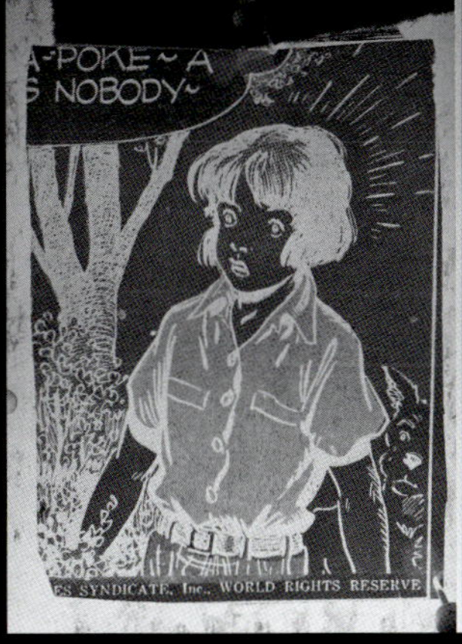

Clockwise from upper left:
Little Annie Rooney comic strip clipping, 3 ½ x 4 ½ in.
Negative made for Henry Darger from *Little Annie Rooney* comic strip clipping, 3 ¾ x 2 ¾ in.
Henry Darger, Untitled (Little Annie Rooney). Photo enlargement (views of both sides) with pencil and carbon, 9 x 7 i
Collection American Folk Art Museum, New York. Gift of Kiyoko Lerner

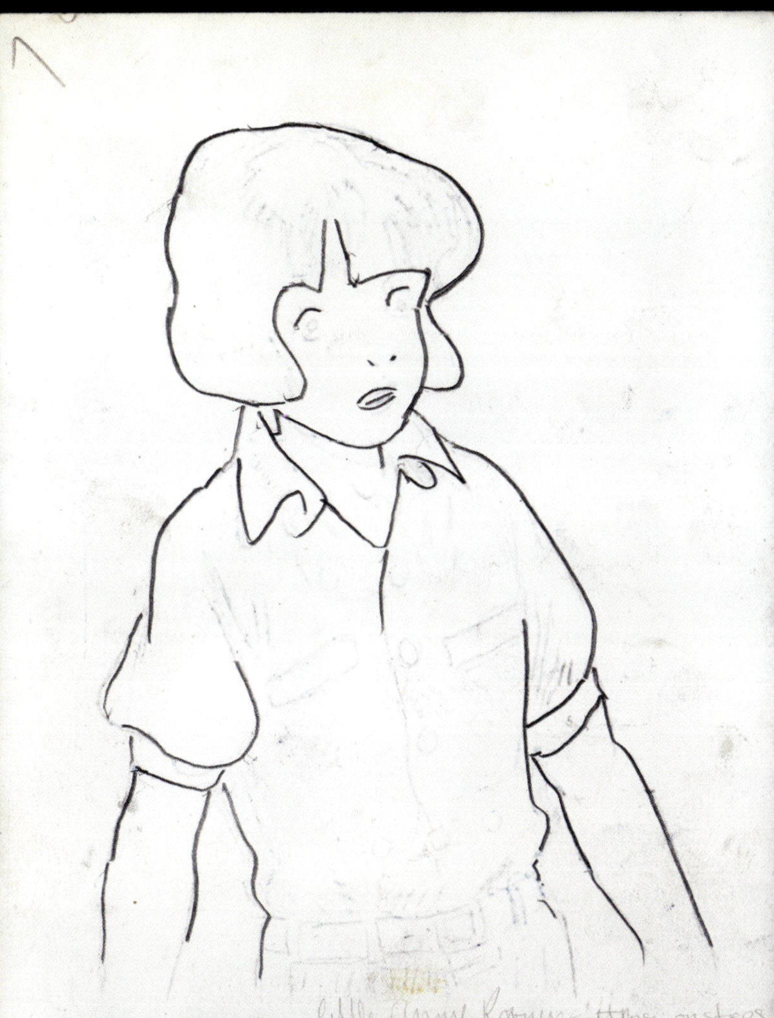

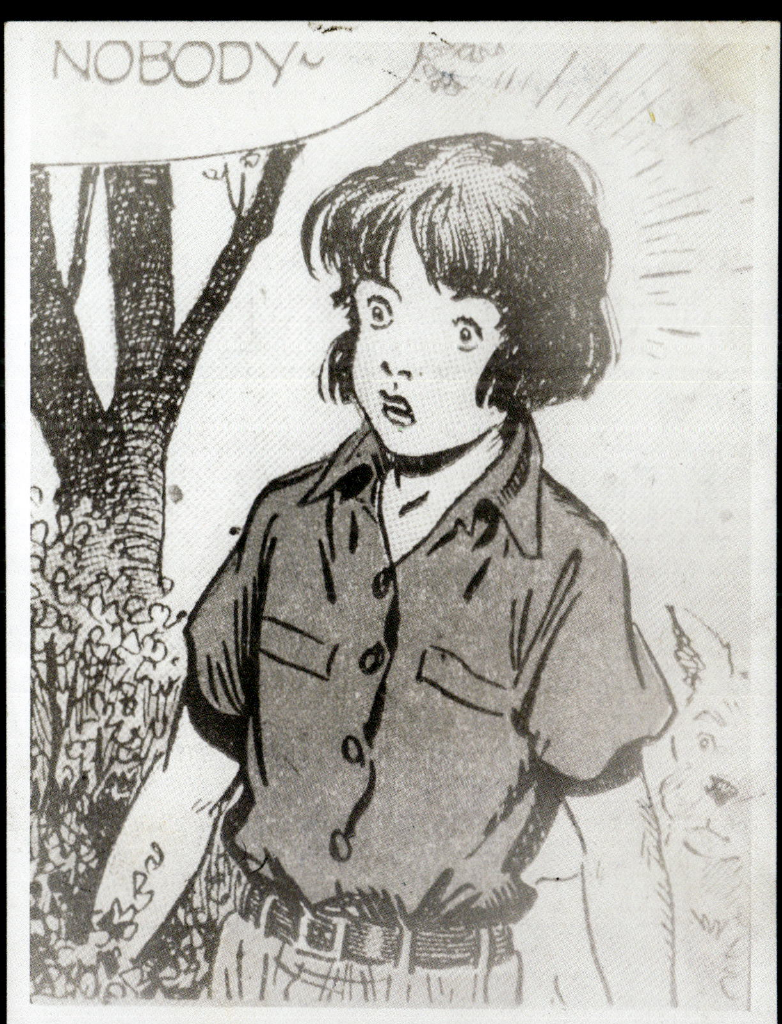

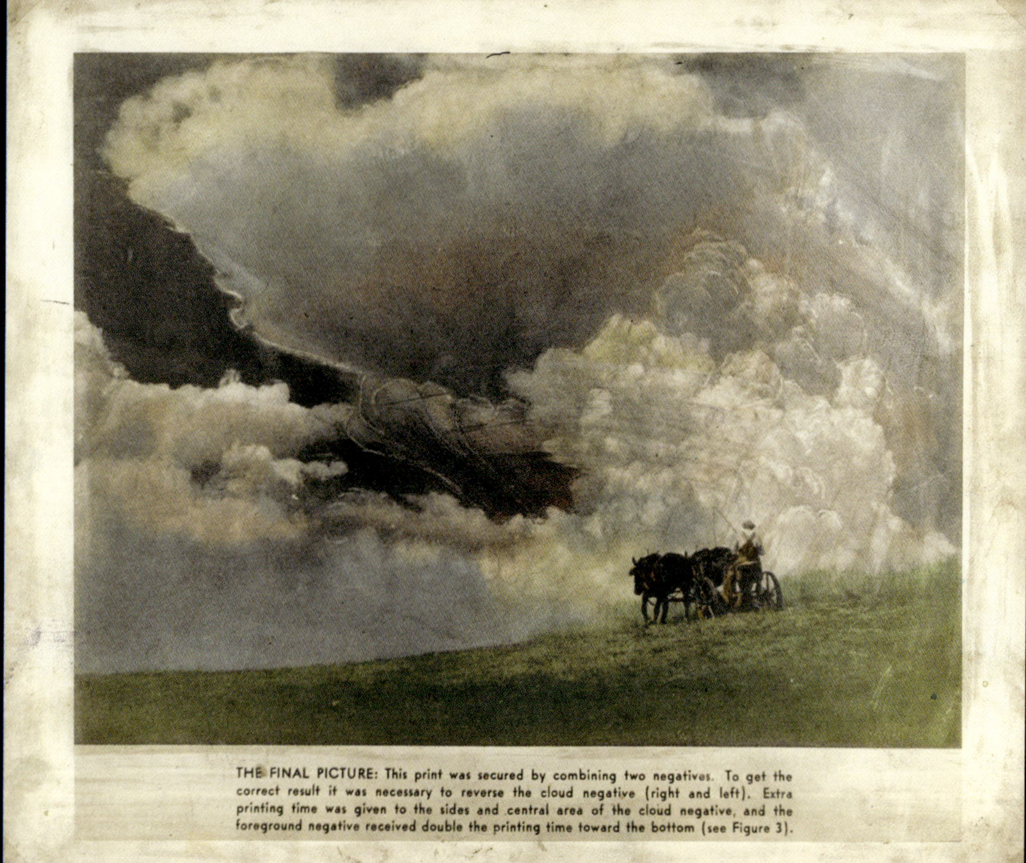

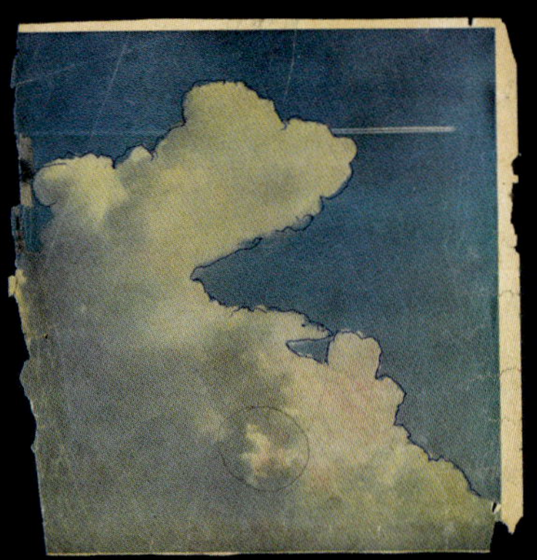

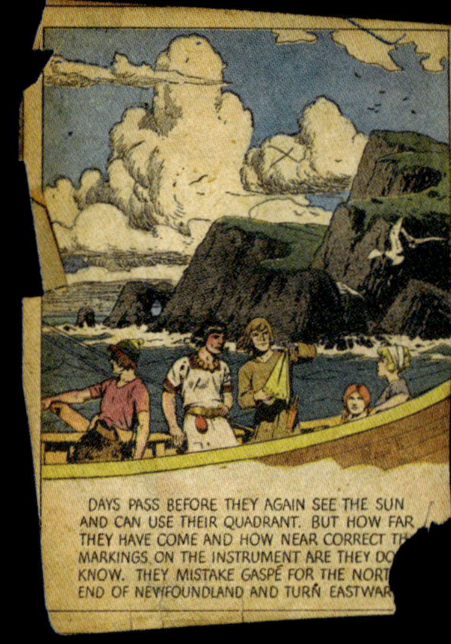

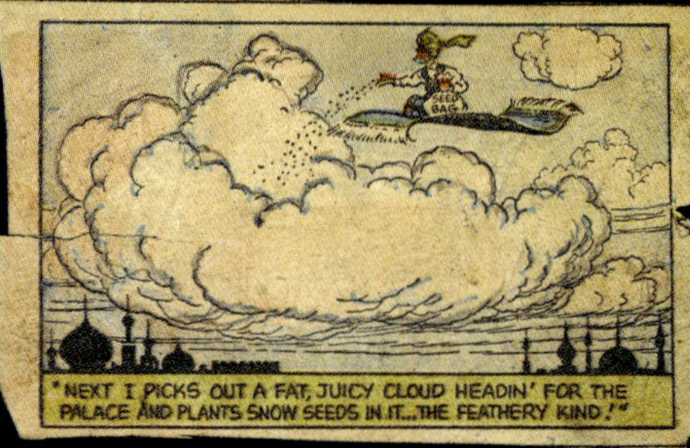

Left: "The Final Picture." Photographic reproduction, mid-twentieth century, with watercolor and pencil tracing by Henry Darger, 11 x 13 ¼ in.
Center: "Days pass before . . . " Comic strip clipping, mid-twentieth century, with pen and pencil tracing by Henry Darger, 7 x 5 in.
Above right: Untitled (cloud). Magazine clipping, mid-twentieth century, with pencil, ink, and carbon tracing by Henry Darger, 10 x 9 ½ in.
Below right: "Next I picks out a fat, juicy cloud . . ." Comic strip clipping, mid-twentieth century, with pen and pencil tracing by Henry Darger, 3 x 5 in.
Collection American Folk Art Museum, New York. Gift of Kiyoko Lerner

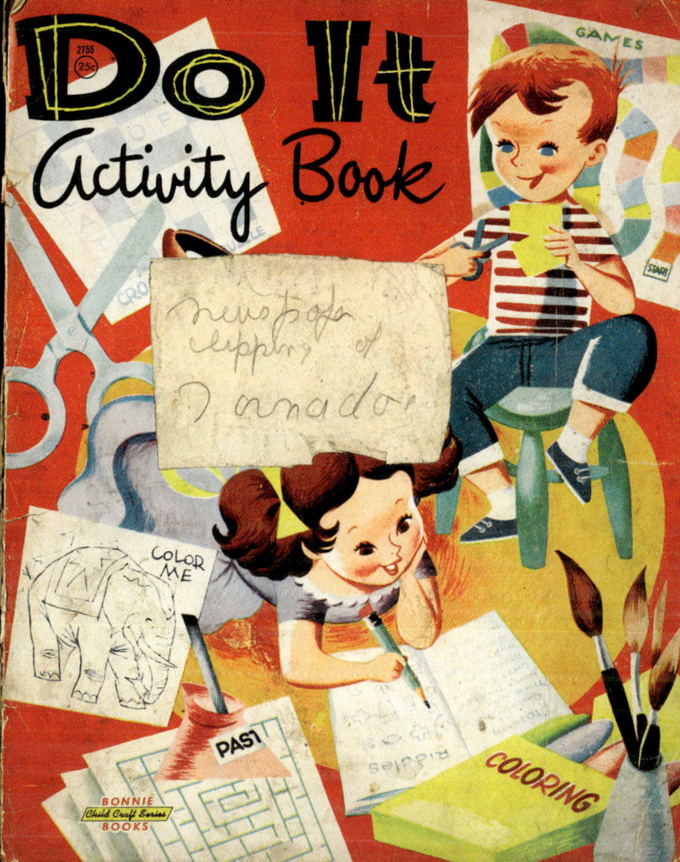

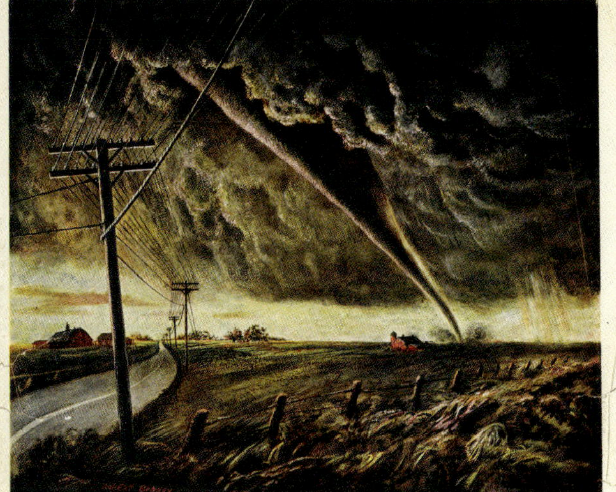

When nature cuts loose!

ANY DAY OR NIGHT, anywhere in this country, storm, flood or fire can threaten telephone lines.

If disaster strikes, Western Electric rushes equipment to the scene at once—wires, poles, cables, crossarms—whatever is needed to help your Bell Telephone company restore service *fast!*

Readiness to meet disaster—as well as daily needs of Bell Telephone companies—is part of Western Electric's job as manufacturer-supplier of the Bell System.

● Western Electric is a unit of the Bell System—has been for 68 years. Our people, who provide telephone equipment and supplies, share naturally in the System's spirit of service that aims to "get the message through" for you—quickly, clearly, and at low cost.

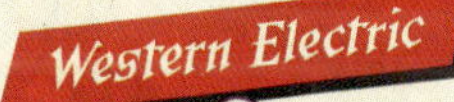

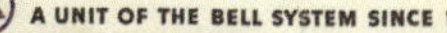

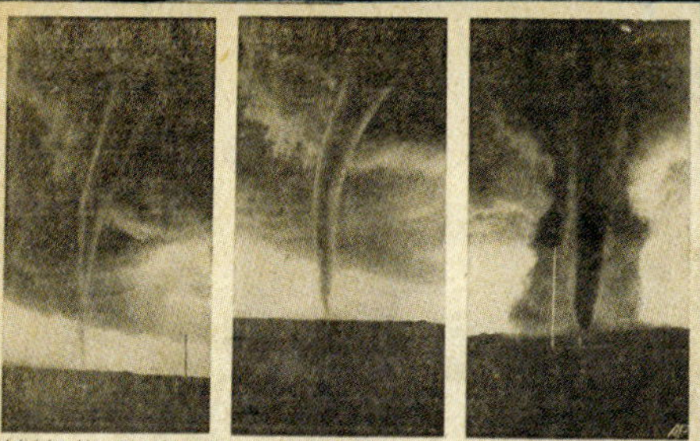

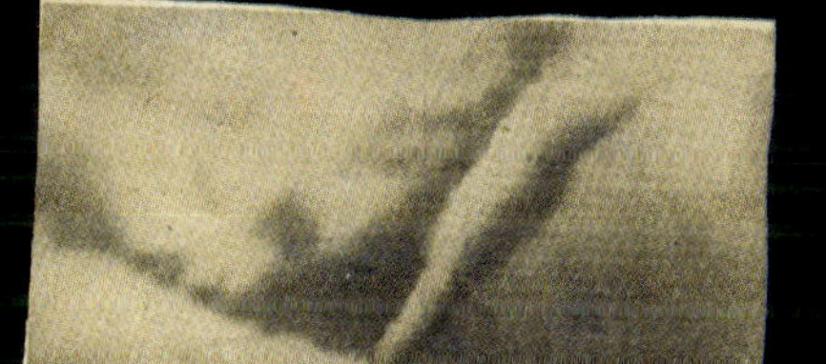

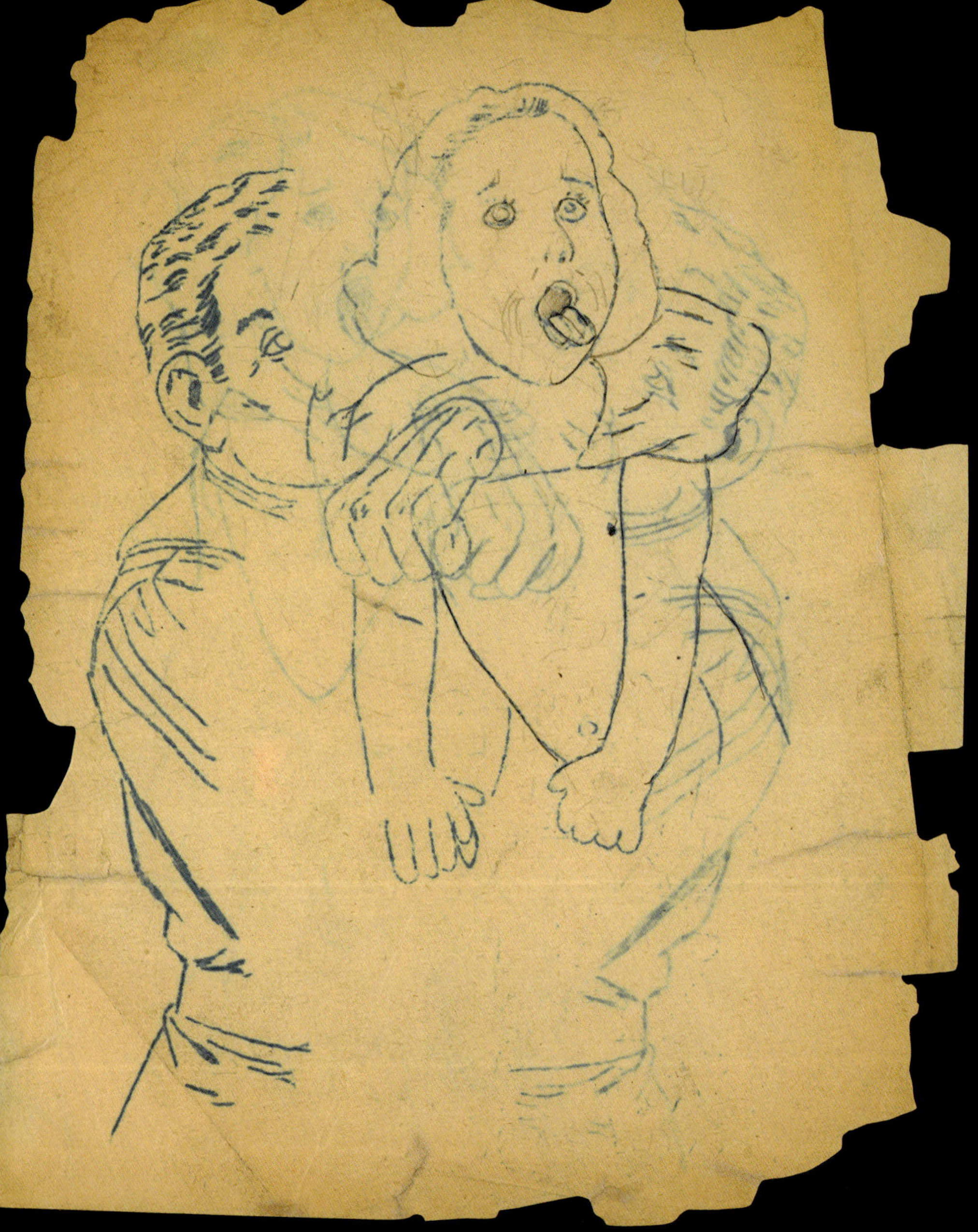

Untitled (man strangling girl). Pencil and carbon tracing on paper,
24 x 19 in. Collection American Folk Art Museum, New York. Gift of Kiyoko Lerner

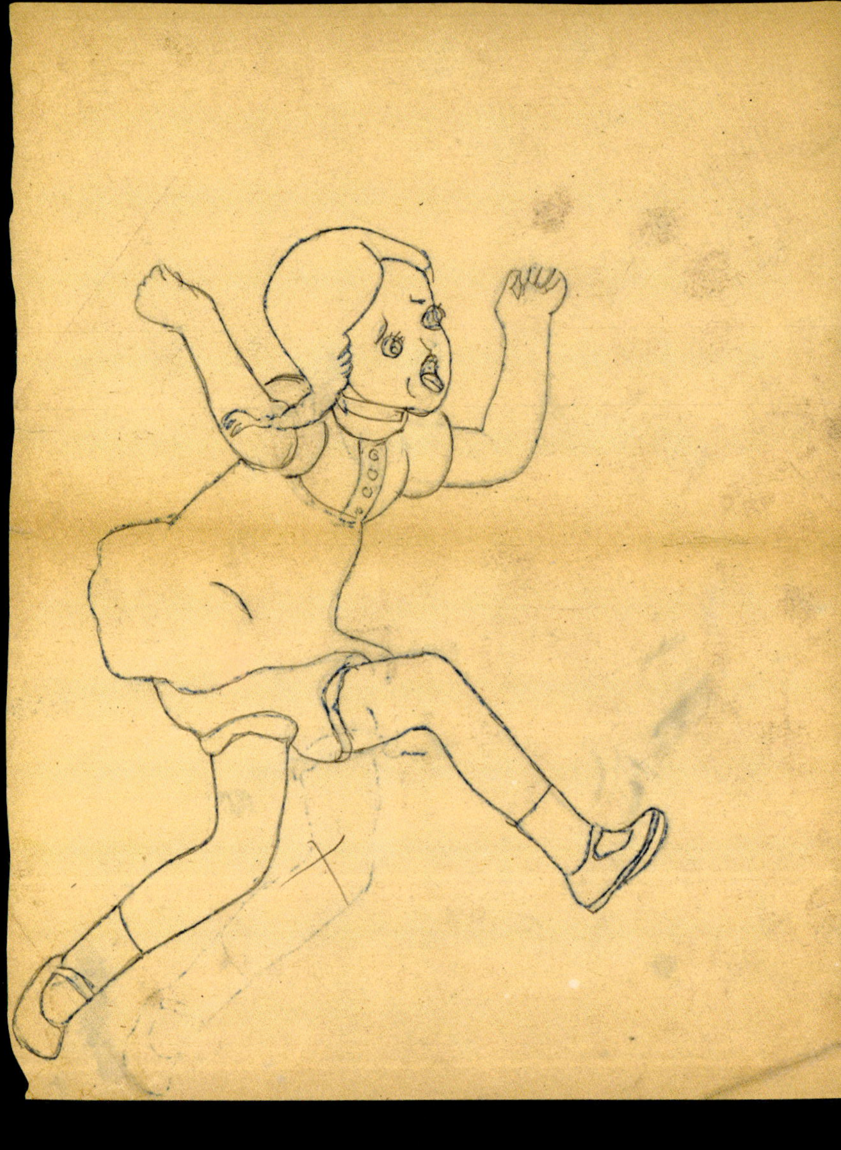

Untitled (girl being strangled while running). Pencil and carbon tracing on paper,
14 x 11 in. Collection American Folk Art Museum, New York. Gift of Kiyoko Lerner

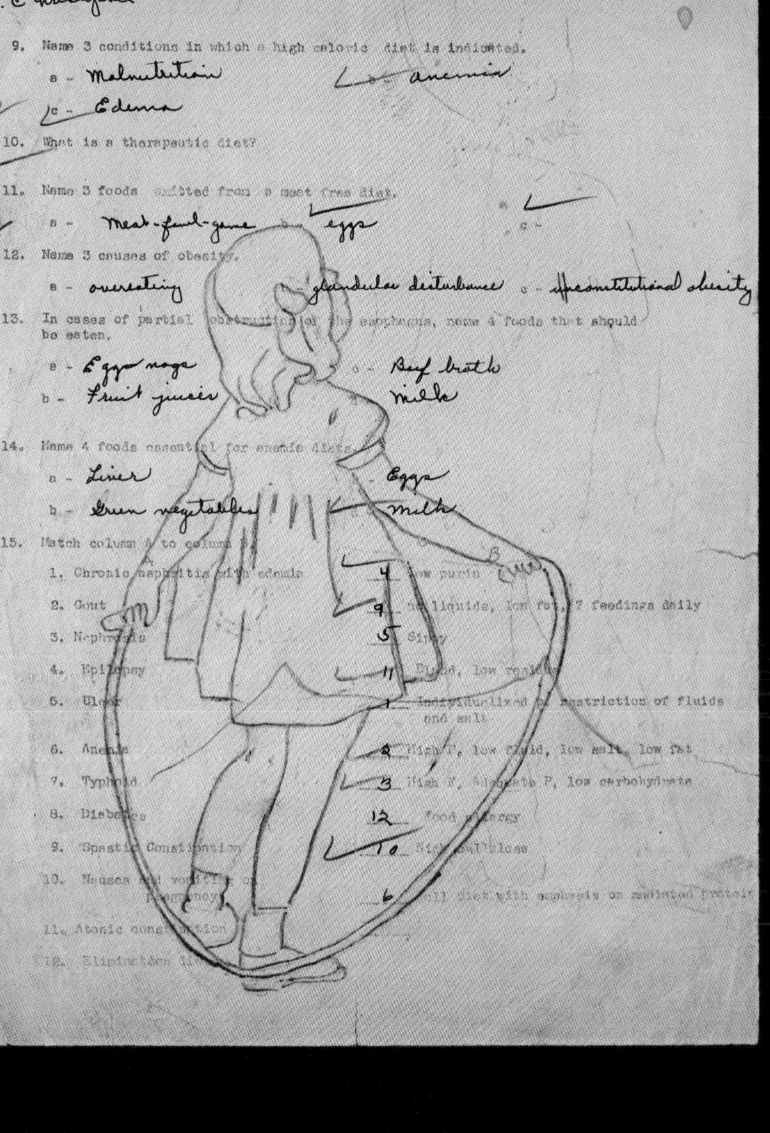

9. Name 3 conditions in which a high caloric diet is indicated.
   a - Malnutrition
   b - anemia
   c - Edema

10. What is a therapeutic diet?

11. Name 3 foods omitted from a meat free diet.
    a - Meat-fowl-game   b - eggs   c -

12. Name 3 causes of obesity.
    a - overeating   b - glandular disturbance   c - Unconstitutional obesity

13. In cases of partial obstruction of the esophagus, name 4 foods that should
    be eaten.
    a - Egg nogs   c - Beef broth
    b - Fruit juices   d - Milk

14. Name 4 foods essential for anemia diets.
    a - Liver   c - Eggs
    b - Green vegetables   d - Milk

15. Match column A to column B.
    A
    1. Chronic nephritis with edema   4 Low purin
    2. Gout   9 No liquids, low fat, 7 feedings daily
    3. Nephrosis   5 Sippy
    4. Epilepsy   11 Fluid, low residue
    5. Ulcer   1 Individualized or restriction of fluids
                   and salt
    6. Anemia   2 High P, low fluid, low salt, low fat
    7. Typhoid   3 High P, Adequate P, low carbohydrate
    8. Diabetes   12 Food allergy
    9. Spastic Constipation   10 High cellulose
    10. Nausea and vomiting of
        Pregnancy   6 Full diet with emphasis on radiated protein
    11. Atonic constipation
    12. Elimination diet

16. What is the ratio of fatty acids to glucose in this diet.

    Carboyhdrates 60 gms.   Proteins 60 gms.

    and Fats 150 gms.

Untitled (study of girl jumping rope). Pencil and carbon tracing on found paper, 11 x 8½ in. Collection American Folk Art Museum, New York. Gift of Kiyoko Lerner.

Untitled (study of Blengin). After 1945. Pencil and carbon tracing on found paper, 11 x 8½ in. Collection American Folk Art Museum, New York. Gift of Kiyoko Lerner.

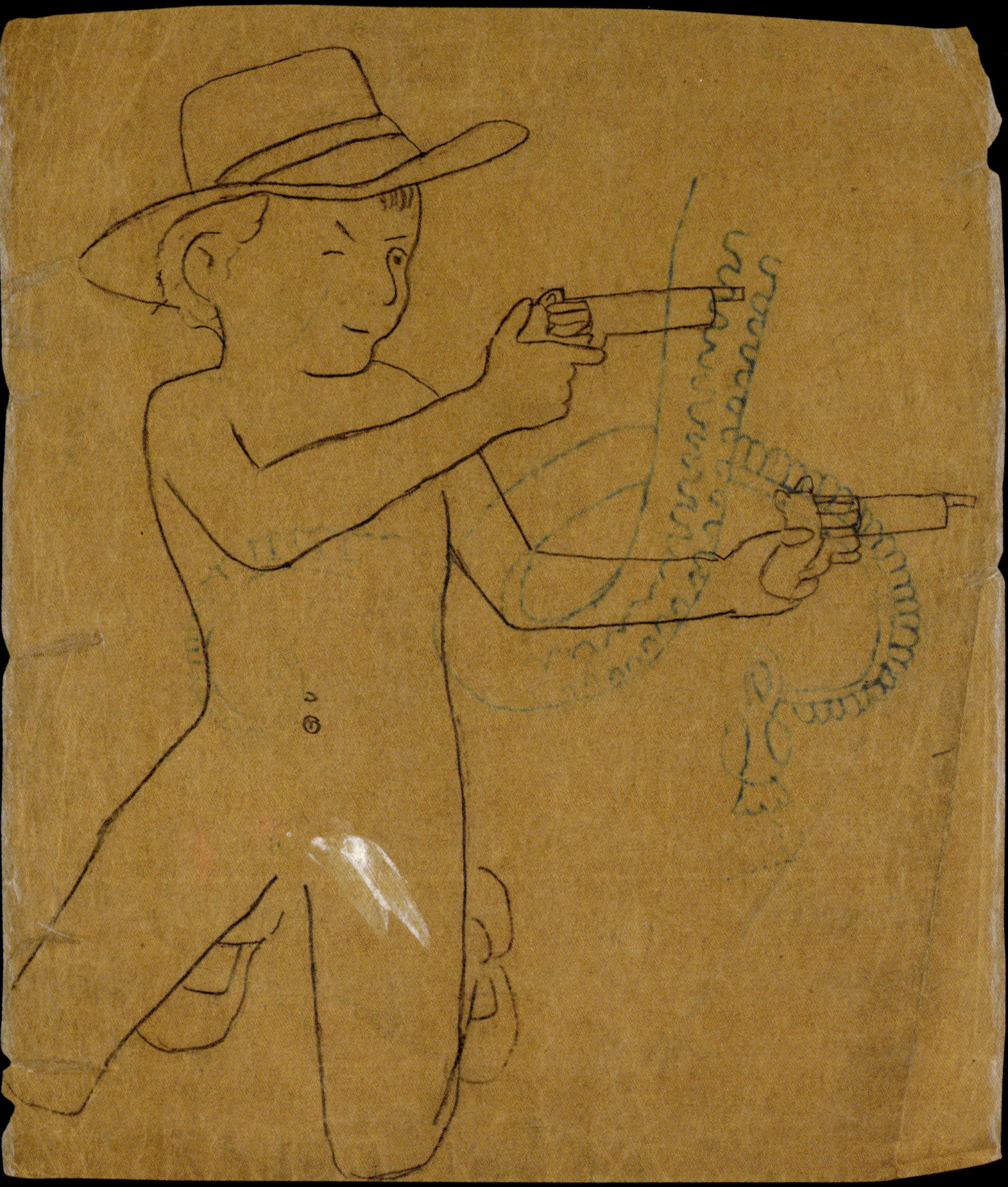

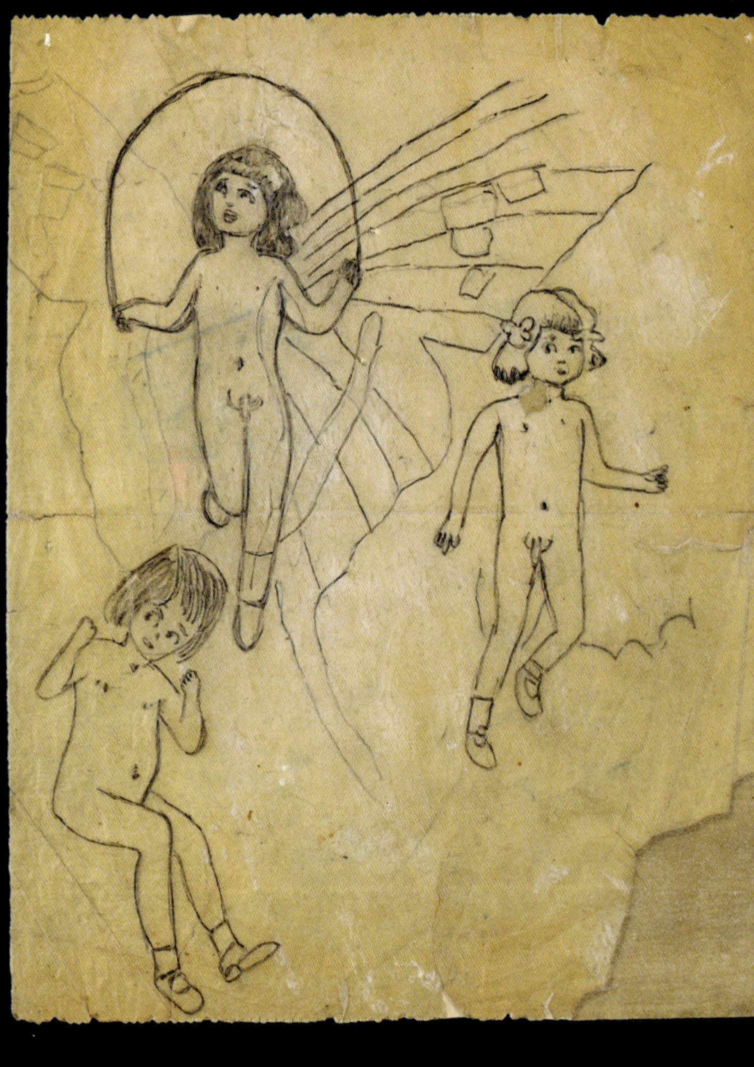

Untitled (kneeling boy shooting two guns / Blengin tail). Mid-twentieth century.
Pencil and carbon tracing on paper, 12 ¾ x 11 ¼ in.
Collection American Folk Art Museum, New York. Gift of Kiyoko Lerner

Untitled (study of three girls). Mid-twentieth century.
Pencil on paper, 10 ⅝ x 8 in.
Collection American Folk Art Museum, New York. Gift of Kiyoko Lerner

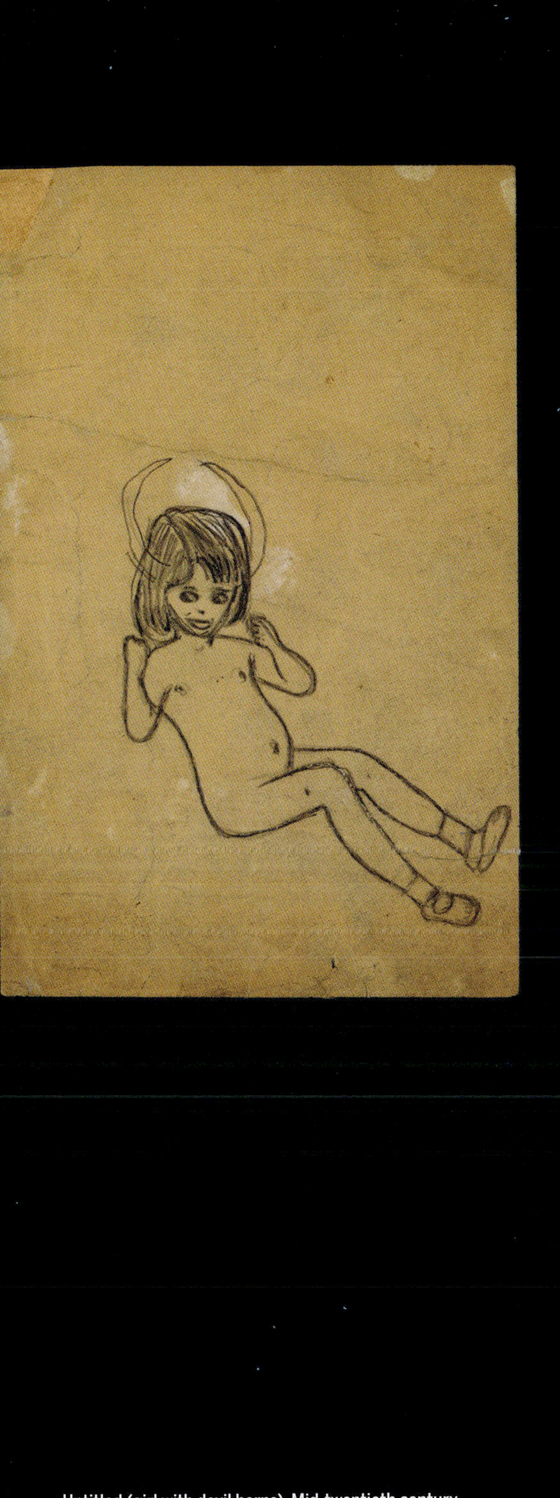

Untitled (girl with devil horns). Mid-twentieth century.
Pencil on paper,8 x 5 in. Collection American Folk Art Museum,
New York. Gift of Kiyoko Lerner

Notes

1. Charles A. A. Dellschau and the Philadelphia Wireman are two self-taught artists whose work was retrieved after their death; it had been discarded in the streets.

2. Scholars, collectors, and dealers have for decades promoted the idea that artists without formal training do not have any core visual vocabulary. This notion originated in a misinterpretation of French artist Jean Dubuffet's definition of Art Brut. He did not assert that Art Brut artists are without culture, but that they lack high culture. The term art brut, coined by Dubuffet in the mid-1940s, literally means "raw art" or art that is "uncooked" by the dictates of Western culture. Dubuffet championed art brut as an antidote to *l'art culturel*—art officially sanctioned by academies, museums, and galleries. In 1949, he defined this new category: "What we mean is anything produced by people unsmirched by artistic culture, works in which mimicry, contrary to what occurs with intellectuals, has little or no part. So that the makers (in regard to subjects, choice of materials, means of transposition, rhythms, kinds of handwriting, etc.) draw entirely on their own resources rather than on the stereotypes of classical or fashionable art." Jean Dubuffet, "Art Brut Preferred to the Cultural Arts," exh. cat. (Paris: René Drouin Gallery, 1949), translated in Mildred Glimcher, *Jean Dubuffet: Toward an Alternative Reality* (New York: Pace Publications, in association with Abbeville Press, 1987), 101–4. The stereotypes surrounding artists like Henry Darger perhaps have benefited the marketplace more than museums and the academy, to say nothing of diminishing respect for the artists.

3. The American Folk Art Museum offers an annual fellowship to graduate students to study the Henry Darger Study Collection.

4. David Berglund remembers that he and Nathan Lerner threw away a substantial amount of of Darger's possessions from his apartment before realizing that they included artwork and manuscripts.

5. These clippings are in the Henry Darger Study Collection.

6. Mary Trent, "Innocence Reproduced: Girlhood in the Art of Joseph Cornell and Henry Darger," Ph.D. diss., University of California, Irvine, forthcoming. Trent considers how Darger and his contemporary, the American artist Joseph Cornell, explored the theme of girlhood in their development of elaborate visual worlds. She argues that Darger and Cornell approach girlhood as an alternative realm in which to celebrate the possibilities for the individual imagination in a mass-media culture and express an alternative modern masculinity.

7. Darger's artistic process has been briefly described by Michael Bonesteel in his monograph, *Henry Darger: Art and Selected Writings* (New York: Rizzoli, 2000), and more fully by John MacGregor in *Henry Darger: In the Realms of the Unreal* (New York: Delano Greenidge, 2002). This topic has been most fully explored to date by Jane Kallir in "Henry Darger: Art and Myth" (New York: Galerie St. Etienne, 2004) and by Juliana Driever in "In the Realms of the Unreal: The Process, Paintings, and Pertinence of Henry Darger," *Research, Writing and Culture: The Best of Undergraduate Thesis Essays,* no. 4 (Chicago: School of the Art Institute of Chicago, 2002–3).

8. Jane Kallir and American Folk Art Museum staff are currently working on a chronology for Darger's oeuvre.

9. MacGregor states that Darger began using photographic enlargement in 1944 (*Henry Darger: In the Realms of the Unreal*, 165).

10. Darger's bank books (in the collection of the American Folk Art Museum) record that his financial savings declined in tandem with his use of film processing.

11. How Darger came up with the idea to create book illustrations on this large scale is something scholars are still pondering.

12. Kevin Miller, a graduate student in museum studies at the City College of New York, is researching an art instruction manual in the Henry Darger Study Center Collection, entitled *A Step-Ladder to Painting*, published in New York in 1939. It includes a chapter about tracing, advocating it as a shortcut to learning to draw the figure. Darger may have used the manual as a learning tool. The author also provides analysis of famous paintings, including works by Constable, Whistler, and a landscape by the American Social Realist William Gropper that is strikingly similar to Darger's work in its use of trees, figures, and simplification.

[Plates]

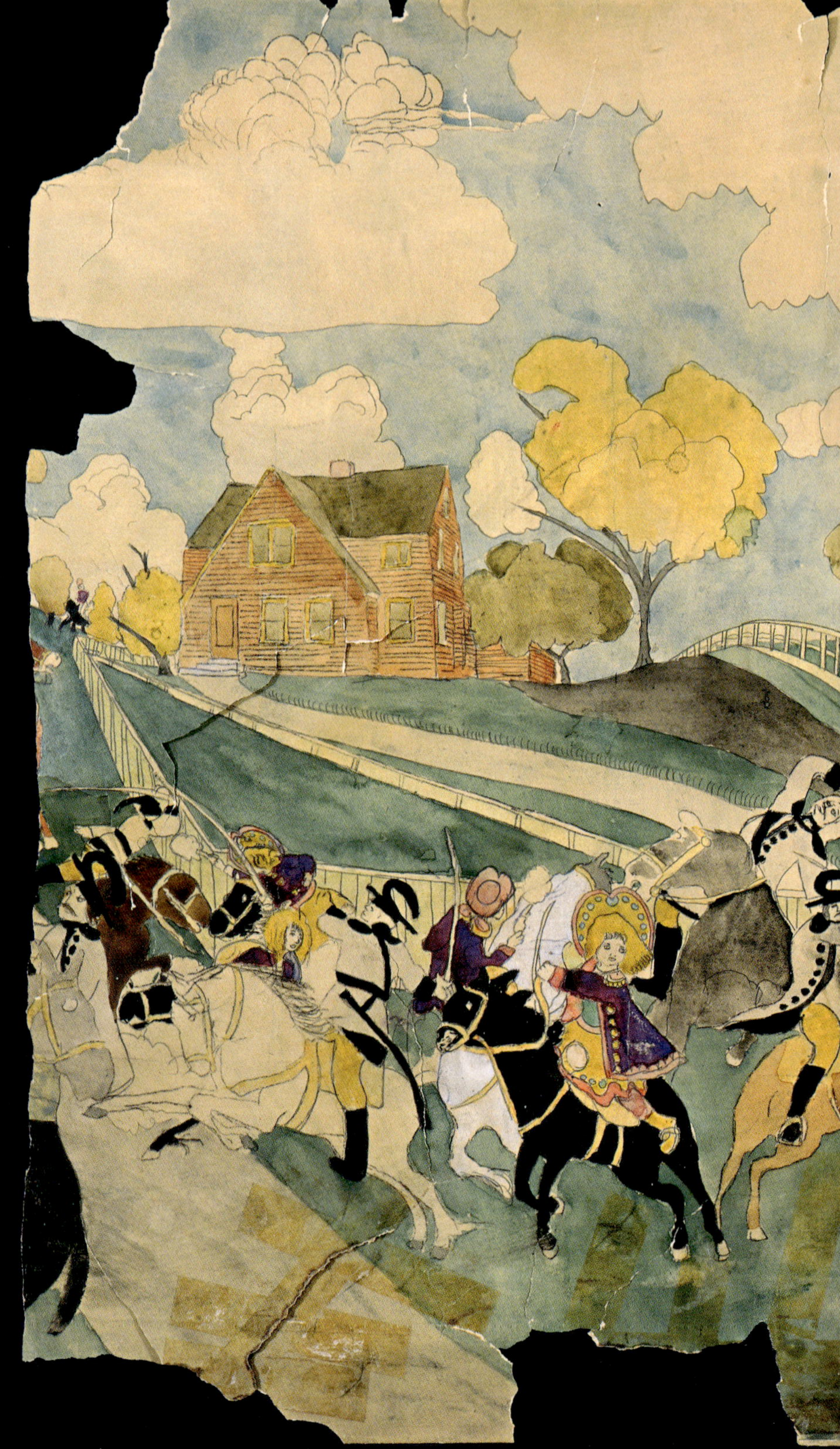

They try to get away with the enemys plans, and some valuable jewelry belonging to themselves,
after setting fire thousands of tents, causing the wildest confusion. Are pursued.
Watercolor, pencil, and carbon tracing on pieced paper, 22 x 42 in. Collection Kiyoko Lerner

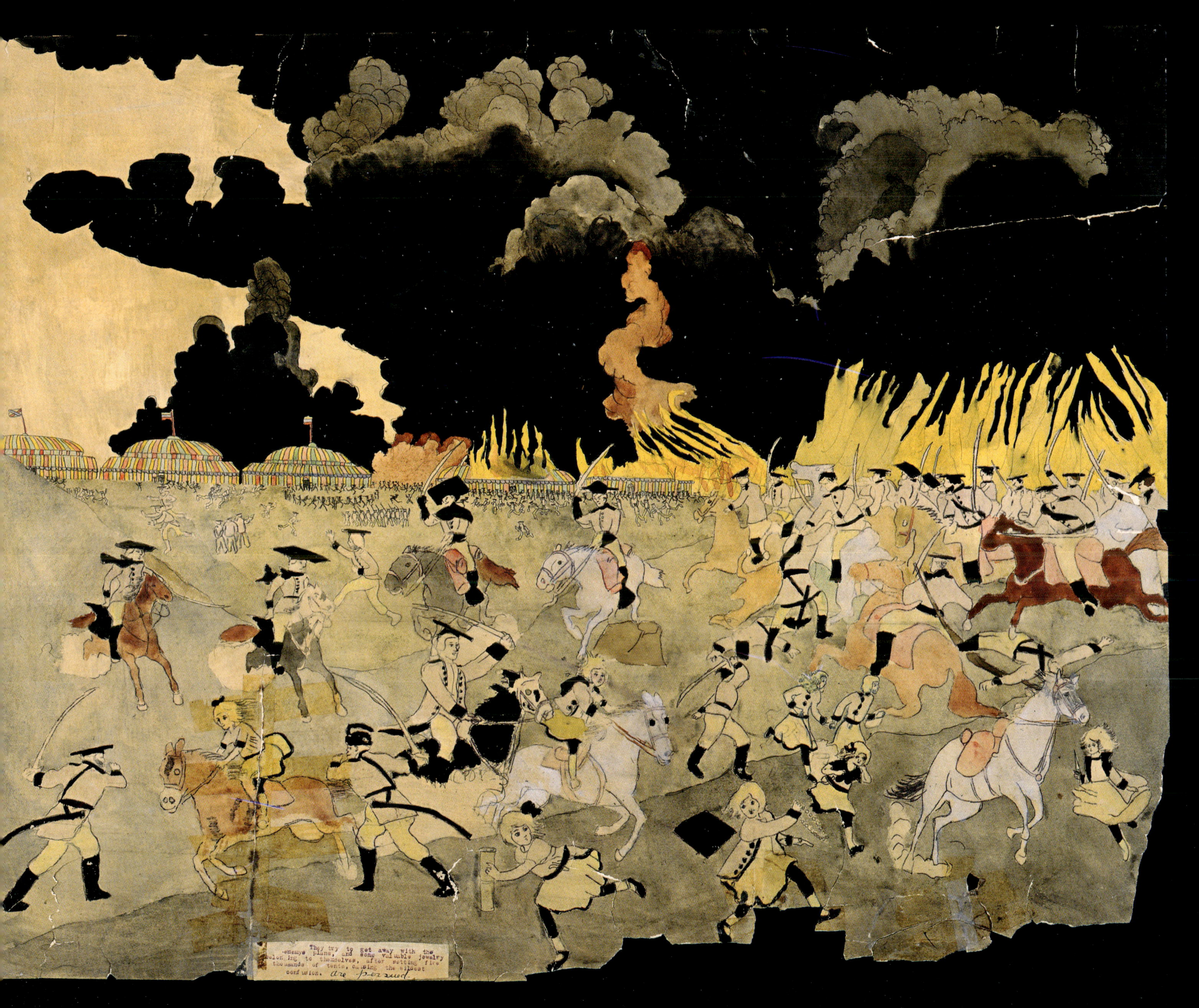
They try to get away with the
enemys plans, and some valuable jewelry
belonging to themselves, after setting fire
thousands of tents, causing the wildest
confusion. are pursued.

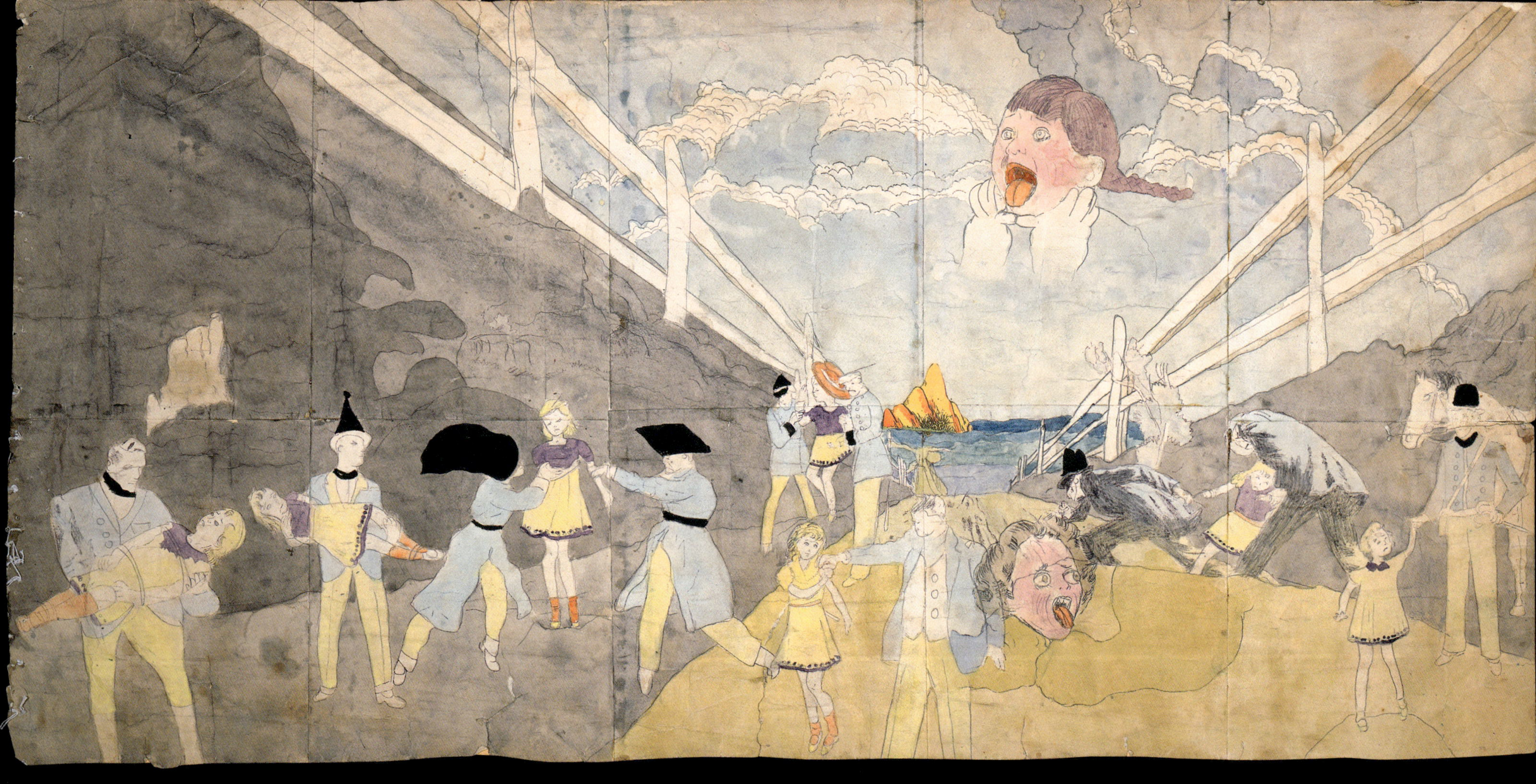

102   Untitled (image of strangled child in sky).

Watercolor, pencil, and carbon tracing on pieced paper,

approx. 24 x 45 in. Collection Kiyoko Lerner

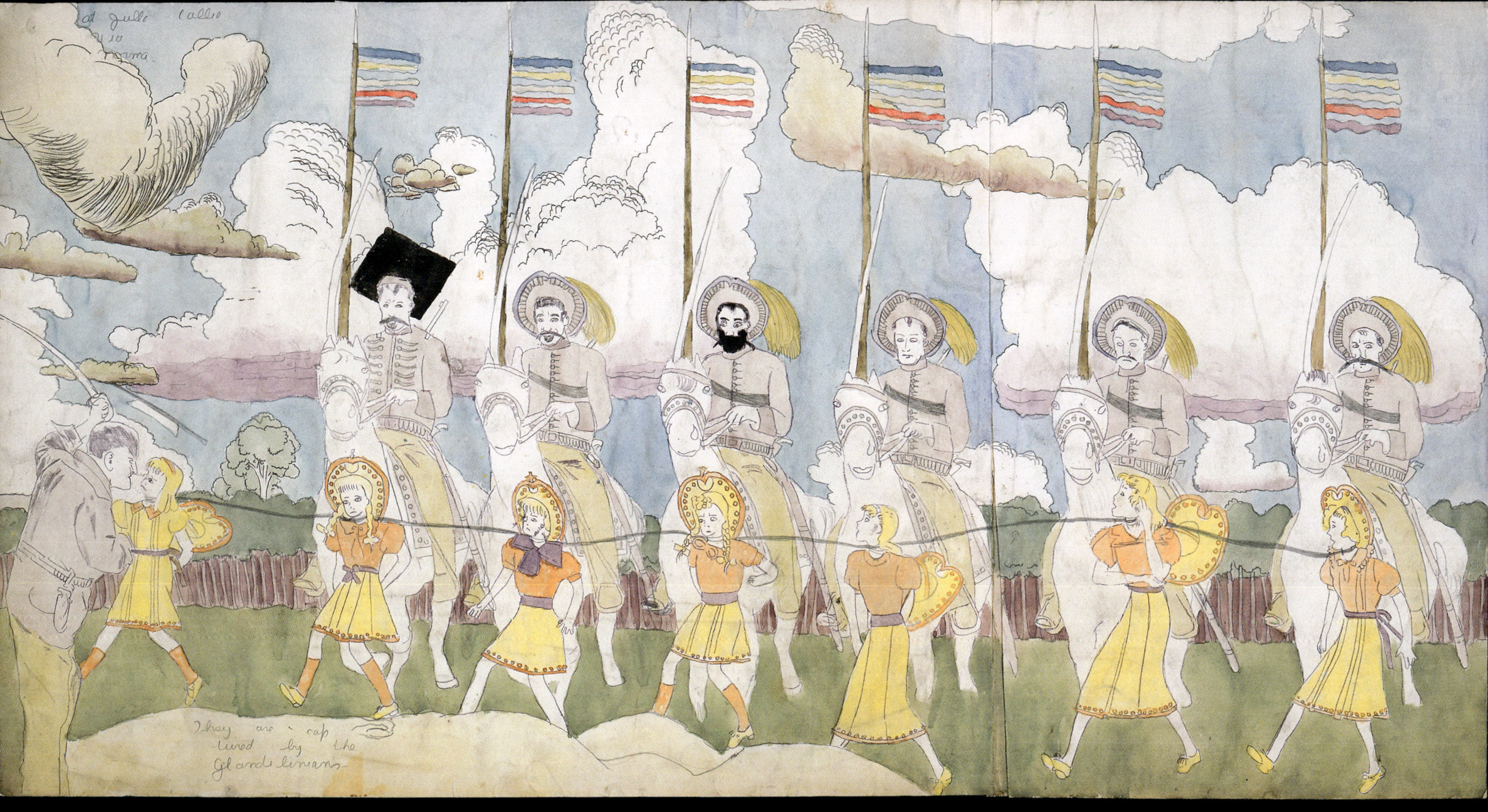

At Jullo Callio via Norma. They are captured by the Glandelinians. 103
Watercolor, pencil, and carbon tracing on pieced paper, 19 ⅛ x 36 ½ in.
Collection American Folk Art Museum, New York

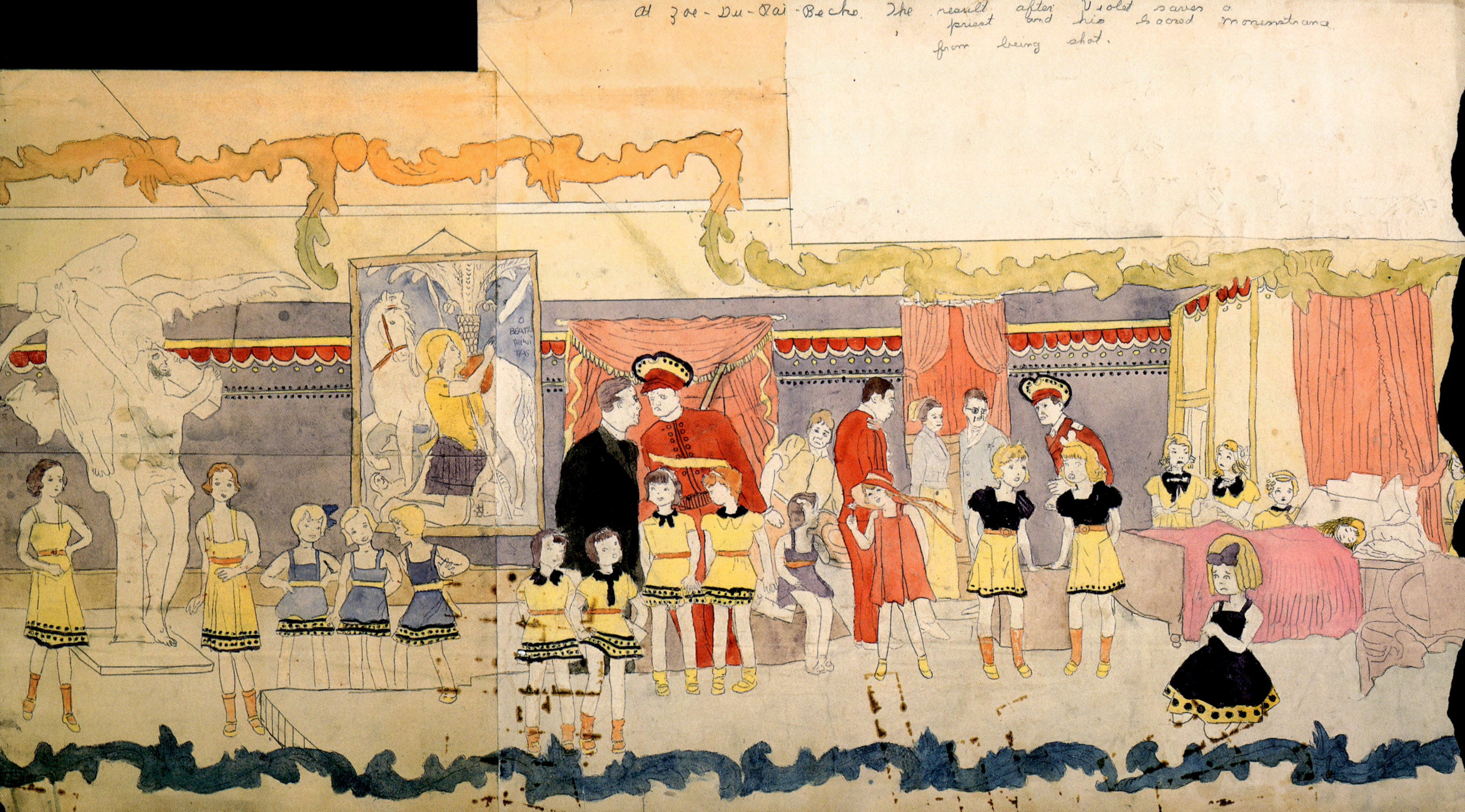

At Zoe-Du-Lai-Becks. The result after Violet saves a priest and his Sacred monstrance from being shot.

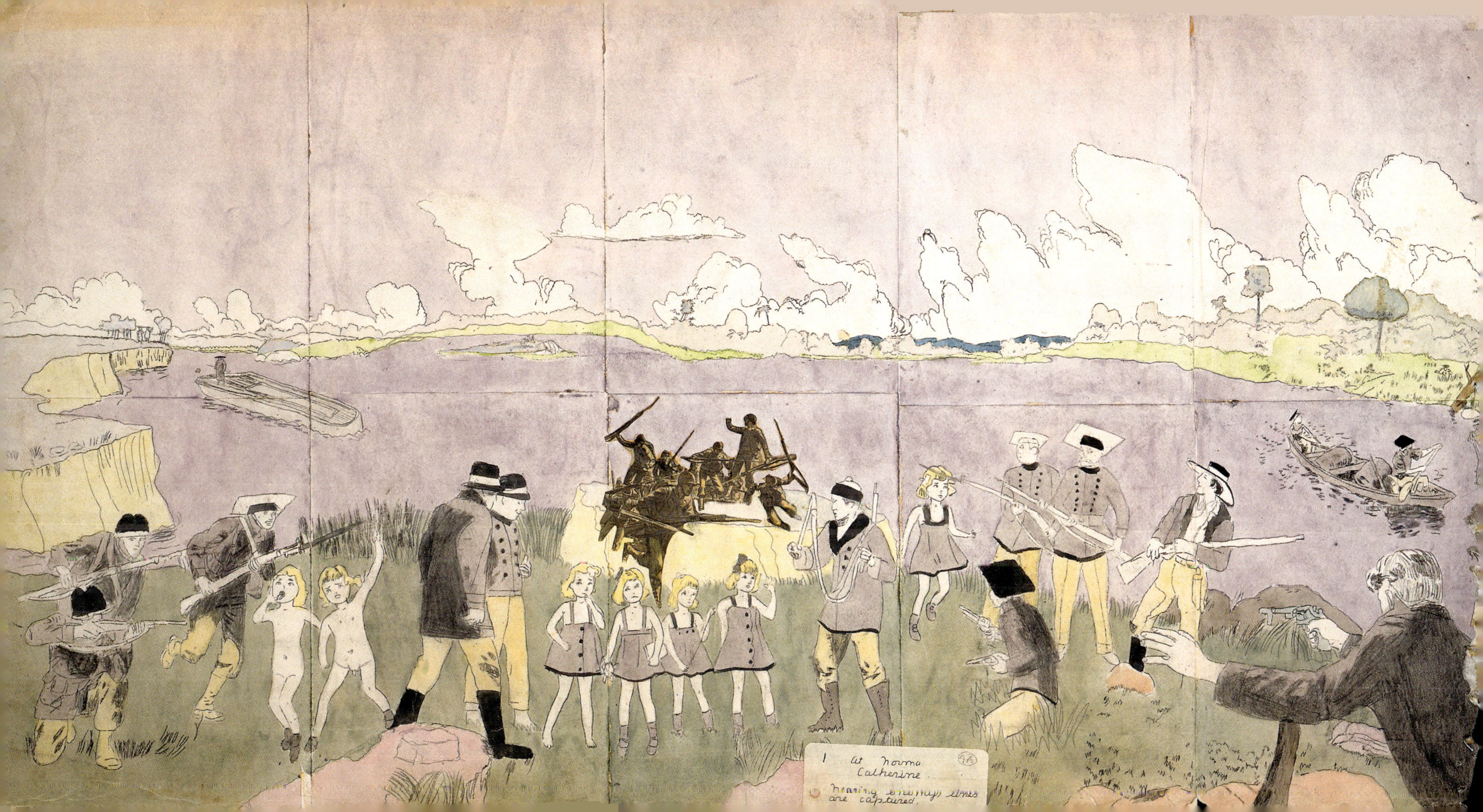
1   at   Norma
Catherine.
enemys elves
are captured.

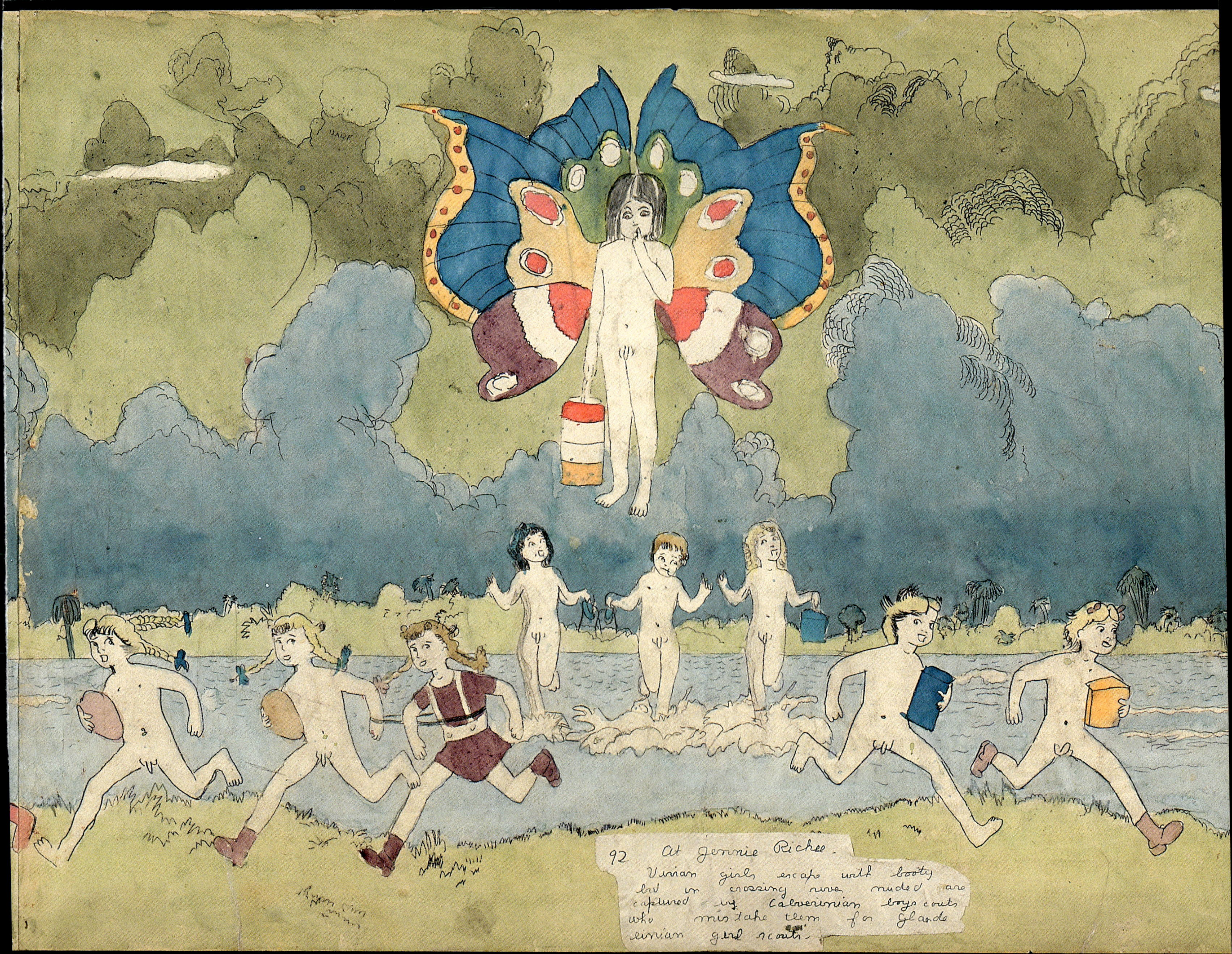

92   At Jennie Richee.
Vivian girls escape with booty
but in crossing river nuded are
captured by Calverinian boys couts
who mistake them for Glandelinian girl scouts.

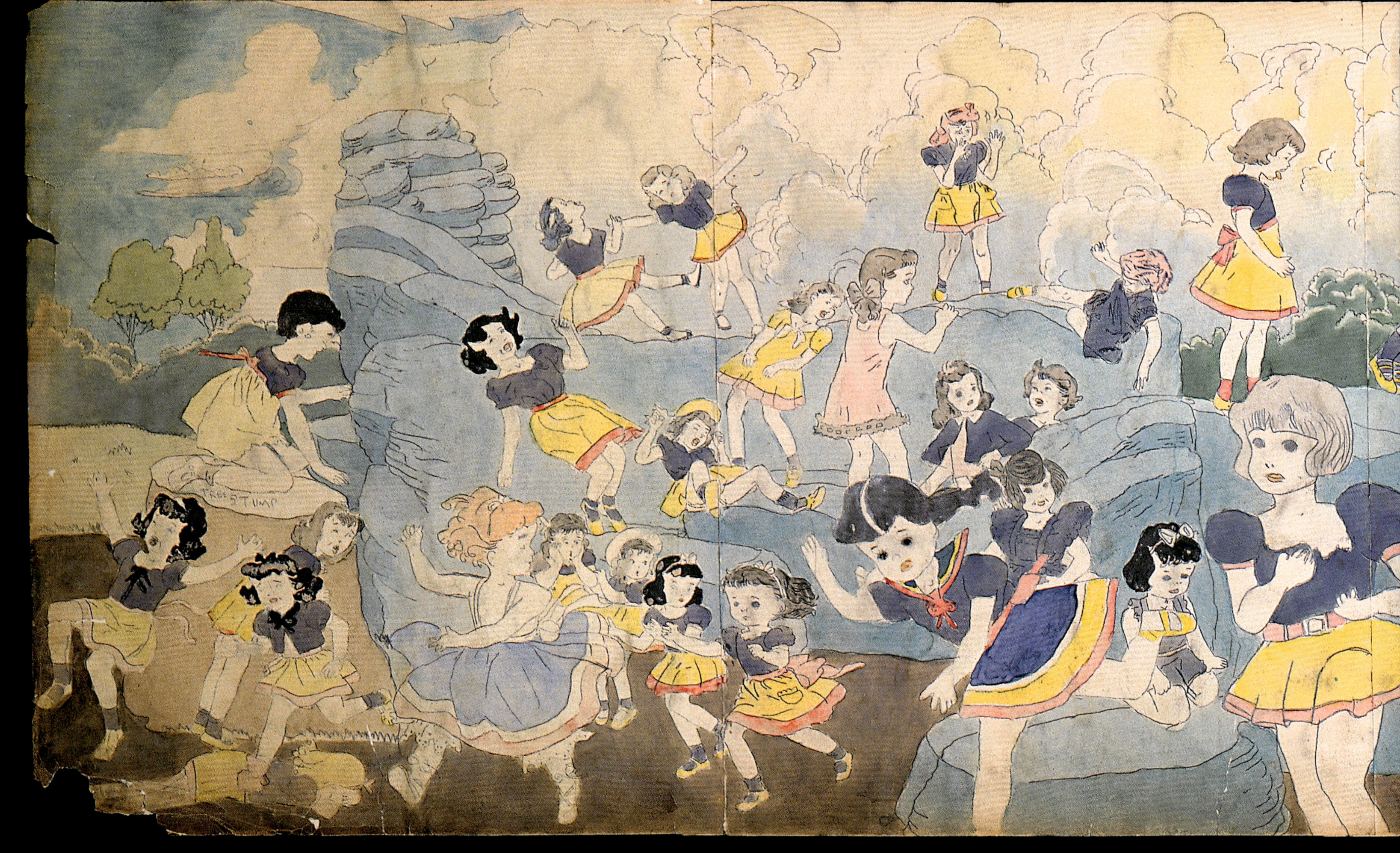

106 | *Part two. Break out of concentration camp killing and wounding enemy soldier guards.*

Watercolor, pencil, and carbon tracing on pieced paper, 24 x 120 in.

The Museum of Everything

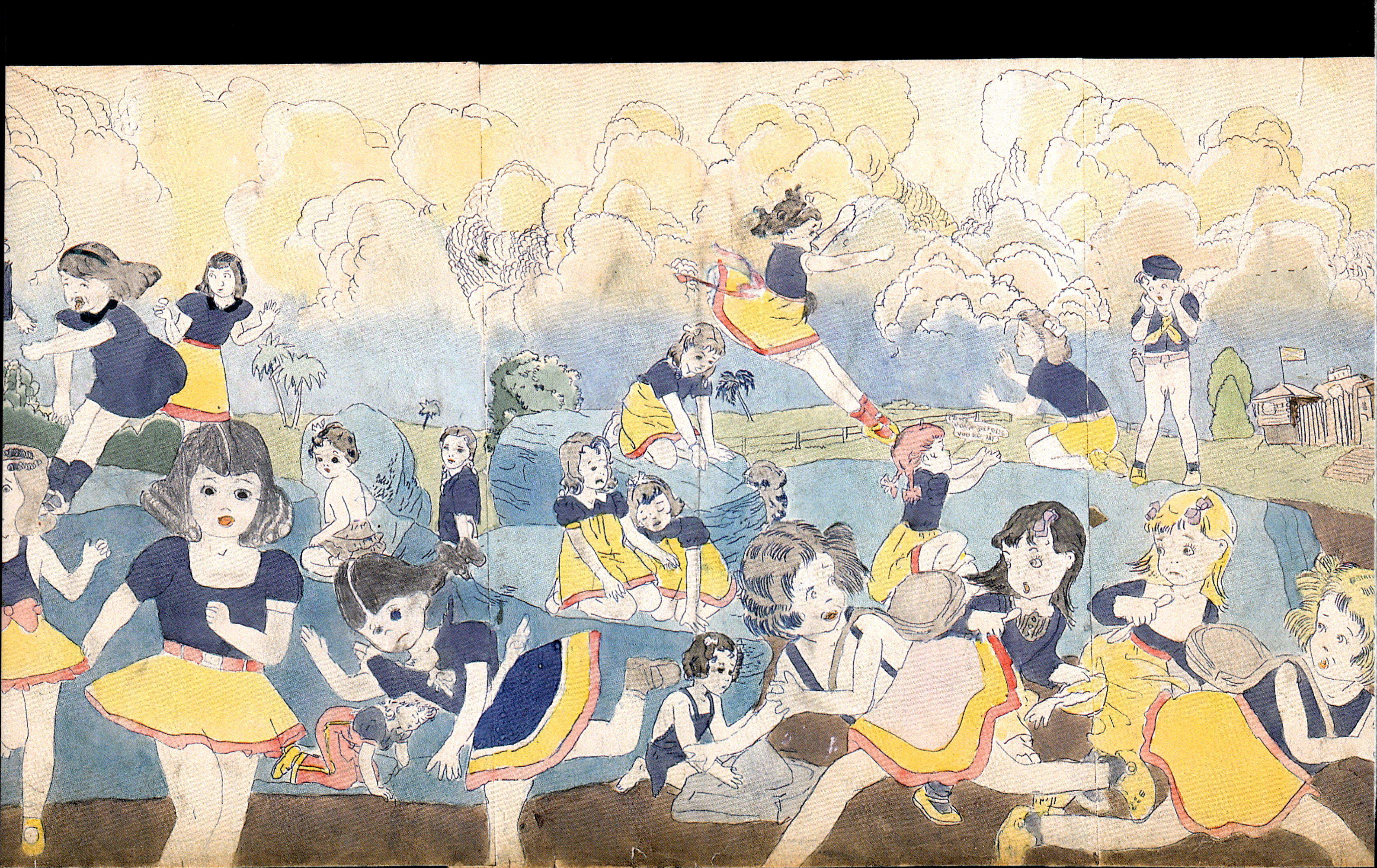

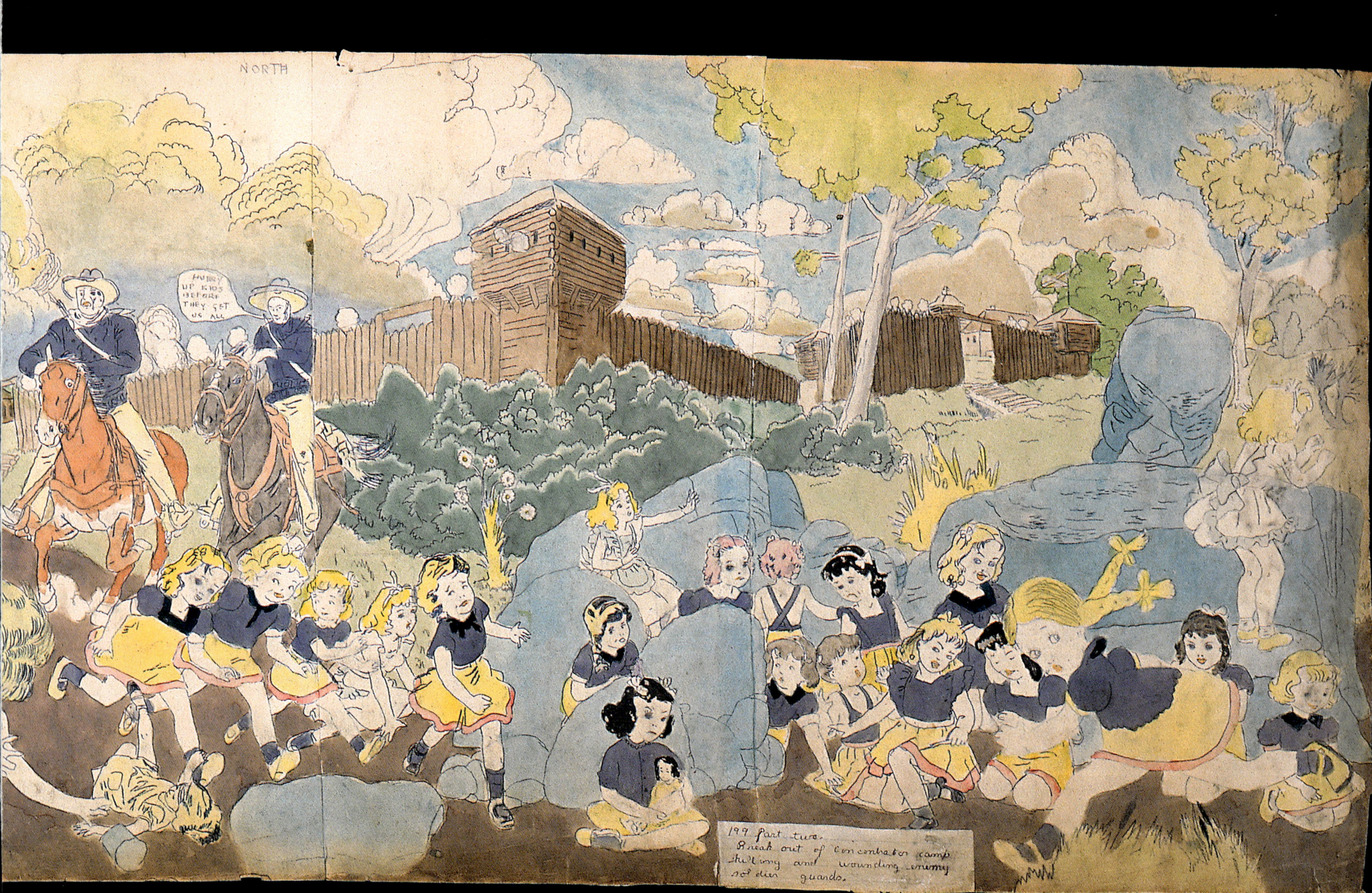

NORTH
HURRY UP KIDS BEFORE THEY GET US ALL
199 Part two.
Break out of Concentration camp
killing and wounding enemy
soldier guards.

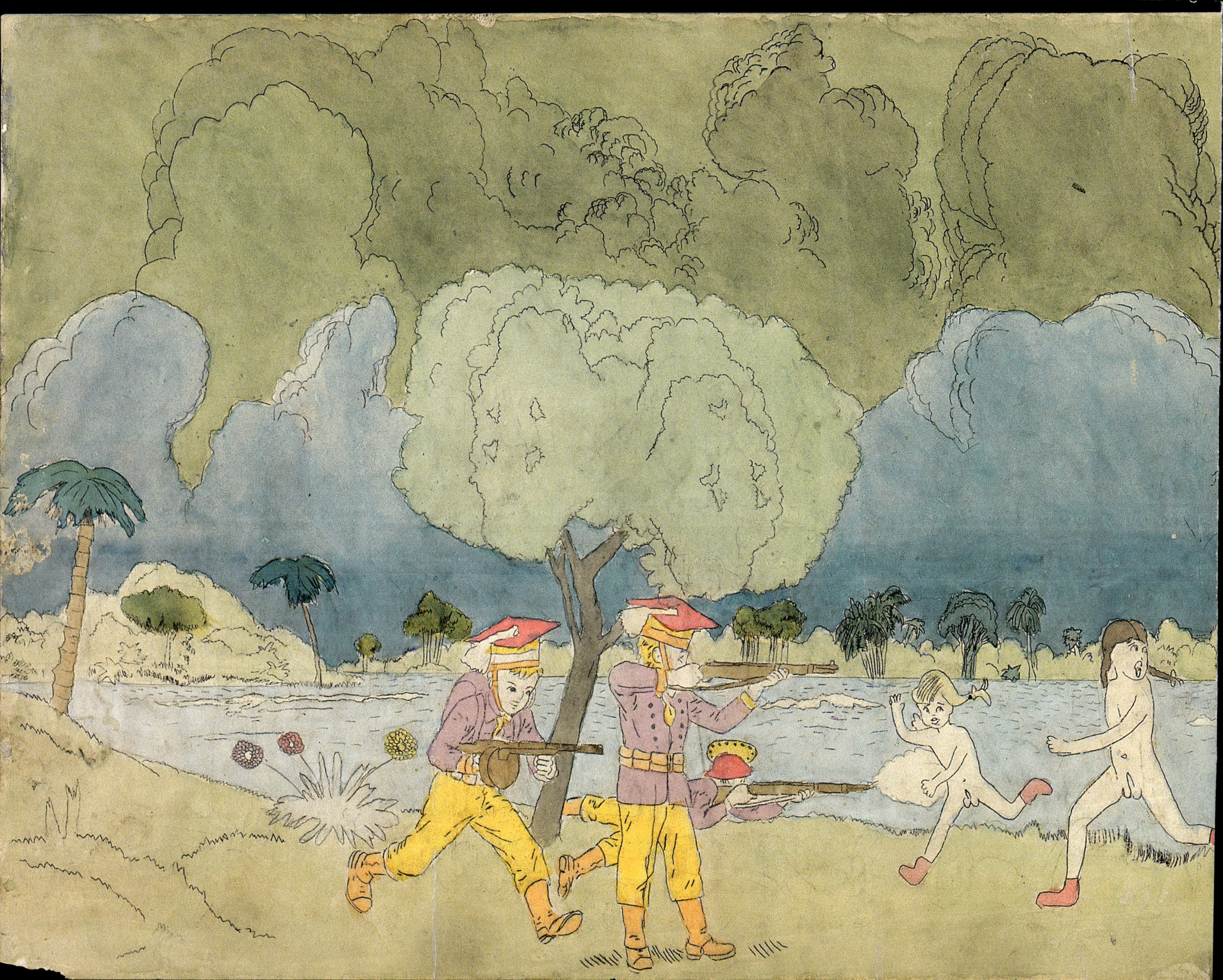

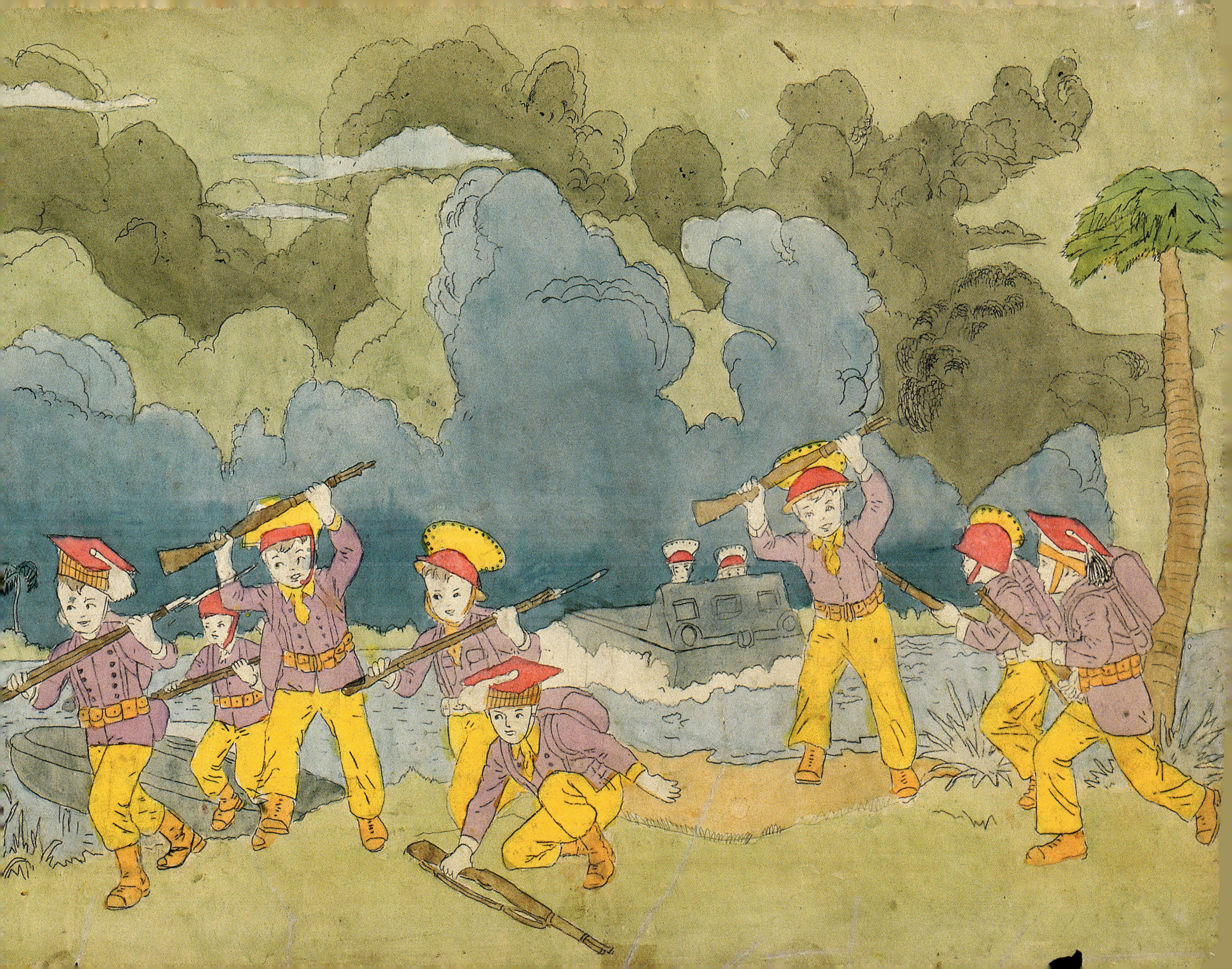

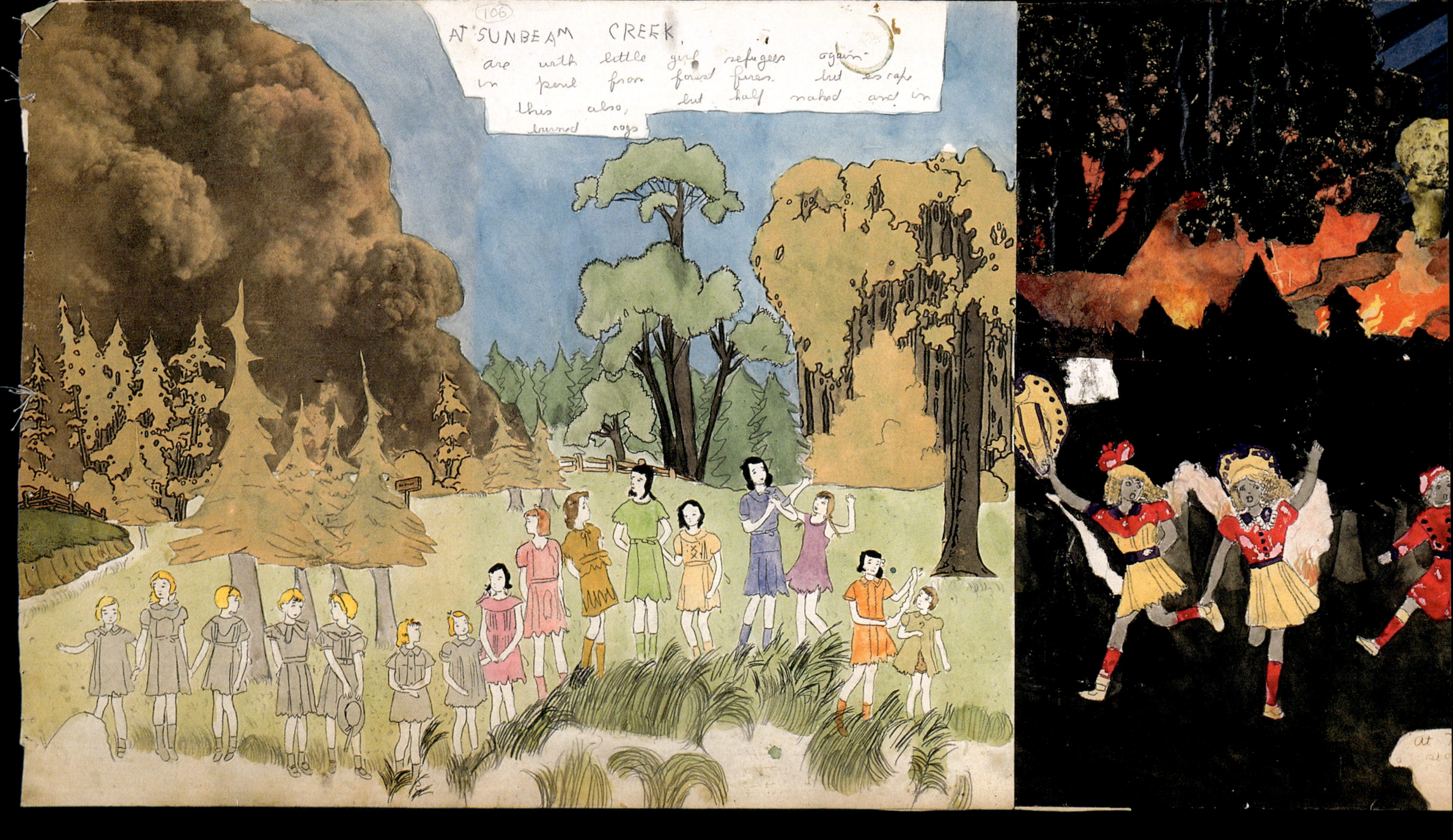

 At Sunbeam Creek. Are with little girl refugees again in peril from forest fires. But escape this also, but half naked and in burned rags / At Torrington. Are persued by a storm of fire but save themselves by jumping into a stream and swim across as seen in next picture / At Torrington. They reach the river just in the nick of time. Their red color is caused by the glare of the flames . . .

Watercolor, pencil, carbon tracing, and collage on pieced paper, 19 x 70 ½ in. Collection American Folk Art Museum, New York. Anonymous gift in recognition of Sam Farber

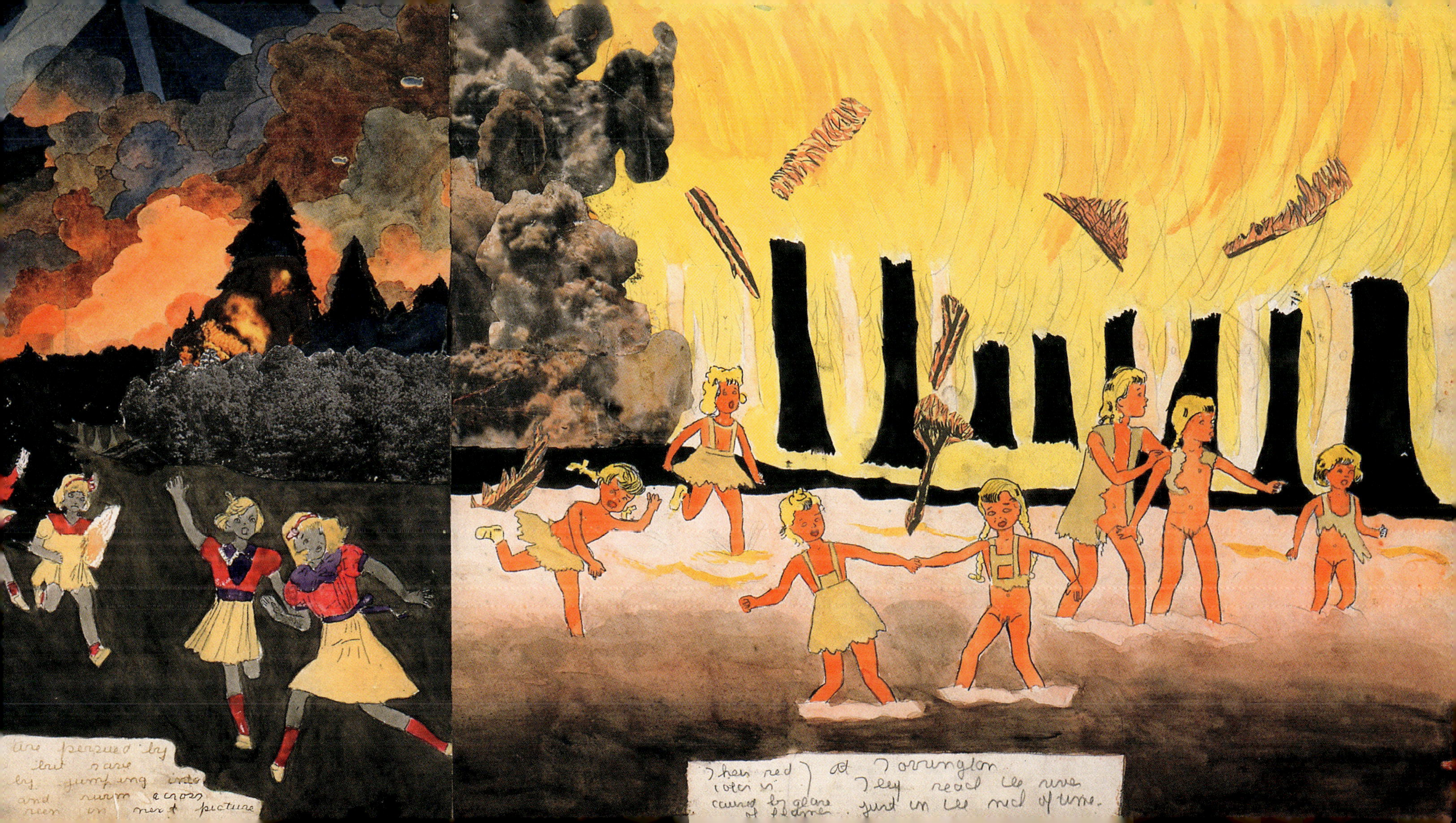
are pursued by
their ... by jumping into
and swim across
seen on next picture
Their red
colors is
caused by glare
of flame.

at Torrington
They reach the river
just in the nick of time.

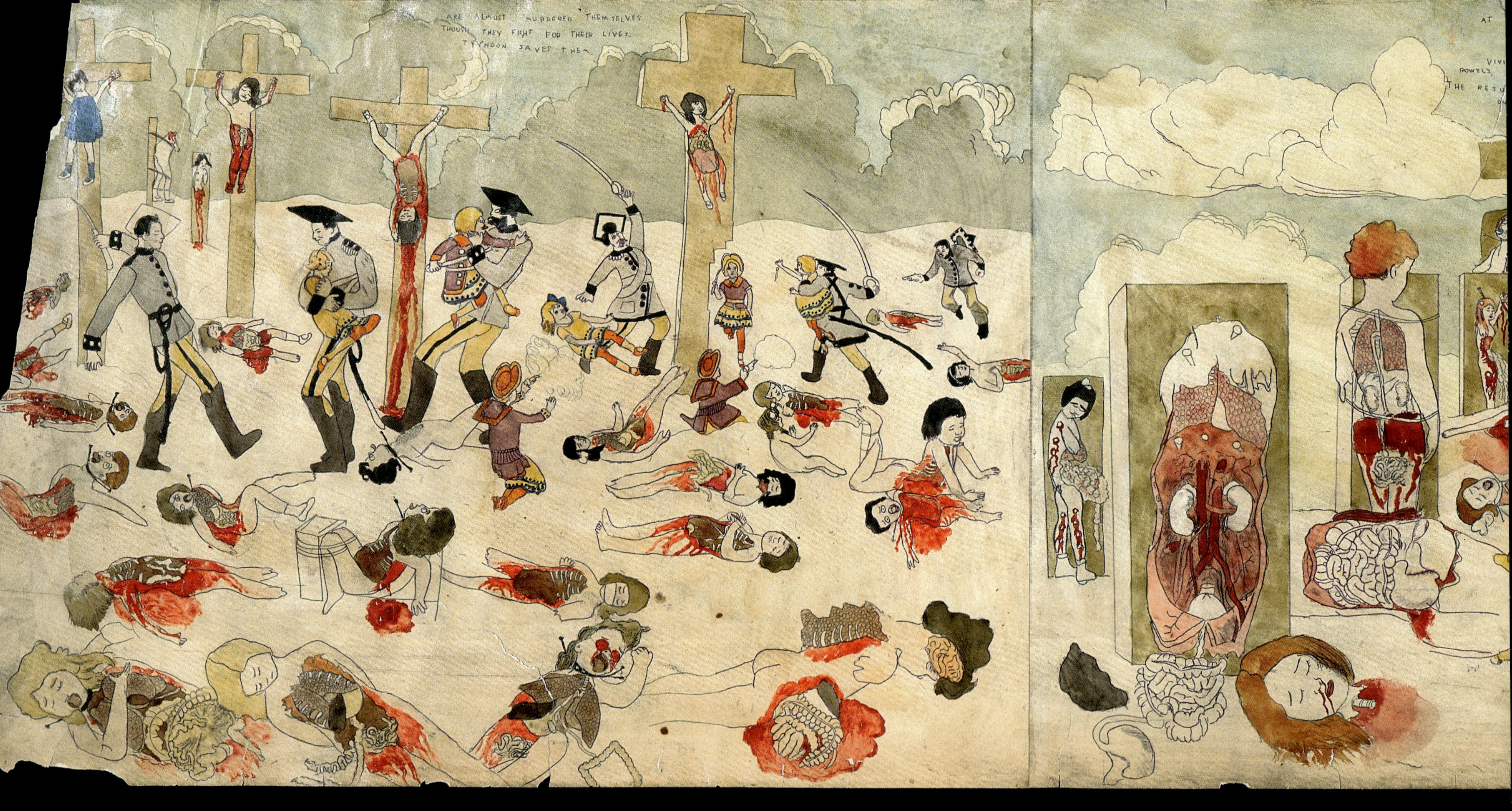

112   Left: *They are almost murdered themselves though they fight for their lives. Typhoon saves them.*

Center: *At Norma Catherine via Jennie Richee. Vivian girls witness childrens bowels and other entrails torn out by infuriated Glandelinians. The result after the massacre. Only a few of the murdered children are shown here.*

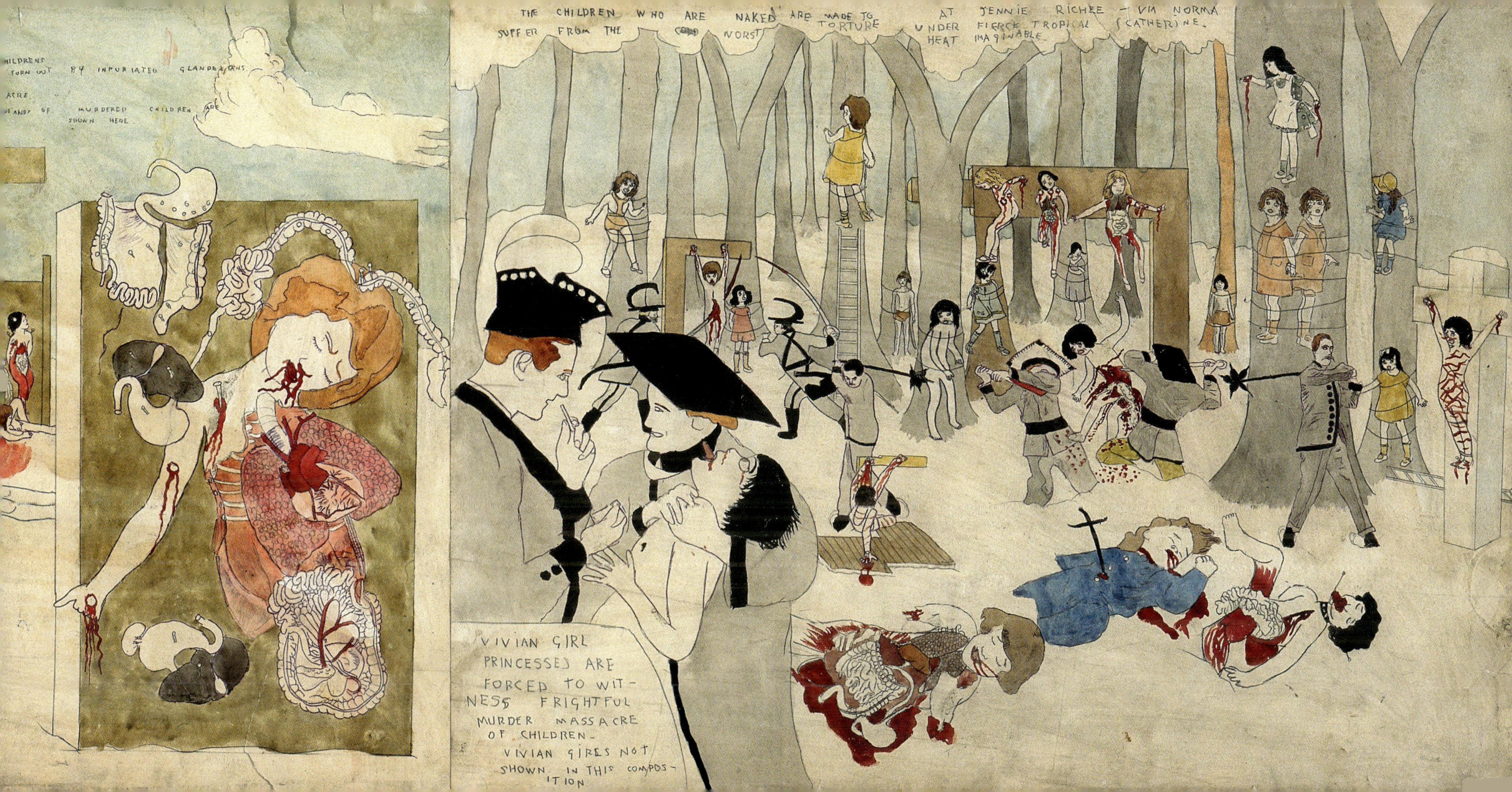

THE CHILDREN WHO ARE NAKED ARE MADE TO SUFFER FROM THE (COLD) WORST TORTURE AT UNDER HEAT FIERCE TROPICAL IMAGINABLE JENNIE RICHEE — VIA NORMA CATHERINE.
CHILDREN TORN OUT BY INFURIATED GLANDELINIANS. ACRE. ISANDS OF MURDERED CHILDREN ARE SHOWN HERE.
VIVIAN GIRL PRINCESSES ARE FORCED TO WITNESS FRIGHTFUL MURDER MASSACRE OF CHILDREN. VIVIAN GIRLS NOT SHOWN IN THIS COMPOSITION

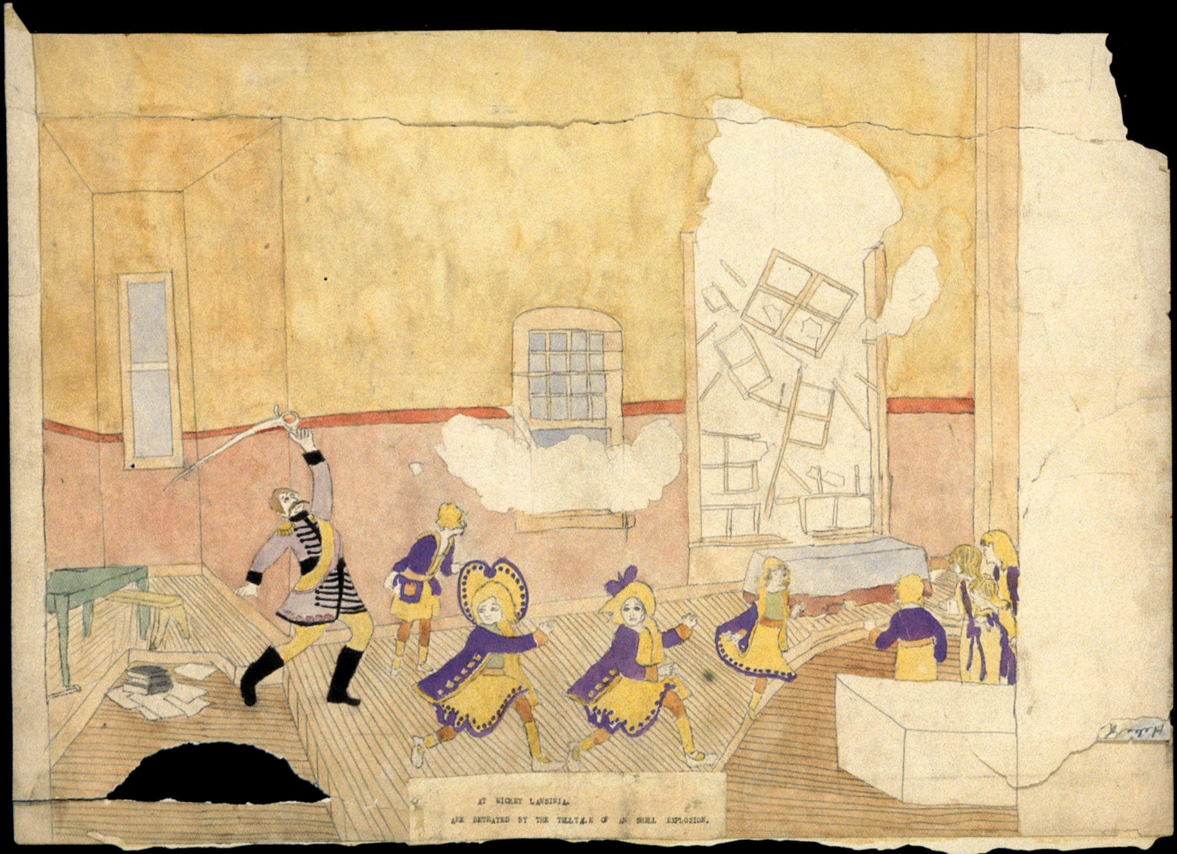

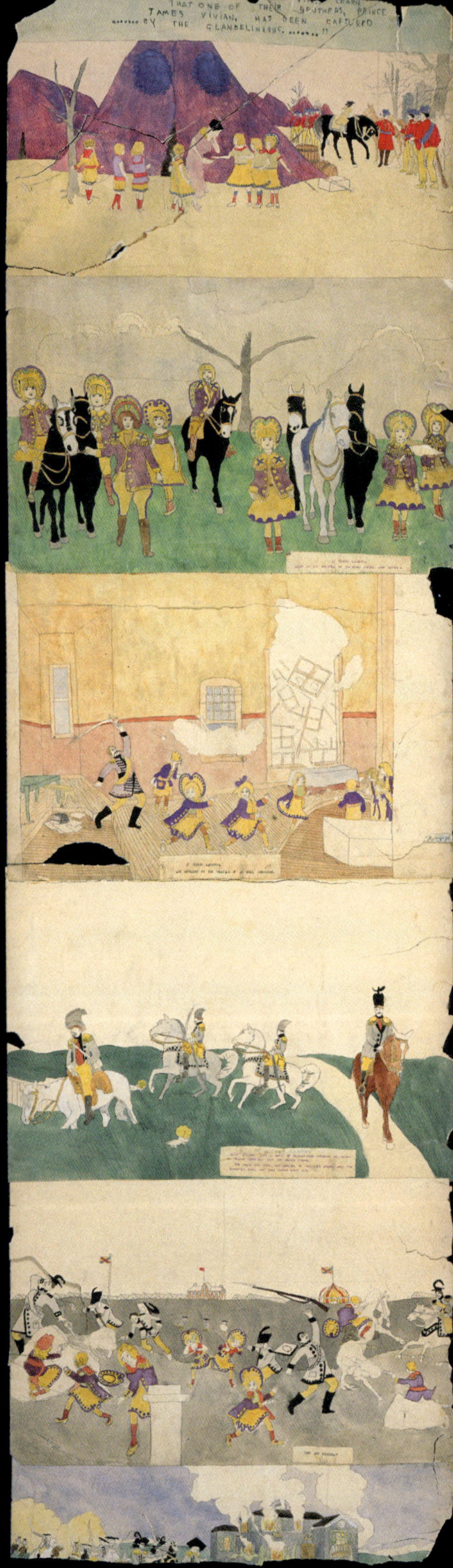

Top: *Vivian girls hear that one of their brothers,*
Prince James Vivian has been captured by the Glandelinians.
Second: *At Wickey Lansinia. Again go out scouting on the enemy during same battle.*
Third: *At Wickey Lansinia. Are betrayed by the telltale of a shell explosion* (detail above).
Fourth: *At Wickey Lansinia. After slipping past a party of Glandelinian*
officers on horseback gain their way in to enemy's lines. . . .
Bottom: *They are pursued.* Watercolor, pencil, and carbon tracing
on pieced paper, 77 x 22 in.
Collection Lawrence B. Benenson

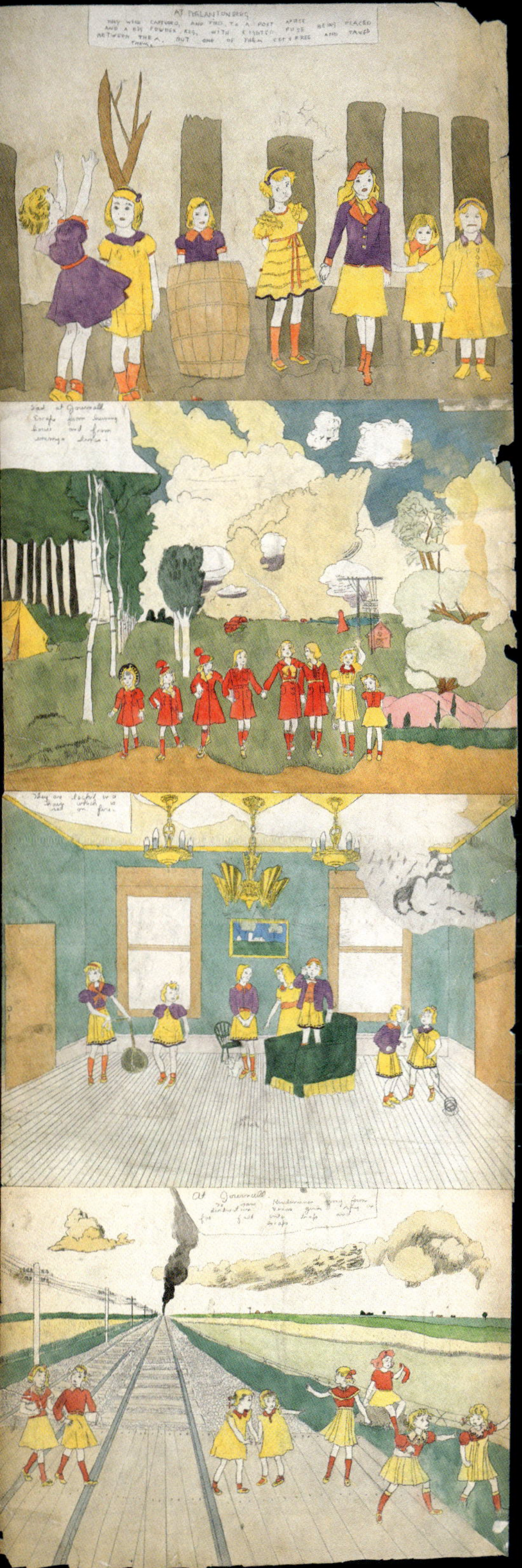

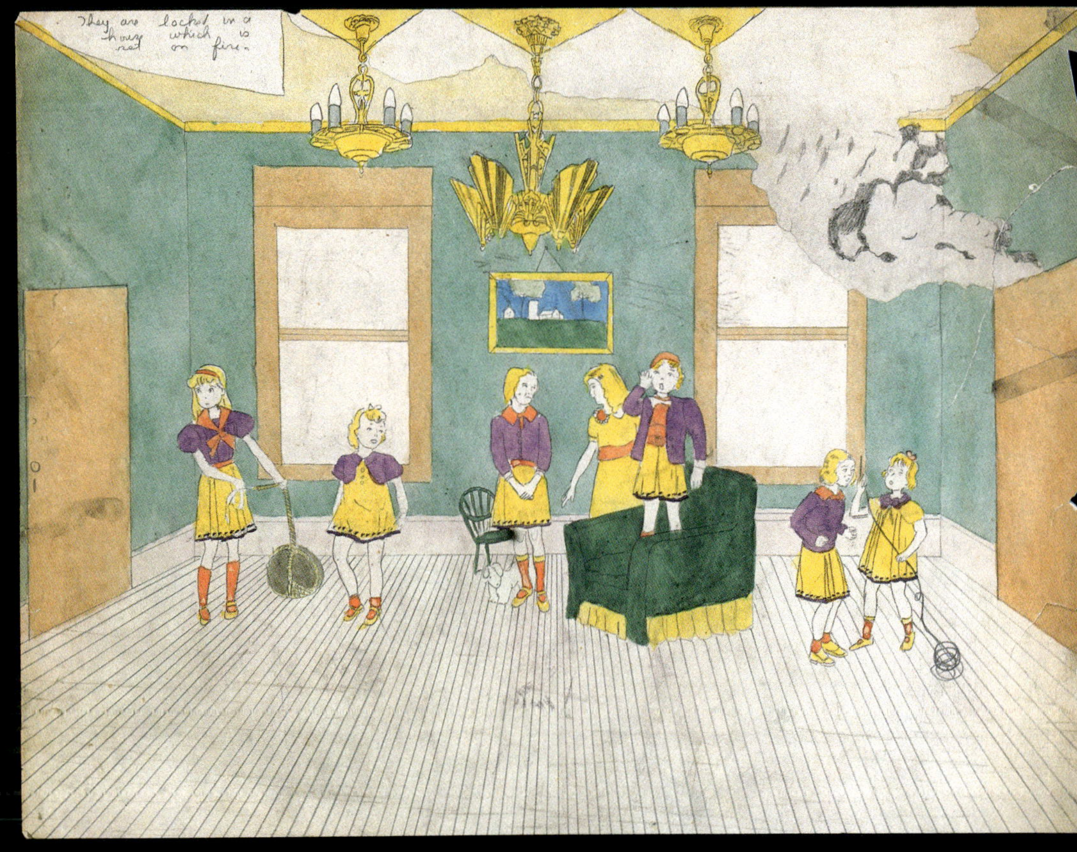

Top: *At Phelantonberg. They were captured and tied to a post apiece and a big powder keg, with lighted fuse being placed between them but one of them gets free and saves them.*
Second: *East at Journall. Escape from burnning house and from enemy lines.*
Third: *They are locked in a house which is set on fire.*
Bottom: *At Journall. To save Reingerring army from destruction, Vivian girls spy on foe fall in to trap and escape.*
Watercolor, pencil, and carbon tracing on pieced paper, 72 x 24 in.
Private collection

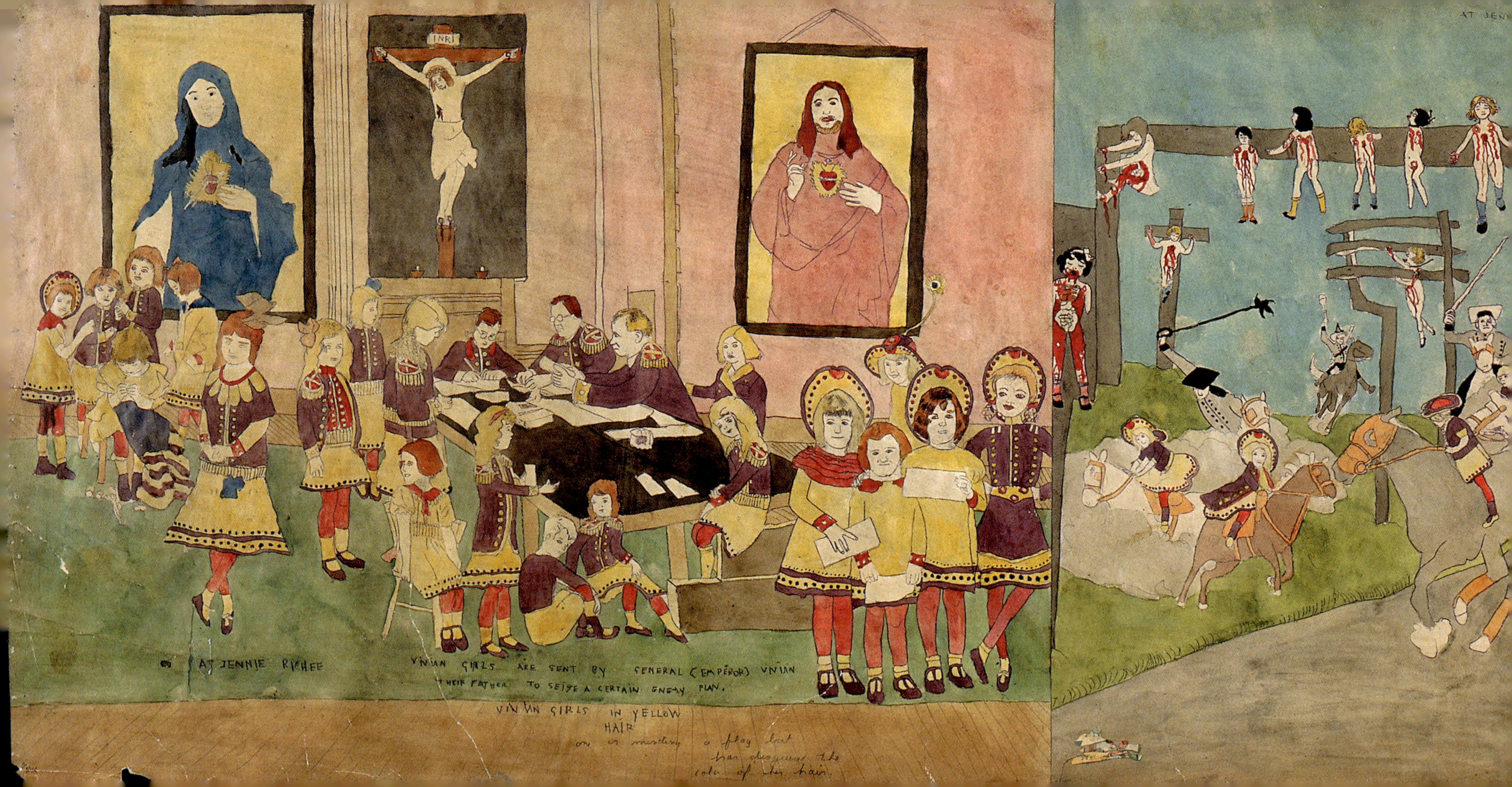

INRI
AT JEN
AT JENNIE RICHEE   VIVIAN GIRLS ARE SENT BY   GENERAL (EMPEROR) VIVIAN THEIR FATHER TO SEIZE A CERTAIN ENEMY PLAN.
VIVIAN GIRLS IN YELLOW HAIR
one is mastering a flag but has disguise the color of her hair.

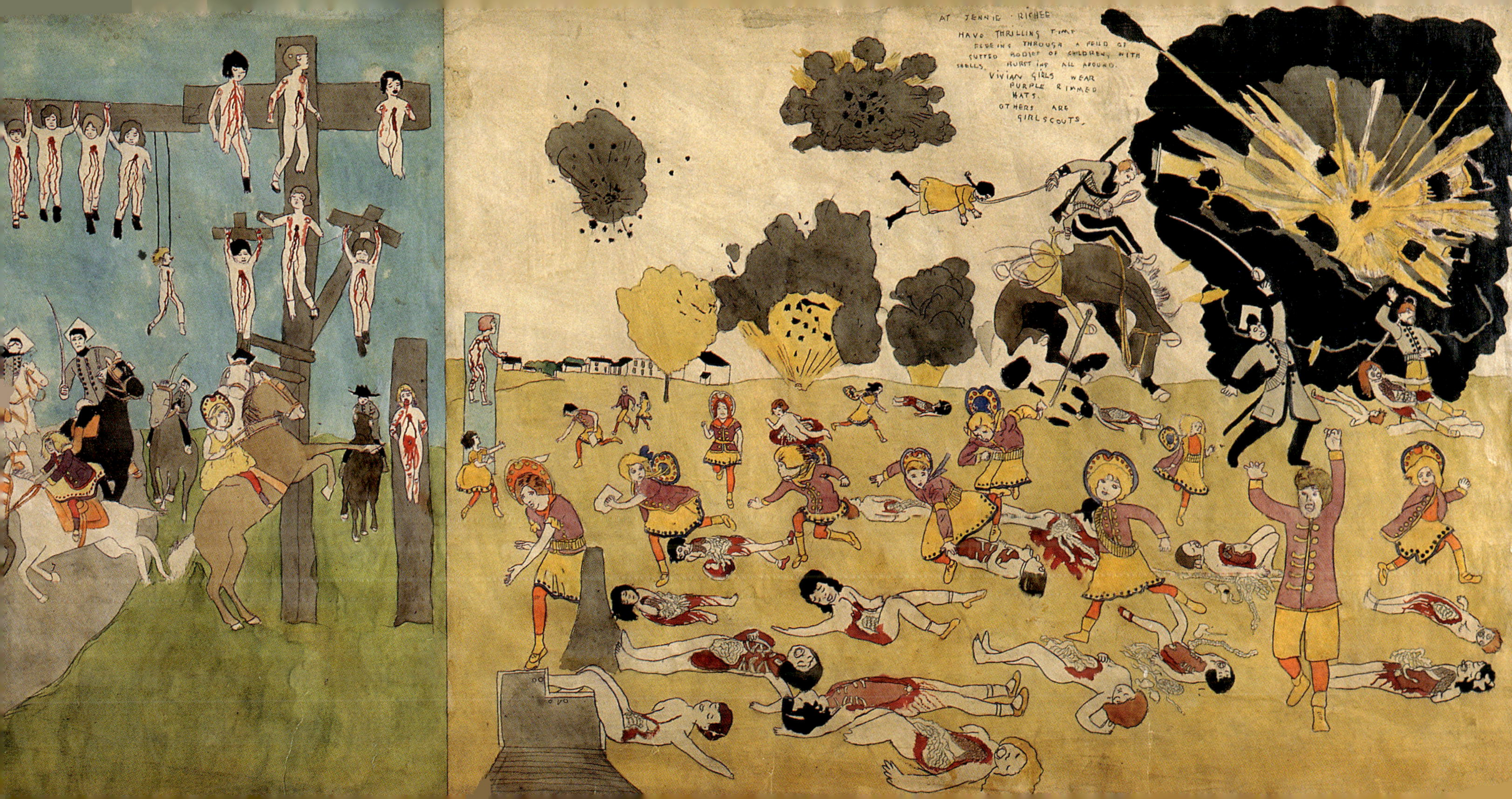

AT JENNIE RICHEE
HAVE THRILLING TIME
FLEEING THROUGH A FEILD OF
CUTTED BODIES OF CHILDREN, WITH
SHELLS BURSTING ALL AROUND.
VIVIAN GIRLS WEAR
PURPLE RIMMED
HATS.
OTHERS ARE
GIRLSCOUTS.

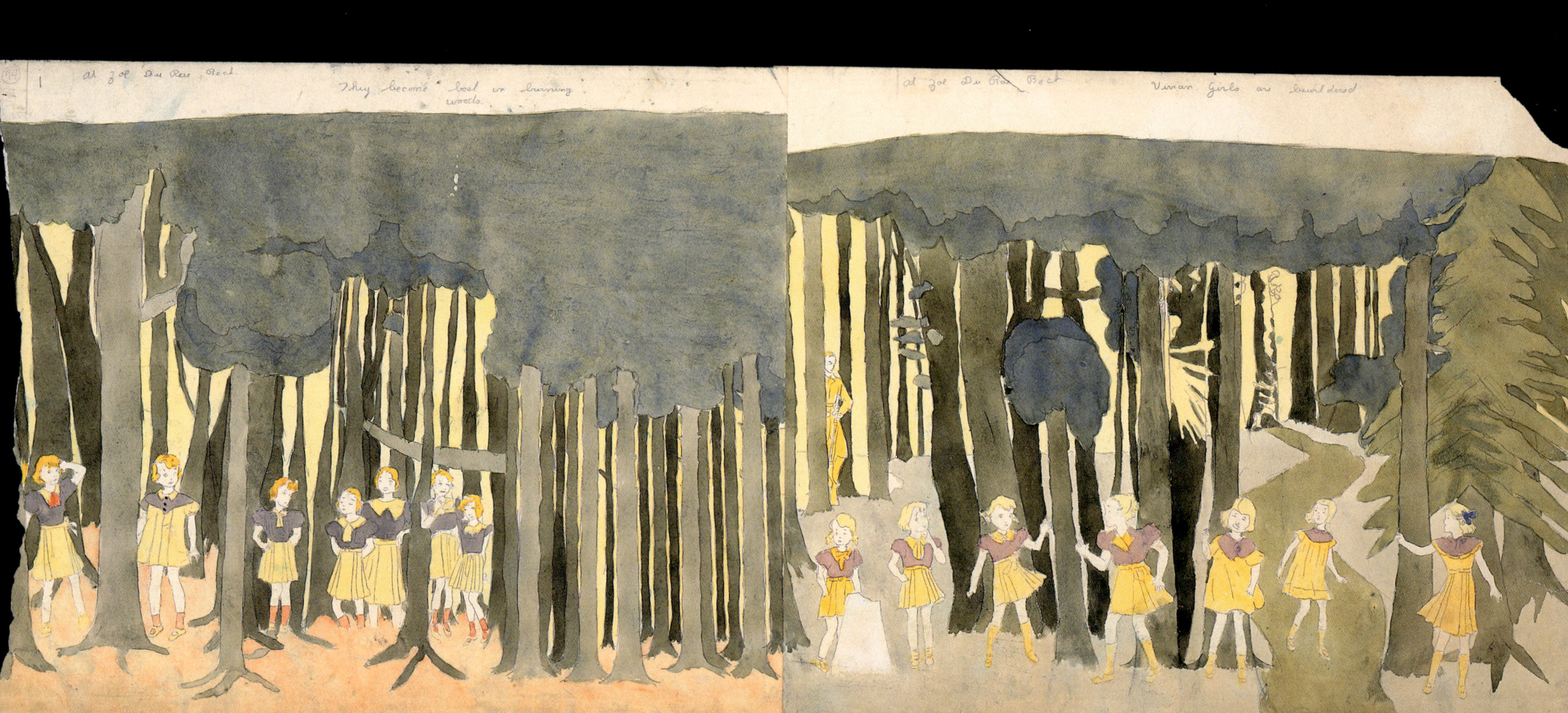
At Jol Du Rai Bect
They become lost in burning woods.
At Jol Du Rai Bect
Vivian Girls are bewildered

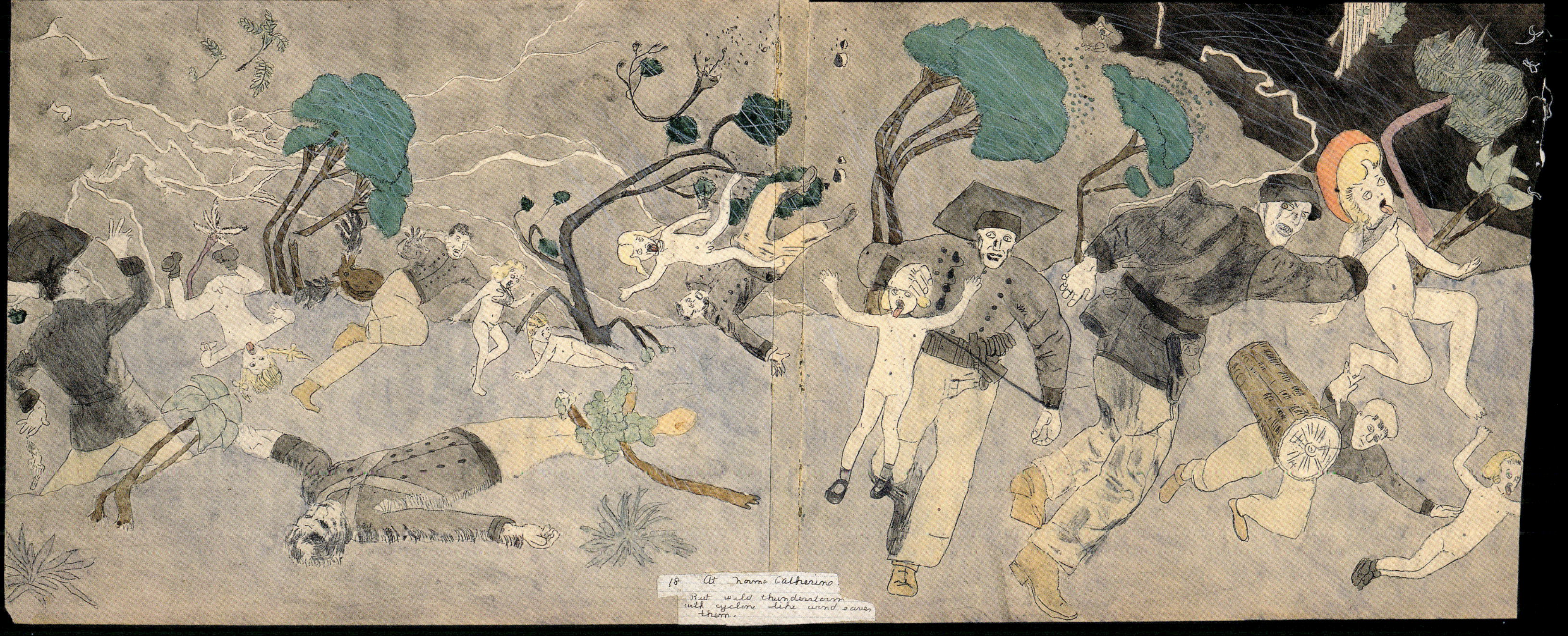

18 At Norma Catherine. But wild thunder-storm with cyclone like wind saves them.   119

Watercolor, pencil, and carbon tracing on pieced paper, 19 ⅛ x 47 ¾ in.

Collection American Folk Art Museum, New York

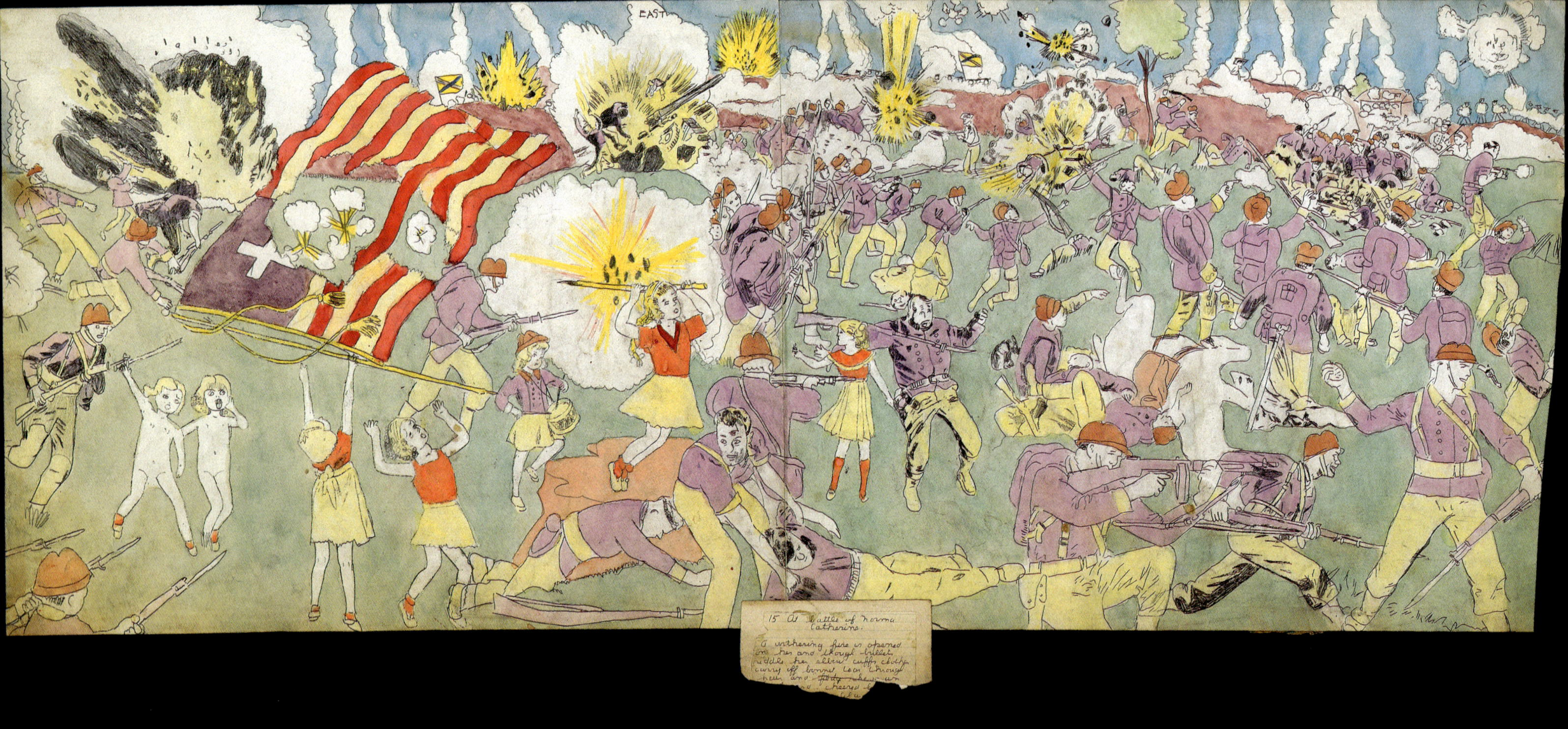

 At Norma Catherine. A Untethering fire is opened on her and bullets riddle her elbow cuffs clothes carry off bonnet Leon through hell and flay . . . Watercolor, pencil, carbon tracing, and collage on pieced paper, approx. 24 x 59 in. Collection Bob Roth

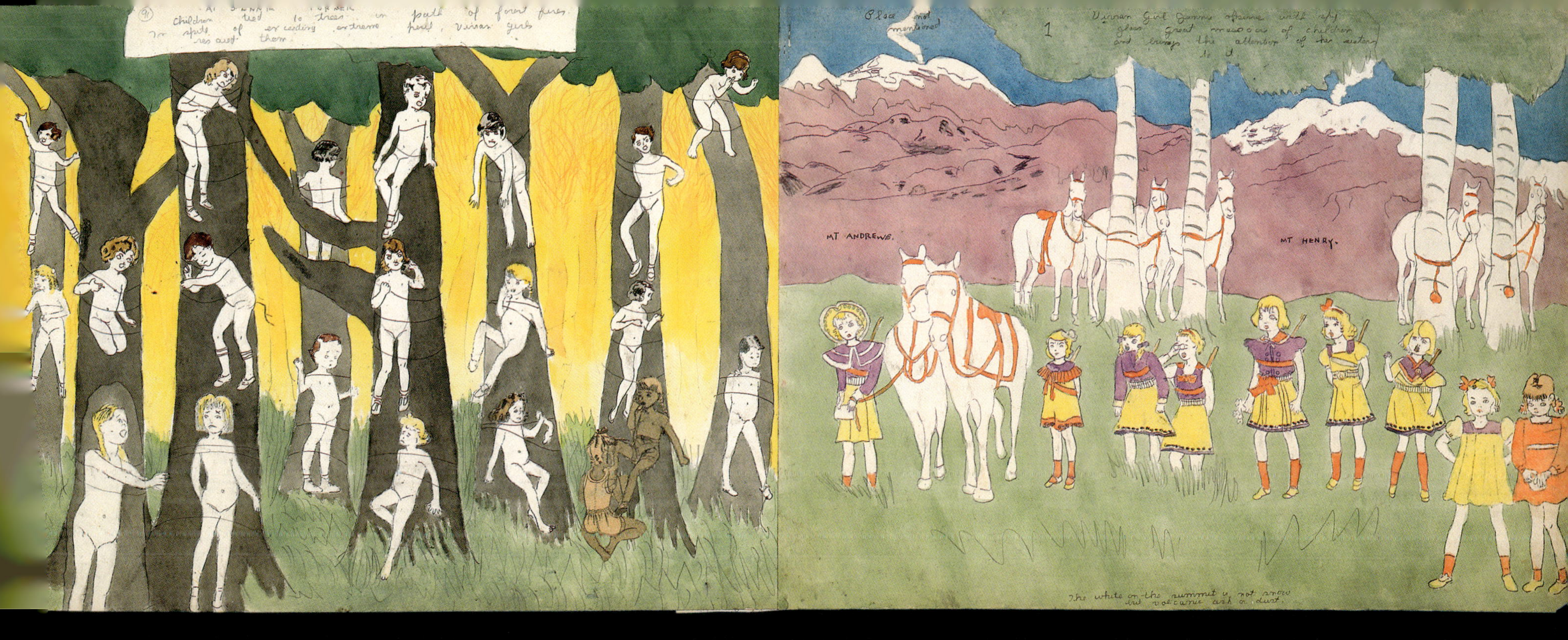

At Jennie Turmer. Children tied to trees in path of forest fires. In spite of exceeding extreme peril, Vivian girls rescue them. / 1 Vivian Girl Jennie observes with spy glass great massacre of children and brings the attention of her sisters to it. Watercolor, pencil, carbon tracing, and collage on pieced paper, 18 x 47 ¼ in. Collection American Folk Art Museum, New York. Gift of Carl Lobell and Kate Stettner in honor of Frank Maresca

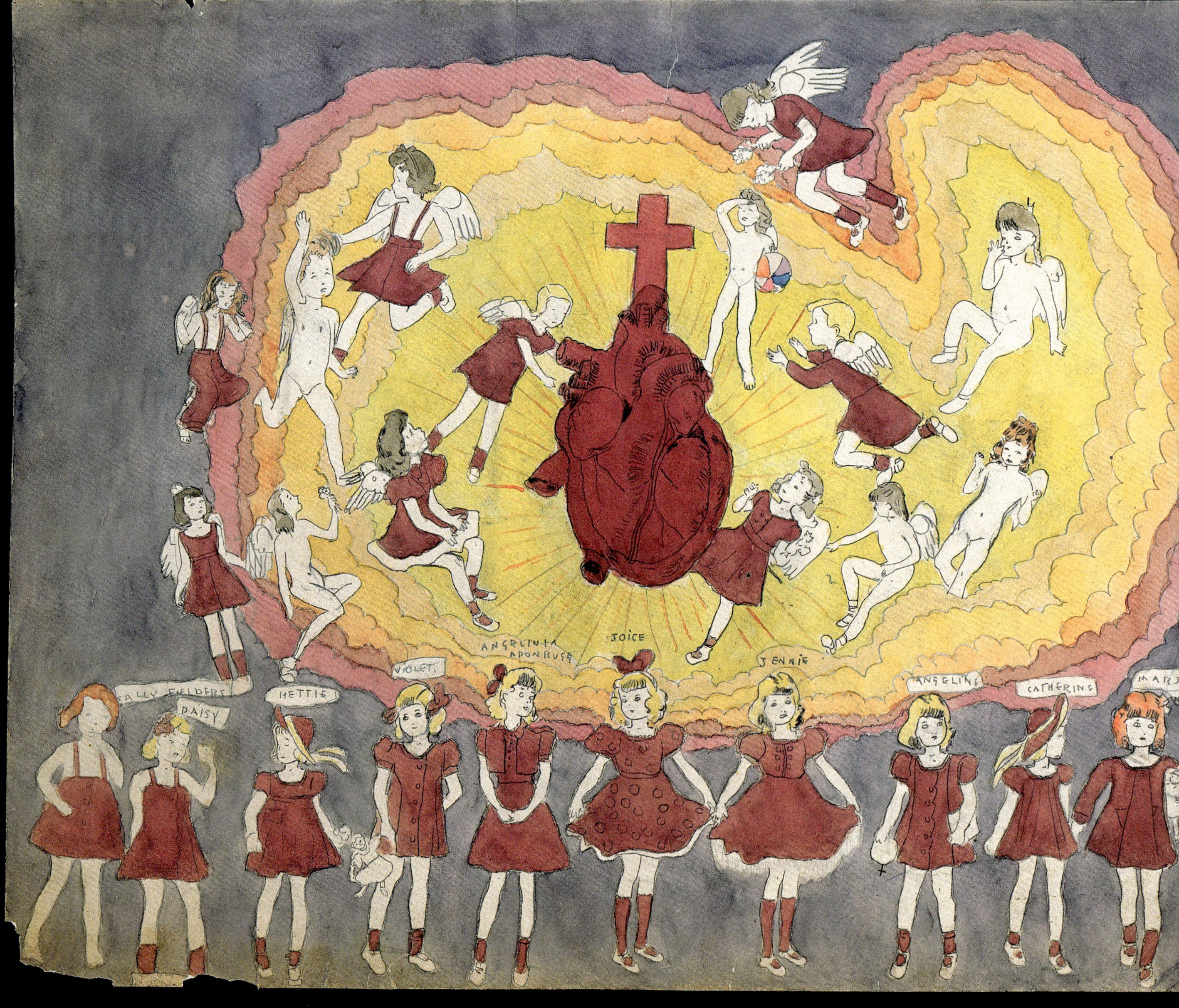

 Left: *Untitled (The Sacred Heart of Jesus).* Right: *At Second Battle of Marcocino also escape from disastrous explosions during battle caused by Glandelinians.*
Watercolor, pencil, and carbon tracing on pieced paper, 19 x 49 in. Collection Kiyoko Lerner

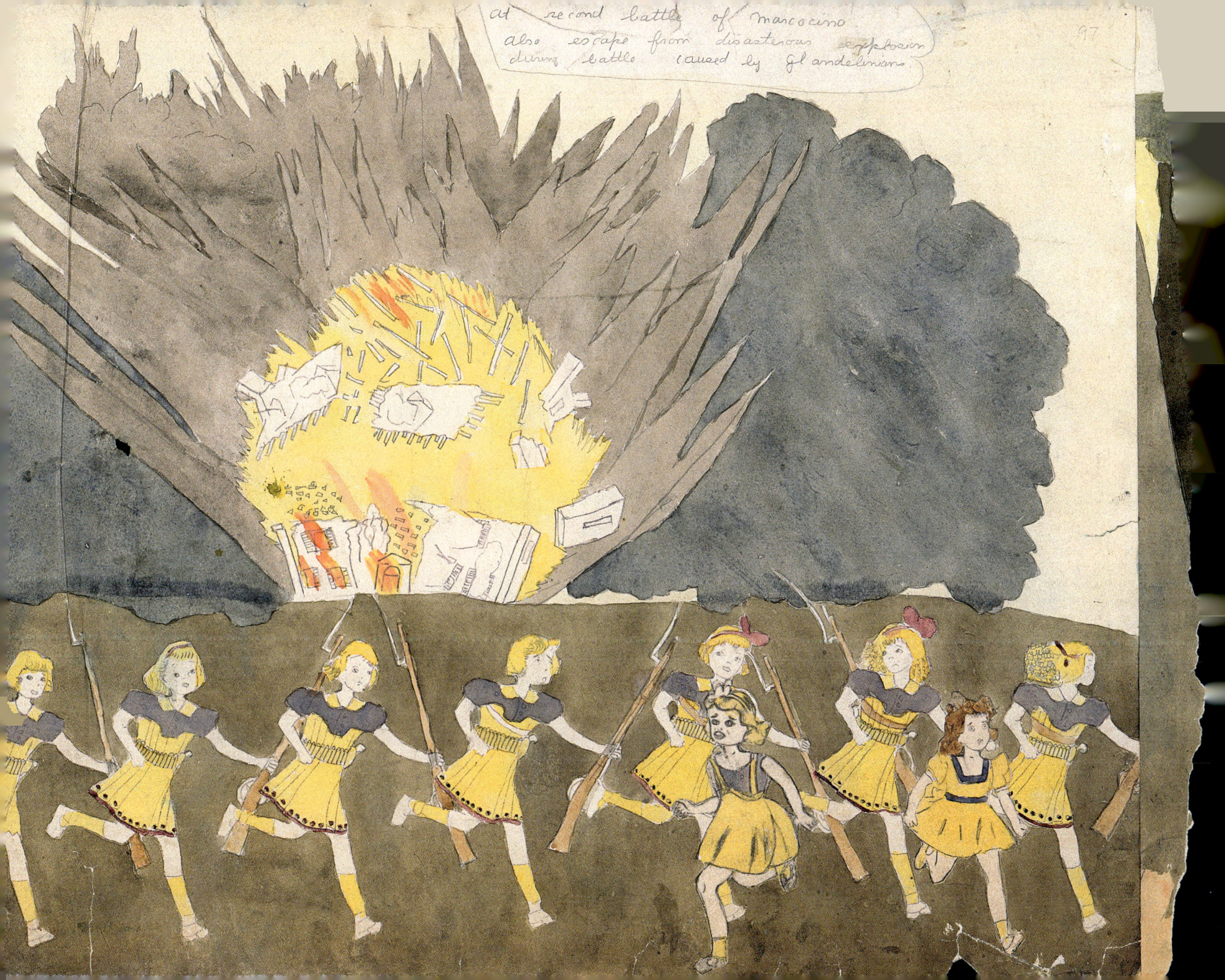
At second battle of marcocino
also escape from disasterous explosion
during battle caused by glandelinians.
97

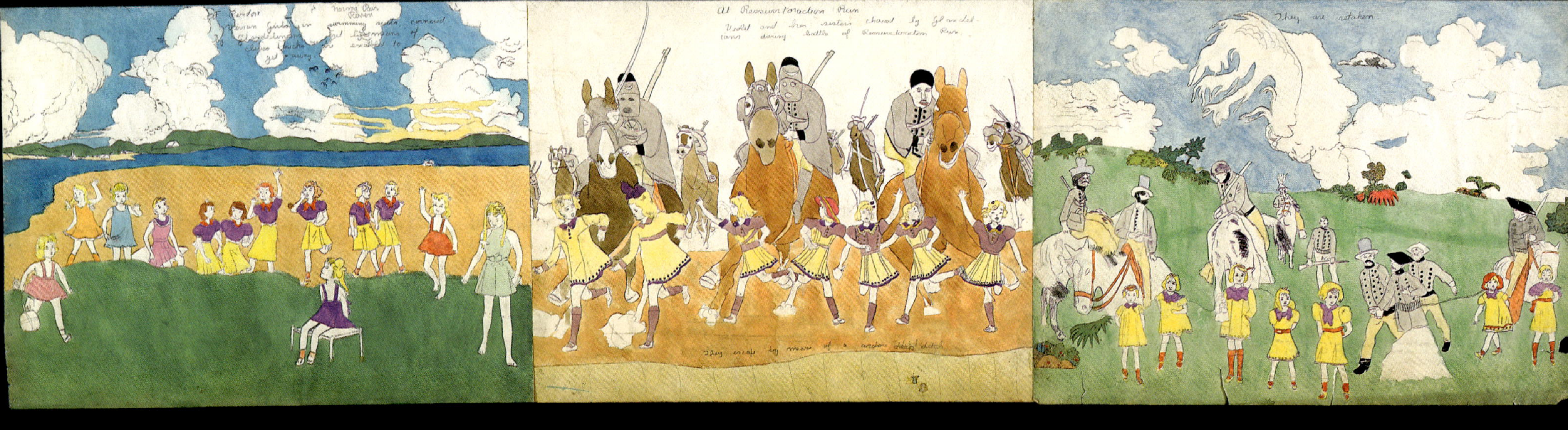

124 | Left: *At Pandora–Norma Run River. Vivian girls in swimming suits, cornered by Glandelinians but by means of clever tricks are enabled to get away.* Center: *At Ressurtonaction Run. Violet and her sisters chased by Glandelians during battle of Ressurtonaction Run.* Right: *They are retaken.* Watercolor, pencil, and carbon tracing on pieced paper, approx. 19 x 75 in. Collection Kiyoko Lerner

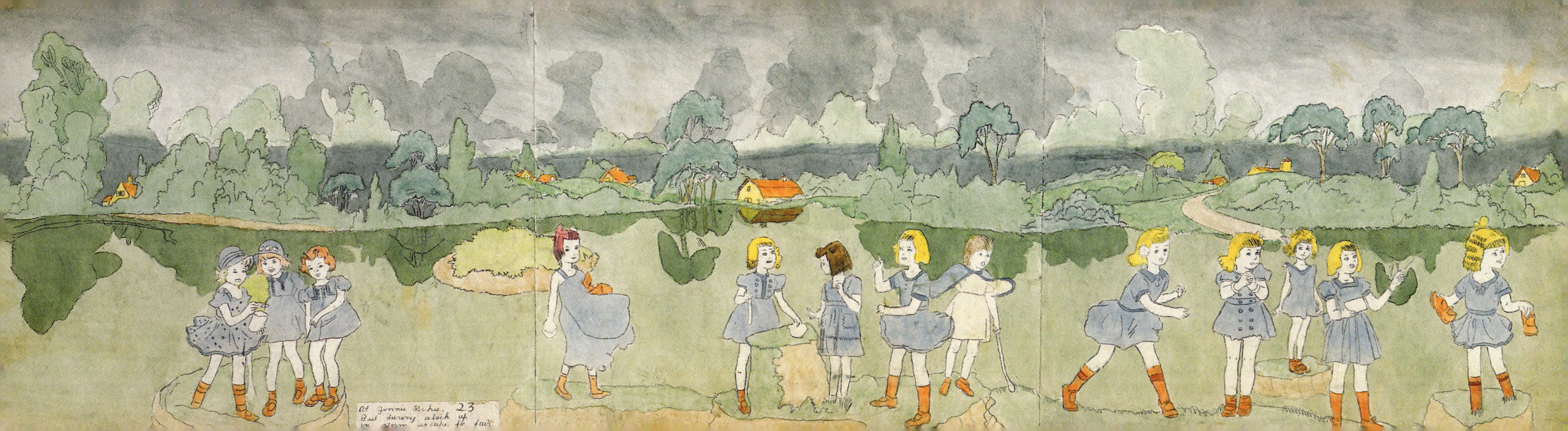
At Jennie Richie. 23
But during black up
in storm we take to fair

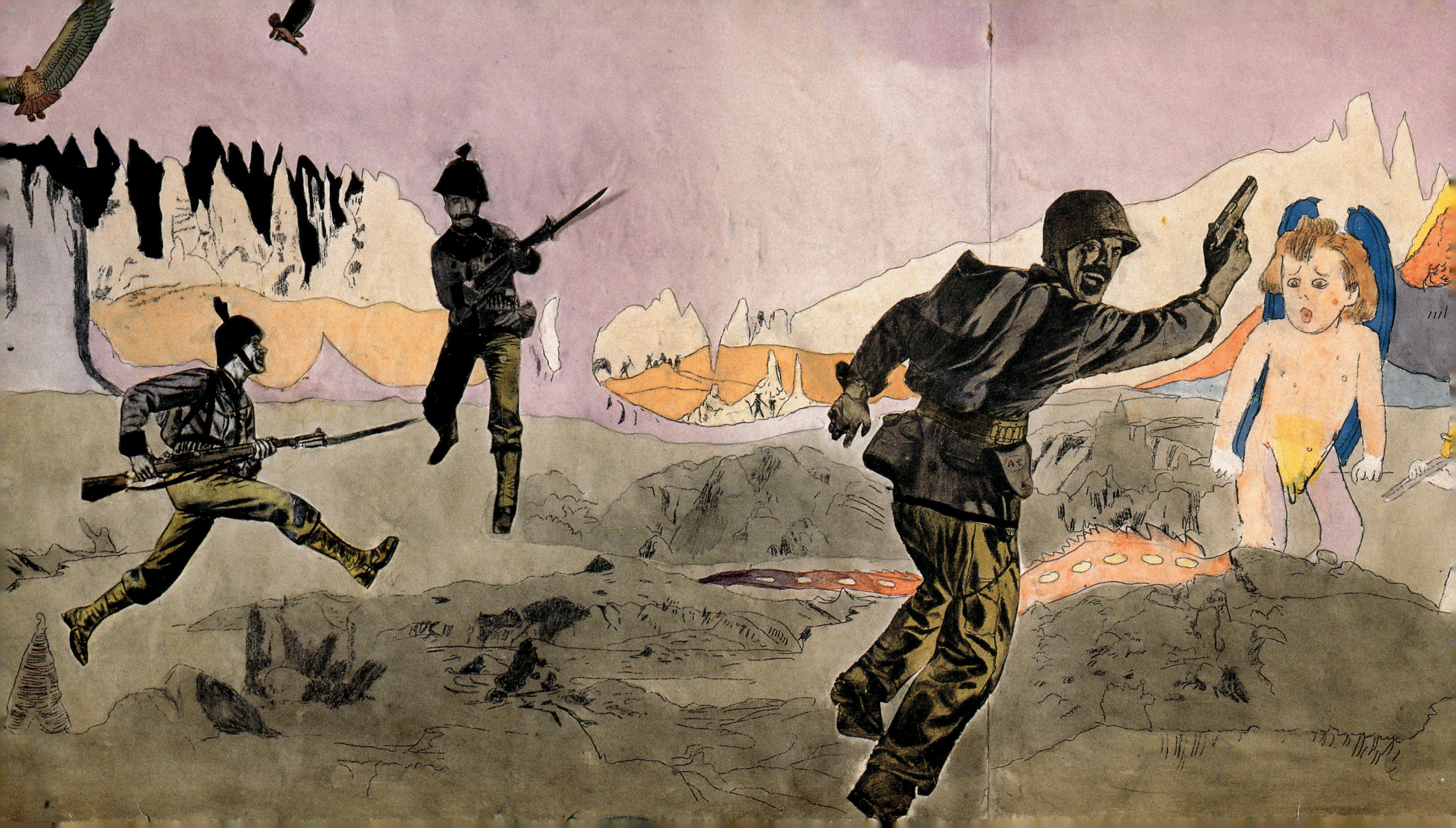

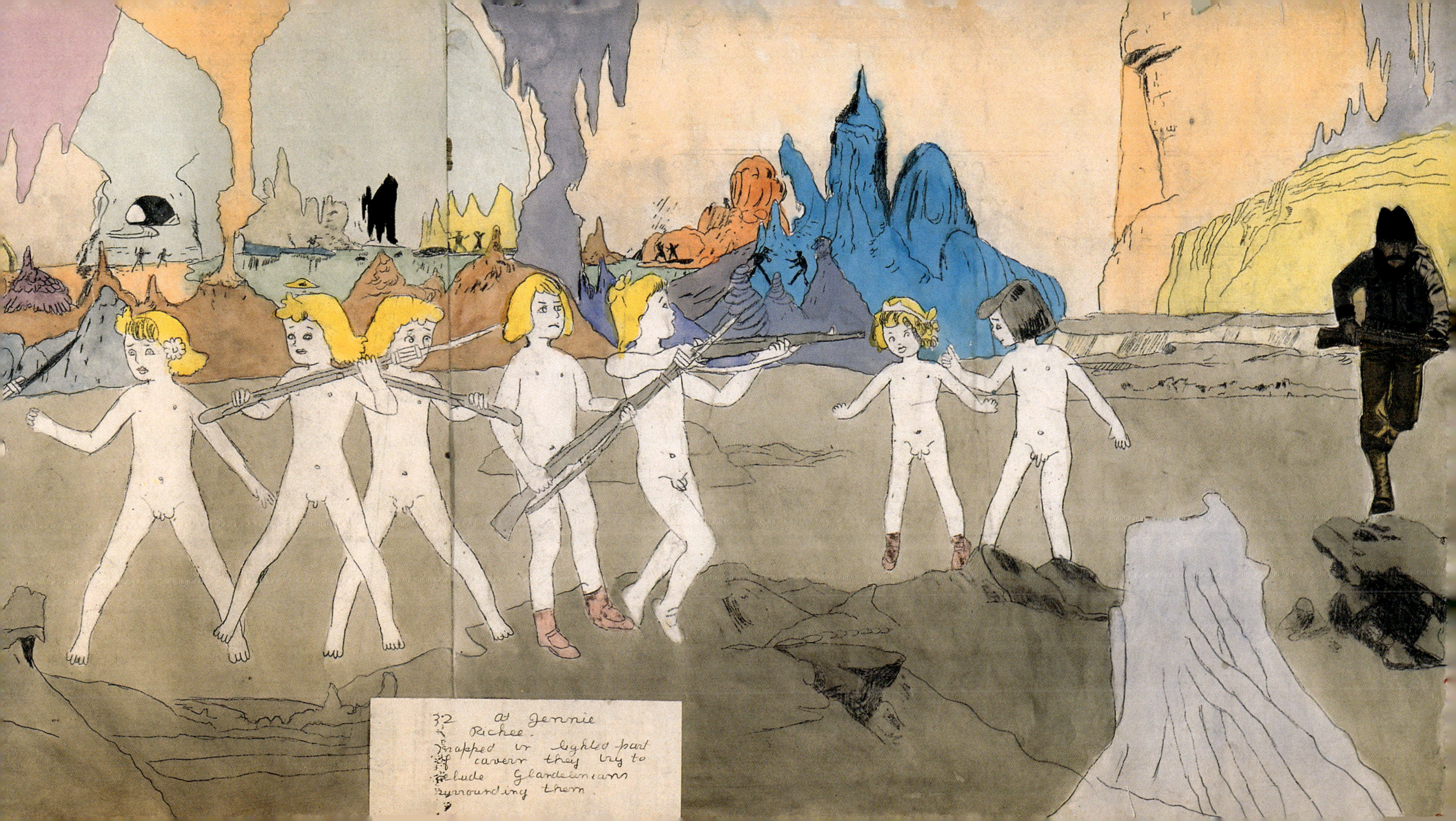

32   At Jennie
     Richee.
Trapped in lighted part
of cavern they try to
elude Glandelinians
surrounding them.

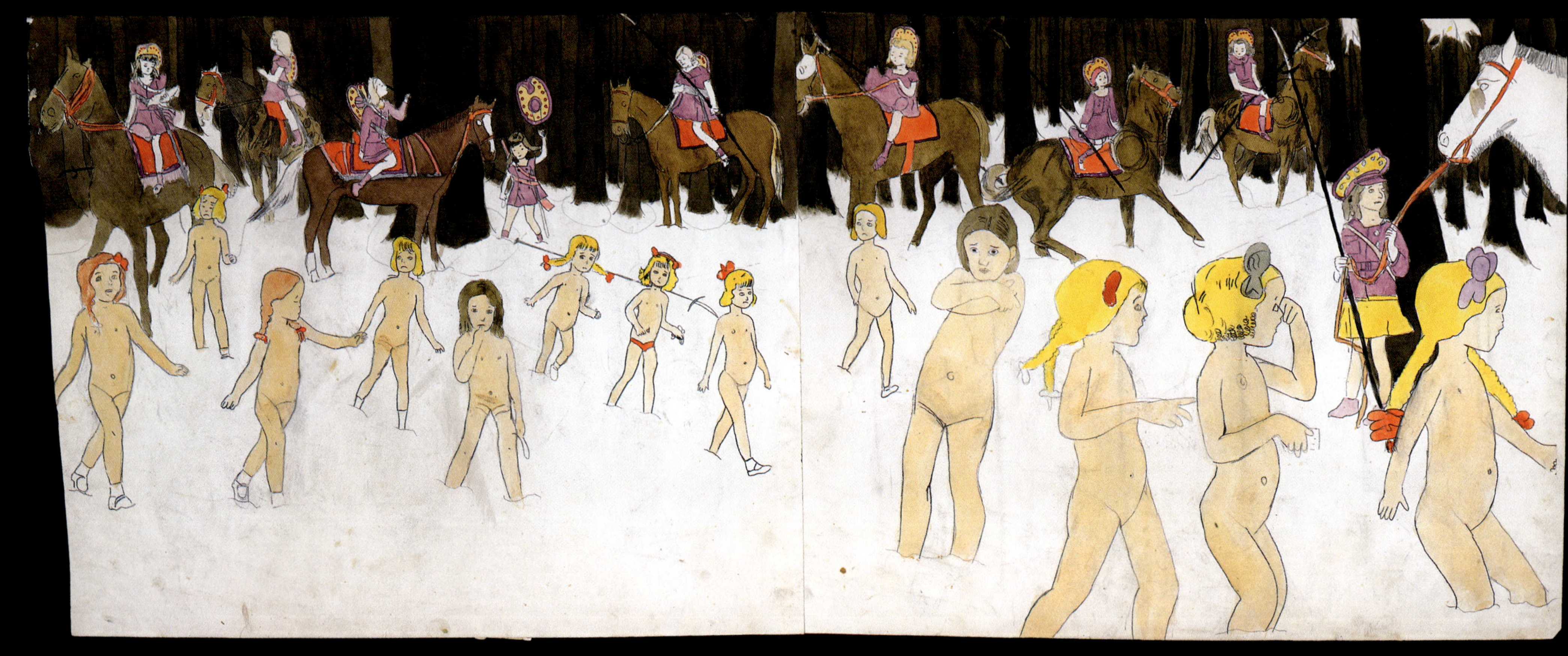

 Untitled (snow scene with rescue of naked child slaves by the Vivian girls on horse-back).

Watercolor, pencil, and carbon tracing on pieced paper, 19 x 46 in. Private collection

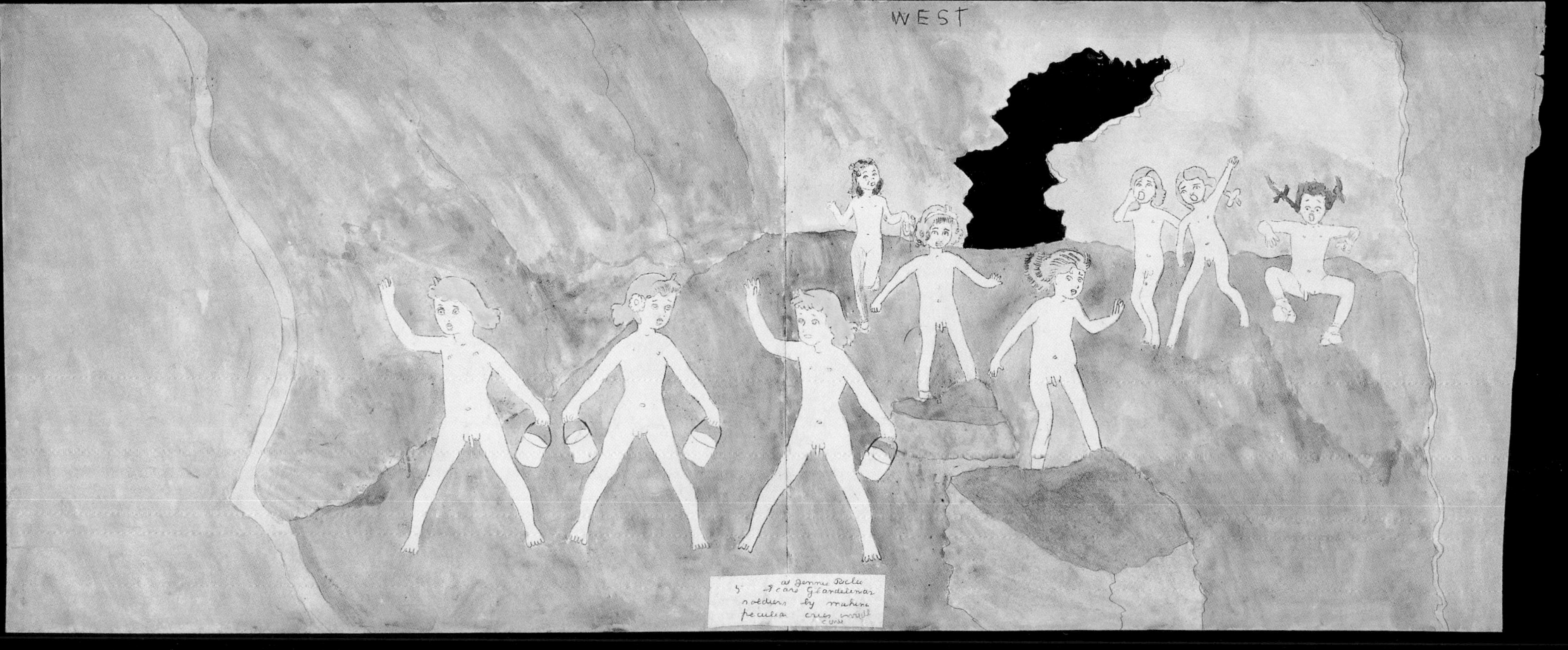
WEST
At Jennie Richee
Scare Glandelinian
soldiers by making
peculiar cries

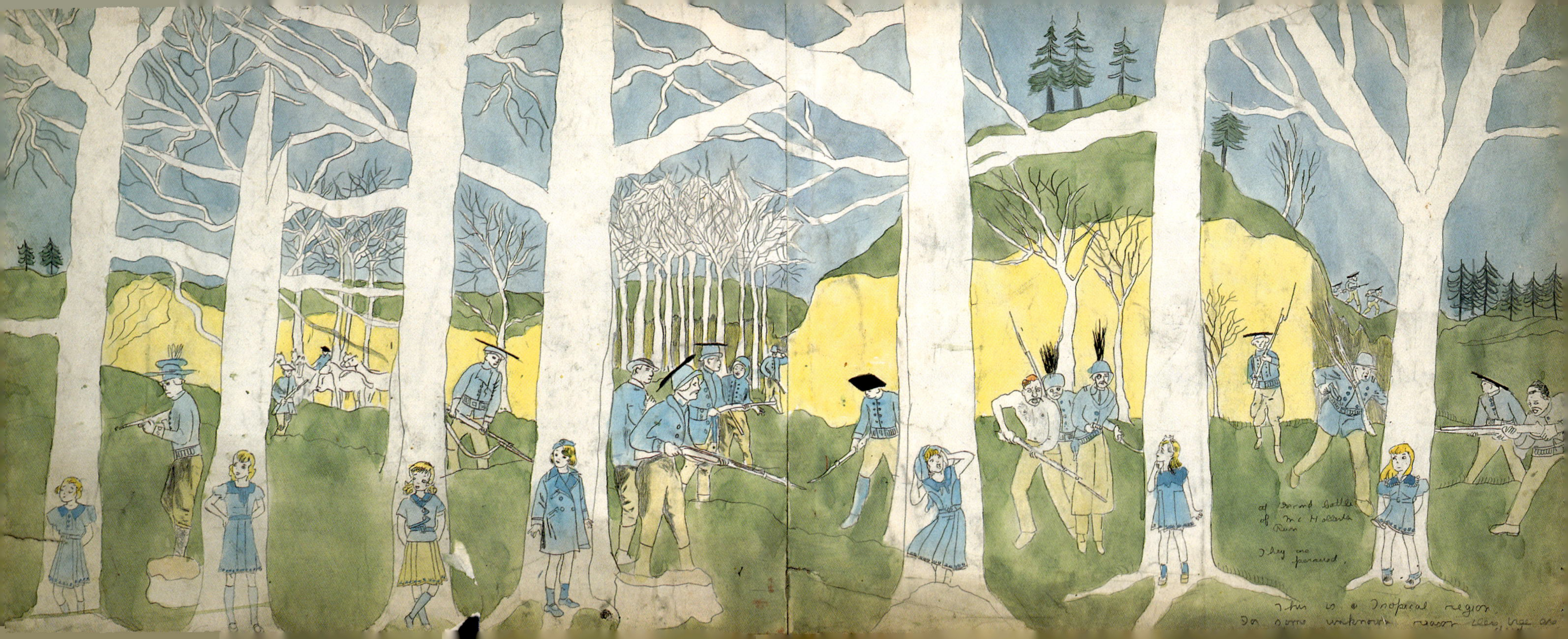

at Grand Battle of Mc Holland Run.
They are pursued.
This is a Tropical region.
For some unknown reason they are

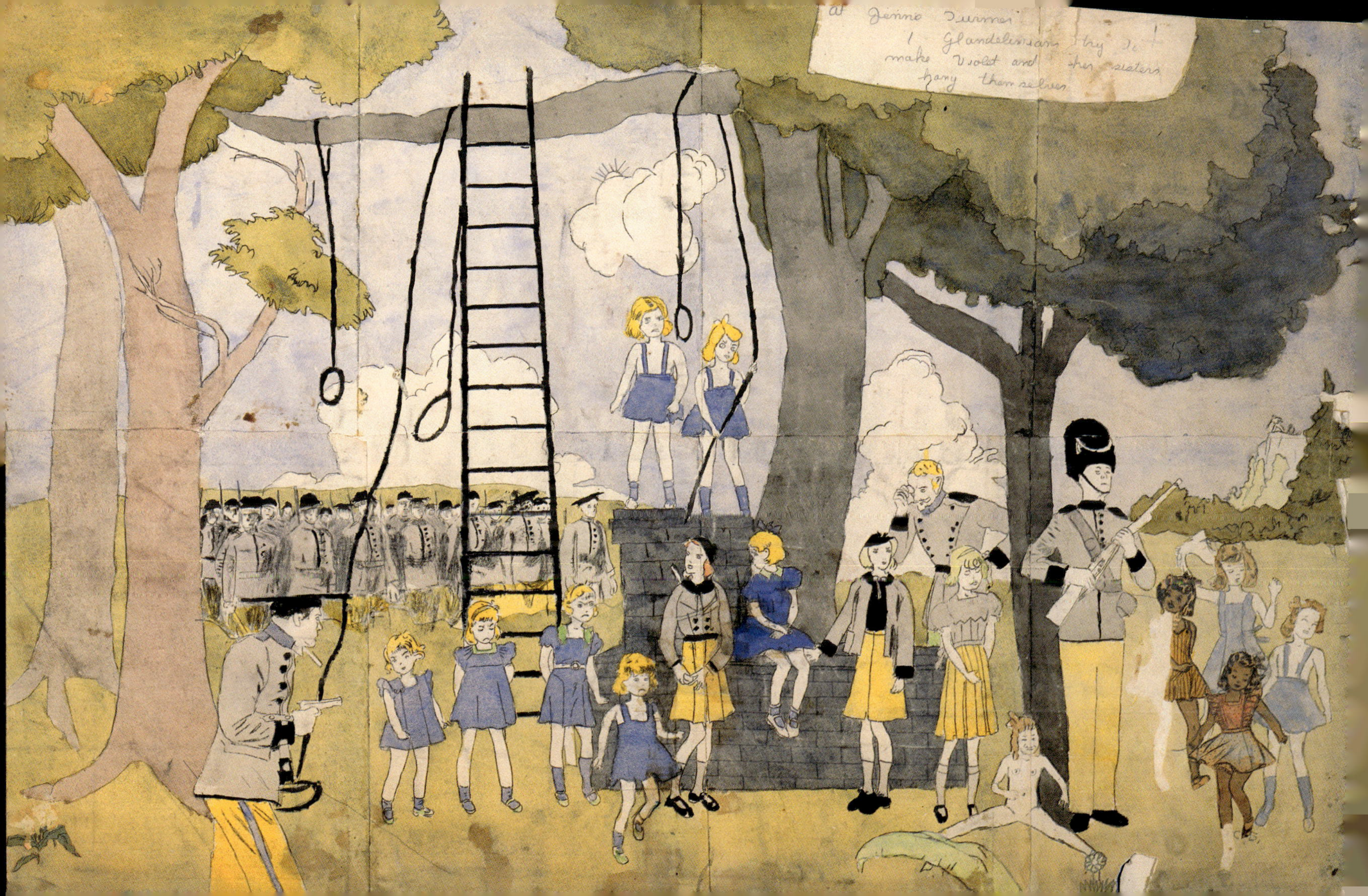

at Jennie Turner
1 Glandelinian try to
make Violet and her sisters
hang themselves

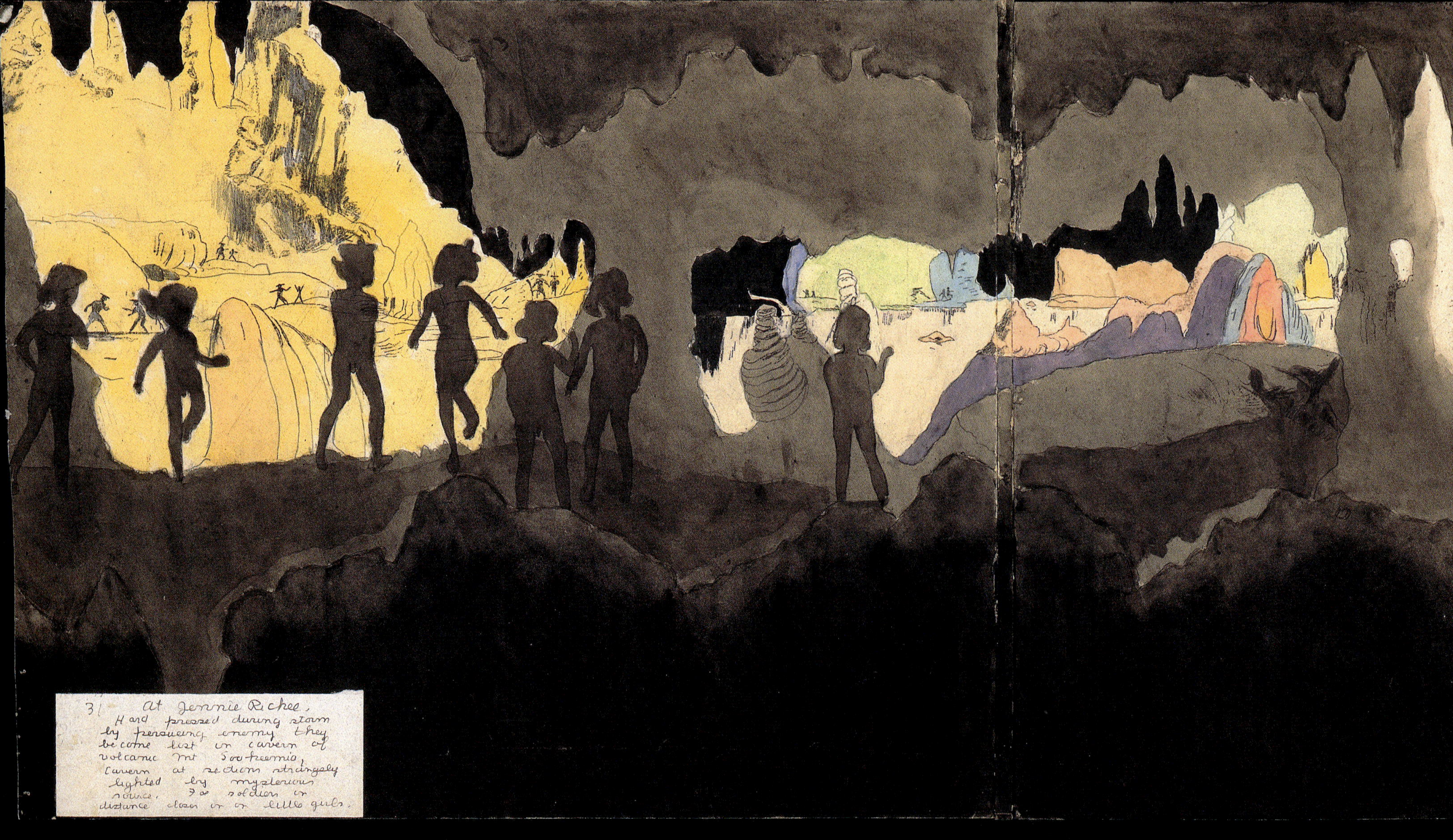

132 | *At Jennie Richee. Hard pressed by persueing enemy they become lost in cavern of volcanic*

Mt. Sootreemia. Cavern at sections strangely lighted by mysterious source. Soldiers in distance closing in on little girls.

Watercolor, pencil, and carbon tracing on pieced paper, approx. 19 x 68 in. Collection Kiyoko Lerner

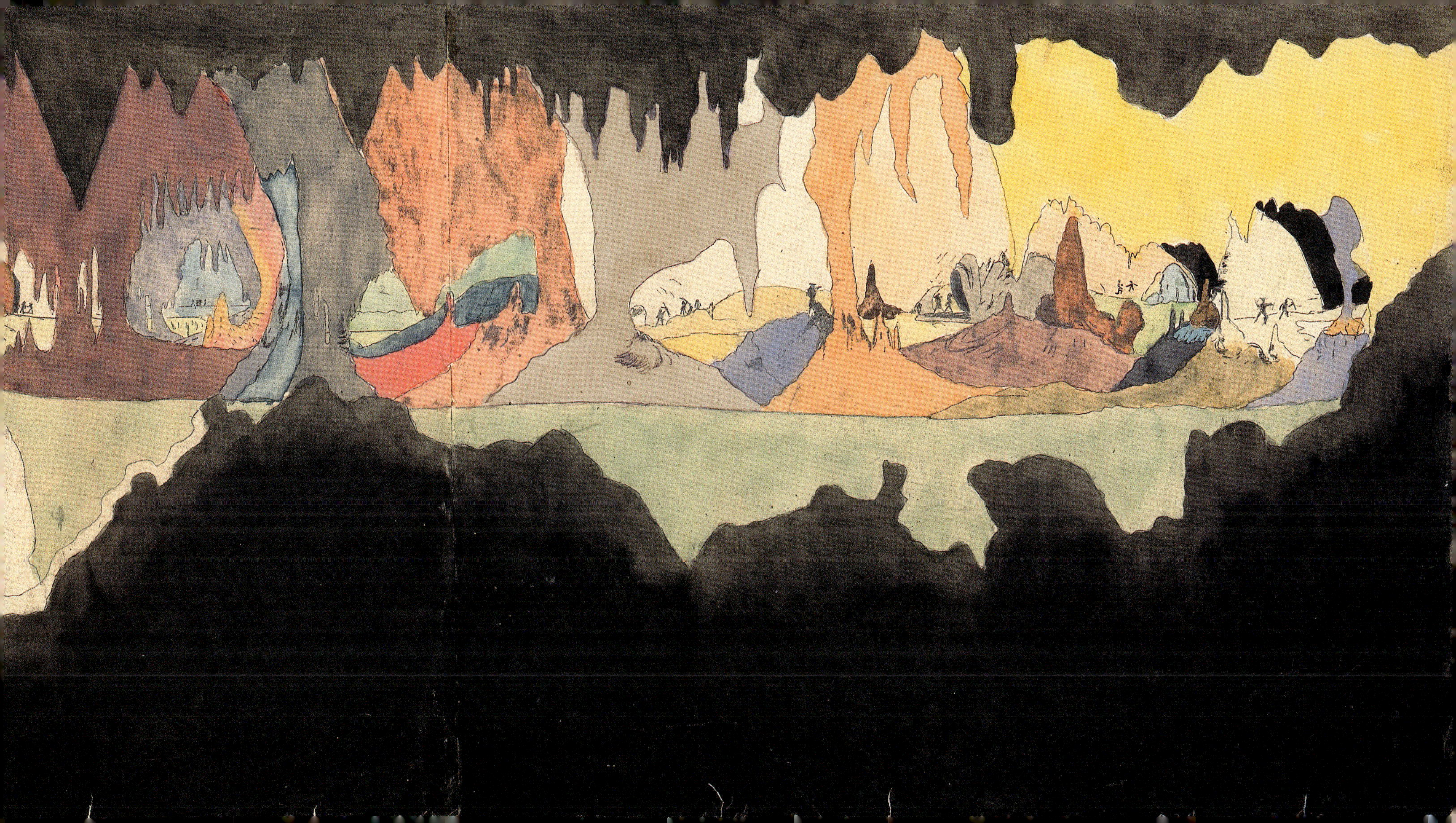

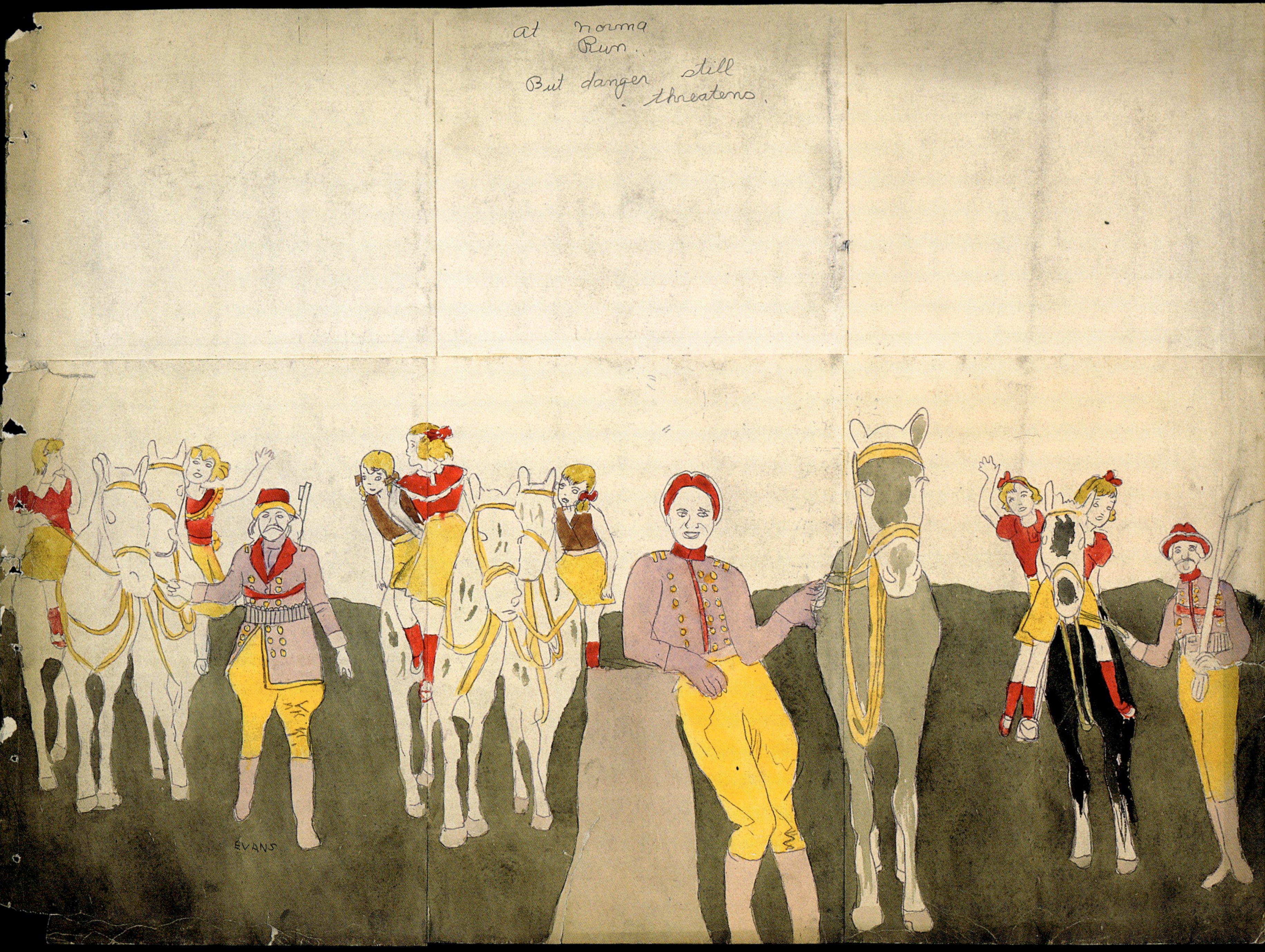

134 | *At Norma Run. But danger still threatens.*

Watercolor, pencil, and carbon tracing on pieced paper, 19 x 26 in.

Private collection, New York

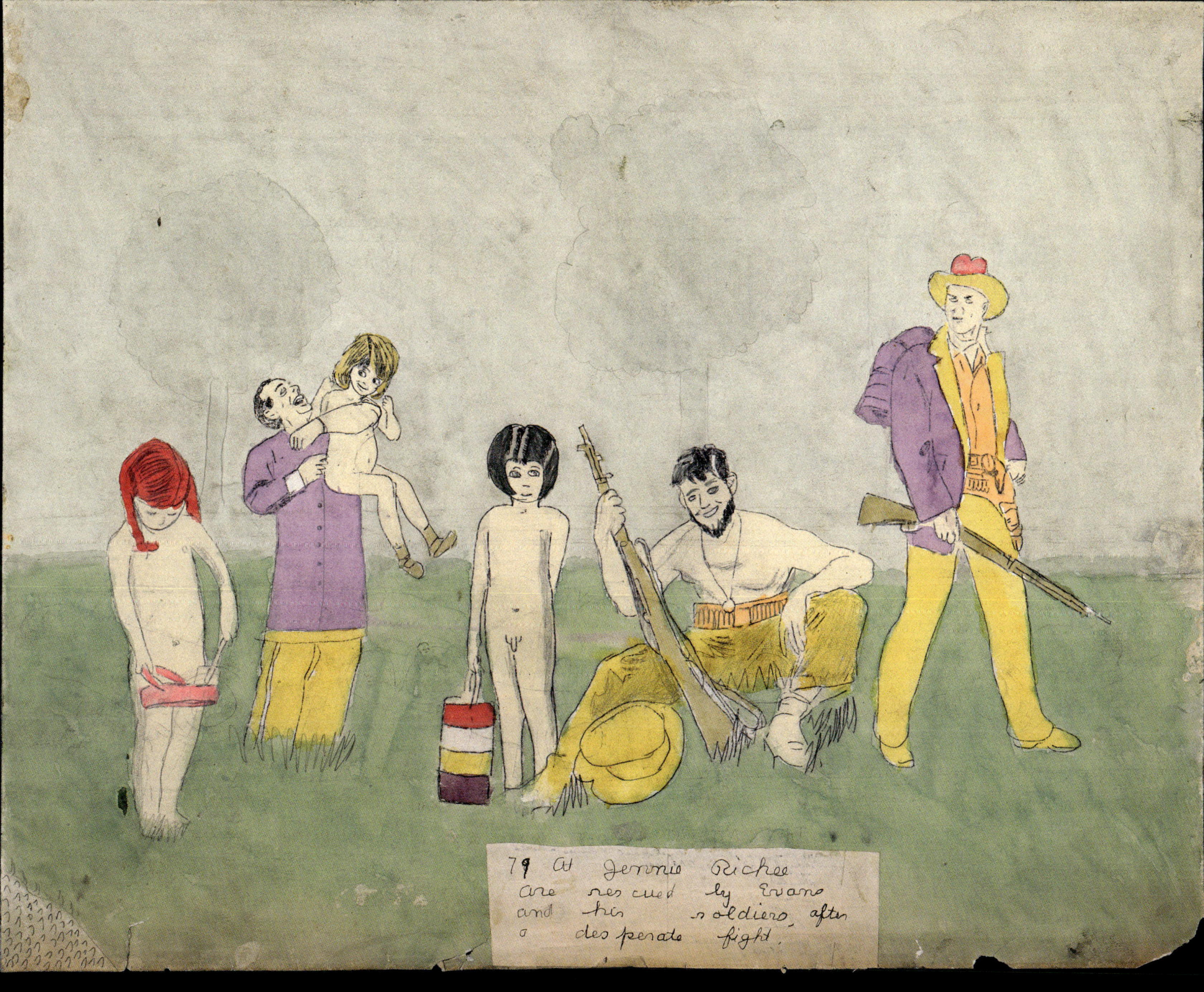

At Jennie Richee. Are rescued by Evans and his soldiers, after a desperate fight.
Watercolor, pencil, and carbon tracing on paper, 19 x 24 in.
Collection Kiyoko Lerner

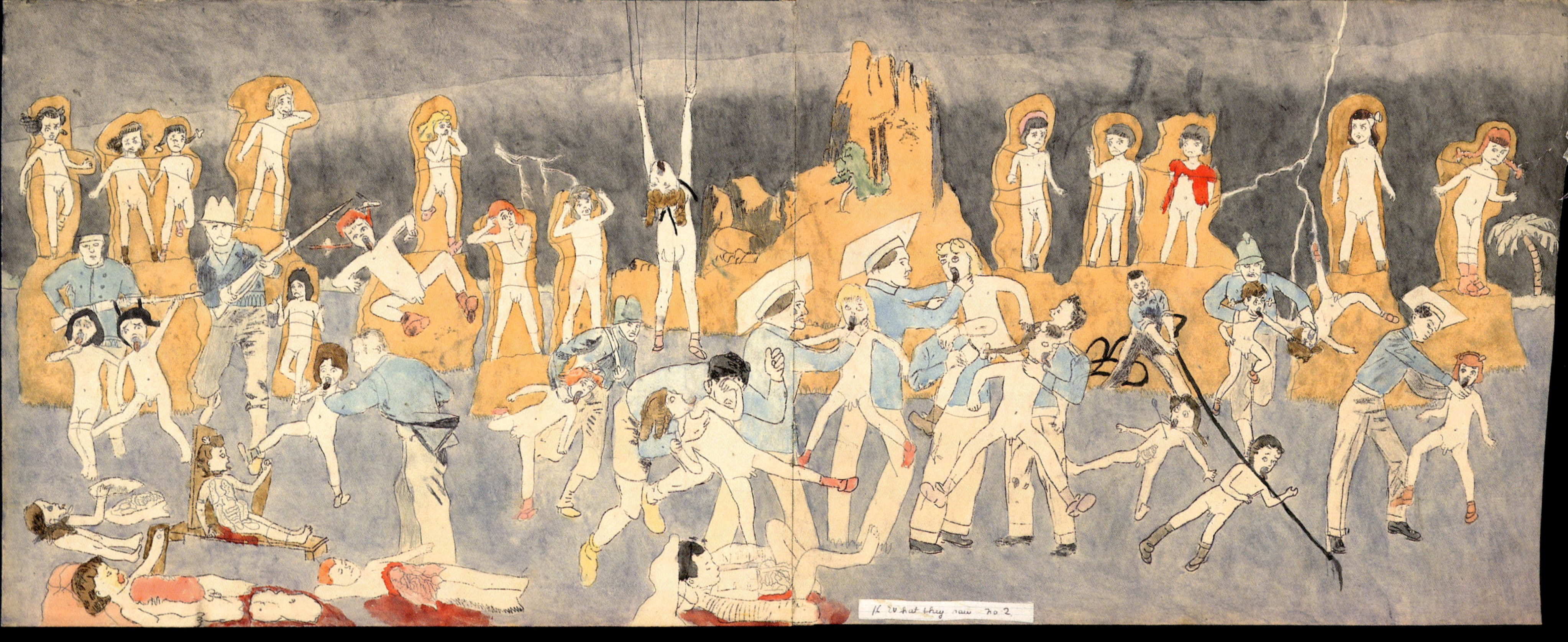

136 | *Phelantonburg. What they saw no. 2.*

Watercolor, pencil, and carbon tracing on pieced paper, 19 x 47 in.

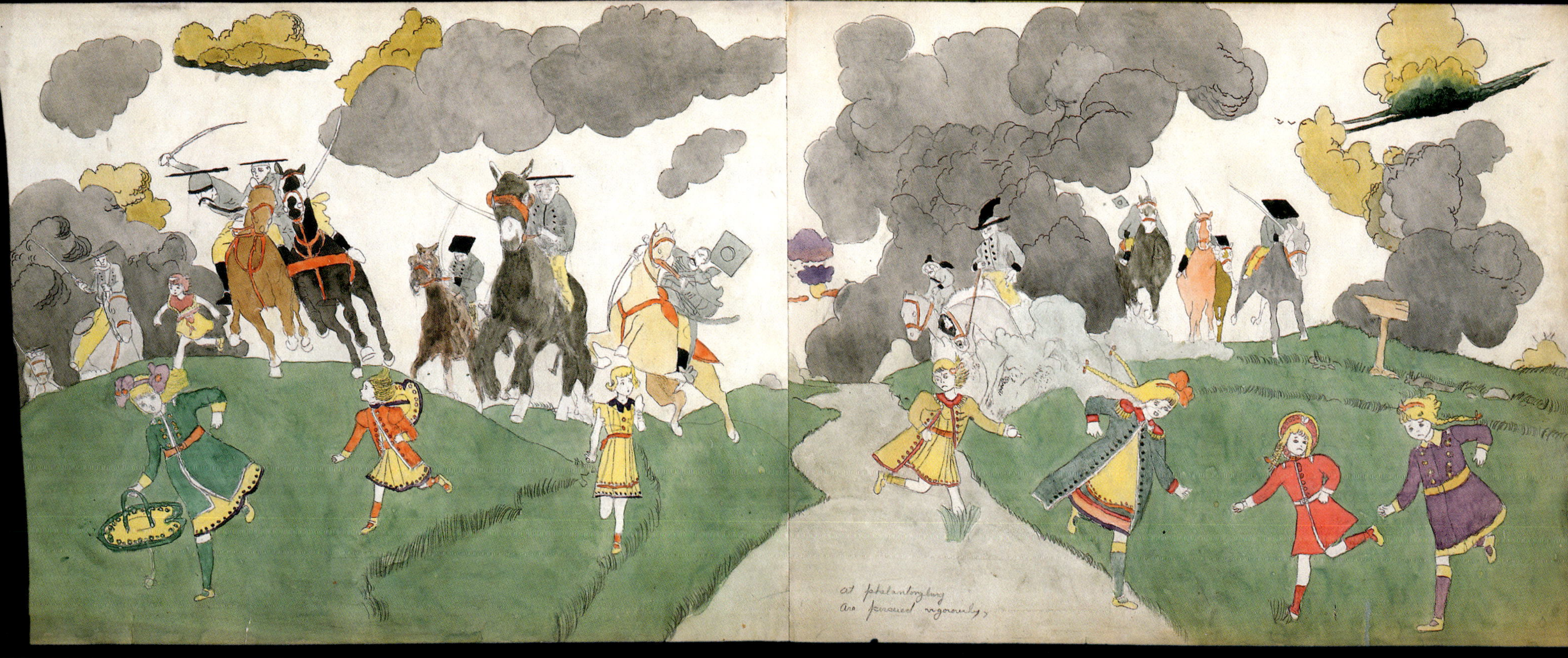

At Phelantonberg. Are pursued vigorously. 137

Watercolor, pencil, and carbon tracing on pieced paper, 19 x 47 in.

Private collection, Tokyo

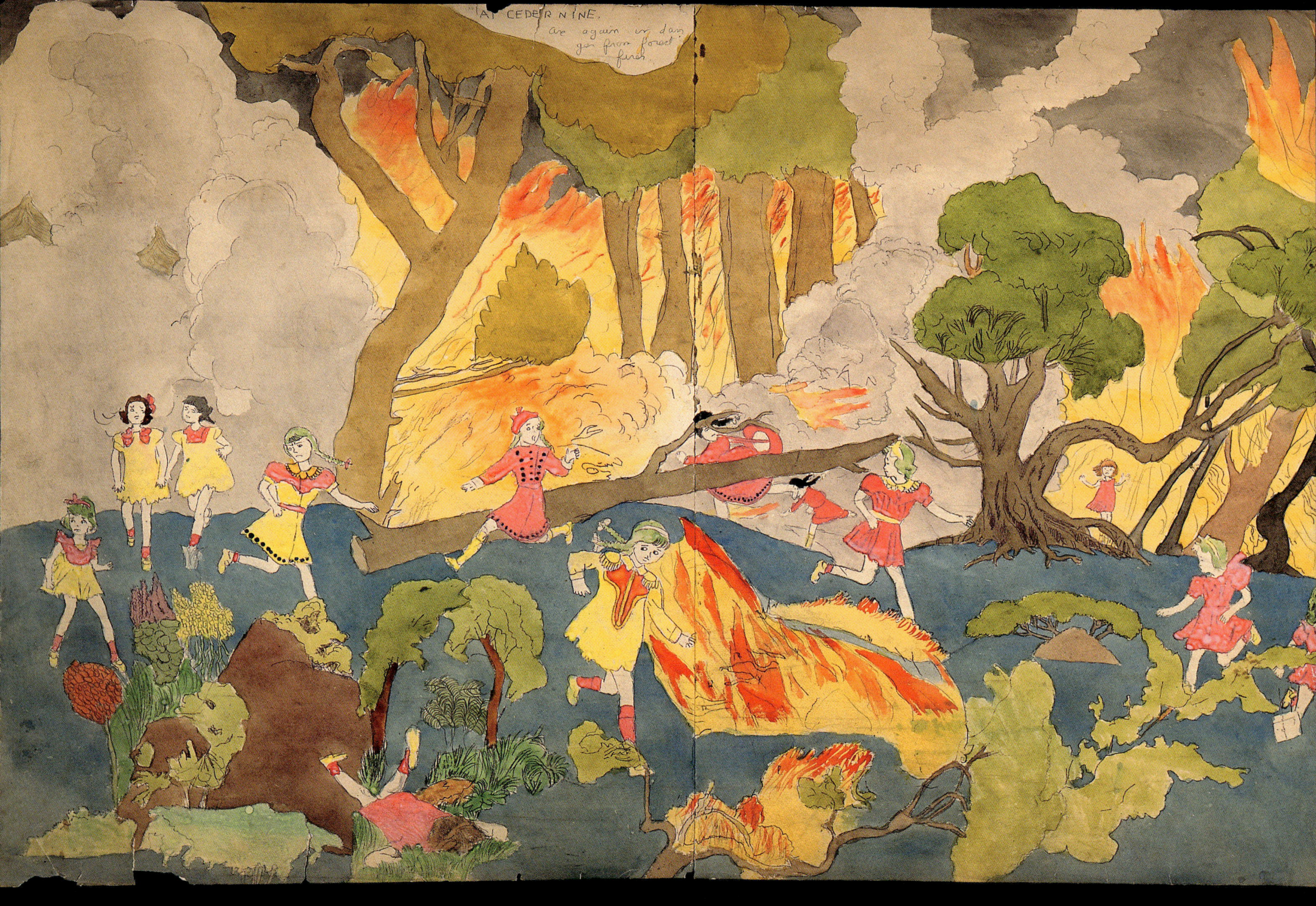

138 | Left: *At Cedernine. Are again in danger from forest fires.* Right: *At Jennie Turmer. Vivian girls being captured by*

Glandelinians they tie them to standing boards and leave one man to hang them. Hanging scene number thirty one.

Watercolor, pencil, and carbon tracing on pieced paper, 24 x 74 in. Collection Kiyoko Lerner

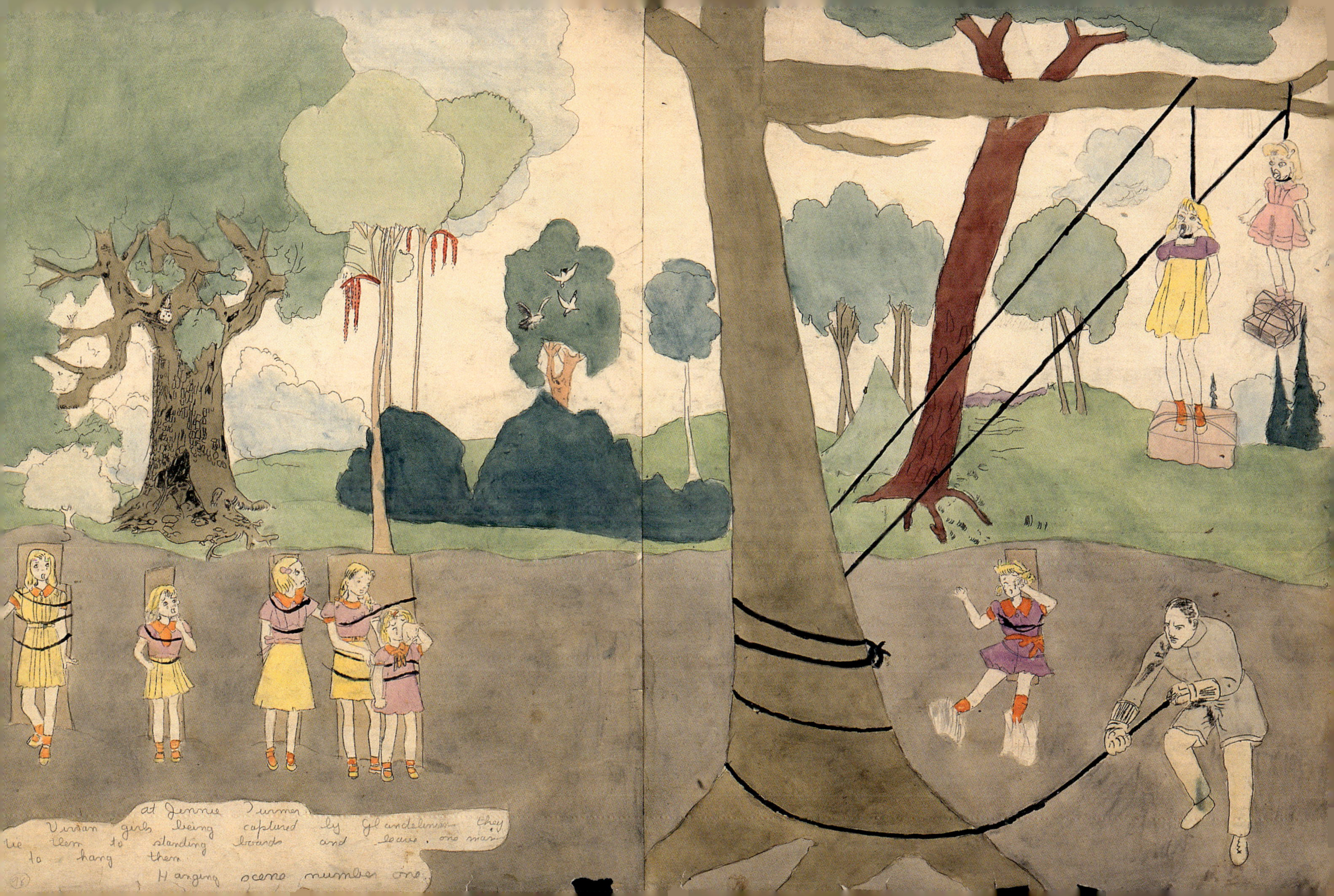

at Jennie Turmer
Vivian girls being captured by Glandelinians they
tie them to standing boards and leave one man
to hang them
Hanging scene number one.

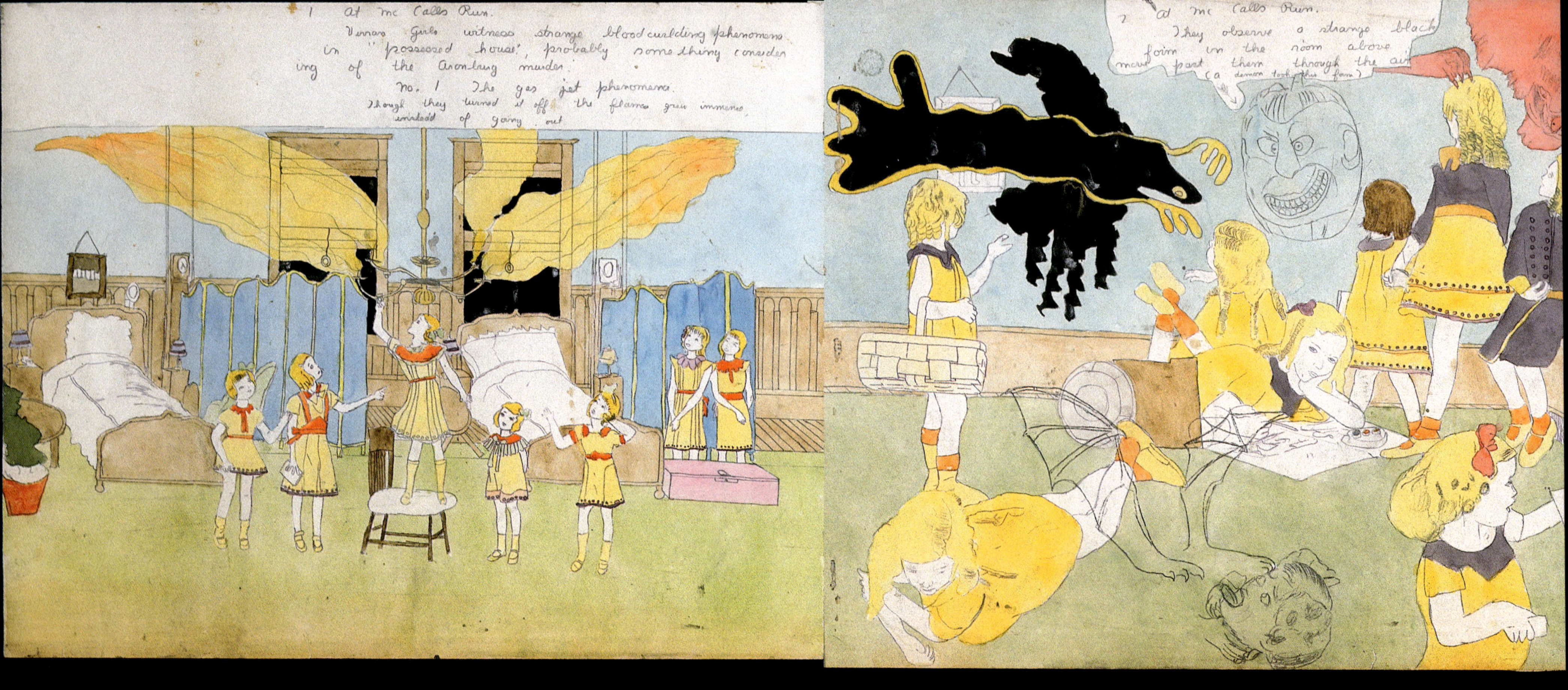

140   Far left: *At McCalls Run. Vivian Girls witness strange blood curdling phenomons . . .* Left center: *At McCalls Run. They observe a strange black form in the room above . . .* Right center: *At McCalls Run. Hands of fire.* Far right: *Imperiled by terrific explosions.*
Watercolor, pencil, and carbon tracing on pieced paper, 19 x 95 in. Collection Kiyoko Lerner

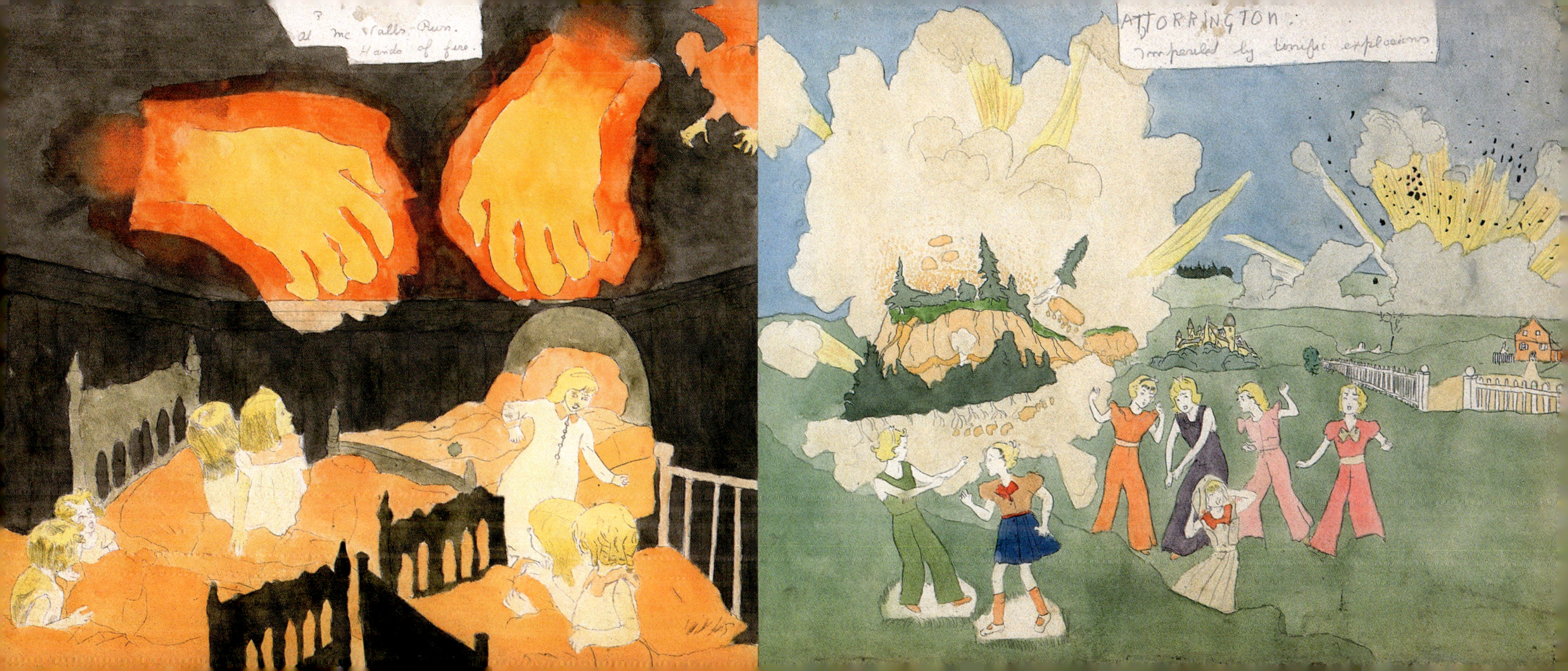
at me Walls-Run.
Hands of fire.
AT TORRINGTON:
Imperilled by terrific explosions

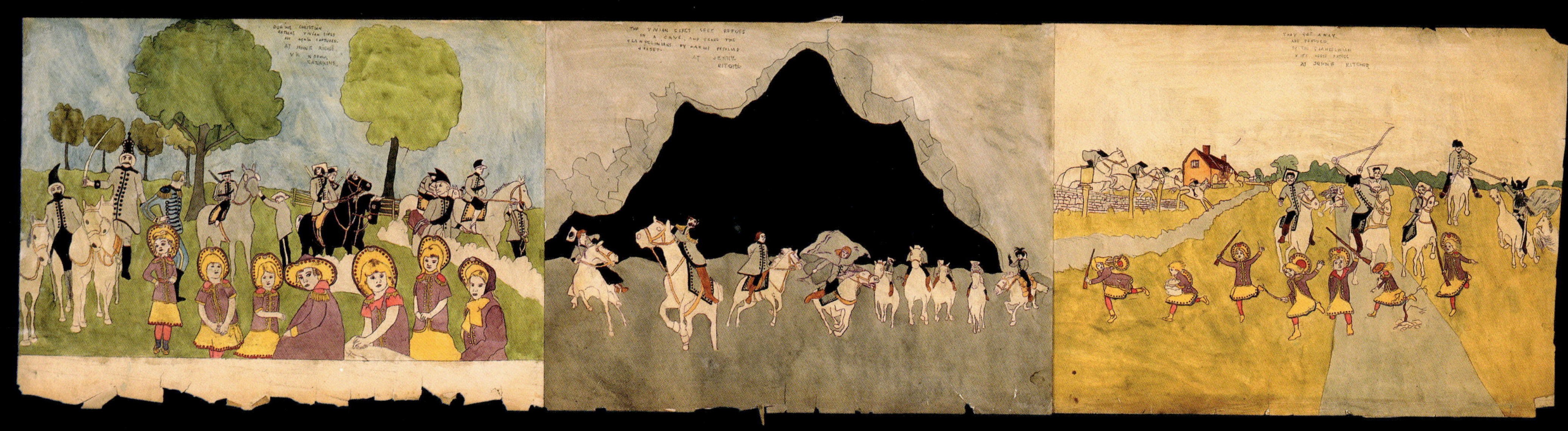

Left: *At Jennie Richee via Norma Catherine. During christian retreat Vivian girls are again captured.* Center: *At Jennie Richee.*
The Vivian girls seek out refuge in a cave, and scare the Glandelinians by making peculiar noises. Right: *At Jennie Richee.*
They get away, are pursued. Watercolor, pencil, and carbon tracing on pieced paper, 22 x 89 in. Private collection.

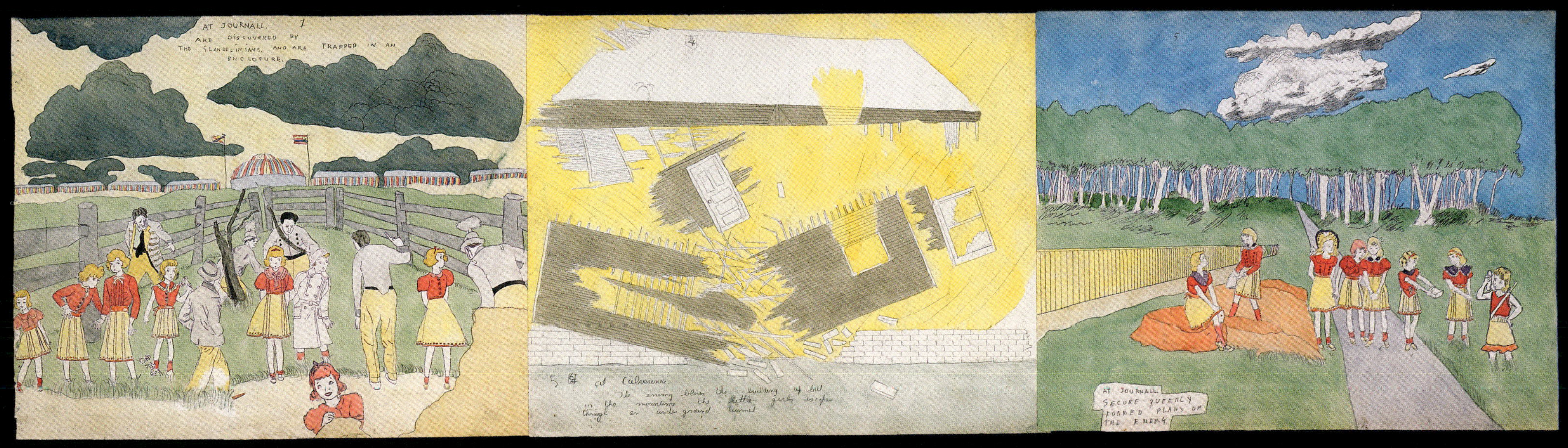

Left: *At Journall. Are discovered by Glandelinians and are trapped in an enclosure.* Center: *At Calverinia. The enemy blows the building up but in the meantime the little girls escapes through an underground tunnel.* Right: *At Journall. Secure queerly formed plans of the enemy.* Watercolor, pencil, and carbon tracing on pieced paper, 19 x 70 in. Irish Museum of Modern Art, Dublin

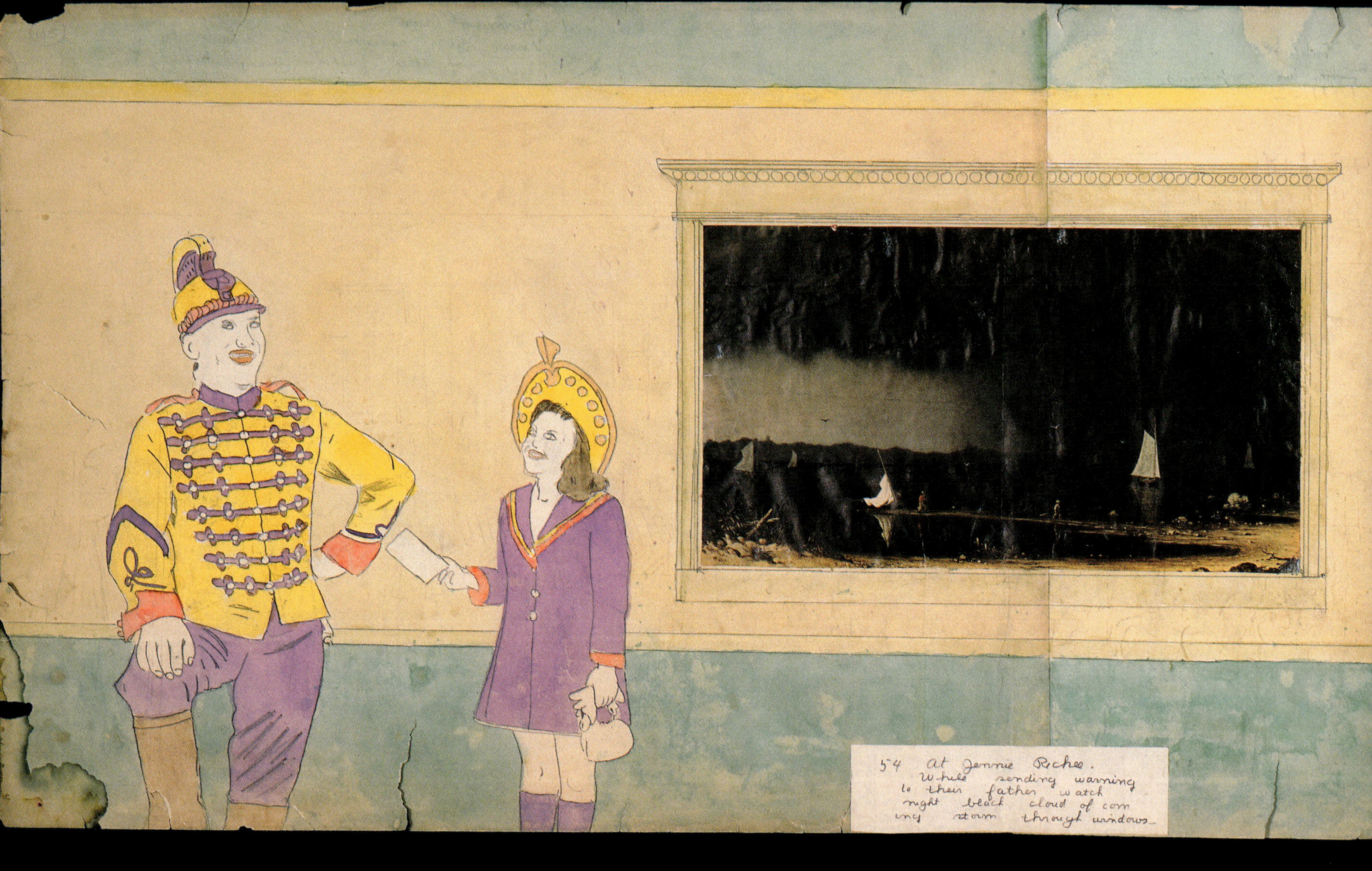

At Jennie Richee. While sending warning to their father watch night black cloud of coming storm through windows.

Watercolor, pencil, carbon tracing, and collage on pieced paper, 19 x 70 in. Private collection, New York

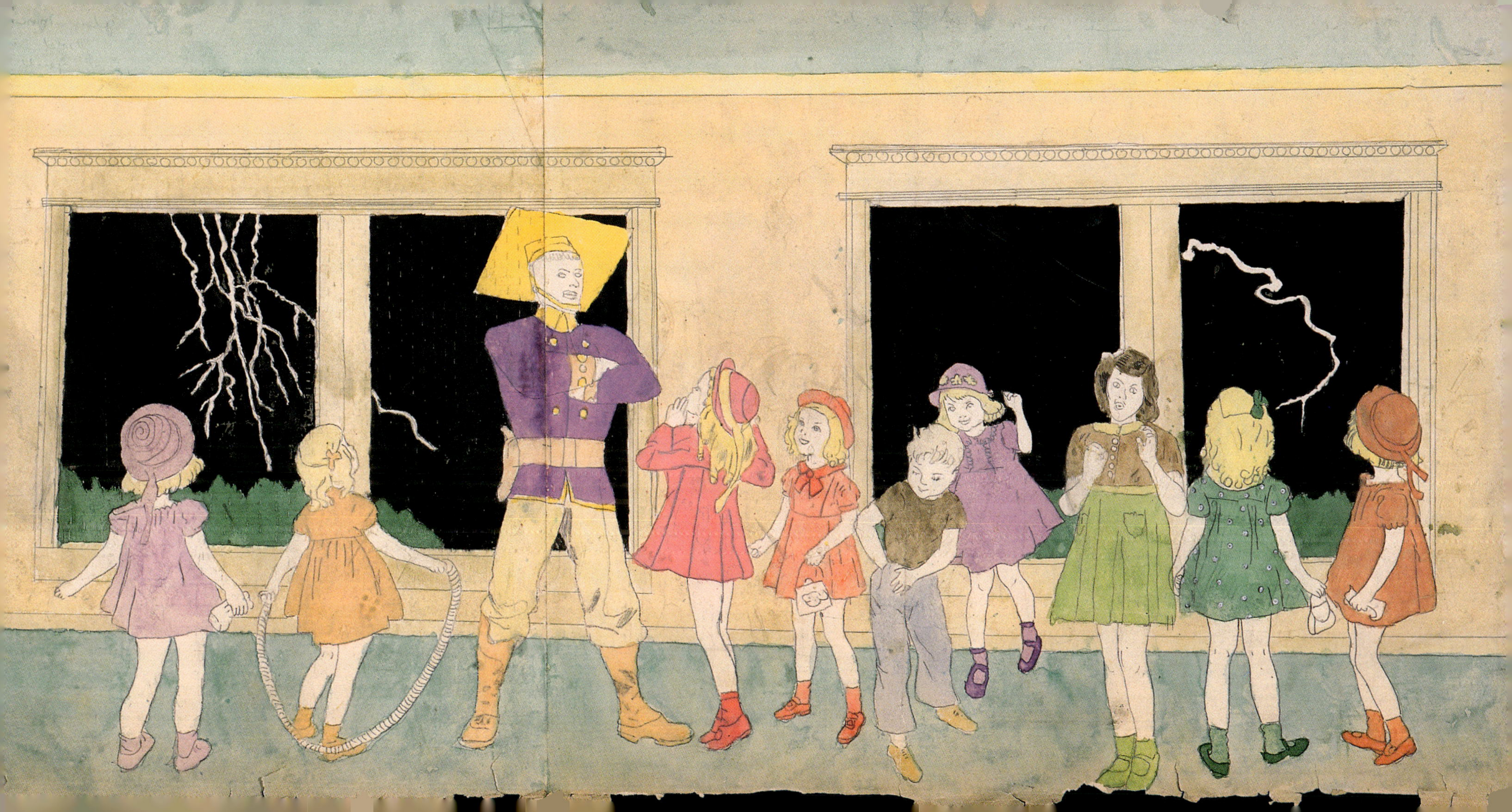

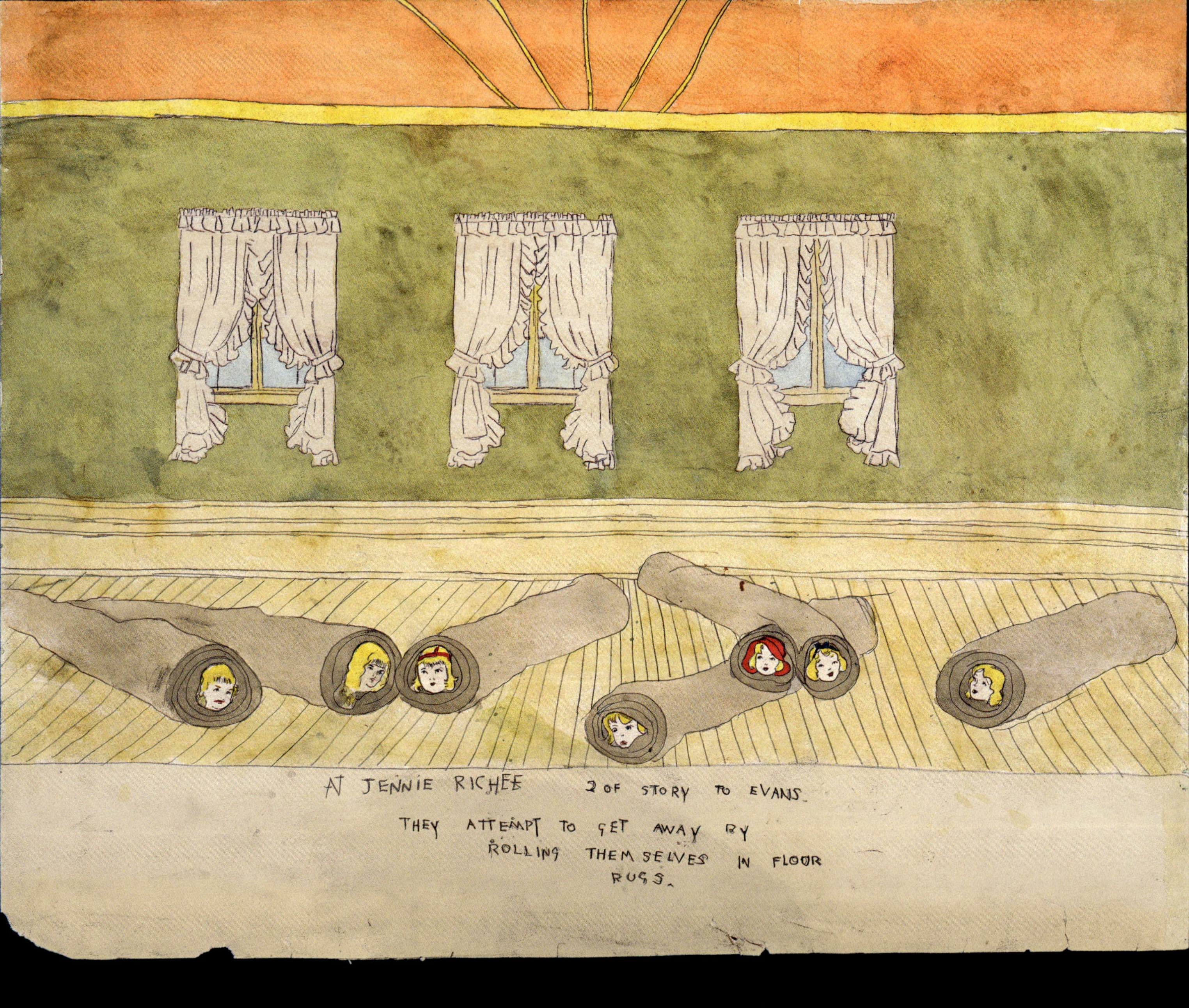

146 | *At Jennie Richee. 2 of Story to Evans. They attempt to get away by rolling themselves in floor rugs.*

Watercolor, pencil, and carbon tracing on paper, 19 x 24 in. Collection Kiyoko Lerner

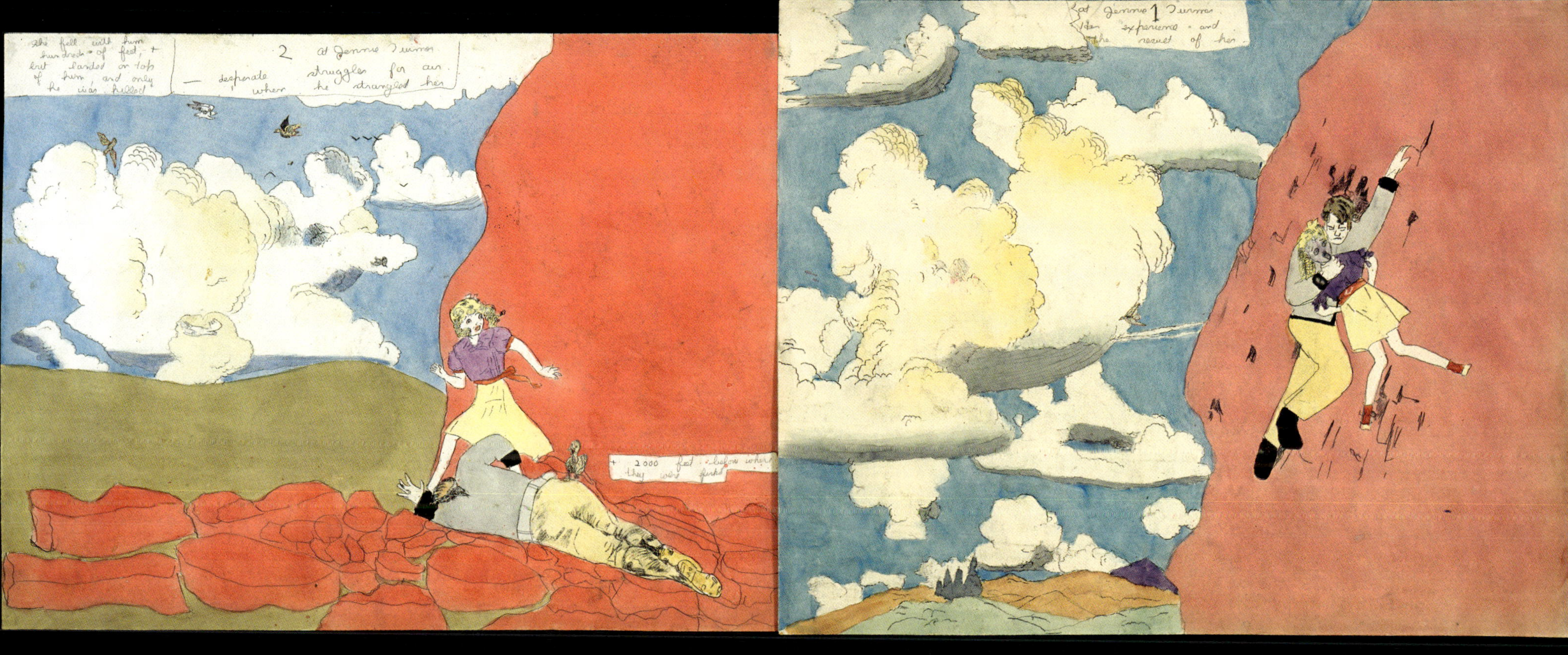

Left: *At Jennie Turmer. Desperate struggles for air when he strangled her. She fell with him hundreds of feet but landed on top on him and only he was killed. 2000 feet below where they were first. Right: At Jennie Turmer. His Experience and the result of her.*

Watercolor, pencil, and carbon tracing on pieced paper, approx. 19 x 49 in. Collection Robert M. Greenberg

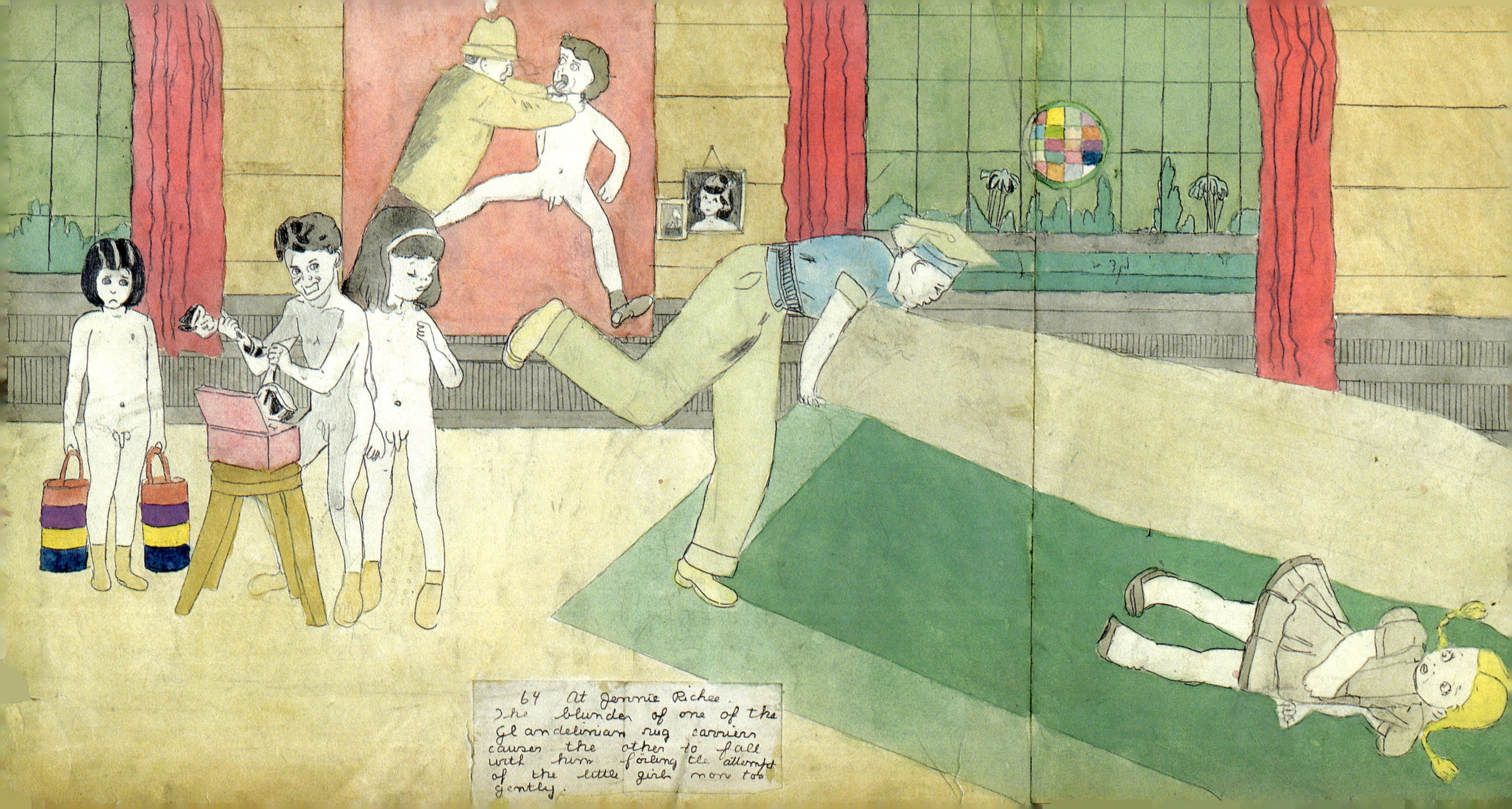

64   At Jennie Richee.
The blunder of one of the
Glandelinian rug carriers
causes the other to fall
with him foiling the attempt
of the little girls more too
gently.

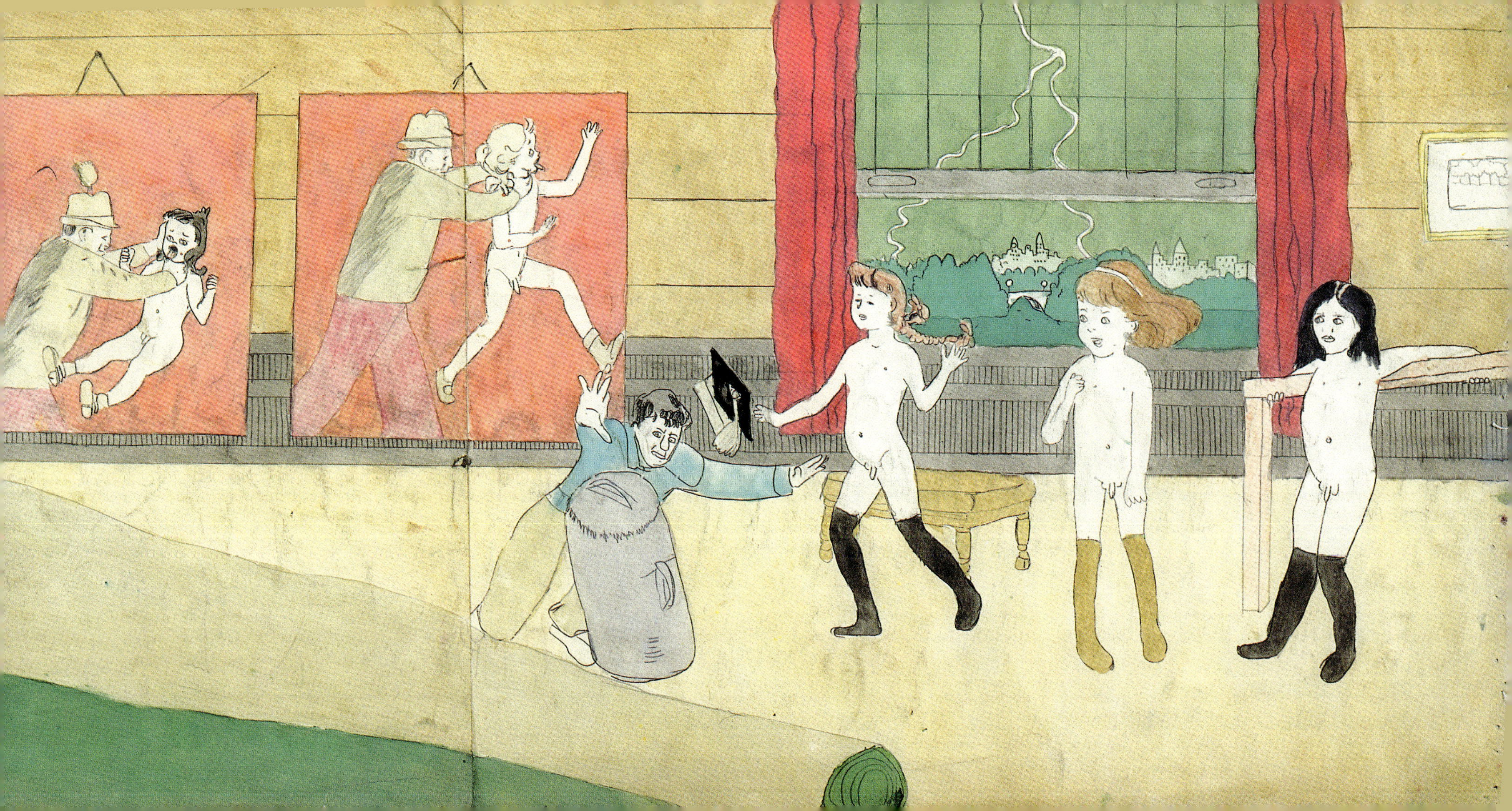

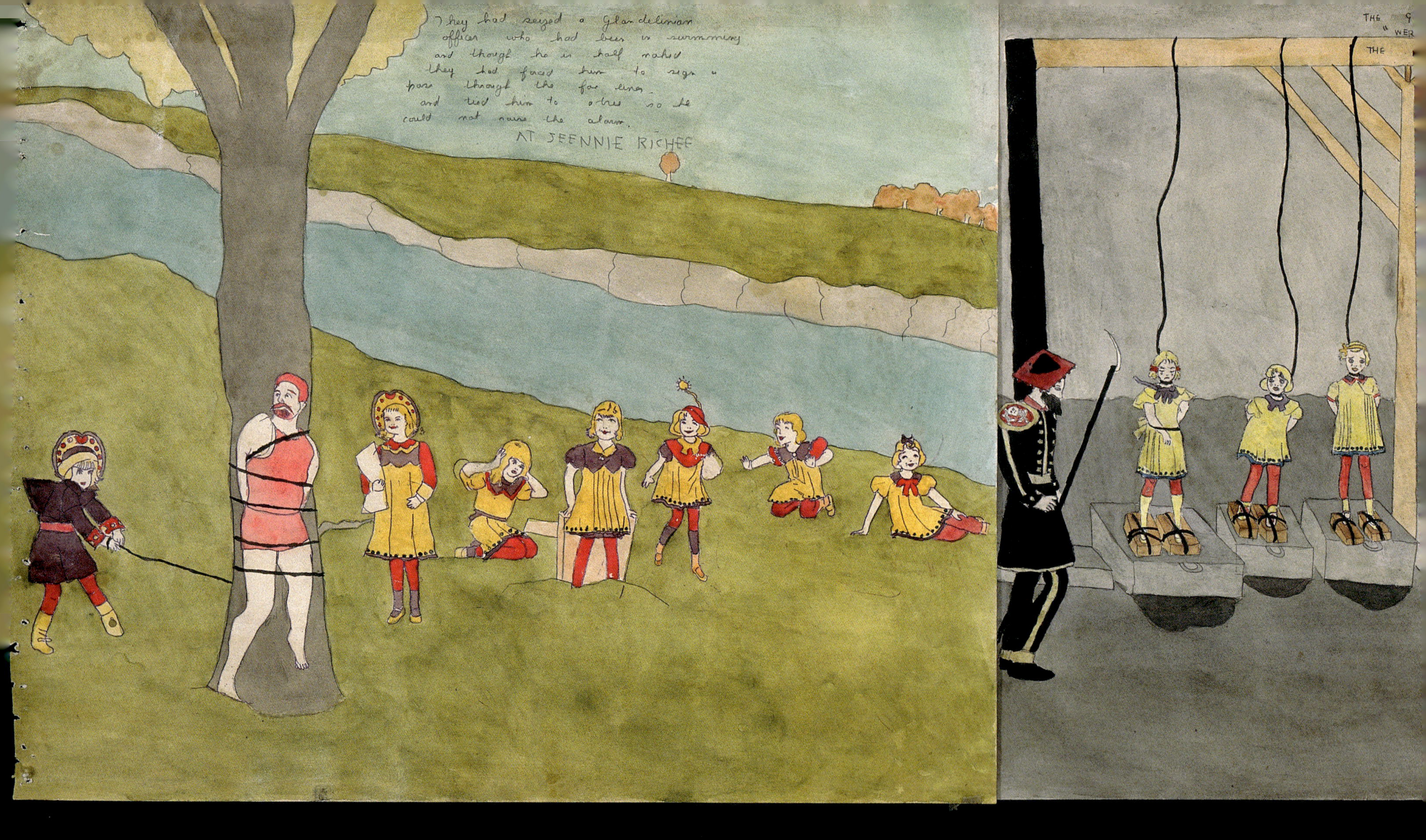

Left: *At Jennie Richee. Seize Glandelinian officer who has been in swimming and though he is half naked they had forced him to guide them through the foe lines and tied him to other so he could not sound the alarm.* Center: *The Glandelinians "were" about to hang the brave little girls. See how they were "hanged" in the next picture.* Right: *They attempt to hide in huge fiddle cases but are discovered because the doors were of glass.* Watercolor, pencil, and carbon tracing on pieced paper, 19 x 70 in. Collection Kiyoko Lerner.

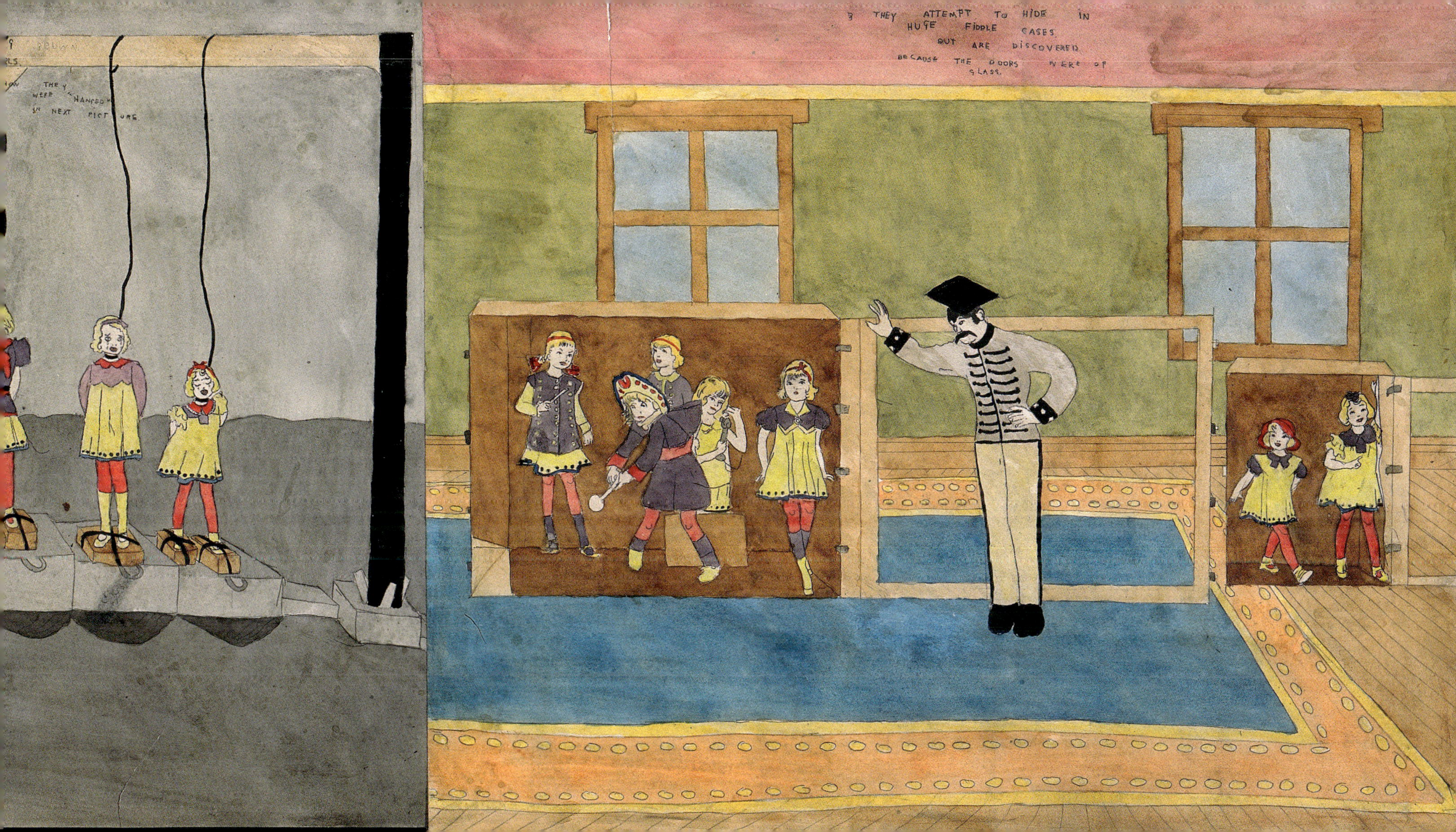
THEY WERE "HANGED" IN NEXT PICTURE
3 THEY ATTEMPT TO HIDE IN HUGE FIDDLE CASES. BUT ARE DISCOVERED. BECAUSE THE DOORS WERE OF GLASS.

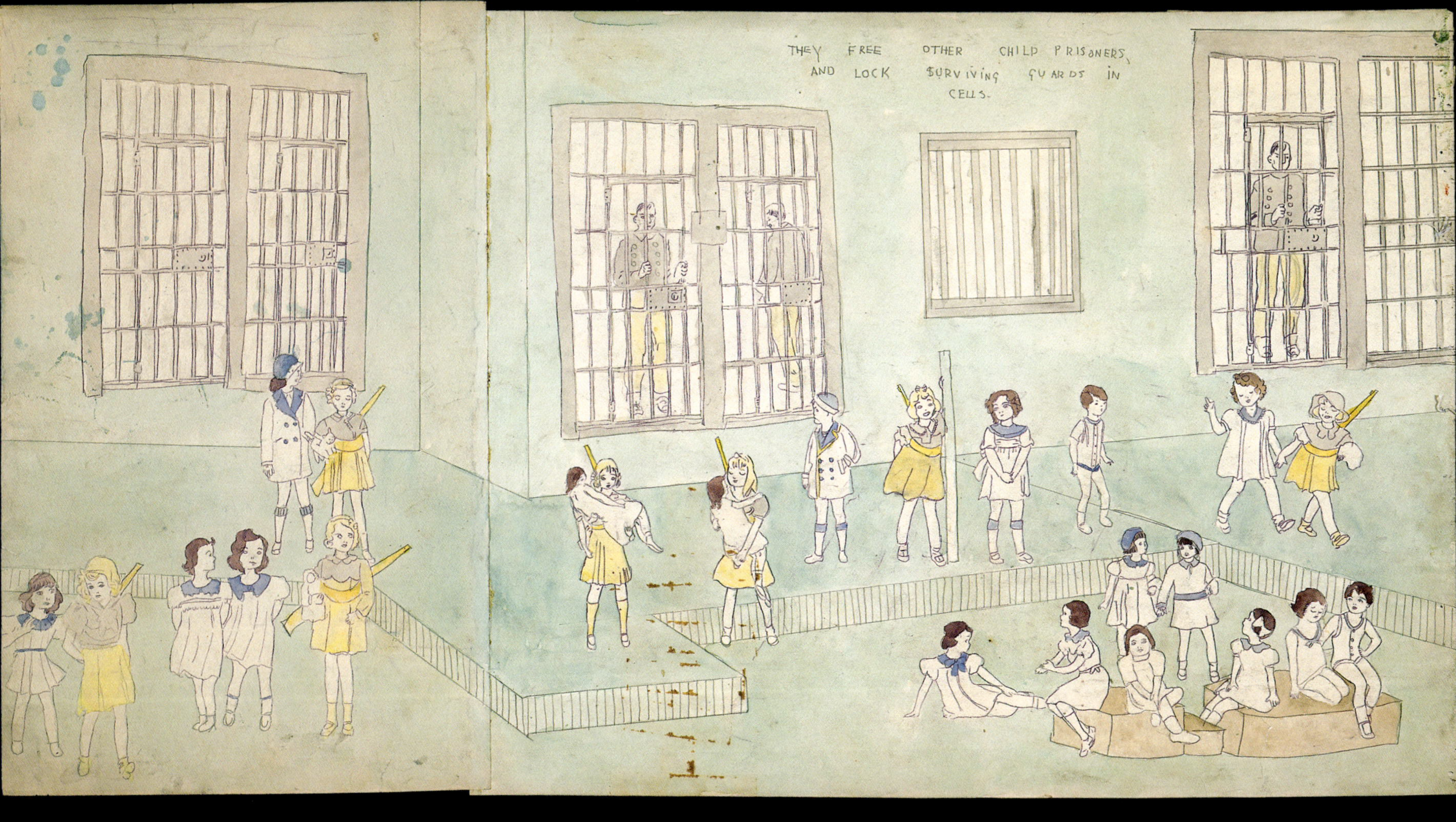

152 | *They free other child prisoners and lock surviving guards in cells.*

Watercolor, pencil, and carbon tracing on pieced paper, 19 x 36 in.

Private collection

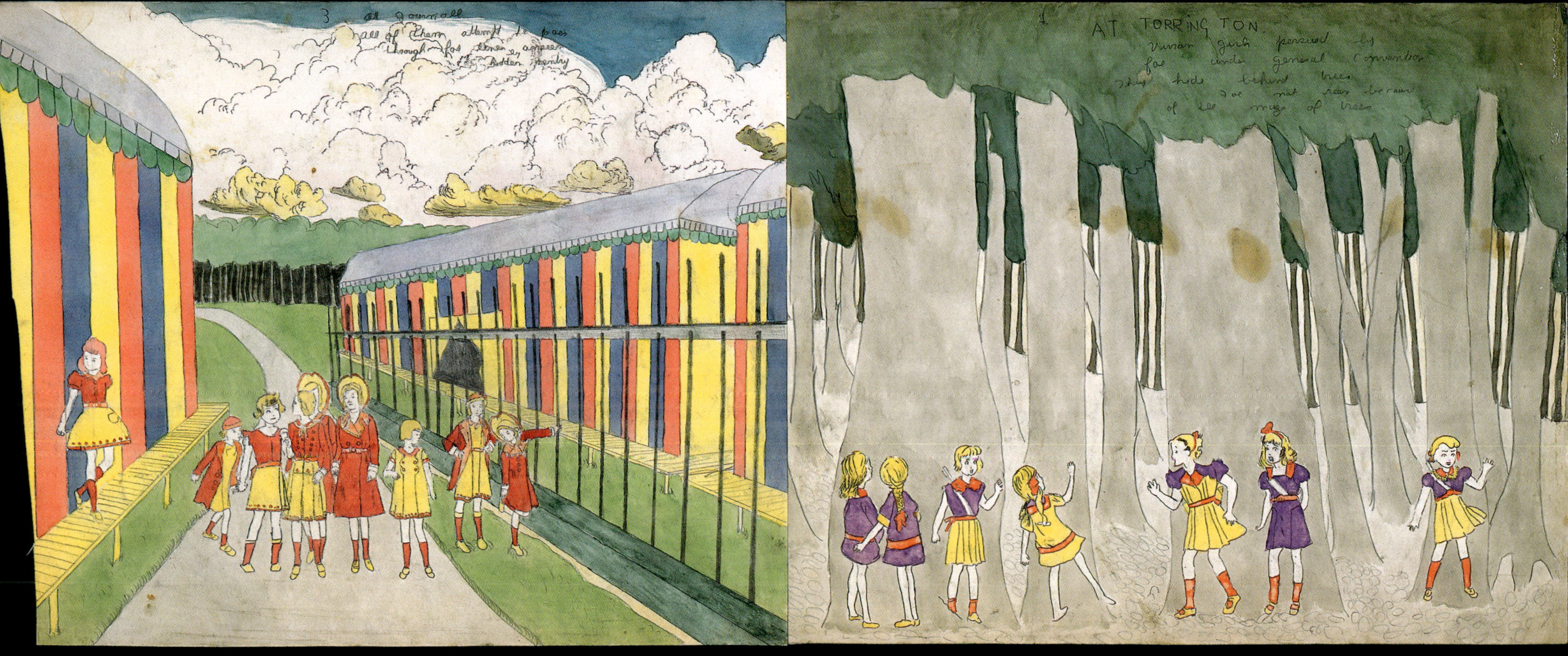

Left: *At Journall. All of them attempt to pass through foe lines unseen by hidden sentry. Right: At Torrington.* Vivian girls pursued by foe under general convention they hide behind trees foe not seen because of the maze of trees. Watercolor, pencil, and carbon tracing on pieced paper, 19 x 46 in. Private collection

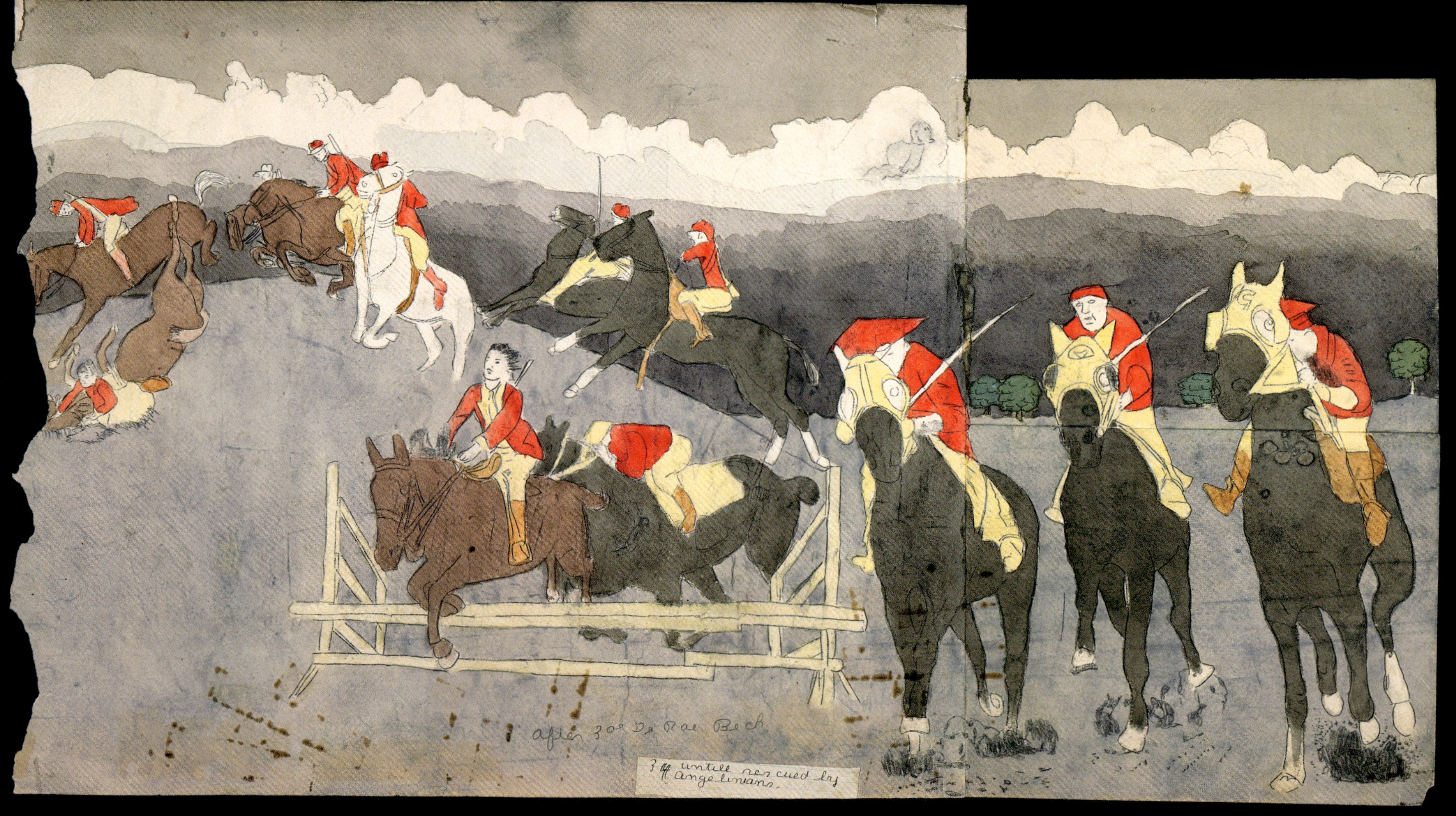

154 | *After Zoe Du Rae Bech. Until rescued by Angelenians.*

Watercolor, pencil, and carbon tracing on pieced paper, 19 x 34 ½.

Private collection, Belgium

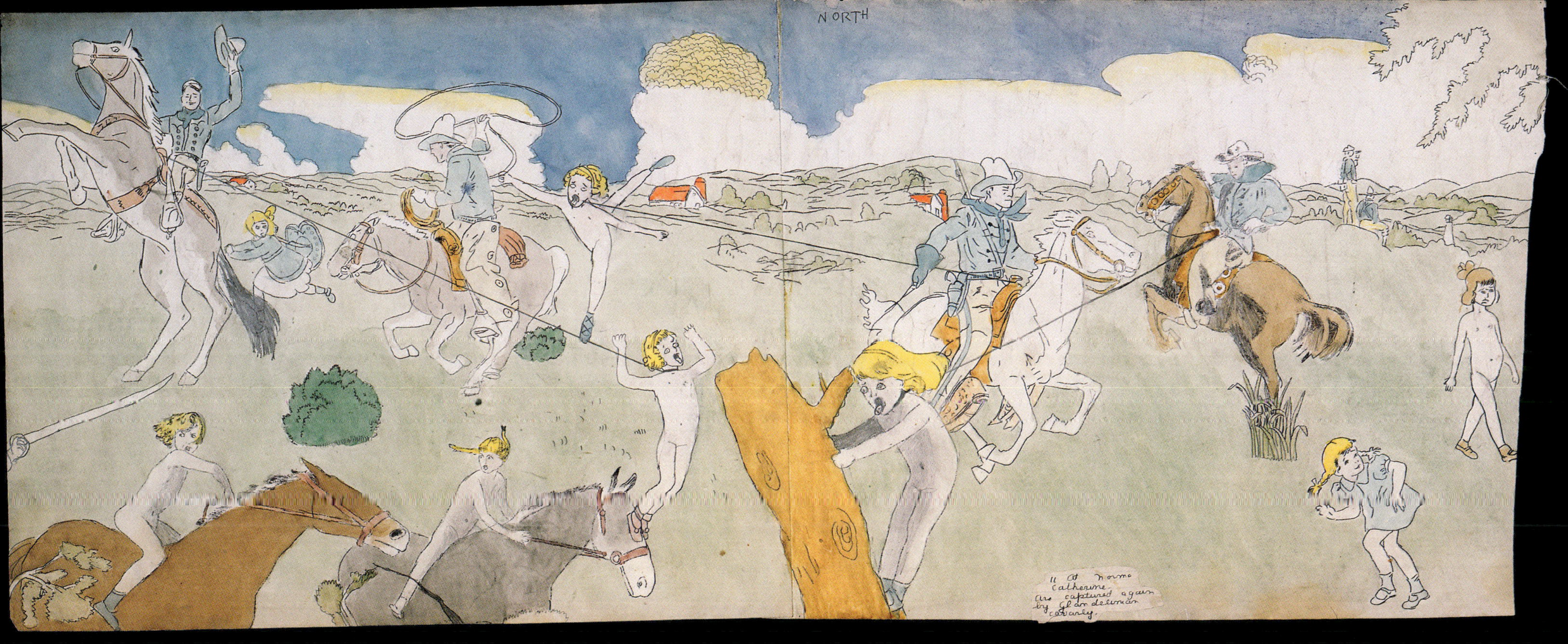

At Norma Catherine. Are captured again by Glandelinian cavalry. 155
Watercolor, pencil, and carbon tracing on pieced paper, 19 x 46.
Private collection

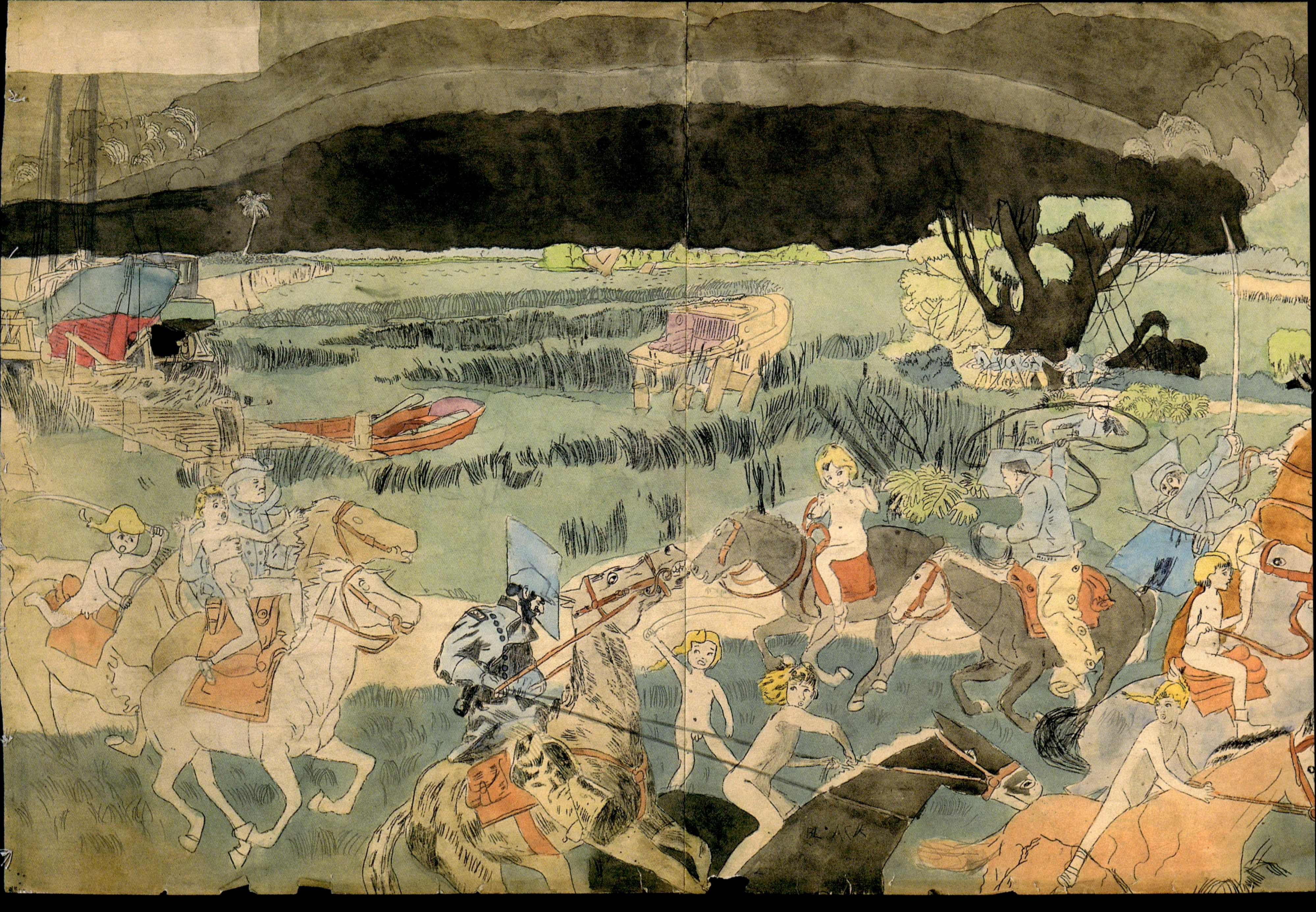

156 | Untitled (battle scene with black storm).

Watercolor, pencil, and carbon tracing on pieced paper, 24 x 74 in.

Collection Kiyoko Lerner

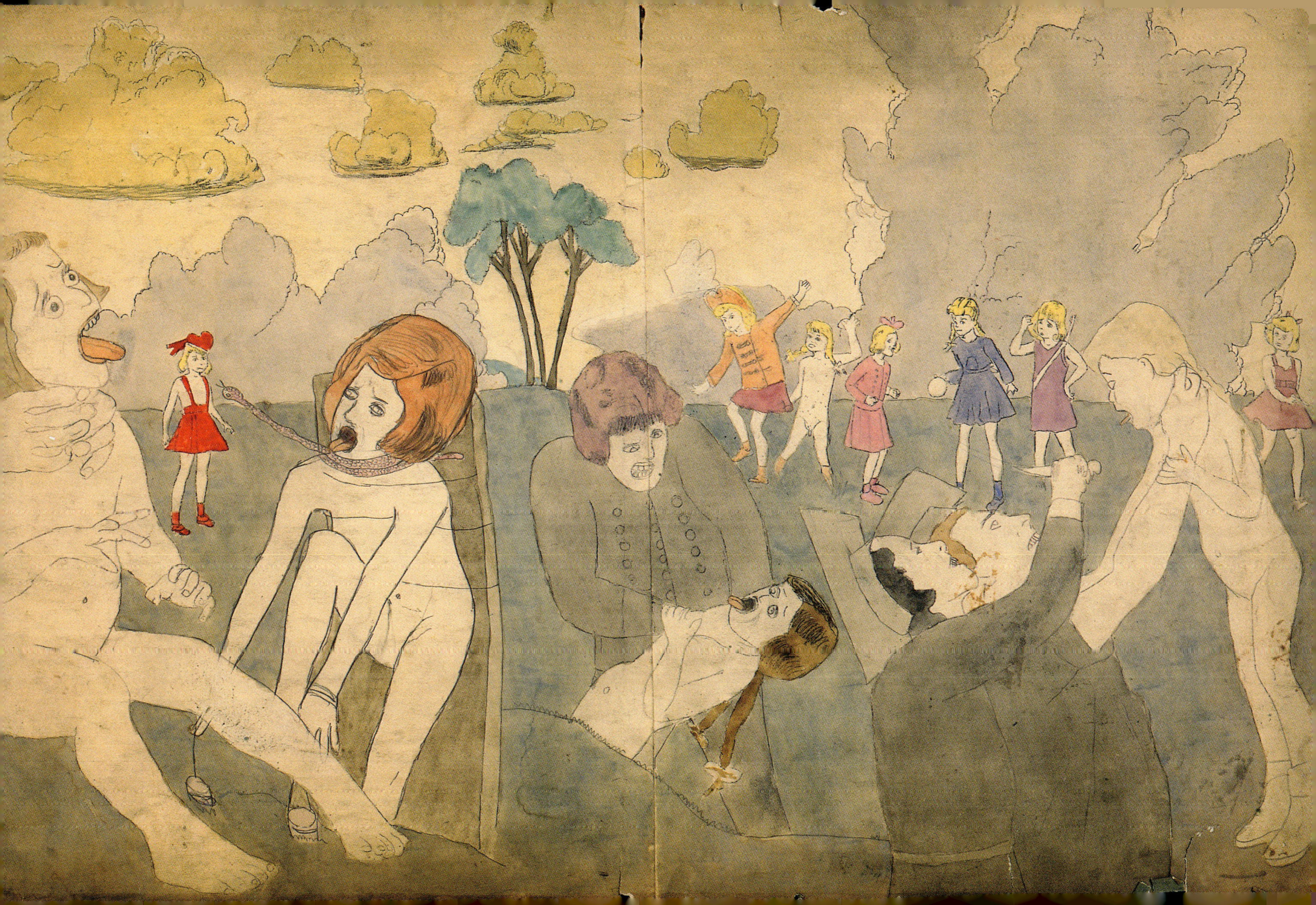

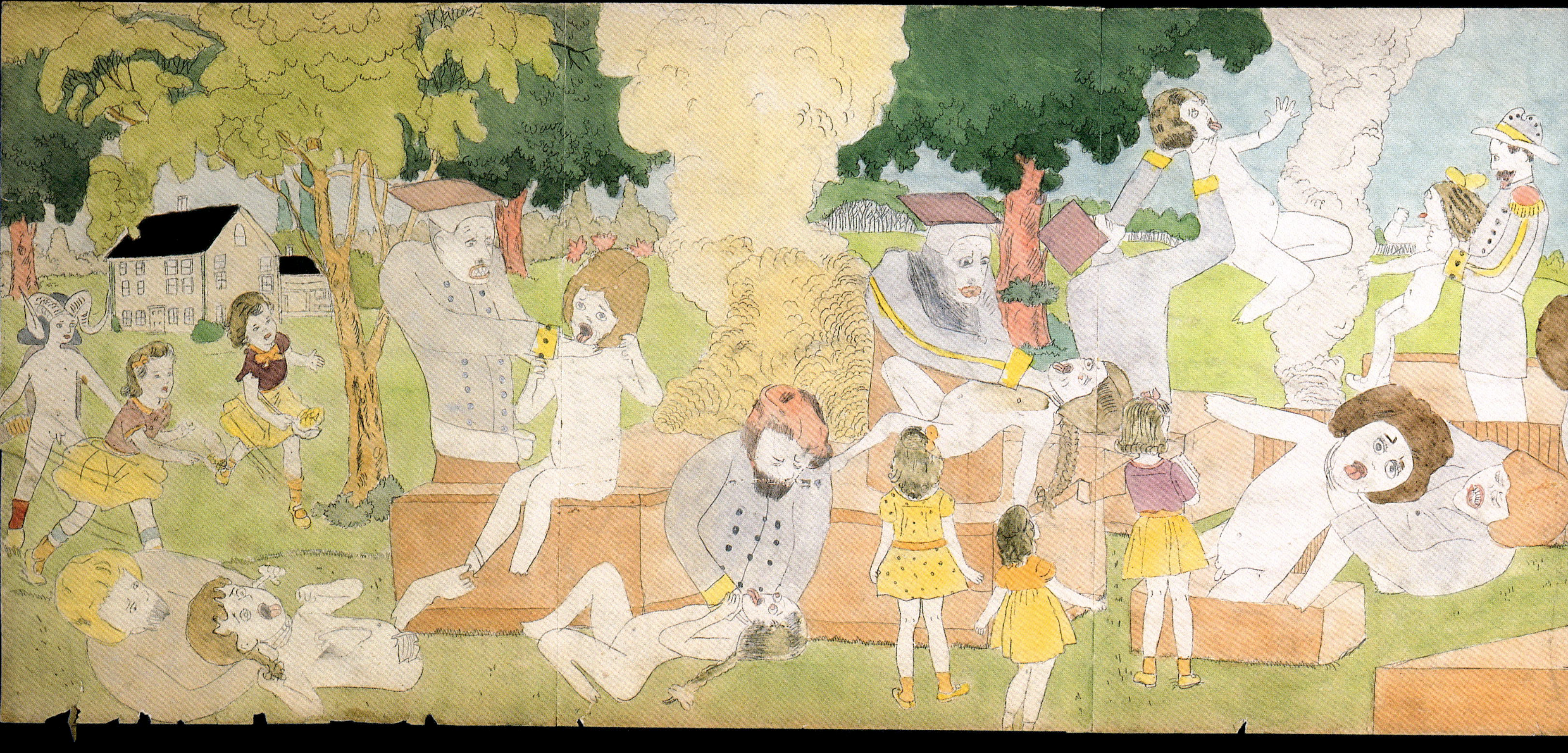

158 | Untitled (statues strangling children).

Watercolor, pencil, and carbon tracing on pieced paper, 23 x 110 in.

Collection Kiyoko Lerner

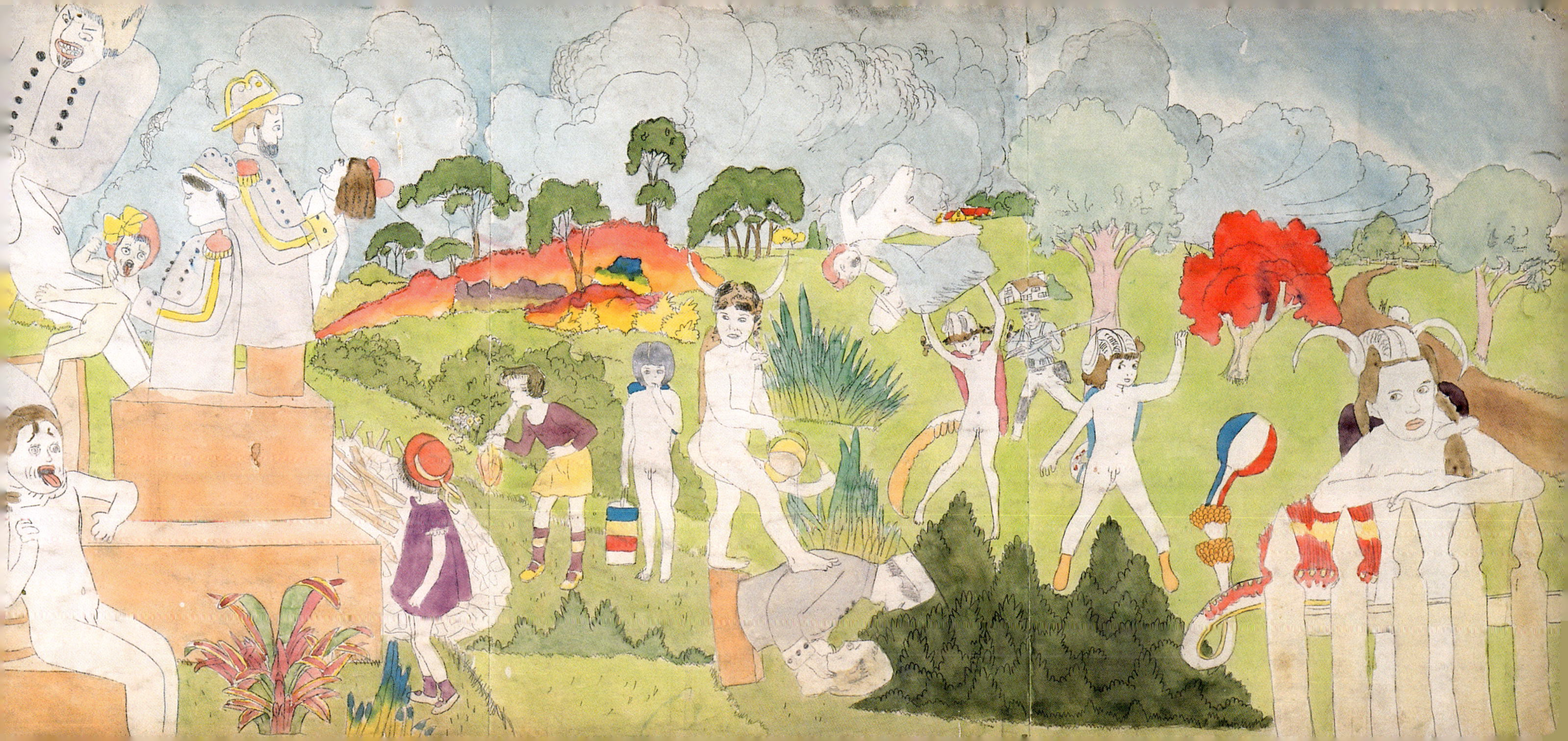

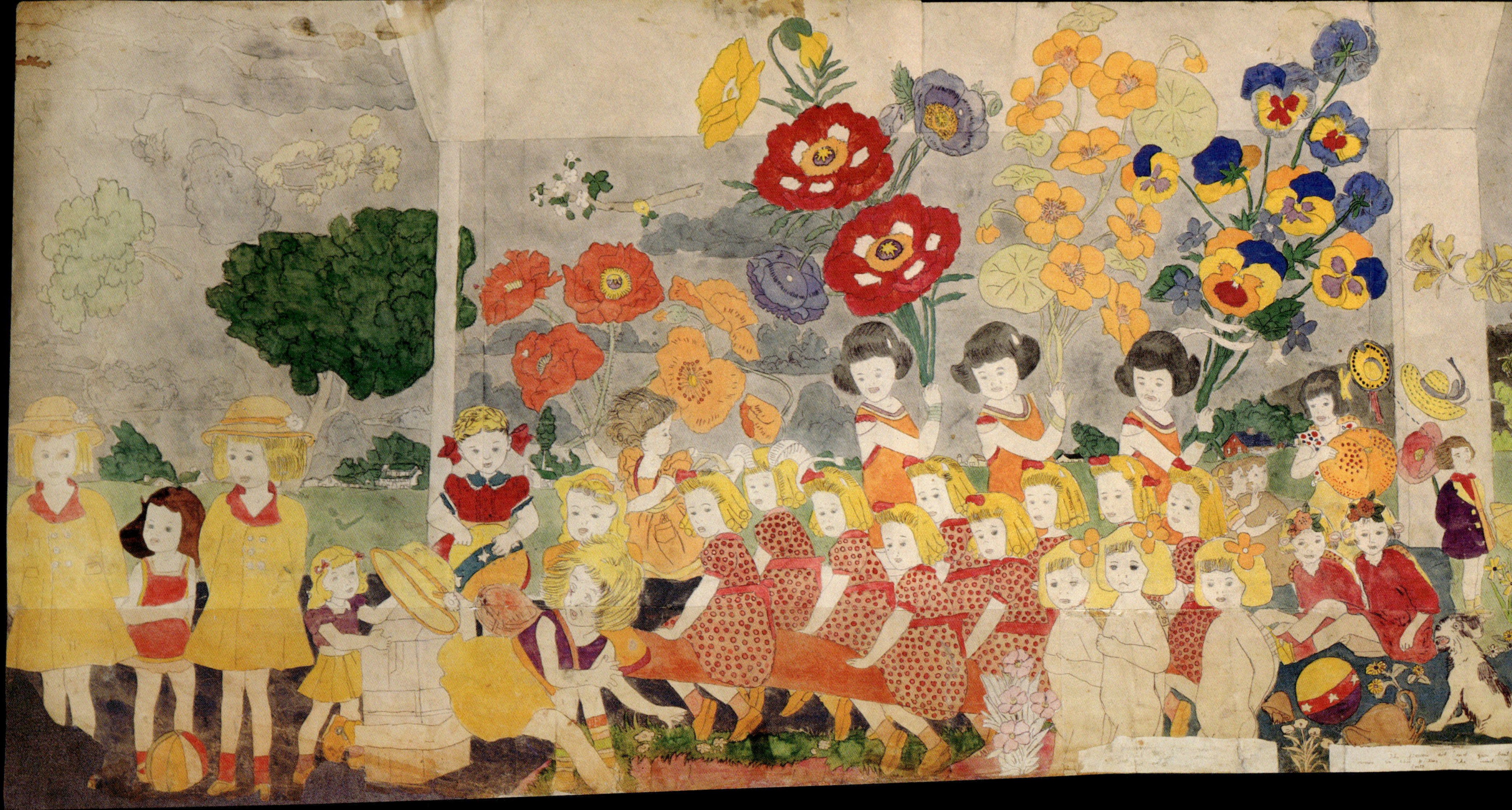

[Storm] brewing. This is not a strawberry the little girl is carrying. It comes from a paradise tree . . .

Watercolor, pencil, carbon tracing, and collage on pieced paper, 30 x 125 in.

Collection de l'art brut, Lausanne

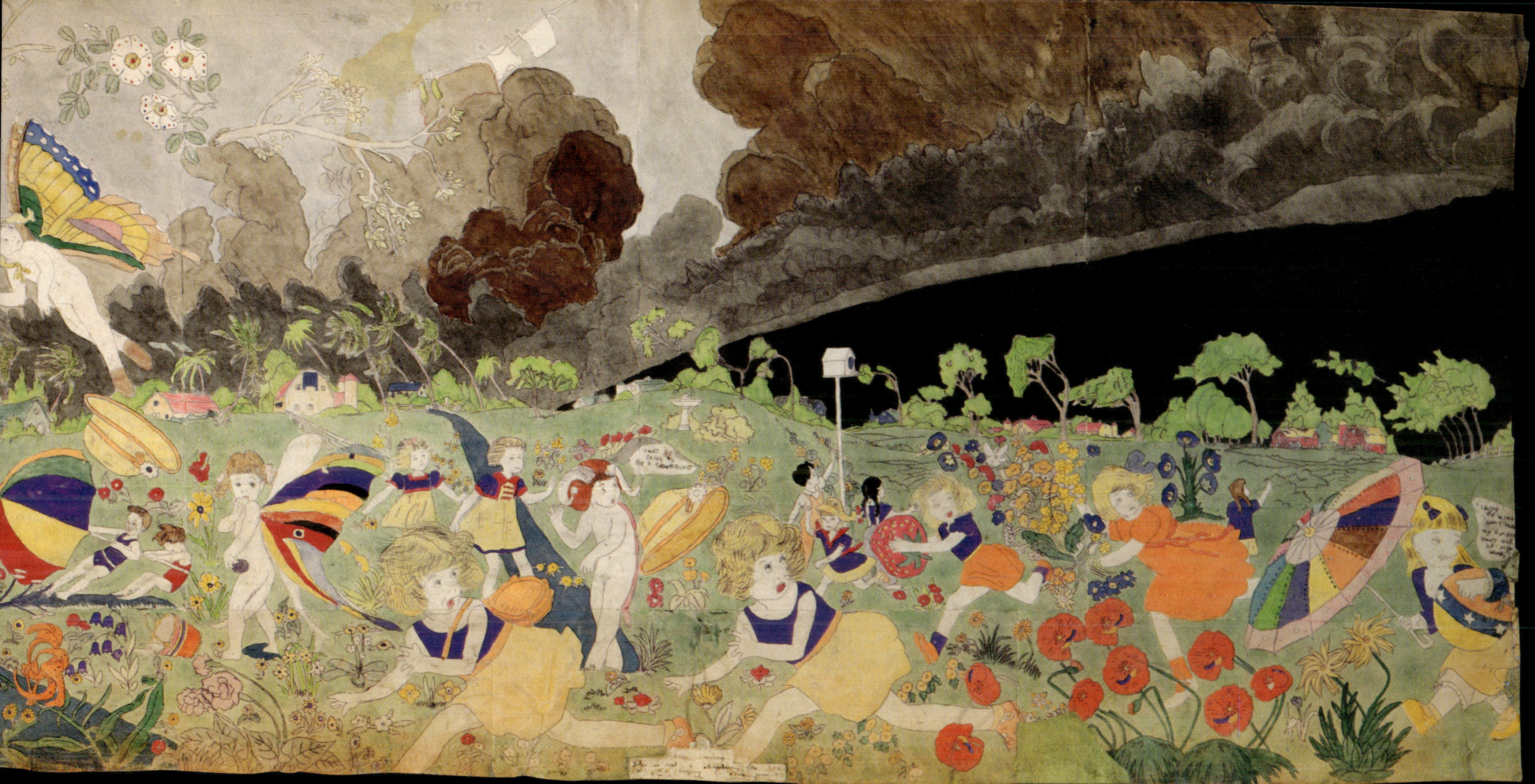
WEST
THAT IS GOING TO BE A CLOUDBURST

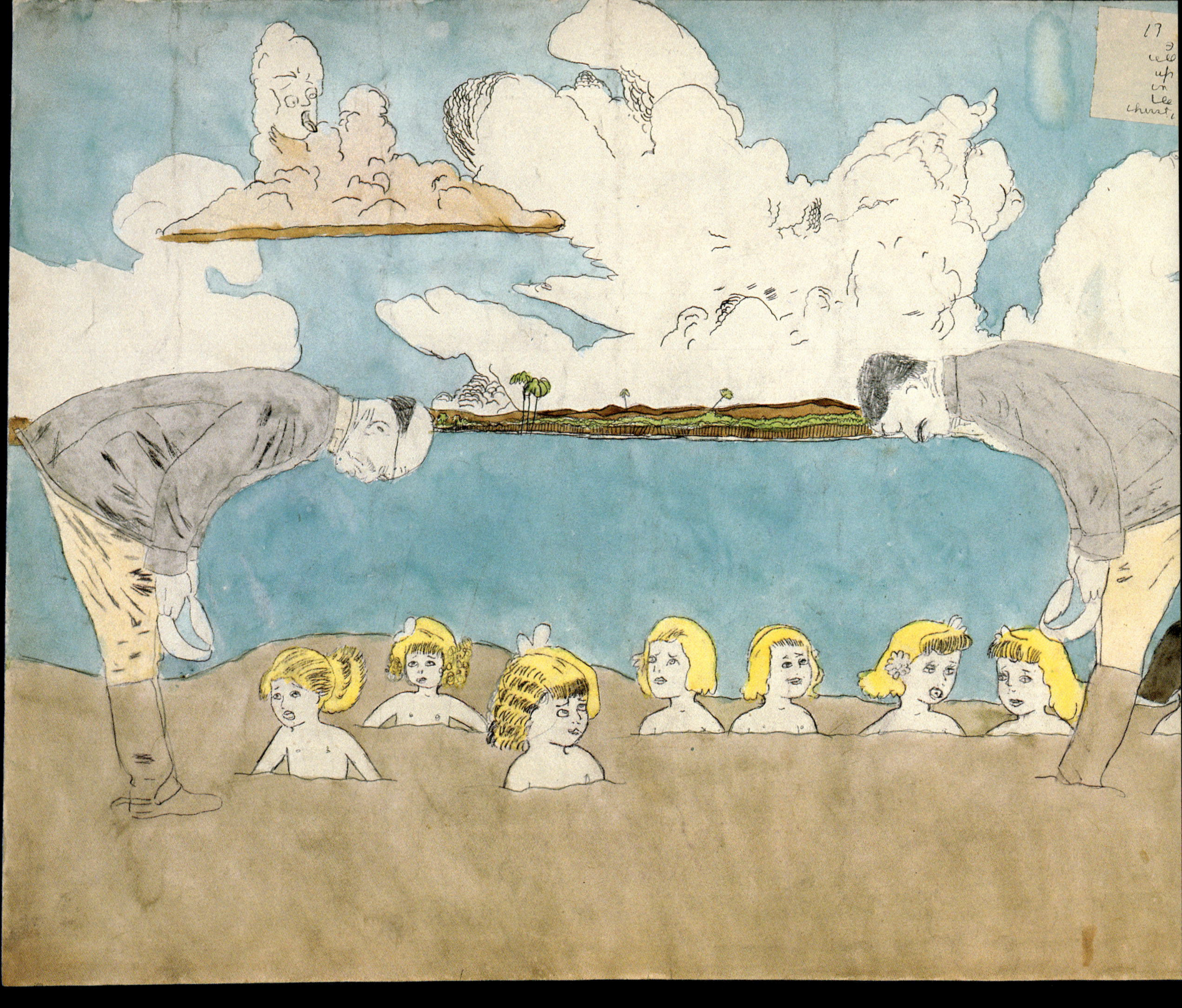

162 | *At Jennie Richee. For refusing to tell they are buried up to their waists in the sand near the river to die of thirst unless they tell. Statuary of Glandelinian strangling child.*
Watercolor, pencil, and carbon tracing on pieced paper, approx. 19 x 47 in. Private collection

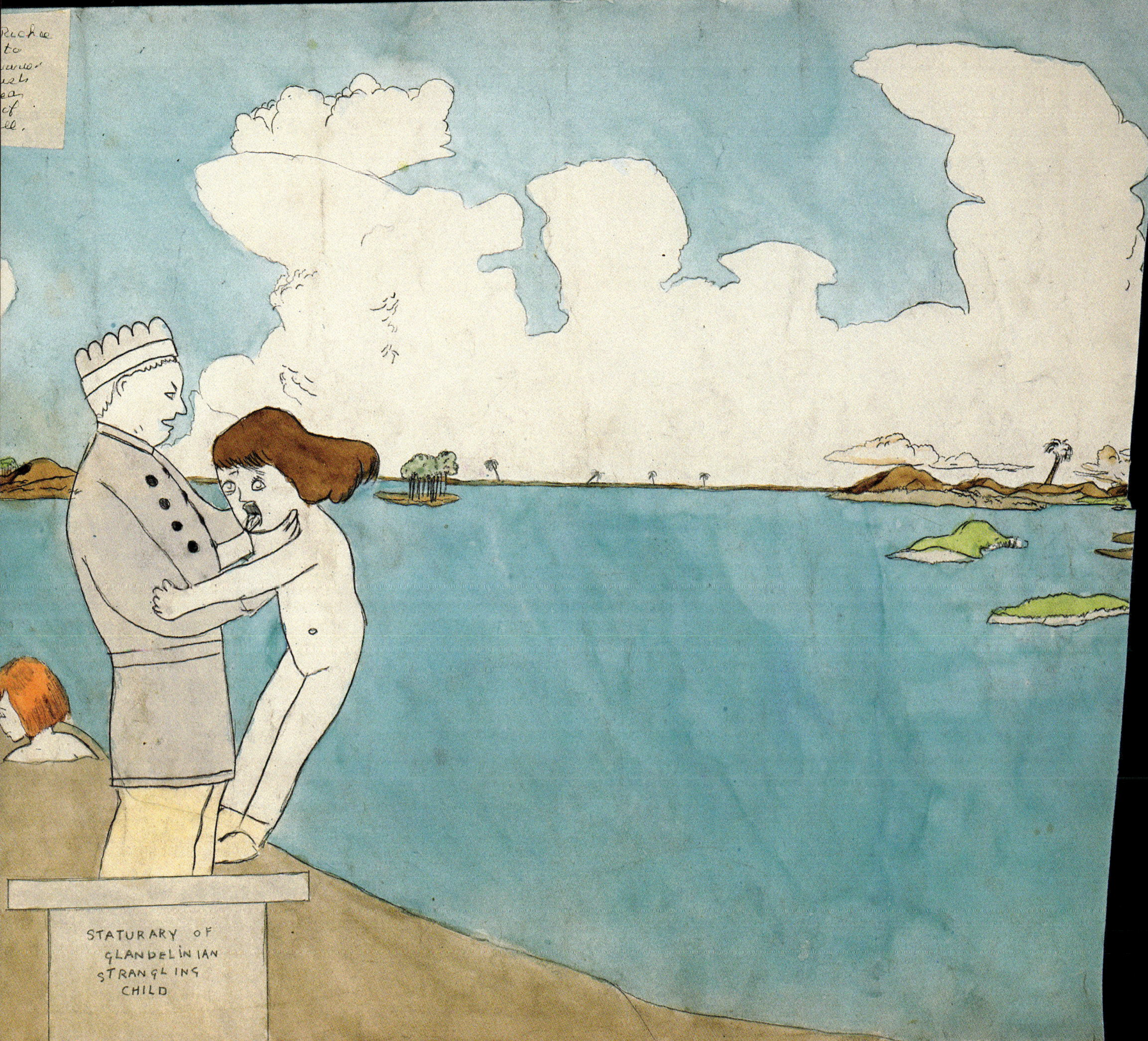

STATURARY OF
GLANDELINIAN
STRANGLING
CHILD

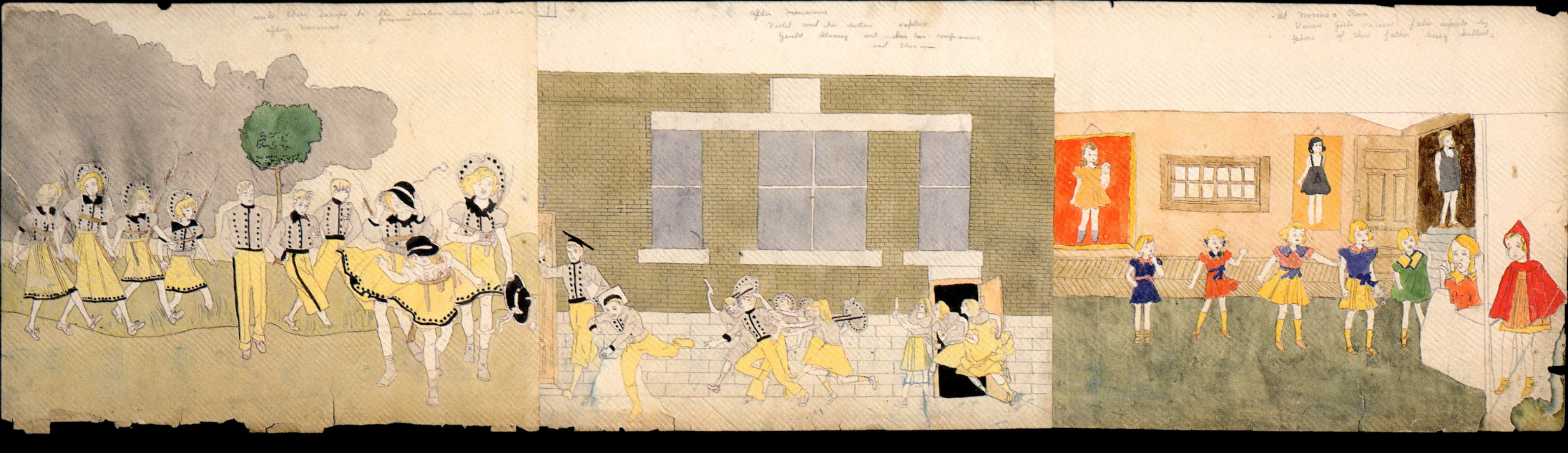

164 | Left: *After Marcocino. Make their escape to the Christian lines with their prisoners.* Center: *After Marcocino. Violet and her sisters capture Gerald Starring and his two companions, and then—.* Right: *At Norma's Run. Vivian girls receive false reports by phone of their father being killed.*

Watercolor, pencil, and carbon tracing on pieced paper, 19 x 71 in. Private collection, New York

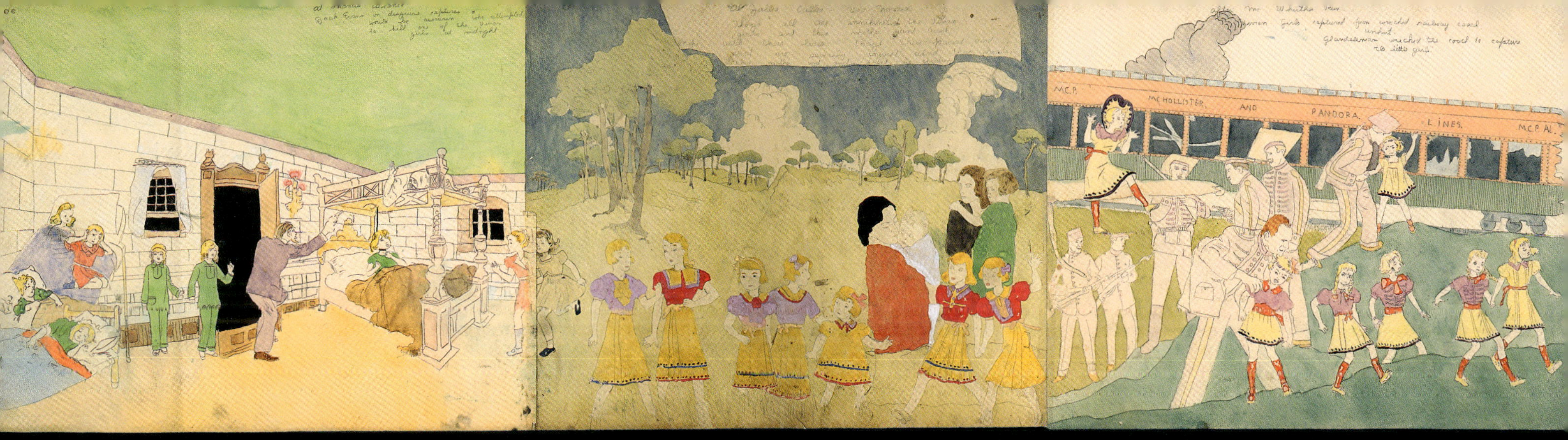

Left: *At Francis Atlanta. Jack Evans in disguise captures a would-be assassin who attempted to kill one of the Vivian Girls at midnight.*

Center: *At Julio Callio, Via Norma. Though all are annihilated, the Vivian girls and their mother and aunt escape with their lives . . .* Right: *After McAllister Run. Vivian girls captured from wrecked railway coach unhurt.* Watercolor, pencil, and carbon tracing on pieced paper, 19 x 71 in. Collection Kiyoko Lerner.

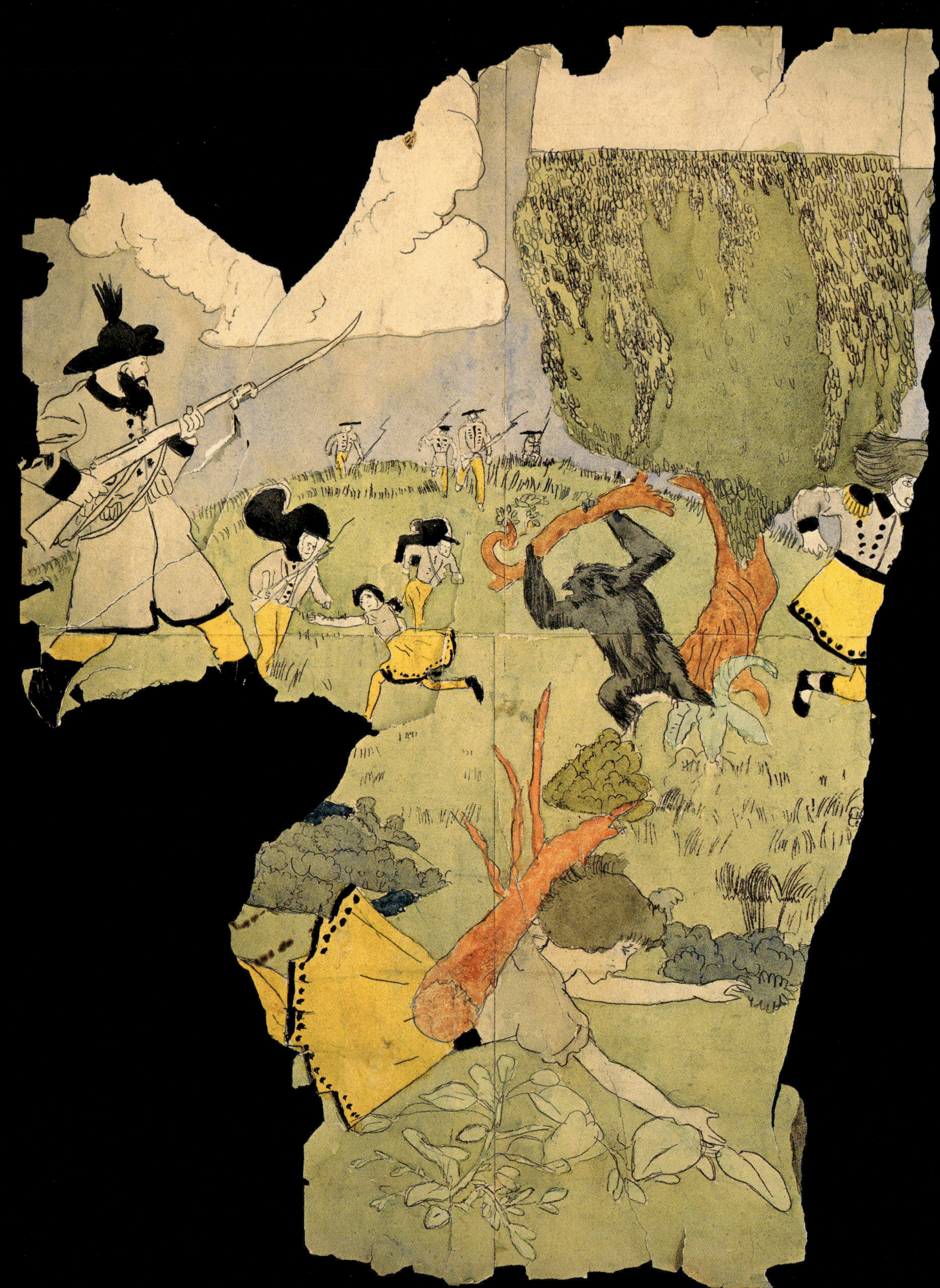

166 Untitled (fragments). Watercolor, pencil, carbon tracing, and collage on pieced paper, dimensions unknown. Collection Kiyoko Lerner

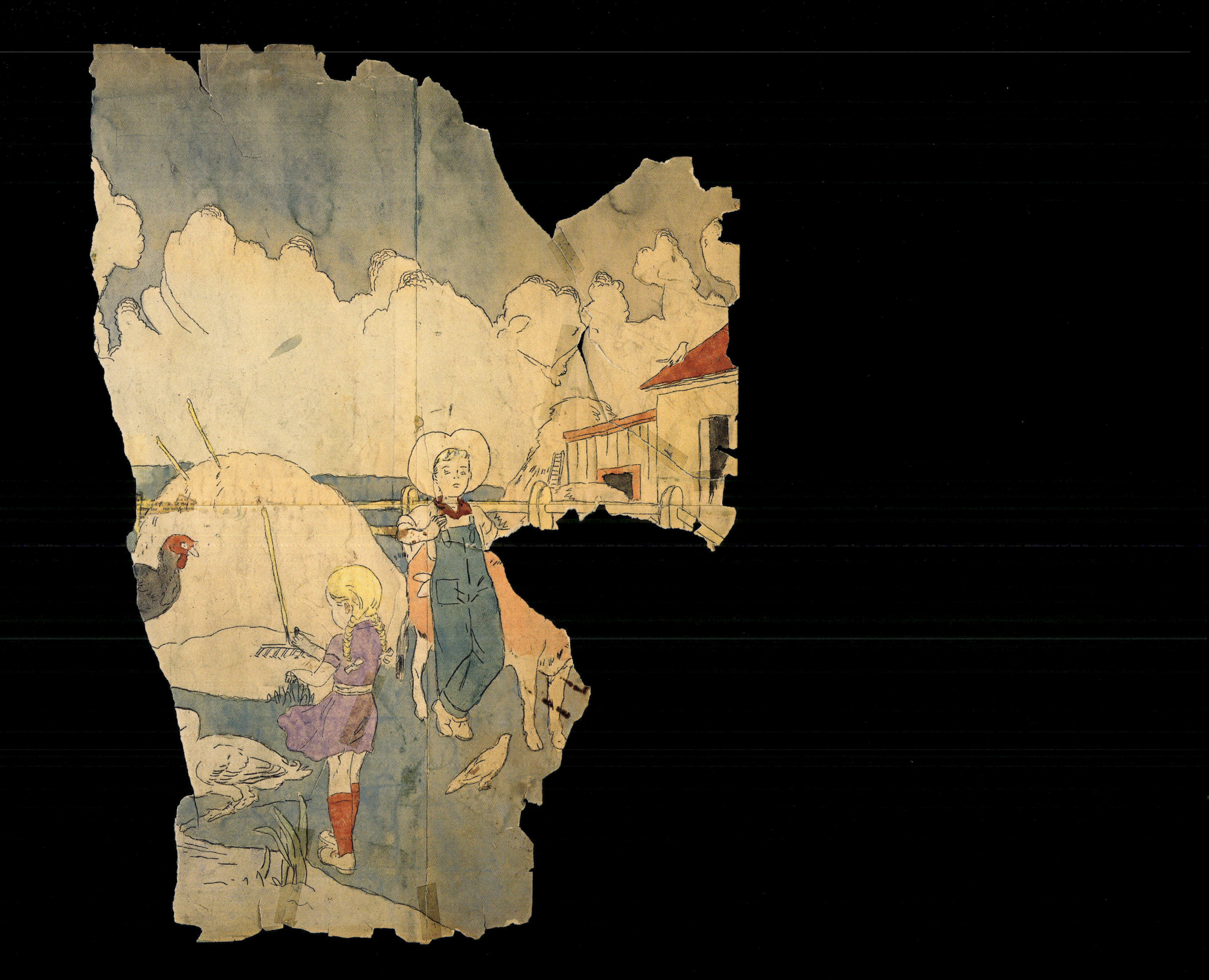

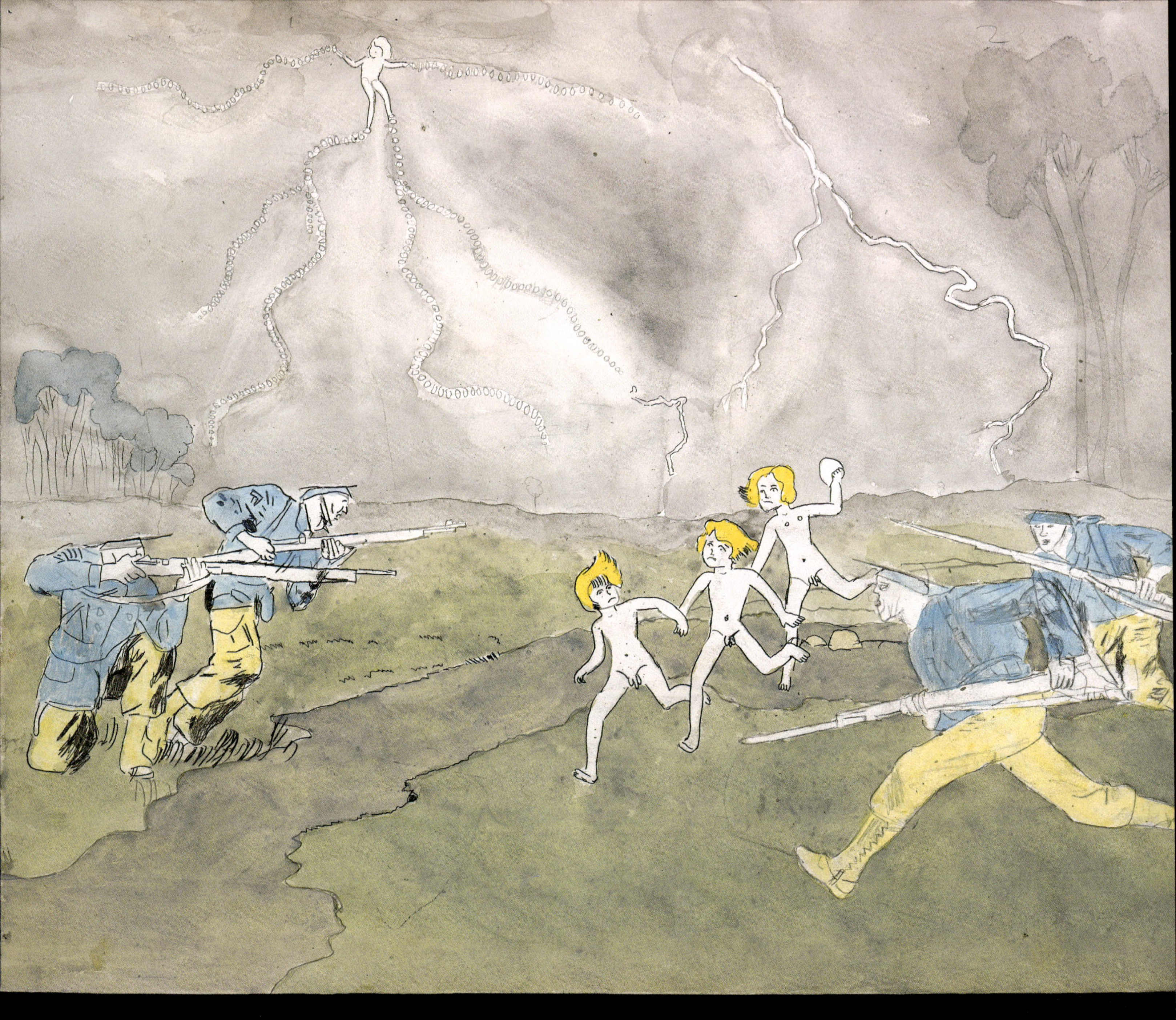

*Are enabled to get away as storm starts though thunder shook the air with quite
the loudest noise any one have ever heard.* Two separated sheets, watercolor, pencil,
and carbon tracing on paper, each 19 x 24 in. Private collections

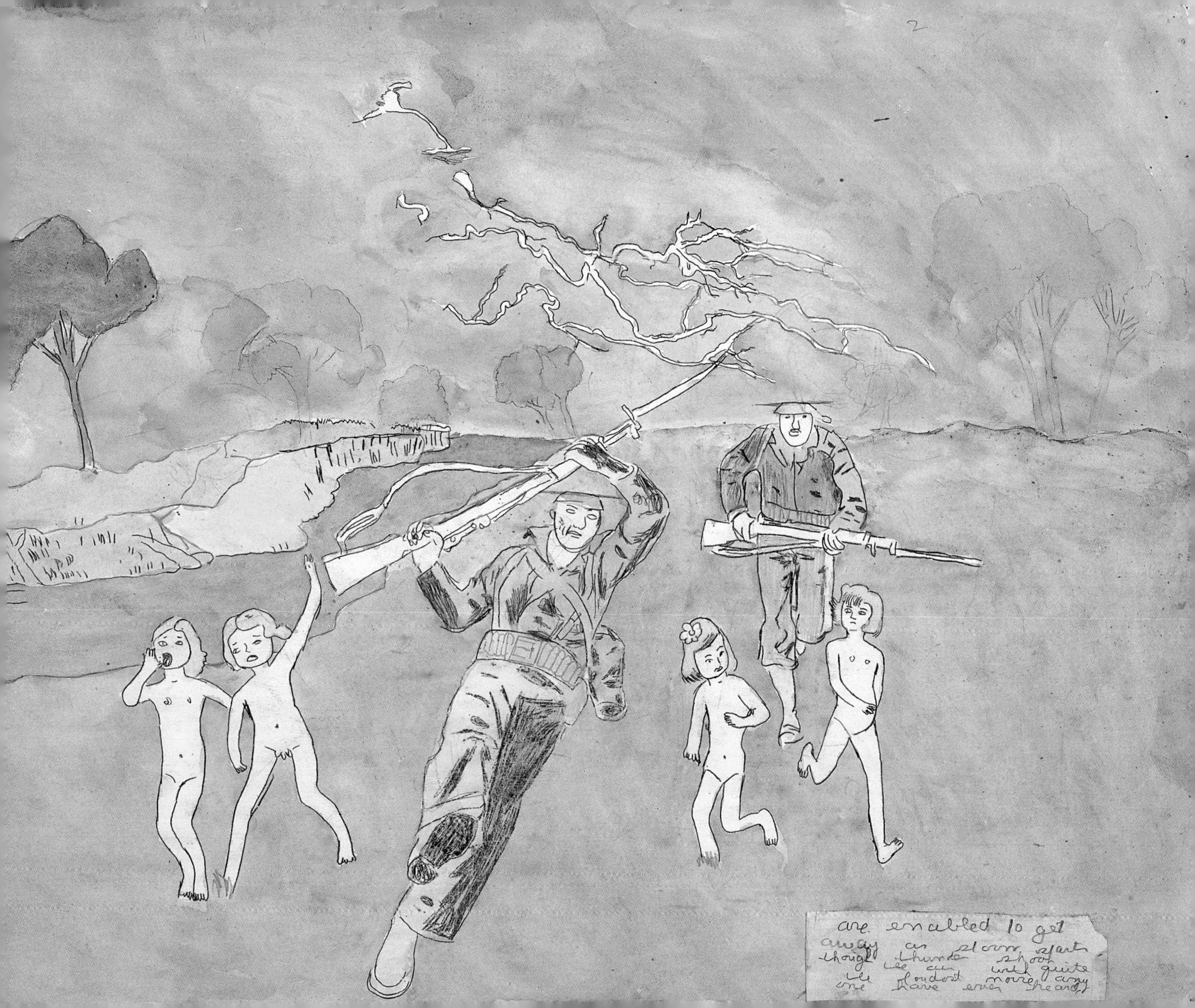
are enabled to get
away as storm starts
though thunder shook
we can with quite
cloudest noise any
have ever heard)

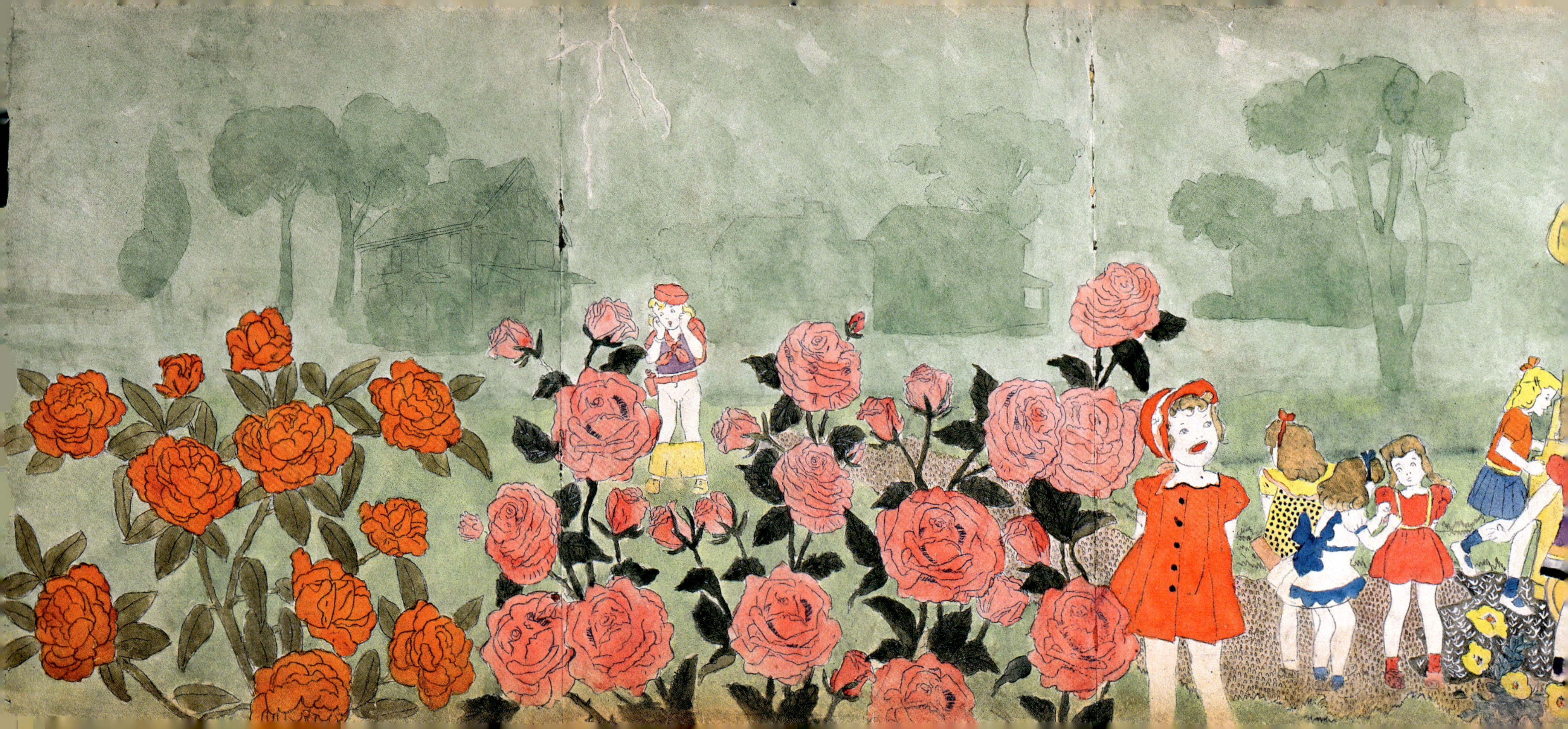

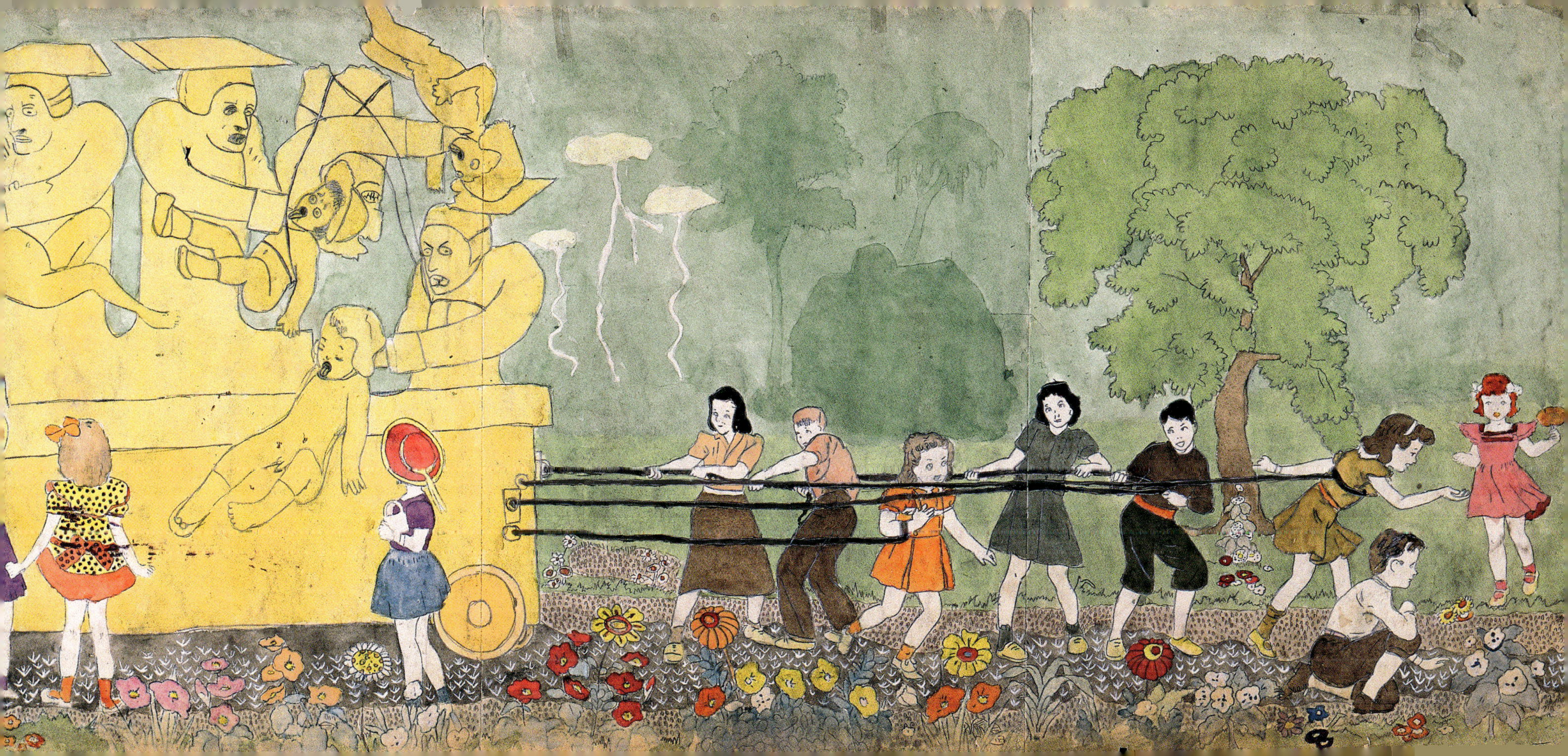

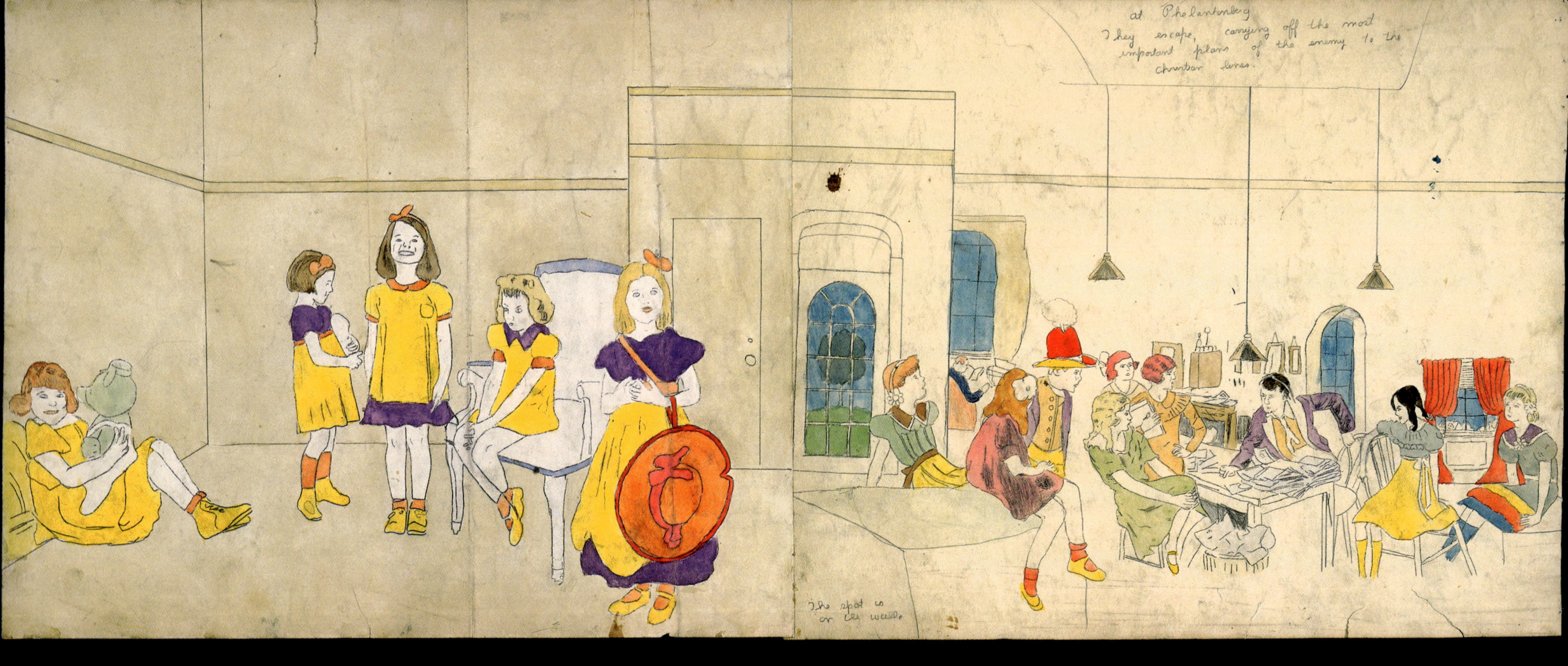

172 | Left: Untitled (girls in room). Right: *At Phelantonberg. They escape, carrying off*
the most important plans of the enemy to the Christian lines.

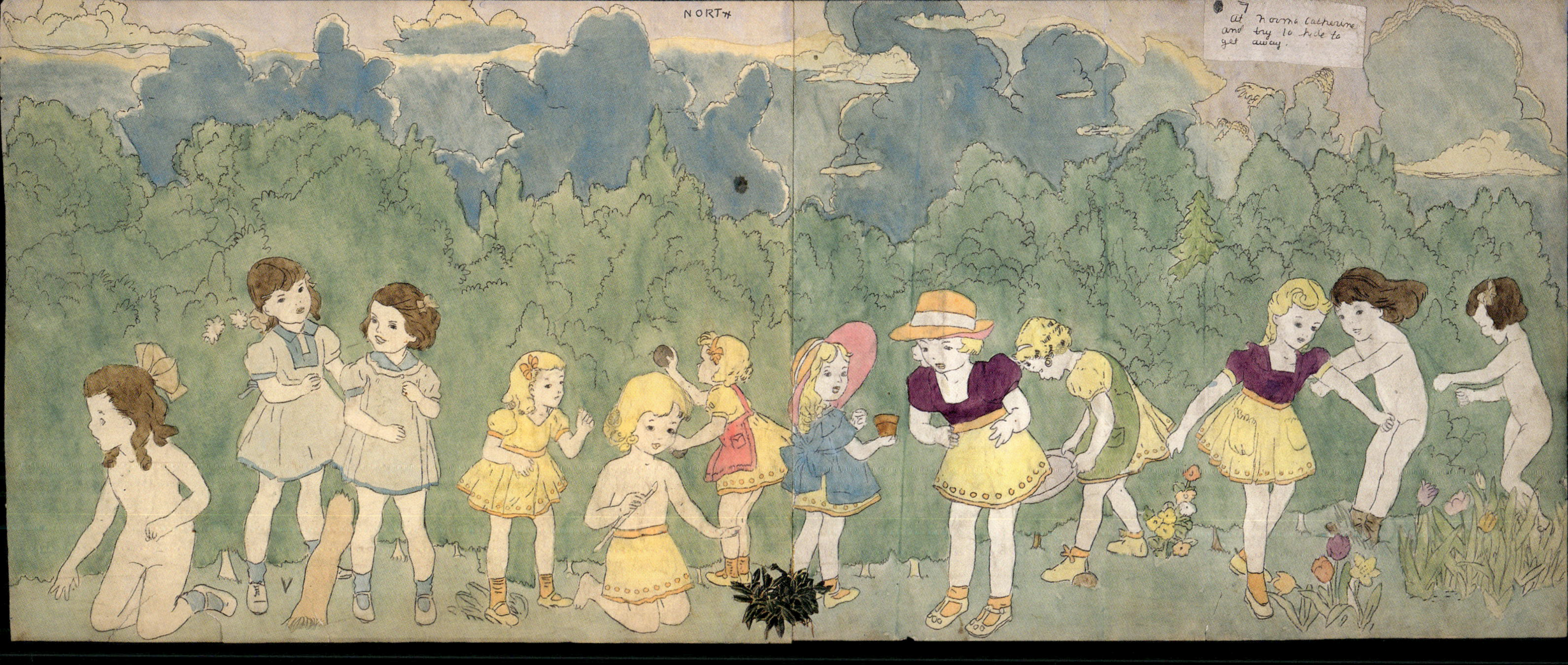

At Norma Catherine. And try to hide to get away. | 173
Watercolor, pencil, and carbon tracing on pieced paper, 19 x 48 in.
Private collection

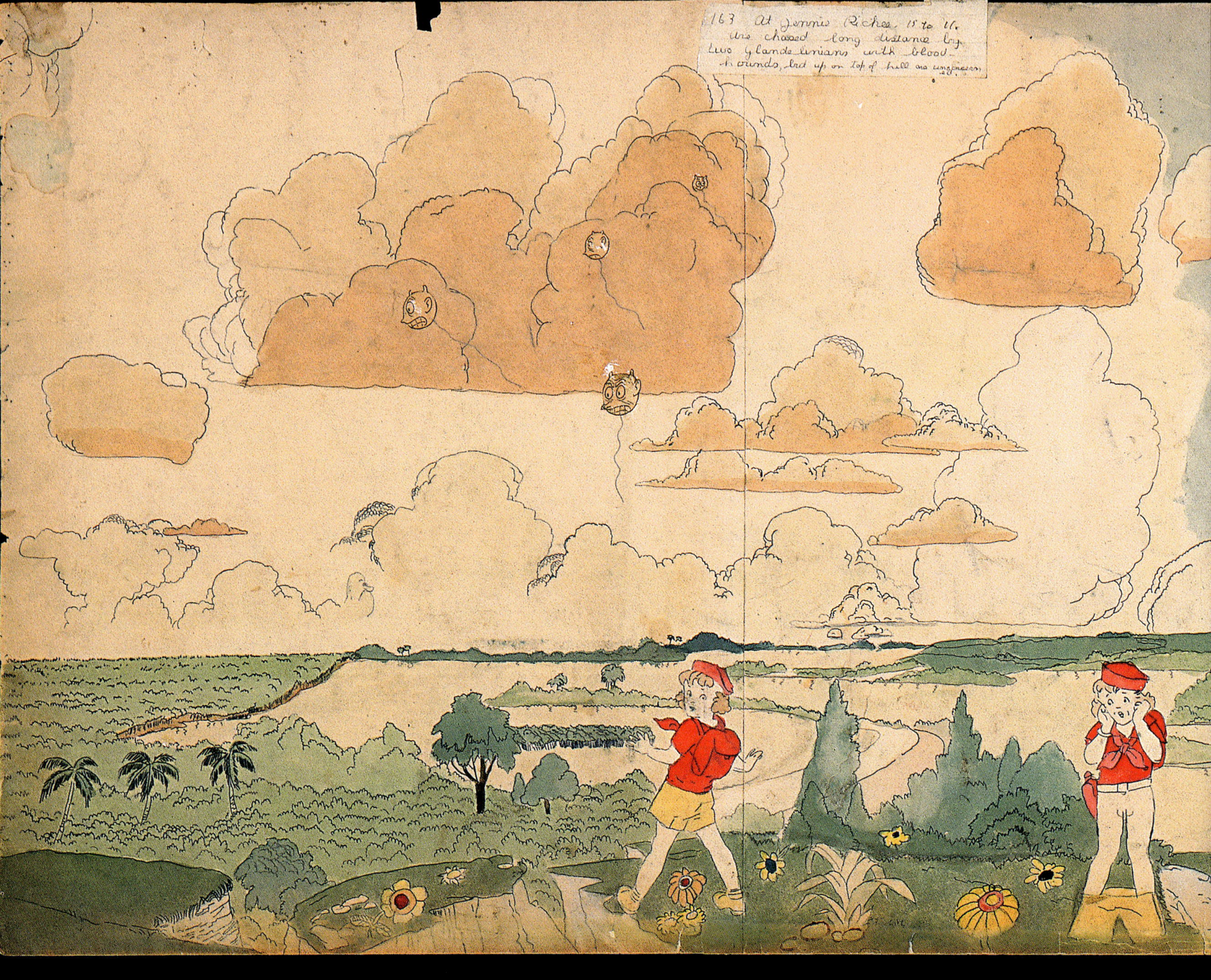

174 | *At Jennie Richee. 15 to 11. Are chased long distance by two Glandelinians with bloodhounds, lad on top of hill are unconcerned.* Watercolor, pencil, carbon tracing, and collage on pieced paper, 24 x 109 in. Private collection

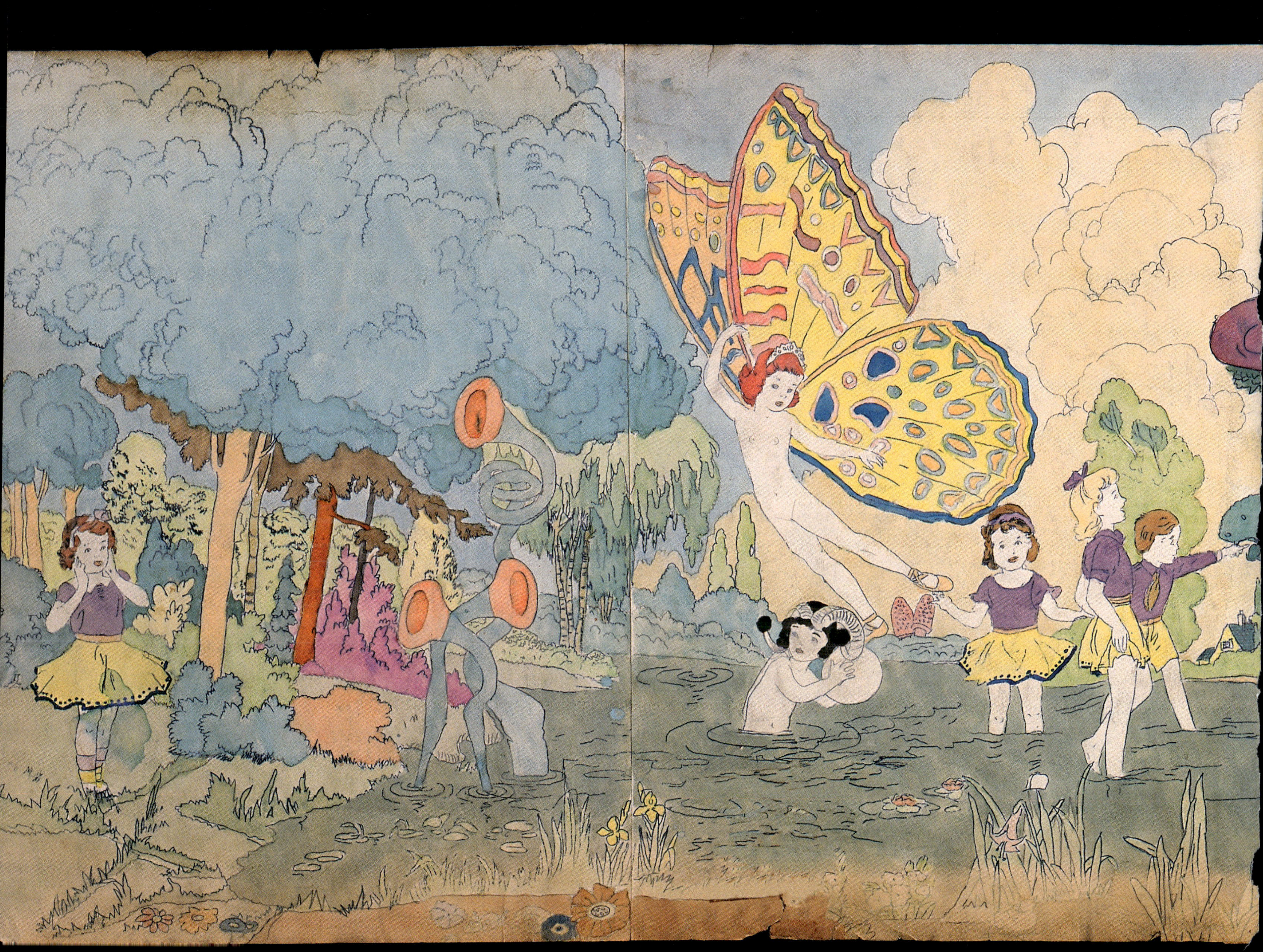

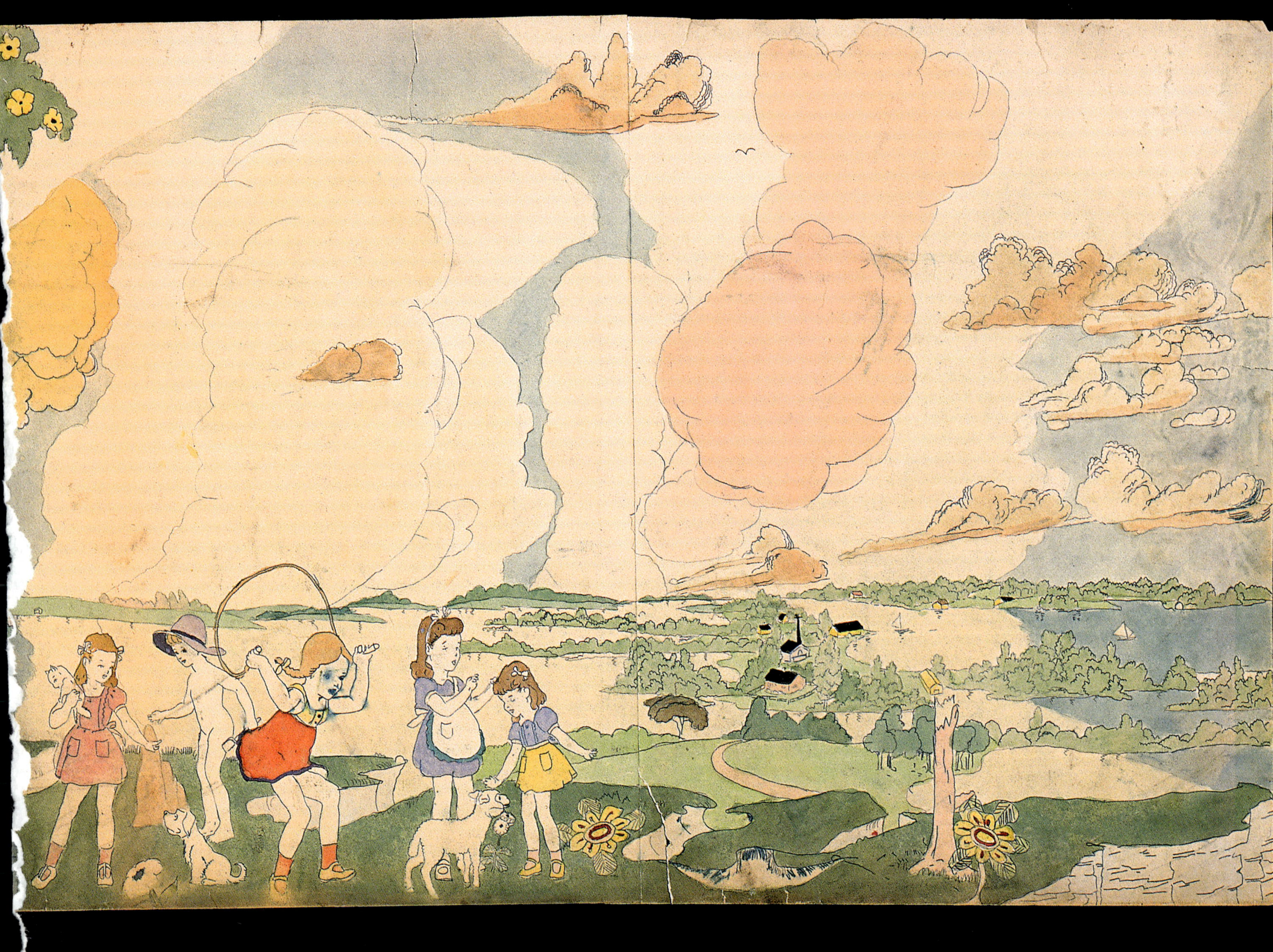

Untitled (goat in center of image, girl watering flowers).
Watercolor, pencil, and carbon tracing on pieced paper, 24 x 109 in.
Private collection

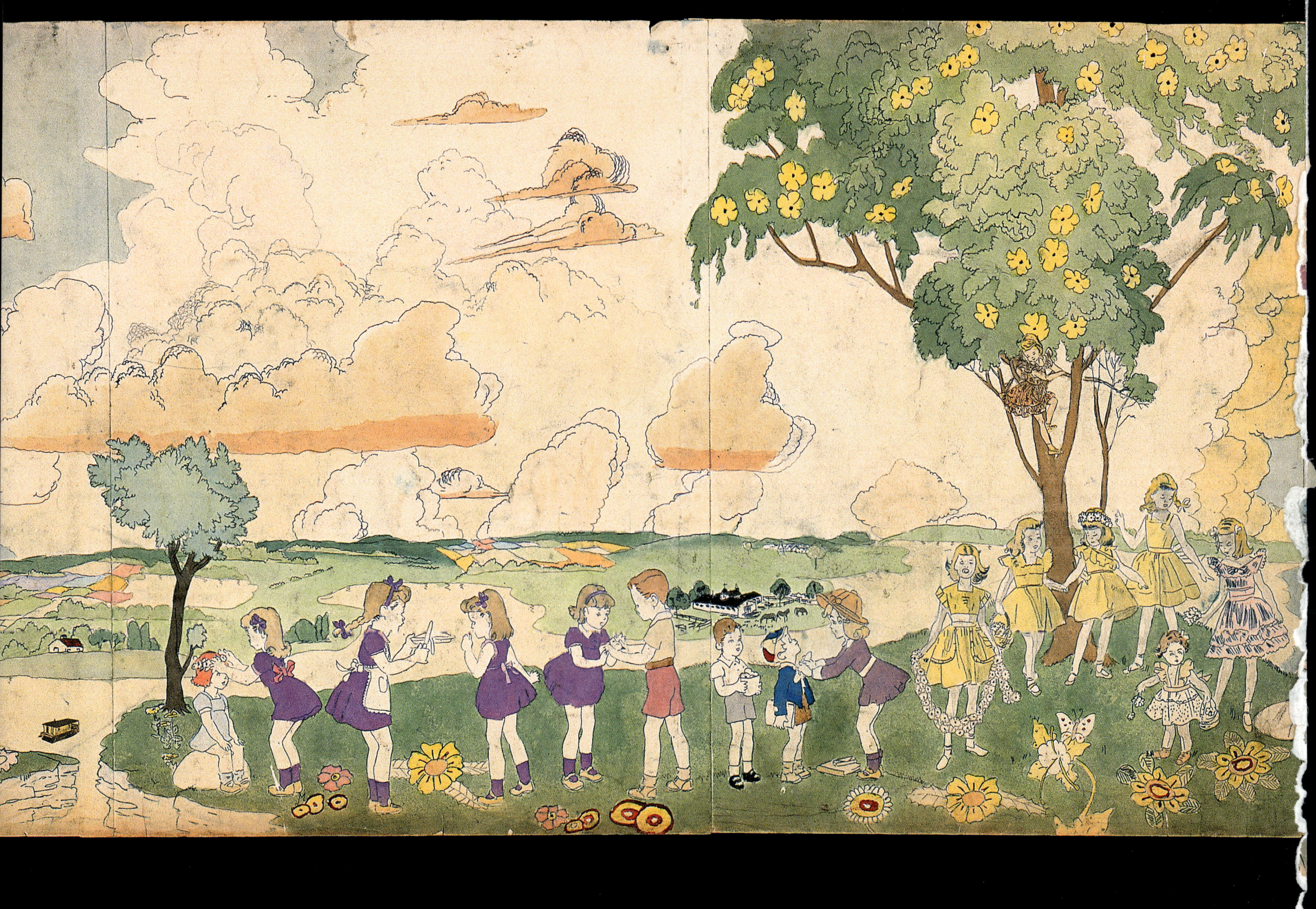

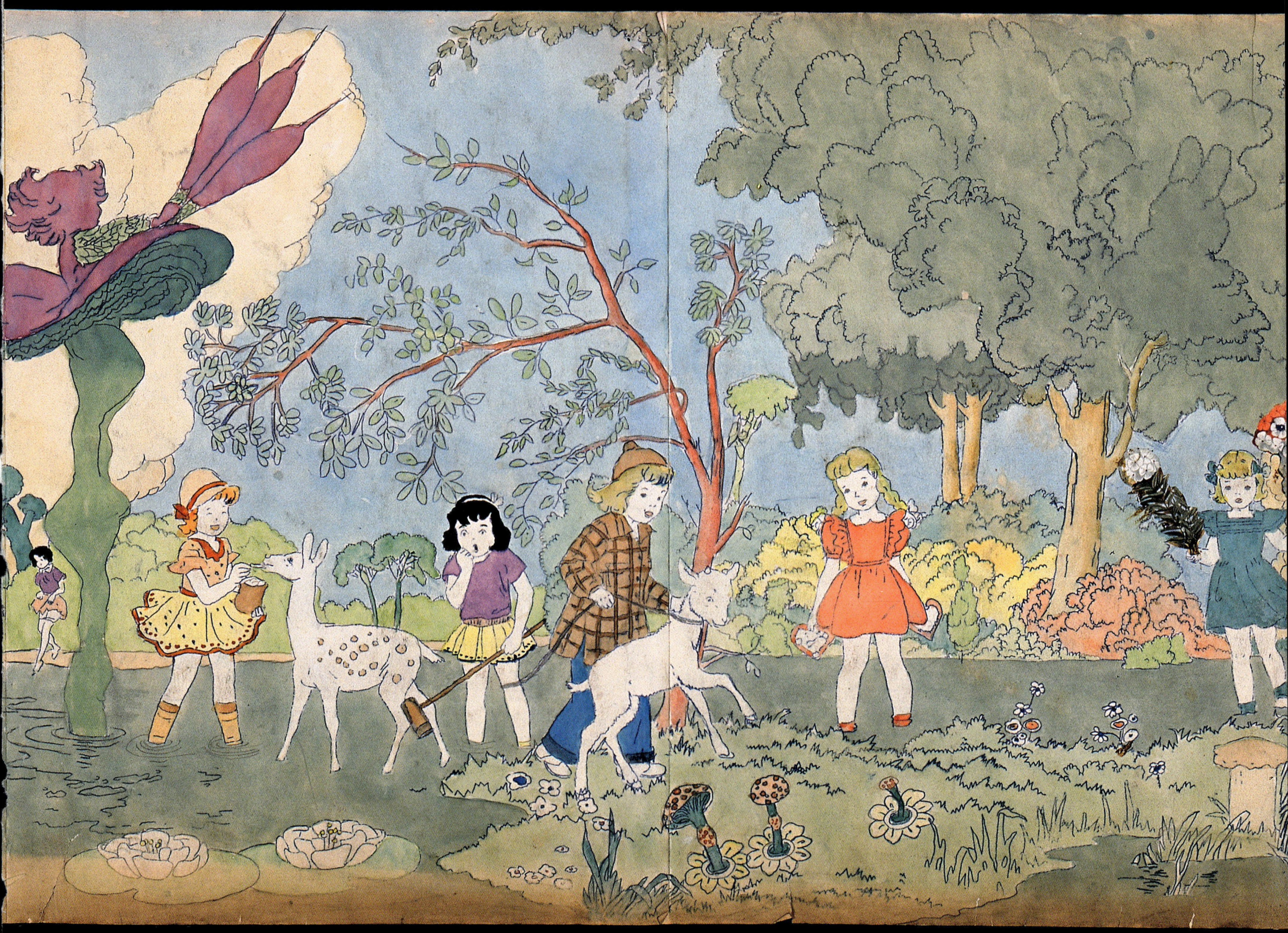

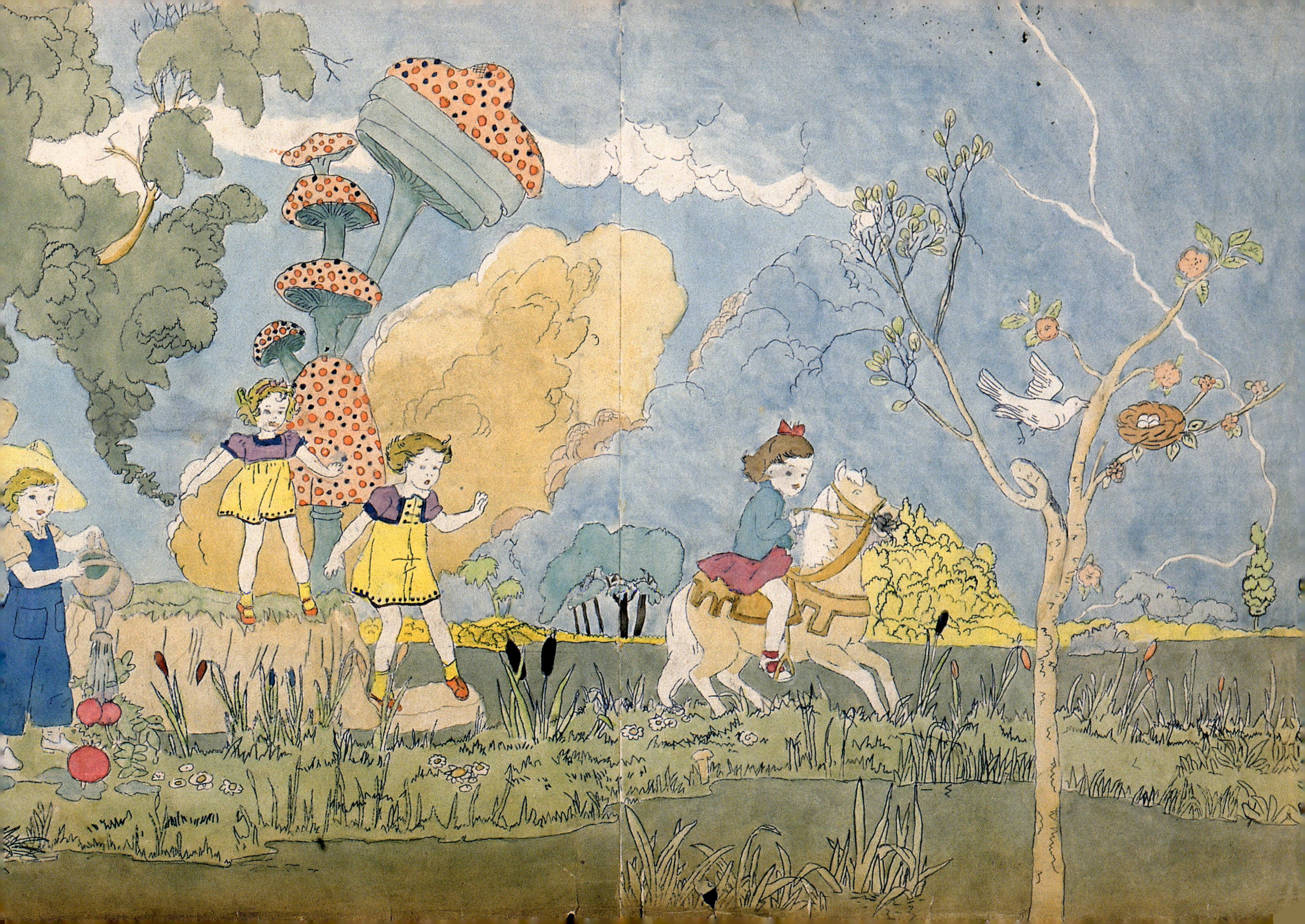

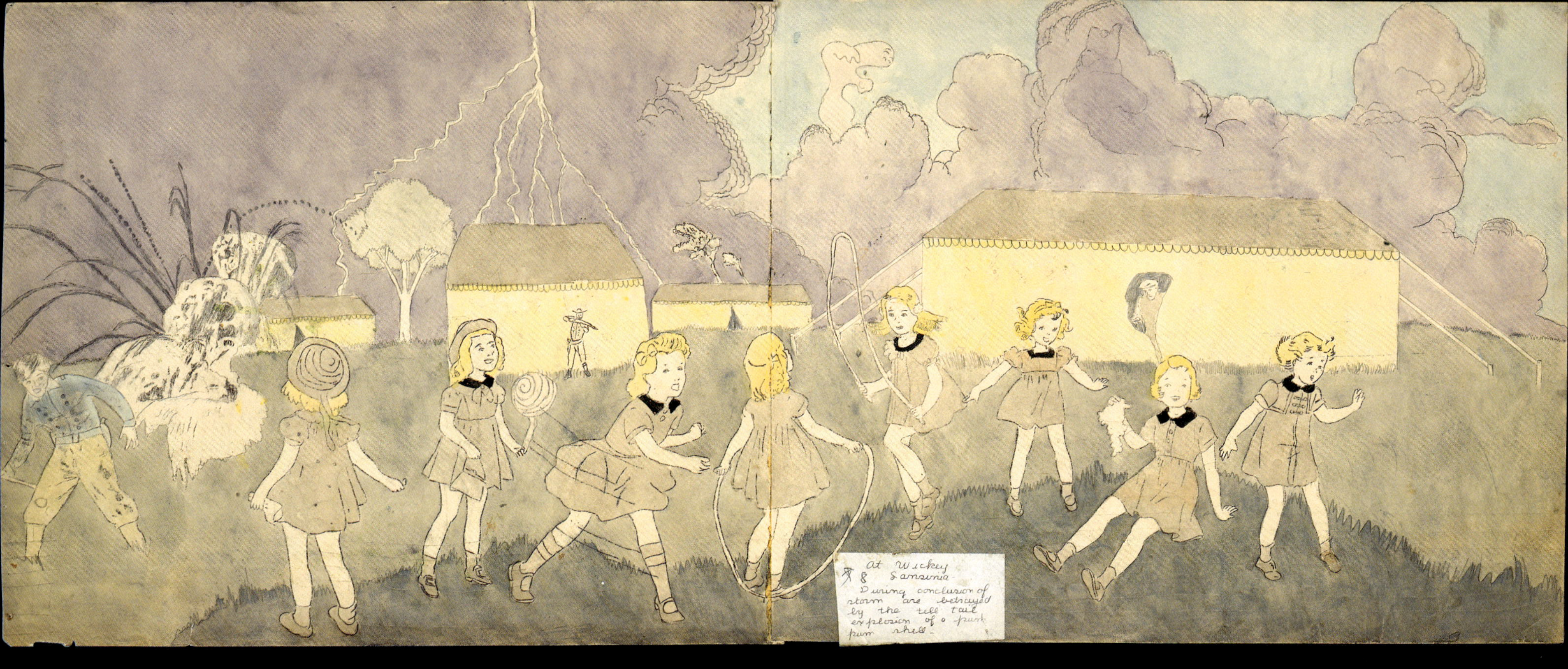

178 | *At Wickey Sansinia. During conclusion of storm are betrayed by the tell tale explosion of a pum pum shell.* Watercolor, pencil, and carbon tracing on pieced paper, approx. 19 x 48 in. Private collection

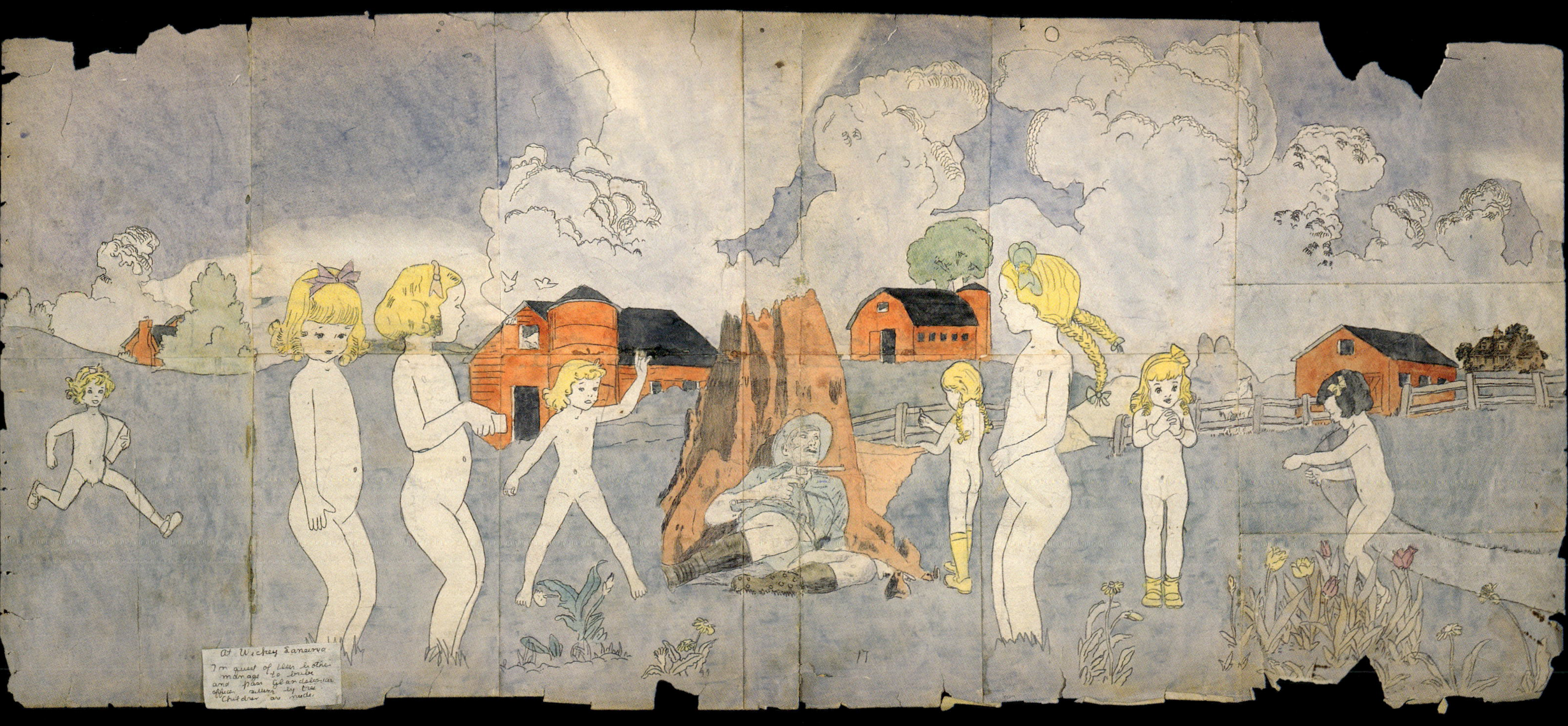

At Wickey Sanevria. In quest of their brother manage to bribe and pass | 179
Glandelinian officer sitting by tree. Children are nude. Watercolor, pencil, and
carbon tracing on pieced paper, 23 x 54 in. Private collection, New York

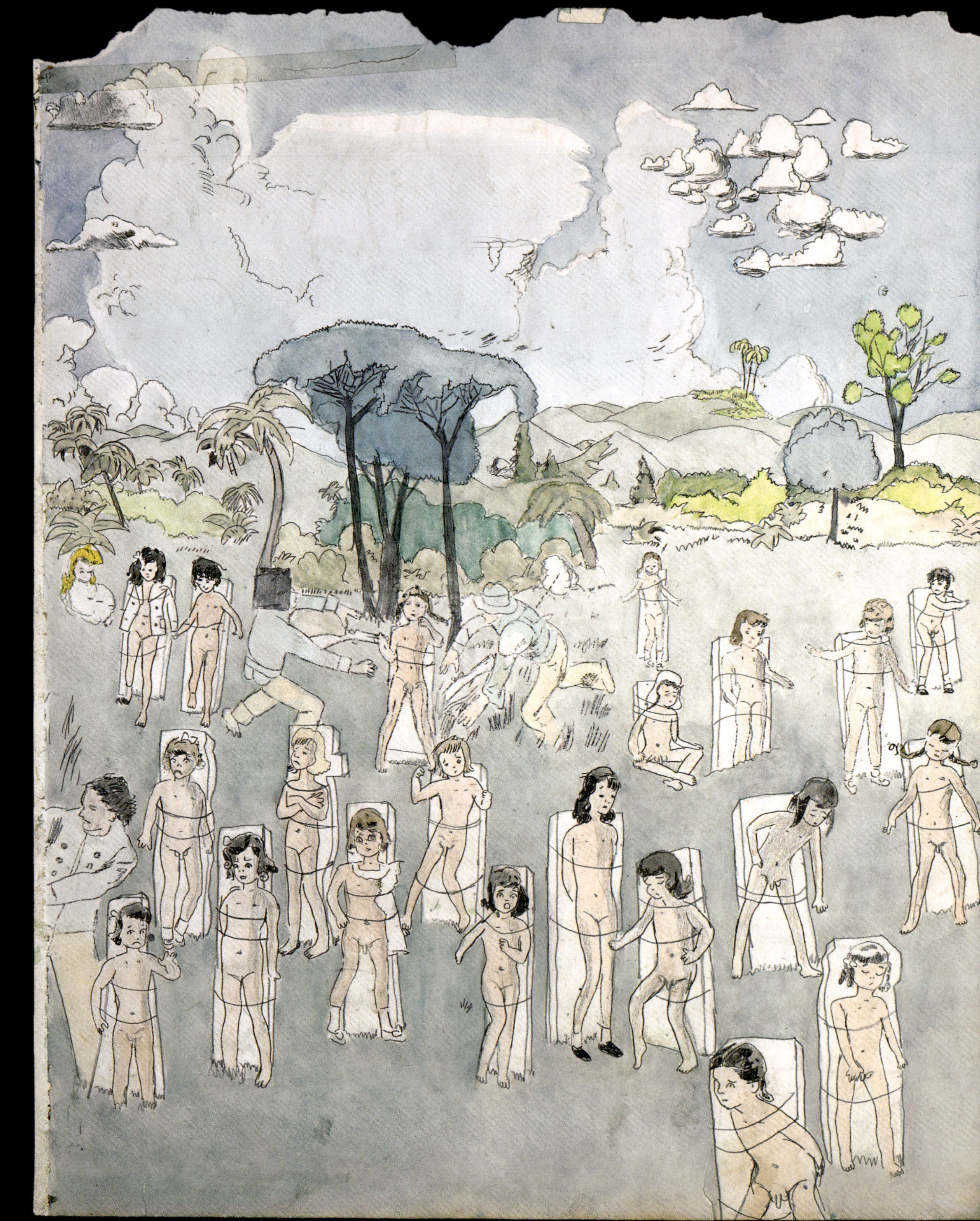

180 | Untitled (girls tied to tombstones).

Watercolor, pencil, and carbon tracing on paper,

24 x 19 in. Private collection.

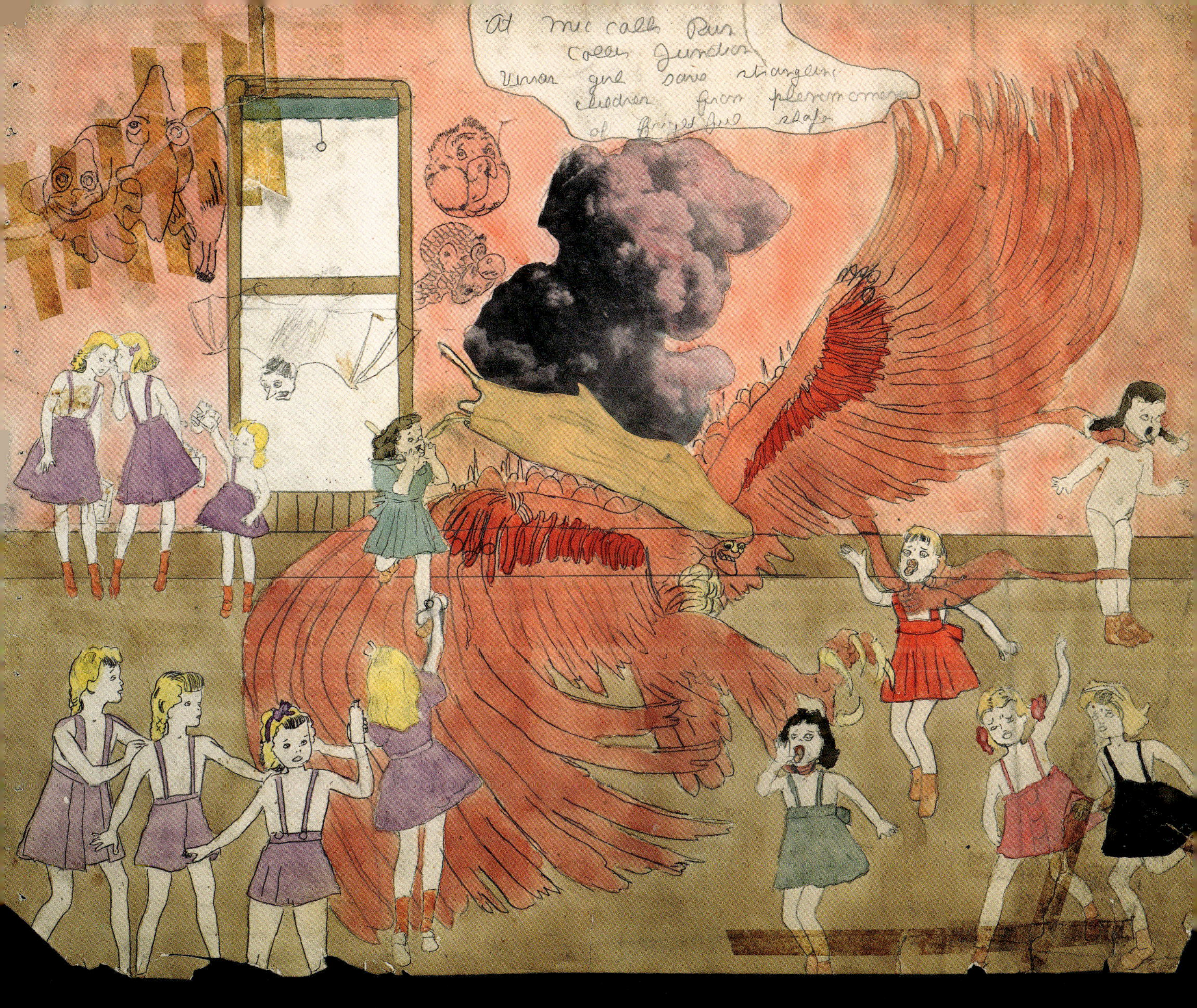

At McCall's Run Colls Junction. Vivian girl saves stranger children from phenomenon of frightful shape. Watercolor, pencil, carbon tracing, and collage on paper, 19 x 24 in. Collection Kiyoko Lerner.

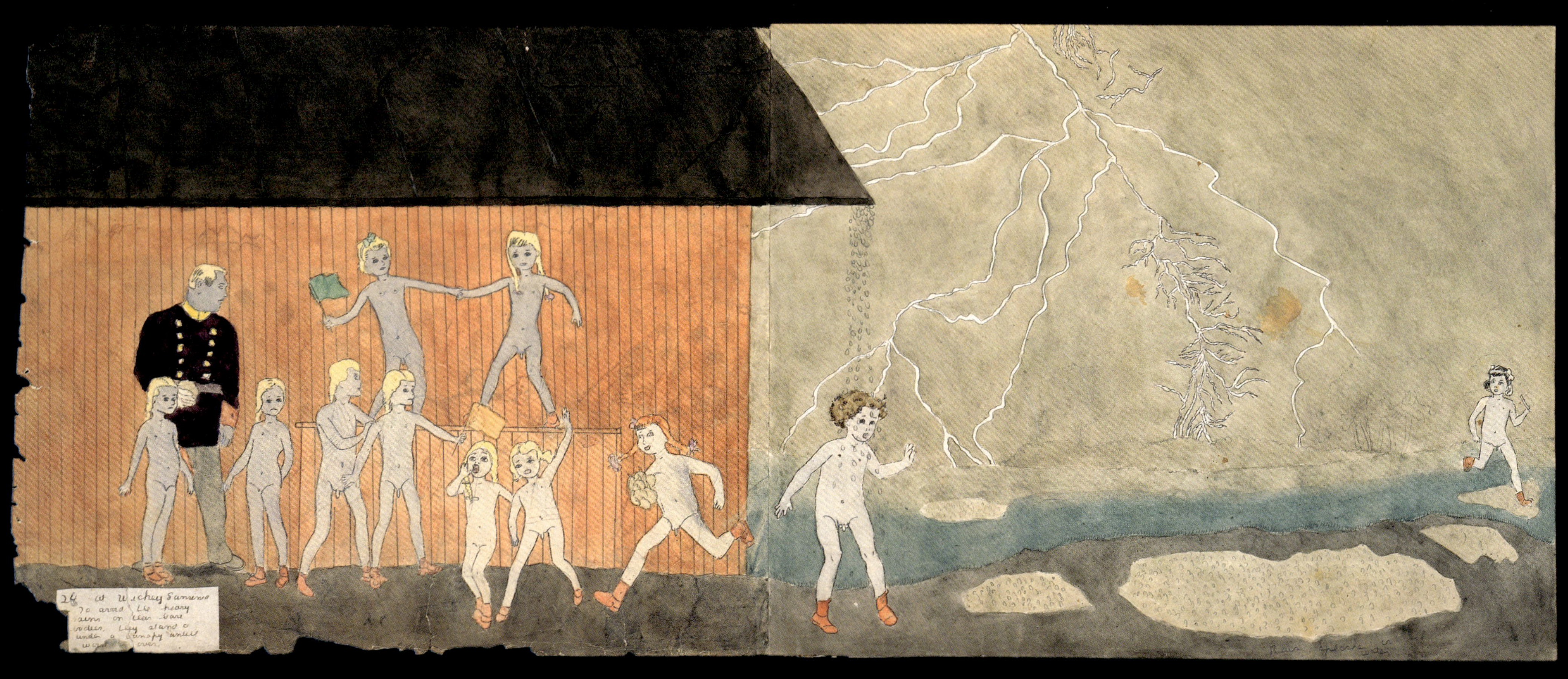

 At Wickey Sansinia. To avoid the heavy rain on their bare bodies they stand under a canopy until worst is over. Watercolor, pencil, and carbon tracing on pieced paper, 19 x 47 in. Private collection

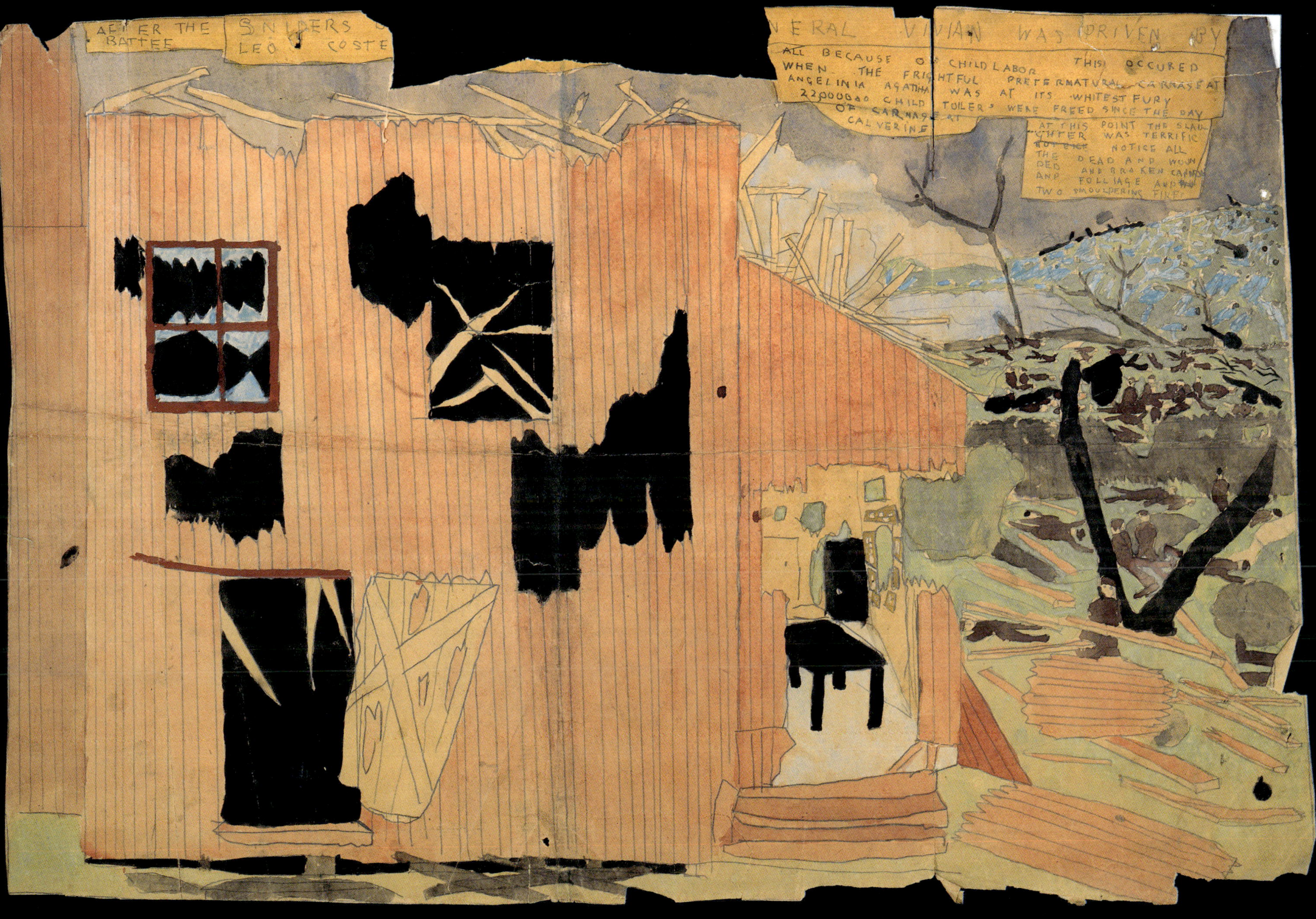

After the [Battle]. Snider . . . Leo Coste . . . General Vivian was driven by . . . all because of child labor this occurred when the frightful preternatural carnage of Angelinia Agata was at its whitest fury 22,00000 child toilers were freed since the day of carnage at Calverine at this point the slaughter was terrific notice all the dead and [wounded] and broken cannons and folliage and two smouldering fires. Watercolor, pencil, and carbon tracing on paper, 19 x 28 in. Collection Kiyoko Lerner

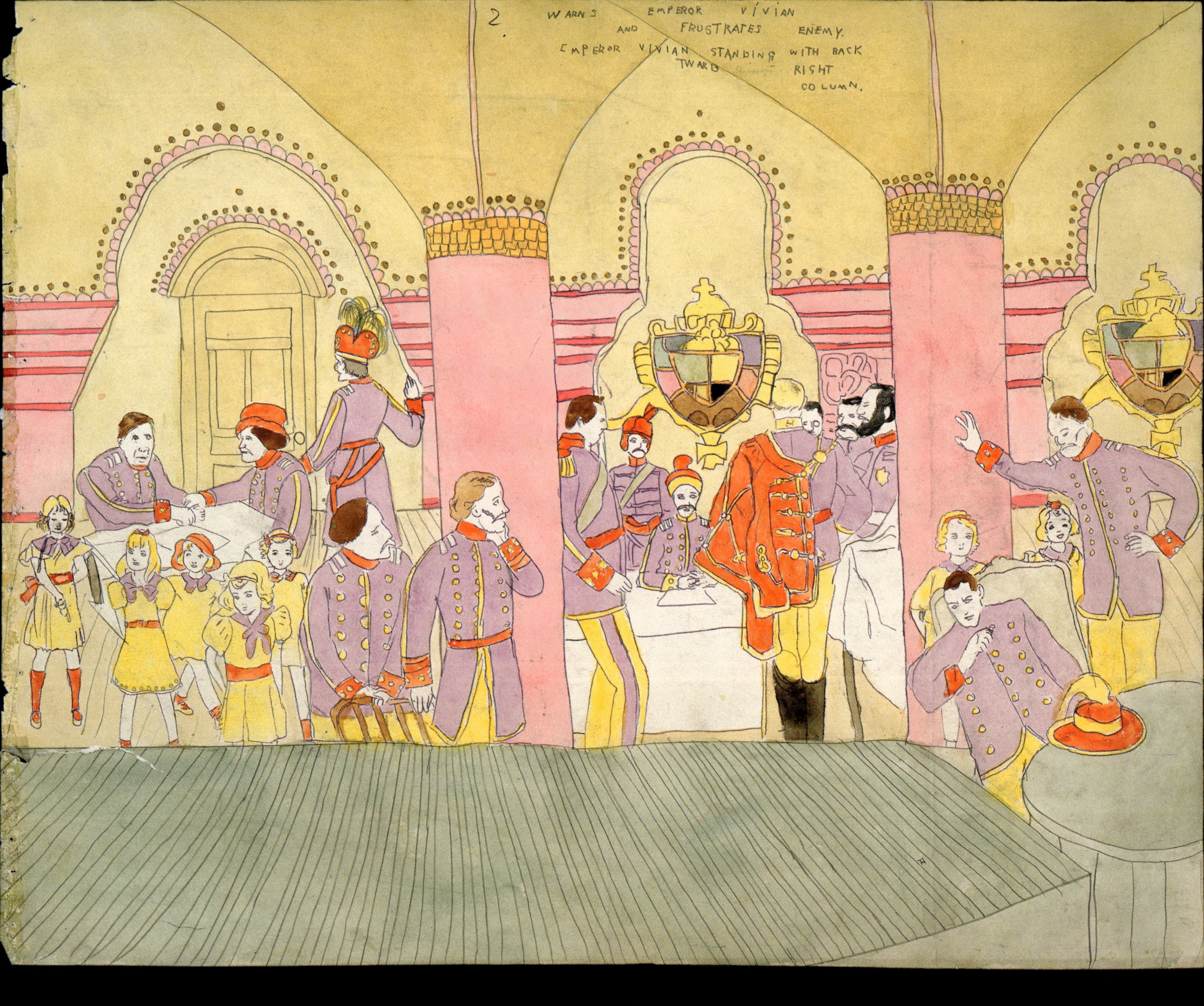

184 | *Warns Emperor Vivian and frustrates enemy. Emperor Vivian standing*
with back toward right column. Watercolor, pencil, and carbon tracing

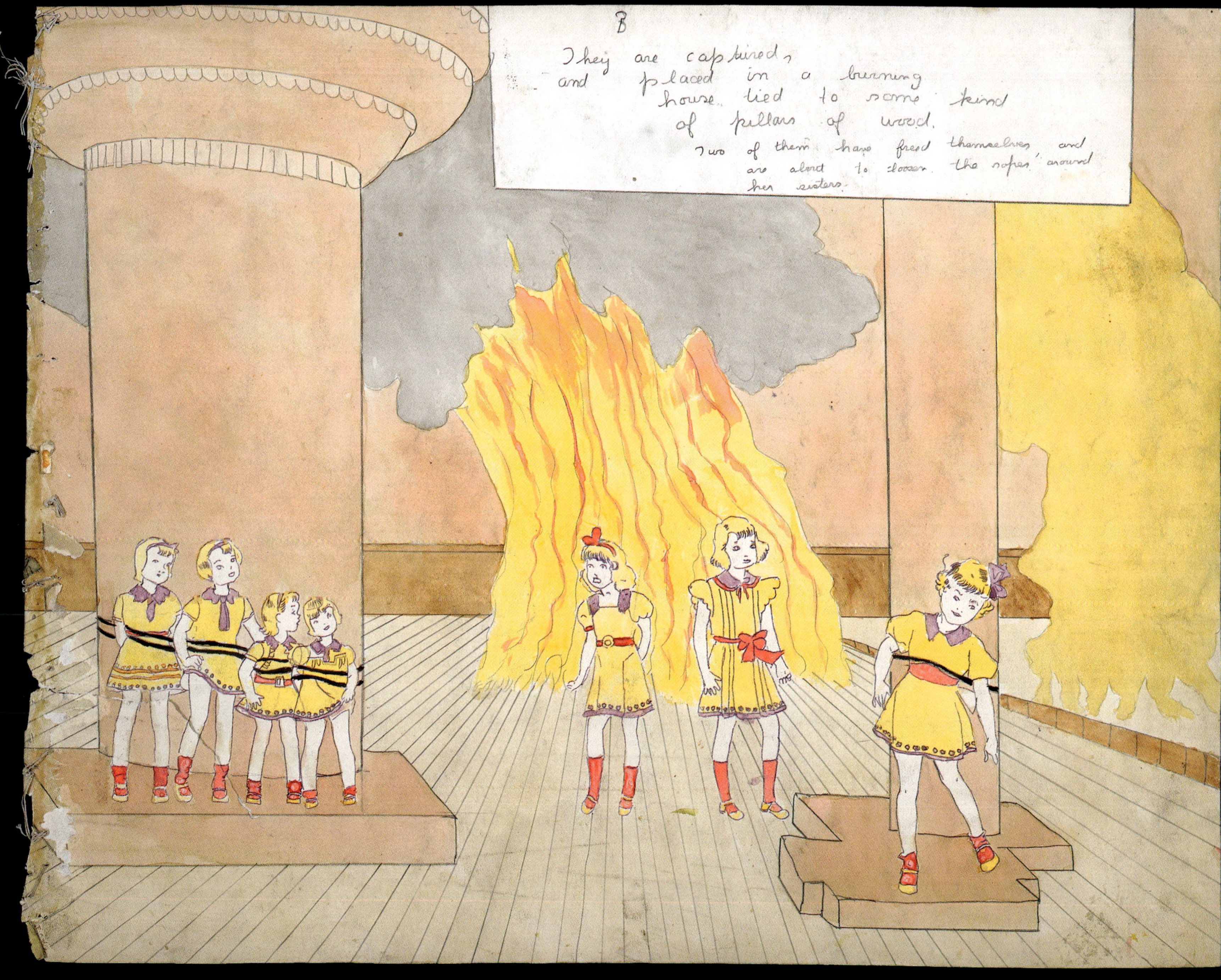

185

Watercolor, pencil, and carbon tracing on pieced paper, 17 x 24 in. Private collection

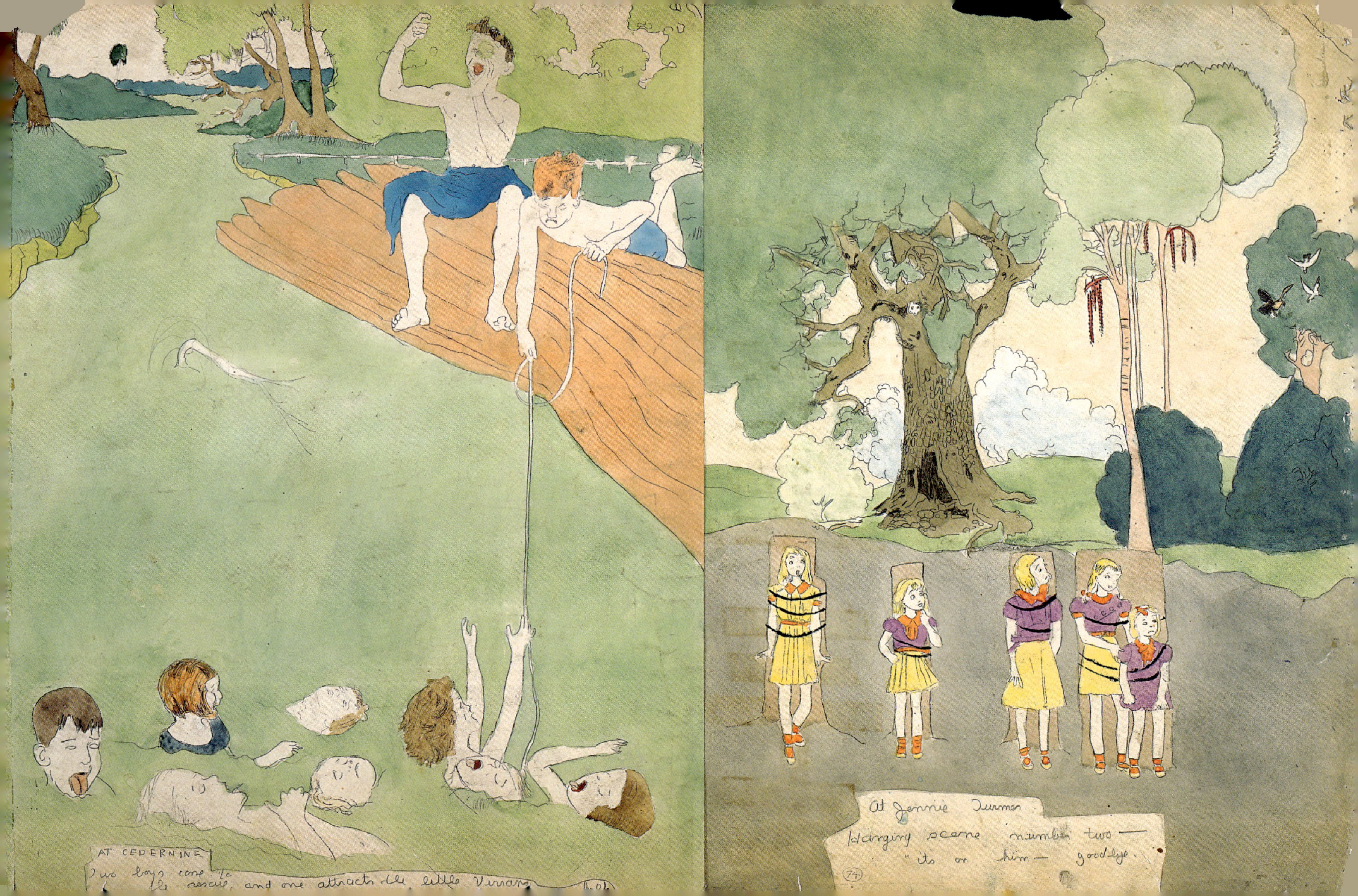
AT CEDERNINE.
Two boys come to the rescue, and one attracts the little Vivians.
A.O.

At Jennie Turner.
Hanging scene number two —
"its on him — goodbye.
74

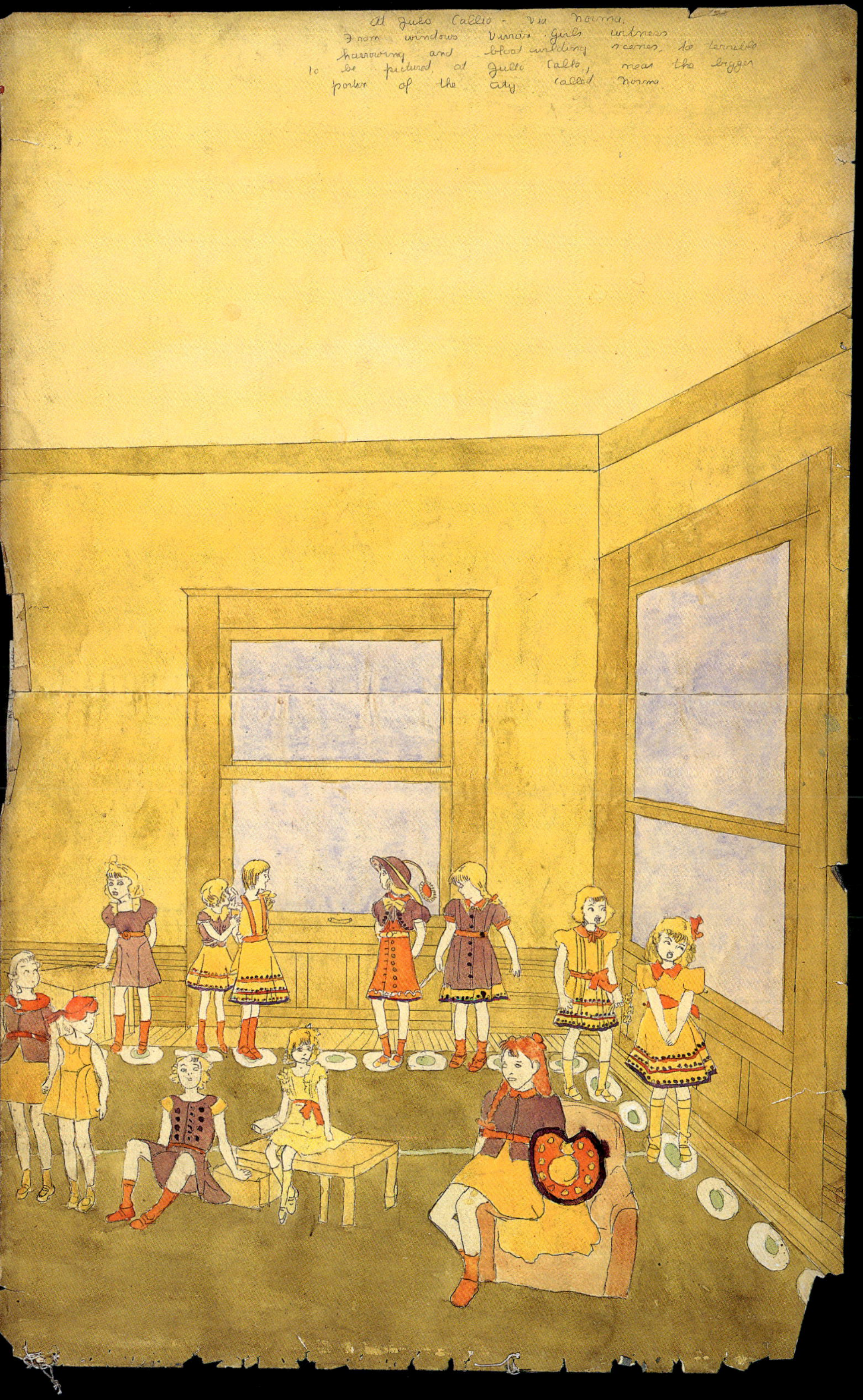

At Julo Callio—via Norma. From windows Vivian girls witness harrowing and blood curdling scenes. Watercolor, pencil, and carbon tracing on pieced paper, 38 x 24 in. Private collection

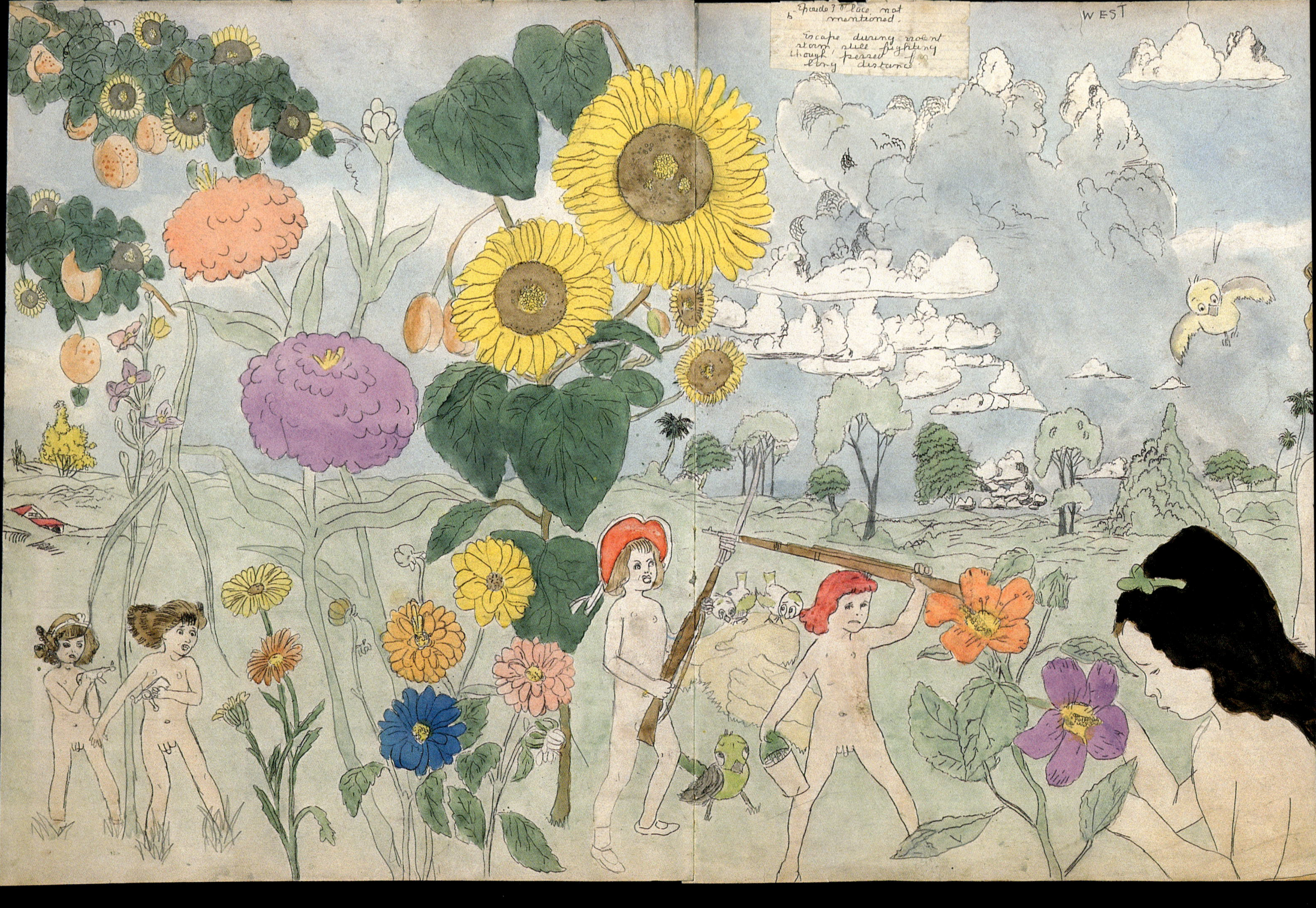

188 | *6 Episode 3 Place not mentioned. Escape during violent storm, still fighting though persued for long distance.*

Watercolor, pencil, and carbon tracing on pieced paper, 24 x 74 ¾ in.

Collection American Folk Art Museum, New York. Gift of Nathan and Kiyoko Lerner

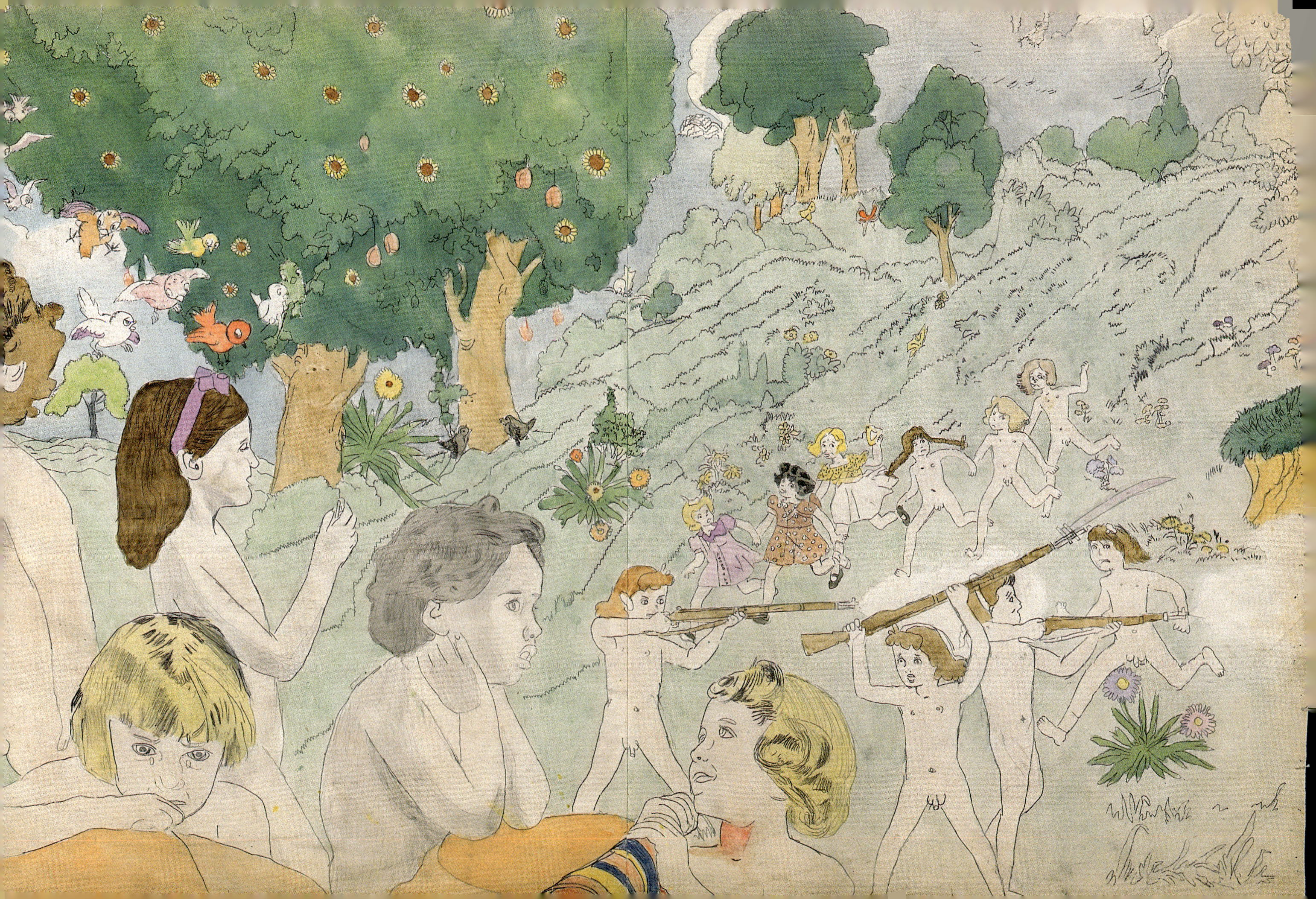

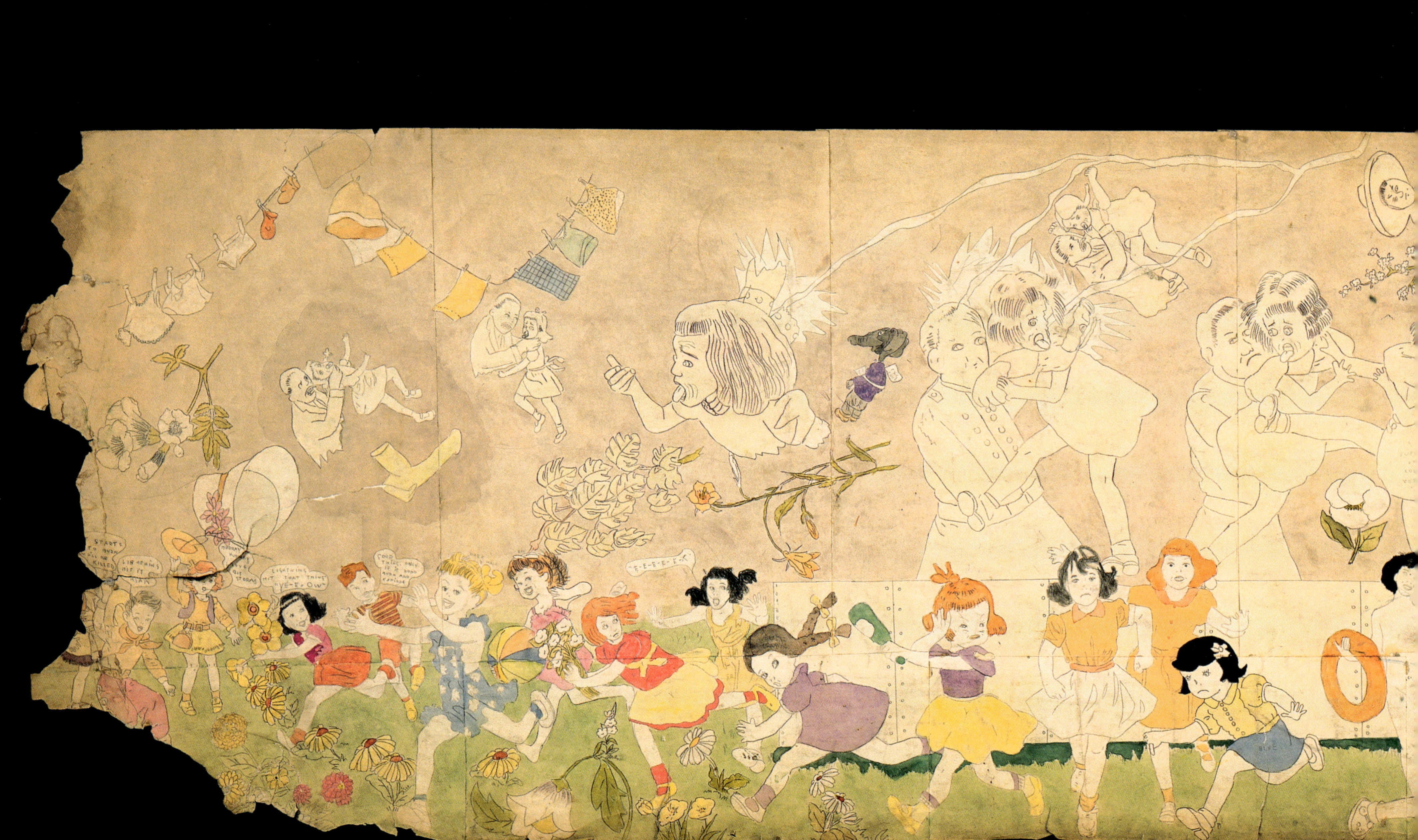
STARTS TO BURN WILL BE KILLED MAN
LIGHTNING HIT IT
HURRAY HOT
BIG STORM
LIGHTNING HIT THAT THING "YE-E-OW"
COULD TIRING ONLY IF IT BURN AND EXPLODE
"E-E-E-E-E"

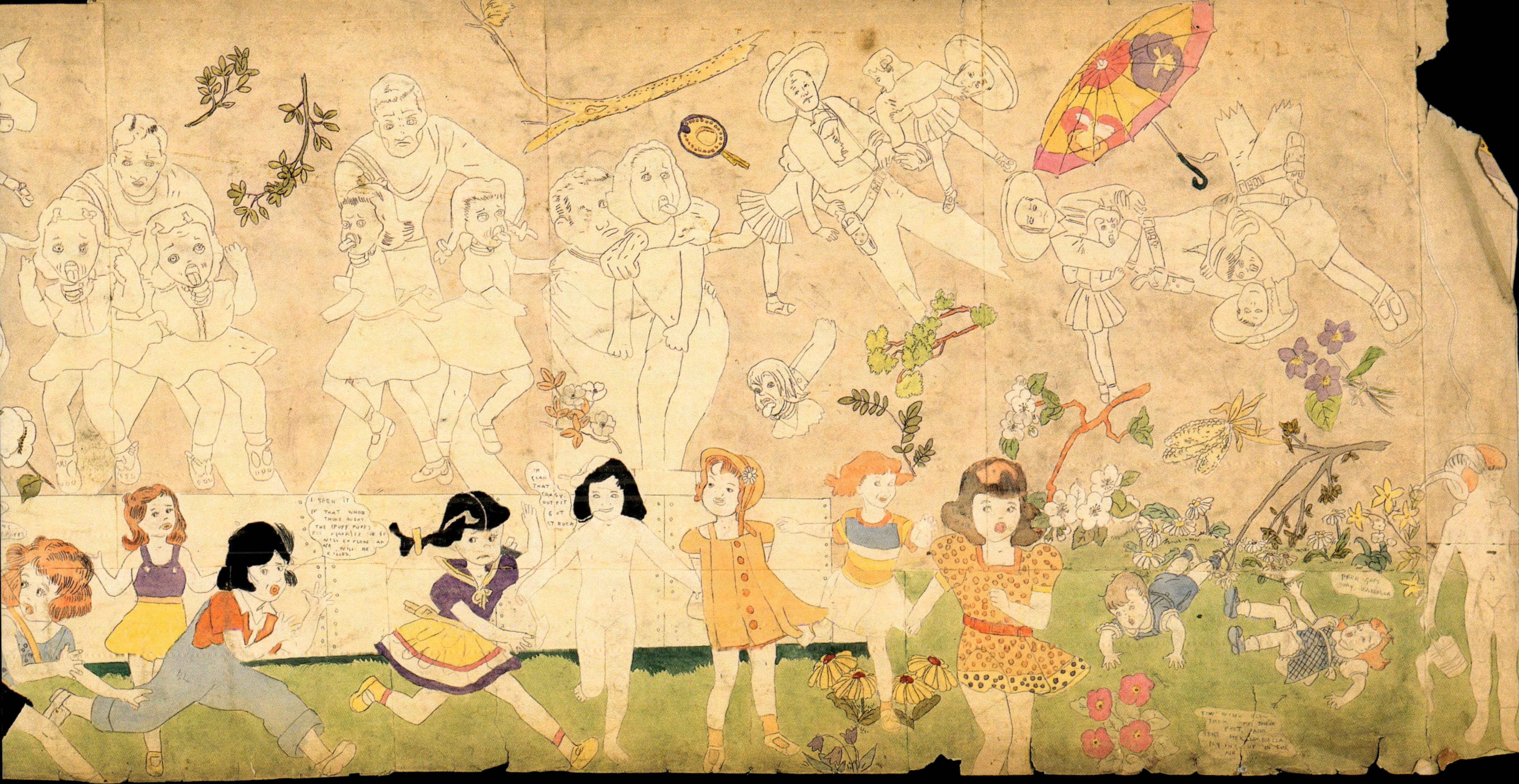
I SEEN IT
IF THAT WHOLE
THING HERES
THE (PUFF PUFF)
FINALES IT SO
WILL EXPLODE AN
WE WILL BE
KILLED.
IM GLAD
THAT
TRASY
OUT FIT
IS ST
ST RUCK
PREE GOD
MY YABELLA

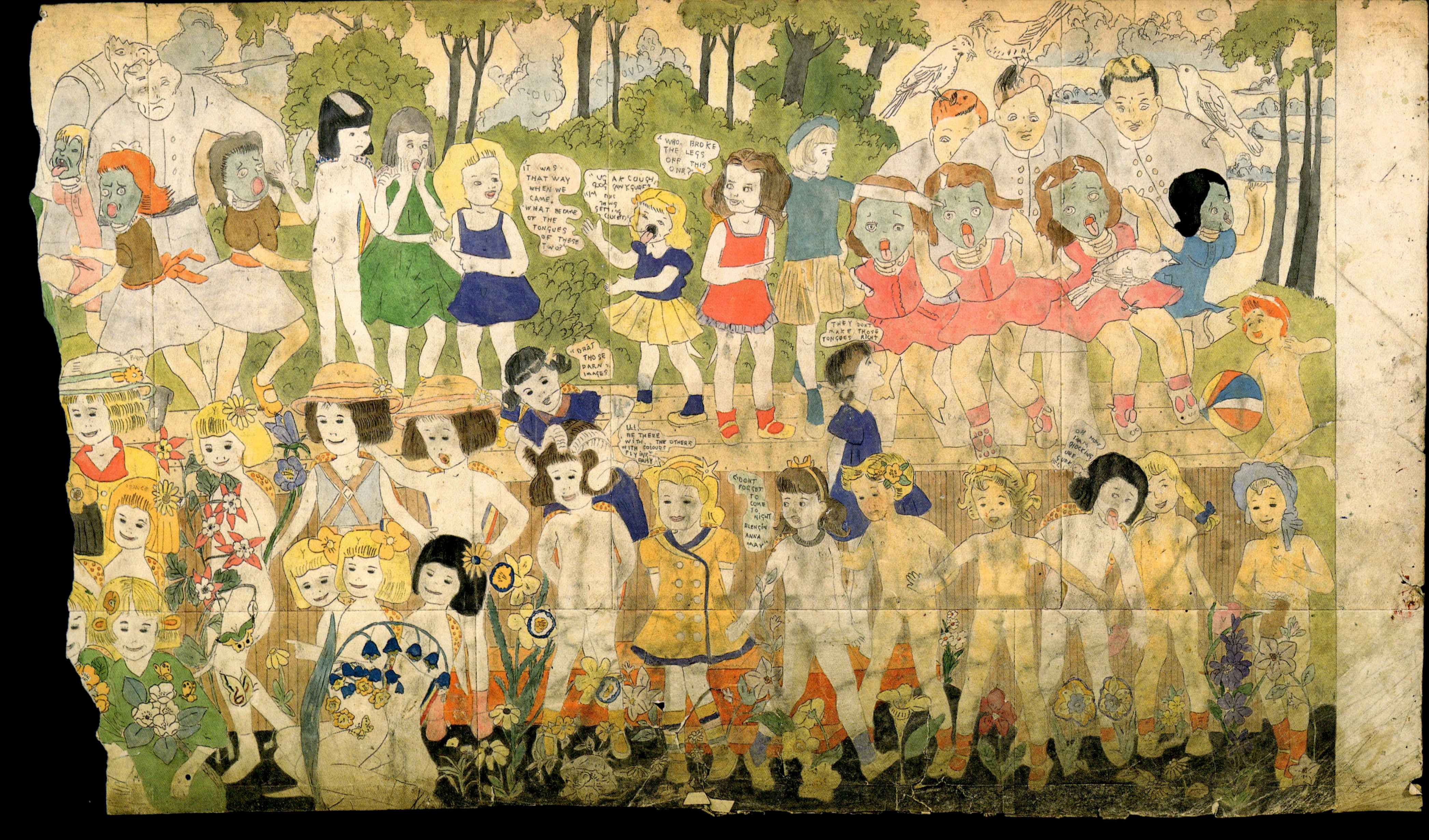

192 | Untitled (girls playing with balls and sitting on fence with Blengin).

Watercolor, pencil, and carbon tracing on pieced paper, 32 x 54 ¾ in.

Collection Kiyoko Lerner

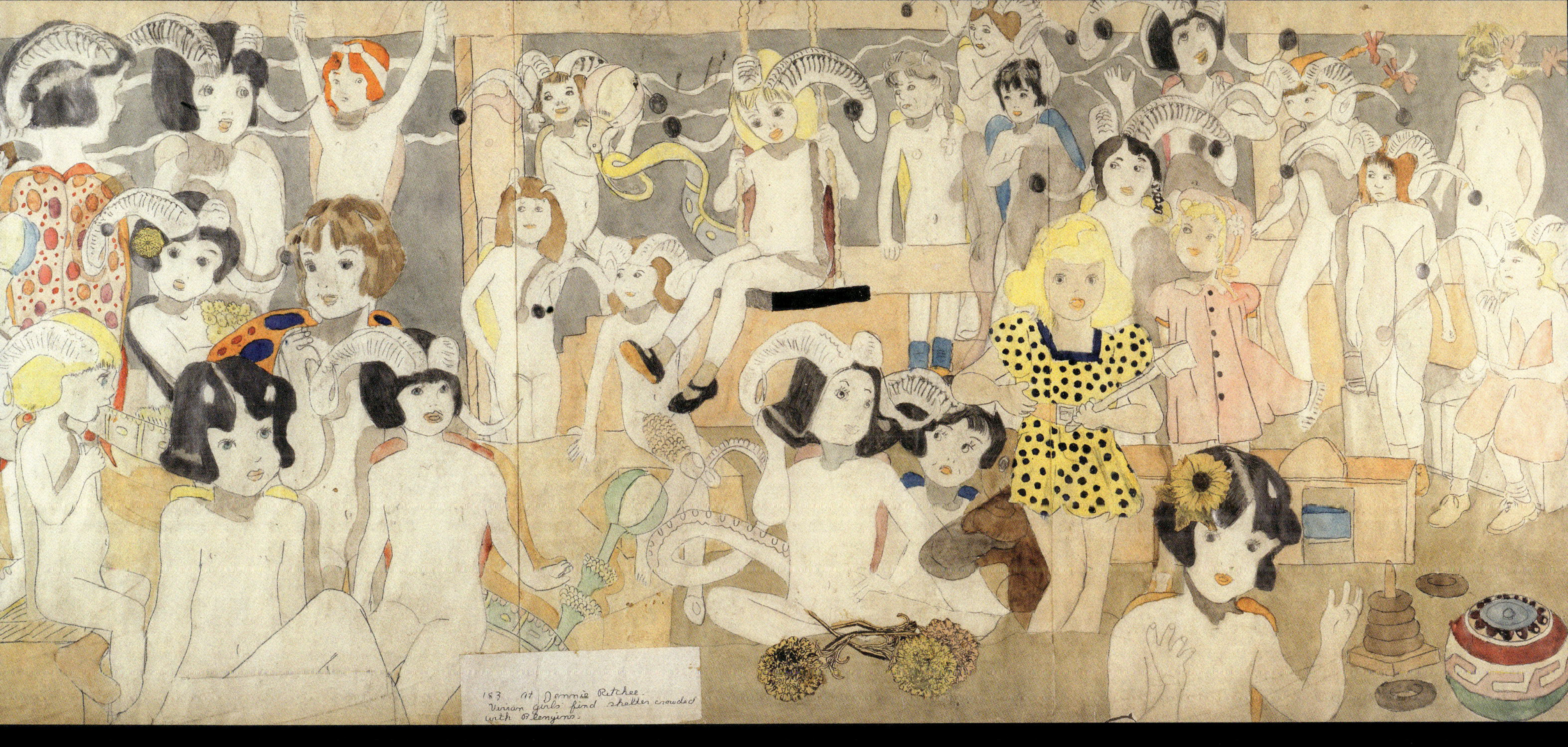

Vivian girls find shelter crowded with Blengins. 193
Watercolor, pencil, carbon tracing, and collage on pieced paper,
approx. 24 x 53 in. Collection of Anne-Brigitte Sirois

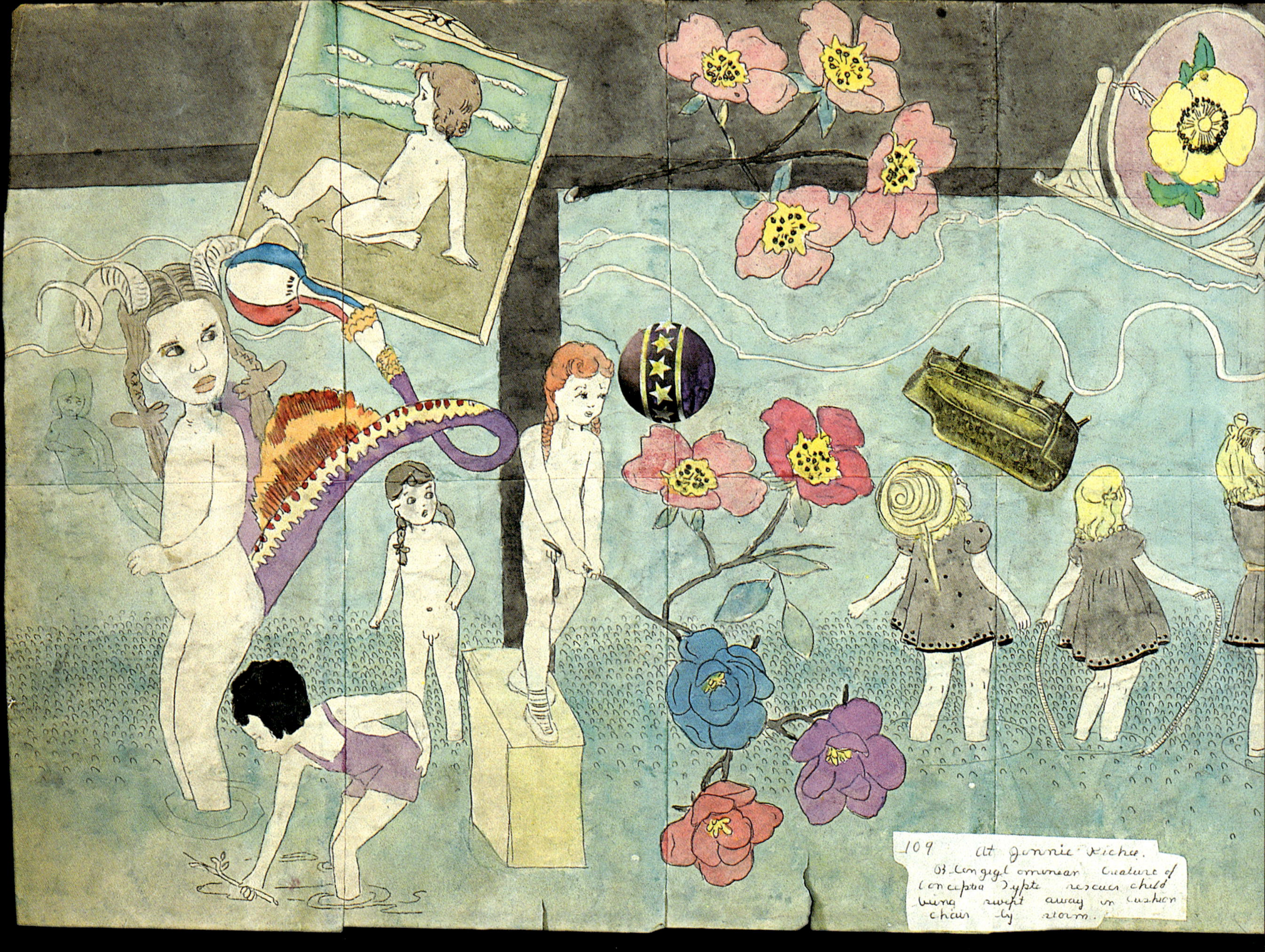

194 | *At Jennie Richee. Blengiglomenean creature of [Conceptia Type] rescues child being swept away in cushion chair by storm.* Watercolor, pencil, carbon tracing, and collage on pieced paper, 24 x 107 in. The Museum of Everything

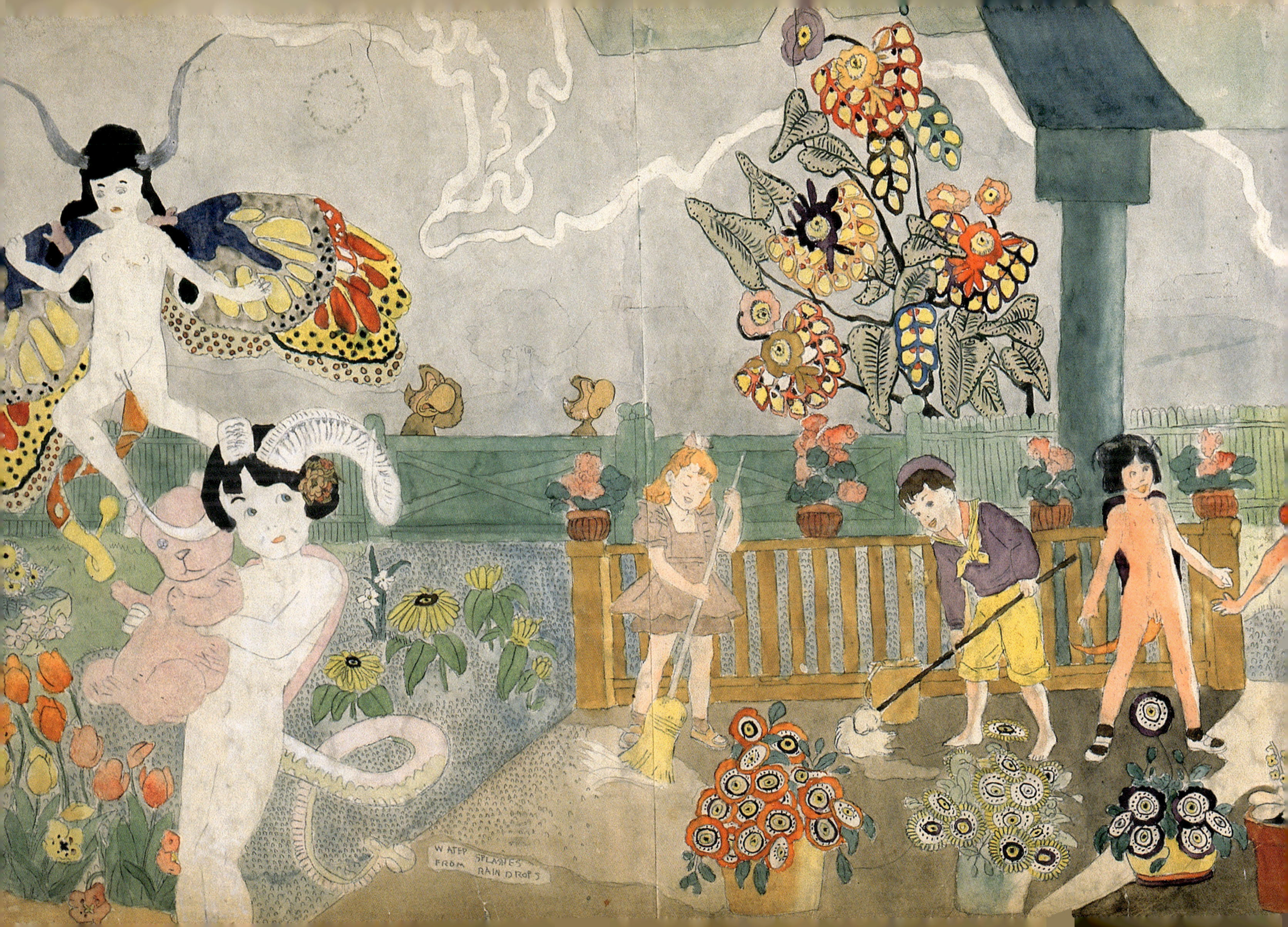

WATER SPLASHES
FROM
RAIN DROPS

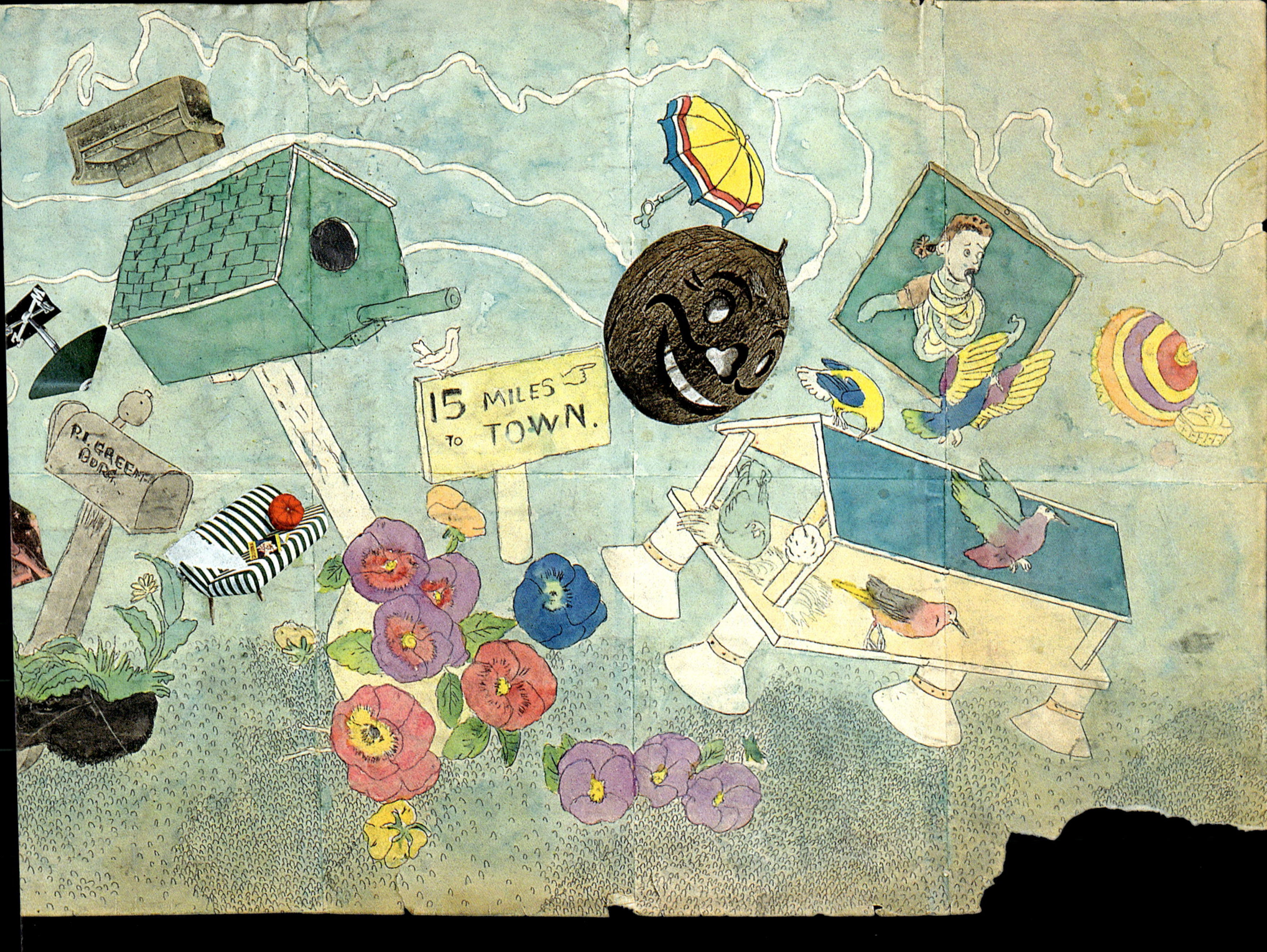

172 At Jennie Richee. Storm Continues. Lightning strikes shelter but no one is injured.
Watercolor, pencil, carbon tracing, and collage on pieced paper, 24 x 108 ¾ in.
Collection American Folk Art Museum, New York. Anonymous gift in recognition of Sam Farber

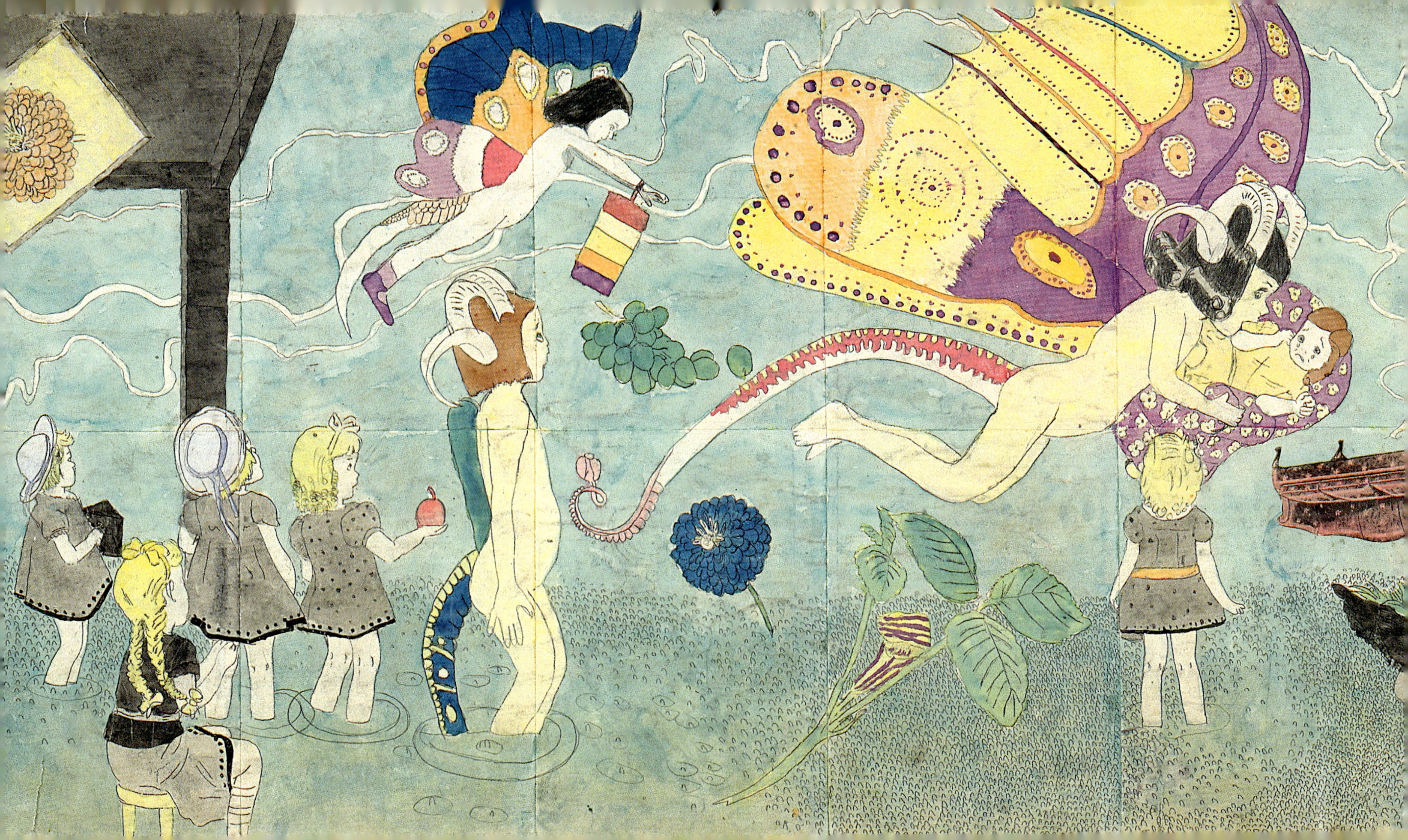

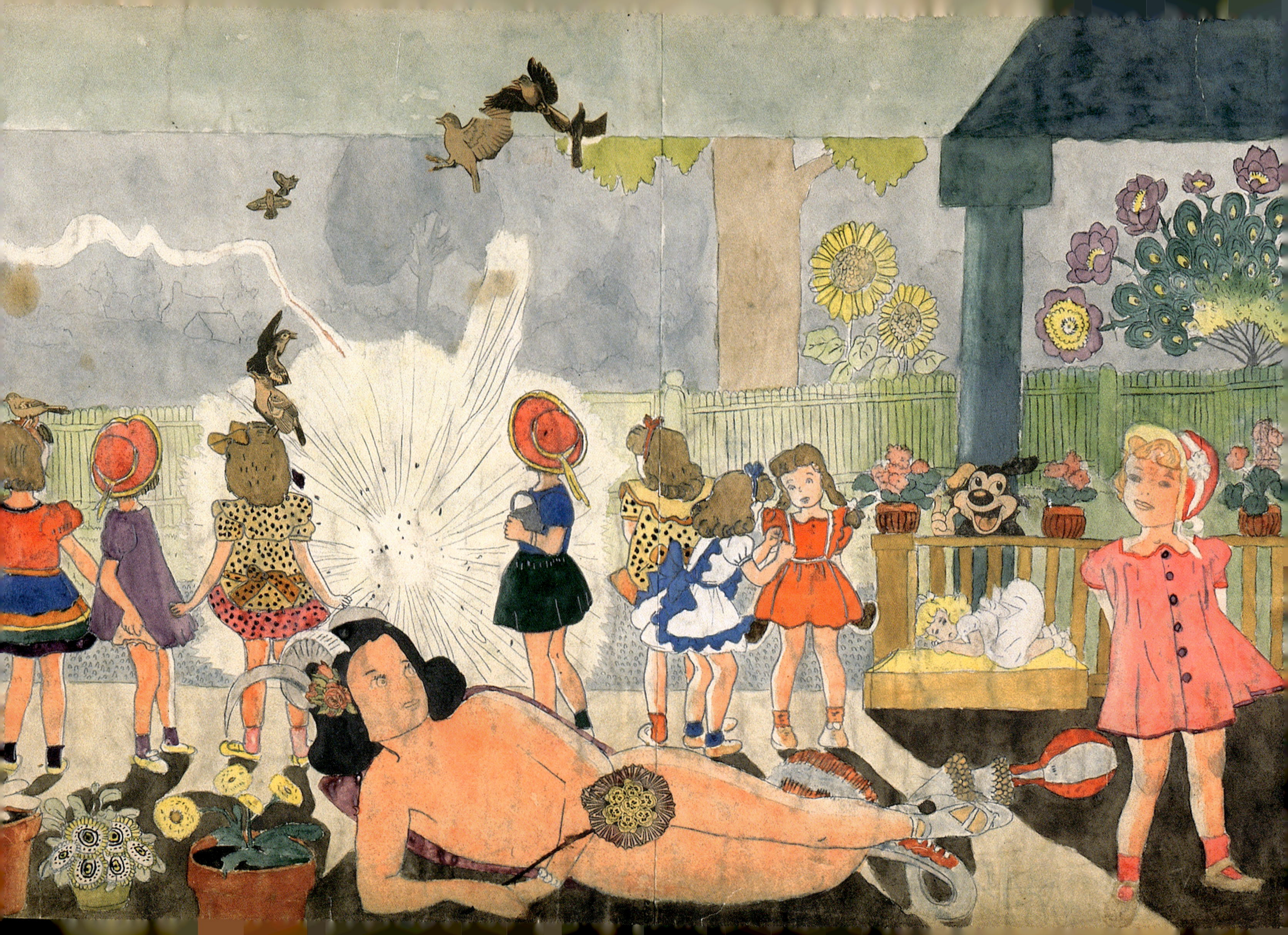

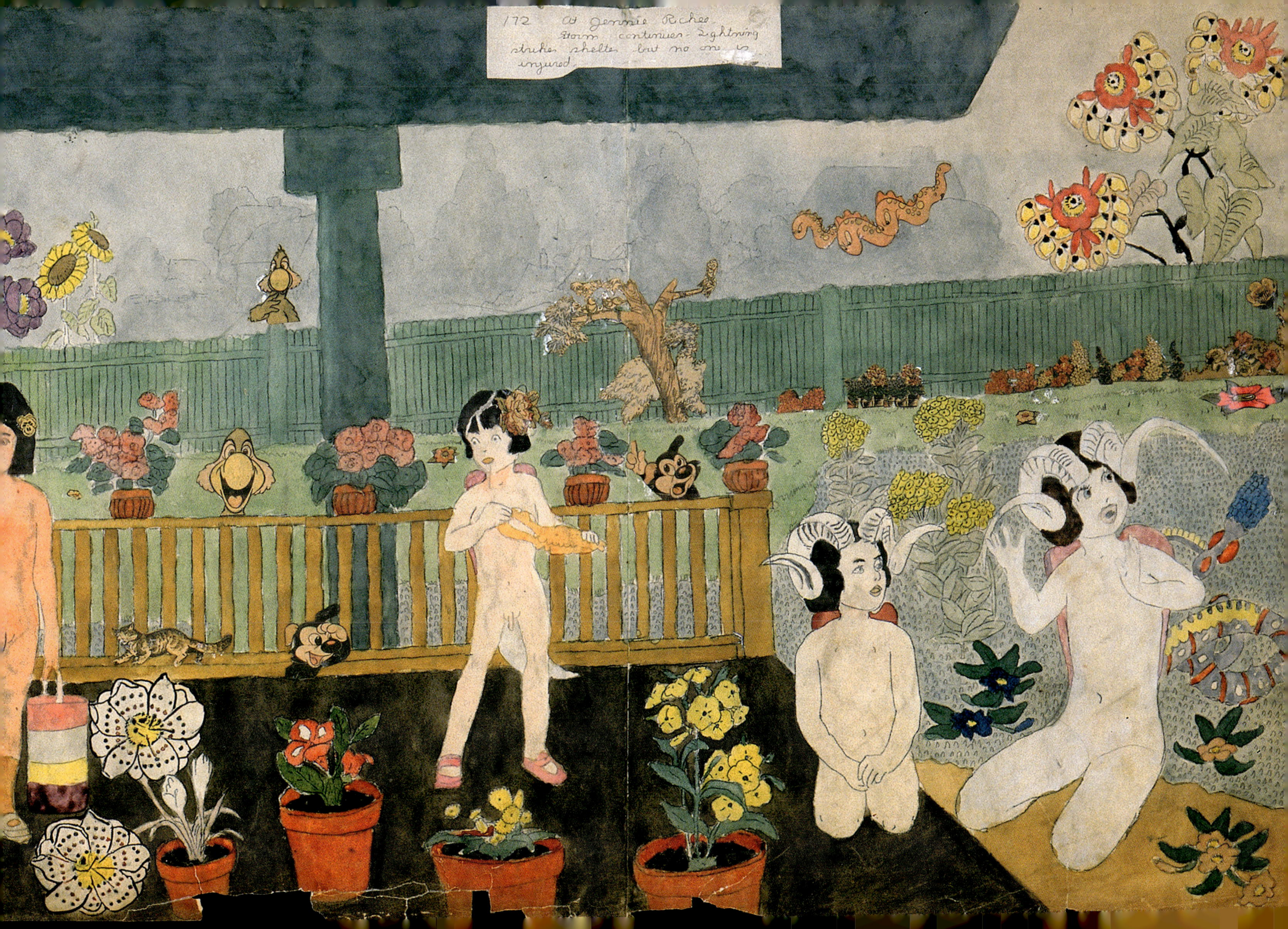
172   At Jennie Richee
Storm continues. Lightning
strikes shelter but no one is
injured.

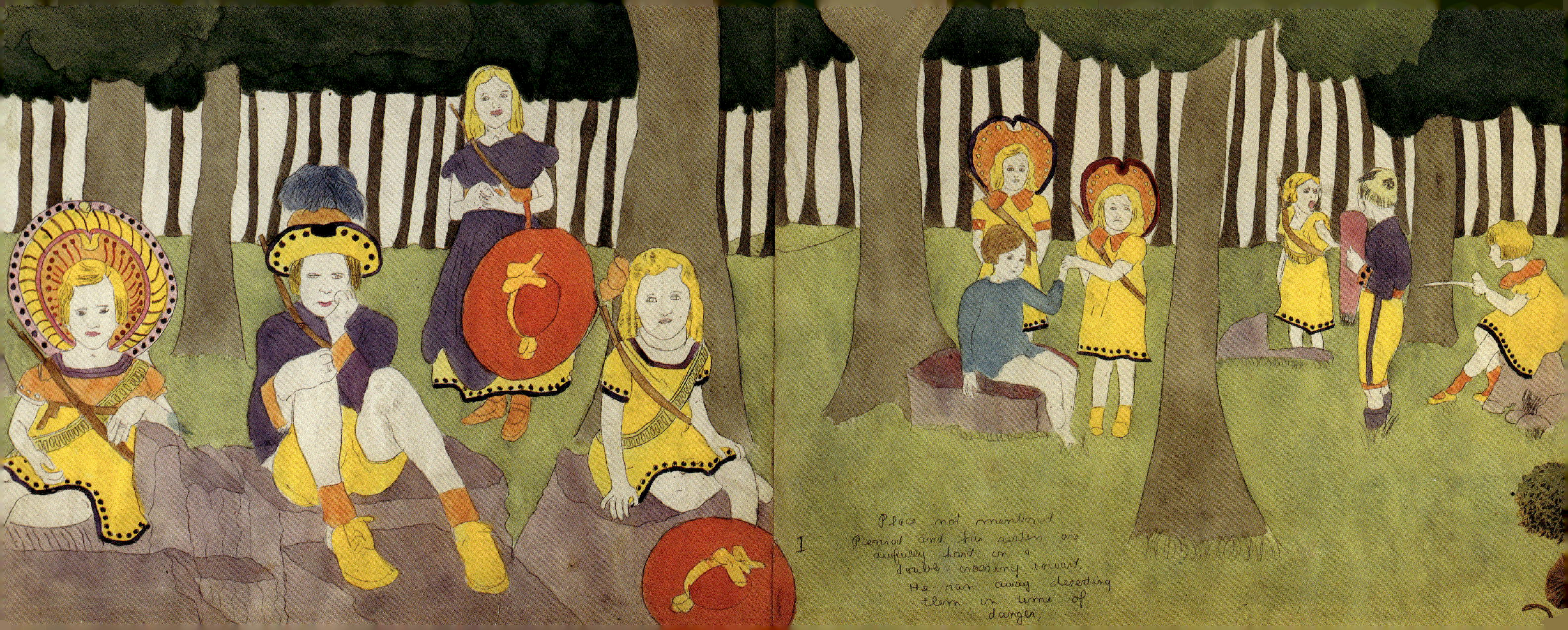
1
Place not mentioned
Pierrod and his sister are
awfully hard on a
double crossing coward.
He ran away deserting
them in time of
danger,

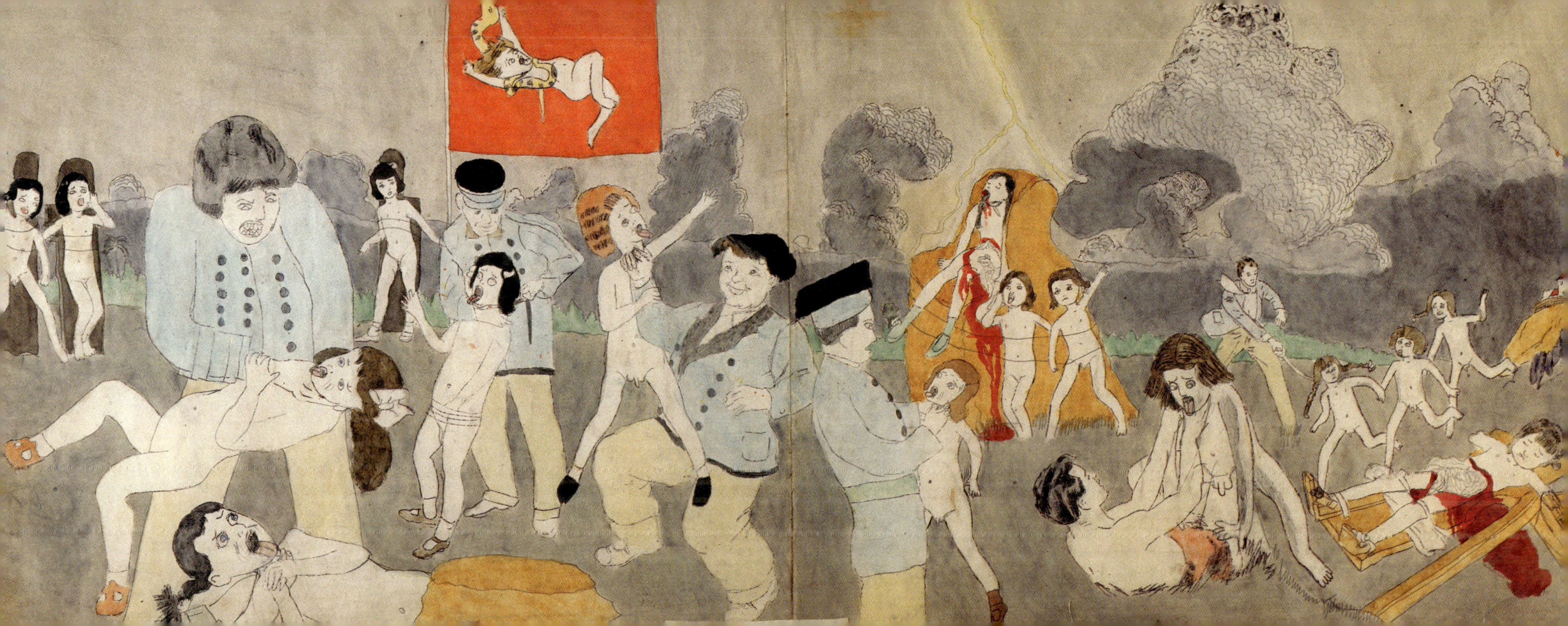

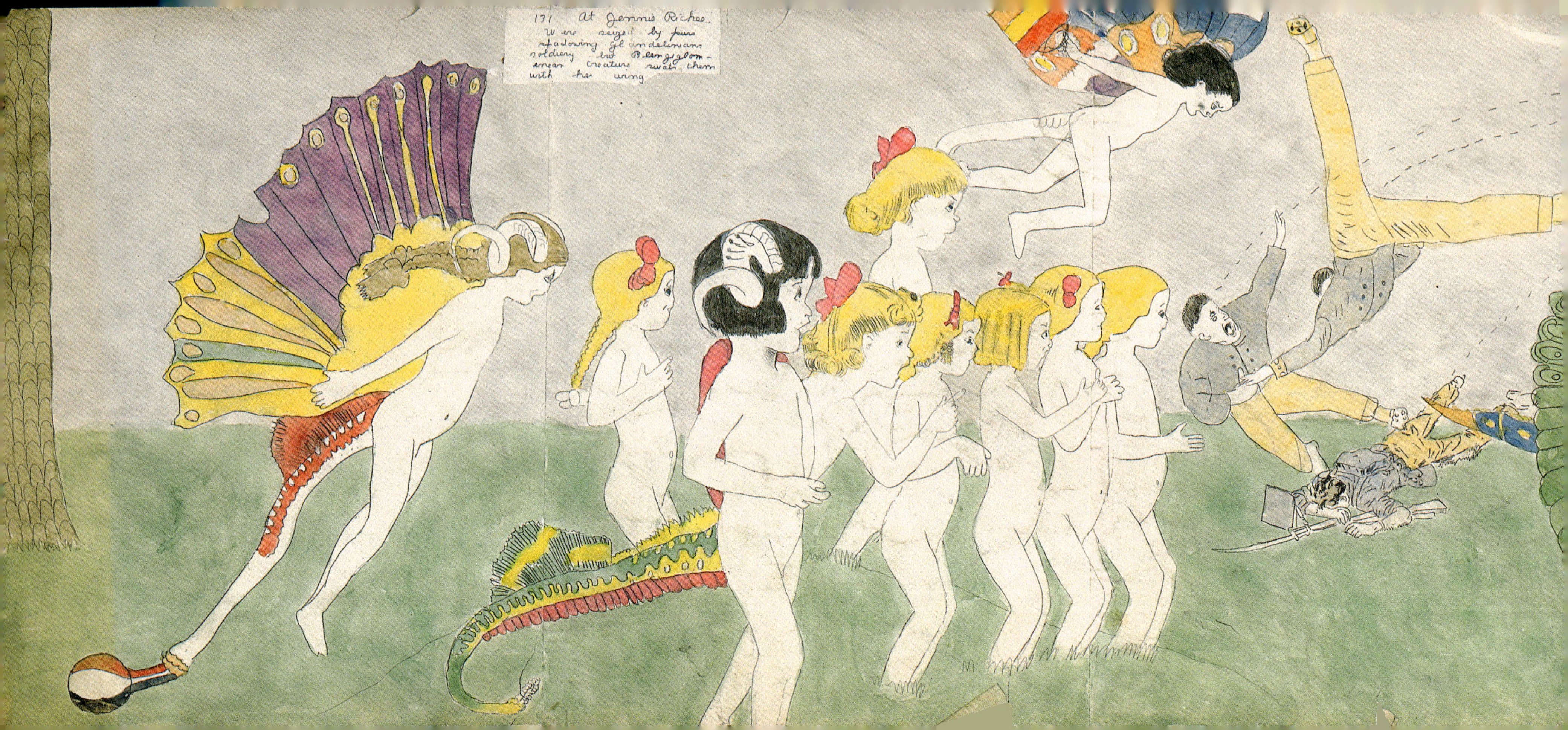
171   At Jennie Richee.
Were seized by pursuing
shadowing Glandelinian
soldiery but Blengiglom-
enean creature swats them
with her wing

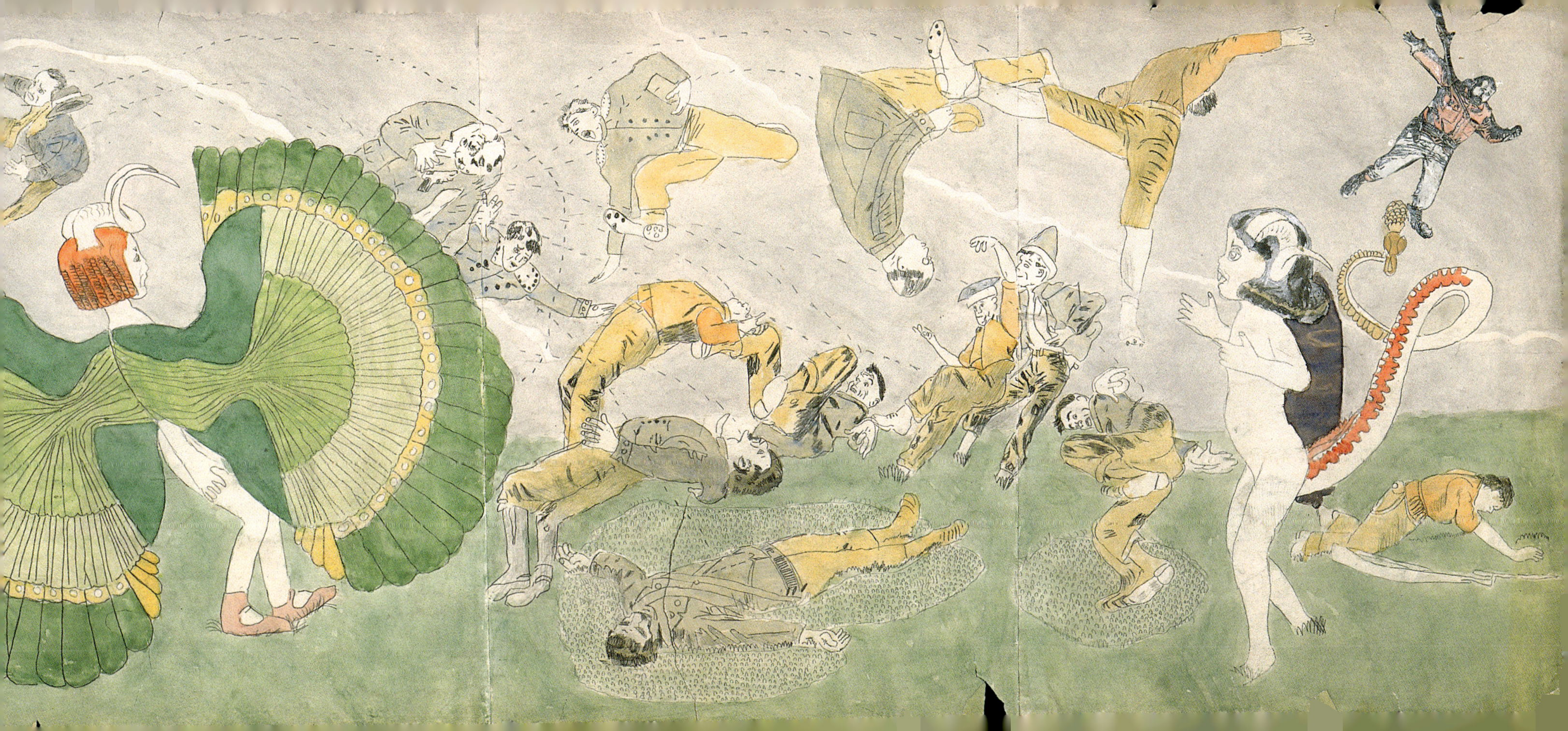

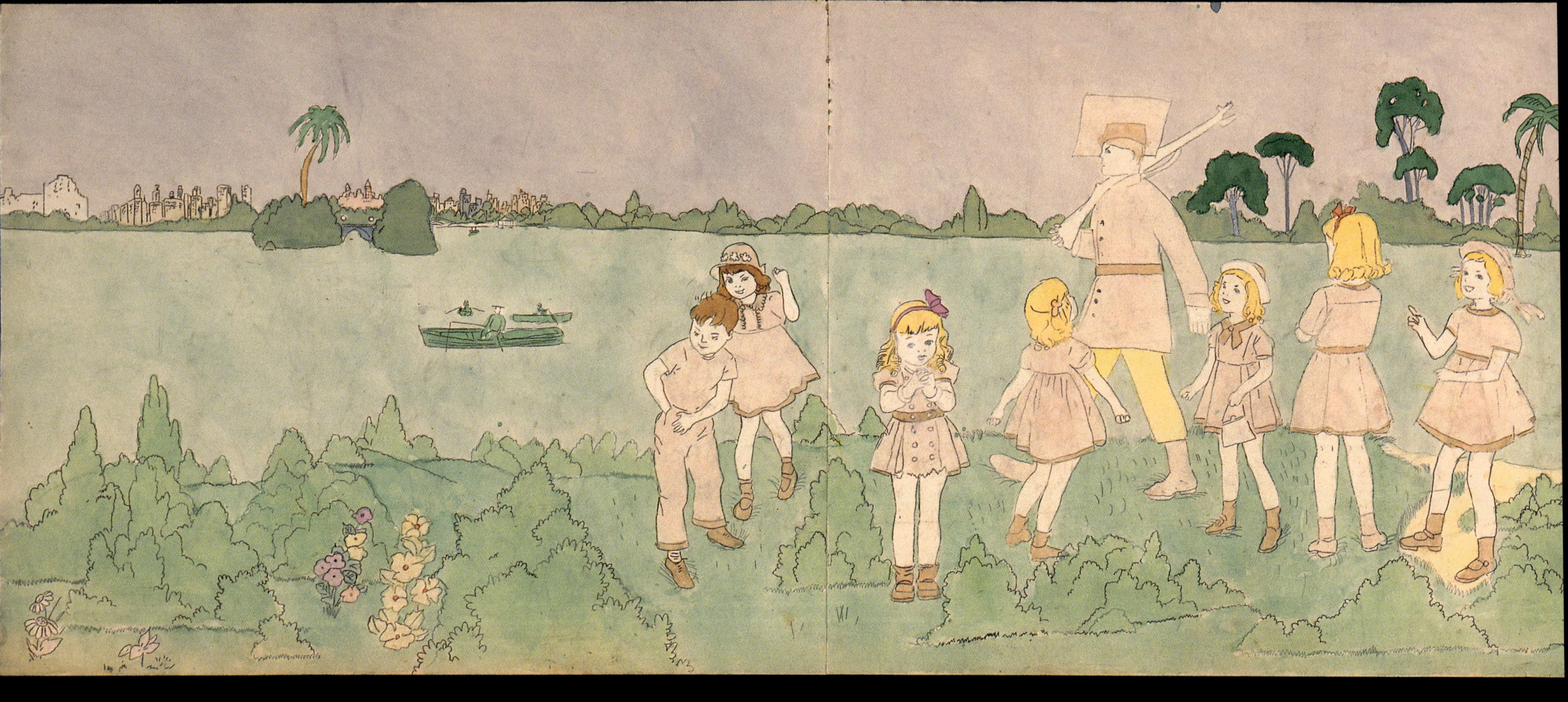

202   *At Jennie Richee. Vivian girls held out until admitted in to Manley headquarters.*

Watercolor, pencil, and carbon tracing on pieced paper, 19 x 95 in. Private collection

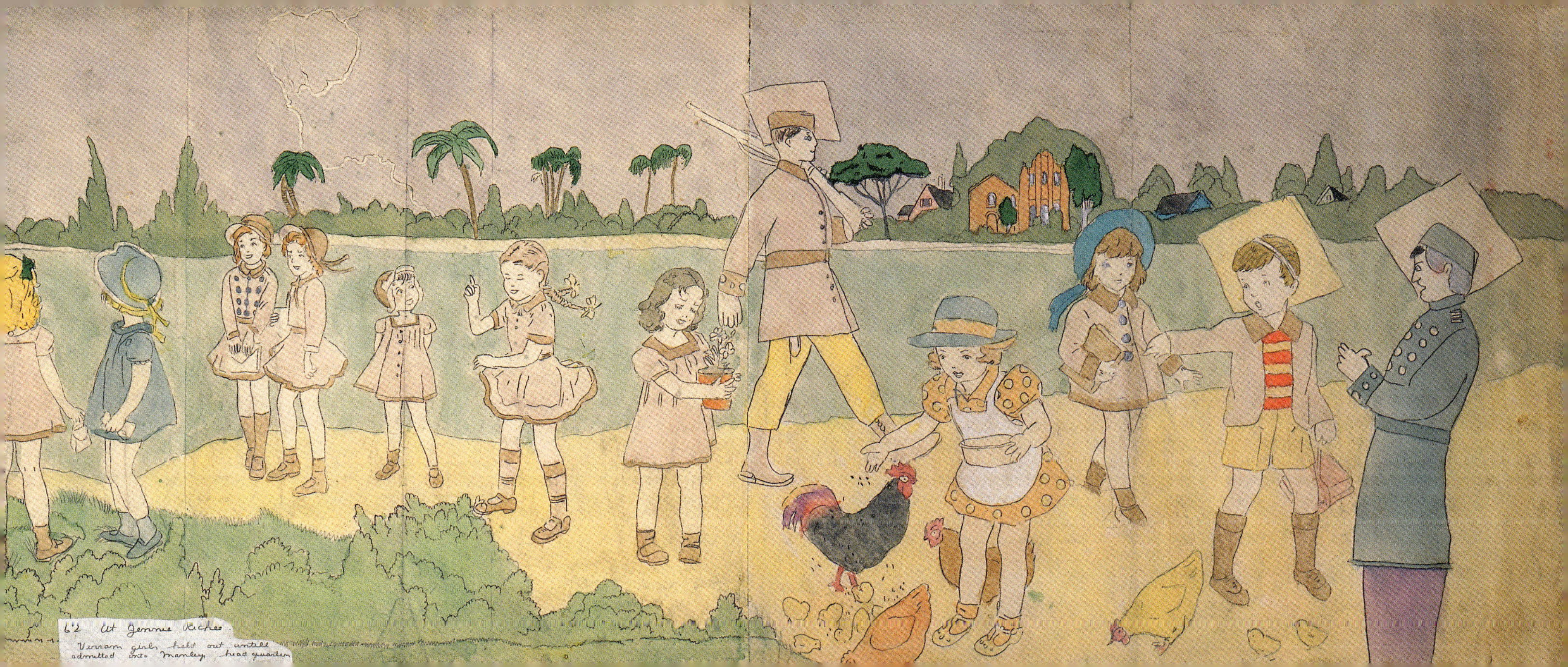

62 At Jennie Riches.
Verram girls held out untill
admitted into Manley head quarters

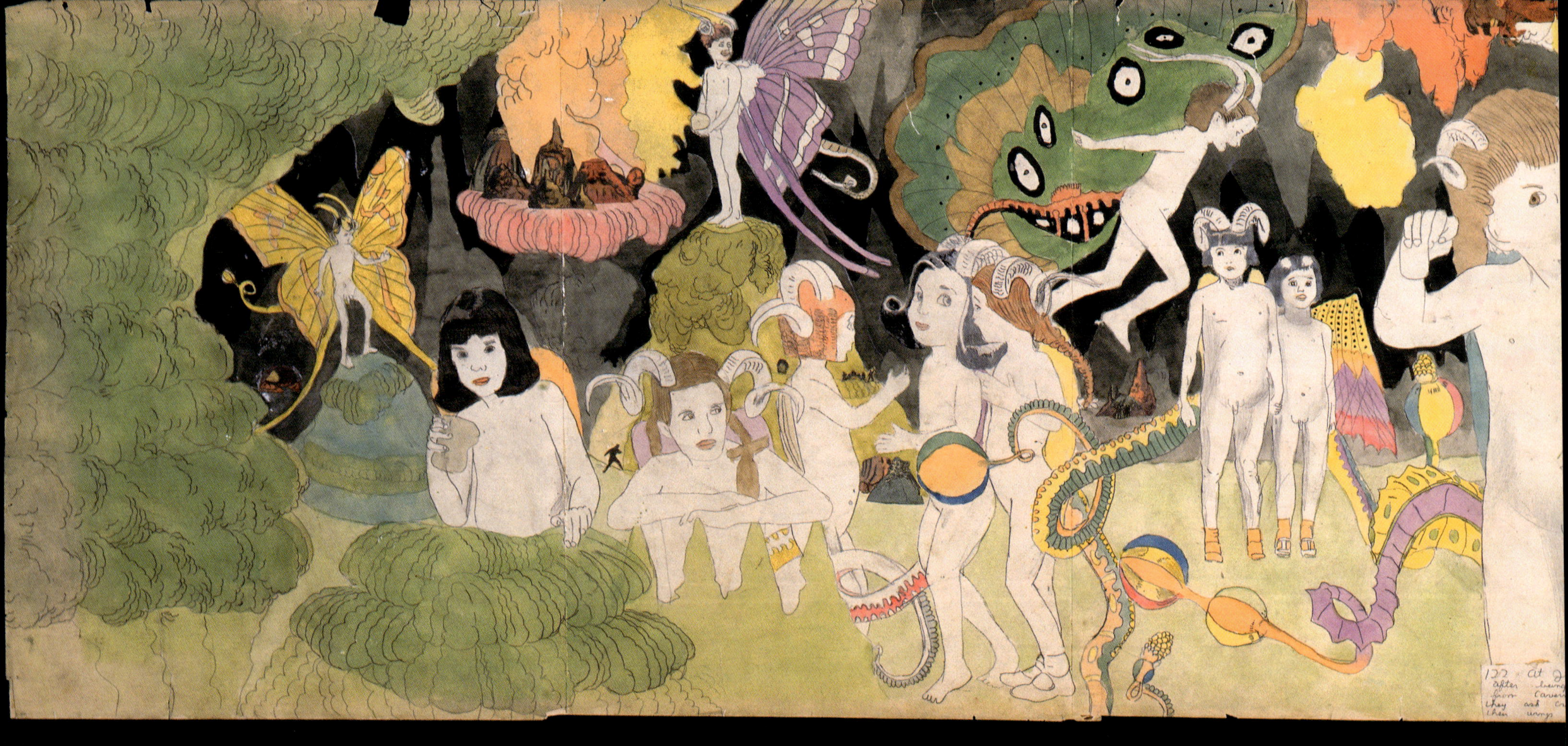

204 | *At Jennie Richee. After being shown how to escape from Guern by their help, they ask creatures to display their wings, which they do.* Watercolor, pencil, and carbon tracing on pieced paper, approx. 24 x 108 in. The Museum of Everything

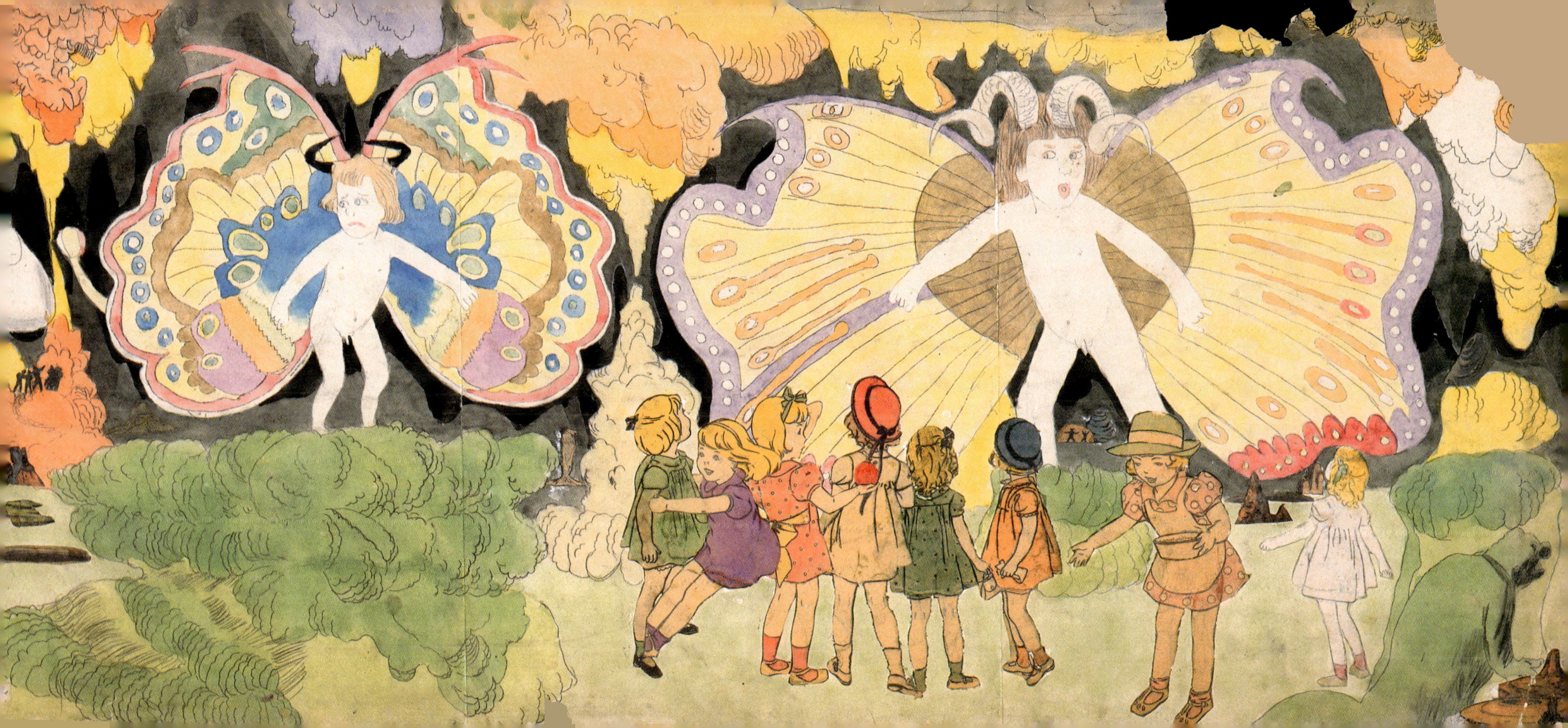

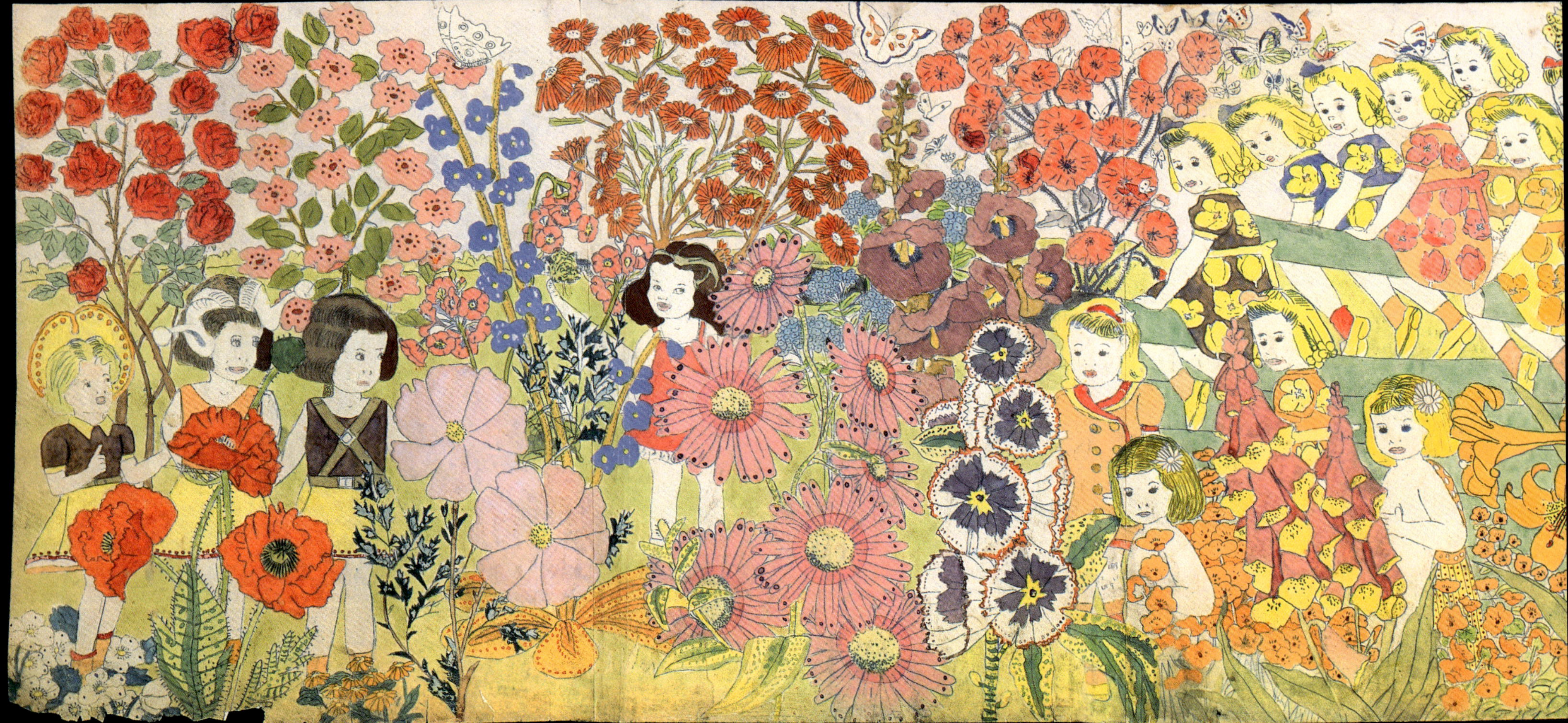

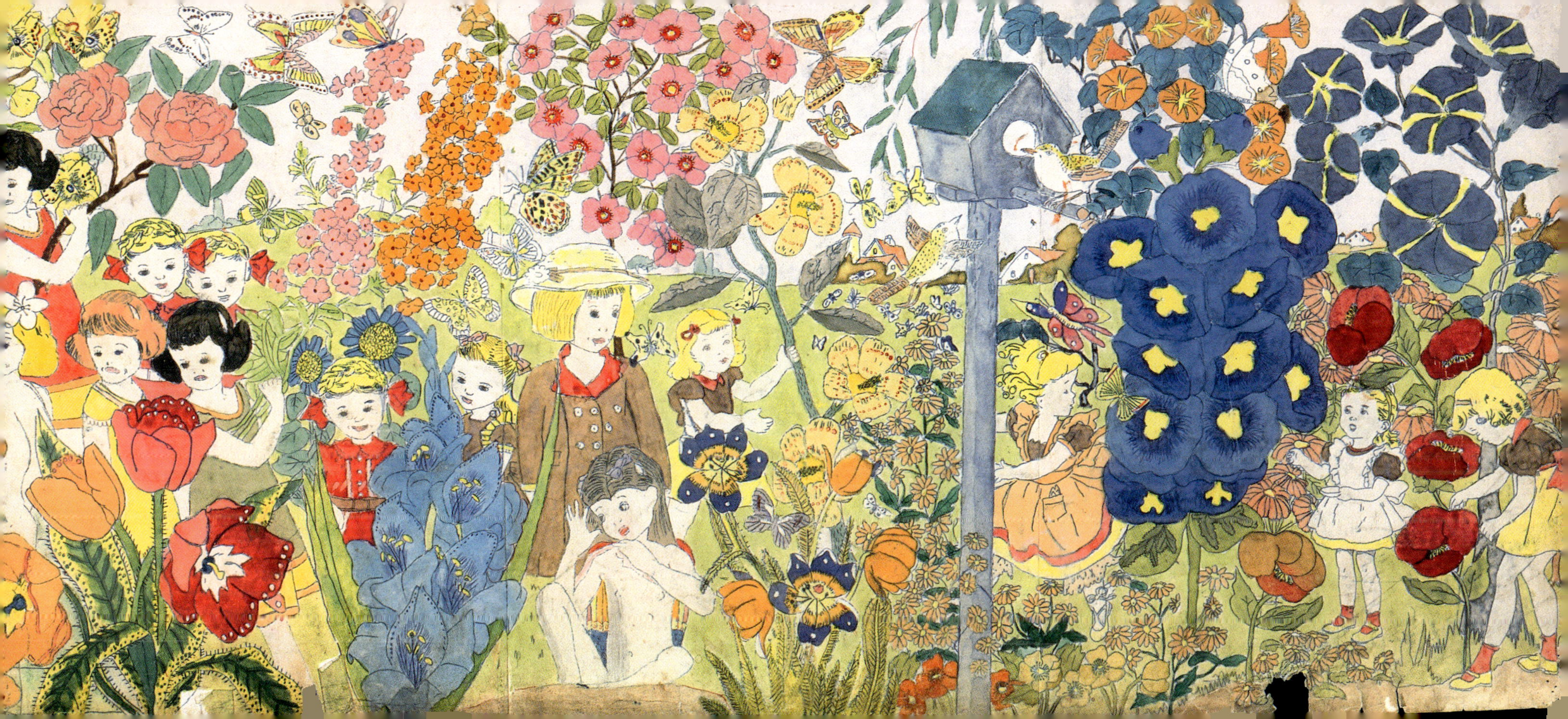

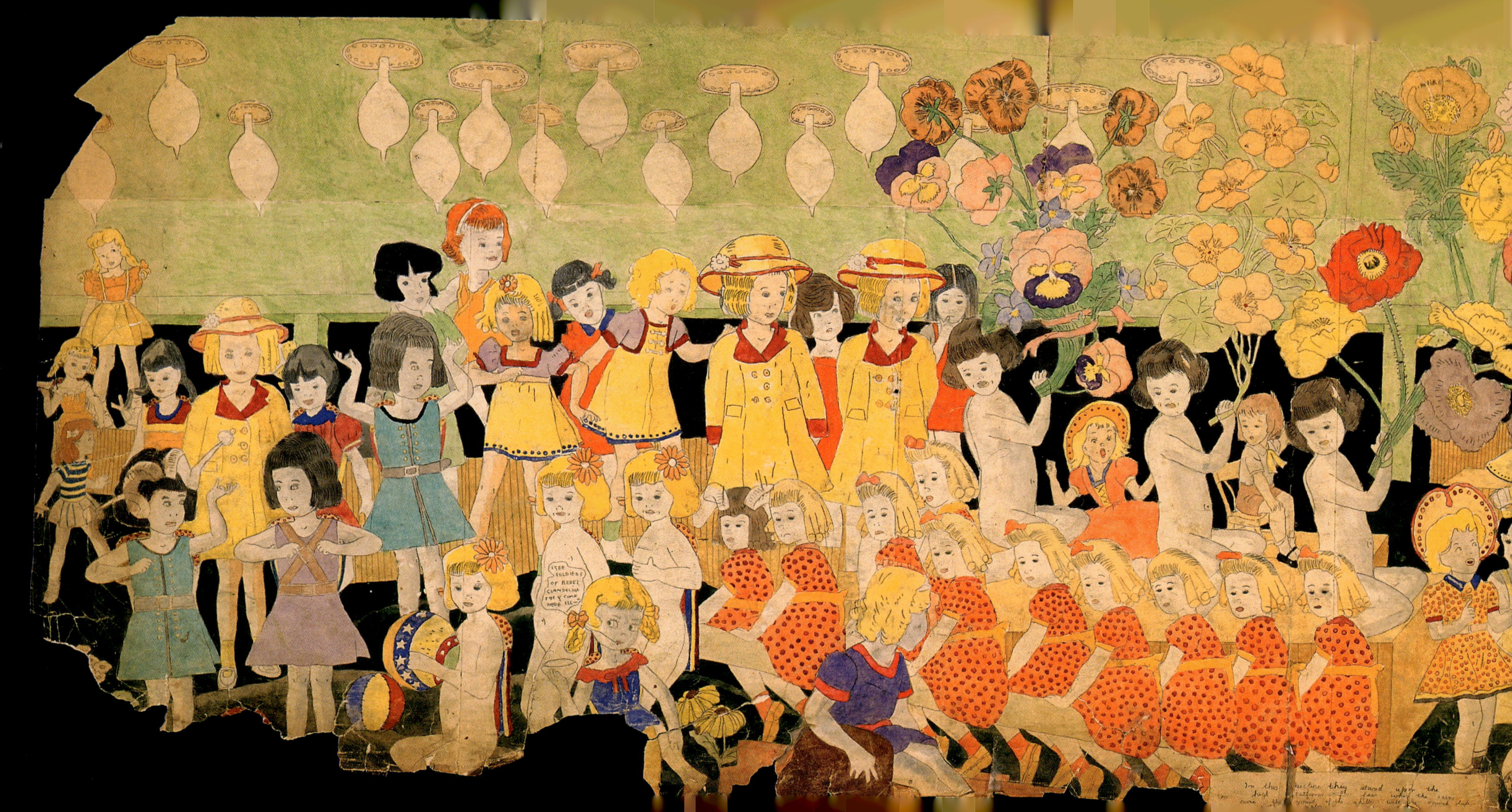
I SEE SOLDIERS OF REBEL GLANDELINA THEY COME HERE ILL—
In this picture they stand upon the high platform

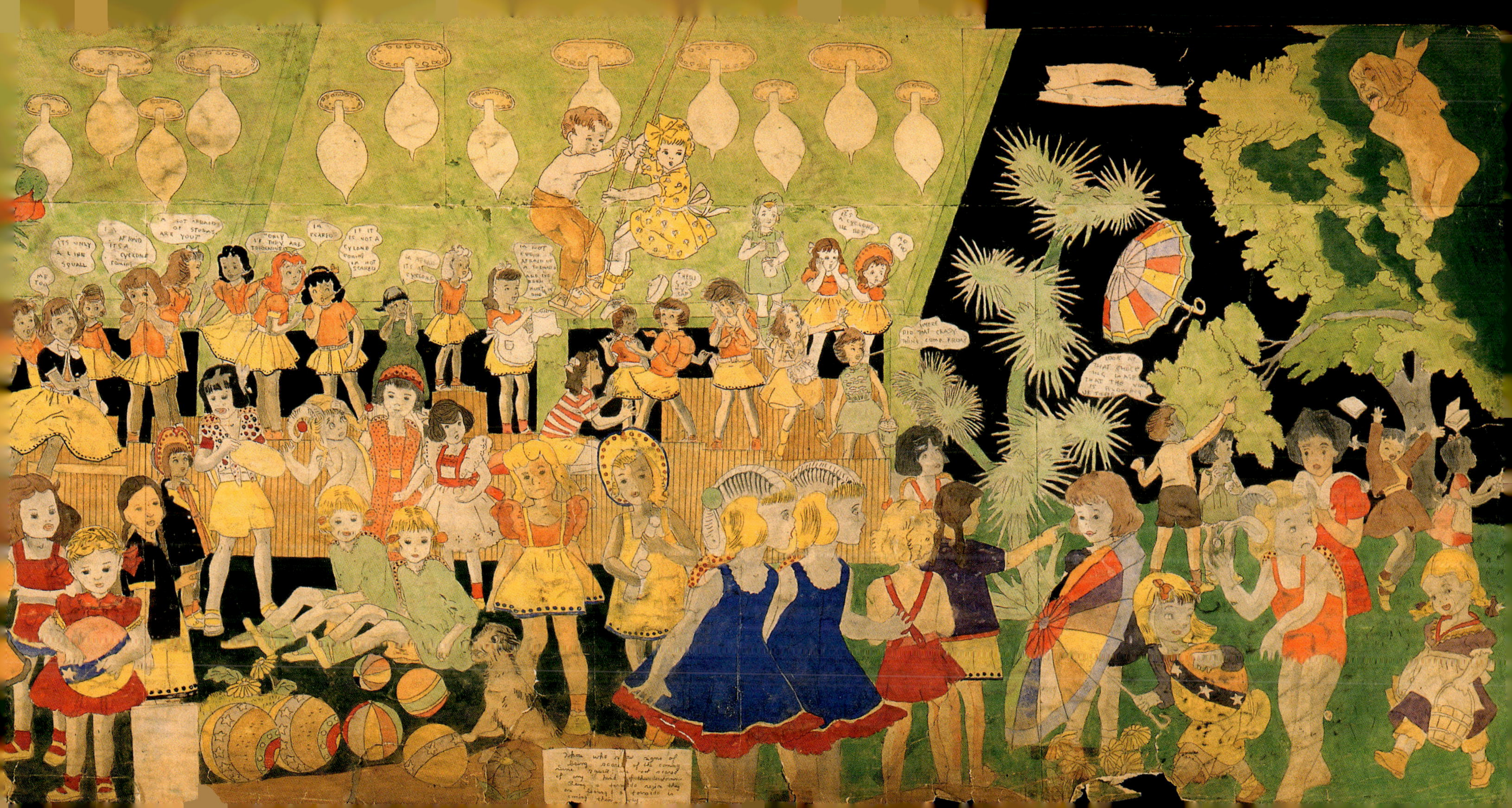

Johns who is now aged of being scared of the coming wind squall am not scared of any kind of thunderstorm. Being a tornado region they on seeing a tornado is coming their way

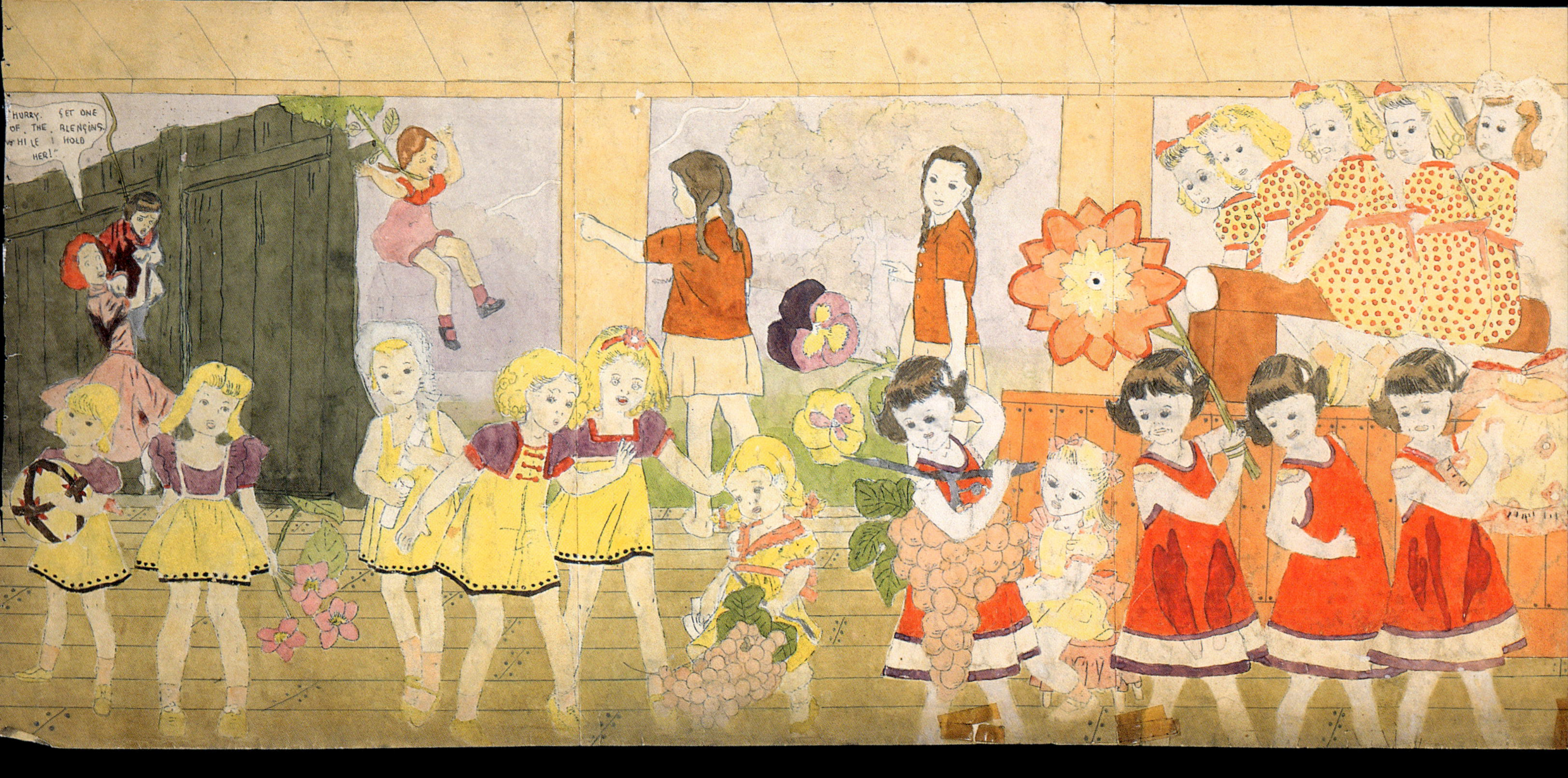

210 | Untitled (vines strangling girls). Watercolor, pencil,
carbon tracing, and collage on pieced paper, 24 x 106 in.
Collection Kiyoko Lerner

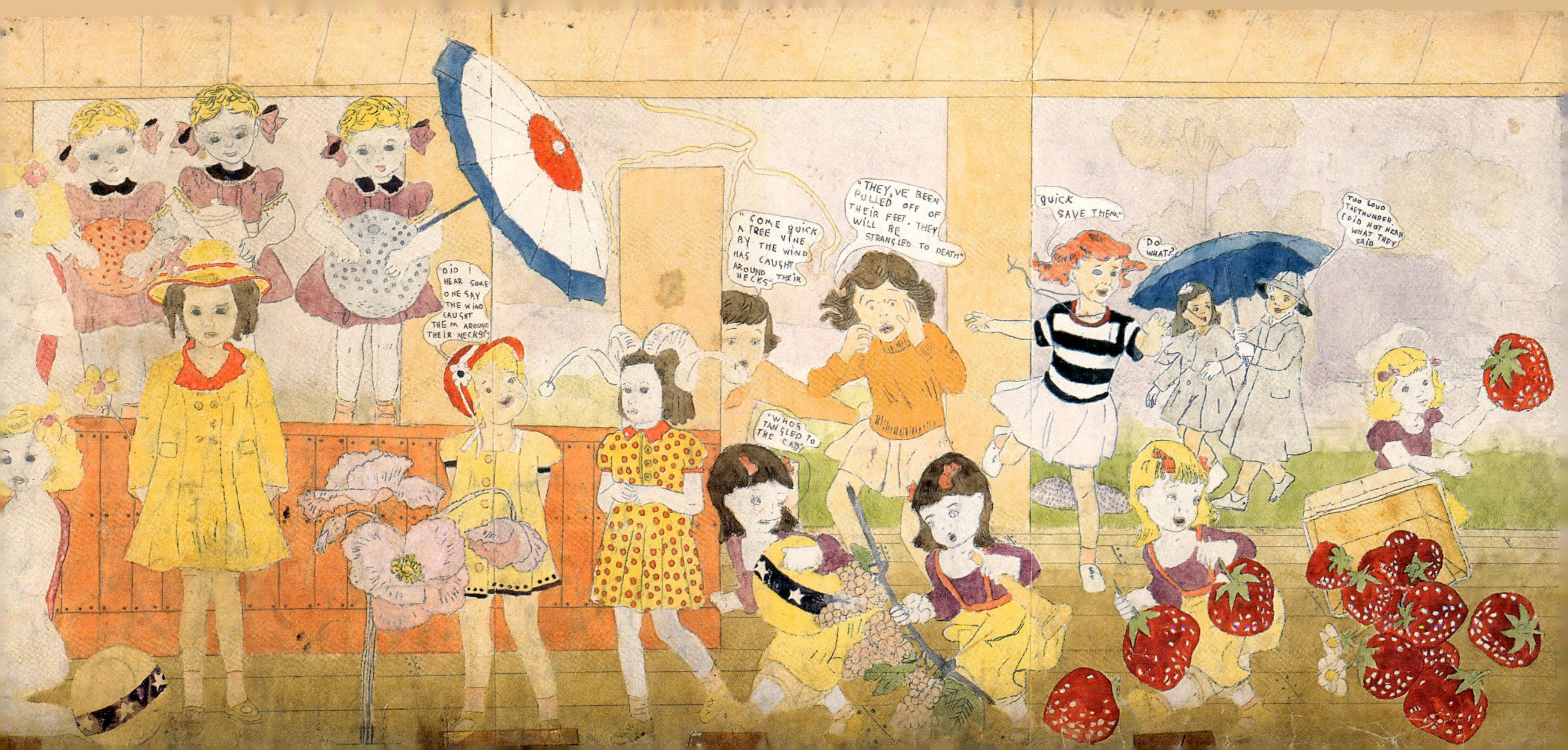

"DID I HEAR SOME ONE SAY THE WIND CAUGHT THEM AROUND THEIR NECKS?"
"COME QUICK A TREE VINE BY THE WIND HAS CAUGHT AROUND THEIR NECKS"
"THEY,VE BEEN PULLED OFF OF THEIR FEET, THEY WILL BE STRANGLED TO DEATH"
"QUICK SAVE THEM"
DO WHAT?
TOO LOUD THE THUNDER I DID NOT HEAR WHAT THEY SAID
"WHOS TANGLED TO THE CAT"

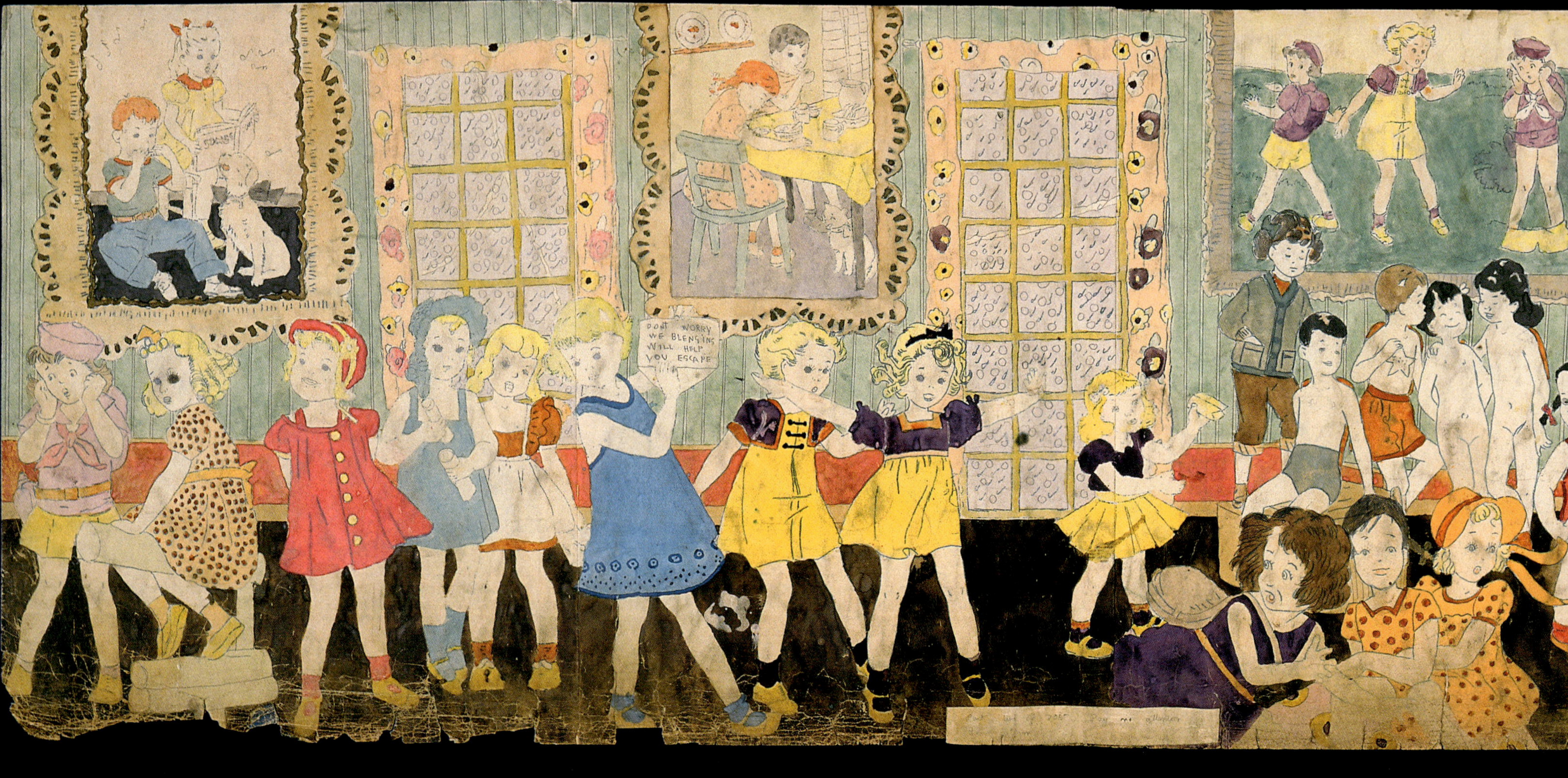

212 Untitled ("Part 2 of 205"). Watercolor, pencil, and carbon tracing
on pieced paper, 24 x 105 in. Private collection

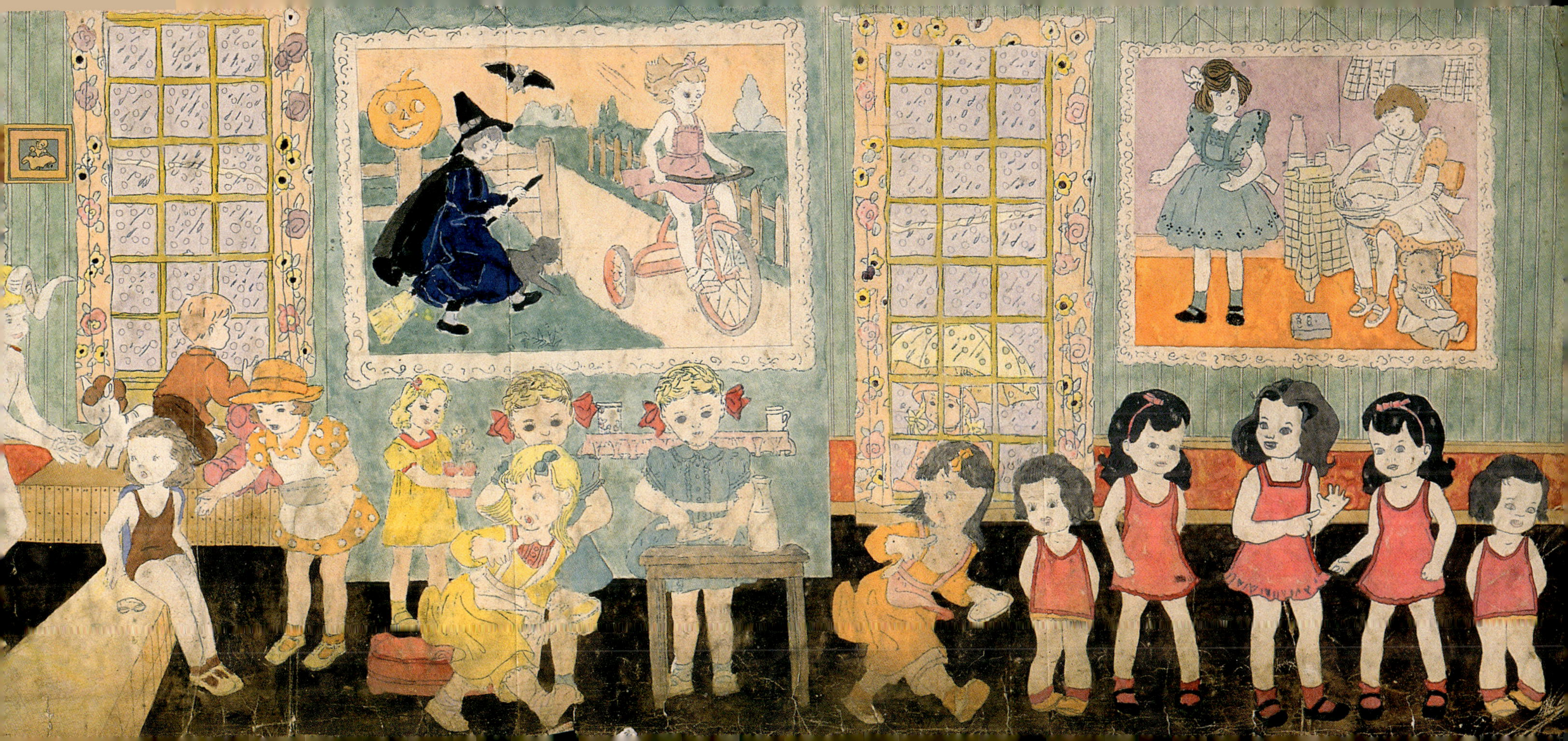

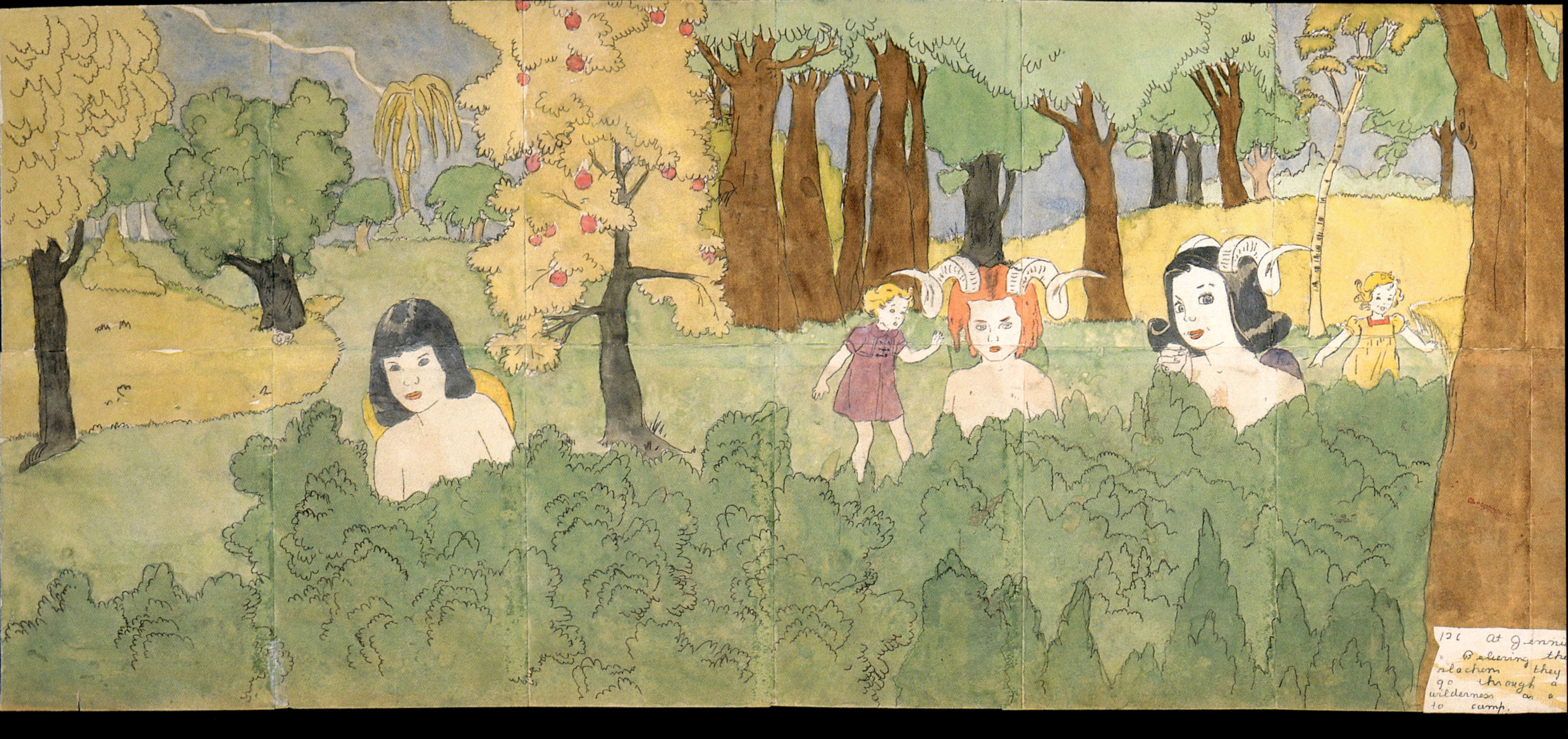

214 | *At Jennie Richee. Believing the storm to slacken they chose to go through a wooded wilderness on a short cut to camp.* Watercolor, pencil, and carbon tracing on pieced paper, 23 x 107 in. Private collection

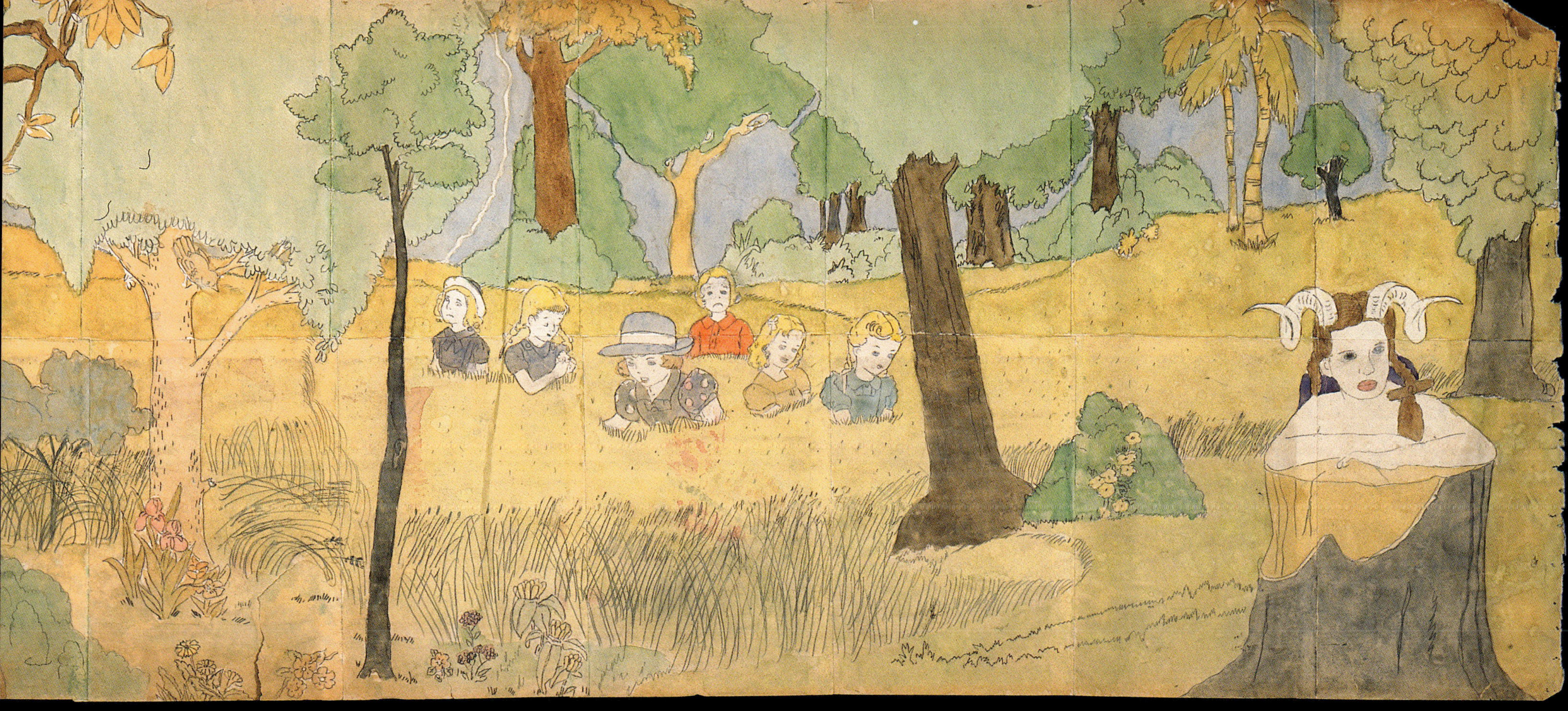

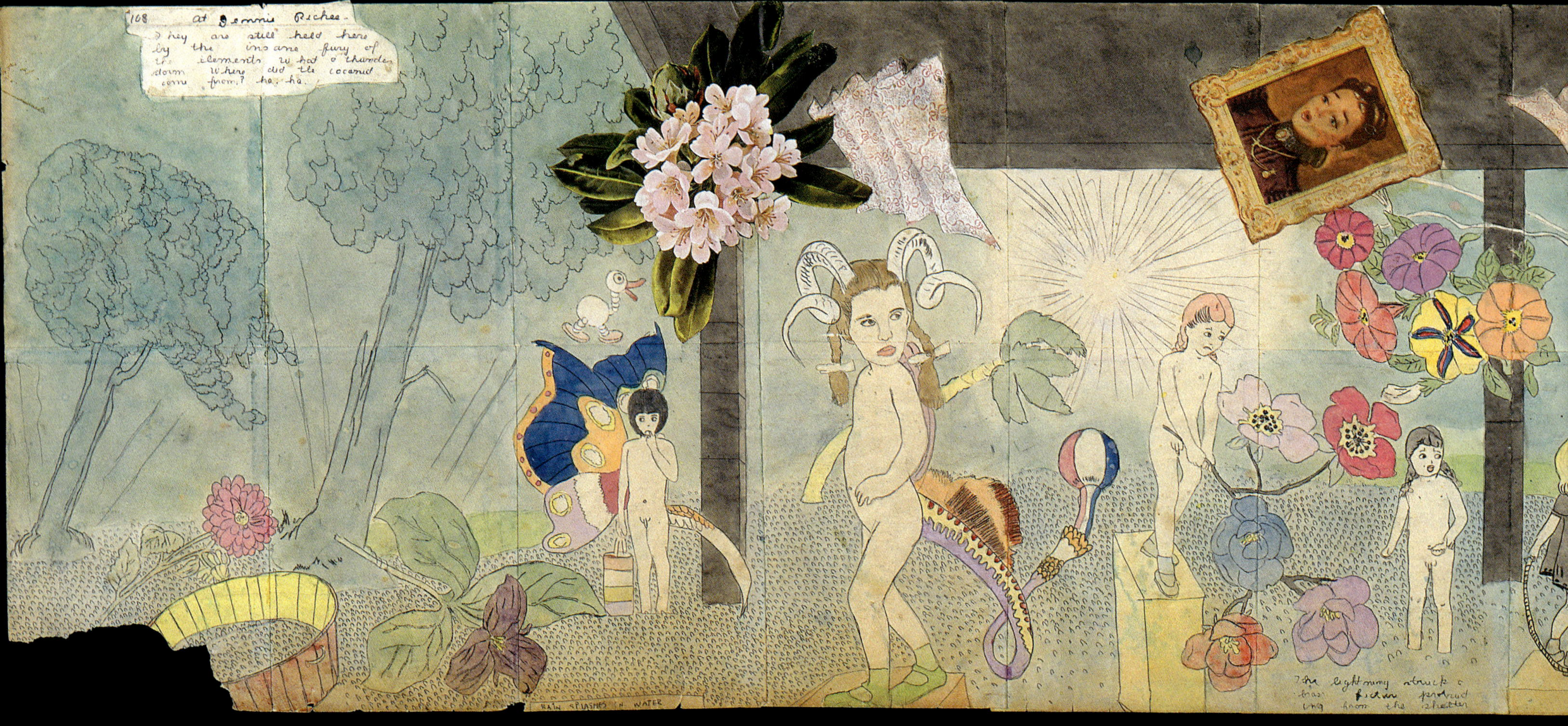

216 | *At Jennie Richee. They are still held here by the insane fury of the elements.*

What a thunderstorm, where did the coconut come from? Ha ha.

Watercolor, pencil, carbon tracing, and collage on pieced paper, 24 x 107 in. The Museum of Everything

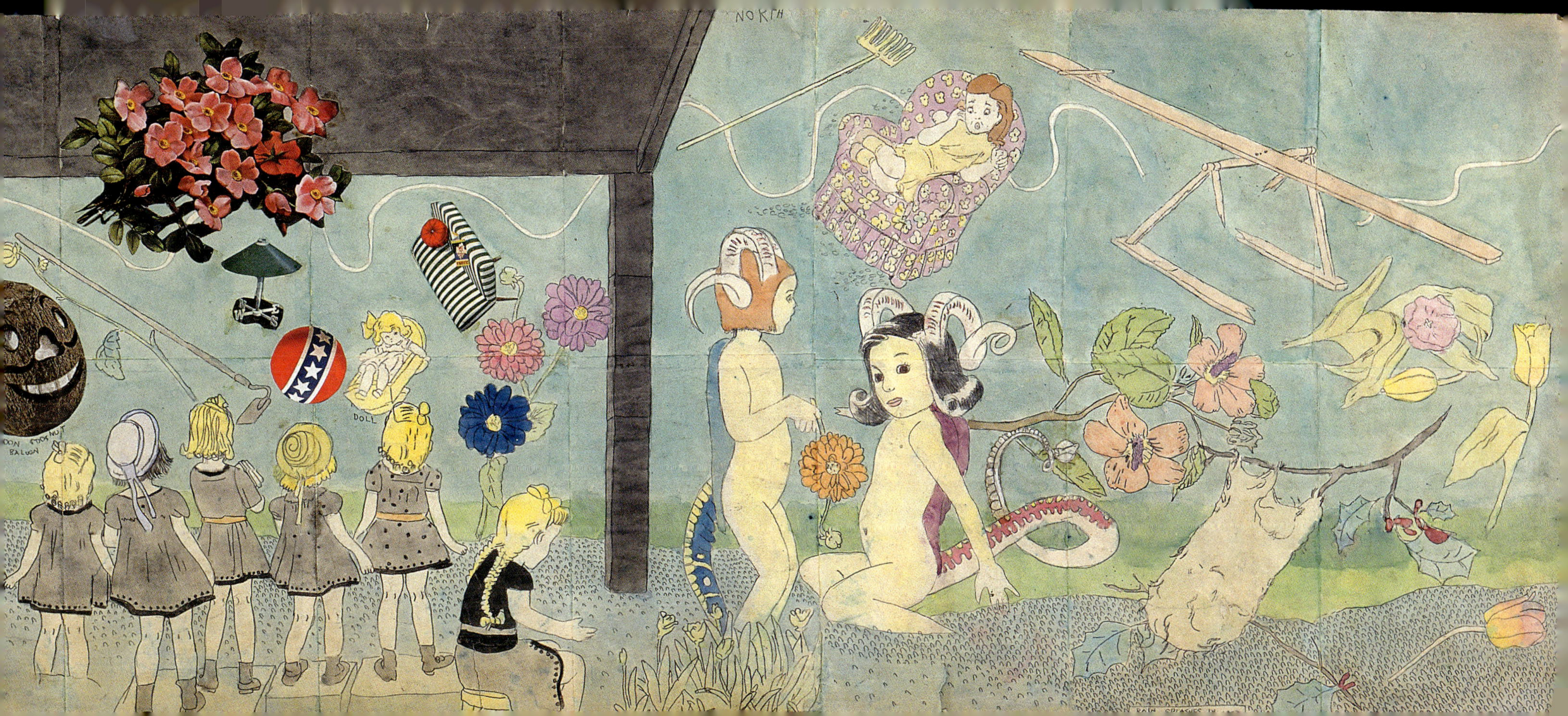
NOKTH
MOON PEANUT
BALOON
DOLL
RAIN SPLASHES IN

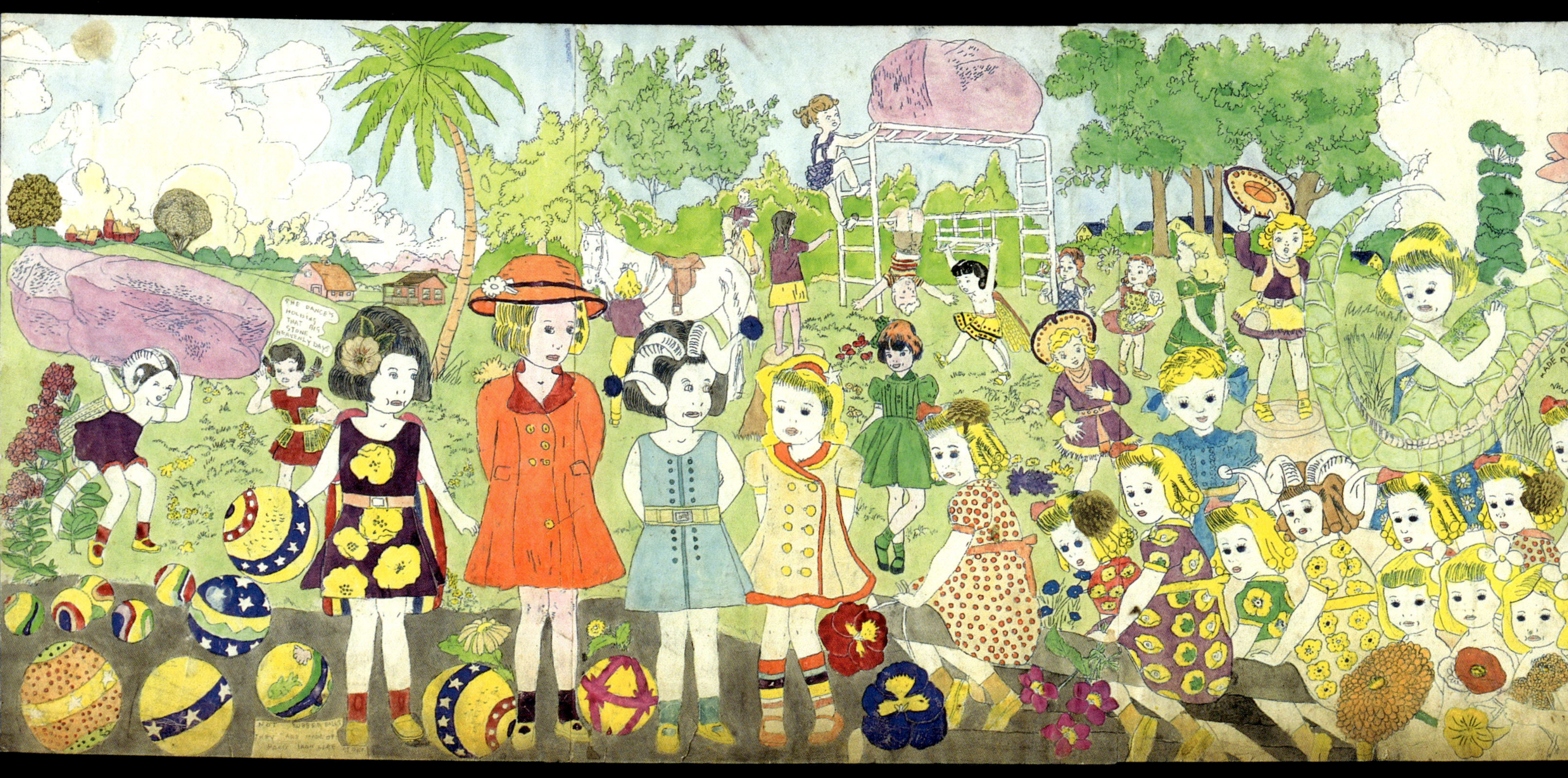

218 | Untitled ("She dances holding that big stone, Heavenly days!").

Watercolor, pencil, and carbon tracing on pieced paper, 24 x 107 in.

Private collection, Chicago

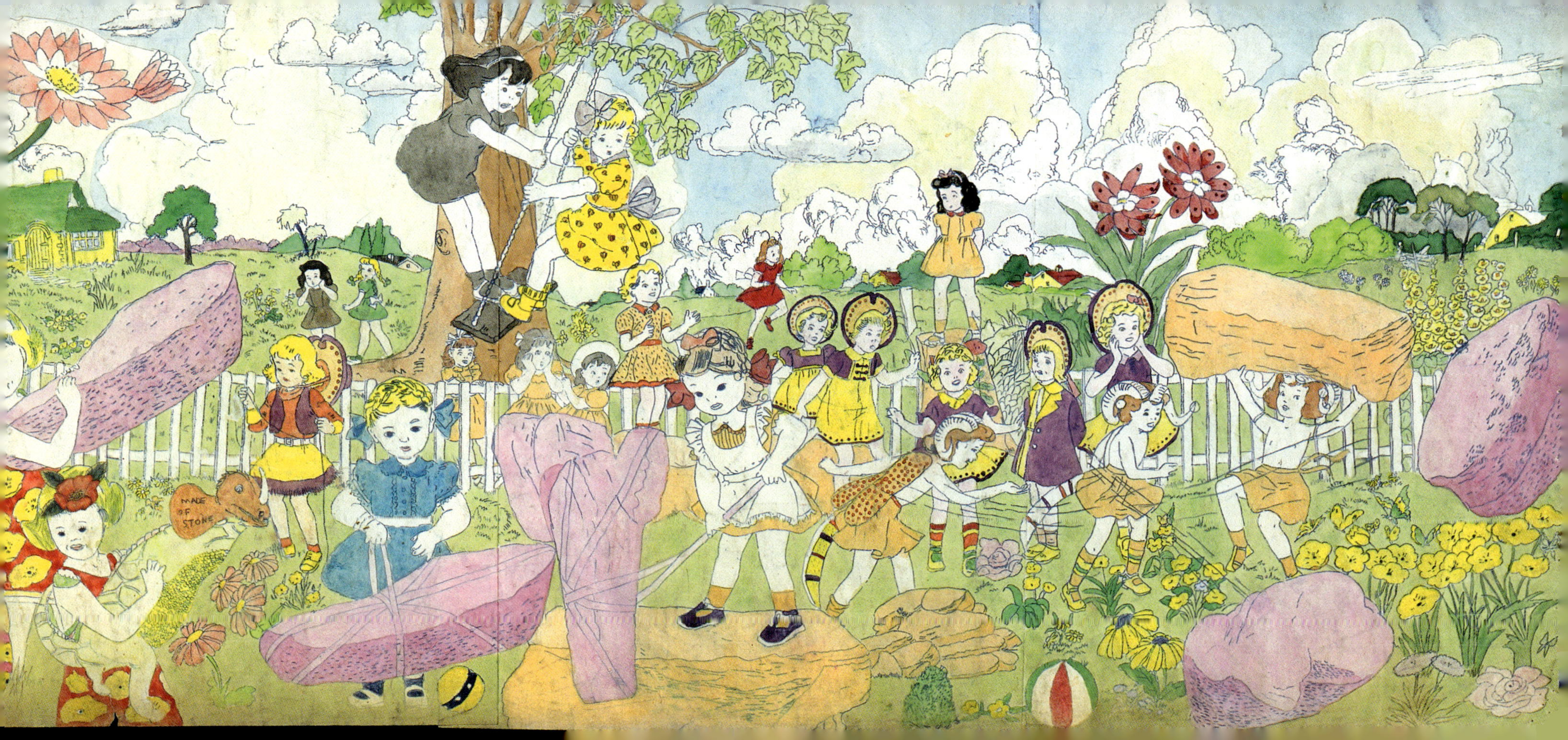

MADE
OF
STONE

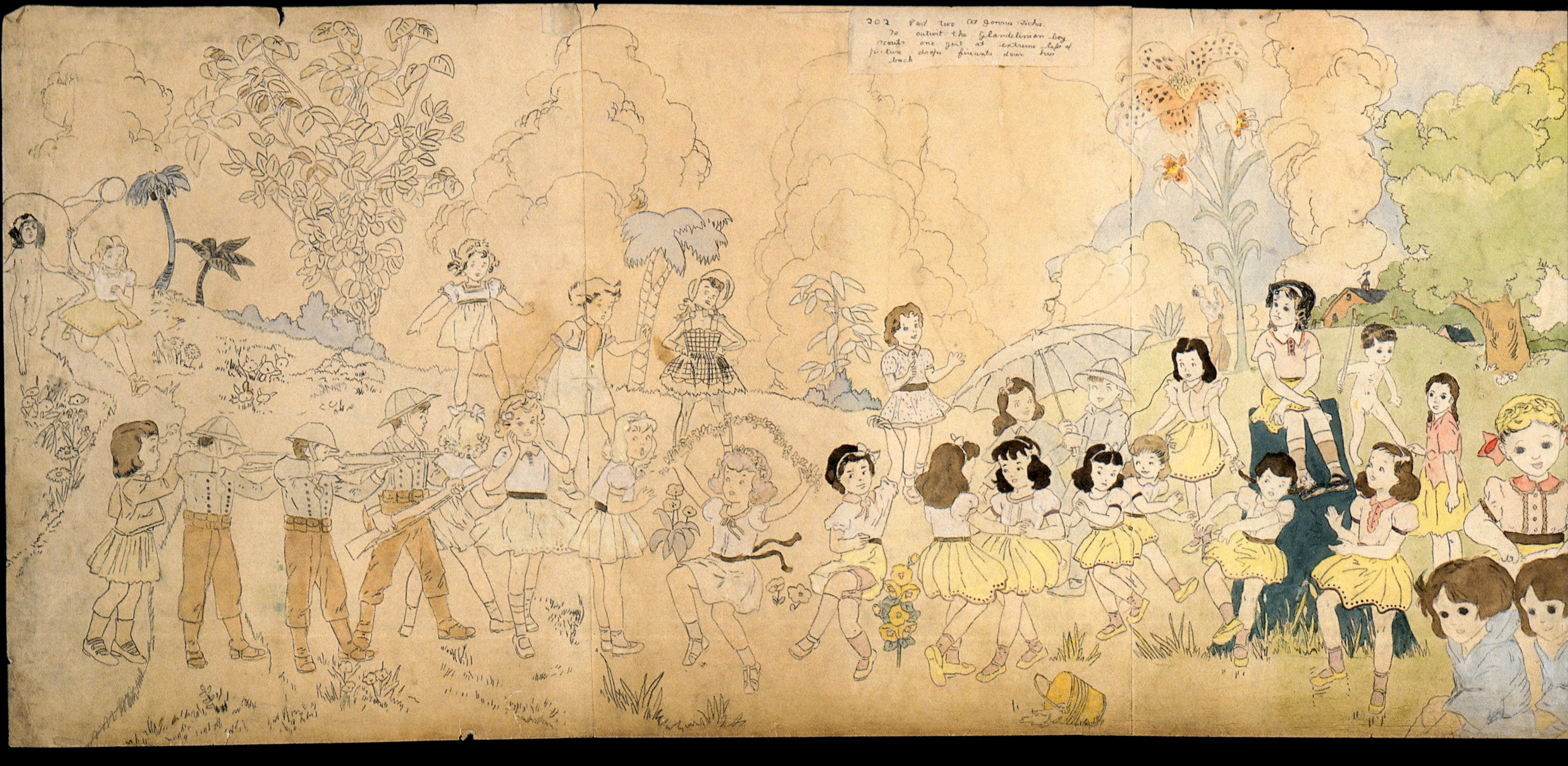

220 | *Part Two at Jennie Richee. To outwit the Glandelinian boy scouts one girl at entrance left of picture drops fire ants down his back.* Watercolor, pencil, and carbon tracing on pieced paper, 24 x 108 in. Private collection, Tokyo

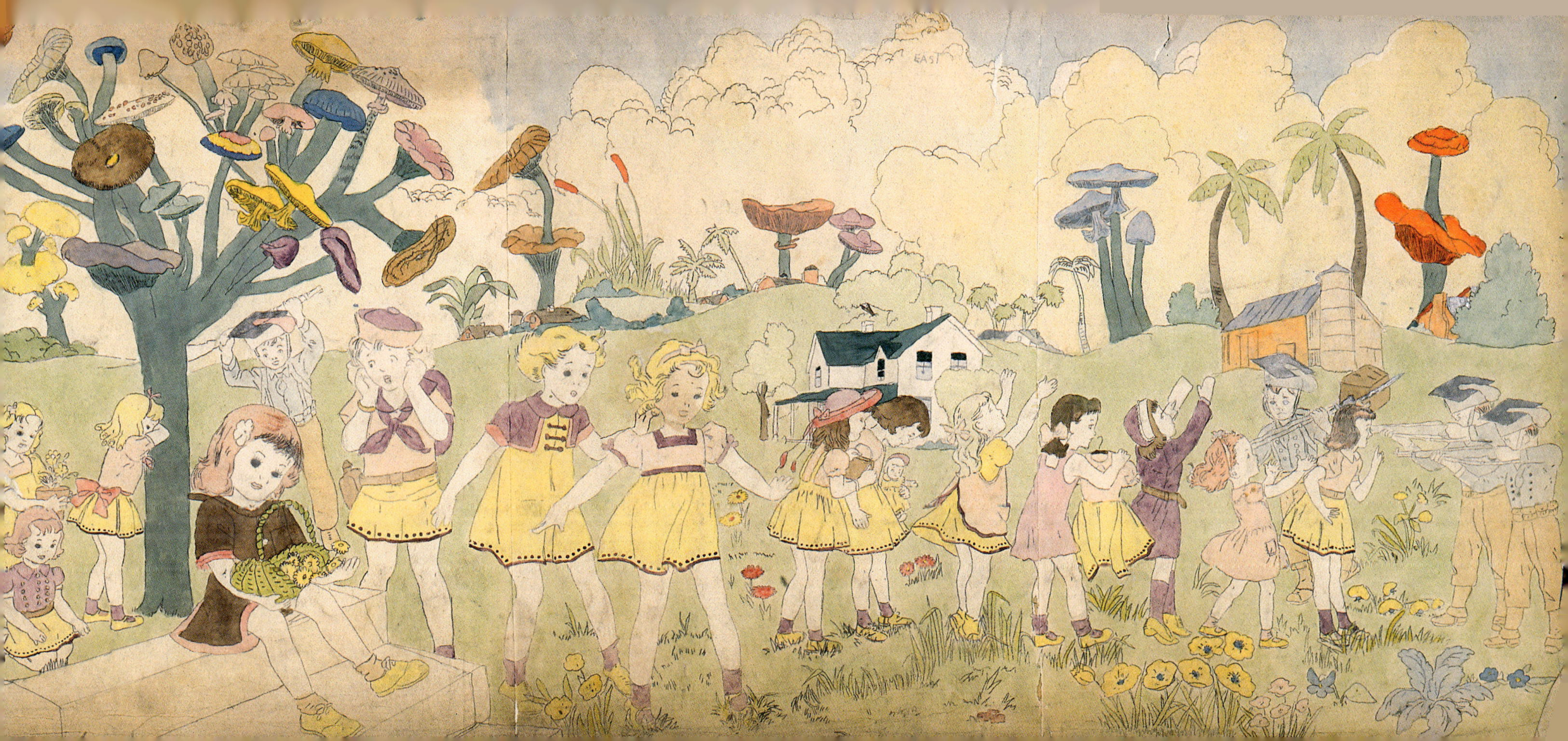

EAST

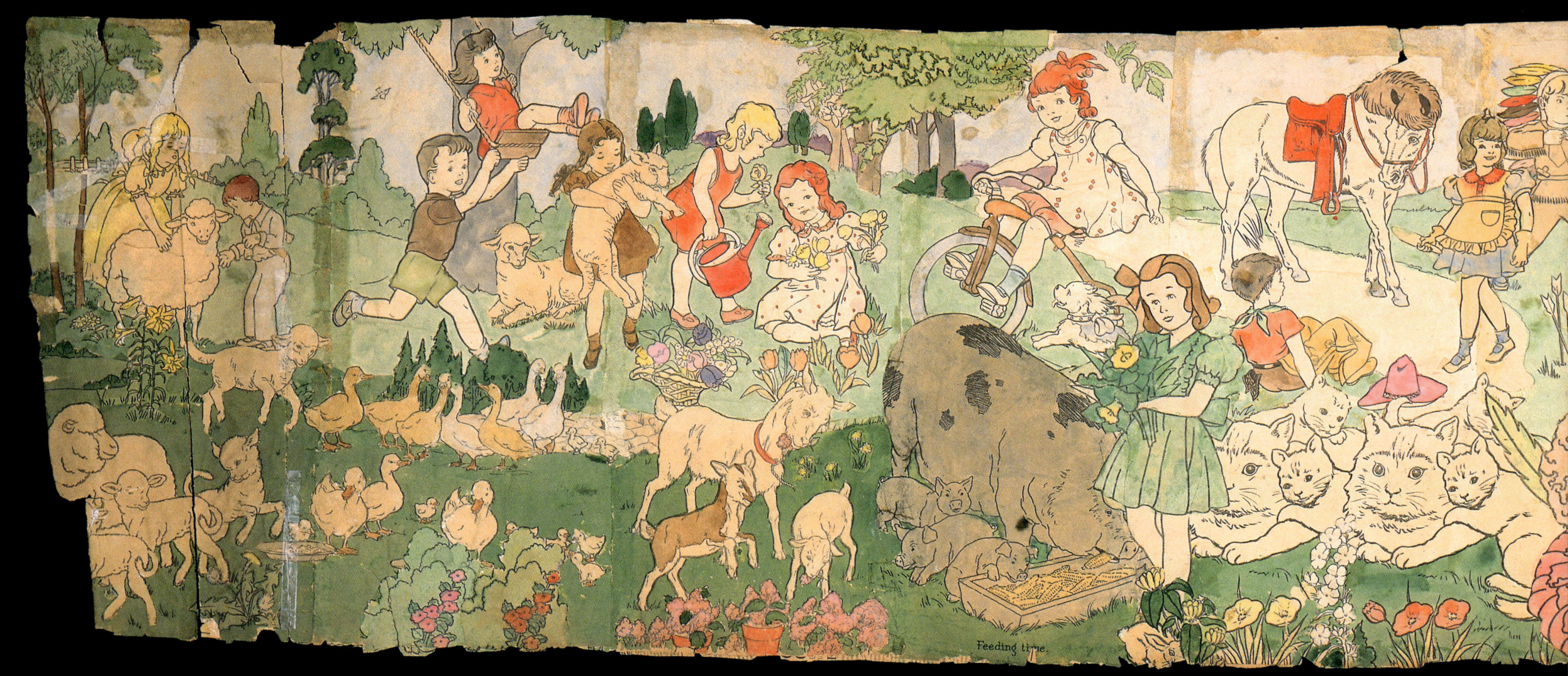

222 | *At Jennie Richee. Some of the children are distrustful and look at them suspiciously.*

Watercolor, pencil, carbon tracing, and collage on pieced paper, 21 x 108 in.

Private collection

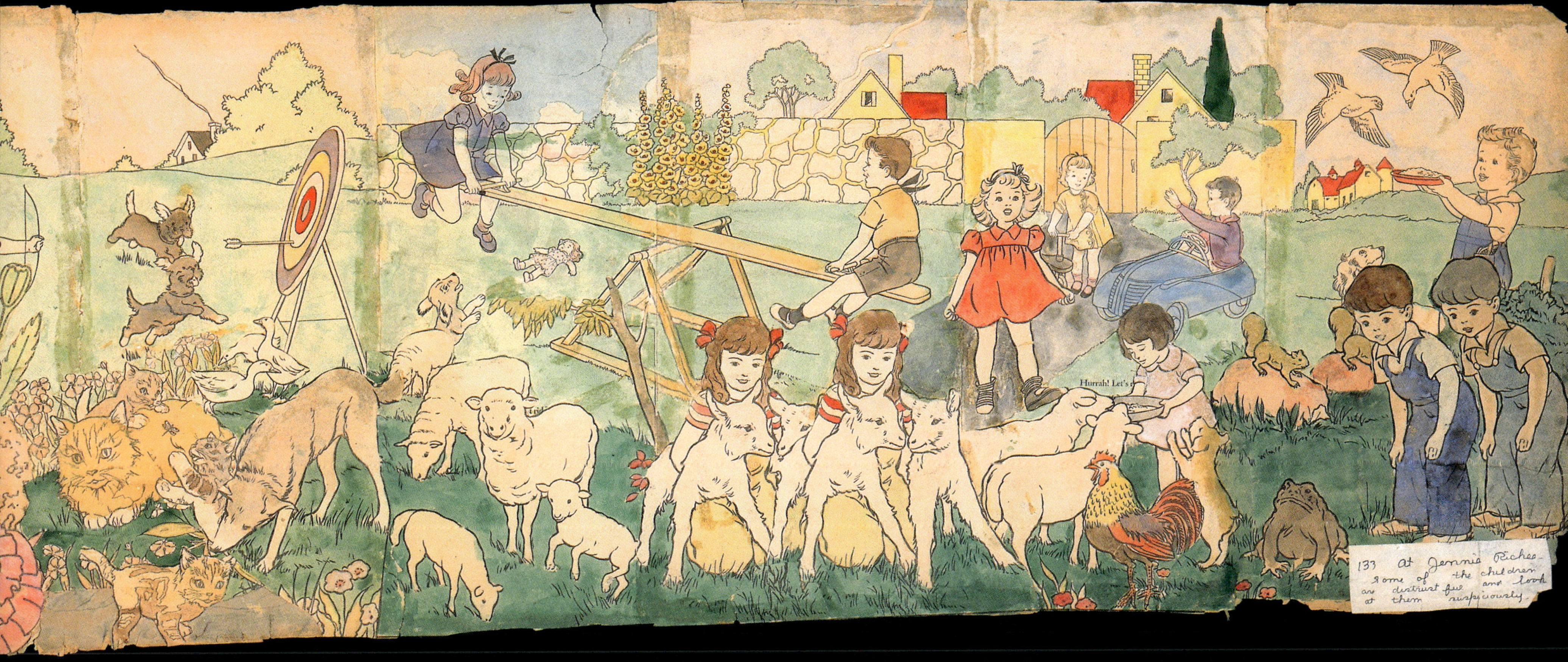

133   At Jennie Richee—
Some of the children
are distrustful and look
at them suspiciously.

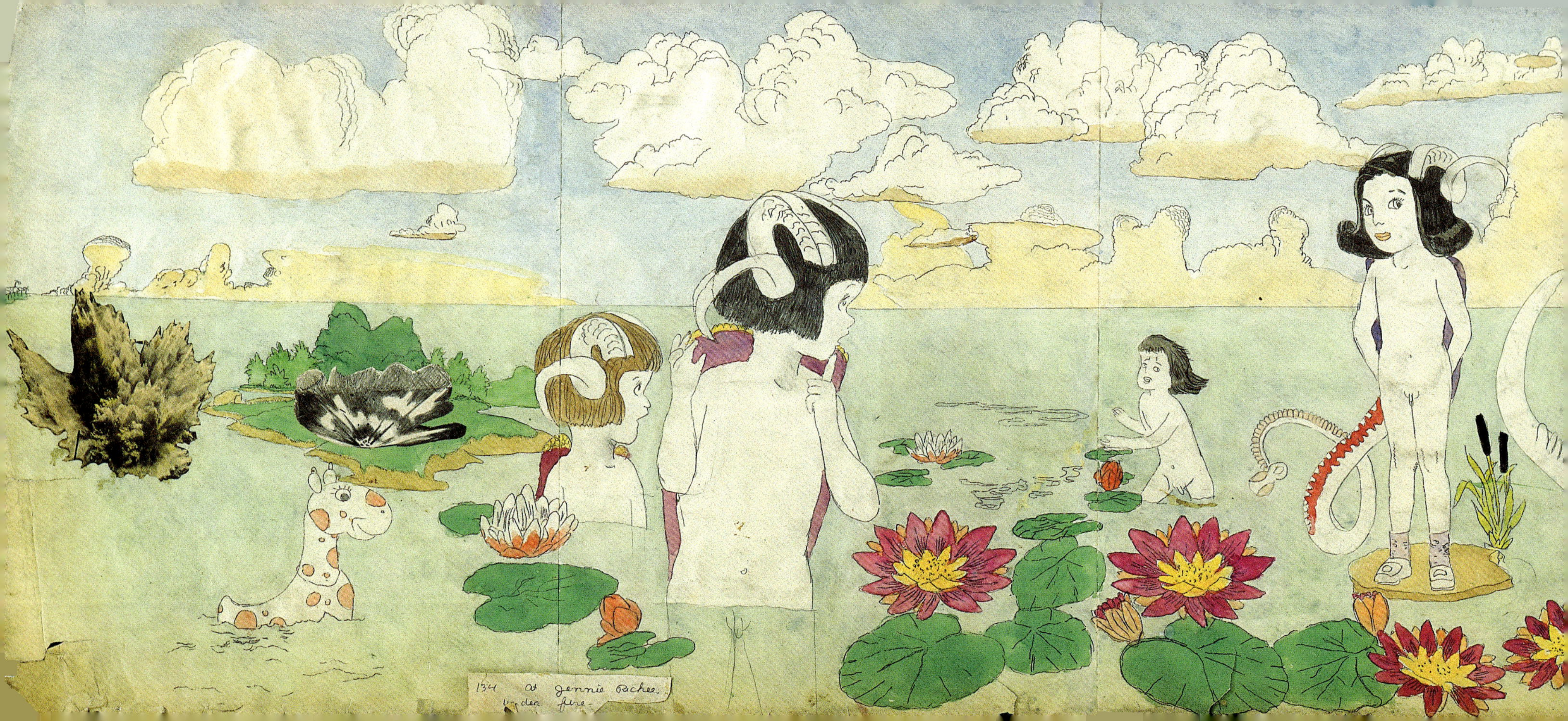
134   At Jennie Richee.
under fire-

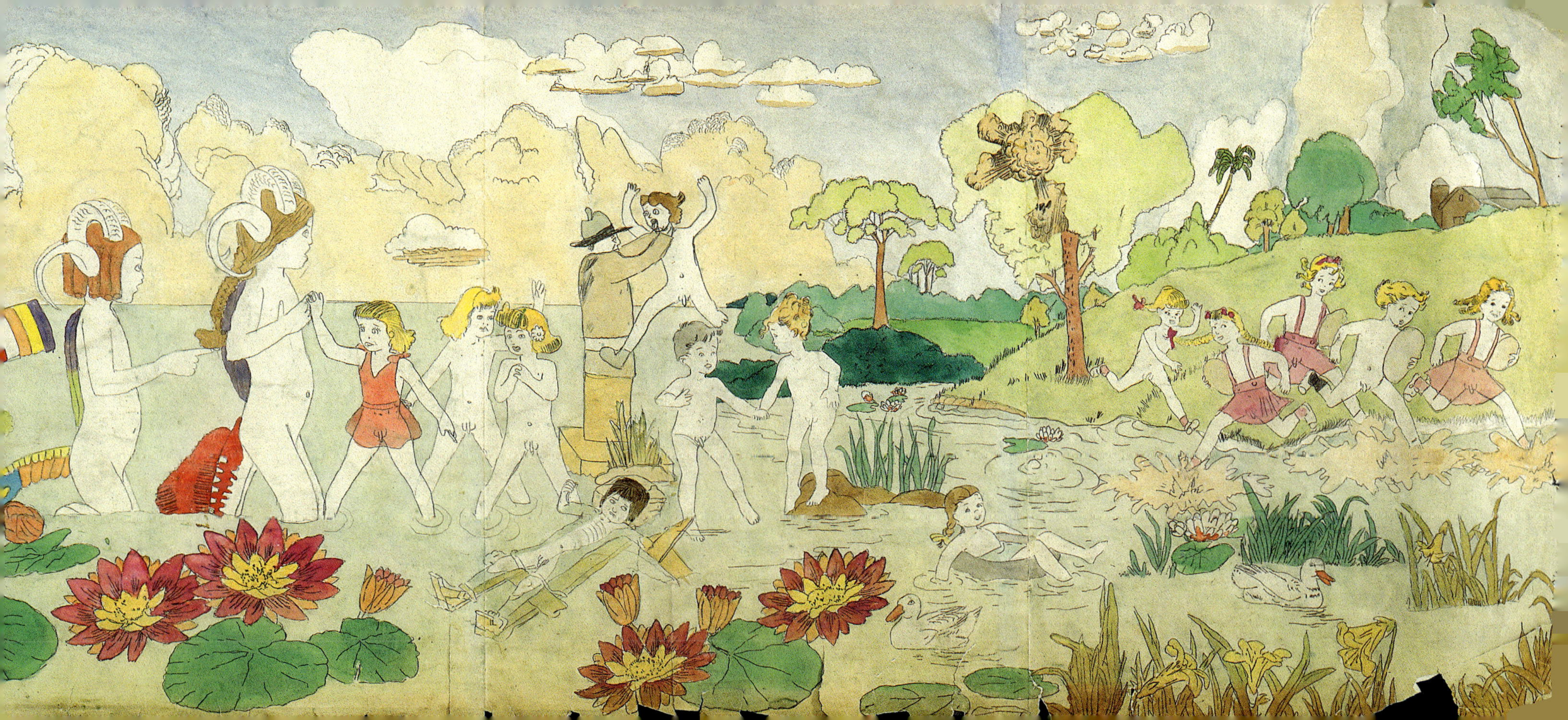

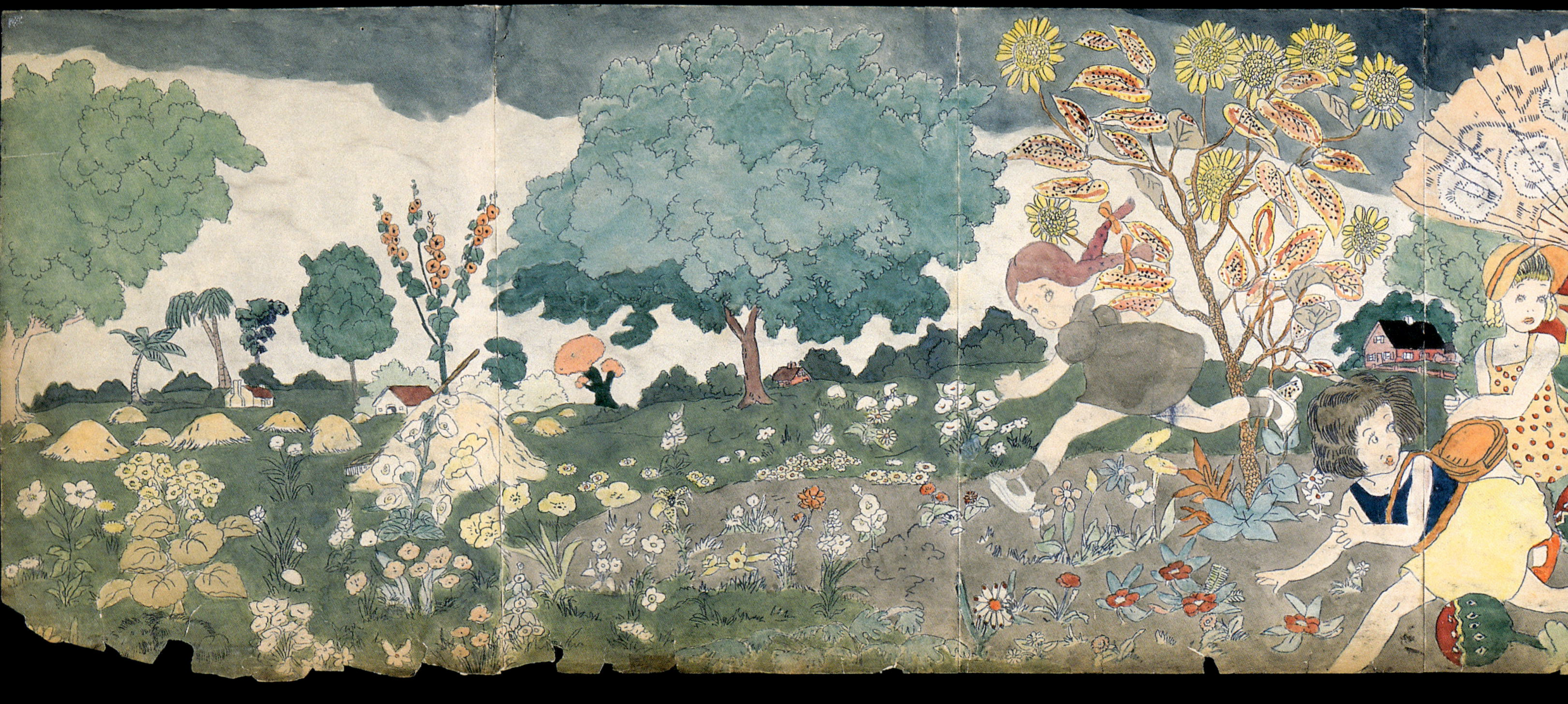

195. Are unsuccessfully attacked by Glandelinian soldiers unseen in picture, naturally escape capture by hiding among Balboa bushes. Watercolor, pencil, and carbon tracing on pieced paper, 22 x 112 ½ in.
Collection American Folk Art Museum, New York

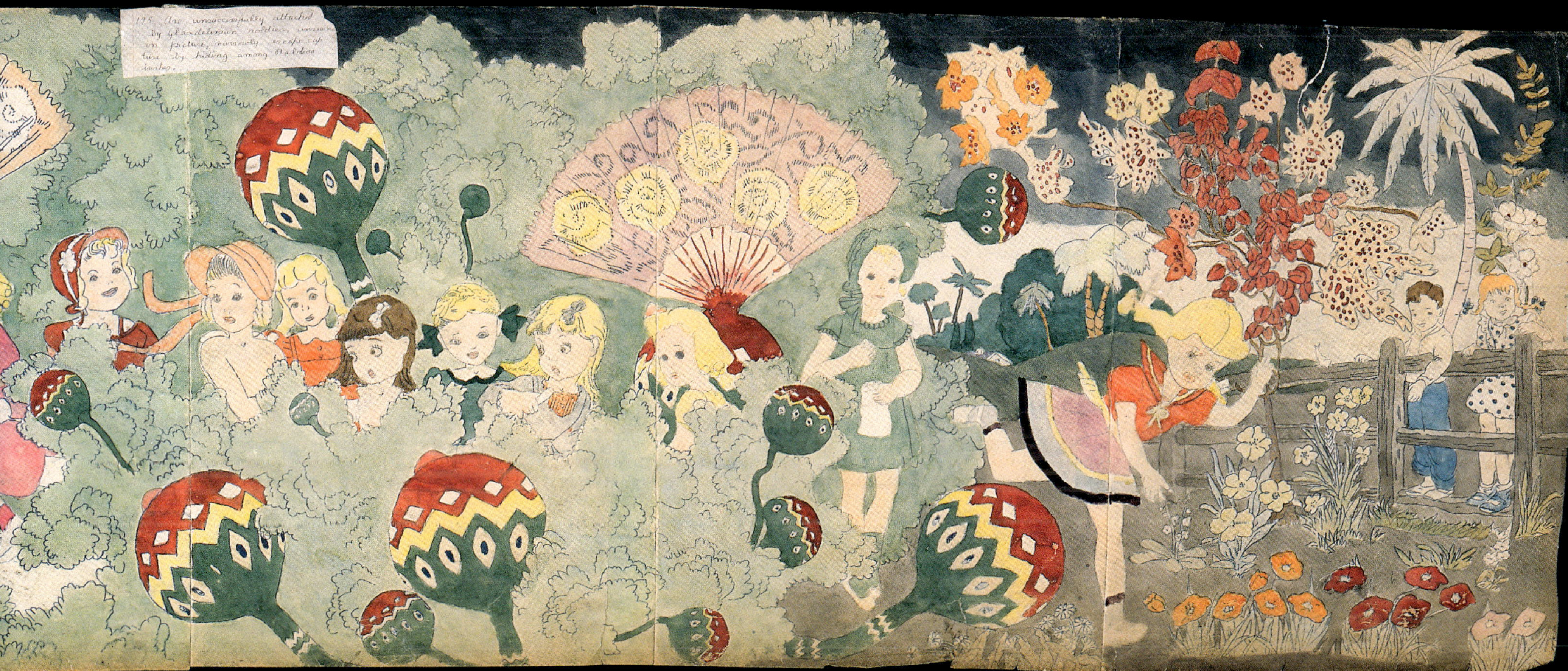
175 Are unsuccessfully attacked
by Glandelinian soldiers unseen
in picture, narrowly escape cap
ture by hiding among flakewood
bushes.

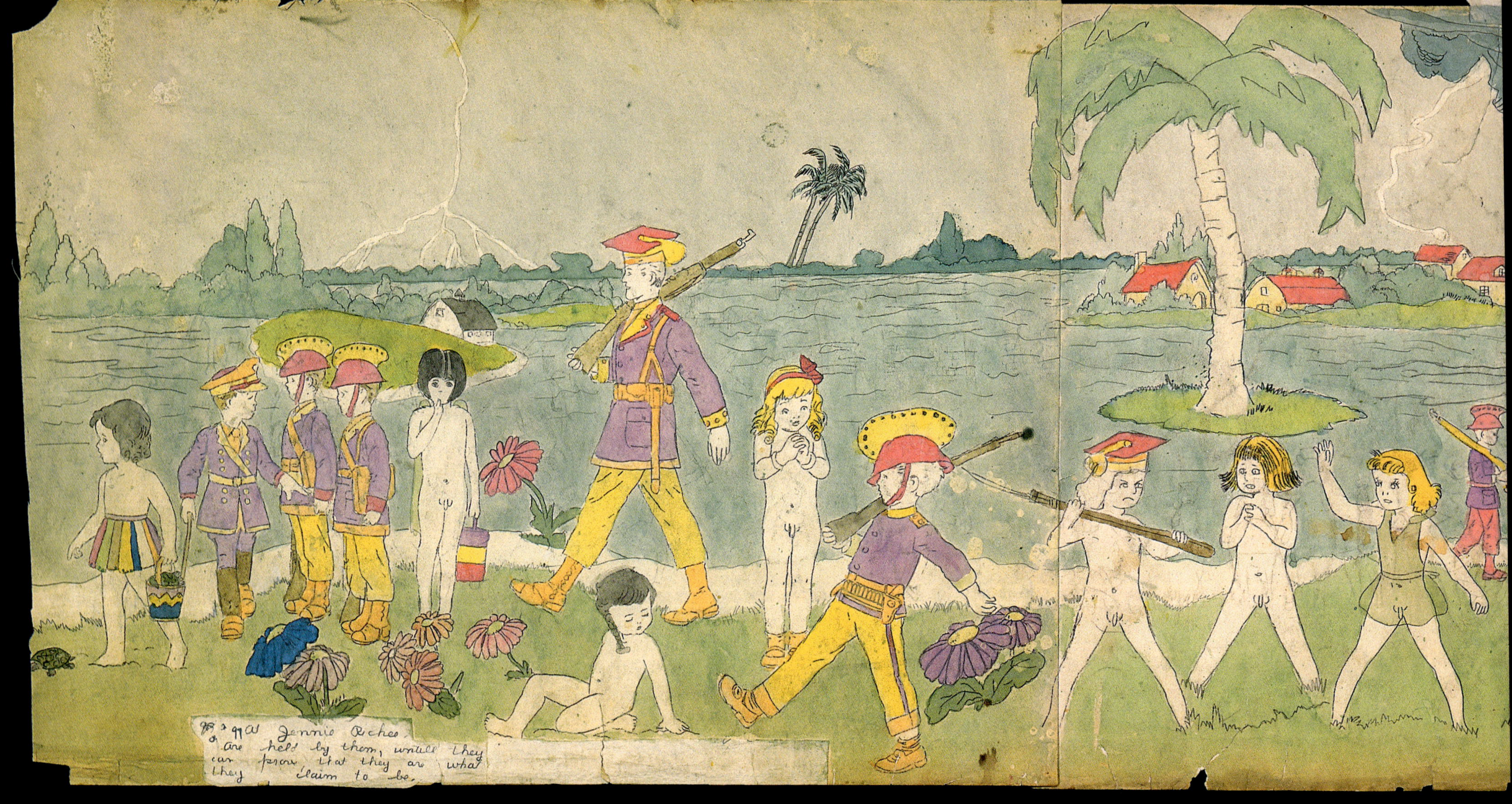

At Jennie Richee. Held until they can prove that they are who they claim to be.

Watercolor, pencil, and carbon tracing on pieced paper, 22 x 89 in.

Private collection

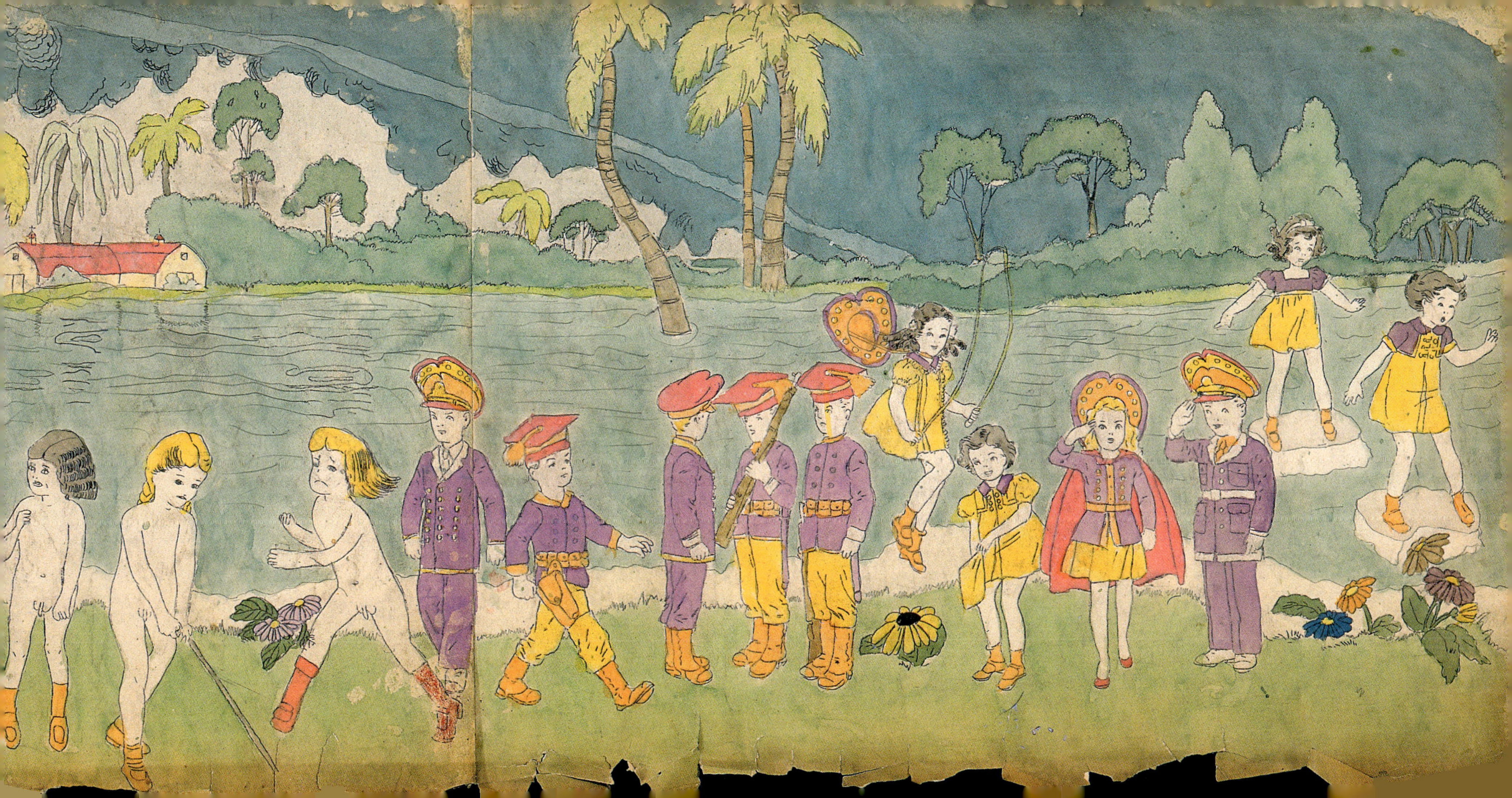

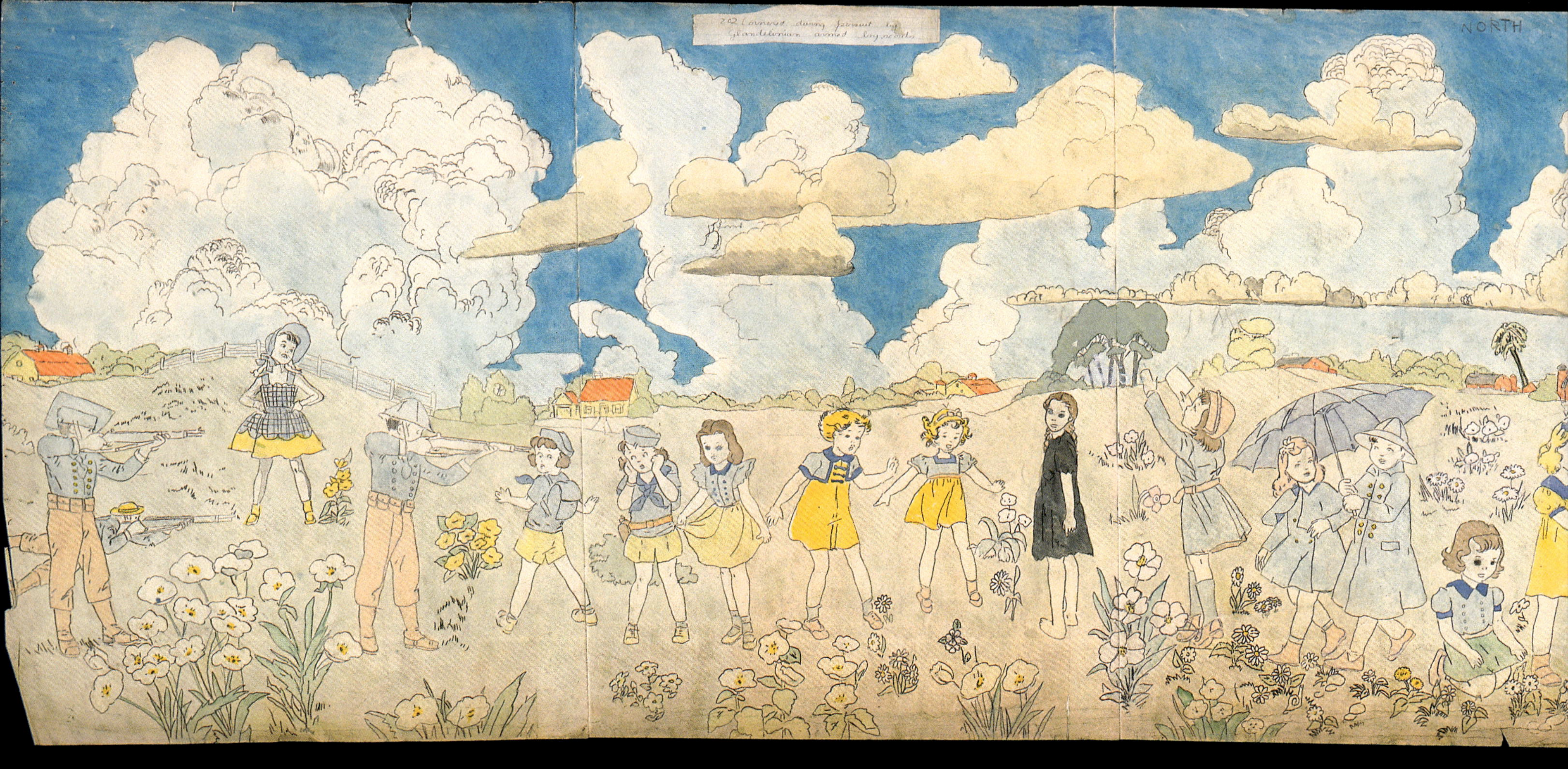

230 | *Cornered during pursuit by Glandelinian armed boy scouts.*

Watercolor, pencil, and carbon tracing on pieced paper, 24 x 108 in.

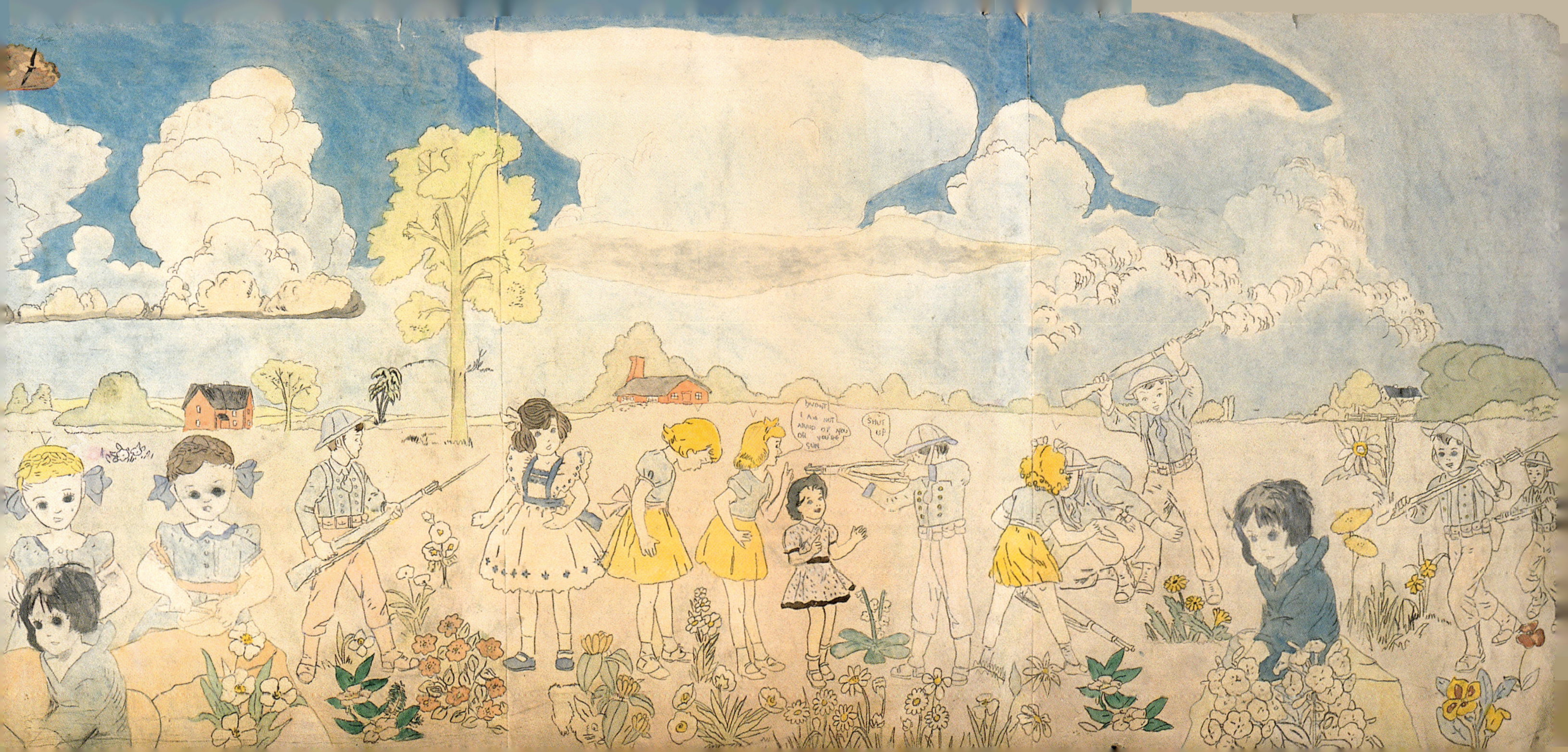

I AM NOT AFRAID OF YOU OR YOU'RE GUN
SHUT UP

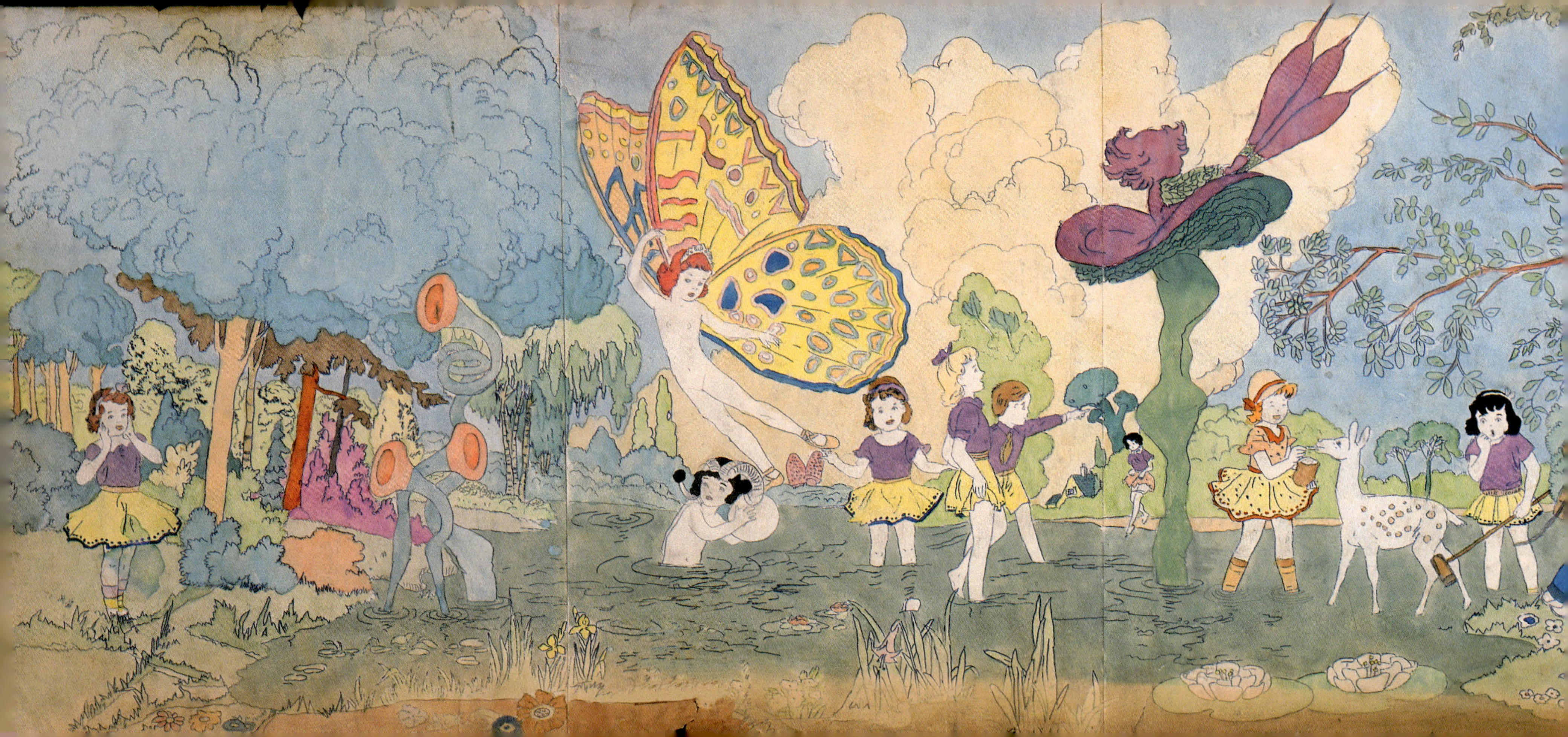

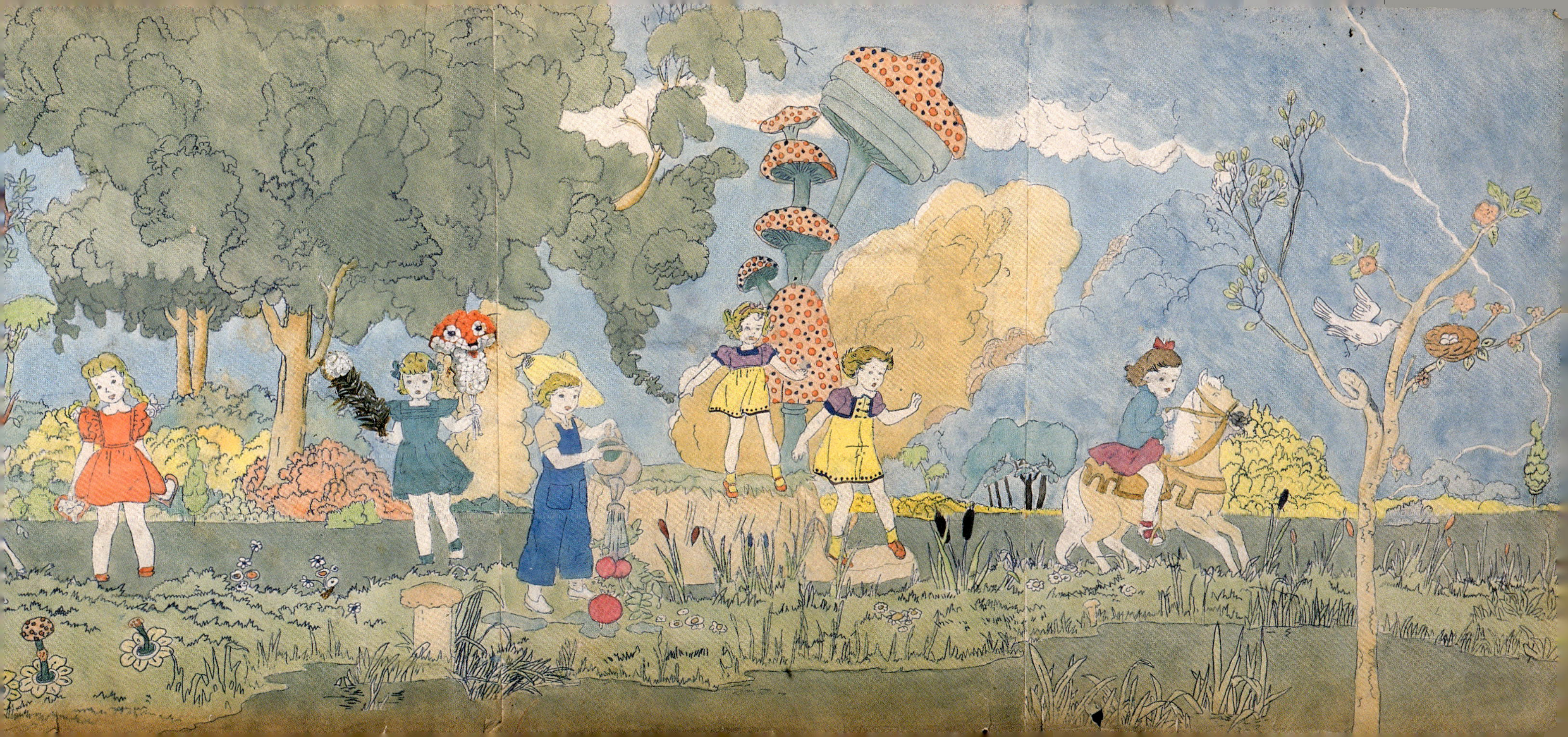

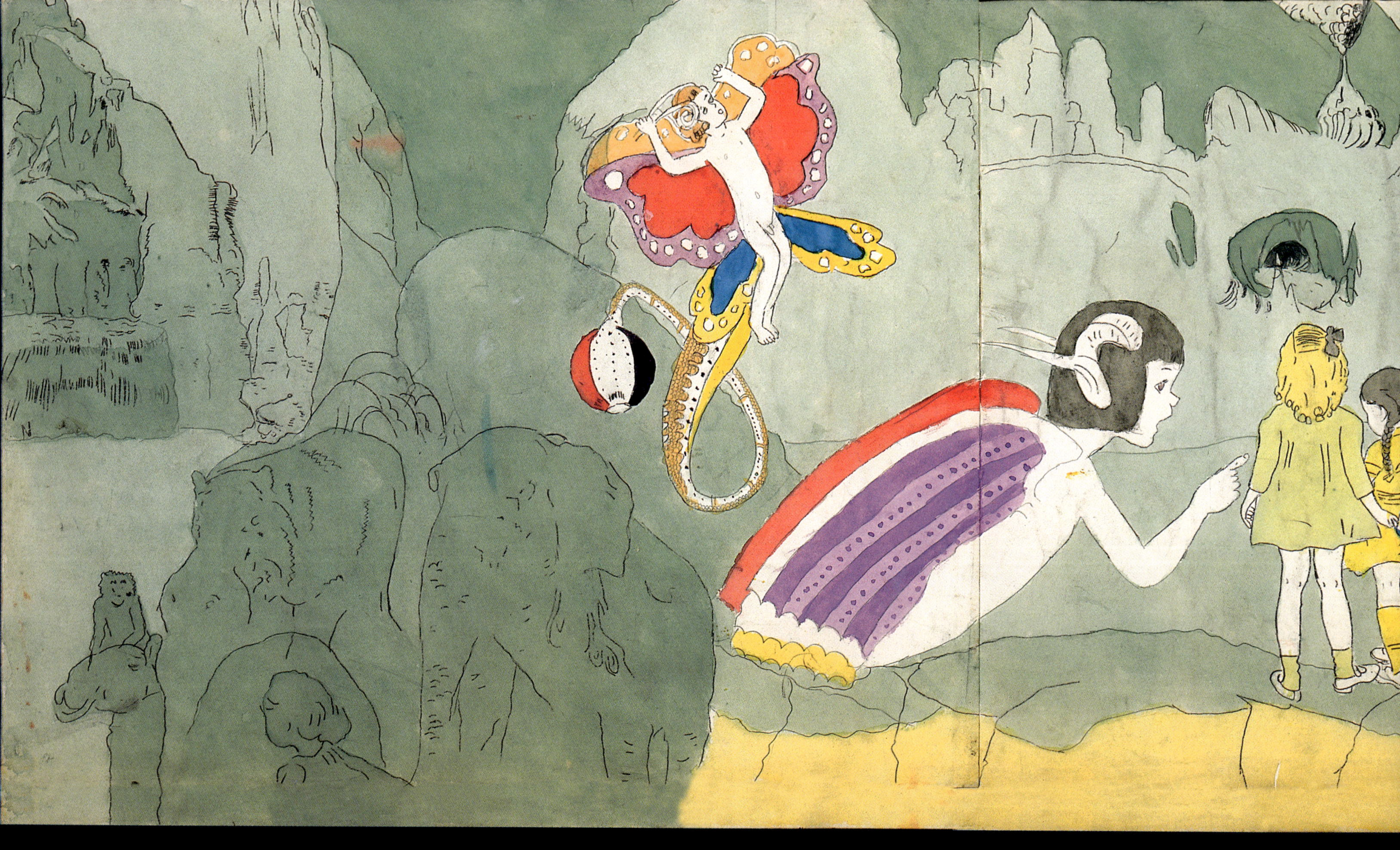

234 | *73 At Jennie Richee Escape by their Help.*

Watercolor, pencil, carbon tracing on pieced paper, 19 x 70 ½ in.

Collection American Folk Art Museum, New York. Anonymous gift in recognition of Sam Farber

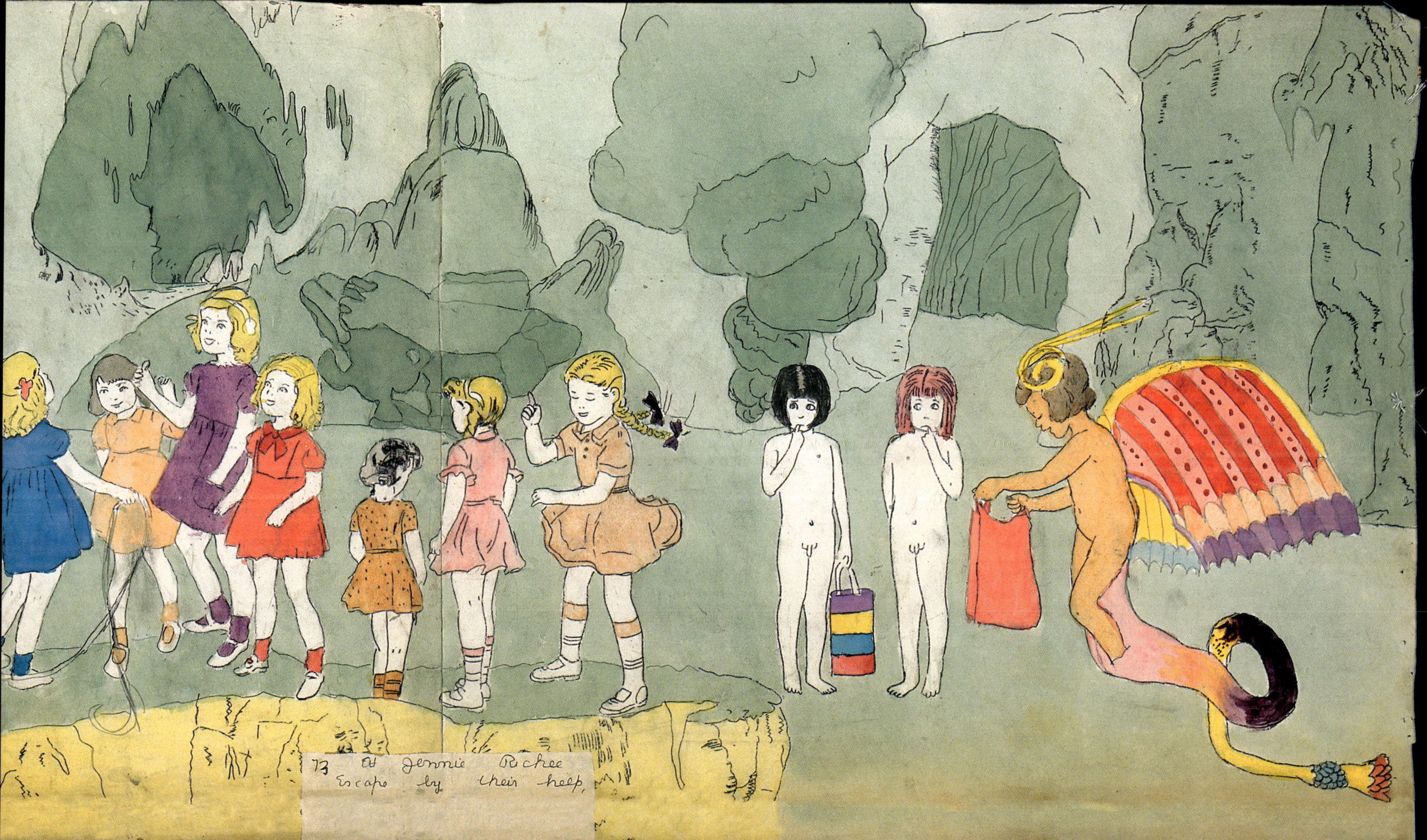

73   At Jennie Richee
Escape by their help.

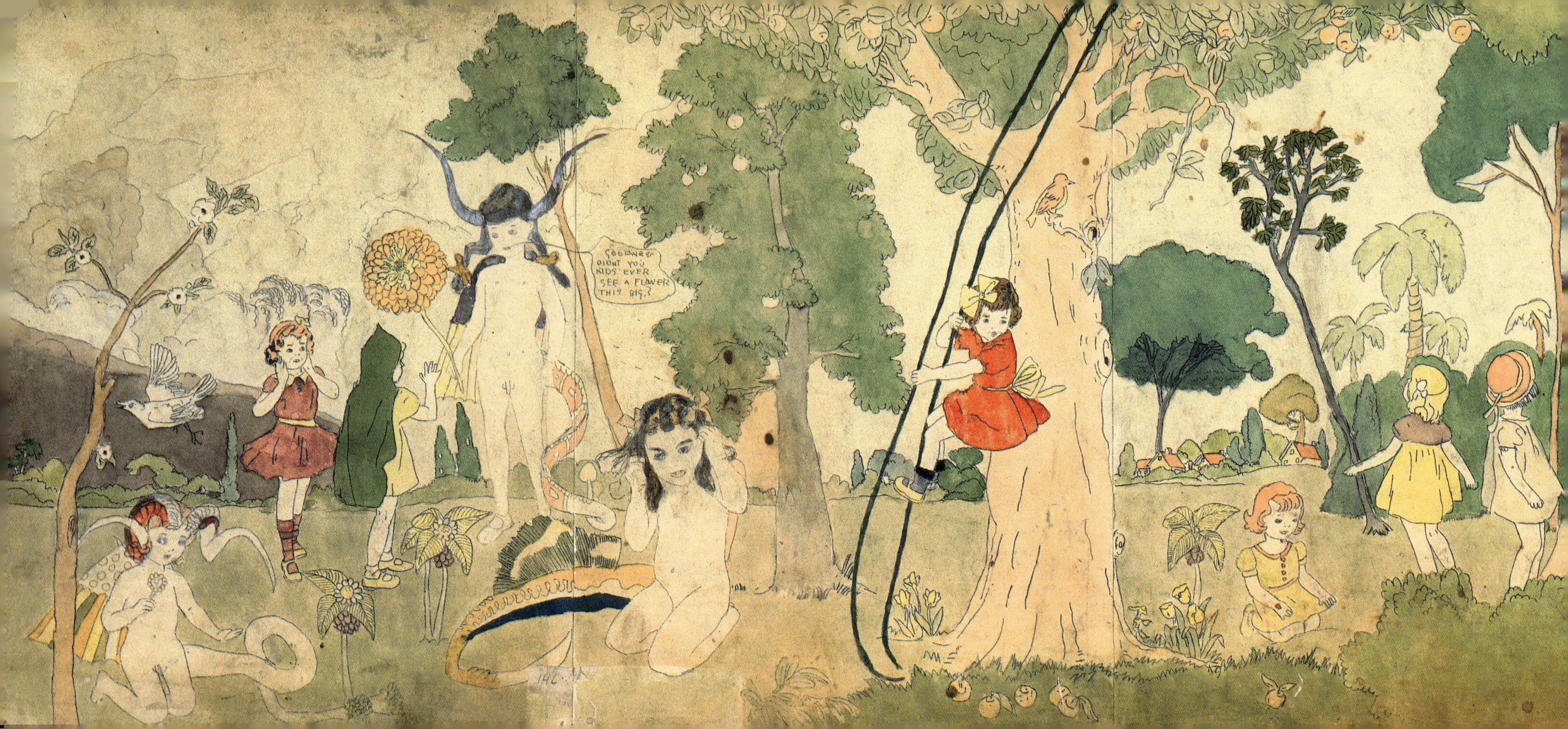
GOODNESS
DIDNT YOU
KIDS EVER
SEE A FLOWER
THIS BIG.?

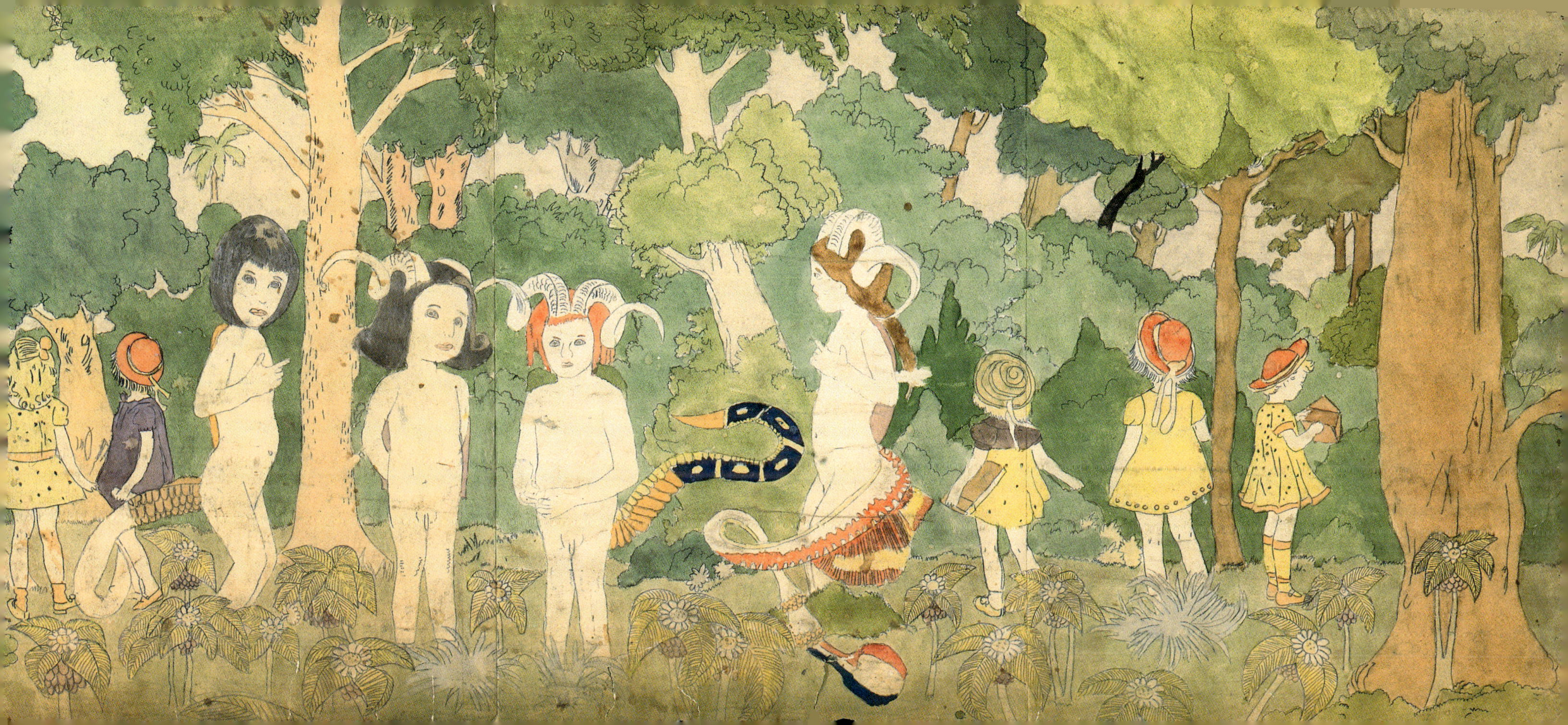

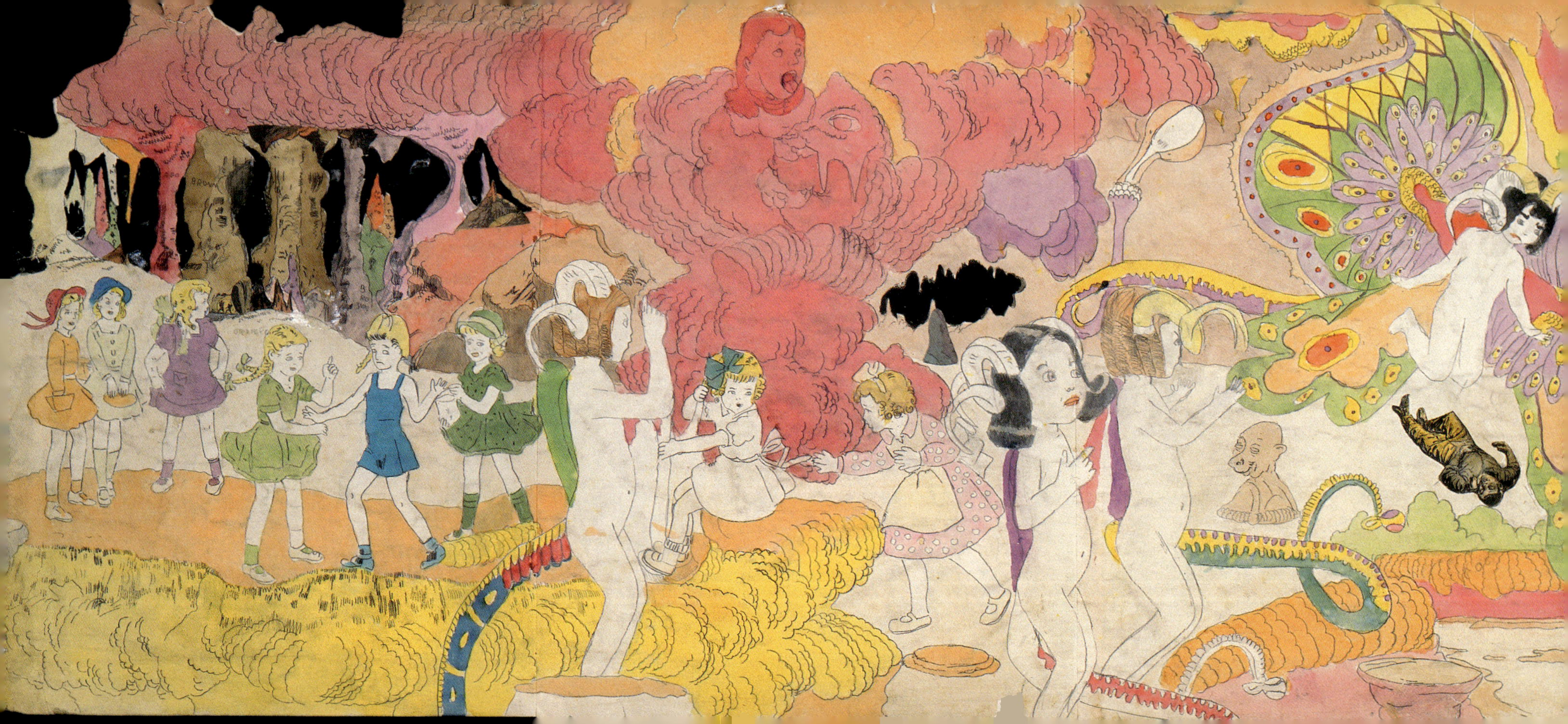

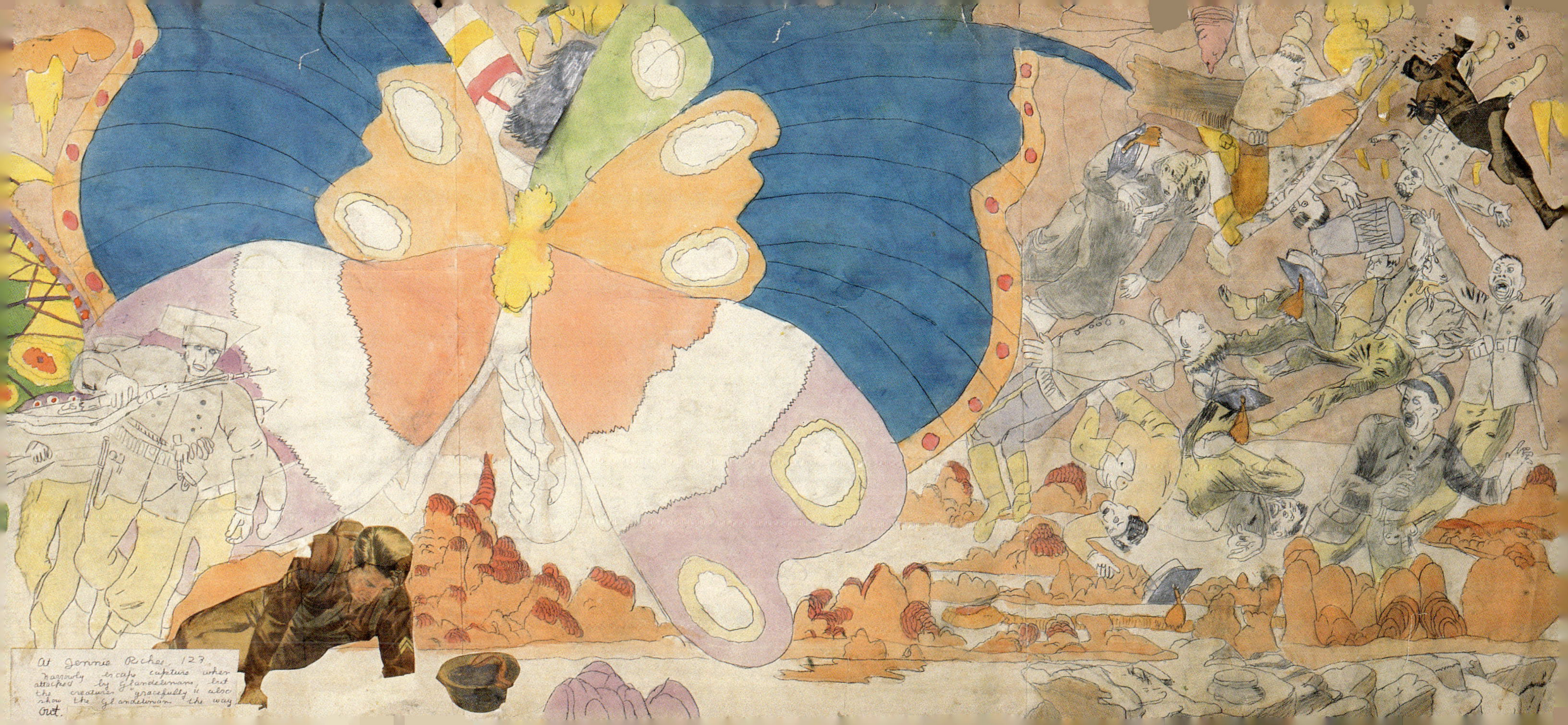
At Jennie Richee, 123.
narrowly escape capture when
attacked by Glandelinians, but
the creatures gracefully & also
show the Glandelinian the way
out.

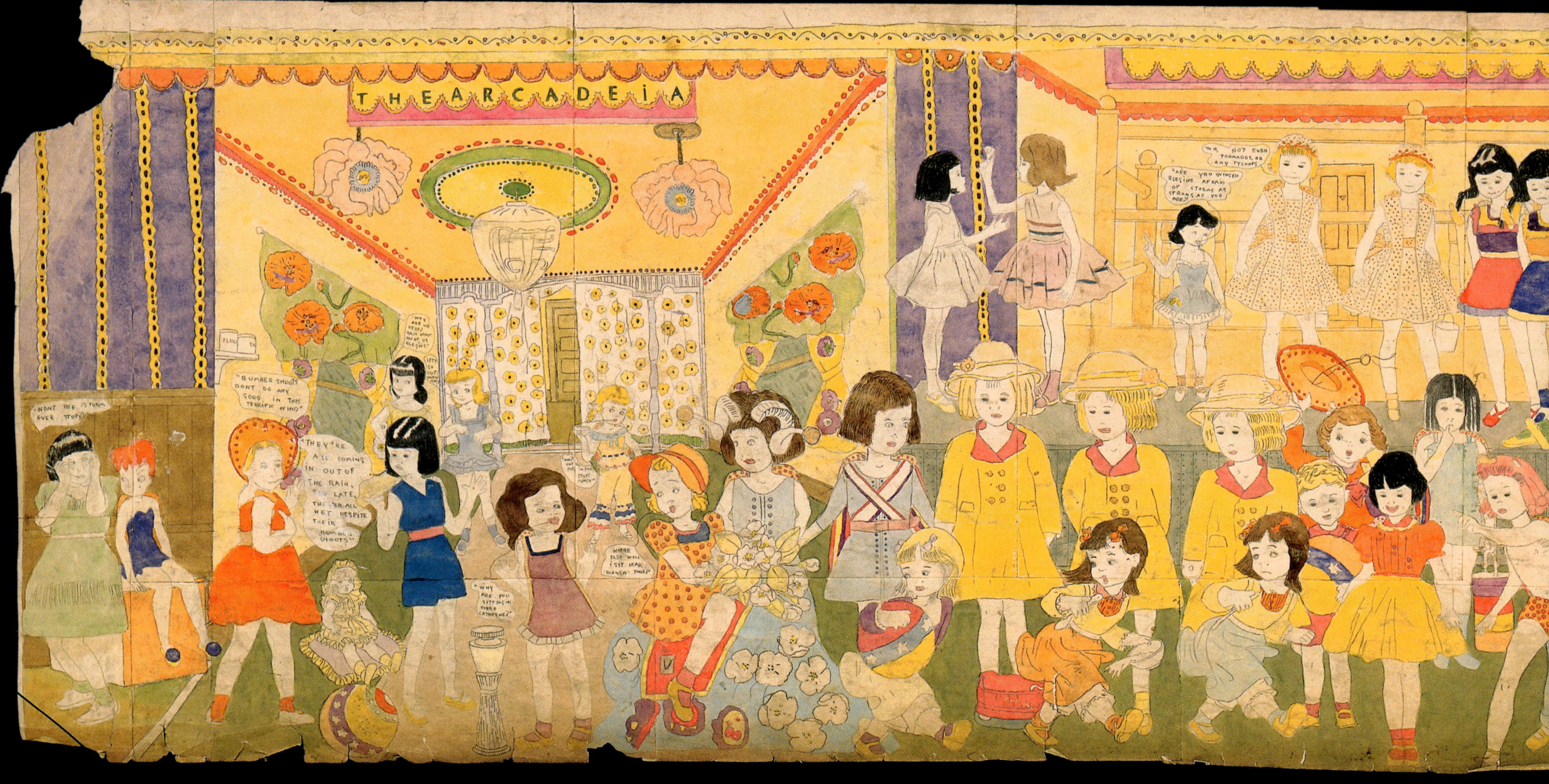

240 | Untitled ("The Arcadeia"). Watercolor, pencil, and carbon tracing on pieced paper, 32 x 132 in. Private collection

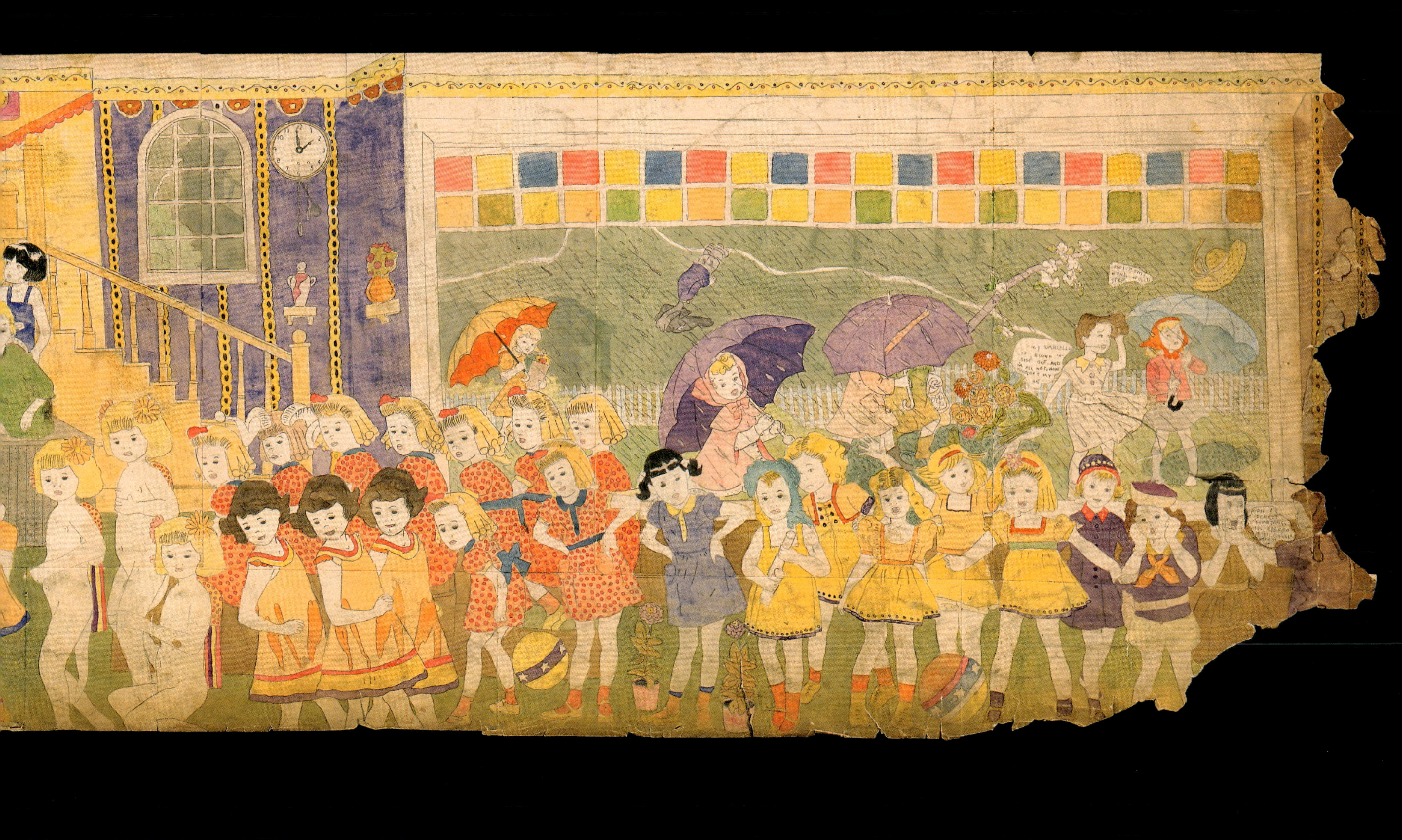
I WISH THIS WIND WOULD STOP
MY UMBRELLA IS BLOWN INSIDE OUT AND I'M ALL WET NOW I LOST MY

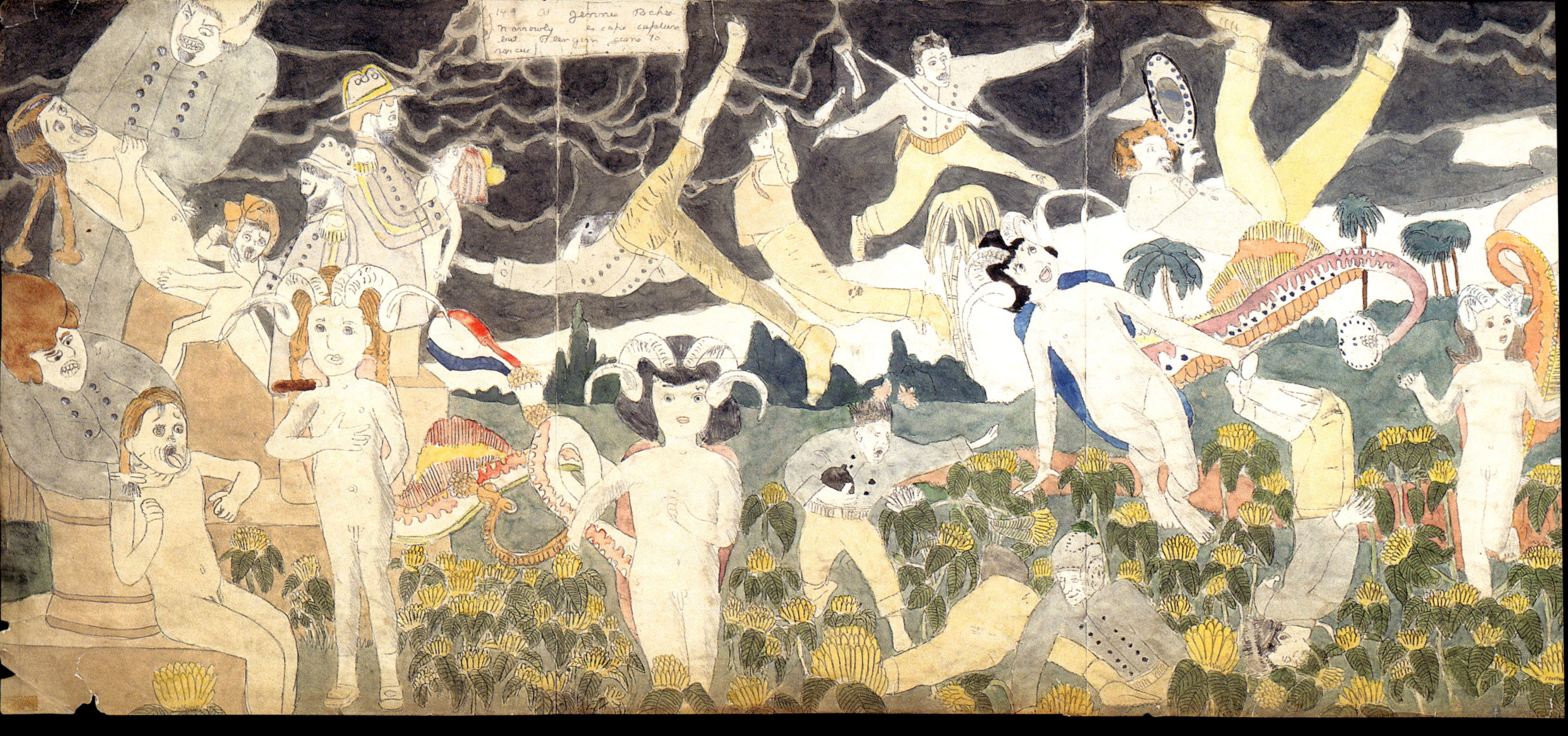

242   *At Jennie Richee. Narrowly escape capture but Blengins come to rescue.*

Watercolor, pencil, carbon tracing, and collage on pieced paper, approx. 24 x 108 in.

Location unknown

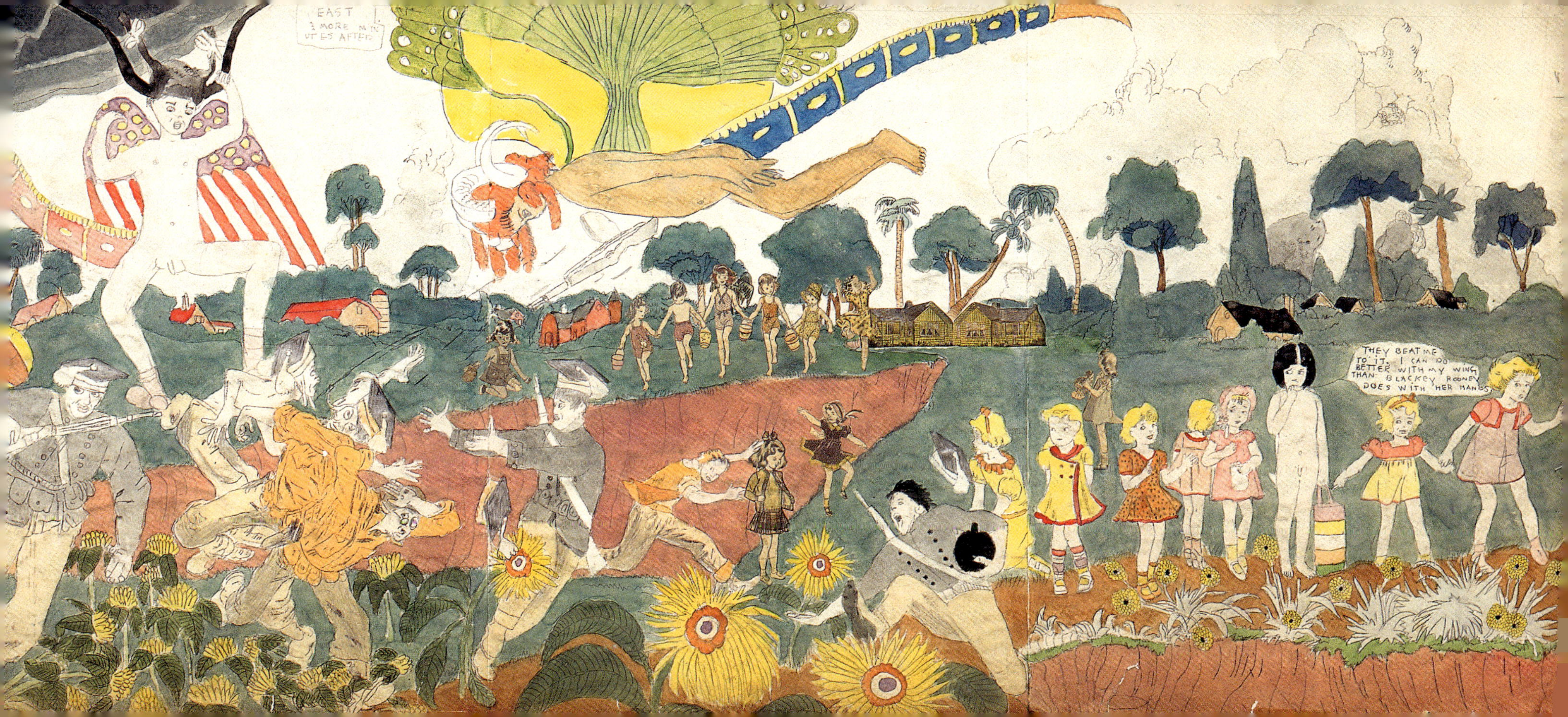

EAST
3 MORE MIN
UTES AFTER
THEY BEAT ME
TO IT. I CAN DO
BETTER WITH MY WING
THAN BLACKEY ROONEY
DOES WITH HER HANDS.

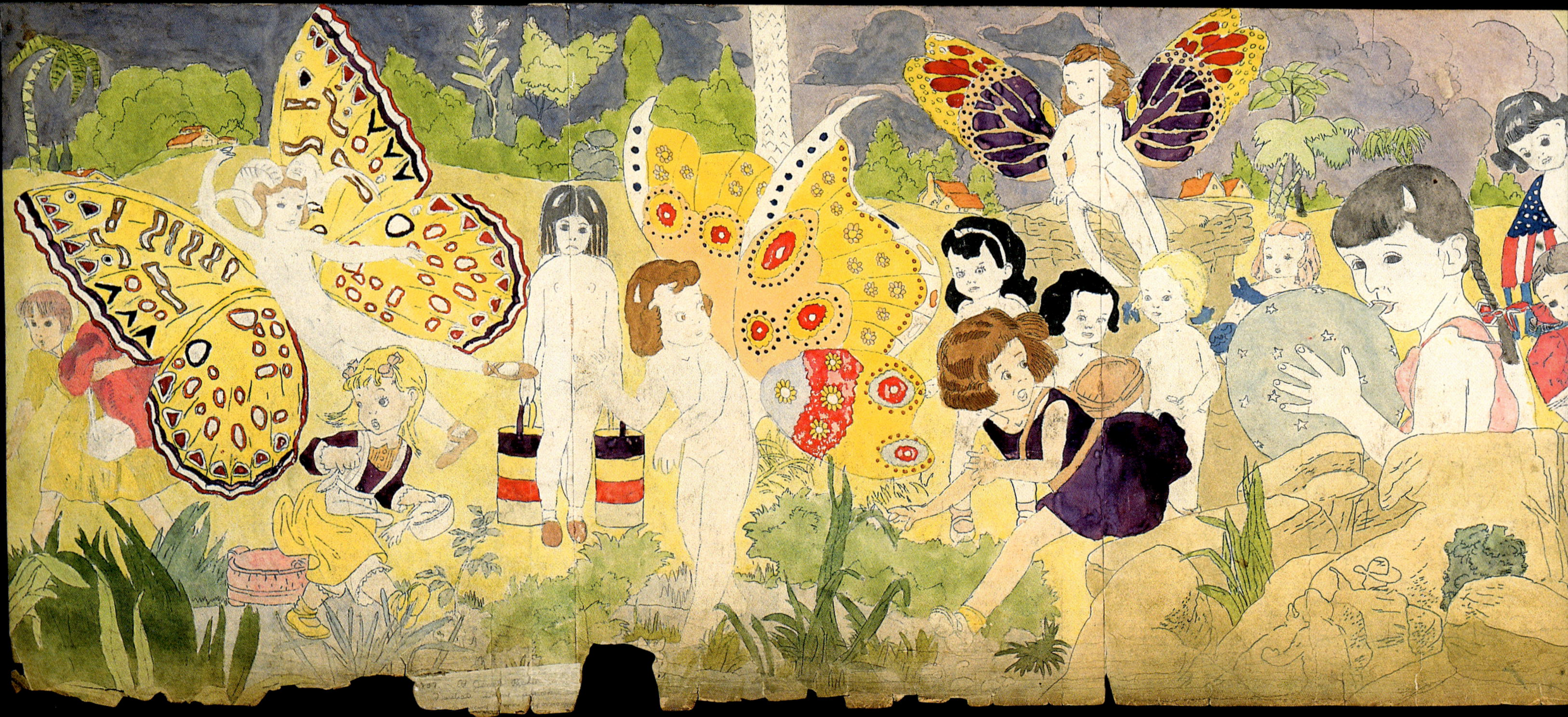

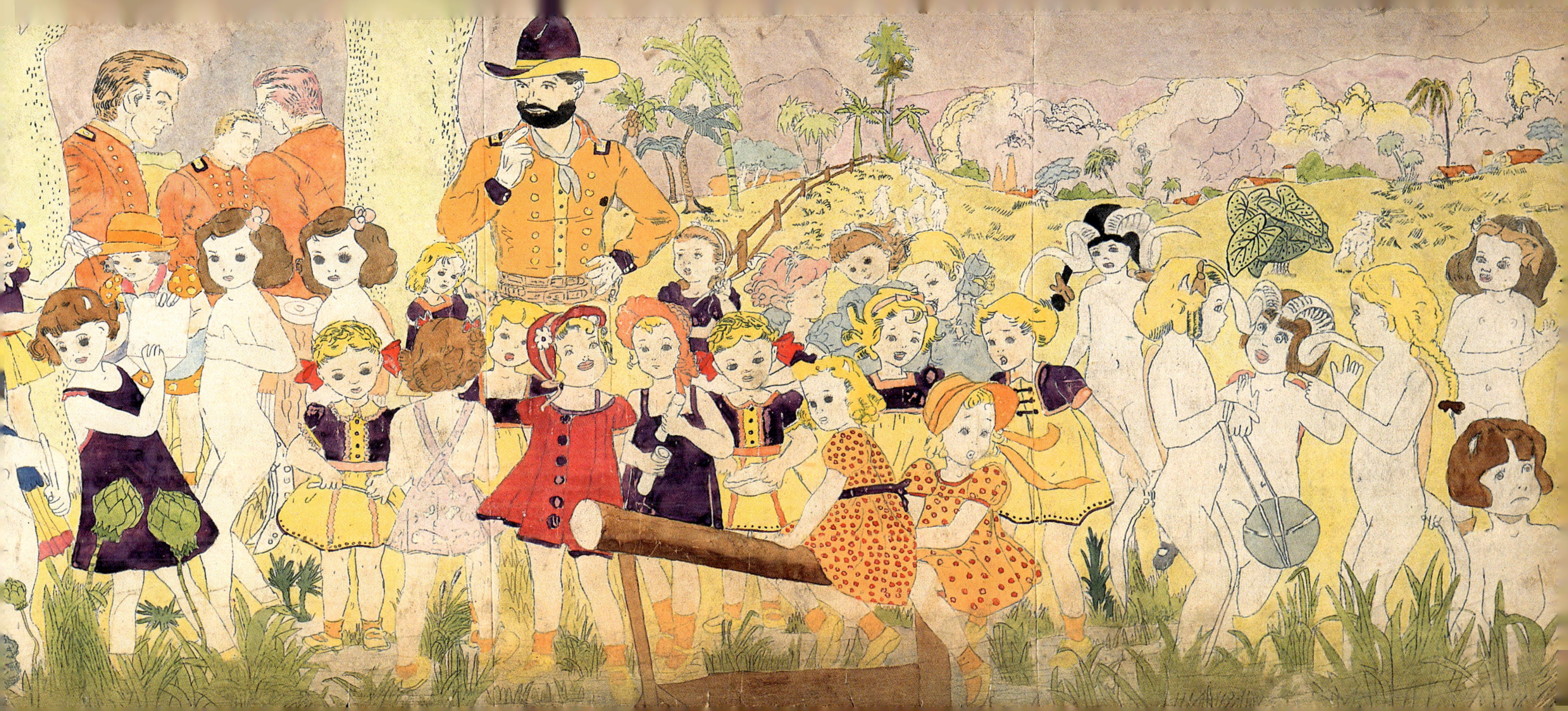

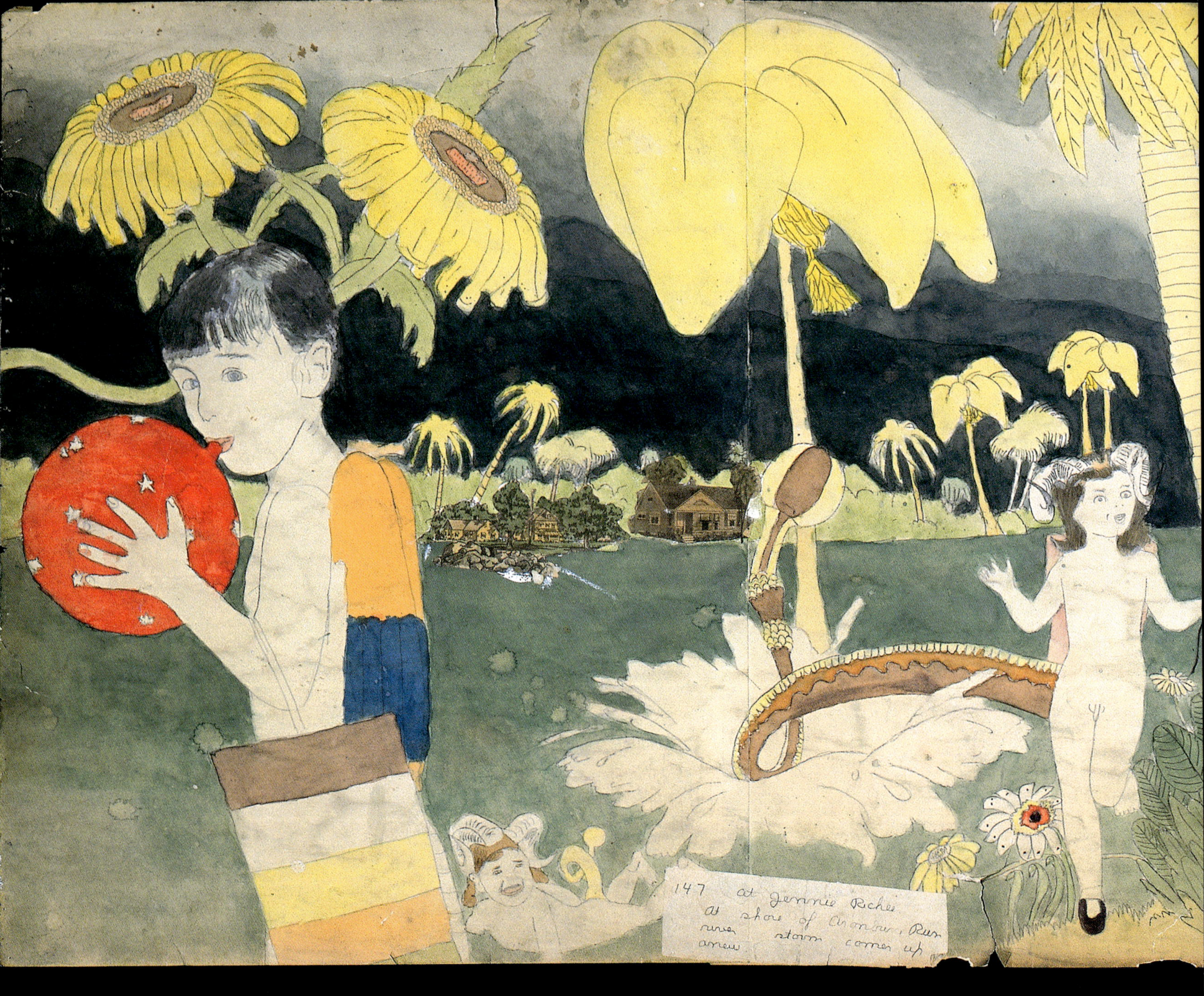

246 | *At Jennie Richee. At the shore of Aronburgs Run River storm comes up anew.*

Watercolor, pencil, carbon tracing, and collage on pieced paper, 24 x 108 in.

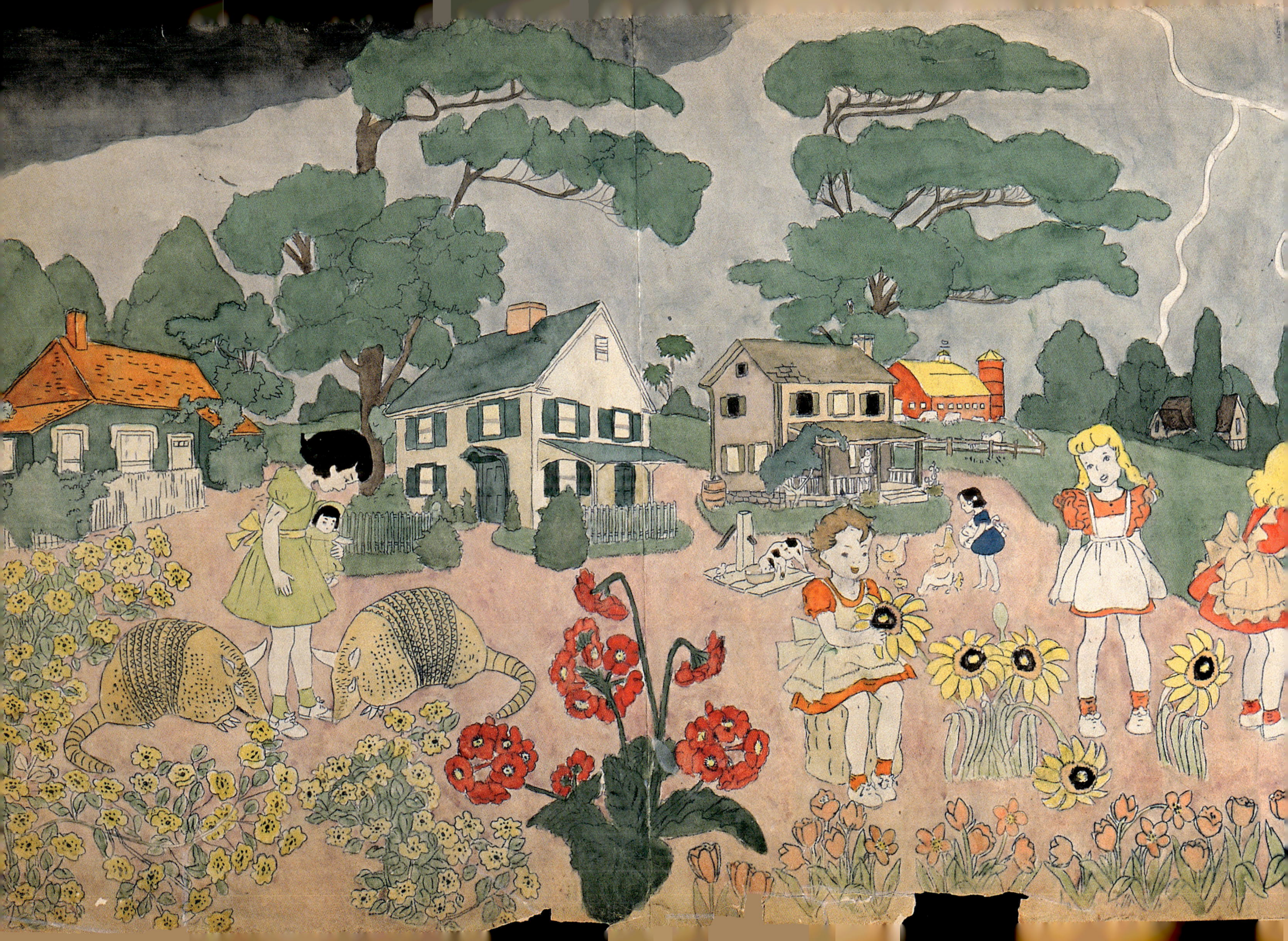

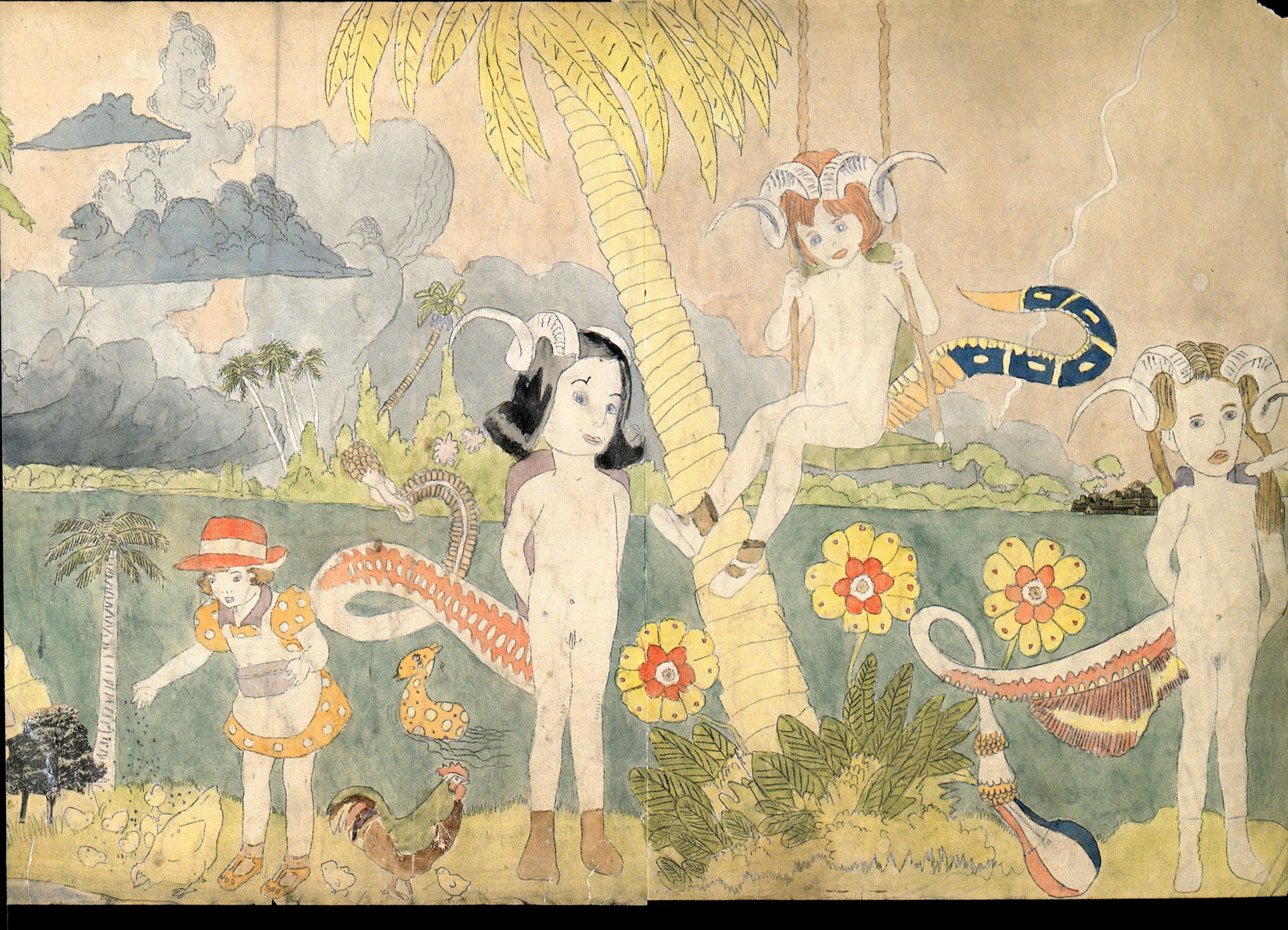

Untitled (Vivian girls watching approaching storm in rural landscape). 248–49 ➤
Watercolor, pencil, carbon tracing, and collage on pieced paper, 24 x 108 ¾ in.
Collection American Folk Art Museum, New York. Anonymous gift in recognition of Sam Farber

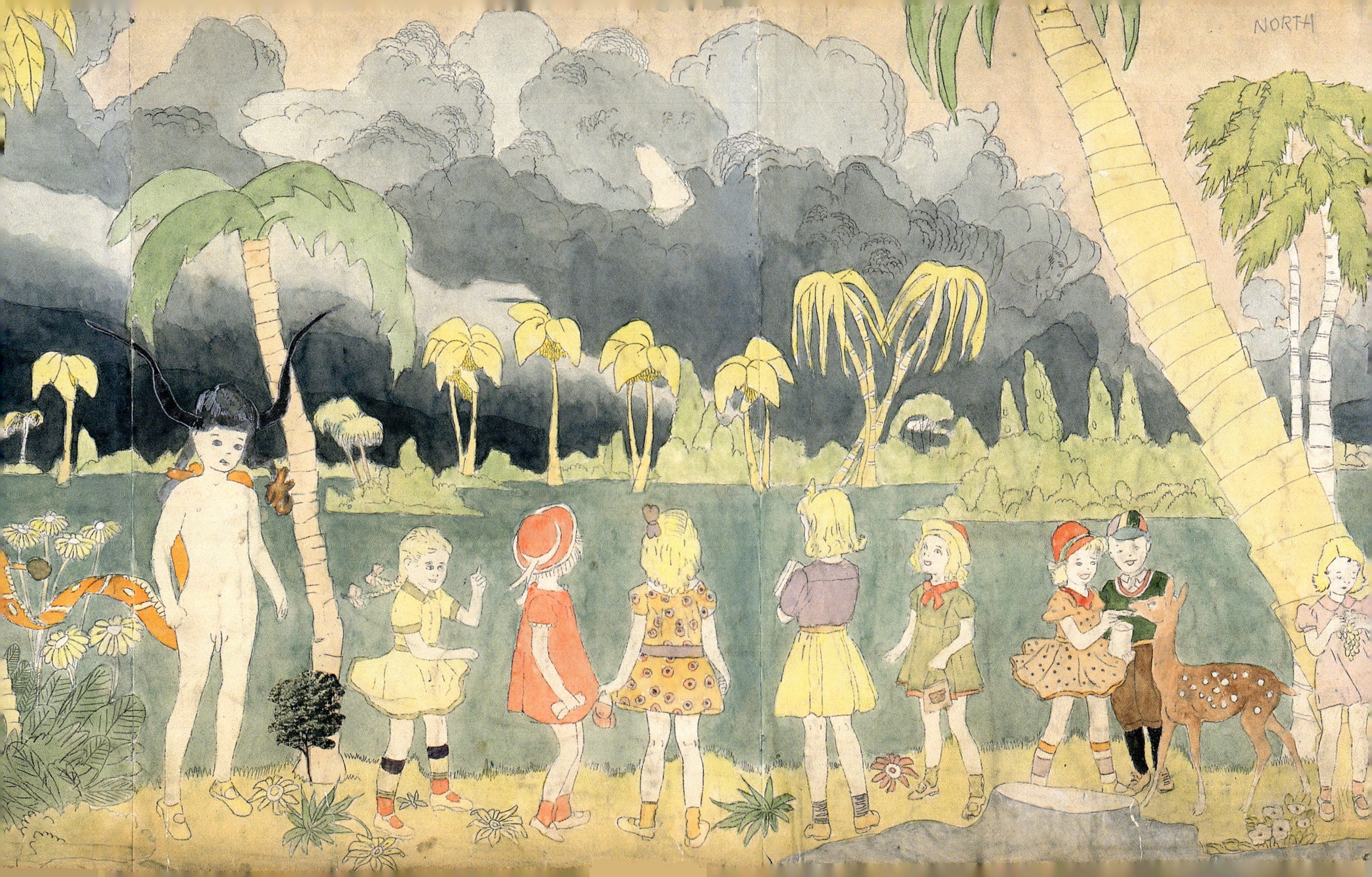

NORTH

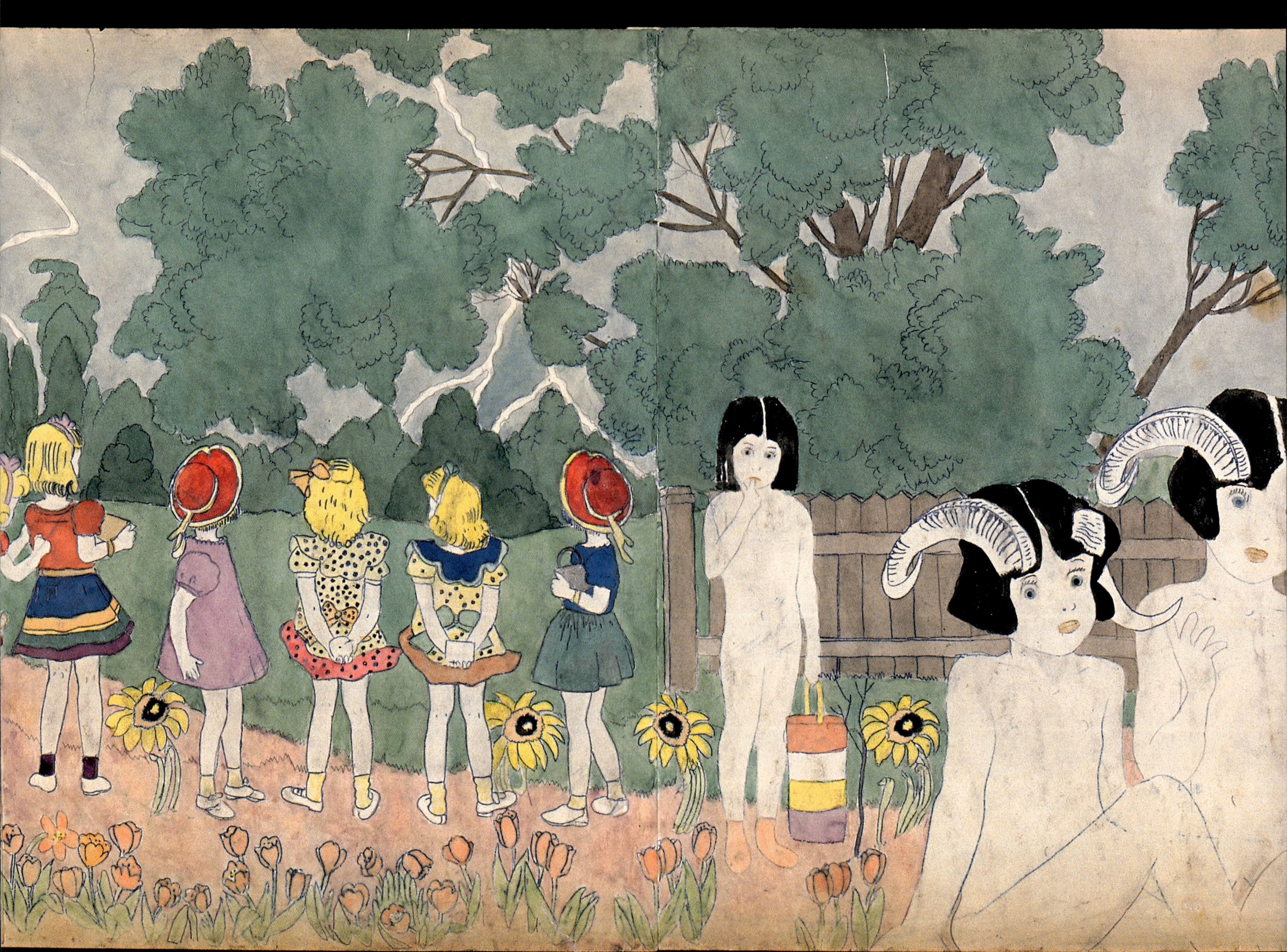

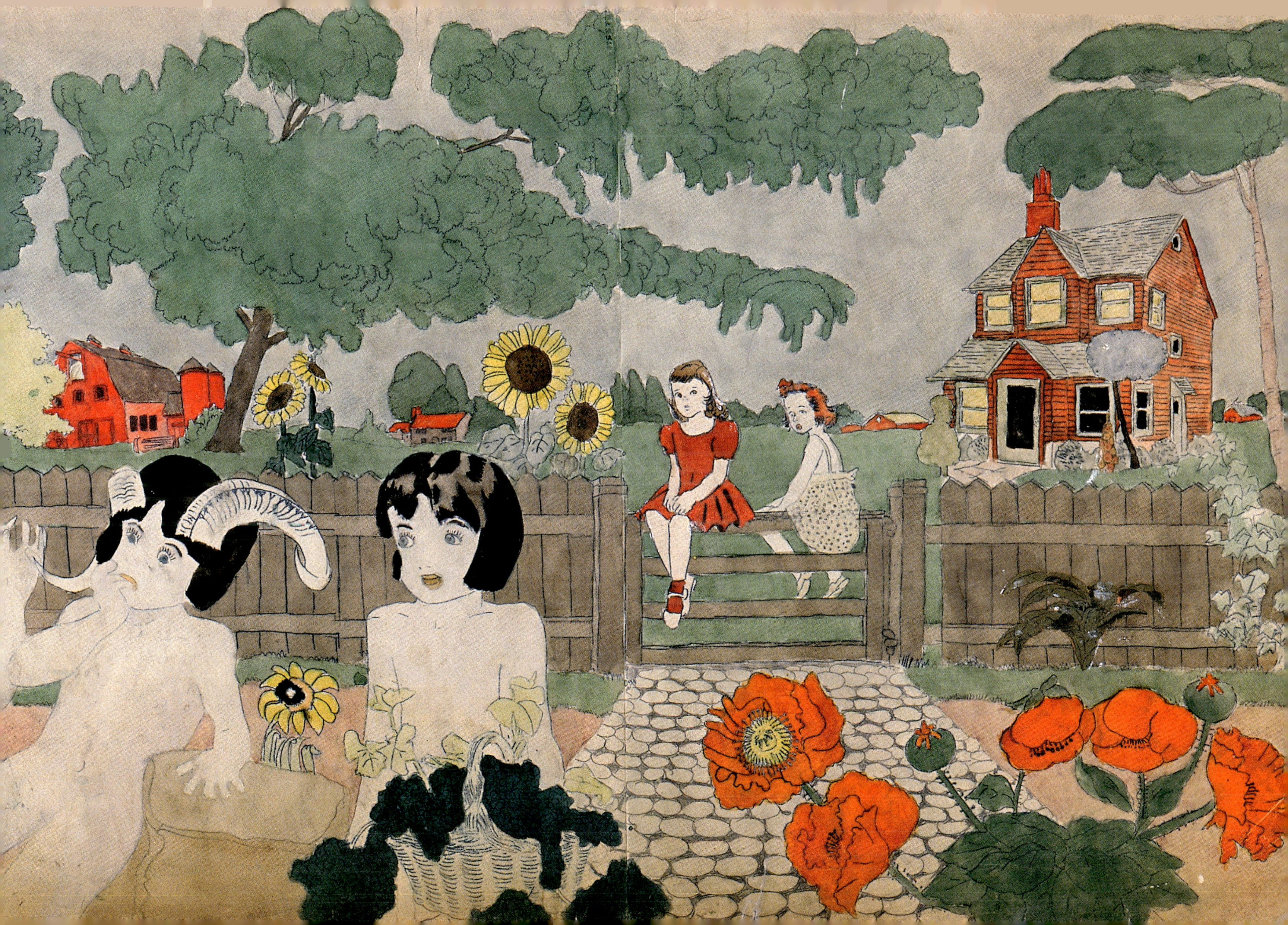

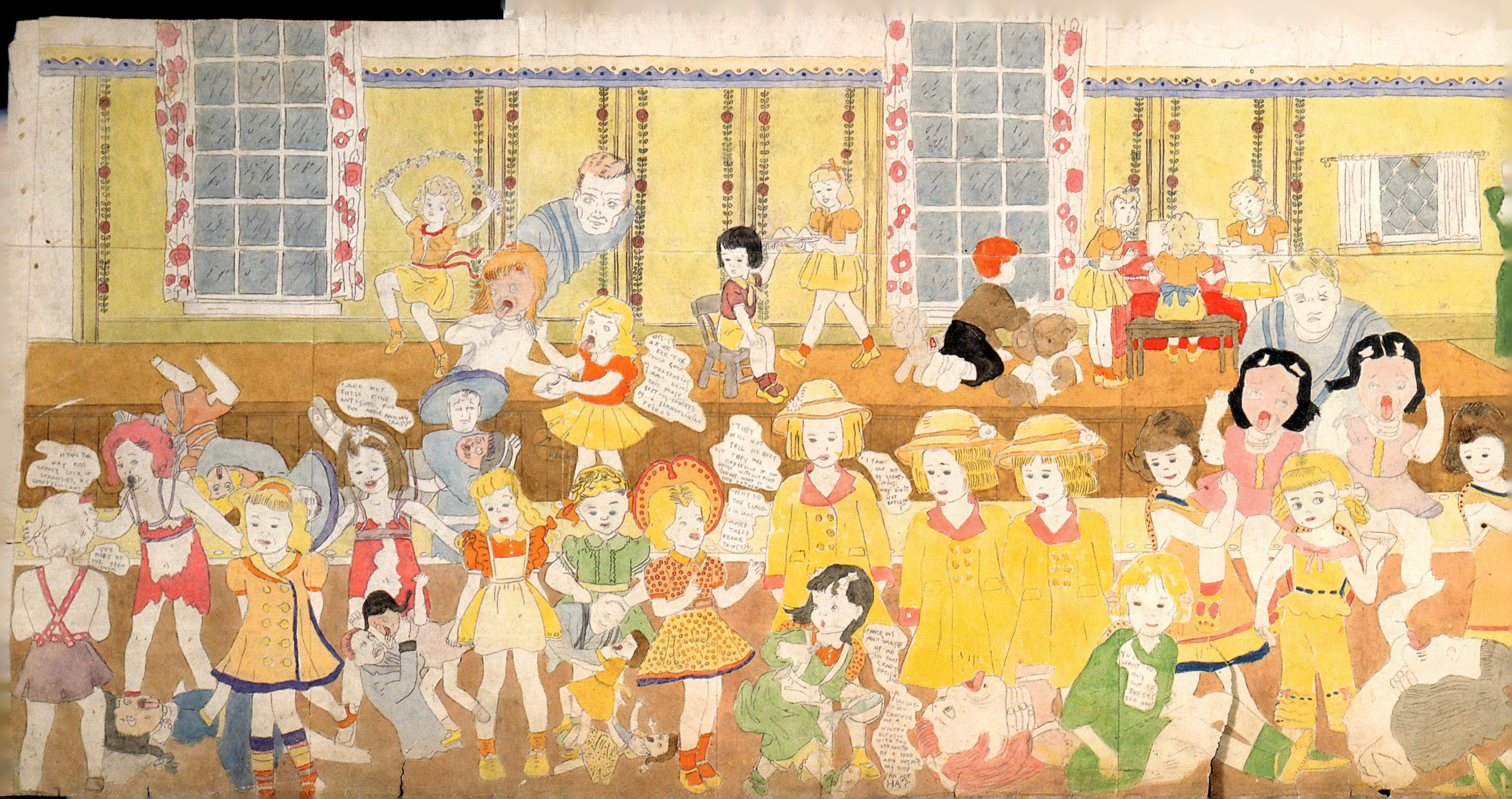

IS THIS THE WAY KIDS REALLY LOOK IF STRANGLED BY GANDELINIAN
YES THEY DO IVE SEEN THEM
ARE NOT THESE FINE ANTIQUES FOR THE ABBIE ANNIAN LANDS?
YES AFTER TOUGH GUID PRETENDING I AM THIS MASS GETTING SHOCKED BY A FLANDELINIAN PERSON
THEY WILL NOT TELL NOBODY BUT THEY ARE DANGEROUS IF YOU MAKE WITHOUT FIRST KNOWING WHAT IS INSIDE OF THEM
WHY DO THE GANDELINIANS MAKE THESE FREAK THINGS?
I SAW ONE NOT BY LIGHTNING. WHY DID IT NOT EXPLODE?
SHOCKING YOUR IMAGE OF ME IN THAT CRAZY DESIGN
... IN IAN SHOCKING ME A WINTER BLEMISH WITH THE STRENGTH OF A 1000 MEN UPON MY SIDE AND SEE HA?!

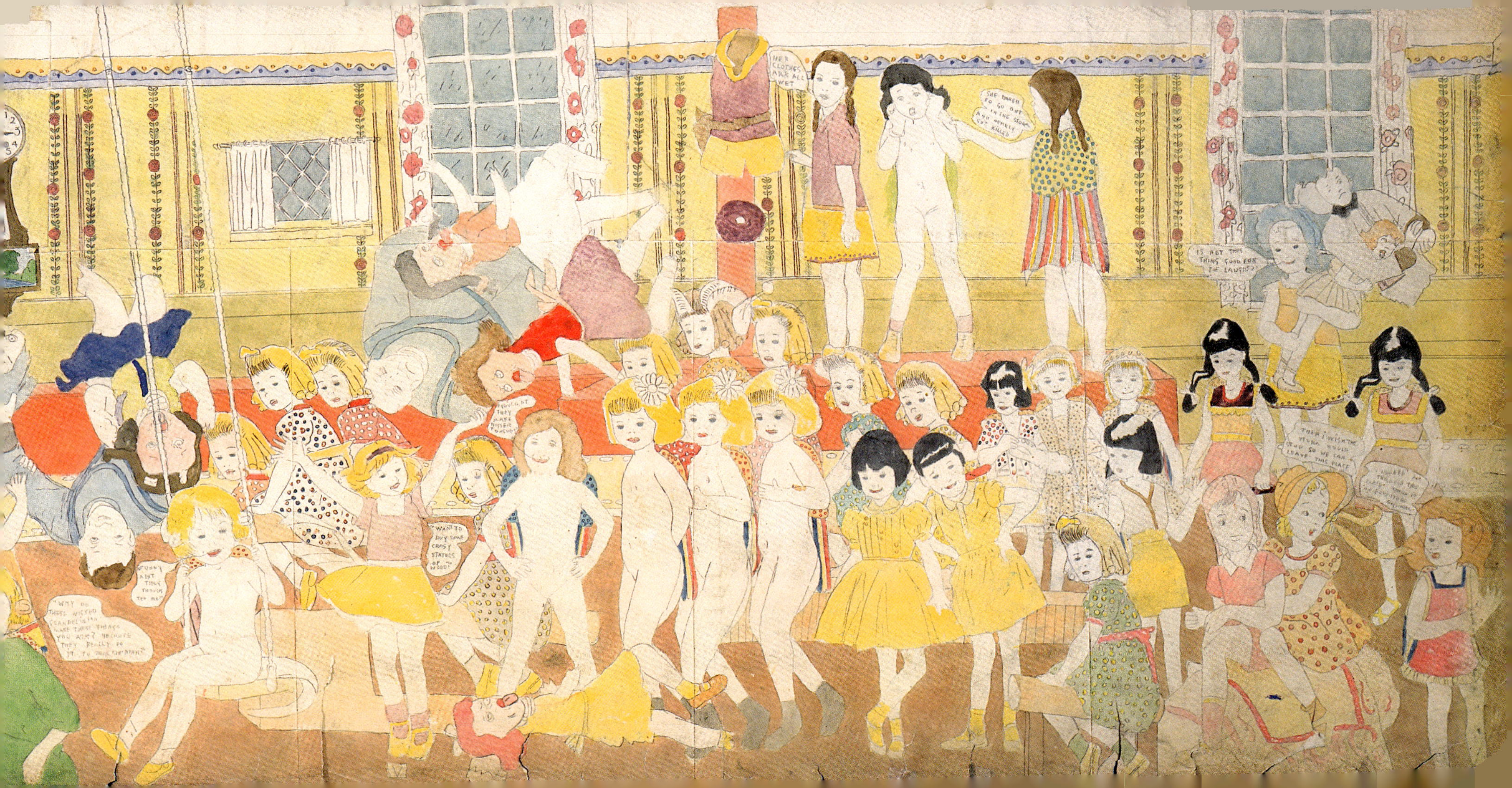
HER CLOTHES ARE ALL WET
SHE TRIED TO GO OUT IN THE STORM AND NEARLY GOT KILLED
IS NOT THIS THING GOOD FOR THE LAUGHS
I WANT TO BUY SOME CRAZY STATUES
WHY AINT THEY THROWN TO ME?

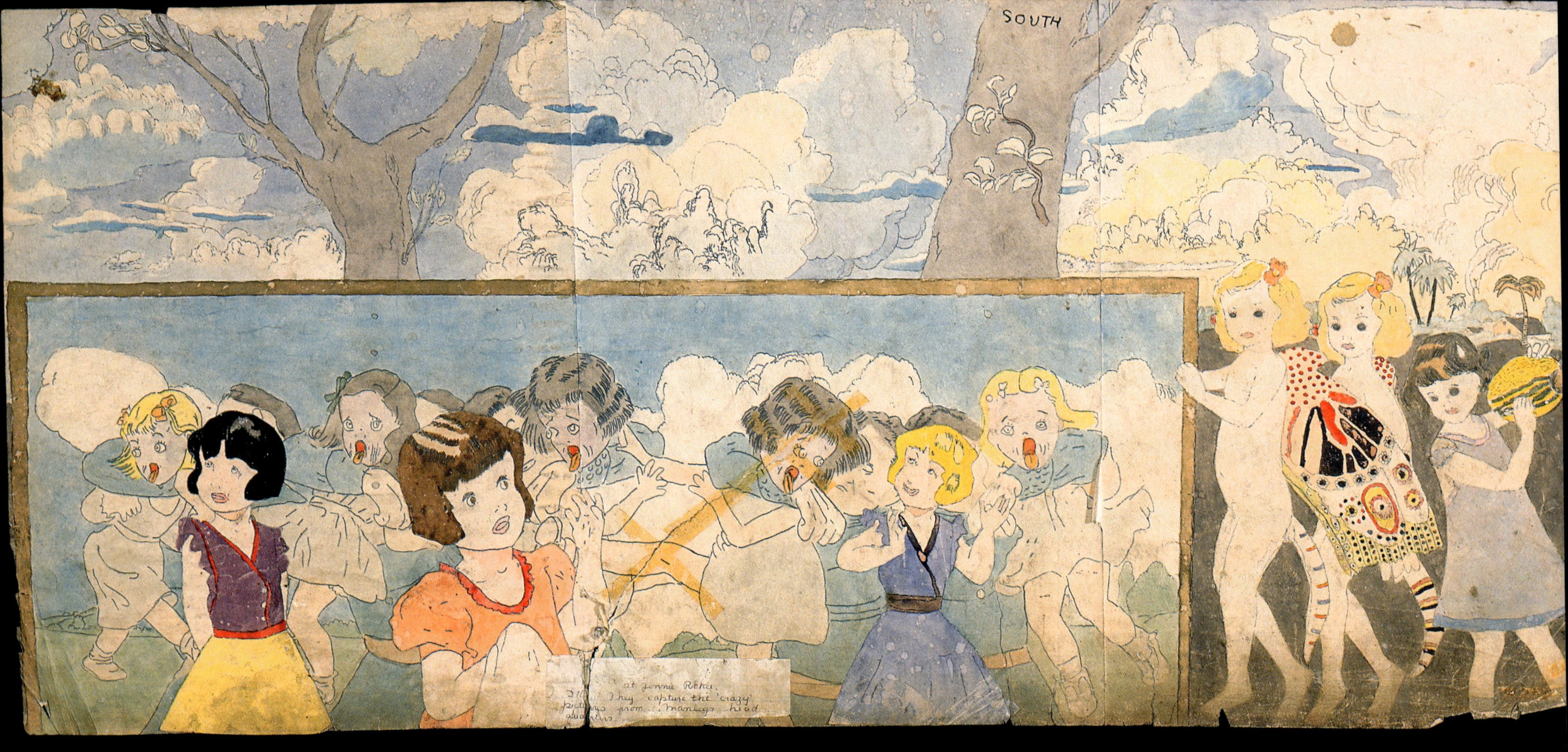

252 | *At Jennie Richee. They capture the crazy picture from Manleys headquarters.*

Watercolor, pencil, and carbon tracing on pieced paper, 24 x 108 in.

Collection Robert A. Roth, Chicago

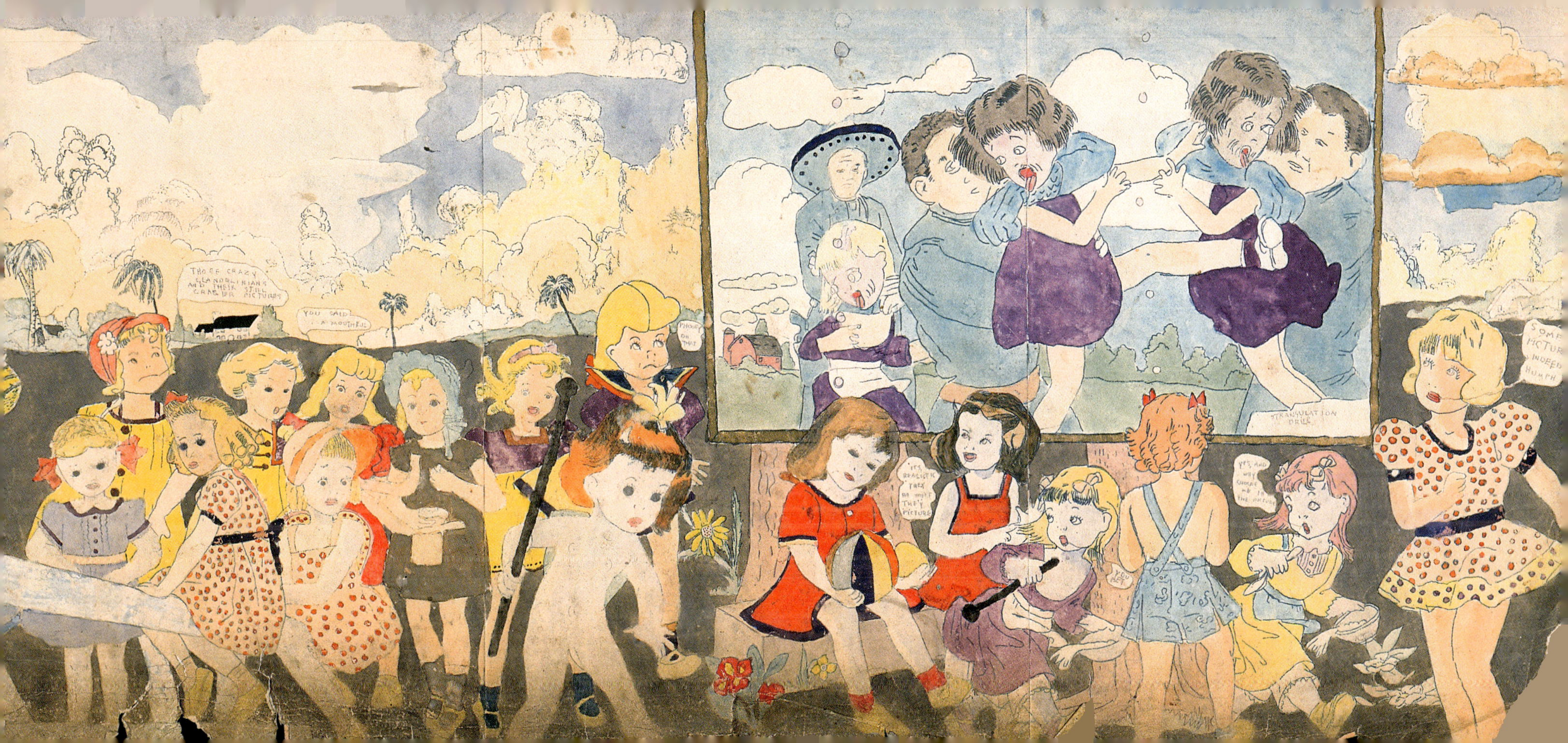
THOSE CRAZY ALABORLINIANS AND THEIR STILL CRAFTER PICTURES
YOU SAID A MOUTHFUL
PHOOIE ON THAT
SOME PICTURE INDEED HUMPH
IT'S REALISTIC THEY AH WHAT THEY PICTURE
YES AND WHY CHOKE ME IN THE PICTURE
YOU BET
TRANSULATION DRILL

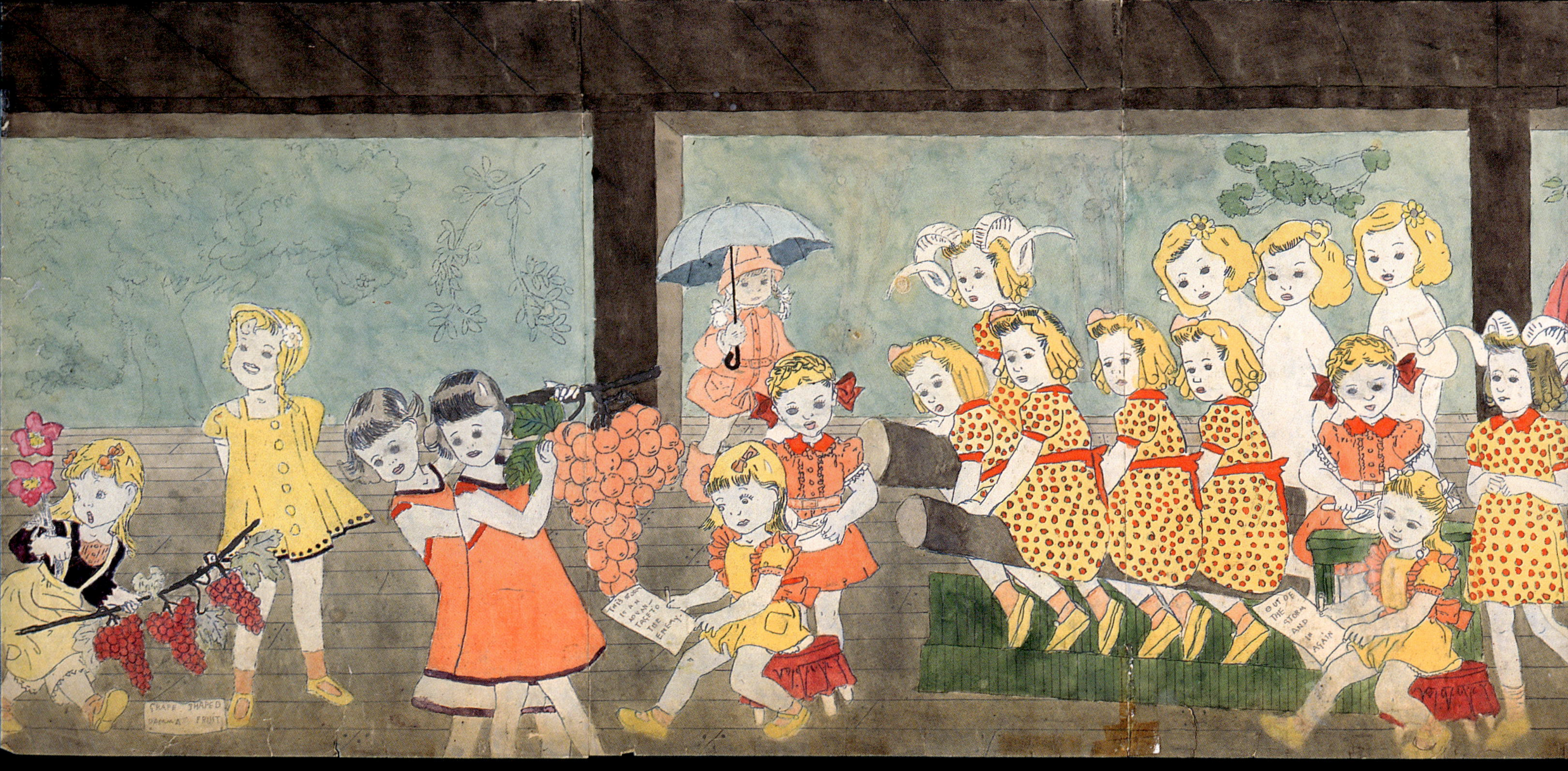

254 Untitled (grape shaped drama fruit).

Watercolor, pencil, and carbon tracing on pieced paper, 24 x 106 in.

Collection Kiyoko Lerner

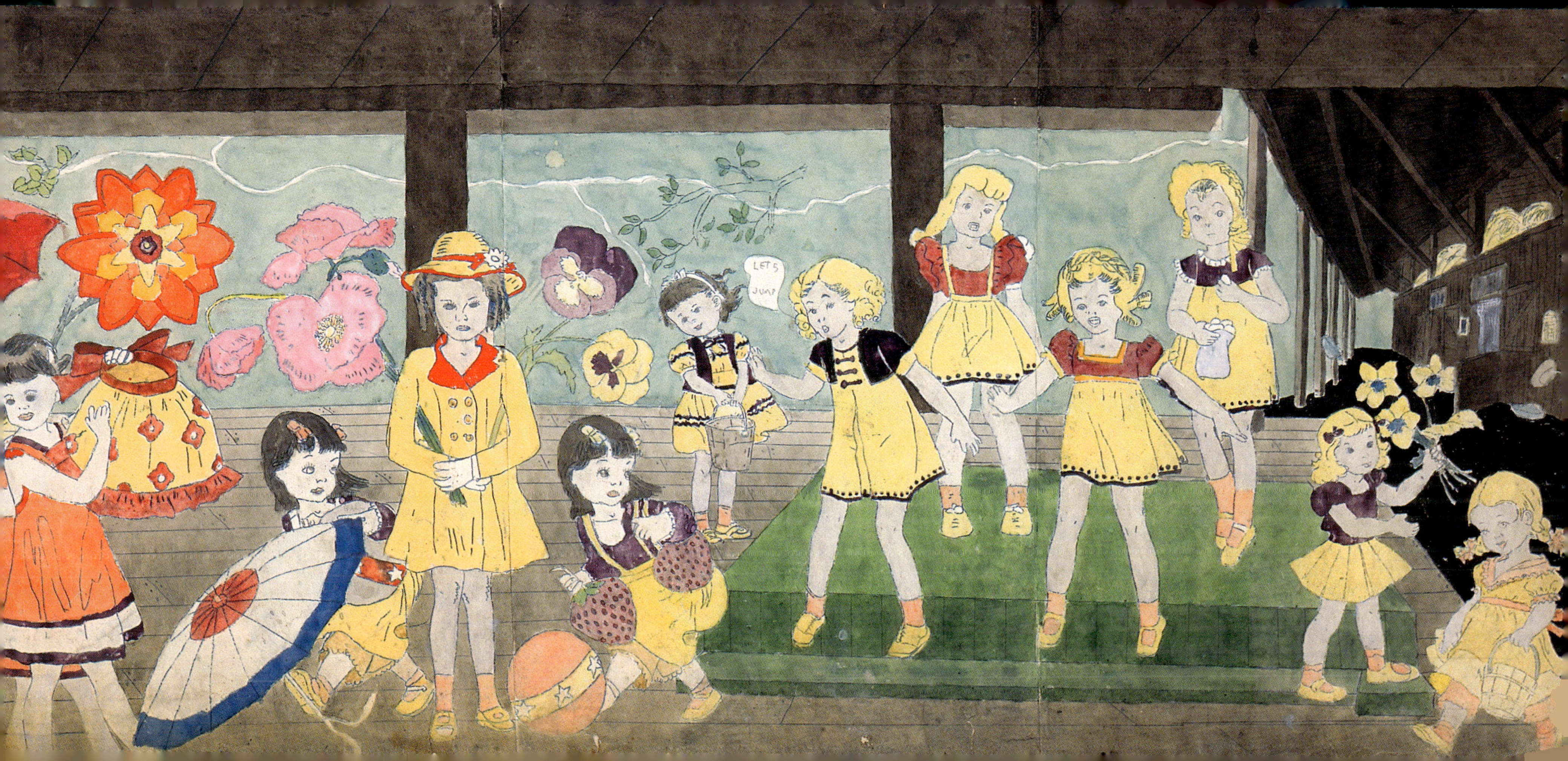

LET 5
JUMP

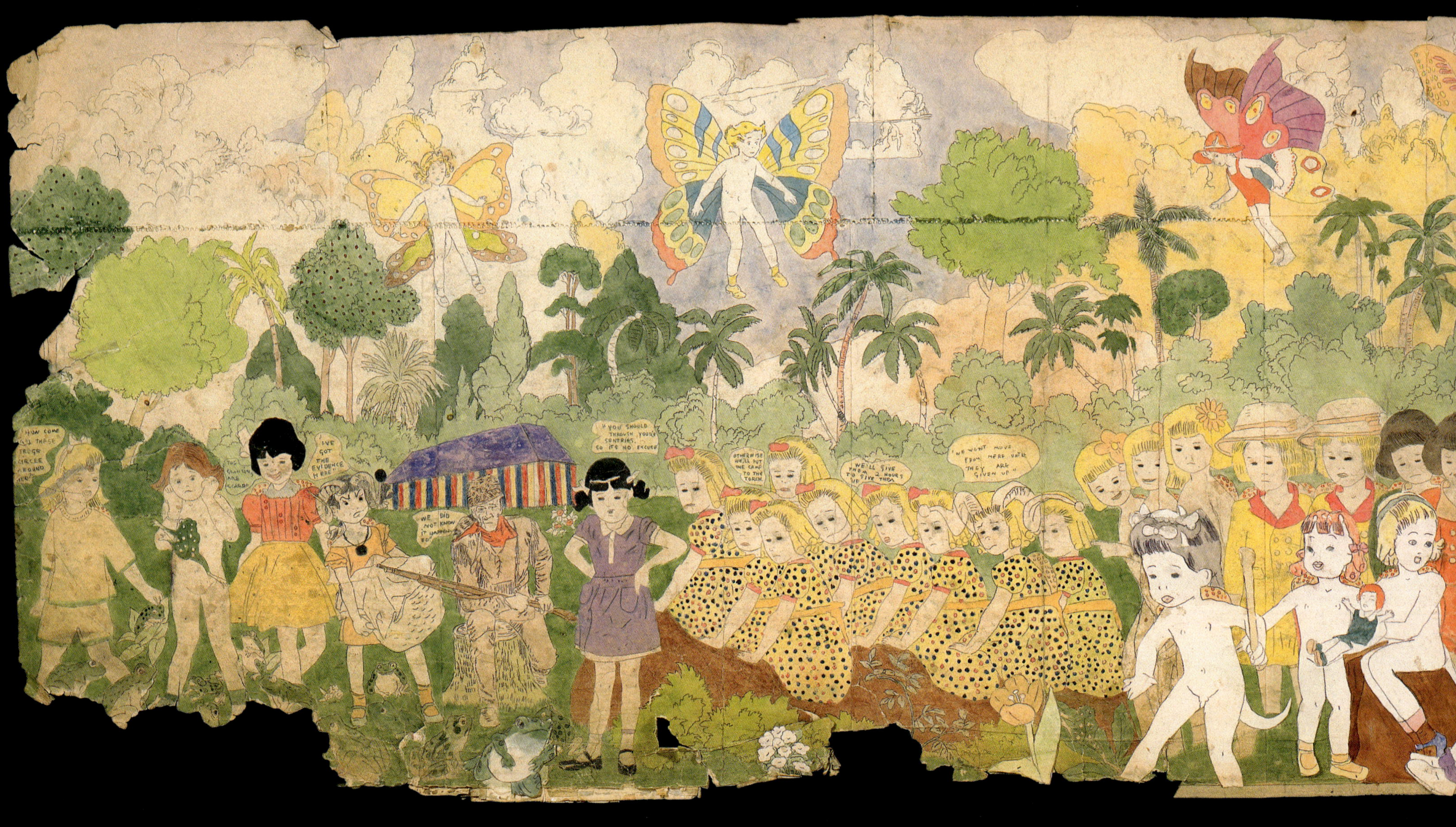

256 | Untitled ("Tell us the jack and the beanstalk fairy tail! We'll believe that more than what you are telling us. This camp is the only one in this territory. Give those bloody murderers up to us, or we'll surely wreck this camp and destroy all of you!! This head proves one of his murders!"). Watercolor, pencil, and carbon tracing on pieced paper, 32 x 125 in. Private collection

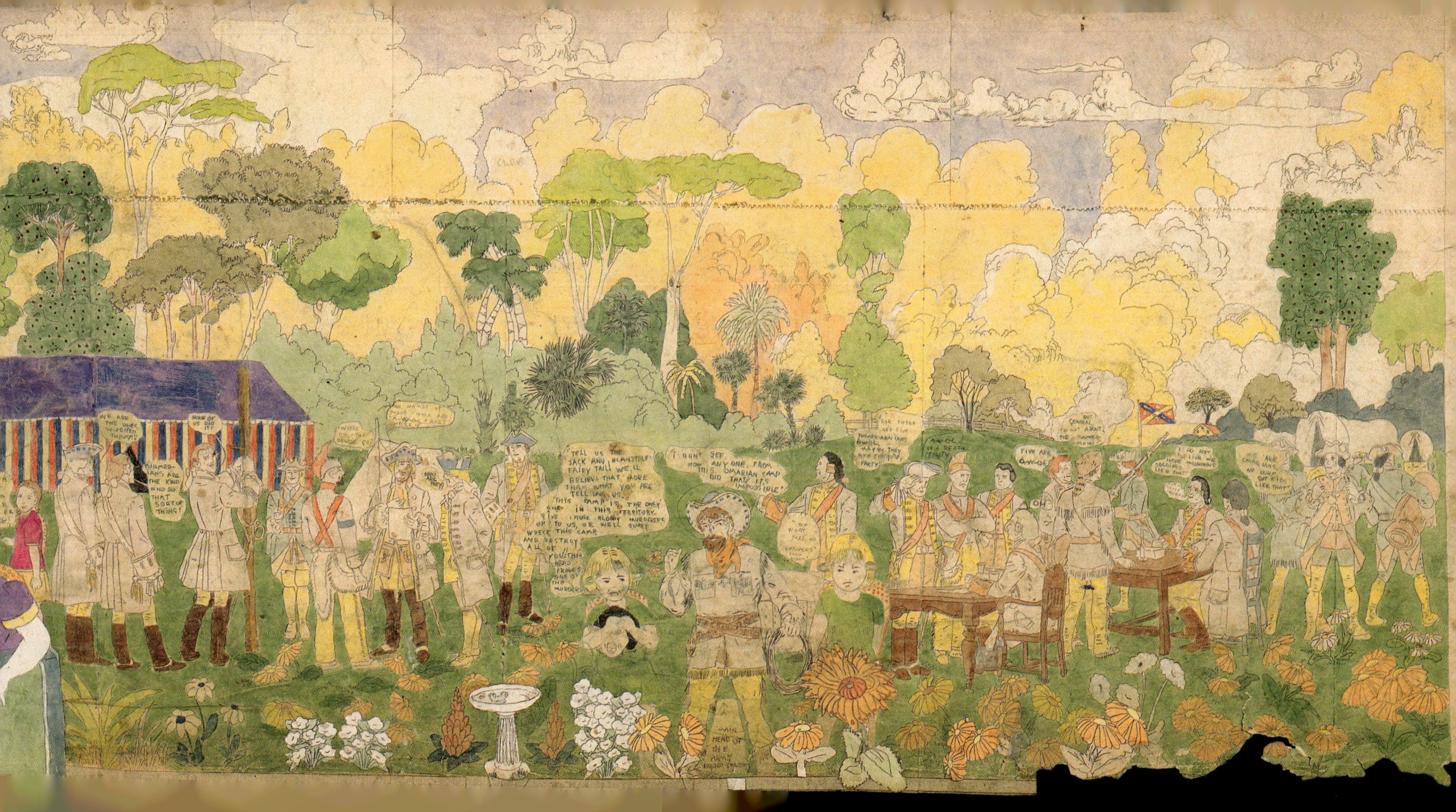

WE ARE THE ONES SUSPECTED THOUGH
HOUSE OF US DID IT?
TURMERIANS ARE THE KIND WHO DO THAT SORT OF THING?
WHO ARE THEY
WHERE ... THE ...
THE HOUSE OF THOSE WHO ARE A-W-OL PLACE
TELL US THE JACK AND BEANSTALK FAIRY TAIL! WE,LL BELIEVE THAT MORE THAN WHAT YOU ARE TELLING US. THIS CAMP IS THE ONLY ONE IN THIS TERRITORY. GIVE THOSE BLOODY MURDERERS UP TO US, OR WE'LL SURLY WRECK THIS CAMP AND DESTROY ALL OF YOU/THIS HEAD PROVES ONE OF THE MURDERS
I DONT SEE HOW ANY ONE FROM THIS OMARIAN CAMP DID THAT? ITS IMPOSSIBLE
SIR THERE ARE FIVE TUSSARIANN FAIRS HERE, MAYBE THEY ARE THE PARTY
AM GL... OF A DEATH FINITY
FIVE ARE A-W-OL
IF YOU WONT TAKE US PRISONERS COME ALONG
I DO NOT THINK WE HAVE SOLDIERS LIKE THAT
WE ARE CHAP LIKE WE WOULD GUT KIDS LIKE THAT?
OH
MAIN HEAD OF THE ALLAN HODDER FAMILY

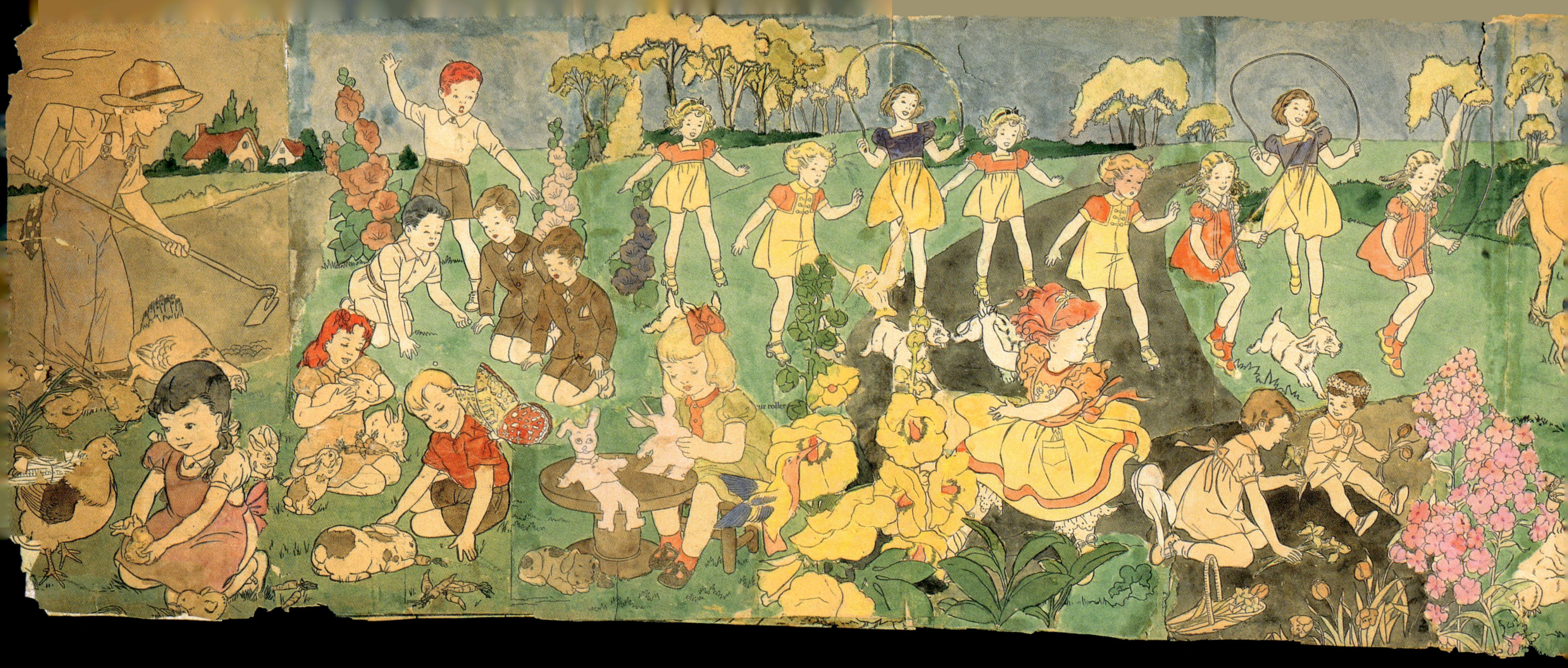

At Jennie Richee. During lull in storm approach adandoned farm where children are playing.

Blengiglomenean and creatures are flying overhead and therefore not seen.

Watercolor, pencil, carbon tracing, and collage on pieced paper, 21 x 108 in. Private collection.

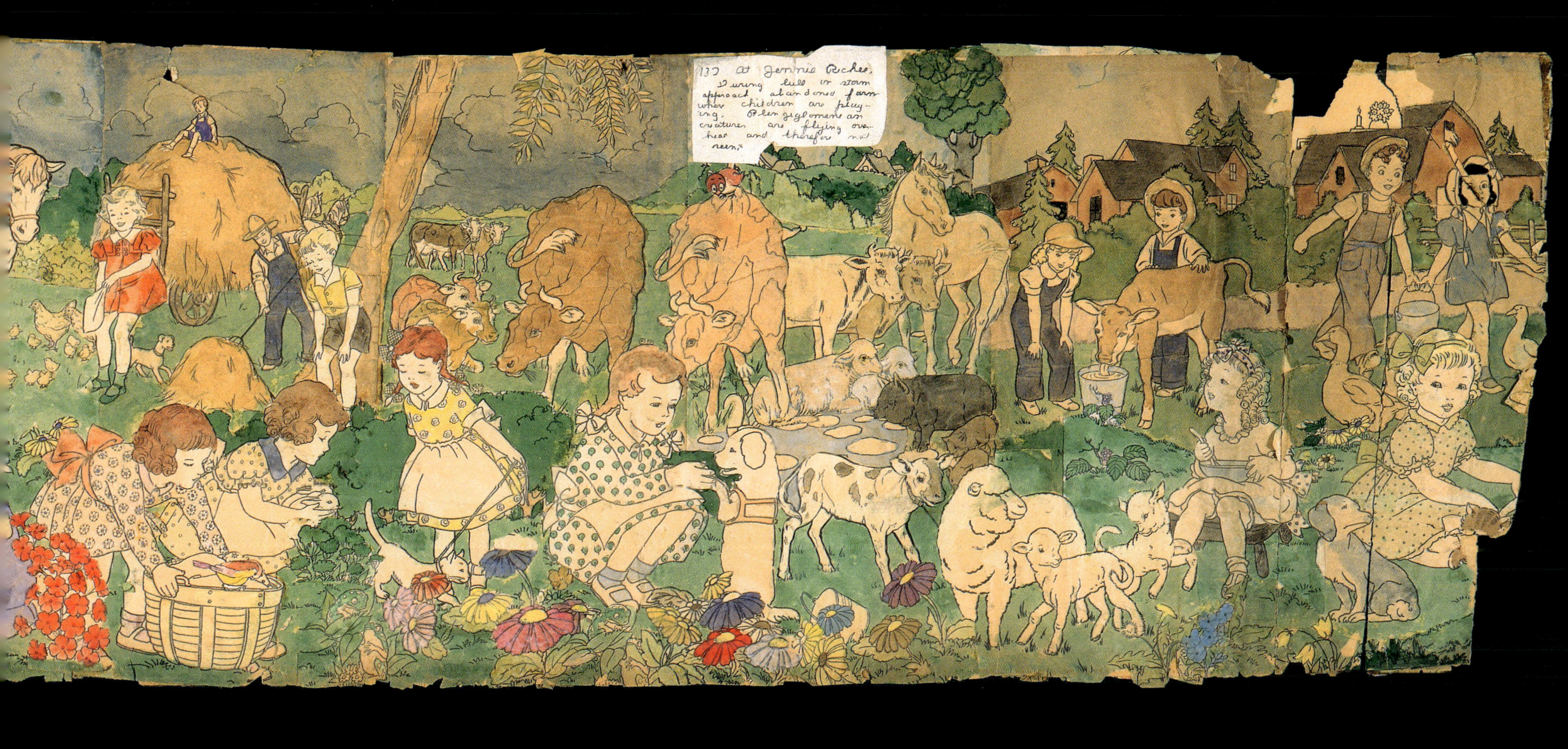
132 At Jennie Riches,
During lull or storm
approach abandoned farm
where children are play-
ing. Plenziglomane an
creatures are flying overhead and therefore not
seen.

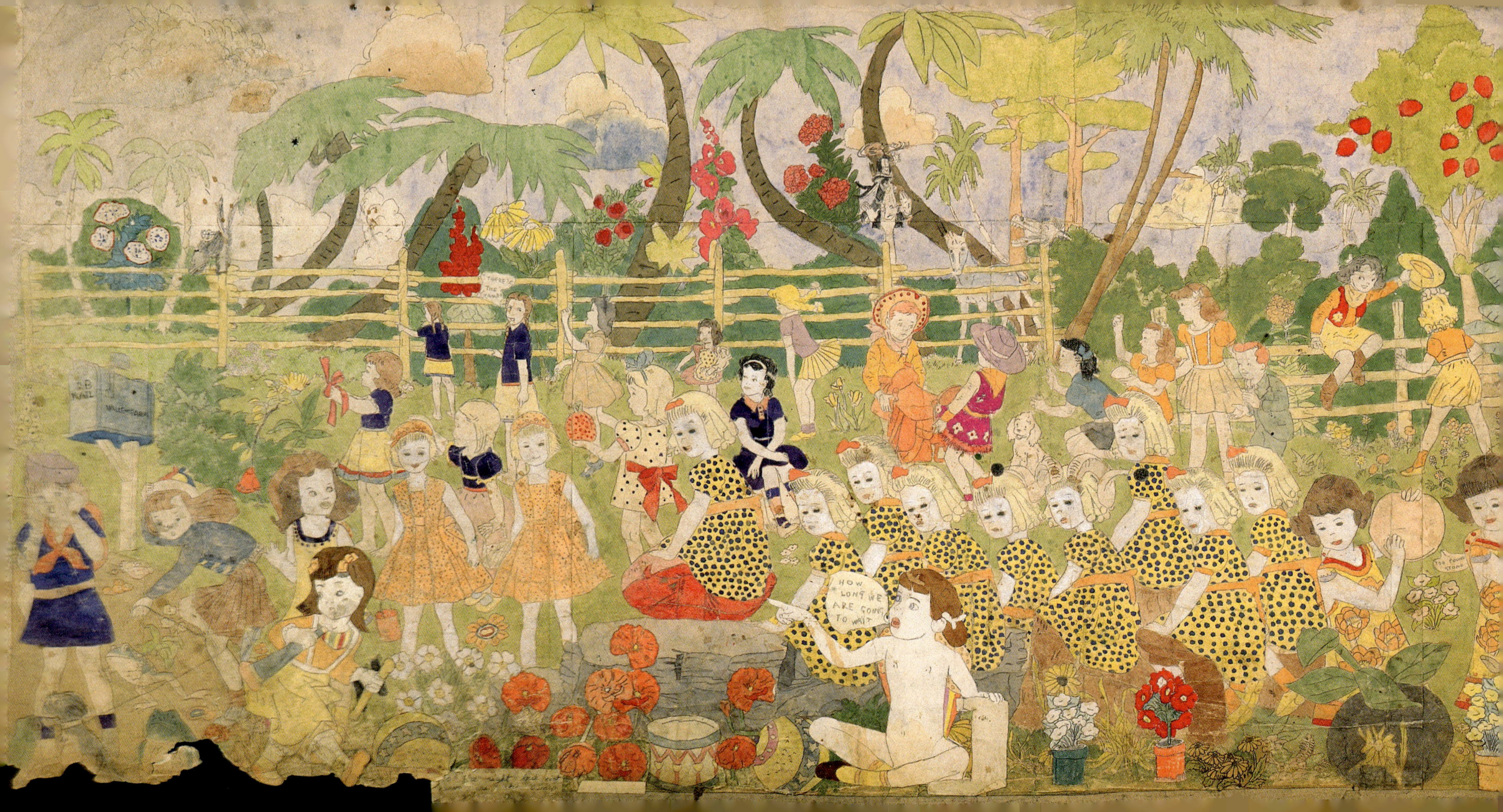
U.S. MAIL
WALLOWARA
THERE'S THE CAMP
HOW LONG WE ARE GOING TO WAIT

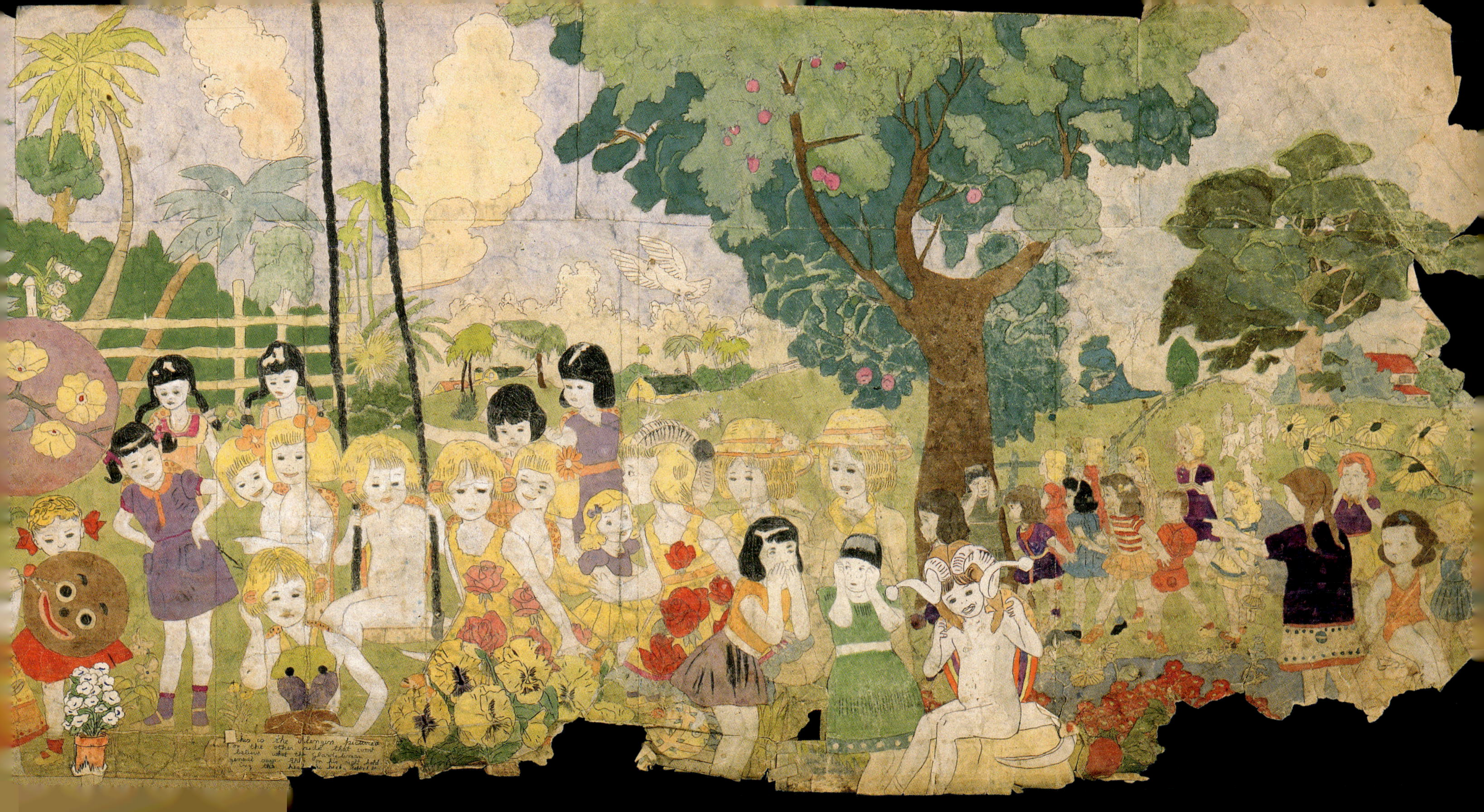
This is the Vivian girls pictured
on the other side that went
believe what the Glandelinian
general over-ran and to the right hold
the heads in back behind

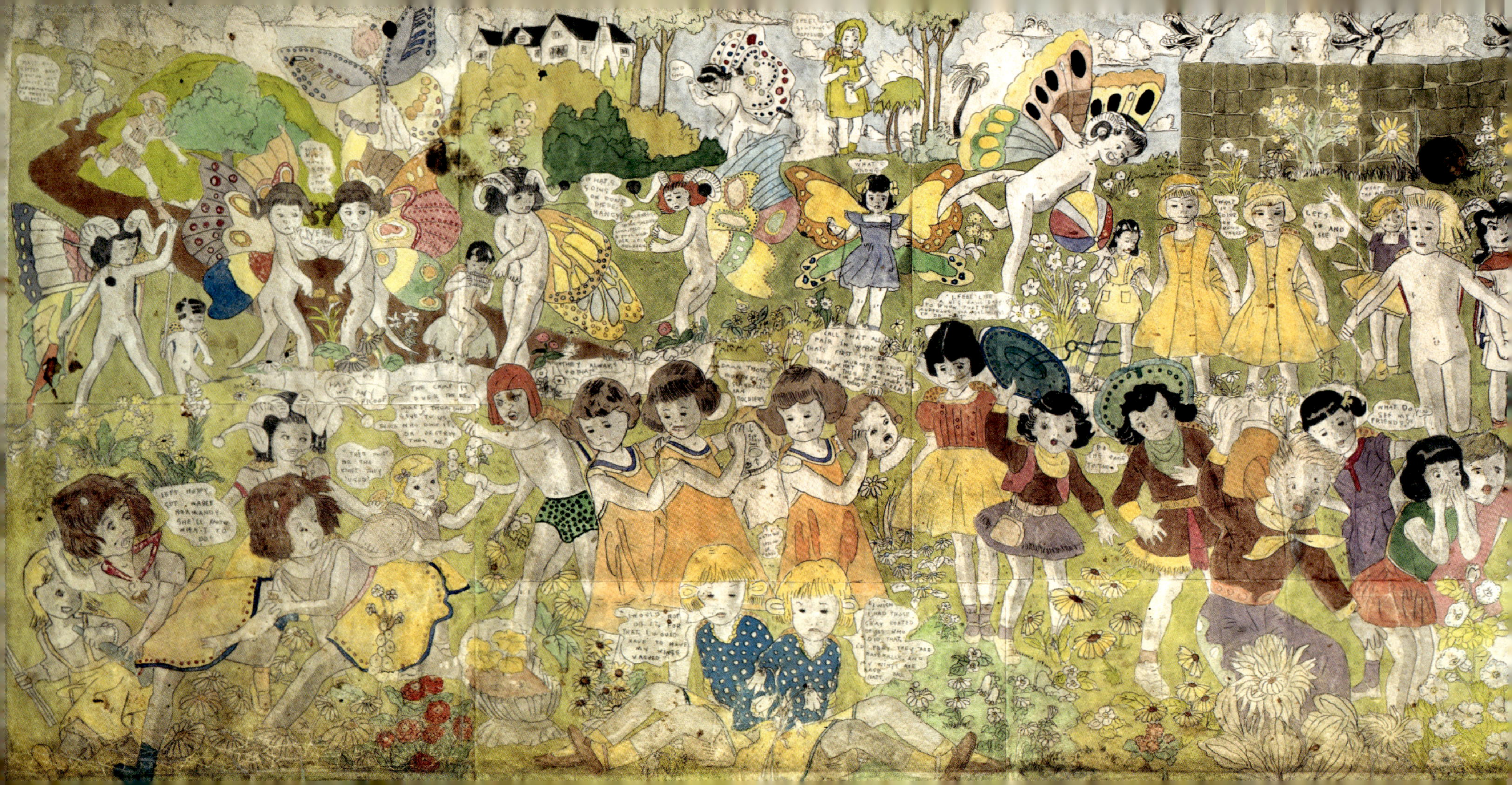

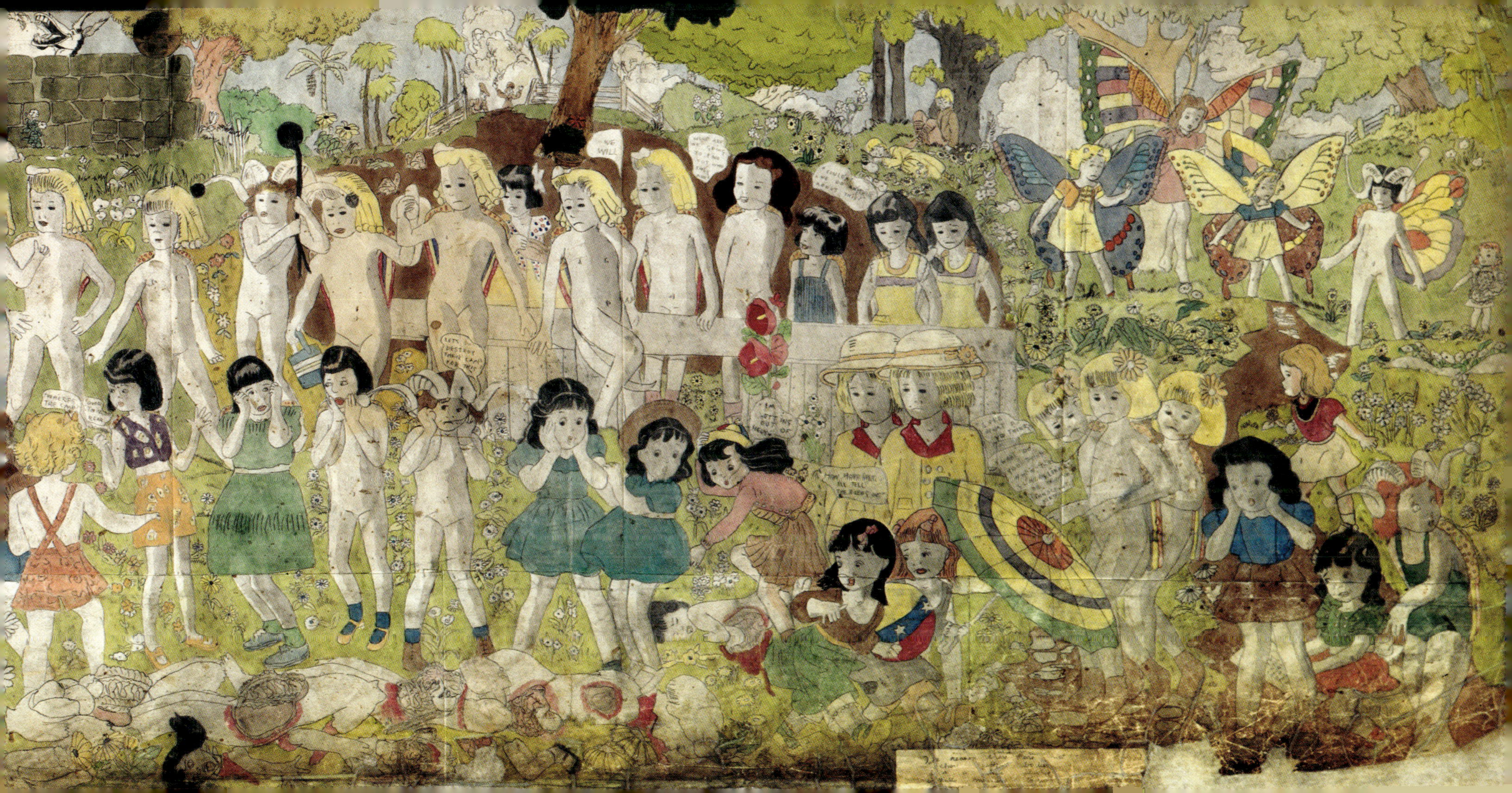

WE WILL

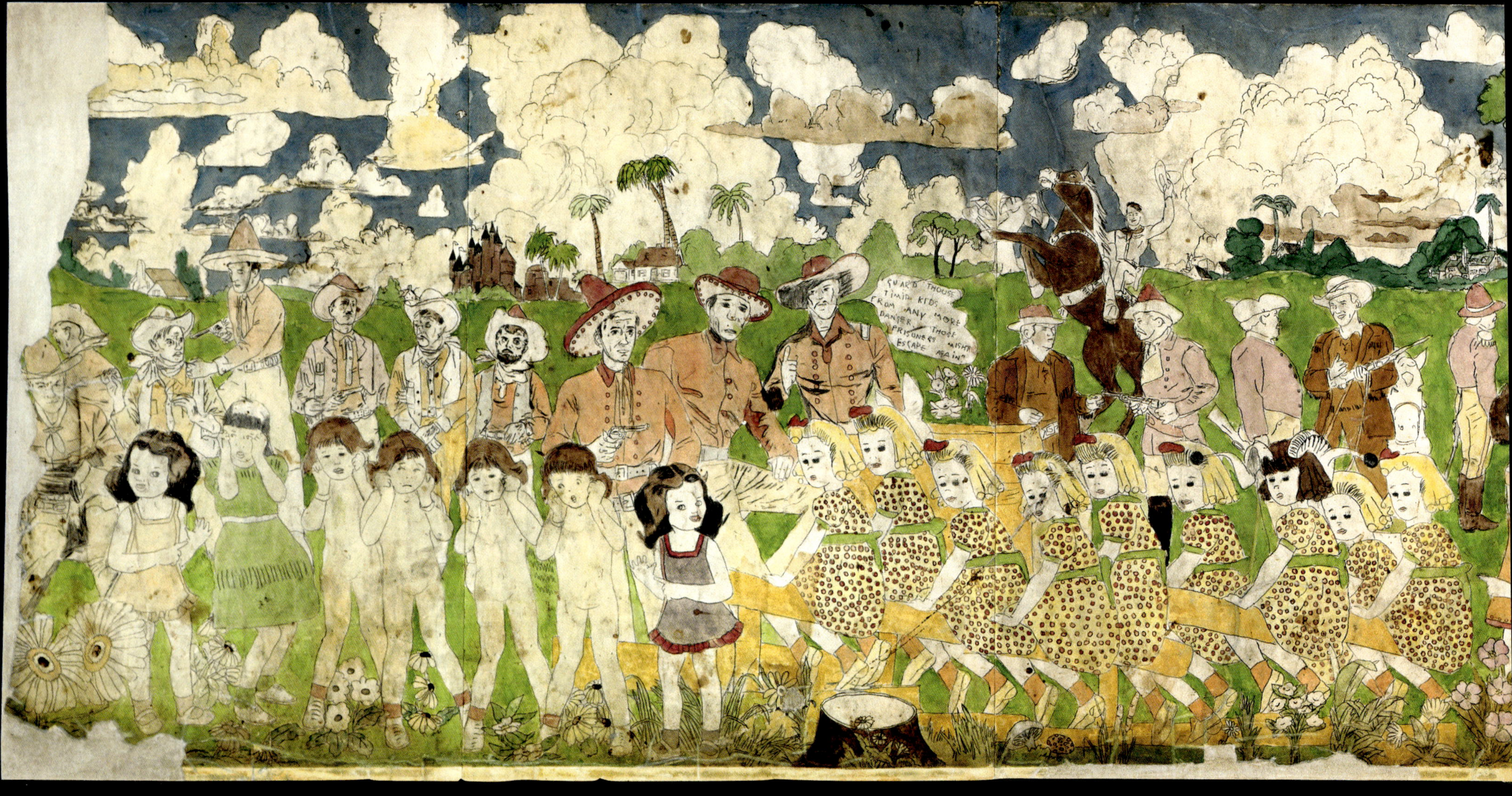

264 | *Guard thouse timid kids from any more danger. Those prisoners might escape again.*

Watercolor, pencil, carbon tracing, and collage on pieced paper, 30 x 122 ¼ in.

Collection de l'art brut, Lausanne

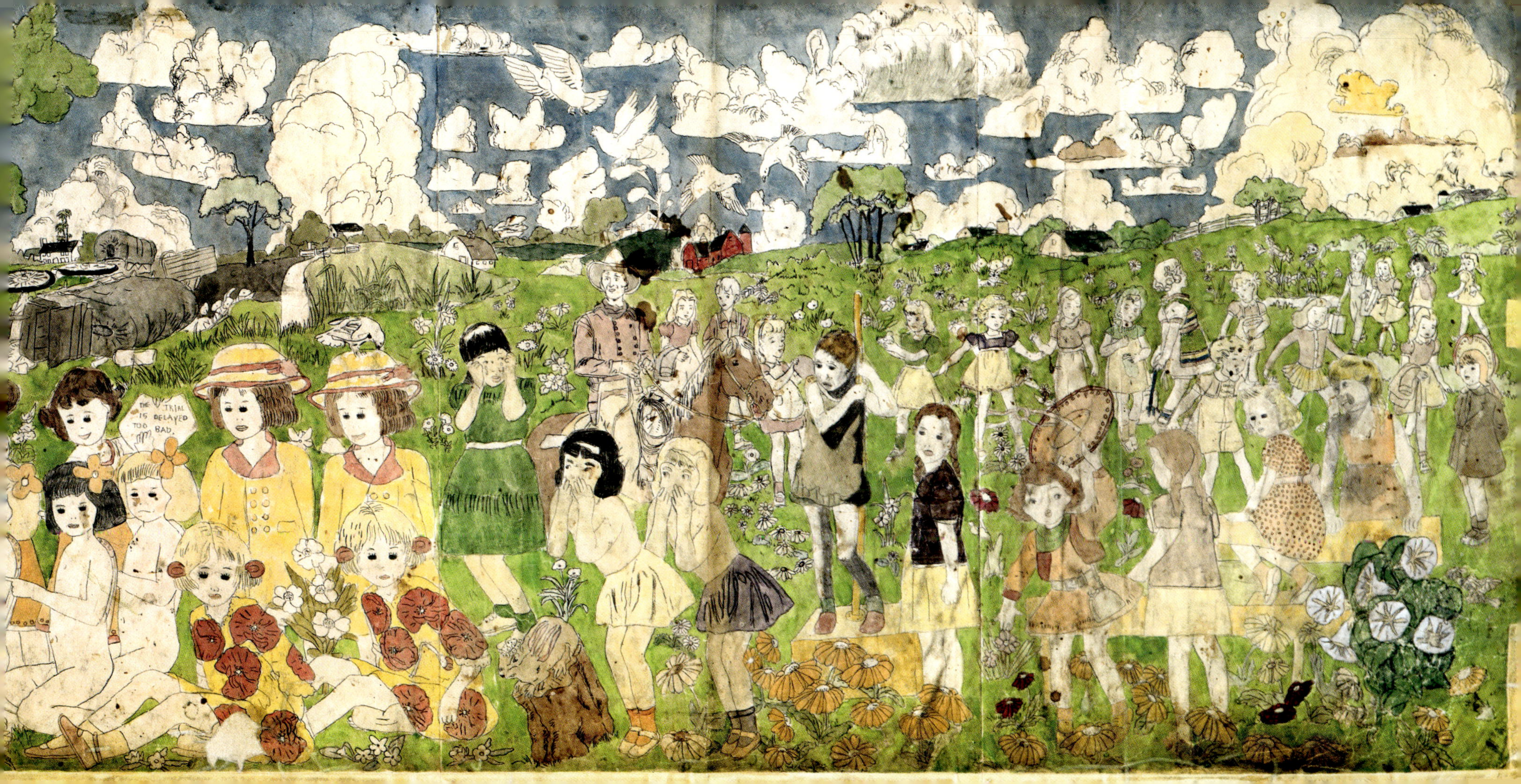

THE TRIAL IS DELAYED TOO BAD.

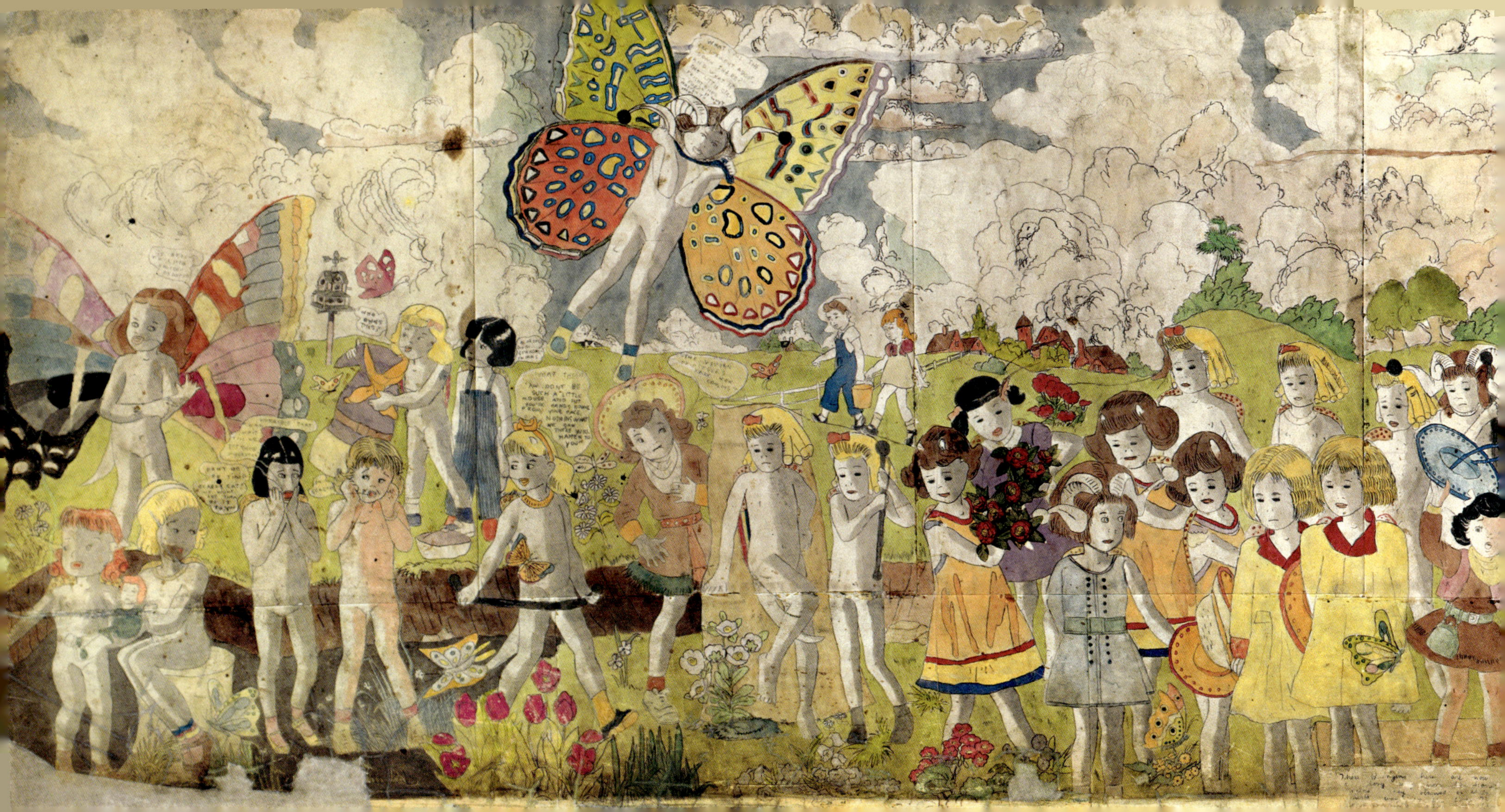

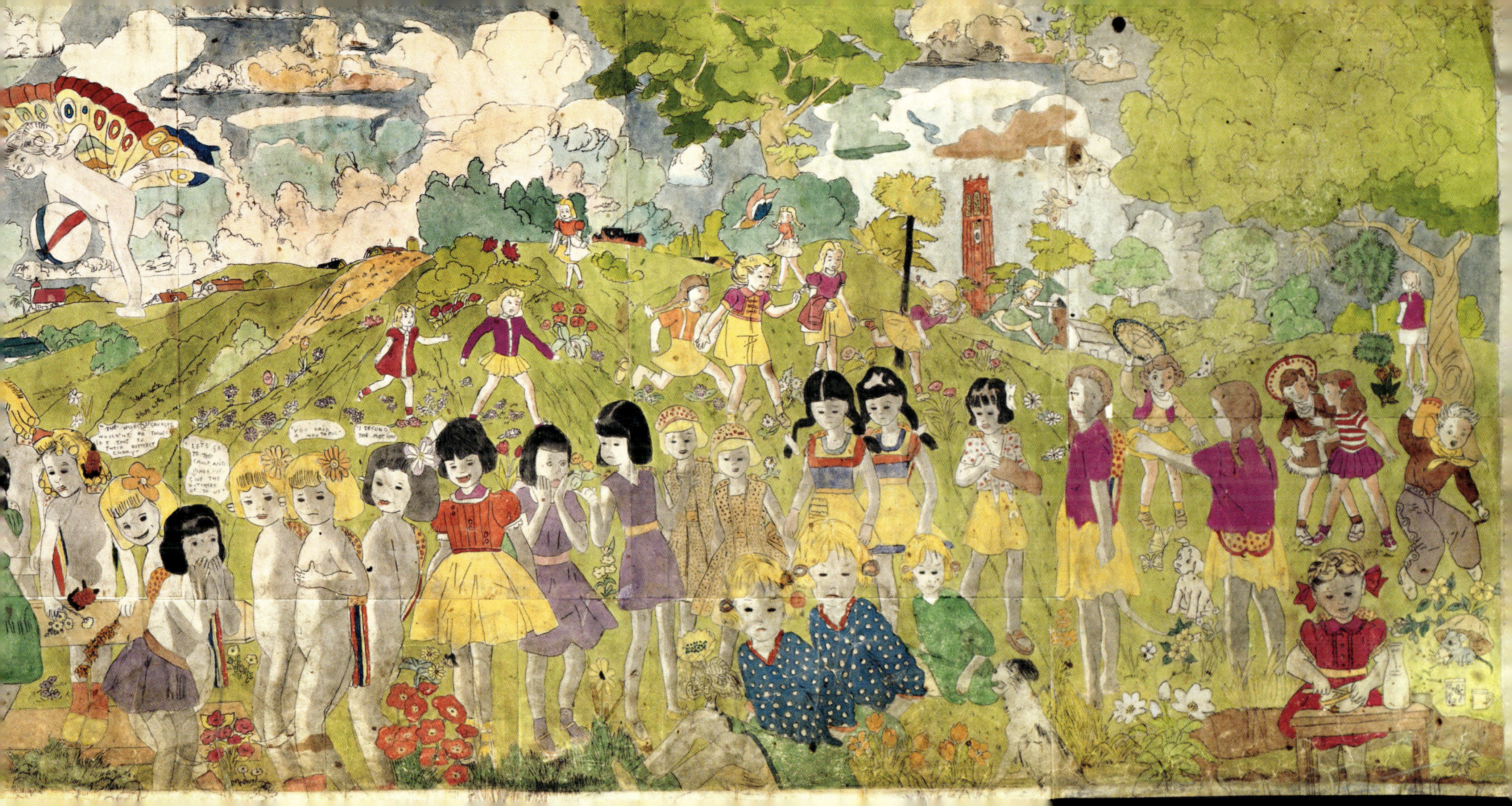
YOU SAID A MOUTHFUL
I SECOND THE MOTION

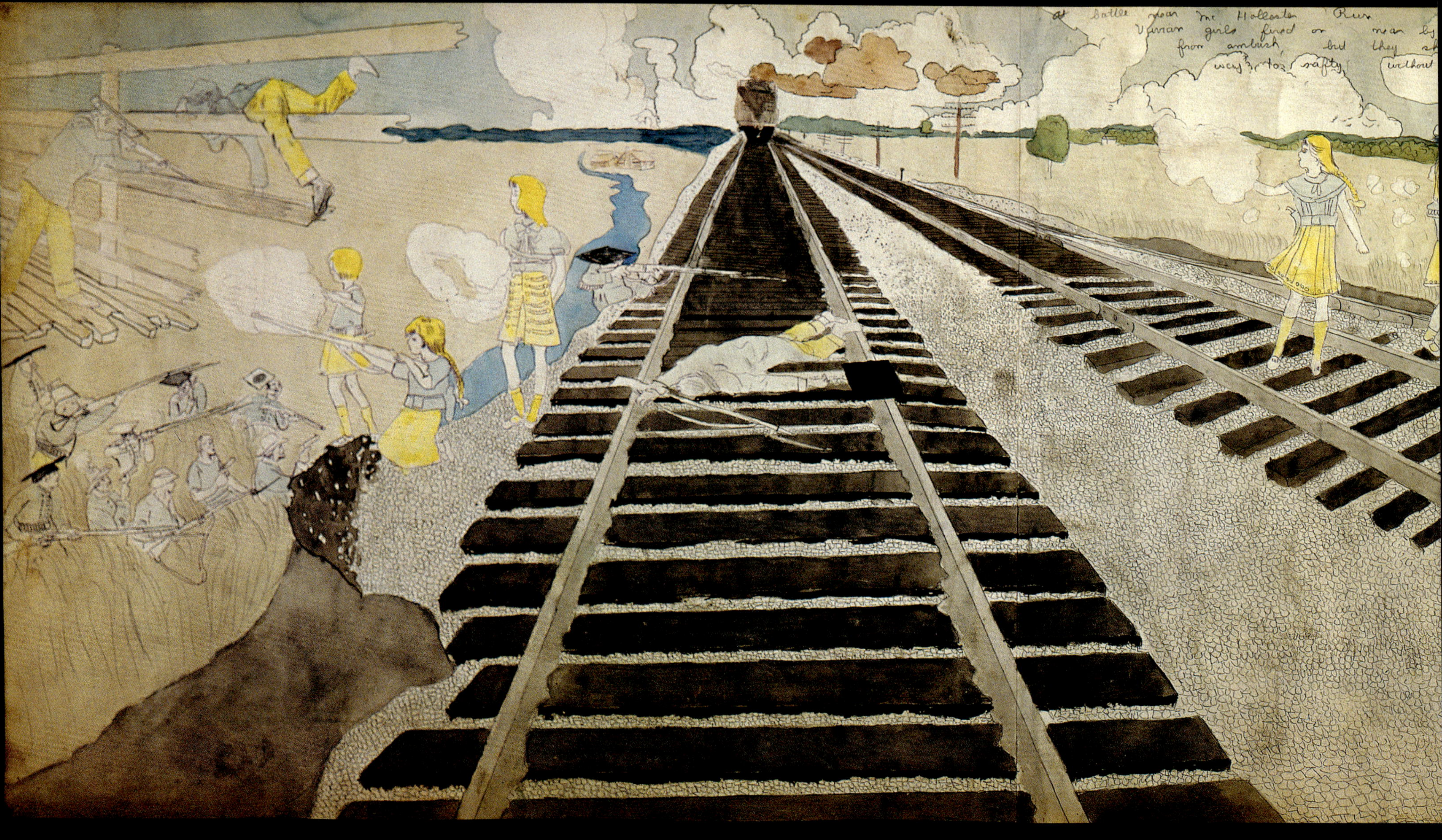

 At battle near McHollester Run. Vivian Girls fired on near by from ambush, but they shoot their way to safty without one being injured.

Watercolor, pencil, carbon tracing, and collage on pieced paper 19 x 47 ¾ in. Collection Robert A. Roth, Chicago

Pages 270–71: *At Norma Catherine . . .* (detail—see pages 120–21)

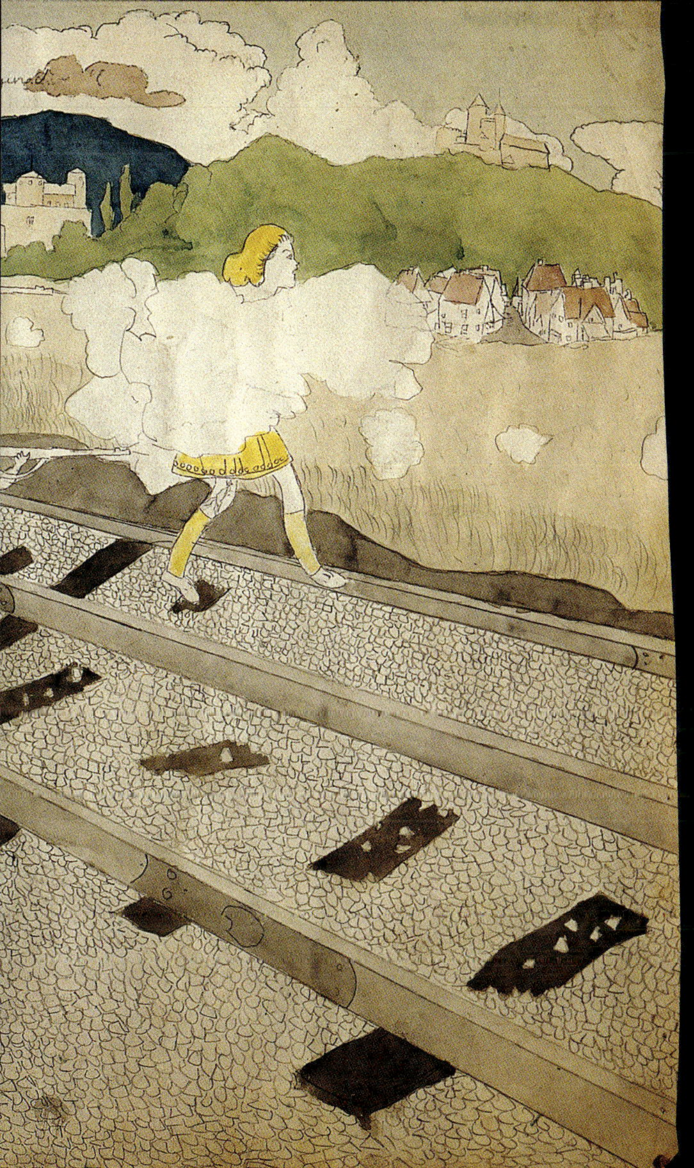

THE LIFE OF HENRY DARGER

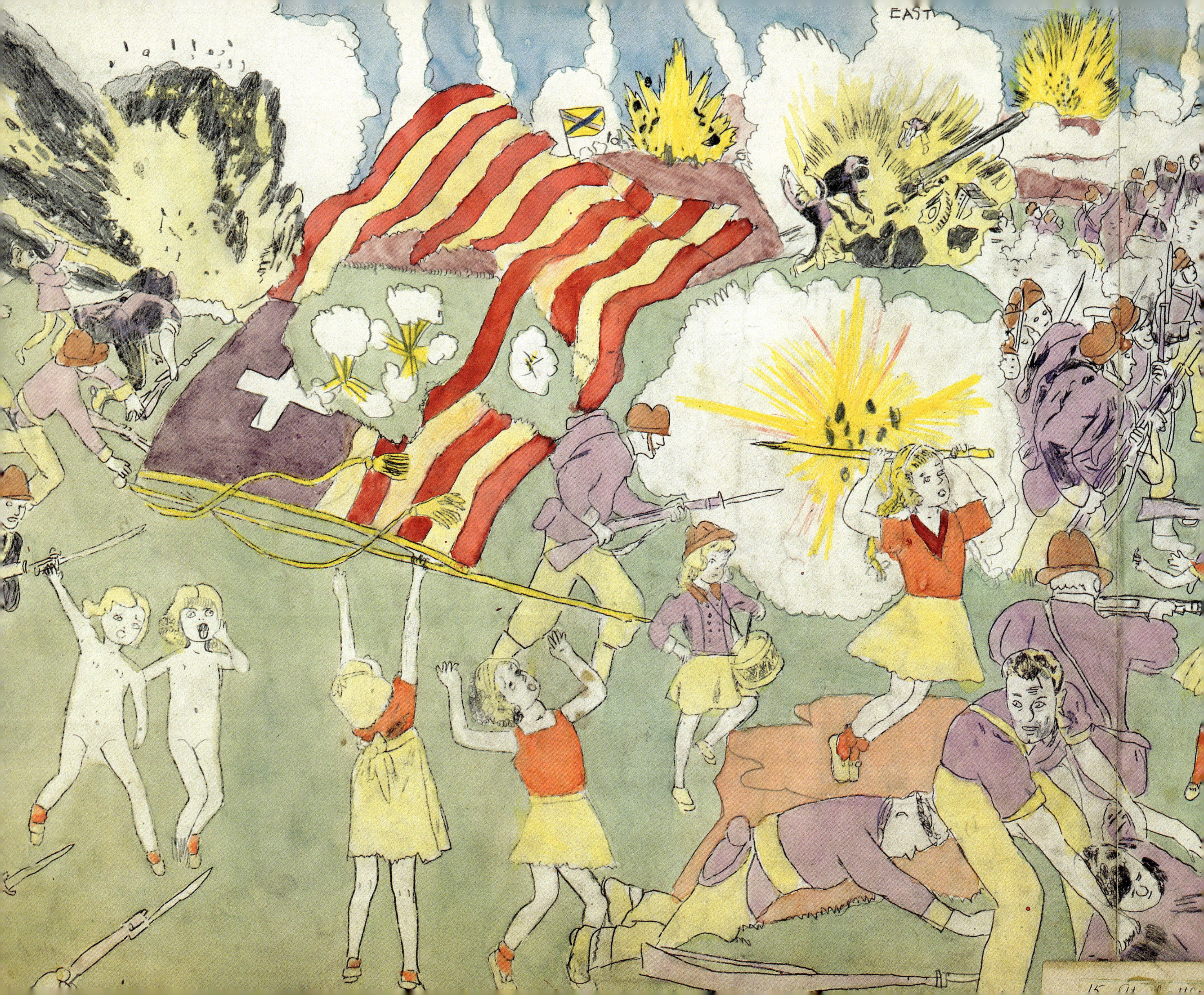

EAST

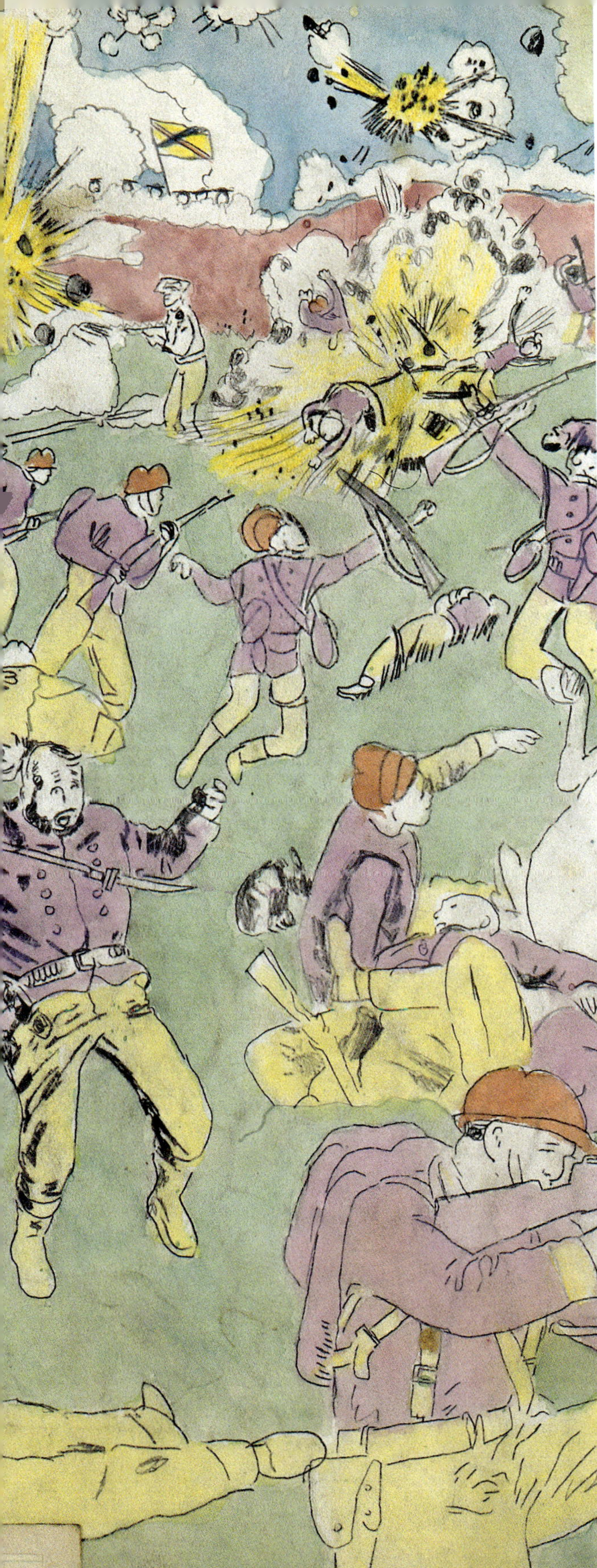

Henry Darger's Great Crusade, Crisis of Faith, and Last Judgment

MICHAEL BONESTEEL

Henry Darger did not like children. Real children, that is. He loved fantasy children, particularly the ones he created in his epic novel, *In the Realms of the Unreal.* In this work, he often based his imaginary youngsters upon real-life playmates he had known growing up. Those real-life children sometimes caused him problems, but his make-believe versions of those same kids provided Darger with a second chance to interact with them. And this time around, for better or worse, *he* would call the shots.

His earliest recollections of interacting with neighborhood kids ranged from pushing them down, getting into fights with other boys, throwing ashes in the eyes of one little girl, and slashing another girl with his pocket knife. He wrote in his autobiography, *The History of My Life,* that when he grew older he came to love baby children and would do anything to protect them, but he did not give any examples of this. He freely admitted: "I hated to see the day come when I will be grown up. I never wanted to. I wished to be young always."[1]

And so he remained, at least psychologically, for the rest of his life. Emotionally arrested in prepubescence, Darger pined for the days of his youth, even though his early years growing up had been marked by trauma and tragedy.

Born the son of a tailor in Chicago in 1892, Darger ex-

perienced his first trauma at the age of four, when his mother died giving birth to his sister, who was subsequently given up for adoption. Darger's father reported that his son was exceptionally intelligent, but also exceptionally "peculiar."[2] Four years later, a second crisis came about when he was separated from his father and placed in a Catholic boys' home. Four more years passed and Darger—who had by now earned the nickname "Crazy" because of his odd behavior—endured another catastrophic hardship when he was committed to the Asylum for Feeble-Minded Children in downstate Lincoln, Illinois.[3] While residing at what he referred to as "that children's nut house,"[4] he suffered various forms of physical, emotional, and, very possibly, sexual abuse.

The last major tragedy in Darger's formative years, the death of his father, took place when he was fifteen and still living at the asylum. These four blows to his increasingly fragile self-esteem molded him into a man who mistrusted the world surrounding him, who kept to himself and built a wall around his psyche. Later, behind that wall, he constructed a new universe—one that he entered as soon as the door to his room closed behind him.

Several hypothetical diagnoses have been trotted out to explain Darger's particular mental condition. Dr. John MacGregor makes a good case for Darger's suffering from

Asperger's syndrome, a form of autism.[5] This condition may have been further complicated by post-traumatic stress disorder and, given his later penchant for depicting little girls with penises in his art, possible gender confusion as a result of childhood sexual abuse.

Following the death of his father, Darger made three attempts to run away from the Lincoln asylum. He succeeded on the last, in 1909. At the age of seventeen, he returned to Chicago and was hired as a janitor at St. Joseph's Hospital, where he also lived until 1922.

Darger's Children's Crusade

Probably in 1912, he began writing the epic novel that was to occupy his thoughts for the next twenty or thirty years and fill some fifteen thousand densely typewritten pages: *In the Realms of the Unreal,* otherwise titled *The Story of the Vivian Girls in What Is Known as the Realms of the Unreal, of the Glandeco-Angelinian War Storm, Caused by the Child-Slave Rebellion.*[6] It's a long-winded, rip-roaring yarn that takes place on an imaginary planet with our earth serving as its moon, and magically traversable by sea cruise. This world is torn by a war between a powerful, demonic nation trading in child slavery and a coalition of Catholic nations attempting to end the evil practice. The seven young Vivian sisters are princesses, daughters of the ruler of the leading Catholic nation. They are blond-haired warrior saints who have characteristics bordering on the angelic. The Vivian girls lend their support to the child-slave rebellion, an army of children initially led by a martyred Joan of Arc figure by the name of Annie Aronburg.

Much of the *Realms* is a pastiche of appropriated literary excerpts and paraphrases from L. Frank Baum's *The Wonderful Wizard of Oz* and its sequels, Harriet Beecher Stowe's *Uncle Tom's Cabin,* Lewis Carroll's *Alice's Adventures in Wonderland,* and many other books. Although it is by no means a well-crafted novel, what gives the saga a kind of artificial life is Darger himself: both literally, as he writes himself

into the story, and behind the scenes, as he becomes the animating force underlying the creation of a strangely familiar and even more strangely aberrant mythology.

In separate works on paper, Darger illustrated his saga, beginning with freehand drawings and borrowed images that he altered, followed by ever more elaborate experiments in appropriation—including collage and pictures traced from source materials, using carbon paper, that he incorporated into complex, monumental compositions enlivened with watercolor. Darger cut out images of young children and soldiers in uniform from newspapers, magazines, comic and coloring books, catalogs, and other sources. These became the basis for illustrations of characters in his *Realms.* He apparently had begun making such images by the 1920s.

A Crisis of Faith

In 1911 or 1912, he lost a particularly prized photograph, clipped from a newspaper, of a little girl named Elsie Paroubek, who was reported to have been abducted and murdered. Darger had planned to use this image as the model for the child martyr Annie Aronburg in his story. This loss was calamitous for him; he invested the missing image of the child with intense emotional meaning, as if he had lost a real child—perhaps his own sister—or as if he had known the real Elsie. This event affected the entire course of the novel for decades, and is referred to again and again in his manuscripts.

As a youngster, he had attacked other children and gotten in trouble. In turn, he was preyed upon by bullies and claimed to have fought back violently in every case. Now the biggest bully of them all—God—was abusing him by refusing to restore the lost picture of Elsie Paroubek.

Darger recorded that at one point he had wanted to adopt a little girl, but his desire came to naught. He took this as another personal affront from God. Over the years, he continued to dwell on these perceived rejections

by God and on the past injuries inflicted on him by others. What might be just frustrations or disappointments to most people were exaggerated far out of proportion in his mind. Once one has experienced a major trauma—like losing a parent at a young age—every subsequent injury is an emotional re-experience of that first trauma.

Darger was a devout Catholic, attending church often. In his anger he gave God ultimatums, threatened to make the Christians in his story lose battles, and increased the scenes of human annihilation in it. Having written himself into the story as a dashing and heroic leader come to help the child slaves, he renounced God and the Catholic church and through various alter egos went over to the Glandelinian dark side. The violence reached horrific proportions, but the missing photograph never reappeared. In the end he relented and, no doubt plagued by guilt, returned to the church with redoubled fervor.[7]

In the Outer Realms

Darger had a couple boyhood comrades at the Lincoln asylum,[8] but as an adult he had only one true friend: a Luxembourg immigrant by the name of Whilliam Schloeder. They probably met sometime during Darger's first few years back in Chicago. Darger and Schloeder would go to Riverview amusement park together and Darger was a frequent guest in Schloeder's home, where he lived with his mother and several sisters. Their friendship was so close that Darger even wrote his buddy—as he had himself—into his *Realms* saga. When Schloeder, who had moved to Texas, died in 1959, Darger took it very hard.

In 1917, Darger was drafted into the army. He was first stationed at Camp Grant in Rockford, Ilinois, and then transferred to Camp Logan near Houston, Texas. It was not a situation he was comfortable with and he was discharged a short time later due to eye trouble, without having served overseas. The only military actions he was interested in pursuing were the ones in his imagination. He had been fascinated with the American Civil War since his early youth and now used it as a model of sorts for his *Realms* saga, as well as bringing in many aspects of World War I, which was being waged during the first years he was writing his novel. Although he did not engage in combat, the newspapers were full of reports of it, offering him much source material.

Darger quit his job and left his residence at St. Joseph's Hospital in 1922 because of his intense dislike of an autocratic nun, Sister De Paul. Shortly thereafter, he was hired as a dishwasher at Grant Hospital and moved to his first apartment, at 1035 Webster Avenue in Chicago's Lincoln Park neighborhood. In 1931, fearing that a new landlord might install a still to make illegal liquor in his building, Darger moved to a boardinghouse two blocks away. In *The History of My Life*, he recounts an episode that he apparently witnessed, in which a still exploded in his neighborhood. He seems to have been terrified by the notion that a still, if installed at his former residence, might also explode while he was living nearby.

The boardinghouse at 851 Webster was owned by a police officer, Captain Walter Gehr. Darger lived on the second floor in a large single room with a smaller attached room. He shared a bathroom with three other residents. Gehr's daughter, Mary Catherine (now O'Donnell) who was born in 1936, and her little brother, grew up in the boardinghouse and often saw Darger.[9] They would sneak into his room sometimes and look at the toys and paints on his table, as well as the pictures of children that covered his walls—especially the works of original art containing figures of little girls. According to Mary Catherine, Captain Gehr was not alarmed by the sometimes gruesome images and simply thought Darger was shell-shocked from the war. After all, that would explain why he always wore the same old army coat year after year; why he was a reclusive loner; and why he didn't like Mary Catherine or her brother snooping around in his room

and touching his things. Darger never had visitors, but guests of the Gehr family and the three other tenants of the boardinghouse would remark that they thought they heard people conversing behind Darger's closed door. Those people were all just Darger—a superb mimic—re-enacting and possibly amending exchanges that had taken place that day or earlier in his life. Mary Catherine and her brother would sit on the stairway leading up to the second-floor landing and listen to him speaking in strange voices and dialects.

Darger had other unusual habits. He attended Catholic Mass three or four times a day. He avoided talking to people, but if addressed, he would sometimes speak in nonsense syllables or mutter something about the weather and then dash away. His room was piled knee-deep in old, bundled newspapers, which he read voraciously, as well as balls of twine that he foraged in trash-hunts through the alleys, collections of busted rubber bands that he "repaired," numerous pairs of broken eye glasses, discarded honey containers and Pepto-Bismol bottles. He kept a large stash of bricks under his mattress, presumably in case he was attacked. He would ritually intone "Ah-bah-suh-duh" in a deep voice before entering the bathroom.[10] He claimed to be from Brazil and because of that, he once explained, he rarely took a bath.[11]

Crisis Averted

It is hard to determine when each volume of *In the Realms of the Unreal* was bound or when Darger finished writing his entire saga. He had begun typing the pages in 1916, transcribing his story from handwritten drafts, which he had begun writing four to six years earlier. Sometime in or after 1932, he hand-bound the first seven volumes.[12] He left another seven or eight bundled volumes of unbound pages as well.

Confusingly, he also wrote that it took him "over eleven years in writing out the long and graphic details,"[13] yet that

would mean that if he started in 1912, he would have finished by 1923. Did it take him another decade or more to sort it all out? The pages throughout the volumes have varied numbering systems, page sizes, and typewriter fonts, all indicating that he was constantly revising and adding to the novel throughout the years. Did he simply give up trying to reconfigure it after binding the first seven volumes or did he continue to write the unbound material after 1932? These questions remain unanswered.[14]

What is fairly certain is that by the time he bound the first volume, he had finished writing the whole tale, for he mentions the outcome of the war in the first paragraph of his introduction to that first volume, apparently written and added at the time of binding. The official ending of the *Realms,* on pages 3544 and 3545 of volume XIV,[15] recounts a Christian victory. But a single unnumbered page follows these, describing an entirely different outcome. It is not really an alternative ending, but rather an optional transition page, featuring a Christian setback that promises to be continued "in next volume." This inconclusive page was perhaps a provisional version to be retained as long as the Aronburg/Paroubek photograph was not recovered, and then ultimately rejected when he decided it was high time to draw things to a close.

Last Judgment

Darger was asked to resign from his job at Grant Hospital by a new supervisor in 1936. He wrote in his autobiography that he did not remember the reason given to him, but he surmised that it was because he had been friendly with the previous supervisor, who was the new one's rival. He was then rehired at St. Joseph's Hospital as a dishwasher.

He discovered a method for photographically enlarging images to be traced into his drawings in 1944 or thereabouts. That is the earliest date noted on the envelopes he saved containing internegatives and original pictures cut from newspapers and magazines. By this time, he had probably finished writing his *Realms* saga and had moved on to an 8,500-page handwritten sequel of sorts, *Further Adventures in Chicago: Crazy House*, which placed the Vivian girls in a more conventional setting. Although he was no longer writing the *Realms*, he continued to make his carbon tracing/pencil/watercolor artworks until the end of his life, though for the most part they no longer referred to specific episodes in either novel, but rather depicted other events or general scenes from his world. Moreover, all references to the war and its atrocities gradually disappeared from the art images, which Darger was now producing as very large, panoramic works. Even the Vivian girls no longer appeared: just happy children—sometimes the same child repeated over and over in patterned rows—cavorting blissfully in a flowery paradise.

In 1947, he was let go from St. Joseph's because the work had become too difficult for him. He was then hired at Alexian Brothers Hospital as a dishwasher, but transferred to the bandage room in 1951.

Once the tales of the Vivian sisters were either completed or abandoned, Darger turned to other kinds of writing. He began keeping the first of six weather journals on December 31, 1957. Always fascinated by the weather, he reported his firsthand observations almost daily until December 31, 1967.

Leg pains forced him to leave his job at Alexian Broth-ers and retire in 1963. It was at some point after this that he began writing *The History of My Life*. It is a selective autobiography at best. He omitted many things, such as his interest in adopting a child and, most conspicuously, the writing of his magnum opus, *In the Realms of the Unreal*. He referred only in passing to the fact that he was also a visual artist. After documenting his memories for some two hundred pages, he launched into a fictitious story about a tornado named Sweetie Pie that occupied nearly five thousand more pages.

Darger was struck by an automobile in 1969 and suffered an injury to his left leg and hip. This, in addition to previous problems with his legs, made it very difficult for him to climb the stairs at his boardinghouse. His landlord, Nathan Lerner, who had acquired the 851 Webster property in 1956, recalls that wallpaper on the stairway to the second floor landing had been worn away where Darger leaned against it for support as he climbed. In 1972, the artist asked Lerner to arrange for him to move to a nursing home, since he could no longer negotiate the stairs. He was admitted late that year to St. Augustine's Home for the Aged—the same nursing home in which his father had passed away.

He kept a diary of day-to-day activities, which consisted of reports regarding his daily church attendance and complaints about his declining health, from March 28, 1968, through January 1, 1972. The last page is dated a little more than a year before he died. Now too crippled and exhausted to rant about his health problems in his diary, and removed from the private world associated with his boardinghouse room, he ceased all written, artistic, or verbal communication, and withdrew into himself completely at the nursing home. He died the day after his birthday in 1973 and was buried in a pauper's grave.

Shortly after Darger moved out, Lerner asked one of his other tenants, David Berglund, to clear out Darger's belongings from the room he had occupied. After hauling away several truckloads of trash and perhaps a wealth of unrecognized artistic source materials as well, Berglund came upon Darger's watercolor works and writings. He immediately told Lerner about them and as they began to examine the material, their awe and amazement grew. When Berglund visited Darger at the nursing home shortly before his death and mentioned the discovery, Darger was jolted out of his reverie long enough to say, "Too late now."[16]

Too late for what? Too late to keep his secret life hidden any longer? Too late to keep the world from running its eyes over the majestic and monstrous landscape of his bloodied-but-unbowed psyche? Absolutely. But perhaps *not* too late for him to realize that he might finally get the audience and admiration he surely wanted. And that his last judgment would take place not only in heaven, but on earth as well.

Notes

1. Henry Darger, *The History of My Life*, manuscript, ca. 1968–72, 14 (Darger's numbering, see page 283).

2. John MacGregor, *Henry Darger: In the Realms of the Unreal* (New York: Delano Greenidge, 2002), 659: "Henry's father states on the application form [for admission to the Lincoln Asylum] that his son began to speak at 'One year.' In response to the question, 'Was the child peculiar from birth?' he replied, 'Yes.' "

3. Ibid., 660. MacGregor cites the application form for Darger's admission to the Lincoln Asylum, where a Dr. Otto Schmidt makes "the rather vague clinical observation that Henry was insane." The application also states that, according to his father, young Darger had indulged in excessive and uncontrolled masturbation from age six to twelve.

4. Darger, *History of My Life*, 43 (see page 287).

5. MacGregor, *Henry Darger: In the Realms of the Unreal*, 656–65.

6. Another manuscript provides the only record of when Darger began to write *In the Realms*: Henry Darger, *Time Book Monthly*, 3, unpublished manuscript with notes for *In the Realms of the Unreal*: "The writing of the Glandco Angelinian war started in June, 1912 . . ."

7. Darger, *History of My Life*, 139–40 (see page 303).

8. Darger, *History of My Life*, 50. Darger writes: "I had only a few special friends, Jacob Marcus, Paul Marcus (no brother of the first-mentioned), Daniel Jones, and Donald Aurand" (see page 288)

9. Mary Catherine O'Donnell, interview with the author, June 1, 2001.

10. Ibid.

11. Nathan Lerner, talk at the dedication of a new grave stone for Darger at All Saints Cemetery, Des Plaines, Ill., November 2, 1996.

12. Where the decorative wallpaper that Darger used to cover the outside of bound volume VII has lifted up to reveal the newspaper lining beneath it, a photograph caption is visible that reads, "Copyright, 1932, International News Photos, Inc." The volume thus could not have been bound before that date.

13. Darger, *In the Realms of the Unreal*, vol. I, 1.

14. *In the Realms of the Unreal* was begun in 1912, according to a note by Darger (see n. 6, above); Darger stopped writing it sometime in the 1930s. (The latest date on a piece of its text is from 1929, but Darger seems to have rewritten and reordered passages for some time thereafter.) The novel comprises fifteen volumes of typescript, seven of which he bound, while eight others are unbound bundles. Although Darger numbered some of the volumes, his system was confusing: The bound volumes are numbered I through VII and the unbound volumes are numbered VIII, X/Part One, X/Part Two, and XI. There is no volume numbered IX or XIII, while three of the bundles have no label. Adding to the confusion, Darger labeled another unbound volume VII, though he also had a bound volume with that number, and it seems to belong to a later point in the tale. Because of the episodic and somewhat fragmentary nature of the narrative, it is not altogether clear how the volumes follow upon one another, nor is the date when Darger wrote each section easy to confirm. References within the volumes to dated fictitious events are guideposts to establishing a likely sequence. John MacGregor and I have each proposed a plausible sequence and dates for the volumes, and agree in most respects:

    volumes I–VII, 1910–13, bound

    volume VIII, undated, unbound

    unbound, unnumbered volume IX(?), 1913

    volume X/Part One, 1913, unbound

    volume X/Part Two, 1913, unbound

    volume XI, undated, unbound

    unbound, unnumbered volume XII(?), 1914–17 (MacGregor has not assigned a location to this volume, calling it "volume Λ")

    unbound volume VII is volume XIII(?), 1915 (MacGregor places this as volume XII)

    unbound, unnumbered volume XIV(?), 1915–17 (MacGregor places this as volume XIII)

MacGregor notes that "the final sequence of volumes and chapters was left unsettled by Darger, with several volumes lacking either a title page or a volume number. Darger often moved huge sections of his manuscripts about within a work, and large fragments were left out, perhaps to be fitted in later. The various numbering systems encountered on many pages provide evidence of evolutionary developments in the writing history of *The Realms*. . . . The identification of [volumes IX, XII, and XIII] is still uncertain, and later studies may yet relocate them in the sequence. Two additional large fragments . . . have not been fitted into the sequence," MacGregor, *Henry Darger: In the Realms of the Unreal*, 666, 709.

15. Or volume XIII according to MacGregor. Darger's numbering system does not correspond to the actual page count.

16. David Berglund, interview with the author, December 20, 1999.

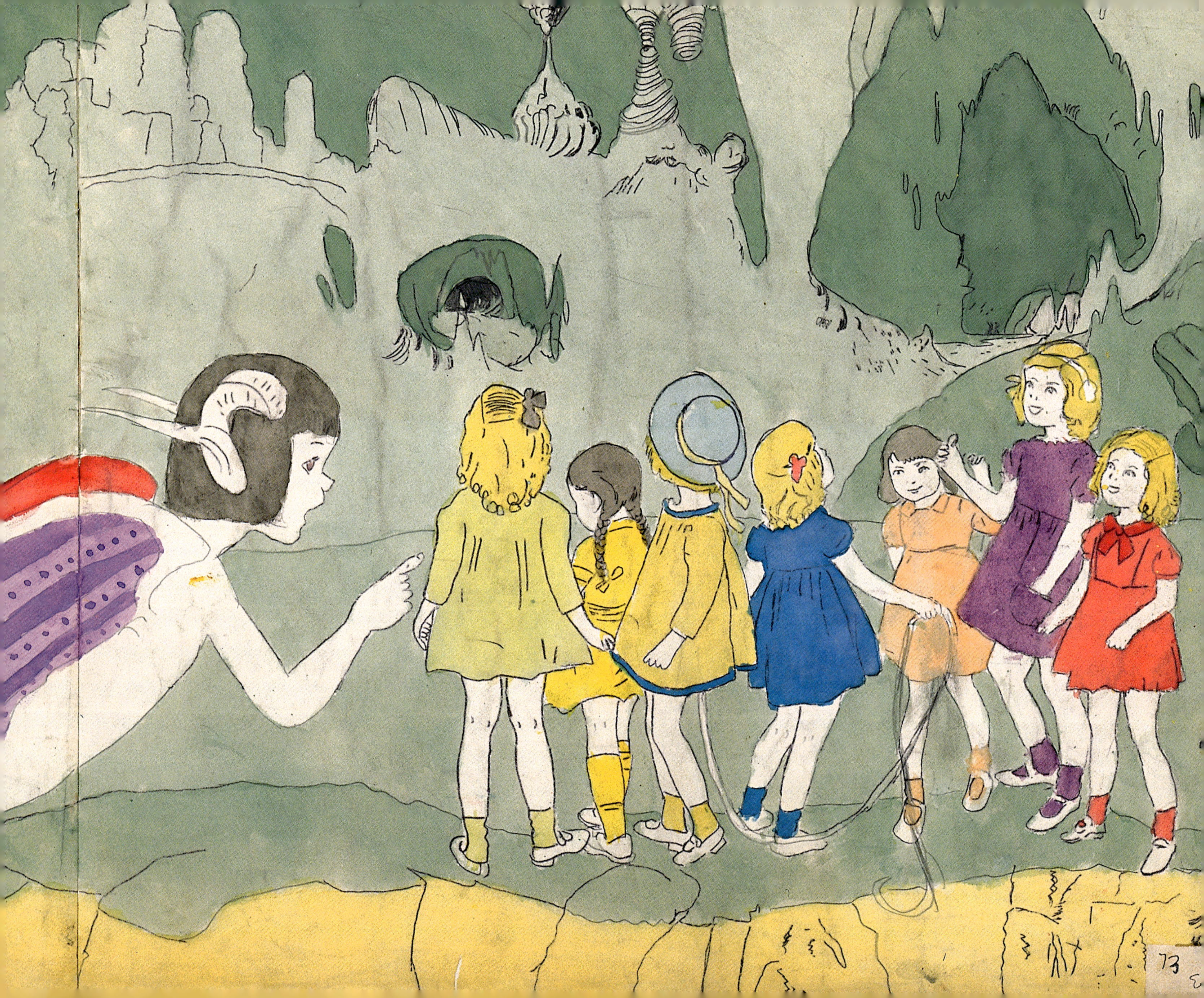

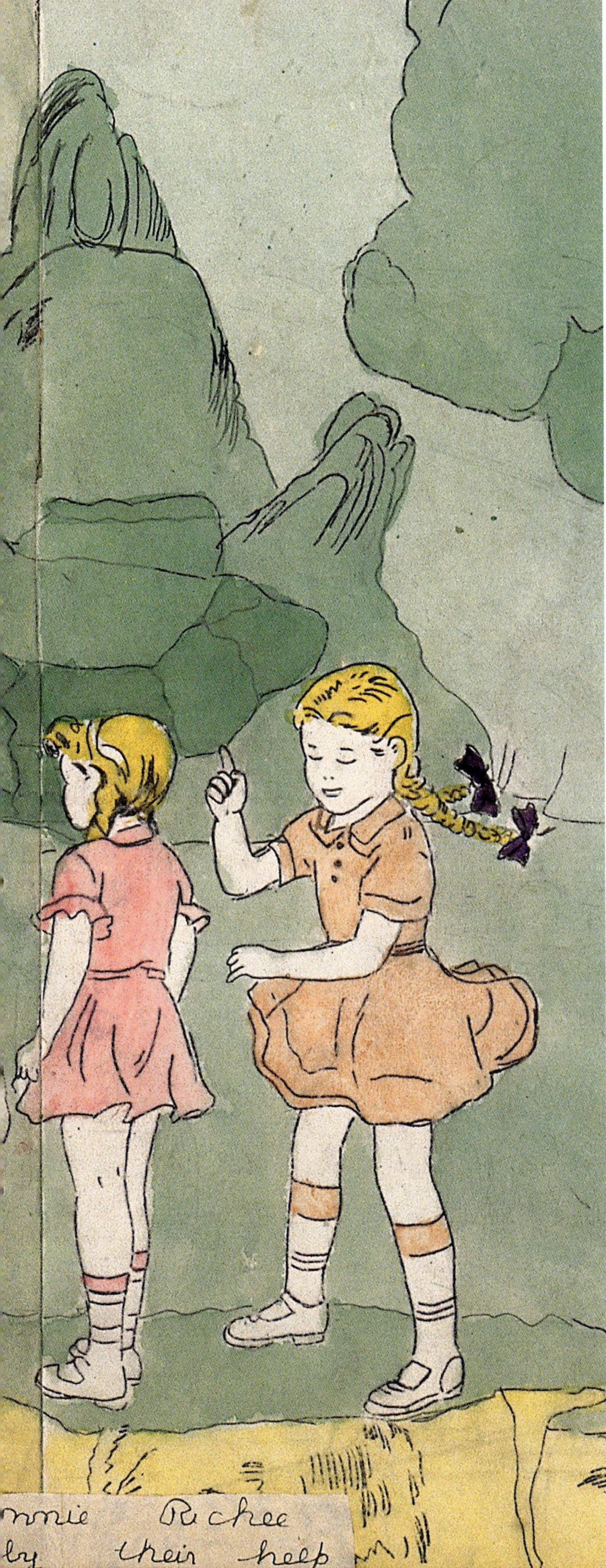

The Metaphysics of Wreckage

Introduction to the Autobiography of Henry Darger

CARL WATSON

The History of My Life is Henry Darger's autobiographical narrative. It was the last of his major texts, begun around 1968 and continued probably until his death in 1973.[1] *My Life,* like all of Darger's books, has a unique physical presence: it is composed of eight bound volumes—school composition and record books of different sizes—tied together with twine. Darger's handwritten pagination is roughly continuous across the volumes; he numbered 5,084 pages. The entire manuscript is actually much longer, due to the circling back and consequent doubling and tripling of groups of page numbers—the bound texts may comprise close to 5,500 pages, and there may be as many as 2,000 additional loose pages.[2] Taken as a whole, the manuscript may be usefully divided into five sections, a prologue and four books, based on distinct breaks in the narrative material: The Autobiography, The Maelstrom, The Inferno, and The Sweetie Pie.[3]

The Prologue has separate pagination and is not obviously consistent with the rest of the work, being thirty-six pages of descriptions of biblical books.[4] The Autobiography is Darger's narrative of his own life and is factual (or largely so), if not comprehensive. The remaining three sections comprise what could be called the catastrophic books, as they recount, via numerous imaginary witnesses, an apocalyptic tornado that ravages central Illinois. Notably, the fictional events of this tale are set in the real world (as opposed to the fantastic world of *In the Realms of the Unreal*). The storm goes by various names until it eventually takes the shape of a "strangle-headed child cloud" called Sweetie Pie. The narrative is made up of endless descriptions of the massive death and destruction this wild turbulence wreaks upon city and countryside alike, savaging zoos, orphanages, supermarkets, and convents. Windmills warp through the sky like flying skeletons, great municipal buildings explode, and bridges buckle like cardboard. The storm ignites thousands of acres of wildfires,[5] which in turn create sinister smolders sending forth poison clouds that spread for hundreds of miles. Witnesses recount the massive movements of men and supplies across ravaged landscapes, applaud the bravery and suffering of entire populations, attend the musings of professors, engineers, and meteorologists, and stand in judgment at the trials of traitors and arsonists, culminating in the trial of Sweetie Pie herself.

Such a synopsis may sound epic, even exciting, but there are, as well, great challenges for the reader. Time is relentlessly cyclical throughout the narrative, events fold in on one another, geography is impossibly fluid, and it is difficult to know who is narrating at any given time. The writing develops no climax, no conclusion, nor any real insight or dramatic tension, but seems to exist only to perpetuate itself in an ongoing metaphysic of wreckage and sublime turbulence.

There is much to fascinate in Darger's catastrophe narratives, but for the reader interested in Darger's life via his own unique perspective, the Autobiography is the place to start. Here, the artist, who seems to claim both a German and a Brazilian identity, provides us with an oddly plotted, unfocused tale of a strange and sometimes brutal childhood followed by an adult life of mundane work interspersed with personal reflections. The reader gains basic chronological and logistic information—most of which seems to be reliably factual—along with indications of Darger's general interests: storms, fires, petty disputes, and personal pains. One may also detect a certain emotional distance, or matter-of-factness, partially attributable to Darger's advanced age—he was in his late sixties at the time of writing—but which is also reflective of a larger missing dimension, that of autobiographical import. In fact, *History of My Life* does not seem to fulfill the typical function of autobiographies as we usually think of them: that is, the portrait of the well-lived life, the reflective life, the life atoned for. Incidents that one might expect to be developed are quickly dropped. Events that normally would seem traumatic or life-changing are passed over with little comment. The deaths of loved ones are only briefly mentioned. Darger does not speak of his landlords, Nathan and Kiyoko Lerner, who were probably the people closest to him during the time of the writing, nor does he mention, except in passing,

his art or his writing, which were his lifelong passions. The reader begins to suspect that much of what is most important or influential is only hinted at or actually absent, lending the narrative a tone of triviality or at least evasiveness, as if the author were hiding, rather than revealing, the relevant truth.

The Autobiography is not totally devoid of emotion, however, as an undercurrent of anger and sadness surfaces periodically. I would stress the periodicity here because as important as any particular autobiographical detail is the structure and rhythm of narration that emerges—themes and patterns that are reflected in astounding ways in the remaining 5,300 pages. For instance, a repeated admission, or consciousness, of unknowing pervades this text. When it is contrasted to what is accepted as *known*, a dialectic begins to emerge that is reiterated throughout the narrative as a tension between control and lack of control, containment and escape, authority and defiance—tensions that are further amplified in the remaining catastrophic books in the form of conflicts between order and chaos, density and explosion, the inexplicable and the limits of human knowledge. There is, as well, a continual chronological backtracking in the Autobiography that often takes the form of something Darger "forgot" to tell us, shoring up not only the chronological integrity of his story, but also his identity. In fact, much of the second half of the Autobiography is a "going back" in which various revisited themes can be seen as attempts at either enhanced self-definition or more willful explanation.

The final return to the forgotten past occurs on page 206, in the last sentence of the Autobiography section: "There is one really important thing I must write which

I have forgotten." No further information about this one important thing is given; instead, Darger turns immediately to a description of the fictional tornado. This return—incomplete, unfulfilled—thus functions as a narrative phase shift into the fiction of the remaining books. We might read it as a retreat from the dissolution of old age and fading memory, as described in the factual Autobiography, to a more fully realized and more meaningful, albeit invented, existence—heroic, authoritative, prophetic. Even if it is fictional, this new phase may hold as much subjective relevance as the autobiography.

Most scholars consider *History of My Life* as two distinct narratives, the autobiography and the tale of the tornado. Darger's intentions in this respect are open to question. We may believe that he was writing an autobiography and simply, unbeknownst to himself, went off track into the fanciful storm drama that had always fascinated him. Or he may have intended to write a fiction all along. It is also very possible he actually did witness a major tornado at some point, perhaps during his youth in rural Illinois. It is almost certain that he read about such a tornado, and he may have later believed or "remembered" having witnessed it. A famously destructive tornado that struck the Chicago area in 1967 may have inspired him to begin this narrative.[6] In his concurrent diary he states that the story of Sweetie Pie is fictional, but then again the name Sweetie Pie does not appear until page 4158, so this may have been a late realization. He headed page 1 with a title, "The History of My Life by Henry Joseph Darger (Dargarius in Brazilian)" and inscribed the tops of the manuscript pages, albeit erratically, with some version of the heading *History of My Life* (or *My Life History*, or *Life History*) for nearly two thousand pages, long after he had ceased to describe his own life story. The heading becomes less and less frequent until its last occurrence on page 1980, better than a third of the way through the total volume of the manuscript and well into Book Three. We can conclude, therefore, that on some level Darger was writing the same book he had begun, even if its purpose had changed.

However we choose to define *History of My Life* as a whole—as autobiography, fiction, creative nonfiction, psychological reportage—it is a unique experience for the reader, an inconclusive, obsessively redundant tale that, in the end, seems to have no real point other than the pleasure of the writer, a delectation gained from intense indulgence in the text's most prominent themes: Catastrophe and Mystery. These may be interpreted as the Catastrophe by which the world is punished and redeemed and the Mystery that underlies every attempt at understanding. From the parades of the destitute, the mad, and the stalwart to the collapse of the highest accomplishments of human engineering, to the strange tangled constructions of violence, to the motives of men and of girl-shaped whirlwinds: "It was all confusion commotion . . . glory majesty mystery and even beauty."[7] This mystery, for us, is readily equated to the mystery of the artist himself, born in Chicago at the end of the nineteenth century, the quintessential unknown man who unexpectedly arrives in the public consciousness out of the whirlwind of anonymous modern life. Perhaps it is some need of our current media-addled culture that desires this storm he brings. As General Henry Darger himself proclaims: "The heart aches at the sight the inconvenience and strange mystery of it all."

Notes

1. The major texts are *In the Realms of the Unreal, Further Adventures of the Vivian Girls: Chicago Crazy House,* and *The History of My Life.*

2. The existence of these loose pages is based on John M. MacGregor's statement. John MacGregor, *Henry Darger: In the Realms of the Unreal* (New York: Delano Greenidge, 2002), 670.

3. Darger does not separate *History of My Life* into sections. His manuscript flows from one theme to the next without identifying breaks. The terms "prologue" and "books" are mine, as are the titles. A brief description follows. Page numbers refer to Darger's handwritten numbering.

Prologue, Biblical Citations (pages 1a–36a): These are brief descriptions of various books of the Bible with the number of chapters in each.

Book One, Autobiography (pages 1–206): Darger's narrative of his own life up until the time he retires. This narration spends a lot of time on some rather trivial events and avoids any major introspection or reflection on the general course of his life.

Book Two, The Maelstrom (pages 206–1809): Darger's narrative of his first encounter with the great tornado. It is told initially through his own voice as a fifteen-year-old boy who quickly becomes an adult named Henry, wielding both authority and expertise. This section uses a great many invented eyewitness accounts of the tornado by farmers, farmers' wives, railroad engineers, etc.

Book Three, The Inferno (pages 1810–2950): The narrative of the Great Wheat Field Fire. First thought to be a result of the tornado, the fire is eventually found to have been set by four arsonists for reasons of jealousy over the marriage choice of a farmer's wife. Much of Book Three is taken up with battle scenes, strategies, and logistics. There are also discussions of dangerous clouds of smoke and of the "smoulder," the underground fire that keeps erupting to the earth's surface in new conflagrations. Throughout this section Henry is an adult, a master firefighter, although numerous other voices narrate events.

Book Four, Sweetie Pie (pages 2951–5084): The narrative returns to the story of the tornado, which eventually takes the name Sweetie Pie (page 4158) and the anthropomorphic shape of a strangle-headed child cloud, i.e., a girl's head being strangled by cloudlike arms, her protruding tongue forming the funnel of the tornado. This section alternates between eyewitness accounts of the tornado and panel discussions and mock trials, most of which have to do with the storm's strange shape.

4. I include the Prologue as a part of the overall work, because I believe this early section sets up Darger's fascination with numeration, which is magnified in the catastrophic books. It also provides a stepping-off point for reading the rest of *My Life* as an apocalyptic vision, similar to the biblical prophecies.

5. The cause of the wildfire changes over time. See the description of Book Three, The Inferno, above.

6. There is much to be said about Darger's catastrophe narratives, of which just a taste may be offered here. On page 206, shortly after the end of the Autobiography section of the manuscript, he discusses a tornado he witnessed "in his late teens" in northern Missouri. (We do not know if Henry was ever in northern Missouri.) Then he says that the second tornado he witnessed was in extreme southern Illinois (he says only that it was a town with a French name). This second instance actually took place earlier than the first, in 1906, when he was fifteen. The rest of the story seems to develop from this sighting. However, the main part of the tale takes place in upper central Illinois, in the area of LaSalle, so there is a lot of dislocation in time and space. Several tornadoes occurred in 1906, but none in the southern Illinois–Missouri area that I can find. But that was the year of the San Francisco earthquake, which was heavily reported in newspapers. Darger seems to have borrowed several accounts of events from earthquake coverage and used them later in his manuscript. It is also interesting to note that one of the greatest tornado outbreaks in history occurred in 1965, which would have been about the time he was beginning to work on *My Life*: forty-seven tornadoes were confirmed across the Midwest on Palm Sunday, April 11.

7. *History of My Life,* manuscript 3121.

8. Ibid, 2969.

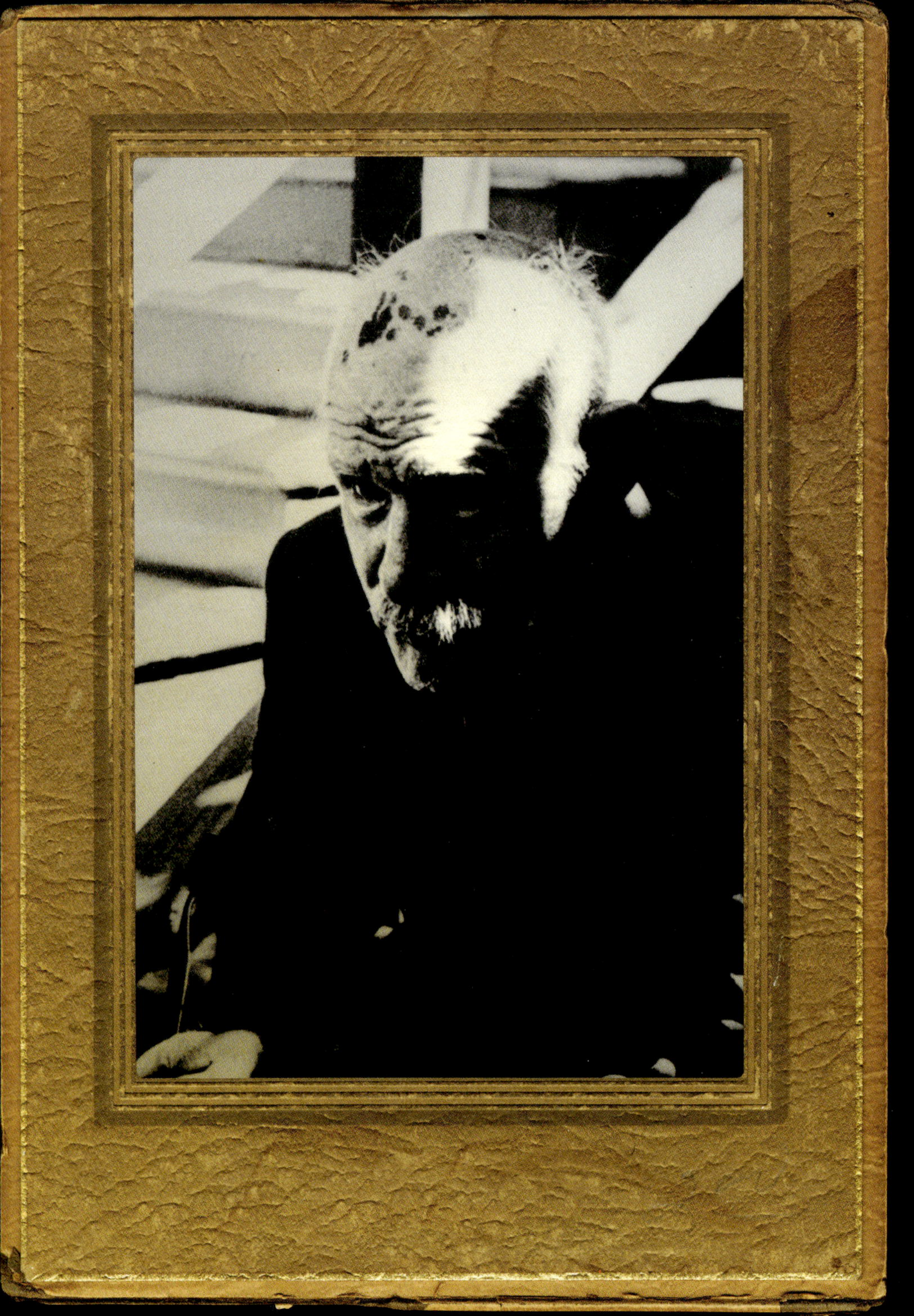

THE HISTORY OF MY LIFE

By Henry Joseph Darger (Dargarius in Brazilian)

851 Webster Ave., Chicago, Ill. Box 14

* * *

[Born] in the month of April, on the 12, in the year of 1892, of what weekday I never knew, as I was never told, nor did I seek the information.

Also I do not remember the day my mother died, or who adopted my baby sister, as I was then too young, nor would my uncle Charles tell me, or did not know either.

My father and I lived in a small two-story house on the south side of a short alley between Adams and Monroe Street.

Across on Monroe on the street's north side were two large high schools, the one a little further west having a high, steep sort of slanting roof, and dark brown walls, and large windows. The one east of it had yellow-white stone instead of brick and a fancy shape; also very large windows. Both were 3-and-a-quarter stories high. The yellow stone one had a water tank on its roof.

Both floors in the house we lived in had only 2 rooms, one a kitchen with a large stove and behind it a bedroom.

The bed was large enough for both my father and I.

The stove was used for heating and cooking. During the hot days of summer we usually ate out in a restaurant.

Our barber was only a block away.

While living with my father, I went to St. Patrick's Catholic on Des Plaines and Adams, first to a Sisters' school and then one operated by the Catholic Christian Brothers.

At our house a staircase on the outside led up to the second floor.

Our living quarters faced north, and the kitchen had only one window. My father was a tailor, and a kind and easy-going man.

I had two uncles and 2 aunts, also easy-going people. My cousin, Harry Darger, was their only son. Their religion, I'm not sure I know. My uncle had a Masonic funeral and burial. His name was Augustine Darger, called August, though. His wife's first name Emma.

Our meals were not scant, and I loved the pancakes the most.

There was, facing Halsted, with the east-rear facing us, a handsome building, three stories high and a quarter-block long. Nearly every day I went on its top floor porch. I was a meany one day when, for spite, I know not why, I shoved a two-year-old child down, and made it cry. No one seen it fall down and the child did not tell on me. This incident happened on that top floor porch.

Once on that porch I observed a big fire east from there on Monroe Street. I did not go to it though, as that day was very cold.

My father, besides being a tailor, was a very good cook.

Once in a while he or I would drink a little beer, especially in the summertime on hot days, but not in the winter. Oh how good the coffee he could produce by boiling. As he was lame, I bought the food, coffee, milk and other supplies, and ran errands.

Though a young boy, I did not hate school, but I did tell my teacher, a Catholic nun, that I "hate" school, when in truth I meant her, because she was so strict, severe, and prim.

I was of the kind that only my father could tell me what to do, and would take no scoldings or authority from anyone else.

I played hooky once for a whole week because of my intense dislike of her.

My father cured her and me both.

When, however, I and my teacher got to understand each other better, there was no more trouble and we got along fine, yet for mistakes in school I would have to write a sentence of words 200 times or more.

For Christmas, I mostly always got colored picture- or storybooks, which I liked, and chicken for dinner. I disliked turkey and still do, but I'll eat it if I can't get anything else.

Once in a while, to paint pictures or anything else, I had paint boxes, but I myself bought them, and other interesting articles.

During my youngest days, before I went to school, and not knowing
any better, I hated baby kids—those, though, who were old enough to
stand or walk. It was caused, I believe, because I had no brother, and
lost my sister by adoption. I never knew or seen her, or knew her name.

I would, as I wrote before, shove them down, and once foolishly
threw with my fingers ashes in the eyes of a little girl by the name
of Francis Gillow.

And her mother and two grown brothers had been very good to me,
and the boys often came to see me. And not thinking I would do such a
mean deed as that.

My father had to pay the doctor's bill. Her mother scolded me
from her open window, but did not punish me.

But she told me that my father would sure have to pay plenty on
the bill.

The night of the same day, my father, coming up the steps, said
to me, reproachfully, "What if she had died?"

I had so forgotten the incident that I did not comprehend what
he was saying. But what I had done I did not know any better anyhow.

My Christmas presents, as I probably remember, that year were
deducted because of my being made to repay his payment on the doctor
bill.

And yet I was too young to feel sorry for what I had done. Later
she and her three children moved away. To my own knowledge she was a
widow. I never heard when her husband had died.

You remember I wrote that I hated baby kids. So indeed I did.
Yet what a change came in me, though, when I grew somewhat older.
Then, babies were more to me than anything, more than the world.

I would fondle them and love them. At that time, just any bigger
boy or even grownup who dared molest or harm then in any way was my
enemy.

I will have to say, all my childhood days with my father, who
was very busy every day, except Sundays and holidays, were sort of
uneventful, except I was very interested in summer thunderstorms
(still am, old as I am) and during winter (cold) I could and would
stand by the window all day, watching it snow, especially if there
was a great big blizzard raging.

I would watch it rain with great interest, also short or long
showers.

Once, not knowing any better, I put lots of newspaper beside the
stove near the wall and set it on fire. I got my ears boxed good and
proper. I got it good, once again, from my father when he thought
from my action that I was going to do it again.

But I had no intention of doing so.

Every 4 of July, I shot off all types of firecrackers and never
was hurt or burned once, I was so overcareful.

I was also crazy about making bonfires, but was so careful I was
never scorched, singed or burned.

I also loved to splash water in pools left by rain, especially
with my hand, to pretend it was raining, but somehow never got wet.

Big or small as they were, I would never run to or go to fires.
At home I'd watch the great cloud of smoke, or the glow in the sky by
night-time.

I was scared of burning buildings on fire, for fear of falling
walls or other debris.

Once on a late summer afternoon, my father took me to a big one
close to home, on the corner of Washington Street, close to Halsted.

We stood watching it across Washington Street on the south side.

He told me it was a tar factory.

It was not a wide building, only 6 windows across, but it stood 10
stories high and was like an inferno from the street to the top floor.

We did not stay watching it very long.

The fire was in the late afternoon but also raged all night,
keeping the sky well lighted up.

It must have been an awfully stubborn fire to resist the efforts
of so many firemen like that.

The fire departments, however, did not have the long snorkels
that we now have, and they had no way to reach the top floors of so
tall a building with their hose streams.

It was still burning the next morning and an awful smoker. All the fire companies I heard were still there. On that morning, the breezes being from the northwest, smoke enveloped our whole district, so thick that we could not stay in our house unless we wanted to be smothered.

Southerly winds came to our aid in the afternoon and drove the smoke to the north.

I did not go near the fire that day anymore, as I was afraid.

I did not remember the year, day or month of the fire.

One thing I must write is that us children in those days were looked on as beneath the dignity of grownups and did not amount to much, whereas, to my opinion or feeling, all grownups and especially all types of strangers and those I did not like were less than the dust or mud beneath my feet.

I also believed that I had read in the Holy Bible that children, especially all good and innocent ones, were more important to God than the grownups, and that He, when on the earth as a man, Jesus Christ, had said that it was better for a man or any person, of any kind, if harming a child, to have a millstone (not feather) to be tied around his neck and be drowned in the depths of the sea. Or the child's guardian angel will witness against the person who harmed a child before God who is in Heaven.

Also, in my boyhood days (I was like a little devil, if called "kid"), I had a very queer way of playing in the snow, by motion of my left hand, which later on got me into some serious trouble, of which I will explain somewhat later.

Do you believe it? Unlike most children, I hated to see the day come when I will be grown up. I never wanted to. I wished to be young always. I am grown up now and an old lame man, darn it.

I do not remember the number of years I lived with my father, but they told me I was 7 years old at the time of the One Hundred Days' War with Spain.

Except when enjoying myself, otherwise my life was uneventful, and during my somewhat later years (believe it or not) I was very good, and I and my father and even the neighbors got along fine, except one.

Other kids had been stealing his wooden fruit and vegetable crates, and he accused me of taking them, which was very unreasonable, as I could furnish proof of my innocence.

In order to get even with him when he was not home (he being a peddler) I took a few of the crates, piled them in the center of his yard, and set them on fire. Then I quickly left and sat on the steps in front of the house, facing the alley. My father soon came out, it being near night, and sat with me.

Just about dark we both noticed a light of brightness which I felt sure could not come from the few crates I had set afire.

I ran over there to see what was the cause. Against the west side of the house the peddler had stacked by three wide an actual wall of the crates.

I could not believe my little bonfire, so far from there, could have caused it, but the shebang, including the side of the house, was one high, towering mass of singeing flame. Some of the blazing crates crashed down, bouncing, and covered the spot where I had made the little one, erasing evidence against me.

There was a number of boys in the neighborhood, but I and they could do nothing, though we worked like mad, my father helping. We could not reach the reach the flames with the pails of water higher up, so it was I who ran to the fire station only half a block away.

They got it out in twenty minutes. What do you say? What did the landlord say? He was the owner of the building and a few others nearby. According to what the firemen told him about what I and the boys did, he was good and friendly to me from then on. The fire only burned the outside. It did not get inside the house.

The cause of the fire was never known, but secretly I found sure proofs that my little revengeful bonfire did not do it.

Before I went to school, however, I could already read the newspapers, which my father had learned me by study.

Because of that, from first grade I was promptly put up to
third grade.

My teacher had been very astonished at this. This happened when
I went to St. Patrick's School.

I also excelled in spelling, but was still rather poor in
figures and geography. History I almost knew by heart.

I once told my teacher, but the one, Mrs. Dewey at Skinner
school, that I believed no one truthfully knew the losses in the
battles of wars (including our Civil War), because each history told
different losses, and I had the histories and other stories to prove
it, and let her see and go over them. I had three histories that told
different losses at the big Civil War battles, including Pittsburg
Landing, Antietam, Bull Run No. 2, Gettysburg and so on. And it is
true. Some claim Shiloh or Pittsburg Landing was the war's bloodiest,
with 24000 dead in the 2 day battle.

I don't care what you might say, but I firmly don't believe it.

As the time passed on, my father grew worse in his crippled
condition and I believed my uncles payed my father's way into the St.
Augustine's Poor House Home on Sheffield and Fullerton Aves.

The place is still nicknamed The Little Sisters of the Poor, yet
many are tall Sisters.

My Godmother, which until now I forgot to mention, who presided
at my baptism at 8 years of age, took me to a place on Jackson
Boulevard, some distance west, that I nicknamed "The Newsboys' Home."

The right name was the Mission of Our Lady of Mercy. The
entrance was on North Jackson Boulevard.

The Home had a home in the rear, or north, called the Playhouse.
It was very large and had all the conveniences necessary.

The Mission of Our Lady of Mercy building was four stories high,
had a steep slanting roof, which leaked a while during storms. The
top floor, under that roof, was our large sleeping room. I never knew
how many boys there were, but there were not many. Our large sleeping
room at times surely had the "beautiful little creatures of a red
colour" known as bed bugs. Got the creeps?

Our building was 50 feet wide, and the windows seven feet high.

The dining room was on the ground floor and the meals were good,
except on Fridays the cook put some horrid-tasting sauce or fish
gravy on the fish and I could not make myself eat it.

When I first came, there was a woman matron in charge of us by
the name of Mrs. Brown. During the time I was there, my Godmother
gave me two dimes, which I did not yet spend for anything, or yet
had time.

A boy whose name I did not yet know, seeing the dimes, accused me
of stealing them.

I got the whacking on the hands with that rubber I mentioned,
but still he did not get those dimes. They were really mine, and I
would not surrender them no matter what the cost.

I notified my Godmother. She came and proved she gave those to
me, and did he get it from Father Meaney, not O'Hara.

He never dared say that to me again, but I never forgave his
frame-up either. He made me his bitter enemy.

In the matron's presence, in the dining room, I let out a big
whopper of a poop, and as I said nothing, she, or most of them there,
did not know who it was. The oldest one there said, "It might have
been 'Crazy,'" meaning me.

She said "if he is crazy, he does not know any better." John
Manley, who sat across from me, said to me truthfully, "It was you."
One time, during a hot day in June, she wanted to adopt me, but I
could not let her do it without my father's consent. He wouldn't give
it. I was walking down the street past her house and she called me
in, to make the request. Though living in the Home, we were allowed
to roam at will.

She was a good woman, though. When she left her job to retire,
for she could afford to do so, there came a new woman by the only
name I knew her by, as Mrs. Gannon.

She had a son with her there by the name of James Gannon.

At that time, being in the Home, I was sent during the days to a
city public school called the Skinner School.

Even now it is still there, with a large north addition of yellow brick. It is the same height. We were sent there for it was way too far from any Catholic school.

The Skinner School was on Jackson Boulevard and Aberdeen Street. The school front was on Aberdeen— that is, the main entrance. The school, both old and new, was a three-story building and was two blocks east of the Home. I don't remember that name of the street the east side of the Home fronted on, but the entrance of the Home was on Jackson.

There were two priests in main charge, Fathers Meaney and O'Hara. Father Meaney was the main head or otherwise top administrator.

They were prime and very severe and because of it I had been tempted to run away from there more than once, but after all I did not.

What boys were not allowed to do there was climb onto the top of their clothes lockers, as they were called.

I was forced to tell on them once when they did so, and after that they—and even prime Mrs. Gannon—were sore at me, and some of the bigger boys told me plenty. They did not hit me, though. I never did that again.

There was one boy who was somewhat friendly and sometimes not. When he got angry at you, you knew it. He was not a bully though, nor tried to be.

But at times he was a snitcher. His name was John Manley.

His parents were Irish. The boys there all had parents, but they could not take care of them.

He wanted my company and friendship but was hot-tempered and aggressive, and I did my best to try and avoid him. He wanted my company, but was bossy. He wanted my company always, for sure, I'll say again, but when I don't like anyone I wanted him to stay away. He would not do so. I knew two others who were brothers, by the names of John and Jim Scanlon.

Most kids there were of Irish descent.

I was of German descent, and I do not know why my father did not learn me the language. My father and two uncles were, as they told me, born in the city of Meldorf, Germany.

My Uncle August told me that in his late teenage he witnessed at a safe distance the battle of Meldorf, at which the French army was beaten badly.

It was during the early part of the year-long Franco-Prussian War, when then the French were invading Germany.

They were soon driven out, but the war then raged fiercely on in France until the main French army was overthrown at Sedan.

What he looked like, I would have been dreadfully scared of my Grandfather, especially because of the awful mustache, horseshoe in shape.

That probably made him look more fierce and stern than he was. He and my grandmother, however, stayed in Germany.

Another thing that happened when I was young was when, without the least expectation, I was taken from my father and hustled off by train to a certain small boys' home at Morton Grove. I was there, however, for a short time when my father came and took me right home— and for good, for that never happened again. And for a good reason. Nobody could fool with my father, not even law officials.

At the beginning of my first term at the Skinner School (my teacher's name was Mrs. Dewey, a distant relative of Admiral Dewey, hero of Manilla), I was good and studious, but not meaning any harm or wrong, I was a little too funny and made strange noises with my mouth, nose and throat in my classroom to the great annoyance of all the other boys and girls.

And I thought they would think it funny, and laugh or giggle. But they gave me saucy and hateful looks.

Some said if I did not stop it, they'd gang up at me after school, and gave me the dirtiest looks. I defied them.

After several months of it, it caused my expulsion from the school.

The children were glad, for because of my silly noises, they were very much annoyed and tantalized. They surely did not like my

crazy noise one bit. They, some of them, did try to beat me up, but I
knew how to defend myself with the long stick I always carried, and
with telling effect.

My teacher had said that they had been otherwise, and still had
been the best-behaved children in any classroom she ever did any
teaching in, and my annoying them caused me being excumicated from
the school.

I do not know, or even remember, how long I was away from school
after being excumicated, but when one of the priests brought me back,
asking to give me another chance, the administrator or principal
allowed me to come back to school.

But she told me very sharply and angrily that if I ever did that
again I would be expelled for good.

As I truly forgot and did not remember what I had done wrong, I
did not really know what she was scolding me for so sharply. I would
have told her off, but Father Meaney warned me with a sharp look to
be careful.

But nevertheless, I was returned to school, and I was so
unusually changed. I remembered still not what I had done out of the
way the first time at school, but believe me and heaven knows, I was
now one of the best-behaving boys in school.

Mrs. Dewey still was the teacher of the classroom and all those
children, girls and boys that I was with now were well-behavers too.
To go back for a while, when I still lived with my father, I knew a
woman by the name of (I do not know her first name) Mrs. Anderson.
She lived in an old wooden three-story house. (A house next to hers
burned down one night.) She had a son and older daughter. His name
was John and her name was Helen Anderson. I knew not their religion,
and never asked, but I and he, without my father knowing it, went on
Sundays to a Salvation Army Sunday School.

I believe they were Scotch-Irish.

Helen sure was a little girl for cleanness, and often washed my
hands when she came to see me.

A bad thing happened to poor Helen when I was with them on a
visit one hot summer day. An ugly thunderstorm, with savage wind,
came on from the almost straight north.

We were having a meal in the evening, and the north window was
wide open because of the heat. Johnnie was shaking pepper from the
pepper shaker, whose lid, not screwed on tight, came off. He was
sitting with his back to the window and so was I.

A squall of wind came in through the open window and sent the
pepper into Helen's eyes, as she was facing the window. Her mother,
sitting alongside, got a little of it.

As he was only across the street, despite the blinding sheets of
rain I ran over and quickly brought the doctor.

I do not know whether her eyes got better or not, because it was
a few days after that my Godmother took me to the Home called the
Mission of Our Lady of Mercy.

Also, before that happened, I used to go and see a night
watchman in a six-story factory building a short distance from where
we lived. That factory is not there anymore, or other building. Even
the fancy school across from us on Monroe is gone.

To me it is a sad remembrance, now, to go back to the home. I had
been there, I believe, for about seven years.

There was a sort of overseer, besides Mrs. Gannon (my Godmother
didn't like her) and the two priests. His name was Otto Zink.

Between him and my "pain in the neck" John Manley, and the two
Scanlons, I was accused before Mrs. Gannon and Father O'Hara of
something, Heaven knows, I never did, but I had no means to prove I
was innocent. It seemed, also, I did not have the brains or courage
to fiercely deny it.

I got whacked by the priest, as often as I was told on, on the
hands with the kind of rubber you put over your shoe.

If I knew where to go, to be elsewhere taken care of, I would
have surely run away.

I hated my accusers and would have liked to kill them, but did
not dare. I never was their friend, and am their enemy yet, even
whether they are dead now, or not.

Yet for other strange things I really did, I was thought of and called "crazy."

Especially for the strange way I threw with my left hand, like pretending it was snowing.

Had I known that, I only would have done it where I was not seen.

It caused Mrs. Gannon, her son, and Otto Zink, and others there who saw me do it, to think I was either feeble-minded, or actually crazy.

In fact, I made far better advance in my school lessons than any of them did.

Her son was a very unusually proud boy, and because he was her son could do things which us other lads could not dare think of doing. I actually had an awful intense dislike for him, and his mother too.

So that, for a time, caused all the boys who disliked him too to leave me alone, or avoid me completely.

My father came to see me during my stay there often, in the winter and the summer.

And especially on the Fourth of July and Christmas. My Godmother also came often to see me. Once, my father brought some woman relative to have me adopted by her, but Father Meaney was not there at the time, and Father O'Hara could not do anything about it. My father would have to see him.

He never did.

My father never came with her again. I had heard that Father Meaney, without a court order, could not grant him the request.

My uncle said I was better off not being adopted by her as she was a heavy drinker and might cause me to become one.

I do not remember the length of time or years I remained there in the Mission of Our Lady Home, but one part of the last year I was still there, I was taken several times to be examined by a doctor, who, on the second time I came, said my heart was not in the right place.

Where was it supposed to be? In my belly? Yet, I did not receive any kind of medicine or any kind of treatment whatever. Yet his office sure had an awful medicine smell.

I did not know it at the time, but now I know I was taken to the doctor to find out if I was really feeble-minded or crazy.

He said nothing about that especially in my presence.

Had I known what was going to be done with me, I surely would have ran away.

Again, I will say he said nothing about what my examination was for, but during a cold, windy, threatening late November day (I know not the day or date of the month), I was hustled into the Chicago and Alton Limited train, and brought to some kind of home for feeble-minded children, outside of, and south of the small city of Lincoln, Ill.

If I had known at the time of the cause of me being sent to that children's nut house, I surely would have never forgiven those at the Mercy of Our Lady Home, and would have revenged it the very first chance I had. I, a feeble-minded kid. I knew more than the whole shebang in that place.

I believe Mrs. Gannon was really responsible. Otto Zink, before I was taken away, was not there anymore.

It surely was a severe blow to me, but after the long run I got over it. I was now one hundred and sixty-two miles away from Chicago and my father. I wrote letters to him, and received once in a while Catholic prayer books and a musical harp.

But I did not know how to play it, or had anyone to learn it to me. I knew a lot of songs and other pieces.

My stay there was for some good number of years and was uneventful but busy, except my schooling and interest in big summer and winter storms.

During my earliest time there, there were two boys there by the names of George Hamilton and John Johnson, whose character was such that no punishment of any kind would change them. It only made them far worse.

One morning, when us boys were in what is called the "playroom," Johnnie Johnson, known as the most bad of the boys, teased or tormented me.

At that time I was suffering from a very severe toothache. The pain and his torment of me roused me to an awful fury.

I went at him so savagely that afterwards he never even dared to come near me again.

Then, also, I remember one morning when I was in the classroom, conducted by a good teacher by the name of Miss Duff (Irish, I presume), there came into the schoolroom door and swiftly down the side aisle, two persons, one a janitor and the other I do not know who or what he was. They sure were handing each other a perfect storm or "cyclone" of fist blows.

The taller one almost right away had the janitor backed against the wall, beside the right side of the teacher's desk.

He held his mouth open wide in a strange, funny way, accompanied with an awful sort of frown during the 20-minutes conflict.

The poor teacher was scared, though, crying, "boys, boys," and us kids were sort of panicky! A fine example for those two grown rowdies to be fighting before us children in the schoolroom.

In my day I've seen many fights, but never like these two fought each other so savagely. The janitor was, however, a much better one with the fist, and though shorter than the other more than doubly stronger. The taller man was getting the most blows.

Still he wouldn't give up, and tried to fight more and more savagely. One of the boys of our class went to bring the school administrator, but she was scared too. She went to her office to call the police.

I never knew or even learned what caused the twenty-minutes fight, but I watched the janitor as he surely swung blow for blow. He had a dangerous look on his face. But when the fight was on its 20 minutes' duration, the janitor, with an extra-hard blow with his right, felled the taller man, who crashed headlong to the floor.

He lay there for a half minute, then got up, his face bleeding badly, but instead of renewing the fight, walked off, his mouth still open that way.

The janitor's name was George Harnford. I knew not the name of the other. Two weeks or so later, he quit his job and we never seen him again.

Again to Johnnie Johnson. This is after the fight between the two men. There came into the asylum a new boy, whose name I never learned. He was good-looking, had blond hair and was a little taller. Stronger too. When Johnnie teased him he would holler very loudly: "Johnnie Johnson, very bad boy! When my papper or papa give me a gun I shoot him." As he appeared to mean what he said, and I for one believed he meant every word of it, Johnnie hereafter left him alone. The boy did look dangerous, yet I could see he was not crazy, for in all his lessons he was ahead of all of us.

That building had two sections, one for girls and one for boys.

I had heard there were at times 1500 children there. The head man there was a professional doctor and surgeon whose name was Doctor Caldwell.

Among all the boys in my section, I had only a few special friends, Jacob Marcus, Paul Marcus (no brother of the first-mentioned), Daniel Jones, and Donald Aurand.

The latter had very bad eyesight. There was a sort of parklike grounds south and extending west, north, and south of the asylum, where we boys had our recreation during the summertime.

It had a tall, rounded sort of fire escape on the east side, which we boys often, for a fire drill, slid down on the inside.

One boy was terribly scared to go and slide down in it. We made him, or else.

What if the asylum had a fire? What would he do then?

Yet scared or not, two of the bigger boys grabbed a hold of him, brought him to the round fire escape, and pushed him down it.

For my part, it was fun sliding fast down on it.

We all retired to bed at eight o'clock in the evening, got up at six AM in the morning and went to the school across from the asylum. It was 200 feet north of us.

Once in a while, in the school hall on the ground floor, we were entertained with shows, training exercises, and church meetings, or

Sunday school on Sunday morning.

Those who could sang hymns and recited prayer meeting.

The minister never gave any sermons, though the other type of services lasted from 8 in the morning until noon.

The one who was over us was a severe, stern man by the name of Henry Aurand. For forgetting to make my bed once, he sure boxed my ears. That made me his enemy for life, but yet otherwise I behaved so well he had no real occasion to punish me further.

Yet because my real descent of my nationality is much against such type of punishment, had we been in Brazil, he would have been killed for boxing my ears.

You cannot there with safety hit anywhere on face or head with the hand. The assistant superior was an Italian by the name of Mr. Bandico. He was very severe too, and somewhat harsh too, but never bothered me.

He thought otherwise: that my behavior was marvelous, and liked me well, I being among all those boys in that section, and yet got along with them all fine. As I mentioned before, my special boyfriend was Daniel Jones. We were great pals.

We had, later on, a tall colored boy come there by the name of Earl Little. He turned out to be a bully, always picking on the smallest boys, who could not fight him. For a good reason he molested me once, for what I did. I'm surprised and glad I did not kill him. Afterwards, he kept away from me.

He also soon met some others too, who put him in his "place," and being humbled and put down that way caused him to run away. He was never seen again. There a little girl there by the name of Jennie Turner. I thought I could be attracted to her, but when I learned from others of her disposition I kept away from her. I had my doubts for a while, thinking they wanted her for themselves and lied to me.

The truth was, Heaven help any man that when she grows up marry her. She was a wildcat and let you know it.

After several years more of my stay there, which sometimes was pleasant and sometimes not so, Doctor Caldwell, the head man, left and a new administrator came in charge.

He was a little, handsome, short man, and had a wife and little daughter.

She was a pretty child, but somewhat bossy, but no one paid any attention to her.

She otherwise appeared to be a very good little girl.

There was also a head boy in charge of us by the name of Whilliam Oneil. He was all right, but sometimes imperious. Whilliam Thomas Oneil was the best-looking boy I have ever seen. He was no bully or exactly bossy, but being set over us by the administrator, we had to obey him and do his bidding. If you did, you and he got along fine.

If you did not, he'd take you before the administrator and you then were in serious trouble.

Finally I had got to like the place, and the meals were good and plenty. But when I was somewhat older, probably in my earliest teens, I was put with a company of boys of apparently the same age to go and work on what was called the State Farm.

It was three and a half miles from the asylum.

The work was not hard. We quit at four in the afternoon, started at eight in the morning, after milking the cows, and off again at 4. We were off on Saturday afternoons and Sundays. We had our baths on Saturdays, before our dinner.

The meals there were splendid, but I believe at breakfast I was a glutton (if not hog) for the oatmeal. I spent one whole summer there, then back to the asylum we went.

I believe that fall a bad plague of measles broke out in Lincoln, Ill., and it spread to most of the kids in the asylum.

Strange, though: I never caught it.

Next summer I was back on the farm again. I liked the work very much, but still I don't know why, but I did object to leaving the home. But as they said so, you had to.

As will be written later, that was the cause of me running away two summers later.

There was on the farm, in one large field or more, a very

peculiar type of crop, yet well-known to all farm growers, if not all of us people.

It is a strange but very beautiful tomato plant called the "Beautiful Lady," or, in Spanish, Belladonna.

The juices of that plant is used by chemists for medicine and other needs. I've once used it for a sore knee.

It really was a most beautiful plant, with most beautiful little flowers, before the tomatoes came.

There is where it got the name "Beautiful Lady." But God help those who ever ate one of those tomatoes. We had very large, easily seen and easy-to-read signs (also electrilly lighted at night), warning tramps or hobos and visiting strangers about eating them, or anything of the plant.

Their original name, well-known by most, is the deadly nightshade.

No hobo or anyone else went near them.

When removing the tomatoes, you had to wear protective gloves, for if one of them was squashed or overripe the juice would cause serious infection, if gotten into a mere scratch or wound.

The juice smelled horrid and sickening.

Anywhere else was also grown, in long straight rows, all crops and vegetation you could think of.

I loved to work in the fields. We worked on the farm only in the summertime. During our working days, we at night slept in a large place called the Dormitory. The farm had a regular boiler and engine room, and motor dynamos or other machinery that produced the electric lights.

The farm was supervised by a man whose known name was Allenberger. He had a wife and little girl. They were very good people.

We boys working on the farm were divided into "gangs," three gangs, I believe, and under a supervisor for each. Their names were John Fox, Whiliam Oneil, and Mr. West. He was the cowboy.

At the approach of late fall, we were returned to the asylum, which Mr. Allenberger termed the bughouse. I loved it much better than the farm. But yet I loved the work there. Yet the asylum was home to me.

While back at the home I received a severe shock.

I got the bad news that my father had died at the St. Augustine home.

I did not cry or weep however.

I had that kind of deep sorrow that, bad as you feel, I could not.

I'd have been better off if I could have. I was in that state for weeks, and because of it I was in a state of ugliness of such nature that everyone avoided me, they were so scared.

Even when back on the farm the next summer, they noticed a change in me.

They heard the sad news, however, and did not bother me. During the first of my grief, I hardly even ate anything, and was no friend to anyone.

I was even very dangerous if not left alone.

I believe I was at the asylum 7 years, and during the summer between that time on the farm.

During the early summer of the fourth year, it was June, and I made my first attempt to run away, but that farm's cowboy caught me in a cornfield, tied my hands together on a long rope, and made me run back all the way at the rear of his horse.

The second attempt was successful. I, with another boy, hitchhiked a freight. He got off at Joliet, where he lived. I rode on to Chicago.

After a storm, I foolishly gave myself up to the police, who had me sent back. I stayed then again for more than a year.

What made me run away? It was my protestation at being sent away from the asylum, where I wanted to stay, as for some reason it was home to me.

During the early summer of the following year, the sixth—I believe it was June—two boys working on the farm induced me to run away with them. We then got an actual work for a short spell with a German farmer.

It was a job driving to the nearest town with a wagonload of something the farmer sold there. At meal times, breakfast, dinner or supper, he said the Our Father and sang some sort of a German hymn before we ate. He asked why we did not join him.

We answered, We do not know any German.

His son and wife answered some parts.

Being short of working conditions, he finally had to let us go, me and a stouter boy. We were paid. He kept the other boy. Excuse me. I do not remember their names.

With me giving a part of my money to my stout companion, we rode on the Illinois Central railroad to Decatur, Ill. While there, I wanted to see Chicago again.

You would not believe it, but I then walked from Decatur, Ill. to Chicago, arriving early in August. Because of unusual warm weather, and hardly able to sleep, I walked also many a night.

I had forgot to mention: the time when I gave myself up to the police, I was taken by train to the poorhouse at Dunning town.

From there, after a month's stay, I was sent to the asylum at Lincoln, Ill.

But this hike to Chicago from Decatur was successful.

I knew her address, so I went and took refuge at my Godmother's and after some weeks there she took me to St. Joseph's Hospital, which was on Burling and then the street called Garfield Ave.

It now is known as Dickens Ave. I prefer it would have retained its original name, as Dickens was an English man, Garfield an American and one of our presidents.

I got a job there as hospital or floor janitor.

I worked there under Sister Mary Rose and later under another Sister, Dorothy. Sister Rose was prime but good. Sister Dorothy was good too, but you could joke with her.

I worked under each of them until I was there for a little over fourteen years. The name of the head Sisters were Sisters Cephas and Camilla.

Both were good, but Sister Cephas took sick and died less than a year after I arrived. At the earliest of my time, because of an old injury to my right shoulder, I had to be left-handed with the sweeping broom and other things.

All Sister's scoldings could not change to sweeping with my right. As my shoulder injury was caused by a fight, I did not explain to her. She gave up nevertheless and let me sweep as I pleased. I sure knew how to scrub floors as clean as they would get, and all on my hands and knees.

And that was not done that way to humble myself. Under no condition would I humble myself, and Heaven help the one who would dare humble me.

One did, and was in a hospital for a year. And somehow I got away with it, too.

But it was on that score 50-50, as I never exalted myself then either.

I do now, and how.

As I said before, and again will write, that a lot because of my injured shoulder I did really find myself unable to use other certain household articles and the sweeping broom brush.

In my younger days, which I forgot to mention, when angry over something I burned holy pictures and hit the face of Christ in pictures with my fist. I wonder, would I have the heart to do so now? I can't say yes or no.

I've got an awful nasty temper.

Sometime or other, for a time Sister Rose, finding out that I came from the home of feeble-minded children, thought I was still crazy.

I believed she got the information from Sister Nina, who was called Sister Leno by others. My Godmother, not thinking of the consequences, told her.

The whole hospital full of persons soon knew. I was then called crazy. I had, I believe, more brains than all combined. None of them, I found out, even knew geography or history. I did. My spelling, figures and reading and writing was more excellent than theirs. My finding it out: there are many cities in this country and the old world they could not spell or pronounce. I could.

Berlin and Dresden are still the most beautiful cities in the world.

Berlin is largest, next to London and New York City.

As I said before, I received admonition from Sister Rose because of my enforced left-handedness, until I could prove it was impossible with my right hand.

Once, in searching for something that got lost from me in a very dark enclosure of the out exit on the ground floor, behind the dining room, by which you go outside by the rear, I scared some young woman (she was cowardly and timid anyway) out of her wits accidentally.

When Sister Rose heard of it by someone telling her, she scolded me good, and said she surely believed that I am really crazy.

But I could see that, while scolding me, she also had a hard fight with herself to keep from laughing over it. Yet afterwards, by many that woman was looked on as a Scardy-cat, and "chicken."

She quit after that. Several times, when scolding me for something, whether I did it or not, she threatened to send me back to the Lincoln Asylum.

I wished then she had. I felt I was a fool for after all running away. I was better off there, and never was scolded. But I knew they would not take me back now, and told her so.

On the Christmas midnight Mass, a cold snowy one in December 1909, I received in their chapel my first Holy Communion. I was to convince them before then that I was baptized Catholic, but in the asylum, I even then knew all things of the Religion but also, in the asylum and on the state farm, they never, even for us all, showed any kind of religion.

They seemed even Godless, even in the school there. The only sign of something like religion was in the asylum's main children's dining room for us, when before and after meals the Our Father was recited by the dining-room matron, only ending the prayer in the Protestant way.

Or on Sunday, some sort of Sunday School, where only some hymn was sung by the best singers.

Otherwise, no sign of religion at all. She said, then I did right to run away. My Godmother had me baptized on the snowy afternoon, in St. Patrick's Church on Des Plaines and Adams Street, Chicago.

The way it was there, as I told her, you'd think there was no God at all. And at first I wanted to stay there. I suppose they had the idea that feeble-minded people could not at all understand Religious instruction.

Then why were they to go to school? The school building, as I wrote before, I believe, was over two hundred feet north of the asylum, and there was an underground tunnel leading to it from the asylum, to be used only in bad weather. All this I told her. I can't say whether I was actually sorry I ran away from the state farm or not, but now I believe I was a sort of fool to have done so.

My life was like in a sort of Heaven there. Do you think I might be fool enough to run away from heaven if I get there? Besides, for doing it the third time, the officials of the state farm would not take me back.

I have to go back for a few words again about my stay at the asylum, because many things slip my mind. I'm telling the truth: there was a night freeze rain, lasting till mid-morning of the next day, followed by the most terrific blizzard storm I have ever seen before and during my lifetime, even now.

I remember the big snowstorms of 1912, March 26 and 27th of 1930, and also, before that, one of 1918. I've seen here also two other big ones, including last January 26. But believe me or not, that one when I was at Lincoln, Ill. had them all put together beat.

It raged all day, all night, and till late afternoon the next day, so thick you could not see a hundred feet away.

But strange, unlike most awfully big blizzards, it had no very strong wind, and was off the straight north.

As I read in papers, Chicago and all other Middle West cities and towns had the worst traffic tie-up I ever imagined. At Lincoln,

too, was a perfect stand—still of traffic, and it looked bad for us
inmates for food and fuel for a time. But we got by.

I would not want to see a blizzard like that again, and all
farmers were marooned and snowbound.

Even the state farm suffered severely. It was, as I read,
near two months before traffic could resume in our town, and all
the snowbound cities. And it was bad on all the stores, as nothing
could be brought to them. The storm was on January 24, 1906. It got
terrible cold after the storm to add to all the misery caused by it.

I had read that the worst blizzards of all come if they happen
to follow a freeze rain, which fortunately seldom happens. The freeze
rain was on the night of the 22 and morning of the 23.

The blizzard was on the 24 and 25th.

Another thing I got to go back on is that while still living with
my father I was out alone, playing on Adams Street.

An old man that had the appearance of what we call now a skidrow
bum appeared as if he wanted to kidnap me. I'm alert and very
dangerous to those kind.

At first I fled him, till I reached the crossing of Adams and
Halsted Streets. He still came after me.

I observed a half brick lying near. I picked it up with the
intention of hitting him on the head with it. If molested, I was a
brick thrower, and there are some big bullies who, molesting me,
can now (if still living at this time) confirm my statement. I never
missed.

But this time I did, and for a very unusual reason. As I threw
it, a streetcar came by and I accidentally threw it through a front
side window of the front of the car.

I escaped him and the consequences of the brick throwing, as no
one had seen who threw it, as I beat it so quickly. At that time, a
streetcar strike was impending and it was supposed that a striker
threw it. There were passengers sitting by that side window, and I
really hoped none of them was hit by the brick, or cut by the broken
glass.

My father heard of it, but as it was in the papers and believed
to have been thrown by a striker, he said nothing about it.

And believe me, I never told him or anyone else I did it. I was
afraid of the results. But I did not mean to do it and also it was
lucky the streetcar came between the man and me.

I never seen him again. I'm sorry, but if there is anything else
again forgotten I will have to write it. It can't be at all left out.

I also remember I said I was at St. Joseph's as floor janitor
for 14 years, first under Sister Rose, only a short time under Sister
Damien, and the rest of my years there under Sister Dorothy.

I had also, all the time I was there, an extra job of carting
away to the engine—house trash firebox lots of junk that came down
into the large receiver through a large five-story rubbish pipe. I
took care of that every afternoon, even Sunday, if it was extremely
necessary.

Twice the trash was mysteriously on fire inside the roomlike
receiver.

Something nurses neglected caught fire, and not thinking of the
results they had thrown the burning stuff down that pipe, which I
called the chute.

It was a heck of a job on the rainy days, or in the cold of
winter. On rainy days or also with summer thunderstorms the trash
got wet, and then I had to dump it into the lot till heat and sun
dried it.

Then I burned it there.

I worked at my janitor job, or out there getting rid of the
trash, even in the winter, when I had my worst colds.

You see, I don't know why, but they would not let me off, when
really I should have been in bed and under treatment! I dared not
take off.

And you call that charity. Afraid I would be behind in my work
and that would cost them (money).

Also, a Sister by the name of Sister De Paul was in charge of
the Sisters' Dormitory, or sleeping rooms. Many a time I scrubbed the

floors of the sleeping rooms, and the hundred-foot-long hall of their Dormitory, on my hands and knees.

You would say that was a good way of doing penance or humbling myself? Ha. Ha. I'll still do it on my hands and knees, rather than cleaning floors with a darn sloppy mop.

That does the cleaning so well as the humble, old-fashioned way. I'll get down on my knees still, with soap, rag, and scrubbing brush.

Yet to me, and I hate to say it, but have to, Sister De Paul was a pain in the neck.

She had nothing to say over me, only Sister Dorothy. Yet she acted as if I was under her too. I will not and never did stand for having two persons over me at the same time.

I hated her and showed it that she had no authority over me at all, only Sister Dorothy. Yet as she did not intervene for me, I think, unless I'm mistaken, that Sister Dorothy was afraid of her.

To Sister Camilla I complained, and the only answer I got was, Don't pay any attention to her. I stood for her froward ways for a year. The trouble was with all my work I had to do. I could not come and clean the Sister's latrine just when she wanted me to come and do it. Sister Dorothy would not let me do it until my work was done, yet she did not defend me against Sister De Paul, because I believe she was afraid of her.

Yet I held my own, but not being able to stand it any longer, I sure argued fiercely with her one day.

One day I told Sister Dorothy and others of the big grain elevator fire I seen at the Illinois Central Railroad siding, and one asked, "Did you set it?"

I said nothing more. My days of agony continued with Sister De Paul and so to Sister Camilla. I pretended I was going to quit because she seemed to refuse to give me a vacation, but truly I was leaving because of what I called "the persecution" of Sister De Paul. Despite all the time I had worked there, she did not seem to protest my going.

Sister De Paul had a bulldog-like face, and seemed to have the disposition of one. I don't really believe any Catholic Sister should have such a disposition. That is not charity or Christlike.

Though she was a Sister, I had a very intense dislike for her and did my best to avoid her. As I wrote before, the trouble was caused because I could not come to the Sisters' bathroom to clean its floor when she wanted me to.

Sister Dorothy was my superior, not her, and I had to obey her in all things first. But as I will say again, she had not the courage to back me up. I heard that most of the others were shy of her. I spoke and complained to Sister Dorothy about it, and yet with me, Sister De Paul would not even reason.

As I wrote before, if not now, I finally could not at all stand it any longer and therefore quit, and even a day later got a new job at Grant Hospital. Some weeks later, Sister Dorothy sent the orderly to my house at Mrs. Anchutz* to ask me if I would like to come back.

My fear of Sister De Paul made me refuse.

For a time at Grant Hospital, which I came to in June 1923, I seemed to have leaped from the frying pan into the fire, for the woman Superior, by the name of Mrs. Stevens, in her nature and prime ways had Sister De Paul way beat.

You could argue and fight it out with Sister De Paul, but if anyone even only tried that with Mrs. Stevens, you got fired right then and there.

Somehow, though, I got along with her far better than with Sister De Paul. Mrs. Stevens was severe, of course, but reasonable. Do the right thing and not argue or talk back and everything was all right. Sister De Paul did not at all appear reasonable.

I do not remember the number of years I remained there, but after Mrs. Stevens left to return to nursing, which before had been her vocation, she was superseded or replaced by a woman (housekeeper) whose name was Mrs. Ilene Joice. She was somewhat severe also, but you could talk back to her and argue too, without being fired.

But out of respect I never talked back to her either, only to Sister De Paul, and I still would contest with her.

During my stay for the number of years I was at Grant Hospital (the dishwashing machine at way at the north side of the main kitchen) there were, I believe, four very, very severely cold winters, with way below zero temperatures.

What I would like to write about was the distance I had to walk to it. The meanest winters I had to walk there were those of 1924 and 1927. The distance was six blocks east to Larrabee Street, then one long block to Grant Place, and three quarters of a block east on Grant Place to the main entrance.

You were not allowed to go out the rear entrance, but you could go in that way. But that was a much longer distance around.

How I put up with the severe cold that distance I do not know, but I did. I did not mind the walk in hot summer weather.

There was a young girl there who took charge of the help in the main dining room on the ground floor. Her name was Johanne Kuback. It seemed strange that every time she had her afternoons off it would, winter or summer, come a heavy long rain. On her half day. Though in winter it seldom snowed. Severe cold weather, however, never spoiled her half days.

I felt sort of sorry for her and proposed that if she and the housekeeper were willing she could for once change half days with her.

She chose the Sunday, June 2, Feast of the Corpus Christi.

My Sundays usually had been sunny. I was to be off the following Monday, which was her usual half day.

I'll have to write this down. Did it rain that afternoon? At two-thirty it came: clouds of black or the color of brown-black and a very terrific cloudburst that lasted more than an hour. Thunder was unusually frequent but not loud. The rain afterwards kept up until late evening as a very heavy drizzle.

As I did not have an umbrella or raincoat, I could not have gotten back to Grant Hospital to work.

I got two hours off in the afternoon every day.

When I got there, the kitchen, where the dishwashing machine is, was so flooded that nothing could be done. The food for the patients had to be brought in from outside. Us help, who could not do anything because of the flood, had to eat outside.

I wondered, because of the rain, where all that water came from. I believe it was caused by the backing up of the sewers in the kitchen At late night there came up another thunderstorm that had loud thunder with one extra awful loud crack, but shorter in duration.

The rain, too, was heavy and the wind blew almost like a hurricane. That flooded all the basement and kitchen again.

In the kitchen on that Sunday afternoon, and the whole basement too, the water was almost up to your knees. No one could work in the kitchen.

The next day, in the morning, I told her truthfully: I was sorry the debauchery of the weather. And she said she knew it might happen because, having been brought up in the country, she knew the tricks of the weather and could tell by cloud formation what would come.

So can I. In the dining room during mealtime there was a man who knew of my exchange with her and made fun of her because it stormed on Sunday afternoon.

I got aroused and told him to shut his "blanky blank" mouth.

He, being chided, got up and went out. He minded his own business after that.

I do not remember how long Mrs. Joice stayed, but one morning she received a sort of scolding from the Supertendant, Miss Watson, for being too severe with the baker, and several months later she left, to the sorrow of us all.

She was replaced by another woman, whose name was Mrs. Larson.

I don't remember the cause, but I do believe because of Mrs. Larson, I was asked to resign, so I left and in a huff. I had been a friend of Mrs. Joice, who was Mrs. Larson's rival over something, and probably that was the reason.

At first, for more than eight days after that I had trouble getting any job, which I desperately needed.

There was one place I applied, somewhere on Webster and Burling Streets, and was insultingly told to go to the poor farm at Oak Forest—and at my young age. But finally, after a day's work in a café across from the Alexian Brothers Hospital I was soon again at St. Joseph's Hospital, working in the dishwashing department. That was the third Monday of August, 1946.

I was under another prime and severe one, Sister Rufina. She had both Mrs. Stevens and Sister De Paul put together beat a mile.

If you talked back to her it would also result in losing your job.

Yet, like with Mrs. Stevens, I got along all right, never talked back, from respect, and knew how to hold my ground. I was not afraid of her, and she could see it. That made her like me. She did not like anyone who was afraid of her. And do your duty and there was no trouble. And she was not like Sister De Paul. Excepting my compelled contesting with Sister De Paul, I was not ever the talking-back kind. I received that sort of training in the "Bughouse" asylum, as they called it.

Whoever talked back to a superior there got the real punishment, and how.

Even there I never talked back. I did not dare.

But I had another pain in the neck while employed at St. Joseph's.

It was a dietician by the name of Mrs. Catherine Nash. Before she got married, her last name was Conway.

Sister De Paul, even if she tried her best, could not equal her. But if you even talked back to Mrs. Nash you'd get fired by Sister Rufina. As there was then an awfully severe Depression on, and it was utterly impossible to get a job with any place, I had to stay there and go through a number of years of misery because of her constant nagging. Once she went too far and I drove her out of the dishwashing room.

She told Sister Rufina, and the Sister told me, Mrs. Nash has as much say as she has. Then what could I do? Nothing. I decided to get even with Mrs. Nash, but when the time came I never did.

I was not the only sufferer. She was a pain in the neck also to all the tray-setting girls and others.

It seemed like Heaven when the time came that, to retire, Mrs. Nash quit to take better care of her property and child.

The new head woman hired by Sister Rufina was Mrs. Wise. She was good, kind and reasonable. She never scolded anybody.

She, however, was a very fat woman. Whether she was a Catholic or not I do not know nor heard. Mrs. Nash was a Catholic, but the way she was at us I do not know how much.

I don't think you could blame her for her nature and disposition, though. She had a strange nervous illness, which made her that way and some years later caused her death.

But when I received the news, I had no feeling or emotion. All her primness killed all that in me.

When I received the news I do not remember if I then worked still at St. Joseph's or the Alexian Brothers.

During my employment at Grant Hospital and St. Joseph's a second time, under Sister Rufina, I roomed at a place at the southwest corner of Kenmore and Webster (1035 Webster Ave.).

It was a three-story wooden house owned by East German people by the names of Mrs. and Mr. Anchutz.

They seemed sort of Godless in their way of living, but were nice people to room with. She went to church with him only once a year and that was Christmas Eve.

The church is on Dickens and Kenmore and is Lutheran.

During my stay there, there were quite a number of roomers who, however, were not steady roomers but come-and-go. After one particular one left, the police came looking for him on some swindling charge, but he had left on short notice, at night, and told no one, not even the landlord, and left no address.

As far as I can ascertain, they never found him or heard of him again.

I was the one, that late morning, to discover he was gone. I took the police up to his room. But he was gone and all his belongins.

Usually, swindlers are very shrewd and clever.

Two of the other roomers, good ones, died, one of an ingrowing goiter that strangled him. The other killed himself, but not where he roomed.

He had his body cremated and some of his ashes he willed to the landlord.

At New Years we celebrated by seeing the old year out, and the new year in. We had ginger ale or other soft drinks.

I do not remember how long I worked under Sister Rufina at St. Joseph's Hospital, but the time came when she died of cancer of the breast.

Her successors were two women matrons, one of the main kitchen and diet kitchen. I don't remember the name of the first one but she was under the dietician, by the name of Mary Ann Knuckles.

The other one of the main kitchen was Miss Casey. Both did not stay long.

I stayed beyond this time there, and was soon under a Sister whose name I could not spell. I could pronounce it, though.

I was then fired, after my three weeks' vacation, on the idea that the work was too much for me because of my age, or something like that.

I really had worked from seven AM to 8:30 PM and never got any time off.

In being dismissed I believe I was better off.

While under Miss Casey I had some superiorship, however, and dismissed one of the girls for misbehavior.

The rest all quit in their sympathy for her.

The day I was dismissed a Sister by the name of Alberta was the Superior. I was not there long enough to know her nature, but it was she who let me go.

But she was nice about it. She told me that I was not fired for any wrongdoing. She said the nurses told her that I was there too long, the work was too much, the hours too long and could cause me to break down in my health.

All too true. With so many patients in the hospital, I got so much work I could hardly find time to eat my noonday dinner.

Though fired, I could eat my meals there yet, until I got a new job. She suggested an easier job and with much shorter hours.

I got a new job, then, at the Alexian Brothers Hospital, during the middle of August 1947, after being out of work for a week. I was put in the place of a man who did not show up. I was under a brother, Fabian by name. He was not severe at all.

But still he was somewhat strict. On my job in the dishwashing room I had to work only six hours. At this job I stayed there for more than 14 years. I was transferred up to the bandage room, under Joseph Harry.

I had a helper, by the first name of Jacob. I could not pronounce his last name.

The job was rolling long, six-inch-wide bandages called hot packs. They were fourteen feet long.

After I worked here for three and a half years, it happened that because of violent pains of a bum leg I was forced to quit and retire, and am retired yet. Even before then, during Christmas and New Years of the years before, my leg gave me severe pain, especially at night. Though it don't bother me so much now, I always need the walking stick to go out with. I am on Social Security and yet get only enough to barely live on.

I have forgot to mention that from the time I was a young boy until even now I always had a very rough nature or temper, always was and still am self-willed and also determined that at all costs, even at the expense of Sin, that all things shall come my way, no matter who might try to interfere or stand in my way.

In that situation, now, because of my sore and lame legs, I am still worse and seem to have no way to control myself. I can blow up like a stick of dynamite.

I had forgotten one thing to describe, about when I was employed for my third year at Grant, I believe October 1923.

While at Sunday Mass, I was off that Sunday morning. The priest from the pulpit announced that on Halloween night the students were

to celebrate with a big Halloween bonfire, with mostly wood that will
make much more flame than smoke.

He said all neighboring fire departments were notified that even
if they did notice a rousing glare in the sky, they need not run out,
because they'll know what it is.

I was at my friend's house, Whilliam Schloeder by name, on
Halloween evening. I was astounded by the fact that enough fire
departments were running out as if to a very big fire.

I saw a glow in the sky and it was exactly in the direction where
the big celebration bonfire was to be made.

I said to my friend and his sisters that they forgot the
announcement made to them and thought it a bad fire. The glow was
surely very bright and getting brighter.

Finally, his sister Lizzie said to me, "They said the wood was
not to make smoke, yet look at that big black rolling cloud. And how
high it rises."

I said nothing in answer, because I was too excited at what I
observed. And how extensive the glow was, mostly too far northwest to
be the celebration bonfire.

I said, "It is a fire, and a big one at that." Lizzie and his
sister Catherine and also his mother thought it was the University
burning, but I said, "The glow is too far north."

I and Whillie went on our way to see where the fire was. It was a
twenty-minute walk, but we got there.

It was the big two-thousand-foot-long and three-hundred-foot-
wide broom factory, the west end of which is on Fullerton across from
the St. Augustine old people's home, whose main entrance is on the
west Sheffield Ave. side.

The burning building was 4-and-a-half stories high. Only a
quarter of the building was then on fire, but despite the fierce
fight put up by all the firemen, within an hour the whole immense
long structure, from street floor to the top, was a raging inferno.
The flames seemed to leap three hundred feet from the roof, amid
great clouds of rolling smoke as long as the building.

The smoke went so high Whillie could not estimate it. The west
end of the old people's home faces Kenmore Ave. So did the west
end of the building, afire. And it ended with the east end facing
Sheffield Ave. on the east, three or four blocks long.

I have seen quite a number of big fires in my day, but this one
had them all beat put together. And the worst of it was that it threw
such a heat, so awful, with the wind direction from the west, that
the firemen on the south side of Fullerton could not face it, and
even their clothing smoked.

O, by means of the firescapes of the old people's home, some got
to the roof and aimed their streams at the top of the building from
there. And the streams then hardly reached, as some parts of the home
is more than thirty feet from the south-side street sidewalk.

And hoses had also to be trained on the walls of the home's north
side to keep them cool.

I mentioned the name of the streets, but one of them crossed
Fullerton, along where the burning broom factory was. It extended all
the way down from Kenmore to Sheffield Ave. The building also extended
from Sheffield to Bissell, a little west, though, of the Elevated
train road crossing Fullerton. The building had a narrow four-story
tower on its east end, and that survived the fire.

When the big blaze started, the place was full of night workers.
It was, I believe, a miracle that at the first alarm, all the
employees, foremen, and the owner got out safely.

The owner himself and the managers nearly got trapped in their
offices.

The head of the fire department said the fire must have started
by spontaneous combustion underneath the high bales of broomstraws.

It was true that the bales of broomstraws were large and many,
piled up high on top of one another. Thousands of them were in large
rooms, piled almost to the ceiling with small or narrow passageways
between.

It was, they say, fifty pounds per bale. Standing too long that
way could start dangerous heat underneath—and how fast they could

burn! Once started, the broom stack piles could not be put out, and spread the fire so fast through the whole length of the huge building.

I was never across the street from the building, but a little west of it, in or near the Kenmore side of the St. Augustine Home. There, I did not feel the heat too much, and avoided most of the smoke. I got a good view of the building, though.

As I was to start my vacation the next day, November 1, All Saints Day, I stayed near the fire til close to eleven PM at night. The fire, being very stubborn because of the size of the factory, was still the same, though reinforcements for the fire departments came.

I did not want to stay up all night, in spitement of the blaze, so I returned home, found I had forgot the keys, and no one was home.

I suspected they too, including the house owners, were at the fire. They were.

Mr. and Mrs. Anchutz came ten minutes after I did, and asked if I had seen the fire. I told them I saw it a little after it began.

They let me in and I went to bed. Yet I was still so excited about the fire that I slept but little and did not stay long in bed either, in the morning. I went to Mass and Holy Communion at St. Vincent's Church, and had my breakfast, then went again hastily to the scene of the fire, where from the Church looking northwest the cloud looked as that from an erupting volcano.

When I arrived there, some of the upper part of the building had caved in; a portion of the south wall a hundred feet in length had fallen across a part of the street, and the building was now like a smoking, blazing volcano. The caved-in portions of the top floors protected the raging inferno beneath from the hose streams, causing the huge rolling clouds of yellow, brown, and black smoke. It looked awful.

All the fire departments were still there. This was Saturday, All Saints Day. It was, I believe, a week from the following Monday before it was all out.

Now to go back to my ill nature and character. I did not and will not bear things going wrong. I won't stand for the slightest

pain anywhere, though most of my pains were very severe, and I want everything under any conditions to come my way.

If things went wrong during any kind of work I do, I'll say I lose my temper terribly, and say things the saints and all the angels would be ashamed of me for.

For what I had said in the past, for my severe face pains when I was employed at St. Joseph's Hospital, I'm surprised, yet relieved, that one of them did not strike me for it.

I really believe it is really naturally in me, as I was that way when I was a small boy and no kind of scolding or punishment could change me. Once, in school, for some kind of cutting up a teacher boxed my ears, and my father had to pay the doctor's bill for what I did to her. I slashed her on face and arm with my long knife. I must say also, when I was aroused I was dangerous.

At least, when going to school after that, my father would not let me take my knife or any other weapon with me.

Outside of that, it was all right.

But I was expelled from that school for doing that. Yet if I could, when a boy I would severely revenge punishments, whether I deserved them or not. Some boy once accused me of stealing his wagon, which I did not.

If I would have, I really had no place to hide it. He hit me on the nose with the palm of his hand. For what I did to him in return, he was in a hospital for a long time. His parents could do nothing against me, or make my father pay my bill because witnesses said, and was able to prove, that he and his gang of followers ganged up on me, twelve against me.

What probably caused the trouble was that I often played on the third-floor porch of the building across from where I lived.

He lived there. Somebody did steal his wagon, but not I. What good would it be to have stolen his darn wagon, when, as I wrote before, I had no place to hide it?

If I had even brought it into the house, my father would have found out who it belonged to and made me give it back, and punished me besides for stealing it. As I had no place to hide it I could have fully proved that I never took it, but still they would not believe me. So I was slammed on the nose, and I believe I nearly killed him.

I was a very dangerous kid if not left alone. A much bigger boy than I, a sort of bully, tormented me in front of where I lived.

I nearly broke his knee the way I hit it when I threw that brick, a half brick. That was my temper then.

At the Alexian Brothers Hospital I was an employee in the main dishwashing room.

While under Brother Fabian I would bring a food wagon down to the main kitchen from one of the floors.

Every morning (except on my day off) I would bring the long, four-wheeled cart or dish wagon full of dishes from the Brothers' dining room to the dishwashing room, and have them washed.

Then I would bring them back to the dining-room man.

But after that, after he was gone, the new dining-room man would not allow me into the living room after them, and tried once to put me out by force.

Then this dining-room man afterwards had to bring the dishes to the dishwashing department and back again.

I would not do anything for him, and told him if I had the chance I'd slash him with a knife. I told him he can't get rough with me and get away with it.

I believe that was one of the reasons I had seen him no more, though I did hear he got into a row with Negro employees in the main kitchen and they chased him out.

His successor had to bring the dishes and wash them too.

During the time or years I worked both at St. Joseph's and Alexian Brothers Hospital and also at Grant Hospital, every evening and Sunday afternoons off (I got no Sundays off at St. Joseph's Hospital), I went visiting a special friend of mine, by the name of Whilliam Schloeder.

I don't know his middle name, but he was a Catholic and so were his folks and sisters. We often went to Riverview Park. I did all the spending. If I had saved all that, what would I have had? He had a

very good, pious mother, but I know nothing about his father because he died not long after I went seeing Whillie.

He had the three grown sisters and a younger but grown brother, Henry. His sisters could boss Whillie, but not Henry.

The names of his sisters were Catherine, Lizzie and Susan Schloeder. In their nationality they were Luxembourger. Susan was very prime and always contesting and fighting with my friend Whillie, and he never talked back. I know I would chase her out of the house if I was him, with my strong independent nature.

His other sisters were not like that. Susan got married, causing her husband to be Whillie's brother-in-law. Their two children, a boy and girl, were his niece and nephew. I forgot the boy's first name but his last name was McFarran. His sister's name was as her mother.

In character, of what kind of family were they?

In spite of being well-to-do, which I would not account with any other. They were very charitable, kind and good. When I had bad, mysterious pains in my face, he did all he could to help me.

What he told me to buy stopped the pain.

I had wished I had children like theirs. They were good.

It was too bad, though, that little Susan so often had such awful toothaches, despite all the dentist tried to do.

And he thought it very unsafe to pull them. To stop the pain he removed the teeth nerves. A dentist did the same for me when I had the same trouble.

After their mother's death, they went to live in the city of Wilmette. I do not know what was the cause, but their sister Lizzie died so mysteriously.

Whillie sold the house soon afterwards, and he and his sister Catherine went to San Antonio, Texas, to live.

I wrote to Whillie often but as he could not write in English, his sister wrote his answers for him.

When in San Antonio three years my friend Whillie died on the 5 of May (I forgot the year) of the Asian Flu, and since that happened, I am all alone.

Never palled with anyone since. Where I worked, I could not get off to go to his funeral. Afterwards, I never could find out where his sister went, for she went somewhere, not leaving any known address. I believe she went to Mexico, where she intended to go anyway.

I do not know where the McFarrans were at the time of Whillie's death.

I just now remember the time, while still working at St. Joseph's Hospital, on the first floor, but then under Sister Dorothy, that I asked some man whose name I need not tell or even do not remember to do me a special, easy favor, which I needed badly.

He refused sternly, saying he had not time to do anyone favors. I'm the sort of person that, if anyone refuses to do any favors for me, do not expect one from me, either. Then, one day he was arrested for speeding, by a speed cop. I do not actually remember what his fine was, but for the full of it he was short of five dollars and fifty cents.

A cop, or two of them, came to me at the Hospital where I worked. They told me why they came to see me.

I remembered the favor he refused me and not out of revenge, but of my way of no favors done for me, do not expect one from me, I refused his request for the five dollar and fifty cents loan.

Therefore, he had to stay those five and a half days in the police station. Because he had been arrested and jailed he could not get his job back. I thought because of my refusal of the loan to him, the Sisters would rebuke me as being mean, but they said nothing. They did not even know of it.

From then on I have never seen him since.

I am still that way, yours truly, and always will be. If I am refused a favor, do not expect one from me.

And if I have been refused a favor, I do feel that the one who refused has got a lot of nerve to ask me for one. The guts of him! Pooh.

But at Grant Hospital, where I worked in the dishwashing department, in the main kitchen, the work was sometimes slack and sometimes too much.

At Grant Hospital I received two half days off a week and two weeks' vacation.

Grant Hospital was, I believe, fifteen blocks from where I lived to the west, at the Anchutzes at 1035 Webster, and it was an ordeal to walk it in bad weather, especially in the winter and during severe below-zero cold waves, and during real hot weather in the summer, and getting caught in sudden thunderstorms coming up, without umbrella or raincoat.

You would ask why I walked such a long distance? It was because there was no way or means to ride there and I could not afford a taxi that distance.

There was a single-car streetcar running on Dickens Ave., but it came only every three quarters of an hour and I could get quicker to my job by walking.

From the Anchutzes' place it was eight blocks to St. Joseph's Hospital, but also an ordeal to walk even there during bad stormy and cold weather, especially the awfully cold winter of 1935, and also of 1936.

I do not remember how long, or the number of years I worked at Grant Hospital, but all that time there were no big, long, blinding snowstorms. There was one blinding snowfall but it lasted only long enough to lay 4 inches.

A March-end blizzard, lasting from March 31 through April 1, I forget the year, only laid ten inches. That snow fell for two days without stopping.

I can't forget the big blizzard of March 26 and 27th, Sat. and Sunday 1930, so late in the year, too. Traffic was tied up for more than three weeks.

It melted too fast under the sun, in the open country, as I read in the papers, and caused the worst flood in the country's history.

Though she was good as a sister, Sister Rufina was a very scolding kind, and I do not remember or recall how many would not remain long working under her.

Yet, too, she was prompt in firing anyone who would talk back to her.

I stayed through the years under her. She died, though, in a hospital in Evanston of breast cancer. So I was told.

Then came the kitchen overseer and when she quit, the Sister whose name I cannot spell. She was very quiet and easy-going.

Work for me those years was way more than I would or could take, long hours, no hours off, but yet a day off, though.

Then, after my last vacation there, after I came back I found I was fired. The head sister, Alberta, said the work was too much for me.

Then, after a week out of a job, I received employment at the Alexian Brothers Hospital. I stayed on the job there until my enforced retirement.

Because there were so many patients at the Hospital, I would at times find work too much; also, I worked in the dishwashing department there, too, but not as dishwasher.

I never ran or operated the dishwashing machine.

I stripped or scraped the refuse off of the dishes and other utensils to go into the dishwashing machine.

When I first came, I had to wash all types of the dishes by hand that had on them what the machine would not take off.

Sometimes here too, the work was slack and other times too much.

One day there came a change in the dishwashing business.

The old machine was dismantled and moved out. The dishwashing room was changed into a sort of medical department, and a new machine put into another room, to be operated by only girls or women.

No more men. That dishwashing room had an electric-driven garbage disposal by the refuse stand.

No need any more to wear out heavy garbage cans. However, a girl had to take out stuff that burns in a container by truck.

I myself got a pot-washing job. Sometimes that job was so slack that you could stand around, waiting for them to come, and at other times there were so many pots, pans and other utensils that you could not hardly manage them without additional help.

However, as the pot-washing room was much too hot in the summer, especially for me, it caused me to have a sort of heat sickness and I had to be on sick leave for more than eight days.

When I came back, Miss Sullivan, the head of the kitchen and the vegetable department, transferred me to the vegetable room for my health's sake.

It was more cooler there. At times there, too, the work was too much and everything had to be on time.

By machine, I peeled potatoes and cleaned and worked on all kinds of vegetables. All these had to be on time and I had to be at work by five thirty, until the brother who came in charge changed it to six thirty and to quit at three thirty.

I did not like that sort of change, because when I came at five thirty I could quit at two.

I was going to quit, but at that time jobs were hard to obtain. So I had to put up with the unpleasant change. I however was soon transferred to the bandage room, up on the fifth floor. There, no one could show any authority over you.

There, you were on your own. Joseph Harry was very good to me and my helper Jacob.

They called him Jake. He had a sort of stomach ailment that made him vomit for any unusual exertion. He would even throw up if he had to walk through deep snow.

The bandage room was an awfully hot place in the summer, with a very low roof which the sun heated dreadfully. It was a very sweat shop, and we shortened our time of work because of it.

In the winter, especially during cold weather, it was like an ice box, even if we had a radiator on.

We soon succeeded in having a second one put in, and it helped a lot.

The heat itself was not so humid as down in the kitchen and that darn hot room.

The heat was caused, as I mentioned, by that sun-heated low roof. I remember that I did mention that I was first, before that,

transferred to the vegetable room, because in the pots room the last
summer I was in there, I got what is called heat sickness, or mild
heat prostration.

I could not understand it, for all the rest of my life before
that, I stood worse heat than that well.

I had suffered no results from the fierce heat of the bandage
room. I stood it perfectly well.

Maybe because that heat was drier. When I got that heat sickness,
it was a terribly hot summer, where for many days eighty-five degrees
was the most lowest temperature. Five days it was over a hundred.

While working at St. Joseph's Hospital and then at the Alexian
Hospital, I got on me a very mean streak, because of prayers not
being answered, and a question over the snow.

Before this happened, I was a daily attendant at Mass and Holy
Communion.

Then foolishly and very sinfully I stopped going to Mass and
Holy Communion and when work was unusually heavy at both places
I badly sang awfully blasphemous words at God for hours without
stopping.

I am surprised that for the words I sang God did not strike me.
But no, he did not.

I believe he knew there was a time coming when I would wisely
change my ways. It did happen. It was while I was working in the
bandage room.

Up there, there were days when the work was so scarce that I
almost had nothing to do.

In some sort of a magazine I read of a young fellow, who, when
losing his fortune, turned bandit and robbed and killed at will.

He was betrayed by false women friends, arrested, and being
found guilty at his trial, was condemned to be hanged.

When he died he went to hell and was tormented horribly by
fiends.

There was not only descriptions of the story, but as many
pictures. The pictures of his torments in the fires of hell, and by
the demons, scared me into repentance, and I stayed good and after
Confession have been going to daily Mass and Confession frequently,
and also daily Communion ever since.

During my long stay at the Alexian Brothers, I was raised in my
pay three times. Then I got partial retirement, and worked part time
in the bandage room with half the pay reduction.

I then received $100 a month with employment taxes to pay.

Yet it was either at St. Joseph's Hospital or the Alexian
Brothers that I was in bed under the care of the main head doctor for
a severe pain on the right side of my belly. Yet what was the cause
of it, I or the Doctor did not know.

Repeated Axrays revealed nothing. The pain however slowly
stopped after I vomited tward the afternoon of the day, which it had
started in the morning early, while at work. But I had to remain in
bed for for six days. It is a long time since that happened, but I
have been walking with a cane ever since.

I'm over 65 years now, but sometimes, off and on, that same kind
of pain returns and goes.

But it so far has not been so severe, except on January 26, a
year ago from this January, it caused me chills while in bed that
I thought would not stop. Then all of a sudden when I did master
those chills, I felt a sudden need to vomit, and go up to do it, but
nothing would come up.

Then, as suddenly, it was all over and I was all right.

I plowed through that deep snow to the grill on Sheffield and
Webster to breakfast. It was Friday the 27th and the storm was still
going strong.

Was it that the blizzard storm affected me that way Thursday
night?

I had slightly suspected my gall bladder. Some of the hospital
employees thought I might have strained the right of my belly
muscles. That too could have been a real possibility, because the
pain does not feel like being inside of me, but on the abdomen.
This happened when I worked in the bandage room, rolling what was

fourteen-feet lengths of what was called hot packs, I as I mentioned
before, with my helper by the name of Jacob Feserl.

He, though somewhat fussy, was a good man. His fussiness made
him somewhat troublesome. If I could not, he did the rolling, after
my turn to get the long-gauge hot pack straight for him.

He would command, "Open."

They are called hot packs because they were wrapped about, where
they were to go around the patient, as hot as he could stand it. Joe
said the hot packs cost fifty dollars per one.

I and Jake and Joe too took turns in rolling them.

It was a sort of pleasure to roll them myself, but when Jake
rolled, I have to say with his complaints and hollering "Open," he
was a pain in the neck.

Otherwise he was absolutely peaceful, friendly and good-natured.
I did the very best I could to please him, and did not understand
what he really meant by "Open."

I missed him nevertheless, when he left to retire. He owned
houses (he did not say how many) and two big watchdogs: a police and
a shepherd dog. He also roomed in a house on Montana Street.

After he left, it would be double work for me and Joe, especially
if there were more than twelve, 12 large bags of hot packs.

And believe me, they were very large back size bags, and held
plenty.

Jake told me the bags were sometimes more than thirty in number
and then he had to work on all of them alone, when Joe was sick in
bed. He too had been sick abed several times when I was there.

The hot packs never were as many as 30 of them while I worked in
the bandage room, but once there came as many as twenty-three and I was
alone with them, too. That happened when Jake was away on his vacation.
There were still that many when he came back. Then it was my turn.

When I returned the hot packs had diminished to nothing. That
was the way with that job. Sometimes too many, and sometimes almost
nothing.

I got Thursday and Sunday and holidays off.

In the kitchen dishwashing and vegetable jobs, I only was off
one Sunday a month, and two weekdays. I sometimes had to work mostly
on Christmas and other holidays and was only off then when my layoff
came on one of them. I know of a country where the employer would
have to pay a thousand-to-10,000-dollar fine to work himself or work
his employees on Sundays, holidays and holy days.

As I wrote before, the bags were large, heavy when full, and
held plenty.

The least number was two of them. I would go get the large laundry
cart they were on. When loaded, the cart was heavy and hard to push.

The work on the hot packs usually had to be done on time, when
the nurses (men) came up for them.

Yet this sort of work caused me a lot of standing on an uneven
floor with my bad leg and the work was worse yet when Joe was sick
and I had to go it alone. Especially if there were a lot of them.

Strange to say, there were always a lot of them when I was alone,
and they were slack when we worked together.

And if he was with me and the hot packs were not many, I was
always able to quit before dinner and go home for the rest of the
afternoon.

I always came at seven thirty.

If I only had him with me and the hot packs were very numerous, I
had to work sometimes to past three o'clock in the afternoon.

Though I could, having a meal ticket, I seldom stayed for supper
but ate out. I was in the Hospital bandage room for a little more
than four years, I do believe, and I and Joe got along fine, no
trouble or nothing.

Then one morning, I believe it was in early November 1958, my
right side (same old belly trouble) and right leg both tortured me so
bad I could not hardly stand, at the same time. I went to a hospital
doctor, who gave me the prescription for some pills for my leg
trouble and told me I got to retire if I don't want to be bedridden.

I was told my side trouble was a permanent strain, and that I
should be careful in anything I do and do no heavy lifting. I came

first to tell Joe I got to retire, and then the personnel manager,
and got the checks coming to me.

Yet to go back a ways, being at the Alexian Brothers Hospital,
I was under Brother Fabian. The rest of the time I worked there,
excepting one occasion, there was no brother in charge when Brother
Fabian left. I was under no one at all.

I did not like that. Then came Brother Hillary. He was all
right, but he did not stay long.

Then in charge of the kitchen came a Miss Sullivan. She had
nothing to do with the dishwashing room. She was somewhat prime but
nevertheless good, social and fair. Do what she said and she even was
your friend. But as I wrote, she had no charge of us.

I forgot the name of the woman who had, but she had so much work
elsewhere that she seldom came around to see how we were getting along.

It just now comes to my mind that she was called Miss Dolgiest.

She was not prime or severe. She too quit, some years later, to
retire.

Then Miss Sullivan was put in her place.

I worked under her in the vegetable room for a certain number of
years and we got along fine and dandy.

I worked under her in the vegetable room until I was transferred
to the bandage room. In the pot room, before that, I was only under
the chef or the main cook. When Miss Sullivan went, I was upstairs
then; I missed her.

During my stay up in the bandage room there were two awfully
cold winters, the one before being below zero for three days, before
we got a morning that was 14 below.

The winter following, I believe it was 1959, there were two
weeks of moderate subzero days, until came a twenty-one-below day.
The day following, was 14 below and then a week more of severe
subzero temperatures, but not that severe. The rest of the winter
also was severely, severely cold, but not subzero any more.

Spring, too, was cold. The following summer was not a very warm
one, and rainy.

Strange for me, the Sunday before I went upstairs to the
bandage room, the Personnel Officer, Mr. Shields, said to take the
Sunday off.

Yet according to Miss Sullivan I was supposed to work that
Sunday, and she asked me why I did not come.

I did not think at that time, that Monday noon, of what the
Personnel Officer told me, and I told her I had been sick or something
like that.

And believe me, I certainly did not feel at all well, at that,
vomiting badly in the early morning. It was not what I had eaten. It
was that darn side pain, off and on. As I had said, I had suffered
from it since the the first time, and had a bad spell again on the
26th of January, the night of the big blizzard, and I nearly did also
vomit that night.

Are you ashamed of me? You ask why? It's because of the pain. I
shook my fist twards heaven, meaning it for God.

I also had a bad spell all day last week, when, near the west
side of the St. Vincent Church, I vomited some green stuff in the
early afternoon.

The pain gradually stopped. To go back to writing about Miss
Sullivan, when I told her I was sick, she excused me. I should have
told her also about the Personnel Officer's permission.

She even for that would have to excuse me, because being only a
dietician she had no say on that, or even over me. I was on my own.

Then, sometime, after I had been working for five years in
the bandage room, the knee pain came again, especially worst after
midnight.

The left leg then took its turn, and then back to the right. It
was very severe. I would get up and apply a hot rag for a time, but
that did not help much.

When I went back to bed, I thought I had received relief, but
half an hour later it was even worse. I had to get up and stay up.
That alone slightly slackened it. It spoiled a Christmas and a New
Year for me.

Since then, though, the pain is now not so much anymore. I had to start walking with a cane.

It's terribly difficult to walk, otherwise. I also discovered how awfully hard it was to walk through that deep snow Friday, January 27, that storm of Thursday and Friday. I dread those blizzards ever since. When I was out to go to Roma Grill on Webster and Sheffield Aves., I walked in the path already made by those gone before me. While at Mass in St. Vincent's Church, I can stand, I suppose, at standing times, or kneel, but do not, and it is at times mighty tiresome sitting all that time.

I go to three morning Masses and Communion, at the seven thirty Mass every day, and one extra Mass on Sunday afternoon at five o'clock, besides the seven fifteen and the eight thirty.

And on Monday, I go to the Miraculous Medal Novena Devotions. It too is followed by a Mass.

What did you say? I am being a saint? Ha Ha. I am one, and a very sorry saint I am. Ha Ha. How can I be a saint, when I won't stand for trials, bad luck, pains in my knees, or otherwise?

I am afraid I was a sort of devil, if I may call myself one, during the bad pain of my knee at night.

I had forgot to mention that in the early part of September 1917 I was drafted into the army, when the United States entered the latest part of World War One.

I found army life far from pleasant, but I was soon transferred from Camp Grant, Ill. to Camp Logan, near Houston, Texas.

Through real bad eye trouble—which, though, I greatly exaggerated— I received my dismissal from the army, and got my old job at St. Joseph's Hospital.

I was working then afterwards there too, under Sister Rufina, in the dishwashing room, and when the Second World War was on. I had to register then again for the army conscription but because of my age I was not called, fortunately. This time, I don't say why, I could not have passed the physical examination.

I sure felt good about it, as I hated army life. But you know, if I had been a draft evader, I would have served a three or four years' term in prison.

And I do not under any conditions like the idea of being a jail bird, as at least that is what all persons will call you.

To go back to my cross of suffering: I would not bear it. I firmly believe there is no one, not even you, my reader, who would, I'm sure. Who would put up with such pains, my past severe toothaches, face pains, and side pains, and other things I don't find time to mention here? The knee pain at night, I must confess, and am not ashamed to tell of it: I actually shook my fist twards heaven.

I did not mean it for God, though, though I felt like it.

What sin it was (if it was one) I do not know for sure, but when I told it in confession the priest was disturbed and admonished me, and gave me a severe or long prayer penance to recite, yet the severe knee pain drove me to it. Yet while working on the first floor at St. Joseph's Hospital, in the main so ward, or rooms, I never found any patients who put up with any severe pains either.

Then why should I? And people who do suffer are usually crabby or hard to get along with.

Yet despite that pain even bothering me severely in the morning, I went to and stayed through three Holy Masses a week on Thursday, Saturday and Sunday. And also to work on the working days. Yet I stood it.

Would you have done it?

But I will write again of that one morning. I was up in the bandage room with Joe, when my right leg began again while I was rolling hot packs, and it became so terribly severe that I could not stand on it, and to add to my misery, my side acted up severely at the same time.

I had to quit and the doctor who examined my leg advised me to retire.

I did so, depending on my Social Security, I retired November 19, 1963. Have been retired since, and I'll say it is a lazy life and I don't like it.

I suppose a real lazy person would enjoy it.

I do wish I could be back working there again. To make matters
worse, now I'm an artist, been one for years, and cannot hardly
stand on my feet, because of my knee, to paint on the top of the long
pictures.

Yet, off and on, I try, and sit down when an ache or pain starts.
I remember when I and a tall man were walking down Webster Ave.
homeward bound at dark in later fall, we saw an auto, driven without
headlights on, strike a dog, nearly killing the animal right there,
and then nearly being hit by a car coming from the west.

I wished we had been motorcycle cops then; we would have
arrested him.

There is one strange thing I have got to write: Even when a young
little boy, I felt insulted being called "kid." I have had peculiar,
willful ways, and a very independent nature.

At that time I never even heard the word "brat," but had I, and if
I would have known what it meant, if any one would have called me that,
that party—boy, girl, or grownup—would have got a rook or brick on the
head. I don't care what would be the result, I would have done it.

But fortunately I never heard anyone call a little boy or girl
that. I was told that anyone calling a child that commits a very
grave sin. Yet too, I'll say again, I won't, under any conditions or
costs, stand for anything going wrong, or bear any kind of trials or
disappointments whatever.

I would not even stand for a snowless winter. I cried once, when
snow stopped falling. And my poor father looked at me so queer. It
must have been unusual to him.

Though they were small ones, I have committed sins because of
these trials, disappointments, and things going wrong or not running
smoothly, and especially all sorts of childhood pains and miseries.
I was very dangerous if teased.

For my part, to go back to my working time at St. Joseph's
Hospital, with your granted permission: I had had toothaches, very
bad ones, and once severe pains, where teeth had been pulled, that
would not stop day or night. But much worse at night.

The pain was on both sides, in the upper jaws. You, I suppose,
would have been ashamed of me because of the terrible language and
blasphemous words I said constantly during this pain.

A friend of mine for a while loaned me the use of his hot water
bottle, but that did not help. It only seemed to make it worse.

Finally, a dentist I went to, to see if he he could find out the
cause, said it was caused by the teeth being pulled at the time of
the pain, and gave me some kind of mouthwash, and after a week of
using it in hot water in my mouth, the pain was gone.

During the pain, the openings where the teeth had been taken
out would not heal or close. Now they did. The dentist knew what my
trouble was. As I was the one who pulled my teeth, I forgot to dig
the hard abscess pus out.

The mouthwash dissolved and cleaned out the pus. Then the pain
was gone.

I also forgot to mention: while working at St. Joseph's
Hospital, there came as a patient an old man who was there for some
kind of sickness, a sort of shaking sickness, but it was not palsy.
Afterwards, he was put in charge of us working men and the hours that
we sleep in, and turned out to be handy for everything, even causing
a man to be arrested on the charge of hitting a man with a hammer
during a fight at night.

He had thrown the hammer out of a window. The fellow was not hurt
much. In fact more scared than hurt.

His name was known as Mr. Phelan, who took charge of things, and
he willingly did his work without pay to make up the hospital pay, as
he had no money to pay his hospital bill.

He had studied for the priesthood, but failed to be one because
of his oncoming illness. When I was in the army during Nineteen
Seventeen, I would write him letters.

Would you believe it? When I received his answers, I discovered
his handwriting was exactly like my father's.

It certainly was.

I also wrote to Sister Camilla, who was Superior at St. Joseph's

Hospital, and in the answer to my letters, she still sent me monthly wages, though I was still in the army.

In late December I was discharged from the army and came back to St. Joseph's Hospital.

I had sent her a telegram, but—I do not know how or why—I got there ahead of it.

That to me was strange. How long does it take to get to Chicago? I know Houston, Texas, is over 3000 miles from Chicago, Ill. Did the train, the Katy Flyer, run faster than the telegram?

I do not know how I even passed the physical examination for the draft, because all my life I had troublesome eyes, and too much sunglass or sunlight made me seem partially blind.

I could not stand the bright glare of electric lights in the hospital chapel, either. I believe my passing the examination was a fraud on the part of the doctor.

I must exclaim something again about army life. At first I was at Camp Grant, Illinois. I would have, in a way, liked the army life, only I was forced to leave behind things I loved too much. That was almost unbearable.

I do believe it is in the Bible that says it's transgressing very severely God's law to force any man into the army against his will.

I don't blame the Amish, the Jehovah's Witness, the Quakers, and so on, to oppose it. None of them will allow themselves to be drafted, even at the cost of the firing squad, let alone imprisonment.

The Bible says woe to the nation that drafts its men into the army against his will. That nation maybe, in due time, will not exist.

I will repay, says the Lord.

At first I was sent to Camp Grant at Rockford, Ill., through which, it is said, the Rock River runs.

I would, however, have slightly liked the army life after all, if not for what I so strongly yearned for, what I had to leave behind, and still worse: getting shots for this and for that.

I dreaded them, because my arm, or where the darn shots go, was so sore for days. Some of the shots even made me ill. The only good part was the canteen, where I could buy all sorts of refreshments and other goodies. I came to Camp Grant on September the 12th.

I do not remember the day or date of the month of November, but then I was transferred to Camp Logan, Texas, with a long trainload of "buddies." The camp was near Houston.

There, I was for several days reexamined for my peculiar eye condition, failed the test, and so, sometime after Christmas there, I received my discharge papers and came back to St. Joseph's Hospital a few days before New Year's, where I stayed until 1922.

I remember, after I came back, the great big blizzard of January 6 and Seventh, 1918. It was Sunday, the Feast of the Little Christmas, and the Monday after.

Sunday had the heaviest of the big storm, especially in the late afternoon and way into the night. I enjoyed the blizzard, though it did tie up traffic awfully.

Then, as I wrote before, because of Sister De Paul molesting me and making my life miserable, I left, and received a job at Grant Hospital.

I believe my first winter at Grant Hospital was one of the coldest I have ever known, except later, in 1936.

The one I am speaking of, though, was the winter of 1924: below zero, far down, and severe too, for more than two months.

I believe, too, it might have been that winter also that a roomer at Mrs. Anchutz wrote a complaint to the Health Department that the landlady did not furnish much heat in her place. It was true, too, because many a day did I spend in my cold room there, in the winters. Yet I stayed, stuck it out and never complained.

But it was her doing, not her husband's. He wanted to heat the place, but she would not let him.

But as it happened, most of the roomers were away to work most of the day, and she said it was wasting the coal and other fuel, and only put on the heat about late afternoon, before they came home.

He, the complainer, was a stay-at-home kind.

Yet as I said before, I myself, coming home earlier than the others, passed many a time inside, and went to bed with my clothes on and never complained. However, the Health Department sent her a warning by mail. I do not know if she could read English (she was from East Germany) or not, but she certainly could not write it.

She asked me to write a reply for her. I did, but she then got no answer. In the warning she was told it was better to buy the coal. She was told it was better to use the money for it than pay the one hundred dollar fine.

When that man reported to the Health Department, he did it after he had moved.

I believe it was a very sneaky thing to do, and I believe I told her so. She said I was right.

I also remember—again, I have to go back to write this—that while I was working in the pot room of Alexian Brothers Hospital I was suspected by a certain person to have twice snitched on him. I was relieved, however, by the main cook and the kitchen employees, who not only said, but were able to prove that I never did. And also, for all the work I did, and also having to empty all that garbage, which was heavy work, I never had time to go "hanging around Miss Sullivan's apron strings."

I would have liked to find out who told him I snitched on him. Well? You can guess there were many knives around the kitchen.

People of my nationality use knives on "framers." I firmly believe he was the real snitcher, and as "you call it," it "hooked" me to "cover up."

I lived for a long time at the Anchutzes. Afterwards, I do not remember the fall of the year when she exchanged property with an Italian on Logan Boulevard.

I'll now tell why I did not remain, when he was to come to take possession of the house.

I found out that he had a sort of moonshine still in his house (it was during the Prohibition or forbidden years), and when he was about to take possession he was going to bring it over to where I was living, at what had been the Anchutzes' house. That scared me into quickly making a change. For that reason I would not stay there. I will tell you why and how.

I remembered the big moonshine still explosion on Webster and Southport Aves. that completely leveled that big, long, wide three-story brick building to the ground, and broke all the big windows of every house for many blocks around.

Roofs were shaken from from houses, even more than a block away.

The terrible blast, said to have been heard six miles away, happened January 30th, 1930, at night, just after I got into bed. A lot of people living there were killed or injured. Some of the bodies lay on the sidewalk across the street and some half a block down Southport Ave., according to the papers. I myself saw the debris lying across and on both Southport and Webster Streets, blocking the middle of the streets.

It was a good thing for all the people living in the houses, where all the window glass went out from the shock, that there was no cold-wave weather.

Remembering this, and seeing all that, made me afraid, and I moved away to a new place: 851 Webster Ave.

I am still there, though this is 1968.

The sound of that big explosion was like some big boom thunder overhead, which I have heard during some thunderstorms, far as it was from my place. Though it sounded overhead, it was way much louder and actually shook our house badly.

I heard Mrs. Anchutz cry out, "It's an explosion."

As I said before, I was in bed when the explosion came, and at first I thought it was one of those big "boom" thunders overhead, which I have heard in some thunderstorms. But it was louder than all of them put together. I wonder what was the size of the moonshine still, to do all that damage?

I never heard or read in the papers whether they ever found or captured the moonshine maker or not. He was never seen again. And proofs were he was not in the building at the time it was demolished by the the explosion.

I read that those who make the moonshine in Kentucky, Tennessee or other states take awful chances with their stills. It is said an explosion of one of them can kill or maim you sixty yards away from it.

He made his moonshine in the basement, unknown to anybody, even the landlord, and during the time when it was outlawed.

Mrs. Anchutz knew right away that it was an explosion, and when the fire department passed by, she followed it to where it stopped.

There was no fire, however; in fact, the explosion by its great force left nothing to burn.

It was at first really hard to say what was the truth, whether it was the still, as many said at first that it was a black-hand bomb.

The owner, however, was able to prove that he received no threatening black-hand letters.

And many of those living across the streets from the destroyed building testified there was no black smoke or smell of exploded powder.

They said the big cloud was white and steamy and had a caramel and brandy smell.

I did not, at that time of night, get out of bed to go to see what had really happened, but the next day, after I was home from work, I went down there.

The scene was worse than what I heard. I had seen and known the building.

It had been a large three-and-a-half-story building. It had been a quarter-block long, and also as wide. Of pink red brick. A very handsome sort of building.

I could not believe my eyes for what I observed. And no exaggeration either: There was nothing at all left of the building but scattered debris.

A lot of the wreckage blocked both streets in that neighborhood.

The building did not have two feet of any of its walls standing, and wooden planks lay scattered everywhere, even on the rooftops of houses nearby, and through broken windows. It seems exaggerating but not so.

There was a sort of brandy smell in the air.

And as I wrote before, wherever I went, I did not see anything but glass gone from the windows, littering yards and sidewalks like fragments of sheet ice.

I even seen roofs of some buildings nearby shaken loose.

Not believing it was done by a black-hand bomb, I went out of my way to see if there was such a thing anywhere as any fragment of the still. I could not hardly believe it, but here it was: a big piece too heavy to lift, in a lot near Fullerton.

It was half round, with riveted parts and a sort of pipe attached, and was big and too heavy for me to lift even at one end.

Neighbors told me it came sailing through the air and landed there.

Because of needed evidence about the cause of the blast, it was forbidden to be moved then.

That proves it was a still explosion, and one with very great force, to hurl such a heavy object so far.

Why it was left there all night and the next day and a week, I do not know. It was full evidence that the blast was from the moonshine still, even though no officials took it away for evidence examination, or proof.

In four weeks it was gone, and to where I do not know.

There had been a few pipes and one pipe elbow also attached to it. This fragment was shaped like a half-rounded tank, eight foot long and half an inch thick. No wonder it was so awfully heavy.

Excepting for a few days, I do not believe January 30 was a terrible cold month, and had only a 10 inch snowfall before New Year's Day. No snow at all for the rest of the month until the 30th. One was on the 18th with 21 below. Then a short time later came 8 below.

All other days, and even in February, I noticed the days were almost warm above normal. March the first had one below zero. The rest of March until the 26, like late January and through February, was almost snowless.

But March the 26 and 27 had a very big snowstorm, which I cannot explain why I really enjoyed.

The paper I bought later in the afternoon (it's a wonder I could get it) said nineteen inches had already fallen and even then the storm seemed to be at its worst, it showed no sign of letting up.

Really, through the whole storm I am sure it got way much deeper, because it snowed severely all night Saturday, and also all day Sunday, and again way into the night.

Late in the year as it was, traffic was tied up for weeks.

But nevertheless, I enjoyed the storm.

Later, as I read, in the open country parts, the sun melted the snow so fast, it caused the most extensive and worst flood in all histories of floods.

When I worked under Sister Rufina, at St. Joseph's Hospital, for that time, the summers from 1930 to 1937 were the most hottest I have ever seen or felt here.

All that time, too, there was very little rain or snow, except there was a sizable snowstorm on March 7, 1931.

The summer of 1934, however, broke all records on July 18. Yet too, 1933 also broke all records, for believe it or not, for three weeks it was over a hundred and three in the shade, but never reached the temperature of July 18, 1934.

The winter of 1936 was the coldest I ever seen here. Not only because of the extremely low temperatures (7 below for 4 weeks was the highest) but also because of the long duration of the cold spell.

This time, it could not be called a cold wave, because for such a long time it did not abate, for 33 days: All severe below-zero days.

It lasted all the three and half weeks of January, not forgetting Christmas week, and through February without a let-up. On the Saturday of early February. however. came the worst cold spell of all, following a ten minutes blinding snowsquall. And during that cold spell it blew awfully strong from the west for 2 days. Those were awful cold Sundays and Mondays, more than 27 below, according to the news. I do not know how I stood it, walking to St. Joseph's Hospital from where I lived two and a half blocks away.

Yet it was not exactly the cold. It was that awful wind. St. Joseph's Hospital is a long distance, considering the length of those blocks.

But despite the severe wind and cold I managed to take it. I also remember the day Sister Rufina died in a hospital in Evanston of breast cancer. At least, that is what I was told it was. Even then, I stayed for a good number of years, and those were my worst years because of the unruly teenage girls they hired for the dishwashing department.

They were the worst or most severe cross I ever bore.

I was in charge, though, and one evening, under a kitchen head woman, I could stand it no more and fired the most unruly one.

In sympathy for her, the rest walked out. "Oh how I cried," ha ha ha.

Older workers came afterwards and my agony was over.

I did not remain long under the other Sister, whose name I can pronounce, but cannot spell. I left by request.

Sister Alberta let me go, saying the work there was too much for me. She was very much right. Yet I was afraid to quit after being there so long. I don't say how much work there was, but I worked too many hours, from 7 AM in the morning until 8:30 PM, and no hours off. Hardly even had time for my dinner.

After I was let go, I got or obtained a job at the Alexian Brothers Hospital, a week after I left St. Joseph's. A few winters were severe too, while I worked there, especially one, when I worked in the bandage room.

I first worked in the dishwashing room under Brother Fabian, then under Brother Bebe, and then under women supervisors. Every one of these were easy to get along with.

That dishwashing room was an awful hot place in the summer, especially with all that hot water in the dishwashing machine, but not near as hot as the dishwashing room in St. Joseph's Hospital. The Brother stripped the dishes. I scraped off the refuse, and the machine operator loaded the dish trays and run them through.

I never had the chance to operate the machine, though I worked

at the receiving end once in a while, removing the clean dishes and
loading the dish cart wagons.

I also took out the garbage, and cleaned the cans. That was the
only unpleasant job: handling and dumping the slop.

I believe I had once before wrote that all my life, ever since
a child, I always had a very willful nature and mean temper, and was
very determined always that all things will and shall come to my
satisfaction, or else.

I would not even put up with or stand for any kind of bad luck,
and I would always have an anger, slight or severe, which made people
say I have fire in my eyes.

I would not even stand for anything going wrong, no matter what
the cost, and am still that way, if not worse, especially because of
my injured legs.

It says in the Holy Bible, "For those who do not bear the Cross
there is no Salvation." I'm sorry to say I defied that, and still do.

Yet if I am that way, what am I going to do, defy or not? It
seems impossible to control myself. Yet I am not that way to persons,
only all sorts of gadgets and other things.

If something I'm working on goes wrong, "I am a spitting
growling, if not thundering volcano." Blow my top too, as you call
it, or hit the ceiling. And do I say bad words and blaspheme. Oh my.

Despite my nature, I have never been mean or hostile to anyone
except one person.

Yet that was not from my mean temper. I believe I wrote of this
before, but won't think it wrong to do so again. I once asked that
man to do me some favor, really an easy one, but he refused me. This,
as I wrote before, occurred at St. Joseph's Hospital.

As I said before, he got into trouble, of which cause I do not
remember, but it might have been speeding. He was fined 50 dollars,
but only had on him 45.

He sent a policeman to me, asking me the loan of five dollars,
but knowing of the favor he refused me, I also refused to give him
the five.

He then had to stay five days in the police station. I believe
you think me mean but, whether you do or not, I am the kind that if a
person refuses me a favor, don't dare ask me to do any.

I'll stick to that whether I'm right, wrong, or even if it is
sinful. There is another thing, too. There is a saying that it's
better to give than to receive.

But with me, I don't give if I don't receive—and receive first,
too. If anyone don't like my idea on that, they can—well never mind.
You know what I mean.

After five days, I really expected to see him come back to work,
but he never showed up. I think being what is called "a jail bird,"
he got fired. But I am not sure. I am now past 65 years old, and I am
still that way. Refuse me a favor, don't expect one from me.

You would say, what would I do if I had granted a favor first,
then afterwards in asking for one, I would be refused?

Let that person watch out.

I had expected that after his five days were up he would come to
me angrily and raise an eruption for my refusing to pay his small part
of the fine for him, but I never have seen him again, since that day.

Some of those, for what I did, especially those in the hospital,
sided against me, saying I was mean and revengeful, and that revenge
is a mortal sin, and I'll never myself be forgiven. And that to hold
a grudge against him, too, is a mortal sin.

I did not commit any mortal sin.

It was not revenge or a grudge on my part at all, or any
intention of revenge.
Such a thing was not even in my mind. And I had no revengeful feeling.
It was for the favor refused me, so then no favor done by me.
And I believe I am in the right.

Ain't I right? Well, I leave it to you to decide.

I remember a night at Mrs. Anchutz, which I really believe she
and her husband would never forget either.

The ceiling of my room in the south end had been gradually
loosened by a leak.

I suspected something might happen, so I pulled the head of my bed, which was in that location, away from under.

But yet I did not lie in bed with my head there, but the other end, with my feet twards the head of the bed.

I'm telling you that section of the ceiling, coming down, created some sensation.

Mrs. Anchutz cried to her husband, "Amiel, Henry fell out of bed." If I did, I must have been awfully heavy to make that terrible noise that was so loudly to be heard by neighbors, who thought it was an explosion. The fire department came, but there was no explosion.

A piece of the plaster, bouncing off the top of the bed's head, hit the top of my right foot toes, and though I was not injured it was a horrid pain I will never forget.

They came up to my room, and I had a hard time to convince them that I did not fall out of bed.

I cleaned off of my bed enough plaster fragments to fill a bushel basket. I almost nevertheless had a difficult time to convince her I did not fall out of bed.

But her husband saw the large vacancy in the part of the ceiling, the amount of plaster fragments on the floor behind the head of my bed, and knew I told the truth.

During the latest time I worked still at Grant Hospital, a disaster occurred which I, or even the hospital baker, will never forget.

There had been a leak from the eastern ceiling of the hospital kitchen. At the north side (also east) of the kitchen was the dishwashing machine.

Lucky for me, I was at the housekeeper's desk that morning. Something I was asking for which I badly needed.

Before I received her answer to my request, there came from the distant kitchen a loud, thundering noise that startled both of us. We hastened to the kitchen and an awful sight met our eyes.

All the ceiling plaster over that part of the kitchen had crashed down. Near the baking oven stretched a long, wide wooden table, and it and the floor were covered with inch-thick plaster. So was the top of the dishwashing machine. Lucky nothing was inside. The plaster falling on that long wooden table made that deafening noise.

The baker had been hit on the head by a big piece of plaster and was hospitalized.

He had more than 30 pies, which he had baked, on that long table, and they were all ruined. They too were covered with plaster fragments.

Had I been by the dishwashing machine at that time I might have got a piece on my head too. The kitchen ceiling, I believe, is 25 feet above the floor.

The main cook was sick from shock at witnessing the disaster.

The ceiling over his part of the kitchen did not fall, however.

Unless I am mistaken, I believe the baker sued the hospital for damages, declared the condition of the ceiling was known, and nothing was being done about it. He had a slight skull fracture and a badly cut head. He was in bed there for a month.

I do not know if he ever collected, as I never heard, but he received his hospital care free of charge.

By hospital workers, more than half a ton of plaster was wheeled out on carts.

There is one really important thing I must write which I have forgotten.

* * *

SELECTED BIBLIOGRAPHY

Art, Atlanta, July 14–October 20; Amon Carter Museum and the Modern Art Museum of Forth Worth, October 31–January 24, 1999; Memorial Art Gallery of the University of Rochester, N. Y., February 20–April 18, 1999; Wexner Center for the Arts, Ohio State University, Columbus, September 19–December 11, 1999

1996

Art in Chicago, 1945–1995, Museum of Contemporary Art, Chicago, November 16–March 23, 1997

1995

A World of Their Own, Twentieth Century American Folk Art, Newark Museum, N. J., January 27–May 14

1993

The "Outsider" Question, Galerie St. Etienne, New York, March 23–May 28

1992

Parallel Visions: Modern Artists and Outsider Art, Los Angeles County Museum of Art, October 18–January 3, 1993; Museo Nacional Reina Sofia, Madrid, February 11–May 9, 1993; Kunsthalle Basel, July 4–August 29, 1993; Sctagaya Art Museum, Tokyo, September 30–December 12, 1993

1981

Transmitters: The Isolate Artist in America, Philadelphia College of Art, Philadelphia, March 6–April 8

1979

Outsider Art in Chicago, Museum of Contemporary Art Chicago, December 11–February 17, 1980

Outsiders, Arts Council of Great Britain, Hayward Gallery, London, February 8–April 8

BOOKS AND CATALOGS

Henry Darger, Throw Away Boy: The Tragic Life of an Outsider Artist, by Jim Elledge (Overlook, 2013)

Darger's Resources, by Michael Moon (Duke University Press, 2012)

Collectors of Skies, by Valérie Rousseau and Barbara Safarova (Edlin Gallery, 2012)

Groundwaters: A Century of Art by Self-taught and Outsider Artists, by Charles Russell (Prestel, 2011)

The Museum of Everything (Mondadori Electa, 2010)

World Transformers: The Art of the Outsiders, edited by Max Hollein and Martina Weinhart (Hatje Cantz, 2010)

Compass in Hand: Selections from the Judith Rothschild Foundation Contemporary Drawings Collection, by Christian Rattemeyer (The Museum of Modern Art, 2009)

Henry Darger, by Klaus Biesenbach with contributions by Brooke Davis Adverson, Michael Bonesteel, and Carl Watkins (1st edition, Prestel, 2009)

Henry Darger's Room: 851 Webster, by Yukiko Koide and Kyoichi Tsuzuki (Imperial Press, 2007)

Bruit et fureur: L'Œuvre de Henry Darger/Sound and Fury: The Art of Henry Darger, by Edward Madrid Gómez, with translation by Valérie Rousseau (Edlin Gallery, 2006)

Henry Darger: In the Realms of the Unreal, by John M. MacGregor (Delano Greenridge Editions, 2002)

Henry Darger: Disasters of War, by Klaus Biesenbach and Kiyoko Lerner (KW Institute for Contemporary Art, 2001)

Darger: The Henry Darger Collection at the American Folk Art Museum, by Brooke Davis Anderson, with an essay by Michel Thévoz (American Folk Art Museum, New York, in association with Harry N. Abrams, 2001)

Henry Darger: Art and Selected Writings, by Michael Bonesteel (Rizzoli, 2000)

Henry Darger: The Unreality of Being, by Nathan Lerner and Stephen Prokopoff (University of Iowa Museum of Art, 1996)

Henry J. Darger: Nei regni dell' irreale, by John MacGregor (Fondazione Galleria Gottardo Lugano, Collection de l'art brut, Lausanne, 1996)

FILM

In the Realms of the Unreal, Jessica Yu, Diorama Films, 82 minutes, 2004

2008

Messages & Magic: 100 Years of Collage and Assemblage in American Art, John Michael Kohler Arts Center, Sheboygan, Wisc., September 28–January 25, 2009

The World Needs a Narrative, Kevin Kavanagh Gallery, Dublin, September 26–October 18

Vocabularies of Metaphor: More Stories, Hosfelt Gallery, San Francisco, September 6–October 18

In the Land of Retinal Delights: The Juxtapoz Factor, Laguna Art Museum, Laguna Beach, Calif., June 22–October 5

DARGERism: Contemporary Artists and Henry Darger, American Folk Art Museum, New York, April 15–September 21

Lots of Things Like This, Apex Art, New York, April 2–May 10

Glossolalia: Languages of Drawing, The Museum of Modern Art, New York, March 26–July 7

2007

The Writer's Brush, Anita Shapolsky Gallery, New York, September 11–October 27

Effigies, Stuart Shave Modern Art, London, September 7–October 4

Beautés insensées, Nouveau Musée National de Monaco, January 11–February 25

2006

Body Politics: Figurative Prints and Drawings from Schiele to De Kooning, Walker Art Center, Minneapolis, December 15–July 15, 2007

Fairy Tale, Myth and Fantasy, Galerie St. Etienne, New York, December 7–February 3, 2007

A Secret Service: Art, Compulsion, Concealment, Hayward Gallery Touring Project, London; Hatton Gallery, Newcastle, September 17–November 11; De La Warr Pavilion, Bexhill on Sea, East Sussex, January 27–April 15, 2007; Whitworth Art Gallery, Manchester, May 5–July 29, 2007

Into Me/Out of Me, P.S. 1 Contemporary Art Center/MoMA, New York, June 5–September 25; KW Institute of Contemporary Art, Berlin, November 26–March 4, 2007; Museo d'Arte Contemporanea, Rome, April 21–September 30, 2007

Parallel Visions II, Galerie St. Etienne, New York, April 5–May 26

Inner Worlds Outside, Fundacion La Caixa, Madrid, January 27 April 2; Whitechapel Art Gallery, London, April 28–June 25; Irish Museum of Modern Art, Dublin, July 26–October 15

2005

Outsider Art, Tate Britain, London, September 13–January 2, 2006

Realms of Creation: Wölfli & Darger, Side by Side, Edlin Gallery, New York, September 8–October 15

Every Picture Tells a Story, Galerie St. Etienne, New York, April 5–May 27

Mixed-Up Childhood, Auckland Art Gallery, February 24–May 22

Dubuffet & Art Brut, Museum Kunstpalast, Düsseldorf, February 19–May 29; Collection de l'art brut, Lausanne, June 23–September 25; Musée d'art moderne Lille Métropole, Villeneuve d'Ascq, October 15–January 2, 2006

2004

The Ten Commandments, Deutsches Hygiene-Museum, Dresden, June 19–December 5

Between the Lines, James Cohan Gallery, New York, May 7–June 12

Andererseits: Die Phantastik, Landesgalerie am Oberösterreichischen Landesmuseum, Linz, April 30–August 29

It's a Wonderful Life: Psychodrama in Contemporary Painting, Spaces Gallery, Cleveland, March 19–May 14

2003

On the Outskirts: Art Brut, Neuve Invention and Outsider Art, Edlin Gallery, Miami Beach and New York, December–January 2004

Splat Boom Pow! The Influence of Cartoons in Contemporary Art, The Institute of Contemporary Art, Boston, September 17–January 4, 2004

2002

Cathy Wilkes/Henry J. Darger, Migros Museum für Gegenwartskunst, Zurich, August 24–October 20

(The World May Be) Fantastic, Biennale of Sydney 2002, May 15–July 14

2000

Disasters of War: Francisco de Goya, Henry Darger, Jake and Dinos Chapman, P.S. 1 Contemporary Art Center/MoMA, New York, November 19–March 25, 2001

The First 10 Years: Selected Works from the Collection, Irish Museum of Modern Art, Dublin, April 10–September 23

Art without Precedent: Nine Artists from the Musgrave Kinely Outsider Art Collection, Irish Museum of Modern Art, Dublin, February 14–May 17

1999

Obsession: Morton Bartlett, Eugene von Bruenchenhein, Henry Darger, Paul Humphrey, Kunstverein, Cologne, October 30–December 23

The Modern Child, Galerie St. Etienne, New York, September 14–November 6

1998

Self-Taught Artists of the 20th Century: An American Anthology, Philadelphia Museum of Art, March 10–May 17; High Museum of

SELECTED SOLO EXHIBITIONS

2011

Henry Darger: The Certainties of War, American Folk Art Museum, New York, November 4–July 8, 2012

2010

Henry Darger, Edlin Gallery, New York, September 11–October 23

2008

Up Close: Henry Darger, American Folk Art Museum, New York, October 7–September 6, 2009

Henry Darger Room Collection (permanent installation), Intuit: The Center for Intuitive and Outsider Art, Chicago, opened January 2008

2007

Drawn from the Home of Henry Darger, Smart Museum of Art, University of Chicago, December 22–March 16, 2008

Henry Darger: A Story of Girls at War, Of Paradises Dreamed, Hara Museum of Contemporary Art, Tokyo, April 14–July 16

2006

Henry Darger: The Vivian Girls Emerge, Edlin Gallery, New York, November 2–January 13, 2007

Bruit et fureur: L'Œuvre de Henry Darger (Sound and Fury: The Art of Henry Darger), La Maison rouge, Paris, June 8– September 24

Henry Darger: Highlights from the American Folk Art Museum, The Andy Warhol Museum, Pittsburgh, February 5–April 30; Frye Art Museum, Seattle, August 19–October 29

2004

Henry Darger, Galerie St. Etienne, New York, January 15–March 20

2003

Henry Darger, Magasin 3 Stockholm Konsthall, Stockholm, October 11–February 22, 2004

Visions Realized: The Paintings and Process of Henry Darger, Intuit: The Center for Intuitive and Outsider Art, Chicago, March 14–June 1

2002

Henry Darger: In the Realms of the Unreal, Watari-Um Museum of Contemporary Art, Tokyo, November 29–April 6, 2003

Studies and Sketches: Henry Darger, Eva and Morris Feld Gallery, American Folk Art Museum, New York, January 19–July 14

2001

Darger: The Henry Darger Collection at the American Folk Art Museum, American Folk Art Museum, New York, December 11–June 23, 2002

Henry Darger, KW Institute of Contemporary Art, Berlin, September 29–March 31, 2002

2000

Henry Darger: Realms of the Unreal, Carl Hammer Gallery, Chicago, October 11–November 11

New Works by Henry Darger, Galerie St. Etienne, New York, January 18–March 11

1999

Henry Darger and His Realms, Galerie St. Etienne, New York, January 14–March 13

1996

Henry Darger: The Unreality of Being, The University of Iowa Museum of Art, Iowa City, January 13–March 10; American Folk Art Museum, New York, January 11–February 8, 1997; Yerba Buena Center for the Arts, San Francisco, September 20–November 30, 1997; The High Museum of Art, Atlanta, December 13, 1997–March 7, 1998; Chicago Public Library Cultural Center, April 4–May 31, 1998

Henry J. Darger: Dans les royaumes de l'irréel, Collection de l'art brut, Lausanne

1987

Henry Darger, Rosa Esman Gallery, New York

Henry Darger, Phyllis Kind Gallery, New York

1980

The Drawings of Henry Darger, Phyllis Kind Gallery, New York

1977

The Realms of the Unreal, Hyde Park Art Center, Chicago

SELECTED GROUP EXHIBITIONS

2014

Social Geographies: Interpreting Space and Place, Asheville Art Museum, N. Carolina, January 18–May 11

2013

Raw Vision: 25 ans d'Art Brut, Halle Saint Pierre, Paris, September 18–August 22, 2014

2012

Collectors of Skies, Edlin Gallery, New York, September 13–November 3

2010

World Transformers: The Art of the Outsiders, Schirn Kunsthalle Frankfurt, September 24–January 9, 2011

2009

Exhibition #1.1, Museum of Everything, London, October 14–February 14, 2010; Pinacoteca Agnelli, Turin, April 1–June 31, 2010; The Chalet Society, Paris, October 17, 2012–March 31, 2013

Compass in Hand: Selections from The Judith Rothschild Foundation Contemporary Drawings Collection, The Museum of Modern Art, New York, April 22–January 4, 2010

American Folk Art Museum, New York

The Art Institute of Chicago

Collection de l'art brut, Lausanne

High Museum of Art, Atlanta

Intuit: The Center for Intuitive and Outsider Art, Chicago

Irish Museum of Modern Art, Dublin

Milwaukee Art Museum

Musée d'art moderne de la ville de Paris

Musée d'art moderne de Lille Métropole, Villeneuve d'Ascq

Museum of Contemporary Art, Chicago

The Museum of Modern Art, New York

New Orleans Museum of Art

Smithsonian American Art Museum, Washington, D. C.

Walker Art Center, Minneapolis

Whitney Museum of American Art, New York

The visionary art of Henry Darger would not have reached to the far corners of the world without the vision of the late Nathan Lerner—and the determination of the concert pianist Kiyoko Lerner, his widow, with whom I have worked closely. I also wish to extend a very special thanks to the artists who led the way—Tony Oursler, who introduced me to Henry Darger, and Dinos and Jake Chapman—and to David Colman, Vanessa Adler, Erica Papernik, Alexander Kauffman, and Christopher Hudson.

Brooke Davis Anderson, Michael Bonesteel, and Carl Watson have contributed their special areas of expertise to this volume, expanding our understanding of Henry Darger's materials and methods and his personal history. I particularly thank Brooke for sharing her thoughts and facilitating our fruitful cooperation with the American Folk Art Museum, New York. At Prestel Verlag, publisher Jürgen Krieger was an early and enthusiastic advocate for this project, which was ably directed by Christopher Lyon. Mark Melnick has provided a splendid design. I also thank Eve Sinaiko, editor; Ryan Newbanks, assistant editor, for his tireless efforts; Claudia Stäuble, coordinating editor, Munich; and Amanda Freymann and Erich Achter, for production and image separations respectively.

Many people have helped to make this book a reality. The presentation of Henry Darger's art and my exploration of Darger's complex role in the art of our time would not be possible without the generous participation of the artists who have shared with me their thoughts and their work, whose names appear below together with individuals representing the many art galleries and institutions that provided illustrations and information, notably Edlin Gallery, which assisted with caption research and arranged for new photography of a major work by Darger.

I extend my deep thanks to Marina Abramović and her assistant Davide Balliano, Andy Avini, Matthew Barney, Tim Blum, Lizzi Bougatsos, Bill Brady, Connie Butler, Paul Chan, John Cheim, Christophe Cherix, the Conner Family Trust, Elliot David, Donna Desalvo, Cheryl Donegan, Corinna Durland, Andrew Edlin, David Frankel, Nina Franz, Andrew Freiser, Larry Gagosian, Marian Goodman, Tim Goossens, Mary Gould, Georgia Haagsma, Kathy Halbreich, Judy Hecker, Alanna Heiss, Gaby Horn, Kyung Jeon, Yun-Fei Ji, Sean Kelly, Min Kim, Christopher Lew, Glenn Lowry, Roxana Marcoci, Ryan McGinley, Gary McGraw, Kate McNamara, Steve Mumford, Laurel Nakadate, Cory Nomura, Neil Printz, Christian Rattemeyer, Peter Reed, Andrea Rosen, Katelyn Sandfort, Jenny Schlenzka, Margaret Senk, Josh Siegel, Amy Sillman, Michelle Silva, Amy Smith-Stewart, Cara Starke, John Steele, Sarah Suzuki, Union Gaucho Productions, Conrad Ventur, and Amy Wilson.

Klaus Biesenbach
Director of the
Neue Nationalgalerie, Berlin